THE
SEARCH
ETERNAL

Frank E. Brower

THE
SEARCH
ETERNAL

FLEMING H. REVELL COMPANY
OLD TAPPAN, NEW JERSEY

Scripture quotations in this volume are from the *King James Version of the Bible.*

Excerpts (about 600 words as scattered quotes) are used from *The Phenomenon of Man* by Pierre Teilhard de Chardin, translated by Bernard Wall. Copyright 1955 by Editions du Seuil. Copyright © 1959 in the English translation by Wm. Collins Sons & Co., Ltd., London and Harper & Row, Publishers, New York. By permission of Harper & Row, Publishers, Inc.

Cloth: SBN 8007-0428-2

Copyright © 1971 by Fleming H. Revell Company
All Rights Reserved
Library of Congress Catalog Card Number: 78-137443
Printed in the United States of America

TO
the memory of my mother
whose frequent use of St. Paul's saying,
Prove all things; hold fast that which is good,
led me on the road to the search eternal.

CONTENTS

FOREWORD

"The major thesis of this book," says the author in an early chapter, "is to show our life on earth as a meaningful experience, and: to present a theory of meaningful eternal life."

With this objective as a basis Mr. Brower applies all the powers of a superior intellect and the skills of an accomplished writer to various aspects of search in an effort to understand all values ranging from man to God, from life currently, to life immortally.

I have become familiar with Mr. Brower's thinking over a period of years and have watched with interest and admiration its distillation into the book called *The Search Eternal*. When one considers the vast range of thought which he attempts within the compass of one volume, the very succinctness required might presuppose some partial if not superficial treatment. But this does not occur at all. On the contrary, we have in this book an extraordinarily mature and in-depth system of thinking, one which at the same time does not require endless reading. Actually it appears that material, sufficient for several works, has been compressed into one book, one that is so full of wisdom and so compelling in its scholarship that it belongs among the truly great documents of our time.

Years of study, wide reading and reflection have gone into the composition of *The Search Eternal*. For anyone who likes to think, who finds ideas exciting, to whom scholarship is a challenge, this book will be absorbing indeed.

It is hardly a work that can be quickly read once and then put aside. This is the kind of mental discipline reading that toughens the scholarly inclined. It contains more vital thought per paragraph than any work I have read in some time and the book is interesting from beginning to end—exceptionally so.

There is a flow of thought through the book that is within itself highly inspirational. And withal, Frank Brower has an engaging strain of practicality. His common sense comes through in an uncommonly attractive manner.

For the person who wants answers about life, for the reader who likes to think, *The Search Eternal* will bring fresh, valid insights and richer meaning into his life.

Mr. Frank Brower is a dear friend of mine and I am pleased that a wide reading public will now get to know this charming and remarkable man through his inspired book, *The Search Eternal.*

NORMAN VINCENT PEALE

PREFACE

No civilization can long endure without hope. A man without hope is a lost soul. Hope is part of the thesis of this book. But how can modern man have hope? This is the cry not only of the average person but also of some philosophers and existentialists.

No nation—in the midst of wars, fear of wars, and economic pressures—can afford to be smug and self-sufficient, not even the two greatest world powers known today.

No individual can feel relaxed in the midst of the many rebellions he sees on every side: revolutions in politics, education, economics, and religion; fear of nuclear destruction, inflation, credit crunches; moral decadence, the generation gap, the use of dope, crime and general disrespect for the law. No sane person can afford to be a "Pollyanna" in such an era; most people see little hope in our present society.

This book is based on hope and faith in the future, but it is not to be interpreted as a sugar-coated presentation of what lies ahead. The fruits of the future won't come as a gift; we will not ignore the weeds and the thistles and the hard work required in seeking a more ideal civilization. The future is in our hands right now.

Why are we so bewildered today? Is modern life really so difficult or is it a question of adjusting our thinking and living to the new universe science has revealed to us?

The mind of modern man is confounded by the macrocosm, the inconceivable magnitude of the cosmos; it is perplexed equally by the complexity and power of the microcosm, as science continues to delve deeper into the nature of the atom. If we cannot conceive of distances spanned by billions of light years, how can we visualize the existence of matter as a reality when its duration is measured by a trillionth of a second? Is there infinity on both sides of the polarity between the macrocosm and the microcosm?

Eugenicists may present new and valuable concepts for man's physical evolution; man's future, however, is not determined alone by amoral science: the quality of our political, economic, and moral concepts may well decide our progress or retrogression.

Although universal education has raised the level of man's knowledge, it has not, necessarily, raised the value level of his consciousness. Neither has it made him happier or increased his capacity for self-control sufficiently to cope with the problems of the modern world.

Until recently psychiatrists have dwelled too much on the past. Man must know his past, but, more importantly, he must accept his past maturely and then act in the present with a strong vision for the future—a future which inspires hope and faith in his search for the meaning of his own life.

Much of philosophy concerns itself with the history of the great thinkers and much energy is spent on the analysis and interpretation of ancient systems of thought or "schools" of philosophy. Again, a knowledge of the past is

14

important; but we must realize that many ancient concepts have been invalidated by modern science.

A great deal of present-day philosophy—especially the popular kind—is a dismal existentialism in which hope and vision are nonexistent. Such existentialism reflects only the discontent, despair, and disillusionment with our disenchanted nuclear era.

Where do we find the hope and faith for a fruitful life? In the churches, perhaps? Alas, no! Modern theologians who cry "God is dead" may, unwittingly, add to the confusion of the Christian churchgoer. These theologians are only playing with words, for they know full well that their so-called God of history never existed, that He was only a symbol serving as a useful focal point for the more primitive concepts of the past.

Because our old concepts of God may be dead or no longer useful to us, does it mean that God has changed? No; it means that *we must change our concepts about Him.*

We must find a new heaven and a new earth; a new and, hopefully, a more fruitful conception of God and man. This transformation will not occur overnight in a miraculous way, but will come about through the logical means of the great evolutionary process of which man is a part. This book does not furnish a blueprint for each detail, but rather an architectural drawing from which men and women may fashion their own abode.

My purpose is not to present a new philosophy or a new religion; my objective is to offer useful answers and ideas for the serious-minded Christian layman. The questions probed in this book are concerned with the secular as well as with the sacred: man is both. The reader, of course, may not accept all of the ideas presented here, but I hope they may help him enrich his own philosophy of life.

15

Man is a searcher. God was a searcher long before man existed, and the *living God is a searcher even today.*

All searches lead to the search eternal. The search eternal is a process, just as evolution is a process. It is in the search eternal that I find my answer to the nature of the universe and the reality of God.

At an early age I was taught the value of religions different from my own. In my home atmosphere, dogmatism did not flourish; a balance was provided which could withstand the onslaught and disillusion brought into the world by two world wars.

I have tried to maintain this balance in my analysis of the mystical and intellectual elements of the world's religions. I have always considered mysticism as salt in the life of man. Without a mystical sense, man's life is barren; with too much of it, he cannot function normally and may destroy the very purpose of his mission on earth.

Our intellects are essential as a *means* of communicating with others, in the development of our culture. Culture results only when there is communication between individuals. When the intellect becomes an end in itself, however, towers of reasoning obliterate our view. A combination of love and reasoning are essential to a proper vision of the significance of life.

St. Paul spoke to our intellects; Jesus to our hearts. I have tried to present the heart of Christianity, as it has been revealed to us in the words and life of Jesus, shorn of all preconceived theological theories and dogmas insofar as is humanly possible.

If the critic or reader asks from which point of view the various searches are presented here, my answer is: from the liberal arts point of view. I make no pretense that the material in each chapter is an extensive presentation of each search. Rather, I hope, the various chapters, singly and collectively, will enable the reader to form his own *conceptualization* of our physical, philosophical, social and spiritual searches.

I have attempted to present here a vision of life, both on earth and throughout eternity, as a *meaningful* experience. To me, this is the great challenge Christianity has to offer the Western world.

Although the outline of this book was completed a few years before I read *The Phenomenon of Man,* the vision of Pierre Teilhard de Chardin, both as a scientist and as a man of the church, encouraged me greatly. Since I am not restricted by the doctrines of any church, his final conclusions may differ somewhat from mine. Nevertheless, I feel deeply indebted to this man of strong vision for his profound insights. The many hours I have spent in the company of his fascinating mind have been most rewarding.

I cannot begin to enumerate the great minds, from ancient times to the present, whose thoughts and deep insights enabled me to write this book. Perhaps the greatest of these was the influence Harry Emerson Fosdick exerted on me in my student days.

I am particularly indebted to Dr. William W. Paul, Chairman of the Department of Philosophy at Central College, Pella, Iowa, who gave a critical reading to the entire manuscript and whose numerous suggestions have been most valuable.

As in previous writings, my wife's advice aided me greatly and she also assisted me with the editing of the manuscript.

Barry Steinberg was my able research assistant and, in addition, I am obligated to him for presenting me with the positive and stimulating views of our younger generation.

In order to maintain my own special point of view, I was unable to accept all of the suggestions made to me by those who have read one or more of the chapters of the manuscript. Therefore, I, and I alone, am responsible for such errors and omissions as this work may contain.

FRANK E. BROWER

The Gods did not reveal everything to man from the beginning, but by searching men find out in time what is best.

Xenophanes

Part I

1

WHAT ARE WE SEARCHING FOR?

Since the beginning of time, man has been an animal searching for something. Man's very conscious awareness of himself—his developing awareness of the possibilities and limits of his experience—is rooted in his search for the meaning of his existence, and, in this sense, time was born and history began.

While no modern thinker would imply that the universe itself is man-centered, only the phenomenon of man (i.e., man observing and analyzing himself and his environment) enables him to acquire any understanding of the universe.

One result of this quest for meaning is that man has tended to attribute greatness to his own existence, an inclination which has been challenged in our modern situation in many ways. Modern technological progress leads us to attribute greatness to human nature and to the culture man has produced. But, revolutionary social problems question man's self-importance and demand that man search for the meaning of his being. Even modern psychology leads to the deflation of man's ego. Theoretical science draws a mathematical picture of the universe which the layman may find beyond his comprehension, and its pic-

23

ture of the cosmos is so vast that human individuality gets lost in infinity.

Scientific theory asserts that the existence of the universe long preceded the appearance of man on this planet and that our earth was actually a late arrival in the formation of the cosmos.

In the beginning, man trembled and was deeply afraid of the unknown. His response to the unknown produced witch doctors and tribal gods. Today, although man no longer trembles, he remains concerned and afraid of the unknown.

Scientific theory has no answer as to why man was born into the cosmos, nor does it know where he is going. For scientific theory—like all knowledge—is the product of man's own mind. But man is a rare animal; he not only possesses knowledge, he has faith, hope and intuition, also.

Man is prodded to explore the unknown by hope, faith and intuition. His mind observes the wonders of the universe—wonders which become magnified as he acquires more knowledge. Knowing that there is no purpose in science *per se,* man, by his faith, senses that there must be a great intelligence in back of the creative processes within the cosmos. Unless a great intelligence is operating the universe there can be no purpose in the cosmos; human life would be meaningless and civilization nothing but a cosmic joke. Our reason rebels against such existential misery and despair.

I am aware that some naturalistic and positivistic philosophers may not agree with me; nevertheless, I begin with two assumptions: *first,* man is all-important in our understanding of the universe; *second,* a greater intelligence than man's is essential to give meaning and purpose to our life in the cosmos. General agreement with the first assumption may be easier than acceptance of the second, but one of my objectives is to show that these two assumptions form a rational whole.

Man was born in ignorance. Hope, faith and knowledge have raised him to his present status, which is only a milestone on the long road ahead. There are those who claim that hope is for the dreamers, faith for the feebleminded, and that only knowledge is worthy of the modern man. Man requires a great deal more than knowledge, however, if he is to qualify as a human being. The long prevalent notion that science presents only knowledge and religion emotion is an erroneous one, not shared by scientists such as Albert Einstein, who, in *The World As I See It,* states that "cosmic religious feeling is the strongest and noblest incitement to scientific research."

In our modern world, philosophy without science is meaningless; and scientists, in propounding their precise theories, are philosophers at best. In our various searches, therefore, we need to combine science and religion.

Unfortunately, the human mind is trained for analysis rather than synthesis. The college student spends one hour in history class, one hour in biology, mathematics, economics, foreign language or philosophy. But nowhere, not even in much modern philosophizing, is the student encouraged to consider the relationship of these various disciplines to each other, to himself and to the world at large. Consciously and subconsciously he increases his awareness of the separateness of all things.

Pierre Teilhard de Chardin said: ". . . *analysis,* that marvelous instrument of scientific research to which we owe all our advances, but which, breaking down synthesis after synthesis, allows one soul after another to escape, leaving us confronted with a pile of dismantled machinery and evanescent particles." [1]

Although analysis is important in the process of human reasoning by itself, it will not lead us to the reality we seek.

A man who searches must have a purpose, a need for and an aim to reach a certain goal. His faith leaps ahead and commits him to the search, in the belief that his goal can be attained.

What are man's needs and what are his goals? They are many and varied. They differ with the state of civilization and the degree of development of each individual within that civilization.

When people are asked what they are searching for, many seem perplexed, and their answers are varied. Among the frequently recurring ones are: peace of mind; happiness; security; success; knowledge; freedom; power. Many think, or have read, that knowledge is power.

Obviously, no book can contain all of the goals for which individuals may search. But the major thesis of this book is: to show our life on earth as a meaningful experience, and: to present a theory of meaningful eternal life.

Since the searches for all goals lead to the search eternal, we need not describe them all. It seems necessary, however, to present those searches basic to the building of a philosophy that will create a life full of meaning; and then to present a theory which will logically point to a continuation of that meaning in eternal life.

Let us begin with *The Search for Existence,* which is basic for every individual in every nation, as developed in terms of Western civilization in the American culture, with its Judaeo-Christian background.

As man grew in awareness, he began to ask more and more questions—even some intelligent ones. Today, many people do not seem to know how to ask intelligent questions, but we are all engaged in *The Search for Answers*. The questioning mind produces *The Search for Knowledge*. Even today, in the midst of our knowledge explosion, our search for knowledge has not diminished.

No civilization can endure without law and order. We think of law and authority, but what about law's values? Is justice served automatically by law? Tell me the laws of a nation and I will tell you what that nation values most. *The Search for Law and Values* is basic to an understanding of our culture.

In the midst of so much knowledge we hear little about wisdom. *The Search for Wisdom* seems a lost art, but wisdom—or the lack of it—decides our fate as individuals and nations.

Fairy stories always have happy endings: the prince and princess "lived happily ever after." Today's television productions for the young end in gunplay and murder. Neither of these extremes pictures true life. Happiness remains basic to all human existence. Its absence dries and withers the human spirit. But is happiness an end in itself? In *The Search for Happiness,* we may need to redefine happiness in order to make it a basic part of our philosophy of life.

In the heart of every man lives a utopia. Where *The Search for Utopias* is lacking, the heart grows cold and hard. But what kind of a utopia can a sane man afford?

Are We Making Progress? In many respects, we are living in a "twilight zone." We are moving away from the old order of things, but it is not yet clear whether the new order will bring progress or chaos. Both possibilities exist. Will we be able to make the rapid changes necessary, during this painful period of revolutionary transition? The answer depends on whether or not we will be alert and decisive enough to seize the unusual opportunities available to us in our rapidly expanding technological development.

Part II starts with *The Search for God.* What is God and how can we define Him? All of the world's great religions have attempted to present a god and some of his attributes. But, what is religion? My definition is basic to an understanding of our *Search for God.*

The Search for Immortality and Eternal Life are almost universal. From time immemorial, past civilizations had some notions regarding immortality and hope for eternal life. This search is especially important to the meaningfulness of eternal life.

The Search for Certainty is another basic search found in the religions and the philosophies of the past. In our time, the cry for security from the cradle to the grave shows a total lack of certainty. Lost in the complexity and confusion of modern life and bewildered by the tentativeness of modern knowledge, the individual is groping for certainty. In which direction should he search?

The Search for Self seems most important to many people. But the self gains its importance only in relation to others. The self participates in two processes: it instigates action and, in turn, it is acted upon. We may endure or suffer life. On the other hand, the shackles of restraint may be broken, and we may act with freedom, power and decisiveness. Man has free choice. However, can we separate freedom from suffering? What *is* the self in the process of evolution? Is there meaning for the self in suffering?

Perhaps the most difficult search of all is *The Search for Consciousness*—the "purpose" of evolution in evolving and emphasizing consciousness. In the words of Pierre Teilhard de Chardin, the chief goal of evolution is "the

28

ascent toward consciousness." But consciousness, as we know it and experience it, is not the final end; it is merely the beginning of eternal life. We are created in the image of that Great Consciousness we call God. Our life's task is to enlarge and to improve that image so that the end of man will turn into the beginning of supraman. Consciousness is more than reason; it includes emotion, will and vision. *Creative consciousness is both the eye and the heart of the universe.* Spirit and matter are but the two aspects of that mysterious thing we call life.

Throughout the ages men have debated the various aspects of reality. Contradictory as it may seem, it is nevertheless true that as we advance in knowledge reality seems to become more illusive. In *The Search for Reality,* we combine the concepts of consciousness and reality as the creative principle of the universe.

The Search Eternal is our final search. Actually, man's searching of whatever nature is based on the search eternal. The search eternal is the backbone of the universe, but it is also more than that. Out of the search eternal came the universe and life as we know it. The significance of eternal life—as we experience an ever-growing awareness and an expanding creativity—is rooted in the search eternal.

2

THE SEARCH FOR EXISTENCE

Basically, the search for existence falls into two categories: 1) the compulsive seeking which relates man to the animals in his need for food and shelter; 2) those searches which grow out of human desires for more than physical existence. In this study, we are primarily concerned with the desires leading man to search for higher goals.

The concept of "man" is fundamental, but what *is* man? This very old question has been answered in many ways and by all kinds of people from ancient to modern times.

To the physicist, man is ultimately a mathematical equation. As Bertrand Russell once said, "If we only knew enough mathematics, we could explain everything." But we don't know enough mathematics and man is still an unknown quantity. To the theologian, we are immortal souls. While this answer may be emotionally satisfying, what, specifically, are souls? And what is immortality? To the educator, we are imitators and fact collectors. If that is all we are—and that is all that education provides—how can we ever hope to solve the problems we have been led to believe education might enable us to master? The historian considers man the child of yesterday and an uncertain pillar of the future. What certainty can we derive from those historians who are still arguing about what caused the fall of Rome? The Freudian psychiatrist looks upon man as the victim of his own childhood. Unfortunately, the authority upon which psychiatric theory is based is now so controversial that schools of psychiatry are becoming as numerous as sects within the Protestant religion. Perhaps a sense of humor will help us maintain a balance between such contradictory opinions.

Greater unanimity of opinion and deeper assurance exist in those areas where the scientific method was introduced. Only when medical men looked upon the body as a machine and applied the scientific method in analyzing its functions was great progress made in understanding the organism biologists call man.

In looking upon the body as a machine, however, science presents us with a contradiction. A machine is a tool which can be *used for a purpose,* but it cannot be said *to have a purpose.* A biologist who abandoned purpose in his study of the living cell would have to abandon biology. This difficulty was overcome by *not* using the word "purpose" in an extranatural or mystical sense; but by defining it as Sinnoth did, "as equivalent to the self-regulatory and goal-seeking factor of protoplasm, the accompaniment of the special organization of living substance," [2] By thus distinguishing the apparent difference between animate and inanimate substance, the problem of dualism was solved. I use the term "apparent" difference because, in reality, inorganic matter is as much an energy system as is organic substance and no energy system can be said to be inanimate. To our senses, however, matter *appears* to be inanimate.

What is man's body and brain in the eyes of science?

Man has a body which is not very different from that of the highest mammals. Although, in some respects, man is one of the animal kingdom's weaker species, he is nonetheless superior. Superior in what way? Bats can hear tones indiscernible to human ears; bees are able to sense polarized light; spiders can spin intricate traps; small humming birds are able to vibrate their wings with incredible speed in order to stay aloft while feeding. Not only do some animals have sense perceptions superior to ours, but the nerves and brain stems of most vertebrates are on a par with those of men.

The advance of man's biological evolution has been in his headward domination of a complex, integrated nervous system, or "encephalization," and of an enormous increase in the size of his brain.

This brain is receiving the closest attention of scientists everywhere and much has been learned during recent years.

The human brain has an immense capacity for adaptation, and without this ability to adapt to change, to explore the unknown, to use his creativity and to fulfill his aspirations, man would not be the creature he is. In studying this highly evolved being as if it were a machine, scientists do not mean to debase humanity. They employ the scientific method, which is based primarily on quantitative measurement, and through this process they find that the difference in quantity may produce differences in quality. It is much easier for a scientist to point out that at a certain pressure of quantity a new quality emerges than it is for him to analyze what that quality is. As yet, we have found no way to measure hope, will, faith, love and aspiration.

Whether a teleological explanation is scientifically valid appears to depend on how we interpret it.

MAN AND HIS ENVIRONMENT

Our environment affects us in so many ways it would be a considerable task to list them. Man, however, is the only animal who is not only affected by his environment but can, to a degree, control and change it.

With all our undisputed development in scientific progress, we often forget how recently all this progress has come. This supercivilization of ours, so amazingly clean and antiseptic, is only 150 years removed from the filth and disease that is still present in the slums and villages of the Far East. People in such undeveloped countries may be said to exist, to *endure* life rather than to enjoy it. But life is not meant to be endured; evolution requires change and growth; life in its fullest sense demands conquest rather than submission. In a primitive society, life may seem to stand still—the poor Chinese peasant or the African tribesman goes out of life very much the same way he came in.

The contrary is true in our Western society. In America, we state openly that the pursuit of happiness is a legitimate endeavor. In the midst of our great wealth and with our constant capacity to produce more goods than our own people can consume, one would think that the millennium had arrived in the USA. Yet never has there been a time when people seemed more afraid of the future and less secure in themselves.

The advancement of modern society, over that of a primitive one, does not depend on greater brain power but on stronger motivation. This motivation has been expressed in our industrialization by constant research, which has resulted in better and more efficient tools. The difference in environments, between a primitive and an advanced culture, is manifested by the complexity and the facility of the tools evolved by each. The incentive towards progress in our culture has been developed through a social and economic structure known as capitalism, and compulsory education has made knowledge of the world in which we live readily available to everyone.

But this nutshell description of our modern culture does not explain our unhappiness. Are we dissatisfied because we see that scientific progress has not enabled us to control our own fate? Do we despair because our understanding of nature and man has not increased our capacity to solve our personal problems? Are we fearful because we have become such tiny factors within the scope of an almost overwhelming social organism that leaves us nearly powerless?

The answer may be that we will have to shift the various levels of our adjustment. Whereas primitive man makes personal adjustments to his immediate environment, civilized man must make social and political adaptations.

AN ANTIUNIVERSE

Each year new discoveries are made by man's exploration of space, probing the atmosphere of the moon and planets and focusing our telescopes on distant galaxies. In increasing measure we are becoming citizens of the cosmos as well as of the earth. Physicists and astronomers are deeply involved in exploring the nature of man's environment.

They are very interested in a recent discovery of Dr. Leon M. Lederman and his associates, who conducted experiments with the world's most powerful atom smasher, the 33-billion electron volt synchrotron at Brookhaven National Observatory, Upton, New York.

These experiments demonstrated the existence of antideuterons. The antideuteron is the first complex atomic nucleus of antimatter to be found.

For every particle within the atom, such as protons and neutrons, there is presumed to be an antiparticle with a different electrical charge or other characteristics.

When physicists break atomic cores apart in atom smashers, they observe that particles such as the proton and antiproton are created in equal numbers from the energy applied.

The antideuteron is composed of an antiproton and an antineutron, which are held together by a strong nuclear force. Its opposite, our "normal" deuteron, consists of a proton and a neutron. Since we have proof that the antideuteron does exist and is as "real" as the "normal" deuteron, there is good reason to believe that very complex atoms and molecules and even organizations or planets of antimatter may also exist.

"It is no longer possible," writes Dr. Lederman, in "Physical Review Letters," "to question the basic physics part of the cosmological conception of a literal antiworld populated by stars and planets . . . and made up of atoms of anti-matter: negative nuclei surrounded by positive electrons.

"It is not possible now to disprove the grand speculation that these antiworlds could be populated by thinking creatures—perhaps now excited by the discovery of deuterium." Deuterium is the earth form of the nucleus of heavy hydrogen.

If the concept that the universe began with a "big bang" explosion of a primeval atom is correct, Dr. Lederman thinks there is every reason to believe that the same number of particles and antiparticles were created.

This new discovery establishing the reality of antimatter makes it possible for physicists to speculate about the existence of an antiworld and even an antiuniverse. Where this antiworld may be located is not yet known, nor is there any evidence as yet that the antiworld mingles with or interpenetrates the known physical universe.

What we do know is that antimatter is the reverse, or mirror image, of matter as we know it. When bits of matter and antimatter meet, they annihilate each other, turning into heat and light.

Considering that if two inhabitants—one from the earth and the other from the antiworld—could meet and shake hands, both would disappear in a flash of light, heat and radiation, it may be desirable to postpone our knowledge of the actual location of the antiworld.

The more we discover and know, the more fascinating the unknown becomes. If such an antiuniverse can exist, without us being able to see or experience it, does it not strengthen our faith in a spirit world—a universe of consciousness apart from our physical three-dimensional existence, a world we can neither see nor experience directly but which exists as surely as does antimatter? Certainly such a belief in the existence of consciousness independent of physical substance seems no longer fantastic. The belief that the existence of the soul and its eternal life is no longer to be considered a mere religious superstition, confronts us with the responsibility for the future destiny of that soul, as well as for its purpose of dwelling in the body.

The meaning of eternal life must somehow be connected with the meaning of our life in the flesh. In our search for the meaning of life, we may find that earthly existence is but a phase in the evolution of the soul's eternal destiny. Thus, we need to develop a value system in our physical environment, in which man's goals for progress will reflect his spiritual values and aspirations.

MAN AND HIS GOALS

Anthropologists have told us that men without tools live practically like savages and that there is a direct relationship between the development of tools and the advancement of material civilization. Modern culture is equally dependent upon *intellectual* tools for the ideological development of its society.

Science is especially adept in quantitative measurement and analysis; it places great emphasis on ascribing the variation in quality to a basic difference in degree. Such a measurement, however, will not work so well in areas where quantitative analysis seems next to impossible. In our society, man exists not only in a quantitative system, but he is very much involved in, and affected by, a quality system.

Quality resolves itself into value, and value involves choice. Choice is at the crossroads of all of our aims and purposes. Nature, as we have observed, displays her purpose in protoplasm. Every living cell acts as if it "knows" where it is going and what it is supposed to accomplish. It divides, differentiates, and adapts to specific functions of the entire organism. But whatever it does, whatever its degree of consciousness may be, it has no choice but to follow a purpose clearly observable in nature's predetermined plan. With the emergence of man's self-consciousness, however, *nature goes into partnership with her own product!*

In developing his scientifically-oriented Western culture, man has done well in making choices generally. His goals—the eradication of many diseases, the industrialization of most mechanical activities, the development of astonishingly fast transportation, the creation of efficient architectural techniques, and many more—have all been met with truly remarkable agility and success.

For man himself, success does not seem so obvious. The goal here seems to be progress without pain—tranquilization has become our motto. Perhaps we should take hope in the words of Margaret Mead, who is reported to have said: "Man's study of man is not new. But, man's *scientific* study of himself is the youngest of the sciences."

Man's adaptation to change has never been easy. An interesting story is told about a young Hopi Indian who had been well educated in the East and who had returned home to visit his father. The old man had been to see the medicine man to ask for help in preventing sore ankles—which he believed he would get if he walked on the tracks of a snake. The young Hopi was indignant and tried to convince his father of the ridiculousness of such an idea. To prove it and to reveal the medicine man as a humbug, the lad walked in the tracks of a snake—and developed sore ankles!

Why? Because in his rapidly changing society, the

young man's *anxiety-inducing factors had outlived his anxi-ety-resolving factors.*

In simple language, even though we may free ourselves intellectually, our subconscious mind is still there to play us a dirty trick—as it did with the young Hopi.

The Hopi Indian story tells us something else. The father's motivation was to avoid getting sore ankles. The son's motivation was to prove his father wrong. The father, by giving in to a superstition, gained his desire, while the son, by proclaiming his enlightenment, was frustrated. Secure as we moderns may be in our own knowledge, we *know* that the father was wrong and that the son was right; nevertheless the results were satisfactory only to the ignorant.

Of course, this story doesn't prove that being wrong makes one the strongest; it reveals the wondrous complexity of the human mind and illustrates how *illusions can be beneficial to us at certain stages of development.* It also shows us that education alone cannot raise backward peoples to higher levels of consciousness, response, and adaptation overnight. Culture involves a long series of adaptations and requires a great deal more than mere book learning—a lesson that seems very difficult for Americans to learn. Since World War II, we have had significant experiences in this area, and we have made many errors. For some strange reason, we seem to persist in thinking that what is best for us must be equally good for all others. Nothing could be further from the truth.

In studying other cultures, we can become more tolerant of other peoples and more objective about ourselves, thus freeing ourselves from the domination of our own culture. There are many ideals common to all men, especially all those of the so-called Western civilization, but our searches are directed primarily to those found in our American culture.

If a nuclear war were to destroy our country's population, leaving only 100 infants in the care of a deaf and dumb couple, all of the children would grow up to be like savages, because language is the basis of civilization. All the culture, all the knowledge held in libraries, all the scientific advancement of which we are so proud would mean nothing! No one would be able to read, to write, or to use mathematical symbols.

While this would be an unlikely occurrence, it gives us a clear picture of our dependence upon one another. *No man is civilized by himself;* he is so only in relation to others.

Our purposes are dependent on our civilization; our motivations must operate within the framework of our own culture.

Desire is the root of all life. Nations, like individuals, have goals and, as one destination is reached, another is set up in its place. As a man reaches one hilltop, he looks towards the next. When he satisfies one desire, he immediately seeks the fulfillment of another. When he stops setting up goals for himself, he dies. His body may continue to function automatically, but "the spirit has gone out of him."

Our modern culture links the will to live with the desire to do things and it is the evaluation of desire in terms of accomplishment that has enriched our concept of existence. Such an enrichment, however, is not the answer to our search. It is only a candle lighting our way in the darkness.

3

THE SEARCH FOR ANSWERS

The first rebuttal used by a very young child is: "Why?" "Why do you scold me?" "Why can't I touch things I want to feel?" "Why must I do things I don't want to do?" "Why are you telling me things I do not understand?"

A little child must wonder a dozen times a day why Mom and Dad will not let him touch all those interesting objects he sees about the house. How can he find out what they really are unless he *feels* them? He cannot understand his parents' reasoning, for the child's understanding and vocabulary must develop together.

Inevitably, the search for answers becomes a basic part of everyone's life and, to a large extent, our search for answers depends on our emotional temperaments and social conditioning.

The ultrabigoted and extremely ignorant man seeks answers in much the same manner as did the primitive man, who had a good reason to be emotional. The unknown impinged on the primitive man from all directions. The powers of nature and the structure of his own body were a complete mystery to him. He could not reach out to the stars and, like a child of today, he had no way of understanding them. But, unlike today's child, he had no parents or teachers to give him the answers.

When his own ignorance could not provide the answer, primitive man called upon the spirits of fire and water, earth and sky, sun and moon to do so. Prompted by his emotional needs, he used his imagination to provide the answers.

Seldom do we remember that all civilizations have proceeded from the imagery of man and that our own childhood is a phase of primitive life. The primitive man asked: "Why are the gods angry?" The child may ask: "Why are my parents mad at me?" Unsatisfactory answers to both questions may bring feelings of guilt.

The child reared in a happy home may overcome his feelings of guilt and frustration, because the love of his parents is stronger than his fear of them, and their example of harmonious living may enable him to force his emotional imageries into patterns of rational thinking and conduct.

The unfortunate primitive man was the first and worst orphan of nature. To appease the angry gods, who were responsible for his misfortune, sacrifice and burned offerings seemed the only answer.

To many students the Judeao-Christian traditions seem full of such anger and sacrifice, and not until the time of Jesus was life clearly personified in love. Yet, even today, aren't most people basing their lives on fear rather than love?

While we do not subscribe to the old statement that the first seven years of a child's life *irrevocably* determine the course of a person's life, there is no gainsaying the fact that these early years are the most important ones for every human being. During the first seven years of our lives, the inner drives, the feelings, the temperament and the basic characteristics represented by our individual genes meet the restraint and direction of our environment. All of these things, together with early educational guidance, may determine the particular manner in which the child—and later the adult—will ask questions for the rest of his life. If his emotional life takes precedence, he will never change from the "Why" questions he asked as a child and, in all probability, he will be slow in his search for *what* a thing is and *how* it works.

Science does not know *why* the universe is; it sees no reason for it having been created. But science does explain, in precise detail, *what* many things are. It also analyzes organic and inorganic matter and formulates speculative theories ranging from evolution to relativity, and about the beginning, scope and probable end of life and the universe.

We should add that these speculative theories of science are always tested, proved, accepted or rejected by experimental verification wherever it is possible; it is in the function of existence, however—*how* the thing works— that the task of science becomes a gloriously fulfilling one. The child's question about the "why" is raised thereby to a much higher philosophical level as we begin to ask for the intelligent *reason* why.

Physicists tell us how matter behaves; biologists tell us how our bodies and all protoplasms function; chemistry explains how one's physical elements react on one another; geology gives us an idea how time beyond the normal experience of man affects the crust of the earth on which we live. Biochemistry shows us how the functions of the organic and inorganic intermingle; psychology and psychiatry reveal *how* the mind works.

43

It is in psychology that modern man meets his greatest and most perplexing challenge. Many of the events with which science deals are predictable, because the data and their measurements are reliable and easily classified. Psychology deals with subjective data, states of consciousness which are not only highly variable and unreliable because they are subject to choice, but which also are never pure. It is never possible for any one of us to enter the mind of another completely and in utter secrecy. Although modern psychology tries to work with overt behavior, it still has to make its inferences about that which cannot be directly observed. Thus, the mental states of any individual are always colored to some extent by the intruder—be he scientist, psychologist, or anyone else. In observing his own mental processes, the psychologist becomes both the observer and the observed. These two functions are not equally scientific. Psychology deals with the imponderable as well as with the ponderable. At times, it is an experimental science, but it is also an art and a philosophy.

In psychology, while the problem of choice can be analyzed theoretically in terms of individual motivation, in practice it remains imponderable. When it is analyzed, the human will may dissolve, like matter, into an energy quotient, unrecognizable to our experience. Perhaps physicians interested in psychosomatic medicine have been most responsible for bringing the human will back into respectable usage. The will to live and the will to die, the will to be healthy and the will to be sick are by no means empty phrases.

We recognize the importance of motivation, but how do we direct and control it?

MOTIVATION, SEMANTICS, AND SCIENCE

Symbols are the apples on our tree of knowledge. We eat them at our own risk.

A civilization without symbols is unthinkable; symbols can also ruin a civilization. By manipulating symbols, Hitler transformed a nation and nearly the whole world.

The ruthless will to conquest motivated Hitler to direct and control mass thinking and action. Hitler's propaganda was successful because it was aimed at developing mass symbolism, as Communism's today. By ceaseless repetition, mass symbolism can be turned readily into mass hysteria, especially when the symbolism refers to hate, revenge, or fear—emotions shared more by humanity at large than are the love and forgiveness of one's enemies preached by Jesus.

Democracies' propaganda is weak compared to that of dictatorships' because it appeals to good neighborliness rather than to hate, fear, and revenge.

Are dictators successful because they appeal to the evil in man rather than to his better nature? Some religionists may answer this question in the affirmative. The answer of both science and semantics is "No."

To the religionist, man is evil because he gives in or is controlled by the demon within himself. In the view of the scientist, man gives in to emotional hysteria because he is controlled by his subconscious mind which, in too many cases, is filled with fantasies based on misinformation.

If we are controlled by our emotions, how will we be able to reverse the process? We cannot control our emotions; but we can, and must, control our thinking, for only by our thinking may we control our emotions—in greater or lesser degree.

What is true of the dictator on a national or international level is true of every salesman or other individual to a lesser degree. All of us are hypnotized to some extent by what we read and by our contacts with other individuals. Therefore, we need to be fully aware of the symbols we use each day, so that we may judge the apples on our tree of knowledge before we eat them.

Our language is not predominantly made up of words about facts, but of words about words. Unless we recognize these differences between facts and words, between symbols (language) and reality, we may create a mental world of fantasy and illusion.

If we are to find useful answers, our questions must be clearly stated. We must be willing to test our own beliefs and assumptions, and we may well do this in a general semantic way by asking, "What do I mean?" and, "How do I know?" If we differentiate between statements of fact and assumptions, we will be able to avoid vague or meaningless questions.

Although we may feel ourselves far removed from our savage ancestors, who projected themselves so crudely in most of their primitive concepts of life, we must never forget that we still project ourselves in all that we say and do. A major difference between those of us who try to practice semantics and primitive man is that we carry out the natural process of projection, highly aware of what we are doing and why we are doing it.

The major purpose of general semantics is to enable one to have "fewer and fewer misconceptions about more and more things until finally one no longer has any delusions about anything." In other words, the prime objective of general semantics is to make us conscious of abstracting in order to escape from the tyranny of words.

46

The mechanics of general semantics cannot be condensed into a few pages, yet a clear conception of language symbols and language structure is most important in our search for answers. We cannot communicate with one another unless we are speaking the same language, in terms of meanings which are understandable.

Science defines reality not as an absolute thing, substance or essence, but as a continuing process of change. All matter can be converted into energy. To the scientist, the entire universe, including man, is an energy system. Reality is a process made up of energy components or energy "flows." The substance-or-essence philosophy has been replaced by a philosophy of process and relativity. Philosophers are no longer preoccupied with such questions as the absolute, the infinite, the perfect or absolute reality.

The general public has not readily understood the trend among scientists and philosophers to accept tentative answers to important questions; nor has this trend seemed an unmixed blessing. Although many people welcome the benefits from applied science, they have not understood why, with so much knowledge of our present world, we seem so uncertain of everything. Today, millions of people expect to find in philosophy all of the answers to satisfy their need for a sense of security. A dynamic life asks questions and demands answers, but any enlightened individual should know *how* to ask questions and should be willing to run the risk of informative but inconclusive answers.

General semantics came into being as an answer to this need. Its founder, Alfred Korzybski, and his followers have shown us that a sane life is based on sane thinking. They have also provided us with techniques to escape from the tyranny of words. The perusal of any good book on general semantics will aid us in formulating scientific questions and in deriving sane answers.

SIFTING OUR QUESTIONS

Our first task is to sift our questions. Perhaps there is no more worthwhile effort than the one of rejecting the wrong questions. As we have observed, science generally neglects to ask "Why" and, while not ignoring the "What," concerns itself primarily with the "How" questions.

Unlike the scientist, our search for human goals cannot so easily discard the "Whys" and "Whats." Like philosophers we shall have to be concerned with the reasons why some are more valid than others. Yet there is much that science can teach us about the manner of asking questions.

The most dramatic illustration of the successful application in science of the "how" questions is in the amazing accomplishment of nuclear fission. The scientist does not know why the atom bomb exists, but he is very much concerned with *what* constitutes an atom bomb chemically and physically and with *how* it can be safely produced, stored and transported. The social scientist may deal with issues concerning *how* the use of the bomb may be controlled and prevented.

To the question "What is an atom?" the scientist may answer: The atom is a useful concept in our thinking, just as the mile or kilometer is a useful measurement of distance. In the process of energy flows, which may be likened to a road stretching indefinitely in both directions, the atom's energy field may flow in either direction from microcosm to macrocosm or vice versa. Subdivisions of the atom, such as the electron, neutron, and positron, are useful mental concepts, which some day may be further subdivided. No one has ever seen electrons, neutrons or positrons, but we can calculate their existence by the *behavior* of this unseen world of energy.

For the scientist, reality is a process of seen or unseen, imaginable or unimaginable events; but events which can be calculated and described in mathematical symbols, and events which may potentially be verified by observation.

Human beings, however, cannot operate as researchers who, in the context of strict scientific inquiry, have no need for questions about ultimate reality or ultimate purpose. Scientists may legitimately act as naturalist philosophers for their method works in the laboratory. But we do not *live* in laboratories.

We are not only physical, we are mental and spiritual as well. This seeming trinity is, however, a complete unity. Man's agelong habit of dividing things into black or white, up or down, physical or nonphysical, seen or unseen, has done much to preserve the either-or philosophy of Aristotle, for more than two thousand years.

We do not need to *prove* the existence of God, nor the *reality* of spiritual laws, if we can show that a *belief in God is beneficial and that spiritual laws work*. Let us use the scientific method, insofar as we are able to apply it to all areas of knowledge, freeing ourselves from dogmatism and the folly that in this ever more mysterious universe we have the last answer to any question whether it be in science or religion. If science cannot provide answers to the whys of the universe, why should religion be embarrassed if it cannot explain why God created the universe?

What we need to do is to study the spiritual laws and

from their content build our concept of the Creator as He may be and how He has structured this universe for His and our purpose.

Such a concept is essential for both understanding and motivation, if we are to reach our highest goal.

I agree that only by observing and analyzing ourselves and our environment do we acquire any understanding about the universe, but I depart from the humanists and the naturalist philosophers because I do believe in a reality outside of ourselves—a power greater than ourselves, a consciousness far superior to ours.

We must accept tentative answers to our own as well as to other people's questions, and we make no claims to ultimate truth. We are aware of our human limitations but, like many scientists and philosophers, we do not believe that we need to limit our assumptions to those which are verifiable by our present knowledge, as long as we differentiate clearly between fact and assumption. If we do this, we can count ourselves in good company for, when Leopold Infeld asked Albert Einstein whether there is any reality outside of us, Einstein answered, "Yes, I believe in it."

I believe in the common sense approach to everyday affairs. But science cannot be understood by common sense; common sense never taught us the rules by which we test our scientific hypotheses. Scientists, who have learned to comprehend the unimaginable, have acquired the habit of thinking in strange new concepts, totally inaccessible to common sense.

In asking questions about the meaning of life on earth and man's journey through the cosmos, we too must be willing to slough off our old habits of thinking and accept new concepts totally at variance with our preconceived notions.

SETTING OUR GOALS

Perhaps two of the most difficult questions all of us ask ourselves, sooner or later, are: "Why do we search for a goal?" "What is our purpose in life?" The third question which flows from these is: "How do we accomplish our purpose?"

Science, in showing us how society operates, does not tell us how we ought to behave nor what our goals should be. For science is descriptive, amoral; while it accepts the universe on physical and mechanistic terms, it provides us with no direction, no purpose for our lives.

We should not blame science, however, for, in being amoral, science fulfills its function. But, in being amoral, man is like a straw in the wind; he may have lost his feeling of guilt and be unrestrained, but he has no direction. Science need not concern itself with the question of whether the universe is friendly, hostile or indifferent to men. But this question is of utmost concern to us, because the assumption of a friendly, hostile or indifferent universe—to man—makes all the difference in the world in his concept of values. A universe without a sense of direction leaves man at the mercy of a force that can best be summed up as chaos. This feeling of chaos is exactly what troubles so many people who, in the midst of scientific advancement, do not feel secure in what appears a purposeless universe.

The assumption of a universe with a sense of direction shapes our attitude toward life and links the purpose of

51

man to a higher goal. Our faith in a friendly universe will provide a sense of relationship with, and unity between, man and his environment.

The mind is like a mirror; it reflects whatever one thinks or desires. Whatever we think or desire is dependent on our motivation. Our motivation is largely determined and controlled by our attitude. Our attitude is all-important, since purpose without attitude cannot exist. If we believe that the universe is directionless, then we shall find no purpose in the universe. If we believe that man and his civilization are hopeless, we shall find no purpose in this life.

Our assumption of a guiding, creative Intelligence in the universe need not chain us to a dogmatic past which rejects the discoveries of science; instead, we shall search for a spiritual evolution of man to be viewed side by side with his physical evolution. We shall accept happily the findings of science, as it probes into the secrets of life; and we shall emphasize equally the importance of our attitude toward life.

What we can do with electricity is more important to most of us than what the nature of its final components may be. What we do with our lives is of more importance to us than what the biochemical solution of the life processes may be. Of all the important things in human life, none is more important than attitude.

Many years ago, I bypassed a counselor candidate, who had a Ph.D. in psychology, and accepted instead a young man who had not quite finished work for a B.A. degree. The former had the technical equipment we wanted, but not the proper attitude; the latter's situation was exactly the reverse. Gradually, that young man acquired degrees and technical background, and today he has become a successful director of guidance in our educational system.

Many universities could provide him with the required technical training; but only he himself could present that attitude which provides the balance between the empathy and the objectivity required in counseling. *

When we take a severe attitude toward civilized man, we may say that history, in a sense, is the running commentary on man's follies, showing how his changing illusions required a new set of crutches from time to time. If we take a more optimistic attitude we may say that history shows that in spite of his many illusions, man has made progress. Instead of making fun of man's crutches, we may consider them worthwhile supports for temporary use, like the scaffolding of a building under construction. The first statement emphasizes man's illusions and follies; the second emphasizes man's progress.

Life demands action. Action involves choice. Our attitudes determine our choices. No man can escape choosing, whether he does so irrationally or with semantically informed and unbiased care.

"Why do we search for a goal?" A goal is prompted by the necessity to promote the fulfillment of our basic needs. The nature of this goal is determined by our attitude toward the universe and all of life.

"What is our purpose?" Our purpose is to set goals that are not contradictory to, but also not limited by science; to present attitudes that will enhance our goals towards a better life in this world; and to present a concept that allows for the presence of a consciousness other than that possessed by men on earth.

An awareness of the eternal, even in the midst of our relativistic world, can provide a steady point of reference for evaluation, as well as a platform for projecting our vision into the unknown and for deriving new concepts for our understanding of this changing world of human experience.

"How do we plan to accomplish this purpose?" The succeeding chapters are our attempt to answer this purpose. It is vitally important to take our first steps carefully. To find a steady point of reference in such a relativistic world as ours may be as big a task as launching a space platform. How do we get the force to start on our way? Just where shall we begin?

We can begin only with ourselves. We can't get that space platform off the ground unless our machinery functions in good order. We can't receive correct answers to our questions until we know what we are doing. We cannot possibly know what we are doing if we are confused. We are confused when we do not have control over our thinking. We can have control over our thinking only if we are honest with ourselves.

Success depends wholly on honesty. Science is successful primarily because it is "honest." Most, if not all, of the problems in our unscientific lives are due to dishonesty: dishonesty to others and dishonesty to ourselves. Of the two, the latter is the greater offender. *How* do we get honesty?

We can achieve the honesty we need for correct thinking, very simply. Each night before retiring, scan the major events of the day and relive for a moment the successes and failures, pains and disappointments, as well as the joys and achievements. If the mind revolts at painful or embarrassing events of the day, recall each situation clearly and face it fully. One may blush freely in the privacy of one's own mind and, in so doing, the emotional pressures will be released and the mind will be calmed. In being honest with ourselves, we pray with all our hearts, minds and strength. The great creative consciousness, which we call God, does the curing and gives the answers.

In our review of the daily events, it is important that we face each and every unpleasant situation, even if the mistake seems trivial or slightly foolish. Only by facing each action completely and by accepting the reality of each occurrence can we truly accept ourselves as we are. Once we accept ourselves realistically (which means with full understanding and forgiveness), we will be amazed how hatreds, regrets and resentments disappear. (This technique requires willpower, and it must be practiced consistently, in order to be effective.)

When our emotional life is bathed in reality, the unpleasantness of the mistakes we have made is burnt out, and no emotional feelings of regret, guilt or resentment can hide in our subconscious mind. Reality needs no hiding place.

It is one of the great contradictions of human life that many people are nicer than they appear to be, although they make every effort to appear nicer than they think they are. Most of us recognize pretense in others; and, poor actors that we are, we think what we really are can be hidden from others. Honesty with ourselves is the basis for all honesty.

Shakespeare said it so well, in *Hamlet*:

> *This above all; to thine own self be true,*
> *And it must follow, as the night the day,*
> *Thou canst not then be false to any man.*

This simple process of facing oneself may be a little painful, especially at first, but there is *no progress without pain*. We use the word "pain" here in the sense of effort,

effort expended in a task which is needful but which may not be pleasant. (The policy of self-evaluation recommended here does not deny that there may be justifiable bases for guilt feelings and situations that call for forgiveness and reconciliation in our relations with others.)

In our various searches, we may face many unpleasant questions which may require relinquishment of old concepts and acceptance of new ones. With our understanding of semantics, the contributions made by the sciences, the use of the scientific method aided by critical judgment; with honesty as our motive and an attitude of willingness to accept whatever our searches may reveal, we are now ready to search for answers. We must be aware constantly of our limitations and be willing now, as in the future, however, to revise our concepts in the light of further knowledge and insights.

4

THE SEARCH FOR KNOWLEDGE

Everyone talks about knowledge, but do we really know what it is? Throughout the centuries great minds have studied the "nature" of knowledge, only to find it as illusive as the nature of the atom.

The study of knowledge is called "epistemology," which *Webster's Unified Dictionary and Encyclopedia* defines as "the study of the nature and origin of knowledge, and especially its limits, and degree of foundation on truth and fact." This study has led to the writing of a great many technical books. Unfortunately, these ponderous volumes have made exceedingly meager contributions to our general understanding. They have been successful primarily in clarifying the "limits" of human knowledge.

Protagoras declared 2400 years ago that man is the measure of all things. This thought may not be too encouraging but, for better or worse, man seems to be the center of all things—at least of those with which he is acquainted. What he knows is rudimentary; until now he has been unable to grasp, understand, and define absolutes. But, by avoiding absolutes and accepting the relativity of man-made concepts, by using semantics and the modern analysis of language structure, I believe we can make successful strides on the road to progress, and advance steadily in our search eternal.

WHAT IS KNOWLEDGE?

If we consider knowledge as an "acquaintance with fact," we must recognize how dependent all of us are on accumulated knowledge—the countless facts that have been gathered through recorded history for our use. The information gathered in our books and libraries does not become knowledge, however, until there is an acquaintance with facts. That acquaintance can be made only by an individual brain.

How do we become acquainted with facts? Before a baby can understand words, he feels. Emotional response precedes cognition, or verbalization, but if the child can't hear, his knowledge of the world will depend, in addition to feeling, on observation, taste, smell, and sign language.

For a child deprived of the senses of sight and hearing, most of his knowledge must come through touch. Helen Keller is the classic example of the difficulties encountered in gaining knowledge through the senses of touch, taste and smell only; nevertheless, she learned to communicate, and even to speak.

Some linguists claim that we do not talk because we are thinking, but that we think only because we are able to talk.

Bertrand Russell was not convinced that there can be no thought without language. He asserted that there is no definite and unambiguous answer to the question: "What do we mean by knowledge?" [3]

Would it not be better to say that before Helen Keller

58

was able to use language her emotional response was a form of irrational thought? And that only by the use of language—aided, of course, by loving guidance—did she acquire the habit of rational thinking?

All of us acquire speech before we learn to write. Language as the spoken word is as old as man. But writing has a short history of only a few thousand years. When we started to write, we learned that speech was not the same as writing. Our introduction to grammar and our assimilation of language structure in writing was so gradual that we looked upon language as consisting only of words. Since writing took more effort than speech and we learned that spelling and other language structures required more precision in writing, we felt a greater reverence for the printed word than for the spoken word. But do we communicate more effectively on the printed page than by speech? Perhaps—if we can say that the writer is more skillful than the actor. The two techniques of communication are vastly different.

The scientific study of language structure is a rather recent development. Linguists explain that communication is more than language. They point out that we do not converse in a vacuum and that bodily motions, as well as variations in the tone of voice, have a great deal to do with our communication system. Our tone of voice, its high or low pitch, its oversoftness or overloudness, and the smile or scowl on our faces may mean just the opposite of what our words are saying.

In order to communicate fully, people must not only speak the same language, they must have the same or a similar cultural background. Culture and language are inextricably interwoven. Culture began with the invention of language; as culture changes so does language.

One of the major difficulties we have had with Russia has been the difference in our two cultures and our different attitude towards the same words. Terms like "social development," "freedom," "democracy," and "peace-loving peoples" have different symbolical meanings for the Russians than they have for us.

Our "acquaintance with facts" is therefore not a simple process, as Lyman Bryson has said so well: "Human knowledge is not only a jungle of facts; it is a well-ordered structure . . . the specific facts in any subject are far less important than the basic concept around which they are arranged." [4] But how difficult it is to remain aware of this as we endeavor to communicate.

Linguists claim that we can get at meaning *only through structure,* but that we cannot get at structure through meaning. They also believe that structure itself may be one of the principal shapers of what we call our thoughts and ideas.

There are two important and practical aspects of the search for knowledge, which we should keep uppermost in our minds: 1) if we could find complete answers to every question easily, we would discover ourselves inhabitants of a static universe too boring to contemplate; 2) our tree of knowledge has many branches and it is growing rapidly. Its roots are lost in the mysteries of its origin—the earth—but we know the *roots are there* and we *have* the tree!

Rather than getting lost in an endless verbalization about the "nature" of knowledge, I will use the pictorial illustration given by Bertrand Russell in his preface to *Human Knowledge*:

Our increase in knowledge, assuming that we are successful, is like that of a traveler approaching a mountain through a haze. At first, only certain large features are discernible and even they have indistinct boundaries, but gradually more detail becomes visible and edges become sharper. So, in our discussions, it is impossible first to clear up one problem and then proceed to another, for the intervening haze envelops all alike. At every stage, though one part of our problem may be in the focus of attention, all parts are more or less relevant.[5]

The search for knowledge is an attempt to extend our intellectual horizon and to increase our understanding of life. It will always be an individual attempt crowned by individual success or failure. Sometimes, we will "see through a glass darkly," and, at other times, the haze will clear a little. But, whatever concepts we create out of the welter of facts presented to us will always be, particularly, our own concepts. They may not always be right, but they will be unique.

HOW DO WE ACQUIRE KNOWLEDGE?

Our brief analysis of the meaning of knowledge shows how uncertain and incomplete all human knowledge is, but because we cannot be dogmatically certain of anything, we must not assume that it does not matter how we acquire our knowledge, or that it is unimportant whether or not we acquire knowledge at all. In the growing complexity of our civilization, the demand for increased knowledge is inevitable. It is important to know our limitations and to realize what the relationship between words and symbols is, between language structure and thinking, and how observation, sense experience and language combine in our communication systems.

We come into this world not as full-fledged human beings, but as helpless little animals in whom the potential of *becoming* human beings resides. We must *learn* to become human beings by acquiring the thought patterns and absorbing the language structures of our human cultures.

An infant learns to smile without understanding any words, and a precocious youngster may have a fair-sized vocabulary by the age of two or three, without fully understanding the meaning of half of the words he uses. He has learned words before he has learned their meanings. This process, in some measure, may continue throughout his life. For the youngster, the real meaning of life comes not from verbalization, but from sense experience. Perceptions through sight and hearing are noticeably important; for the child, like a dog, watches the expressions on the faces of his elders and listens to the tonal inflections of the words used.

Thus, early in life we acquire a sense of duality between what is said and what is meant. This meaning, in terms of emotional content, attaches itself gradually to some words, until it becomes an integral part of these words, although in actuality our emotional meaning has no valid relationship to either the word used or to the thing it stands for. Our emotional responses toward our culture in general, and to our immediate environment in particular, are well-developed before we reach school age.

One of the important sense expressions we seem to underemphasize is the sense of touch. Babies put everything into their mouths—from forks and spoons to bolts and nuts. We smile when the baby tries to eat his shoe, but a little later we shout: "Don't touch!" The poor, confused child tries to understand his environment by feeling it. Society demands that children be prevented from examining objects that come within their observation and, in learning to be "nice" little boys and girls, some of us succeed so well that we lose interest in examining things ever after. We become content to accept whatever is offered us. Fortunately, this is not true of some courageous souls, who continue to be obnoxious and to analyze everything that is presented to them.

A great deal of controversy has swirled about whether our schools should place their major effort on *what* to think or *how* to think. For the simple acquisition of knowledge, content is most important, but knowledge is more than factual content or *what* we think. For decision making and for research, which is the discovery of new facts, we must learn *how* to think. Both what to think and how to think are important; and we should concentrate on applying both and in applying them at the right time and place.

A culture like ours could not continue without constant drilling on what to think. Memorizing French irregular verbs; correct pronunciation of German; grammatical structure of English; chemical formulas; laws of physics and biology; the learning of trades such as carpentry, mechanics or bricklaying depend primarily on parrotlike imitation. In acquiring any of these facts, the emphasis is on the *what;* but to apply them concretely, as when the bricklayer must build a curving wall, a rounded ceiling or a fancy fireplace, or the young chemist seek a new formula to cure a disease, the *how* becomes all important. A civilization without creative faculties to provide stimulus for progress would soon wither and die. On the other hand, a civilization that does not know what to think would stop automatically.

Americans are proud of their educational system, and rightly so. Yet, we are often confused in our evaluation of the educational processes and more than vague in our educational philosophy.

One of the greatest, if not *the* greatest, challenge for our educational system of today and the future lies in the proper direction of the emotions. And where can this challenge best be met? Not in college, not in high school or grade school, but in the nursery. If I had my way, we would spend a few billion dollars of federal money, which is now wasted on granaries filled with rotting food, on obsolete weapons and battleships collecting rust, or on pork barrel money for our congressmen, on training teacher-counselors of nursery schools throughout the land. In these nurseries I would include three- as well as four-year-olds. Instead of allowing children to waste time at home trying to amuse themselves or being restrained by tyrant mothers who nag, "Don't do this" and "Don't do that," these tots would become acquainted with a few fundamental aspects of their lives.

First, they should be made *aware* of their senses, through lessons in hearing, seeing, smelling, tasting, and touching. Models of animals and other objects would be provided for the children to feel and to name; then the names of these objects should be written on the blackboard. Gradually, the child should learn that the model of a *cow* represents the cow, and that neither the written nor the spoken word "cow" *is* a cow, but only a symbolic representation of one of the species cow.

What I am suggesting is that school psychologists devise means of instruction and play in which, *at the earliest possible age,* children are made aware of the difference between their objective and subjective selves. They should not be restricted from thinking in terms of fantasy, but they should be made to realize that they are indulging in fantasy and not in fact. Indulging in fantasy should be treated as a game, never as a reality. In our present system, from the time little Johnnie is six and enters the first grade, he is told to accept facts and more facts. His dream life and his emotional nature are left to drift until they come into conflict with the normal teaching procedures of the school. When this happens, Johnnie is reprimanded or punished. Gradually, he learns which words will please his teacher and how expressions of agreement will improve his position in the classroom, and perhaps his grades.

In spite of all the advances psychology has made in the study of the brain and the mental processes, the relationship between the physical brain and the subjective mind is still a puzzle. In other words, psychology is unable to describe mental activity concretely. Body and mind are one, says the scientist. The psychologist does not disagree with this statement, but so far no scientist has been able to define any subjective experience such as feeling, thinking, or deciding, except in its own terms. To think, therefore, is but to think, and to feel is but to feel.

Basically, we are subjective in nature; that is, all of our knowledge and all of our experience relate to ourselves. Our senses reach out to the objective world around us, but our brain alone receives the impulses and our mind alone interprets them. Paradoxically, the more we abandon our subjectivity and the more we embrace objectivity, the greater our freedom becomes and the greater our capacity grows to accept truth within ourselves.

Although there has been no definite answer to the question of how we think—from epistemology, language structure, or modern psychology—we have learned a great deal about our objective and subjective selves by indirect means. And, even though we may not know *what* knowledge, mind, or the self is, we have learned a great deal about them. Our educational institutions owe a great debt to the development of intelligence tests. Perhaps "performance" or "learning to perform" or simply "learning ability" may be better terms than "intelligence tests," since we do not know exactly what intelligence is, unless we accept the facetious definition that "intelligence is that which is measured by intelligence tests." What is usually implied is that we infer the level of an individual's intelligence from his performance in school. Ignoring theoretical differences, the proper application of intelligence testing has proved to be of great assistance to educators and school administrators. These tests for intelligence, along with many others which try to determine interests, aptitudes, appreciation, suggestibility, plus the Rorschach personality tests, have been extremely valuable in giving us a glimpse of the subjective selves of others.

Little Johnnie, growing up and entering the university, will need to pass a number of intelligence tests. If he studies physics or chemistry, his use of mathematics and his dealing with unemotional facts will strengthen his objectivity in this field of endeavor and may provide him with a stable professional life. But what about Johnnie's home and community life? When he leaves the laboratory and enters home life, his actions will be determined, not by the facts he has acquired nor by the scientific method he has employed in his profession, but by his control or lack of control over the emotional responses he has developed, suppressed, or modified since the day he was born. Johnnie may now be a scientist, but there is no assurance or guarantee that he may not need a psychiatrist to help him deal with his domestic or personal life. Above all, there is no certainty that Johnnie will find the meaning of his own life.

Here is a summation of what I believe is needed in acquiring knowledge, from nursery school to adult education:

1) Early arousal of a specific sense awareness, either in the home or in nursery schools.

2) A supervised guidance system to create constructive attitudes in relation to emotional responses, or to produce what we might call a well-ordered language structure of emotions.

3) A consciously-directed transfer of the child's sense perception to the first level of abstraction—identifying objects with spoken words and visual images.

4) A further development on higher levels of abstractions presented in numbers and written words.

5) An explanation, on the child's level, of the difference between fantasy and fact—fantasy being presented as a game, played only for occasional and conscious participation.

6) A proper emphasis on acquiring, through repetition, association and memorization, the basic tools of civilization, such as languages, mathematics and history, which form an integral part of our culture.

7) An introduction to elementary semantics, an analysis of language structure and an introduction to the scientific method.

8) Proper respect for conceptual thinking or the "how" of inventiveness and decision making.

9) Equal respect for the "what" in education, the feeding of information for memorizing.

Numerous other items could be added to this list, because education is a continuous and never-ending process.

In *Education and Ecstasy,* George B. Leonard's description of nurseries in the year 2001 seems decidedly far out, but I share his belief that eventually our children will learn all the basic stuff of present-day schooling in less than one-third of the time now required.

Student unrest and riots clearly indicate that changes in our educational system are inevitable. Modern technology will aid in speeding up the required reforms. We know from past history that human conduct changes slowly; and I will not be so bold as to predict whether our educational utopia will arrive in 2001 or 3001.

We may be entering one of those periods, however, when transformations will occur more readily. And, if we succeed in liberating and improving the emotional behavior of children in modern nurseries, Mr. Leonard's hope that education may become an ecstasy rather than a chore and a bore, may eventually be realized.

The Search Eternal is based on the concept that human consciousness will expand forever. Forever has no time limits. Will man's level of consciousness be elevated *in our time?* The answer depends entirely on us.

5

THE SEARCH FOR LAW
AND VALUES

Civilization without law, order and values is inconceivable. Laws are made for the protection of rights, to promote orderly procedures in the social and economic affairs of men, to preserve the peace and to protect individual life.

Without going down the dusty road of legal details, our purpose here, as elsewhere, is to look at the essentials: those principles and concepts which may become building blocks in our own philosophy of life.

The philosophy of law is as complicated a subject as is the study of epistemology. Fortunately, in order to ask the questions and receive the answers we need to know about the law and its values, we do not have to be thoroughly familiar with civil, criminal, corporate, tax and insurance laws, or divine law, moral law, natural law, Mosaic law, Anglo-Saxon, Roman, constitutional and international law, just to name a few.

What we need to know is: What is law? If there is no complete answer to this question, we should know the major limitations to any attempt at definition. Law is based on authority, but what is authority based on? Or, "Law on whose authority?"

Law, like language and culture, is as old as man.

For our understanding of American law, it is necessary only to know that it is rooted in Anglo-Saxon law and that the values on which our Founding Fathers based our Constitution had their origin in English tradition. American and Anglo-Saxon laws are similar but *not the same*. A unique part of American law, which every American citizen ought to know, will be discussed in the section dealing with constitutional law.

WHAT IS LAW?

The question as to what constitutes law is as difficult to answer as are questions regarding religion, knowledge, or philosophy. The difficulty lies not in the lack of an answer, but in deciding which of the many available answers is the right one.

Oliver Wendell Holmes said: "The prophecies of what the courts will do . . . are what I mean by the law." This statement might puzzle us, if we speculate as to why Holmes should link prophecy with law. But, if we consider this statement in the context of the eminent jurist's experience on the Supreme Court bench, we realize that he spoke of the law, not in terms of precisely written statutes, but as the fluctuating and uncertain decisions of nine Supreme Court justices. Used in such terms law becomes a living, dynamic process, actuated by human beings whose values and opinions are changeable.

Then we have the statement by Austin that ". . . law is merely positive morality" and the definition by Thomas

Aquinas that "law is an ordinance of reason for the common good. . . ."

Philosophers could argue for years about the meaning of the terms "positive morality," "an ordinance of reason," and "the common good."

In *Advancement to Learning*, Francis Bacon said: "There are in nature certain fountains of justice, whence all civil laws are derived but as streams. . . ."

By implication, Bacon's statement tied justice to authority and placed both of them in the lap of nature.

In dealing with the law, it would seem that we must include authority, reason, positive morality, justice, and enforcement. The inclusion of enforcement, which is usually thought of in connection with putting laws into practice, is necessary because the problems arising from law enforcement are very revealing about the nature of law itself.

The common view of law enforcment has not changed in centuries as Bacon observed in his *Apothogems*: "One of the Seven was wont to say: 'that laws were like cobwebs; where the small flies were caught and the great break through.' "

This view coincides with that of the man in the street, who ties enforcement with power—power in terms of personal or political influence or in terms of wealth. The poor man cannot pay for an extensive defense and he may lack the funds necessary for an appeal to a court of higher authority. Theoretical equality before the law is negated by the inequality behind the law, that is, the economic or political difference between the opponents in the court case.

For practical purposes, we should ask three things about all laws:

1) Whose authority determines the verdict?

71

2) What values measure our justice?

3) How do we enforce the law?

The first question, if pursued far enough, leads us to the "why" of the law. Authority assumes a maker of law. Why did God or the king or the state make a law?

The second question points to a consideration of the contents of the law in terms of desired objectives. The final question concerns the functioning of the law.

THE AUTHORITY OF THE LAW

We cannot deduce that God made law, unless we first believe in God. If we believe in nature, we cannot explain why there is a natural law except by deducing that without a natural law there would be chaos in the universe, and we would not be here to observe it.

In early tribal life, the chief's authority was linked very closely with that of the witch doctor or priest, which made it easier to understand the later development of the king's authority by "divine right," linked with and supported by the power of the church. The authority of the tribal chief and the prophecy of the medicine man are *not the same* as the authority and the prophecy of Oliver Wendell Holmes. But we should realize their similarity and bear in mind two distinct views that still prevail in our American culture. The first one, held by the church, was given centuries ago by Sir William Blackstone when he stated:

The law of nature being coeval with mankind and dictated by God, Himself, is, of course, superior in obligation to any other [law]. It is binding over all the globe, in all countries, and at all times; no human laws are of validity if contrary

72

to this [the natural law]; and such of them [human laws] as are valid derive all their force and all their authority, mediate or immediate, from this original [natural law].[6]

And Cardinal James McIntyre said: "If a law is not in conformity with natural law, it is not a good law." [7]

Both those in the church and those outside agree that natural law is discovered and not made. The same does not hold true of man-made laws. Roscoe Pound takes up this point by saying:

> . . . perhaps we must distinguish law and laws, the law and a law. A law is a rule of policing. It proceeds from authority and has political or established power behind it. The law is a body of principles of justice proceeding from reason and having a sense of right and justice of civilized mankind behind it. We say a law is made. The law is found.[8]

From a philosophic point of view, a great deal can be said about this differentiation between laws and the law; but, when we feel certain that "the law" is found, whose authority or what authority stands behind it except that of reason? We may say that a 91 percent income tax is unreasonable, but can we say that it is against the will of God?

It would be more realistic to examine the authority of our own national laws. Every high-school student is familiar (I hope) with the American Constitution. If asked what the final authority in American law is, the majority of students would respond: "The Constitution of the United States." Some might say, however, that the authority is vested in the Supreme Court, echoing the famous remark:

"The law of the land is what the justices of the Supreme Court say it is."

Our Constitution is such an amazing document that many Americans ascribe a sort of divinity to our Founding Fathers. Actually, they were a realistic group of men, who blended theory with a great deal of practical experience they gained in the ebb and flow of an evolving society and nation.

One of the signers of the Constitution, Gouverneur Morris, was well aware of this when, as Minister to France, he told LaFayette and Louis XVI that the French people and their customs were very different from the Americans; the American Constitution would not work for them and they must devise another legal instrument for their own use.

Is our Constitution still serviceable? Today, our nation is quite different in composition and customs from what it was nearly two centuries ago. In popular thinking, the expression frequently runs, "Let's go back to the good, old Constitution." But, we "can't go home again." It has been said that no country can be permanently imprisoned in the straitjacket of a written constitution. This jacket has been stretched by judicial interpretation and, before our answer is complete, we shall have to ask where this interpretation may lead us. For better or for worse, it is this judicial interpretation that has kept our Constitution alive for nearly two centuries.

In Article VI of the Constitution we find the statement: "This Constitution. . . . shall be the supreme law of the land."

Although lawyers like to start from authority, if you were to ask an attorney what he considers the final authority in American law, most likely he would answer in two words: "Due process." The due process clause is written in the Fifth Amendment and is repeated in the Fourteenth. The Fifth Amendment has been a bone of contention in public opinion because Communists used it—frequently to their own advantage—and the public has not always understood the Supreme Court decisions upholding the rights it sanctions. What many people do not realize is that this same amendment also guarantees that no citizen shall "be deprived of life, liberty or property without due process of law." Furthermore, "due process of law" is the principle on which all our federal and state courts operate: offering anyone bail, trial by jury, assignment of defense counsel, appeal to a higher court, and such other standards as are "reasonable." The due process clauses in state and federal constitutions, however, set no standard by which to determine what is arbitrary and what is reasonable. The courts are free to set their own standards, as well as to apply them.

All laws in the United States originate either in Congress or in local legislatures; the Supreme Court does not initiate any. Only when there is a dispute in cases properly presented to the Supreme Court, do the justices decide by majority vote the "undue harshness" or "reasonableness" of the statute of Congress, the act of a state legislature, or the ordinance of a municipal council. The local law is considered final, if the Supreme Court refuses to review a case.

JUSTICE AND VALUES

We say that nature or God is no respecter of persons. The rain falls equally on the just and the unjust. The Constitution of the United States makes every citizen equal be-

75

fore the law, but the verdict that comes as the end result is not always impersonal. The eloquence of the defense attorney or prosecuting attorney, the conduct and interpretation of the presiding judge, the opinions and decisions of the jury, and the majority opinion of the justices of the Supreme Court are not as unchangeable as natural law nor as certain as Francis Bacon's "fountains of justice"; they depend on the personal evaluations of individuals. We speak of justice tempered with mercy, but we behold justice partially measured and inadequately administered. Yet, certainly we do need a measurement of justice that will better express our cultural values.

Valuation is primarily subjective, and in spite of science's contribution of more or less objective measurements—lie dectectors and opinions of psychiatrists, skilled in objective analysis—the legal relationship between individuals and groups within our society, as it comes before the court of justice, is best expressed as a measure of "fairness" or "reasonableness." In many cases, this reasonableness is nothing but a pragmatic application of our cultural ideals in terms of their workability. And, as our cultural ideals change, so does our measure of "reasonableness."

When the courts determine and apply their own criteria of "reasonableness" and the Supreme Court has the final say on this "reasonableness," we must look to the decisions of the Supreme Court to see whether its interpretations and major decisions are in accord with the changes in our social ideals.

In 1923, in the case of *Adkins* v. *Children's Hospital,* the Supreme Court declared the Act of Congress, authorizing the Wage Board for the District of Columbia to fix mini-

76

mum wages for women, an infringement upon the "due process" clause of the Fifth Amendment and, therefore, unconstitutional.

This decision was a blow, not only to the District of Columbia, but to the twelve states that had passed, during the preceding decade, minimum wage laws with rates of pay based on cost of living. By an evenly divided decision of the Supreme Court, these laws had been sustained as a valid exercise of the police power of each state. This police power, in turn, was based on "reasonableness" and fairness in relation to the protection of women and minors from sweatshop conditions.

Under the authority of the Constitution in 1923, the justices of the Supreme Court did not declare what was good or bad economics, nor did they deal with social questions as such. In his dissenting opinion in the *Adkins* case, Chief Justice William Howard Taft said: ". . . it is not the function of this Court to hold Congressional acts invalid simply because they are passed to carry out economic views which the Court believes to be unwise or unsound."

The fact is that the "written" Constitution did, and does today, guarantee the economic principle of property rights but not the social principle of human needs. Accordingly, it is not strange to hear Justice Holmes, in his dissent on the *Adkins* case, say that "the criterion of Constitutionality is not whether we believe the law to be for the public good."

Public opinion accepted this statement of Justice Holmes without complaint, apparently because of the generally rising trend of wages after 1923. Today, it seems hard to believe that in the prosperous year of 1929 ten million families had a total income of five billion dollars, or an average of less than ten dollars per week per family. In those days, people had not yet acquired the habit of looking to the government for financial help. The great depression of the 1930s changed all that.

Enormous unemployment and conditions of poverty caused governors and state legislatures to pass new minimum wage laws, hoping that the courts would sustain them this time. The New York Minimum Wage Law was held invalid by the New York Court of Appeals, and Chief Judge Crane said: "We should follow the law as given and not speculate as to the changes which have come or are supposed to have come to economic conditions in the last decade, which may move the Supreme Court to a further consideration of its ruling." (In the *Adkins* case.)

When the Supreme Court upheld the decision of the New York Court of Appeals, the storm broke loose. "The Supreme Court is out of touch with the people," the *New York Times* of January 14, 1937, quoted Senator George Norris of Nebraska.

There was a great deal of agitation to "curb the Supreme Court," to "educate" it, or "pack" it with liberal-minded justices, or, if need be, to amend the Constitution.

In his address to Congress on the state of the nation on January 6, 1937, President Franklin D. Roosevelt said:

During the past year, there has been a growing belief that there is little fault to be found with the Constitution of the United States as it stands today. A vital need is not an alteration of our fundamental law but an increasing enlightened view with reference to it. Difficulties have grown out of its interpretation; but rightly considered, it can be used as an instrument of progress and not as a device for prevention of action. . . .

78

The Judicial Branch also is asked by the people to do its part to make democracy successful. We do not ask the Court to call non-existent power into being, but we have a right to expect that conceded powers or those legitimately implied shall be made effective instruments for the common good.

Although President Roosevelt was unable to "pack" the Supreme Court with liberal-minded justices, his criticism of the "personal economic predilections of the Supreme Court majority" added to the attack from many sides concerning the Court's antisocial attitudes and may well have persuaded the majority of the judges to favor social legislation.

Before the year 1937 was out, a body of New Deal social legislation, including a new minimum wage law, was declared constitutional by a majority of the Court. The measurement of justice in our land now included the socioeconomic needs of man as well as his property rights. But were both in equal proportion?

There is a tendency, especially in the United States, for the pendulum to swing from one extreme to the other. The Supreme Court, which maintained tradition throughout the Great Depression by insisting that due process in our Constitution had nothing whatever to do with social and economic needs of the people, has emphasized the other extreme today, by giving the benefit under the due process of the law to every kind of criminal. Some day, public opinion may revolt at the kind of interpretation which protects criminals at the expense of decent, law-abiding citizens.

More and more we must equate the balance of justice

inherent in our Constitution with the balance of values operating in our present culture. Obviously, the values of the 1930s were different from those of the 1920s. Neither are the values of the late 1960s the same as those of the 1940s. Whatever these values may be they cannot condone the corruption of the criminal elements in our midst. The control of legitimate business by gangsters, the blackmailing of decent, hard-working people, and the continued existence of the Mafia are a disgrace to our democratic society. The billions of dollars extracted each year by these criminals could well be used for advanced nursery schools and for the education of the underprivileged.

In 1937, just before the Supreme Court's decision regarding New Deal social legislation was made, I wrote a paper on this subject which ended with the following statement:

> Perhaps capitalism as we have known it is ending. The movement of events, the destiny of the human race, may be on the way to state socialism. But even if it is and even if our desires to have it otherwise may not change the course of events, it would be well to know what is happening to us.
>
> We are facing today the issue whether or not these changes in emphasis in interpreting the fundamental law of the land from property rights to human rights, based on need, may not be the means of leading us into a new social era in which government control and regulation may yet become more cumbersome than beneficial.

Our president, as well as the public, seems convinced that "the fountains of justice" have been buried under the mountains of bureaucratic administrative law.

THE ENFORCEMENT OF LAW

Unjust laws create disrespect as well as resistance and circumvention of law. If government agencies wrote and legislated better and more carefully prepared laws, they would create more respect for the law. They should also clean house regularly. Some of us may smile at the "blue" laws of the Puritans, but are the people of the State of Kansas aware that in 1962 they still had a law on the books which reads: "When two trains approach each other at a crossing, they shall both come to a full stop and neither shall start up until the other is gone"? What legal genius had the brilliant insight to establish perpetual immobility by law?

House cleaning is an urgent necessity not only in the legislative halls, but in all the bureaucracies as well. The growing pile of paper work may eventually suffocate us. Certainly, it creates indifference, if not disrespect, for written directives.

Before the criminal can be jailed, the Supreme Court has ruled that he must be briefed on his "rights," even though he has violated the basic rights of society directly and dangerously. The arresting officer must be careful that he not make the slightest technical mistake, or the offender will go free. What is the matter with a civilization that values the rights of the criminal above the security of society?

It is easier for me to understand the revolt of youth in our colleges; many changes in our educational system that students request are necessary. But the average student has had little experience with the practical requirements of society, and his pendulum between the subjective and objective, the real and the ideal, swings wide. Many of us have gone through this phase of life. Unfortunately, in today's affluent society, students have much less contact with the "realities" of life, because they have been used to luxurious living and have never experienced the self-discipline and self-denial which come from hard times. Like their elders, students suffer from a lack of personal involvement. If the student's education is to mean something more than a lecture and library reading course, there must be closer communication between the student and the professor. The universities themselves must find answers to these problems: give sympathetic hearings to the young idealists, and show no mercy to the small number of hard-core radicals who are interested not in bettering the status quo, but in total destruction of both university and society.

While the revolt of youth is emphasized, we must not overlook the restlessness and unhappiness of the older generation, who are worried by the increase in crime, taxes, inflation and the growing impersonality caused by bureaucracy.

The general public's restlessness is partially due to awareness that our present social values are not what they should be. Out of this feeling of frustration, and spurred by the demand to start a reevaluation of the ingredients comprising our culture, perhaps a responsible leadership may arise and place an emphasis on self-discipline rather than on permissiveness.

It is high time for us to realize that educating the intellect alone will not solve our problems. Unless we educate the emotions and establish high standards of conduct relative to our advancement in science and technology, progress will be impossible. When we undertake this task of major reconstruction, laws can be formulated which will be respected and obeyed.

Each one of us can help in electing men of strong moral character to positions of power within our state and federal governments—men who will not be afraid to espouse unpopular causes, in the interest of the common good.

In the last analysis, we can drift along with the tide towards greater lawlessness, or we can try to improve the values of our culture. Perhaps, if we try hard enough, we may help our weaker brothers to strengthen their self-discipline. Unless we do, our civilization will rot from within and disappear, as others have in the past.

6

THE SEARCH FOR WISDOM

In the ancient days of Greece, philosophy literally meant "the love of wisdom." Socrates personified this interpretation of philosophy. Preserved for us in the *Dialogues of Plato,* his discourses and questions about the meaning of life, of man, and of the cosmos went in all directions. If we had asked Socrates how to search for wisdom, probably he would have given his famous reply, "Know thyself."

Nearly everyone believes that he "knows himself," but psychiatry demonstrates that irrational individuals have false ideas about themselves as well as about others. Wisdom requires deep understanding of human nature, as well as insight into the motivation of one's own desires and purposes in life.

The famous story of the two women, who each claimed to be the mother of the one child, illustrates the wisdom of King Solomon. His discernment in saying that he would divide the child in two so that each woman might have her half was based on understanding of a mother's heart.

At one time, moral values were the most important part of philosophy. But, to some eminent modern philosophers like Ernest Nagel, the task of philosophy is not to provide a moral code; that is the task of moral and religious systems. At best, the philosopher may rigorously examine the ethical questions presented by the moral systems people value. Primarily, however, the task of philosophy is to examine the underlying structural elements of knowledge, not in order to provide a unity or continuity of knowledge, but to present a tentative and shifting system of secular, scientific knowledge based on logic and sensory perception. By the use of the scientific method, the modern philosopher functions as the critic of the assumptions made by our natural scientists and, likewise, expresses his view of the universe in descriptive terms, void of all purposes and transcendental meanings. The only purposes he recognizes are the ones man puts into his universe.

This philosophic view, known as positivism, is an excellent one for science and I would no more ask anyone to discard it than I would wish to do away with the sciences. But, while I may subscribe to this view as *one* of the important functions of philosophy, I would not limit the task of philosophy to this activity alone.

I agree with the naturalists and the positivists that we may regard human needs as the ultimate base for values, but only if these human needs include man's concern with the unknown and his own relationship to the cosmos. And this relationship between man and the cosmos, between man and God, must be a twofold one: giving purpose to man and demanding responsibility from him. Only on such a relationship can we build a concept of moral values that will be stable without being static.

The assumption that there is no purpose in the universe because we do not see one is just as unprovable as is the one that assumes a friendly universe because we desire it. The difference in the attitude of the man who feels a

85

kinship with the universe, however, and that of one who thinks of his environment as indifferent or hostile is of great importance to society as well as to the individual.

Our sense of direction of the universe may be dim and our expressions of what "ought to be" will most likely be inadequate, but they will spell the difference between hope and despair.

A concept of the universe demanding no responsibility from man cannot present a logical base for moral action. When measured only by man's purpose, knowledge, law, justice, and values may be used for evil as well as good. The use of power may make or break a nation. Law, values, knowledge, and power, as they "ought" to be used, are the only rational means to deliver us from our irrational society. Our concept of God, or the directive power of the universe, may change as we grow in spiritual as well as in physical stature. But, without a concept of a power greater than ourselves and an intelligence transcending ours, we shall reap a civilization composed of man-made cross-purposes, which will inevitably decay.

We must change not the universe, but our concept of it. We must modify not the function of religion, but its present-day naïve concepts of the universe and of man's place in it. We must rectify not the function of philosophy, but the attitude of philosophers so that they may be willing to provide a synthesis of the moral, spiritual, and physical characteristics of the universe to which modern man can respond with all his creative desire and intelligence.

THE QUEST FOR UNITY

In our search for knowledge and law we find many different ideas. Nor do we find unanimity of answers to the question: What is philosophy? This lack of unanimity is frequently disconcerting to those who have studied little or no academic philosophy; they expect that somehow philosophy is the essence of wisdom and should provide answers to all the basic questions of life. College students find such a dream of unity and certainty rudely shattered when they begin their study of philosophy. Instead of finding certain knowledge and comforting wisdom, they run into a series of conflicting systems of thought, each logically pursuing its own basic assumptions. In all probability, the student will find that philosophy does not place its emphasis on the meaning of life nor does it present a way of life; he finds that philosophers have explored the meaning of meaning and have presented their voluminous researches in works on epistemology and ontology which, for the greater part, are either discarded today or are practically useless.

The professor of philosophy should exhort his students to the realization that what philosophy presents is not a system of thought in itself, which is finished once and for all, but that it is a stimulation to thinking and a scientific method for questioning all ideas, including his own. We hope that the professor will indicate that the questioning life need not be a fractured one and, by example, show that unity which is essential for an integrated human being.

Unity is one of the essentials in my concept of wisdom. Wisdom should include goodness, unity, values, intellect, experience, and certainty. Unity and certainty are two elements seemingly lacking in our modern age.

Because pictures sometimes can give us a clearer idea than words, let us try to visualize the concept of unity in picture form.

Draw a circle large enough to contain a man, and visualize him with hands and legs outstretched touching the circumference. The circle represents our accumulated knowledge of the world and man, firmly grasping the circumference, can be seen in full control of it. We may even say that the world is his oyster. Such was the view of man and his knowledge, in the days of Socrates.

Now, visualize that circle extended a thousand or ten thousand times. Man is still located there in the center but his hands are useless to him now. No longer can he project by touch; only by abstract thinking can he project himself to the circumference of the circle where his mind wanders among the innumerable branches of knowledge, and where some men have built strongholds of intellectual abstractions that they protect in ivory towers.

In this view of the modern world, man appears to be floating helplessly in the center of things, now himself an oyster—a captive rather than a conqueror, generally useless and purposeless rather than in control of his environment.

"What is man that Thou art mindful of him?" asked the Prophet. The mystic answers it by saying that since God is a spirit only the spirit of man matters; the intellectual may shrug his shoulders and reply that we should not ask such silly questions.

Let us draw another picture, remembering that this picture does not represent truth, but is used only as an aid in our understanding.

Students in high school know that our bodies are made up largely of water, plus other chemicals, and that water is H_2O. But let us visualize man now as being personified by water, i.e., he *is* water. Man, then, is made up of two elements, but instead of calling them H_2O we designate them as matter and spirit. Water, however, is different from either hydrogen or oxygen. It has a quality of its own. So man has a quality of his own, which is a combination of both matter and spirit. Water, put under the pressures of heat or cold, reveals its two aspects. Intense cold produces ice, intense heat produces vapor. Man (representing water) sees his material desires turn into solid ice (the products of the cold logic of science), and his spiritual desires turn into vapors (the faith that extends beyond reason). The solid ice can easily be demonstrated, controlled and measured; some of the vapors may be felt or seen, but most of them are not seen. They are too difficult to measure and control.

The ice-cold logic of reason may seem irreconcilable with the vaporlike qualities of faith, imagination, and intuition, but, like ice and vapor, they are different manifestations of the same substance.

How solid the ice looks; we can walk on it and, if it is thick enough, we can build on it. How vague the vapor seems, but, if we direct the steam, what power it produces. Steam, however, condenses in time, and ice melts away eventually; only water remains. The unity between ice and vapor is no greater than the unity of matter and spirit I have described as the two aspects of man. To see man as a whole, to synthesize his different aspects is a task far more complicated, but in principle, it is the same. As the thermometer's index moves up and down, there is a difference in degree. The difference in degree may produce a difference in kind or aspect. At the lower end of the thermometer's scale, water (action) solidifies so that no movement (purpose) remains to be observed. At the upper end of the scale, water becomes less and less solid and movement (purpose) becomes all important.

The desire of scientists to deal only in reason (ice) is neither more nor less valid than the desire of spiritual leaders to deal only in faith (vapors). I think both are necessary, but in various degrees. The desire of those who assume the universe to be friendly, however, is no less rational than the desire of those who cannot—or in some cases will not —see a purpose in the universe beyond their own because they will deal only in ice.

THE TYRANNY OF ABSOLUTES

Certainty, that other ingredient of wisdom, is in even more disrepute than unity. Various aspects of certainty will arise in our forthcoming discussions on the meaning of life, so it may be useful to discuss the revolutionary changes academic philosophy has undergone regarding its concept of certainty.

Man as body-mind has two aspects: the objective and the subjective self. Our bodies receive sensations and our minds reflect and interpret these sensations correctly or incorrectly as the case may be.

While man is a sorry spectacle without the use of his senses, we know that his senses cannot be trusted in every instance. While neither our reason nor our sense impressions are to be trusted as irrefutable truth, we still need both to arrive at some stability. This stability is increased when we compare a series of mental reflections based on the same or similar experiences. Scientists dealing with inanimate matter can use the same experience over and over, which makes them feel rather secure in the reflection of their observations. Their reasoning is based on inductive logic, reasoning from particulars to a general rule or law.

The great philosophers of the past, who endeavored to present a consistent body of thought and principle, did so primarily by deductive logic. They reasoned from the general to the particular. Particular errors were errors, because they were not deduced from right principles. They started out with general principles and assumptions and deduced their theories from them. The point of reference for a scientist may be one event or datum, at which he may arrive either by observation or by methodical calculation. The point of reference for the ancient philosopher was either a stated or implied absolute. Ultimate reality, infinity, oneness, truth, eternity, and perfection were abstractions, which were as much definite points of reference for philosophy as absolute love of God was for the theologians. Truth, Reality, Infinity, and Oneness were four basic and indestructible concepts; they were written in capitals, signifying that they were absolutes. Only absolutes are indestructible. God, as the First Cause, is the First Absolute. The four abstractions of ultimate Truth, Reality, Infinity, and Oneness are only four aspects of God the Unknown. Since no one could know God, no one could know these four perfect aspects of God. They were considered, nevertheless, as real as God Himself.

As long as man acknowledged that God created the heavens and the earth, no one questioned these absolute aspects of God. When evolution was introduced as a process of natural development by trial and error, the "perfect" creation of God was cast into doubt.

In philosophy a considerable revolution took place. When Charles Darwin made clear that species were not immutable, William James attempted to unseat the absolute by substituting a pragmatic relativity. He got rid of Oneness by replacing it with plurality. John Dewey followed this example by dethroning the kingly noun "Truth" to an adverb and doing likewise to the noun "Reality."

Albert Einstein introduced space-time as a new concept, thus further emphasizing the relativity of time and space.

Are there then no absolutes? We can only believe or disbelieve that they exist just as Einstein believed, and others may disbelieve, that there is a reality outside of ourselves.

In an essay on philosophy, Ralph Waldo Emerson gave this interesting definition: "Philosophy," he said, "is the account which the human mind gives to itself of the constitution of the world. Two cardinal facts lie forever at the base . . . 1. Unity, or Identity; and 2. Variety. We unite all things . . . by perceiving the superficial differences and the profound resemblances. But every mental act—this very perception of identity or oneness, recognizes the difference of things. Oneness and otherness. It is impossible to speak or to think without embracing both."

What is the point of reference in this unity between the one and the many? It is: "the law which pervades them."

We may not be as certain in defining the law of gravity as we once were. In taking things apart and separating various aspects of single units, the human mind can analyze almost everything away. But whatever we may call that force, which we recognize in a practical sense as gravitation, we realize that it presents cohesion between the forces of affinity and repulsion—the one, and the two —and thus we have our operating solar system. Likewise —only in a manner much more difficult to comprehend— we see the same principles at work in the smallest components of matter or what we may now term energy forms, energy fields or energy flows. Without this cohesion or unity our bodies would not be walking on the earth.

I reject dualism as a metaphysics. Body and mind are one, *and* two. Hot and cold are one (scale and temperature) and two. We have two eyes and one vision. Unfortunate are those with double vision.

Logical reasoning is one, inductive and deductive logic are two. Inductive logic goes uphill and deductive logic comes downhill or, if you prefer, they are the two halves of the same circle.

The human intellect shows its greatest cohesion when the analytical and synthetic processes have both been fully utilized. I believe in one evolution with two major aspects: the physical and the spiritual.

It is my aim to present a synthesis of these two aspects, but we cannot do so without analyzing or understanding some of the major tenets of knowledge available to us now.

THE ROAD TO WISDOM

In the past 5,000 years of history, the lives of many wise men have been recorded: Confucius, Lao-Tse, Gautama Buddha, Socrates, Plato, Pythagoras, Aristotle, Jesus, Mohammed, St. Francis of Assisi, and many others. Most of them were religious leaders or were interested in presenting a moral-physical system.

Some wise men were recognized; some were appreciated during their lifetime; others did not do so well.

Socrates was not poisoned because he knew too much, he was poisoned because his contemporaries were too ignorant. Secure in their illusions, they could not endure the truth.

Jesus was not nailed to the cross because He was too unselfish and loved His fellow men too much; He was crucified because the people were too selfish and did not love their fellow men enough. They preferred the security of their lifelong prejudices and could not endure being disillusioned by a living example of the truth.

"And the truth shall set men free." But many do not desire this freedom. Multitudes still prefer the certainty of their superstitions to the light of truth.

The great search of life (and evolution) is the ceaseless discovery of more truth, power, consciousness, and reality. This *is* the purpose of life.

I do not hold with philosophic idealism, because I do not believe that ideas are the only "real" things, nor do I think that reason alone will ever reveal the reality we are seeking.

Frequently, the importance of reason has been overemphasized in philosophy. The other faculties of man should not be overlooked. On occasion, reason may be illumined by intuition—not the intuition which is the Alpha and Omega of the mystic, but part of that comprehension in which reason plays a necessary part. Using reason and intuition can be compared to the use of both our eyes. We do not ask which eye is better; we realize that the use of both eyes provides better and steadier vision—if they focus correctly.

Wisdom must have the qualities of goodness, unity, value, intelligence, experience, and certainty. And a wise man should also have intuition and a deep awareness of truth. Intuition will provide him with that sense of unity which Emerson pointed out as basic to all of life. Certainty and truth he must find within himself. First of all, the wise man is honest with himself. He reduces self-deception to a minimum. By being sure of himself in a sense that no Hitler or Stalin could ever be, the wise man prepares the soil in which to grow the fruitful tree of life. Goodness flows from wisdom as naturally as rain falls from the sky.

I do not restrict the term "wise man" to those recognized as "geniuses," renowned philosophers or great religious and ethical leaders. The wise man is anyone who has strong convictions without corresponding prejudices; an open mind to changes without trying to be all things to all men; an attitude of sympathy without being sentimental; an attitude of honesty without being self-righteous. In knowing himself, the wise man can accept himself and life courageously. And, knowing his own weaknesses, he will be tolerant of his fellowmen and will temper his justice with mercy. He knows that the fundamental meaning of life is the living of it and, just as life is an eternal *now,* so his search for truth, beauty, joy, justice, and an increasing awareness of the powers of life will be a continuous *now.* He will not worry about the past, he will be living in the present with his vision on the road ahead of him as he continues his journey.

7

THE SEARCH FOR HAPPINESS

Basically, there is only one search: life's quest to find its own meaning. Or, we may state this another way by saying that the search for the unknown is continuous. The root of all happiness lies in understanding this search as we participate in it.

Probably, no search of the human heart is as universal and as vague as the search for happiness. Everyone wants to be happy. But, in a world where one crisis succeeds another, the best most people dare to hope for is "a little peace of mind." This peace of mind seems to be visualized as a state of contentedness, a form of mental and emotional relaxation which is characterized by passivity and freedom from worry.

In our universe, which is basically an energy system, I do not think it wise to embrace a philosophy of passivity and escapism.

Peace of mind does not come from denial; happiness does not appear merely by wishing for it. Neither comes as a gift; both have to be earned.

In stating that among the inalienable rights of man are life and liberty, Thomas Jefferson added "and the pursuit of happiness."

Many people pursue, chase, and hunt happiness, as if it were a thing in itself. Inevitably, disillusionment results from such a pursuit. Happiness is a by-product of life. The question is: how do we pursue life to find happiness?

HAPPINESS IN PERMISSIVENESS?

Freedom from restraint is one of our strongest basic desires. It begins in childhood and remains with us to the end of our days. The polarity between freedom and self-discipline may be the most difficult one each of us must face throughout life. Its complexity confuses both young and old.

The daily news is full of stories regarding revolts against traditional authority expressed in both peaceful and violent demonstrations. Police, once society's respected representatives of law and order, are called "pigs." The administration of our society is called "the Establishment." Its progress in social welfare, as well as in economics, is ignored. In certain circles, belonging to the Establishment carries the same stigma as being a member of the Mafia.

What has caused this situation? Let us not be too hasty in putting all the blame on young people. If they are not well-acquainted with the inseparable twins—freedom and restraint—it may not be their fault. Because psychiatrists of twenty-five years ago blamed all emotional disturbances of children on their parents, many well-meaning parents developed a strong feeling of guilt. Such people embraced the psychology of permissiveness as the one most likely to make their youngsters happier and more stable.

Many parents embraced the new freedom of permissiveness for another reason. They used the system both ways:

freedom for the children and freedom for themselves. The first freedom made children do things on their own, or shift for themselves. The second freedom gave the parents the logical right to "live their own lives." Children were showered with toys and expensive gifts unknown to previous generations. Teen-agers received generous spending money and cars. This freedom aided every member of the family to lead his own independent life, but it short-changed the young people in personal attention and love.

To love means to give—not material things but of one's self, even to the point of self-sacrifice; for to give attention to another member of the family means to care about him. Love demands the occasional surrender of one's own desires to the needs and wishes of another. A totally selfish person is incapable of love.

The permissiveness of the family has spread to the permissiveness of society. Switching couples for sexual purposes is all right, said one housewife, as long as the children do not know about it. But children learn mostly by example and are fast learners in the field of permissiveness.

What causes the unhappiness of youth? They need direction rather than indulgence. Where can they find that direction in our society of self-centered and impersonal individuals?

Youth revolts against the hypocrisy of the present society, without fully realizing that their parents were raised in an era of similar hypocrisy. They revolt against the terrors of nuclear war as it threatens their existence, without understanding the suffering endured by the older generation during two world wars.

Youth is exceedingly conscious of the generation gap. The idealism of the young is a recurrent process and modern youth has no monopoly on it. When I was young, I was painfully aware of the generation gap, but I made no public protest. I can sympathize with the students' problem regarding lack of personal contact with teachers. There are three aspects to this problem. One is the overemphasis placed on research at the expense of teaching. The second is a lack of inspired teachers; even in the good old days there was one inspirational teacher for every three traditional instructors who never moved an inch from the educational *status quo*. The light of creativity was not in the latter, but what a difference those few inspired teachers made in the life of a student!

The third aspect is one of growth. Young and old alike suffer from the population explosion. Cities become more crowded and impersonal each year. Year after year, our universities increase their enrollments. As a college trustee, I have watched my college administration promote greater student attendance as one way to increase the budget and justify plans for new buildings. This insatiable desire for expansion places the emphasis on quantity rather than quality. What is the answer? When Woodrow Wilson was president of Princeton University, he instituted a tutorial system. Students in a given course would assemble once a week in a large auditorium to hear a lecture. Twice a week this crowd would break up into groups of ten or fifteen students and meet informally with their teacher in a small room, thereby gaining the chance for personal contact. Can we afford to have such a system today?

Considerable research would be required to properly evaluate the influence of modern permissiveness on the morals and values of the young; it is easy to note their relationship.

Youth is correct in bewailing the hypocrisy of society's

standards and conduct, yet they seem ignorant of the fact that hypocrisy has been one of the major defects in the conduct of men and women for ages. Nor is youth honest in downgrading the material values of their elders while accepting luxuries from them. The double standard of morality practiced by their elders does not give young people the right to dismiss all restraints on their own potent sexual desires. Promiscuous sex relationships and sex orgies do not produce values for a better society.

Americans tend to go from one extreme to the other. Puritanism reigned our land for too long. Our middle-class morality was in need of a change. But freedom from puritanism does not mean turning to licentious hedonism.

Drugs and the psychedelic atmosphere are not reality; they are an escape into illusion and forgetfulness. Prolonged drug abuse weakens the nervous system and the will to be creative. Habitual indulgence in sex orgies will make sexual impotents of our young men before they reach middle age.

Sooner or later, all of us must learn that nothing in the universe is absolutely free. The price of total freedom is self-discipline; the price of permissiveness and self-indulgence is deterioration and decay of moral character.

Regardless of how close we may feel to others, a sense of loneliness will overwhelm us from time to time. During my happy college days, I experienced the feeling of aloneness many times. The gaining of knowledge can be a painful process, for knowledge may restrict as well as assist in communicating with others. The law of the universe demands that we learn to stand on our own feet, as individuals. The perfect example of a man standing alone is Jesus in the garden of Gethsemane.

Students complain that college administrators do not

listen to them. I sympathize with them for I had this experience, too. Once, I approached the president of one of the colleges I attended with a proposal that I thought truly creative and inspiring. Also, it would bring students and faculty closer together. The president looked at me as if I had lost my mind. Quickly, he turned me over to the dean of men, who listened sympathetically. Nothing, however, was done about my recommendation. So it is today. Faculty and administrators should have open minds and sympathetic attitudes towards students' suggestions, indicative of needs born of their changing time. Not all proposals made by students will be practical or acceptable, for various reasons, but they should not be swept callously under the rug of indifference.

Youth's desire for peace, insofar as it is more than an escape from the draft, is encouraging. It would be wonderful if war could be outlawed.

If youth desires a better world, they should spend less time and energy trying to destroy the old, and concentrate more intently on the specific issues vital to building a stable and progressive society. Self-control as well as self-reliance remain inescapable requirements. Lowering the quality of education and creating a climate of general permissiveness and self-indulgence will bring neither progress nor happiness.

Above all, youth needs a vision of a better world and the motivation to use all of their minds, hearts and souls in assisting to bring this about. In this constructive effort they will find happiness and self-fulfillment.

HAPPINESS IN UNION

If youth is frustrated and unhappy, what about their elders? White- as well as blue-collar workers have gained steady wage increases and benefits since the end of World War II. Their only complaint concerns the higher cost of living. Businessmen are pleased with greater profits; their complaints center on increasing wages and fringe benefits, rather than on higher prices.

The unhappiness of adult individuals is not restricted to general inflation, higher taxes, and the disrespect of youth. It is deeper than that. There seems to be no direction in a completely materialistic world. Why not?

Man is a spirit, inhabiting a physical body. In the past, the need to sustain the physical body took most of his time. Now, he is freed from economic bondage to a degree never experienced before. He has time to think, and when he realizes that there is an emptiness, a lack of meaning in our purely materialistic society, he becomes disturbed and dissatisfied. When the older generation sees the values and the structures of the old order disappearing and cannot visualize what will replace them, they become as restless as their descendants.

Man is created in the image of the creative spirit whom we call God. Therefore, man is meant to evolve toward spirituality. But we develop slowly. When we realize, however, that the meaning of earthly life is part of the meaning of eternal life, our perspective widens. As long as man remains on earth, he is compelled to develop his physical and spiritual selves side by side.

The tremendous changes going on in the world indicate that we are suffering the pains of a rebirth. As the customs and values of the old order break down, we must not make the mistake of equating self-fulfillment with self-indulgence. If young people do not know how to construct a new and better society, it is up to us older ones to present the blueprints.

102

Unfortunately, often grown persons are emotionally immature. The increasing rate of divorces is not due to a well-founded recognition that *sometimes* it is better for people to part than to endure an unhappy existence together. All too frequently divorce results from an unwillingness to sacrifice one's own ego, interest, and pleasure for another. Every marriage requires mutual adjustment of both partners.

Marriage and the family have been and, in spite of many upheavals, still are the backbone of our society. Enlightened attitudes in this field should be welcome. Because the blacks and whites of our various concepts and codes have been changed into grays, we should not erroneously assume that our choices have been made easier. If we do, we are only adding to our self-deception.

For instance, we eat to live and we eat for pleasure; we have sex for procreation and sex for pleasure. The danger lies in overemphasis on pleasure. If we eat *with* pleasure to satisfy the natural needs of our bodies, the result will be beneficial. But, if we eat only *for* pleasure, we turn into compulsive eaters inflicting disastrous results on our bodies. Nor is our life enriched when we indulge in sex for its own sake.

Sex happiness cannot exist without love; sexual indulgence has nothing to do with love. Sex experience may be the result of erotic stimulation, or it may be the outlet for pent-up sexual energy which seeks escape rather than union.

Sex happiness is that union in which the spiritual qualities of love blend with the physical act. Restraint, control and concern for the other person are integral parts of sex happiness. In our search for "realism" we must never lose sight of the more sensitive qualities of man, or we shall move from morbid puritanism to ribald hedonism.

The philosophy of balance is not a neutralization of the extreme right or left; it is a positive procedure of giving due consideration to the needs of both body and mind. This task is not easy, because in marriage we come to delicate adjustments of two body needs and two different temperaments. But, only insofar as we achieve an approximate balance will we experience sex happiness.

When this equilibrium grows weak, the union with our life partner is threatened. Frequently, we seek escape in extramarital relations or divorce.

Marriage and divorce are regulated by the state. Perhaps we should change the law to make divorce available only to those who have sincerely tried to restore the balance with the help of a professional marriage counselor. Divorce would be granted only on the advice of such counselors, and not until a divorce had been recommended would attorneys step into the case. The role of divorce lawyers would be limited to financial settlements, and they would have no part in arguing about emotional conflicts preceding the divorce.

Happiness in union will be the continuing search of us all. Life affords many unifications in various fields, such as social work, education, and others. Such unifications appear to contribute to true happiness only to the extent that they make possible one's self-actualization. This can take place on different levels: physical, social, ethical, aesthetic, spiritual. In marriage, however, union may occur most completely and satisfyingly.

HAPPINESS IN DIVERSITY

Without cultural diversity, civilization would lead to universal conformity and boredom. Our interests are stimulated by variety. In spite of the American tendency toward mass production, cultural conformity in sports, movies, television programs, and national advertising, civilization still presents us with such an array of diversity—if we seek it—in science, art, religion, and philosophy that we may feel lost trying to find unity.

The phenomenal expansion of population and the unprecedented growth of knowledge have deflected our attention from the local American scene to the diversity of interests, needs, social progress, traditions and cultural achievements on a planetary basis.

Whether we like it or not, our outlook on life, as well as our attitudes, are affected by the problems of the world we read about in the newspapers or see on television.

The arbitrary division between the free world and the totalitarian systems of the communist countries, which has resulted in the cold war, has separated the extreme political left from the extreme political right. During the 1968 presidential election, we saw the beginning of this political polarization in our country. The disturbances and riots in our universities have added to this polarization. We do not know what a severe economic recession or depression may do to add to the flames of political polarity, but we cannot ignore the possibility of being faced with the choice between an ideological monism of the right and one of the left. The never-ceasing emphasis on *bigness,* whether in business or government, is placing a heavy strain on the ideological pluralism of our democracy. Bigness leads to control; control involves the wise or unwise exercise of power. Our choice between ideological monism and ideological pluralism may well determine whether we will yield to an insane culture like that in Aldous Huxley's *Brave New World,* or whether our psycho-social evolution will generate the sanity necessary for the development of a socio-democracy on a planetary level, in which diversity within unity will be possible.

THE NEED FOR LOVE

Statistics on infant mortality in orphanages have indicated clearly that the high death rate is closely associated with emotional deprivation and the absence of mothering.

Everyone, regardless of age, needs to be loved. In turn, we need to love someone; for without giving love, the self grows inward and becomes selfish. The more we love, the more we are able to love. The less we love, the more selfish we become. What should be emphasized is that love is a necessary ingredient to the achievement of unity in the midst of fragmented diversity. Love is a bond that can lead to happiness in life, uniting the self with others and giving to the self a higher sense of purposiveness.

It is interesting to note that scientists are changing their positions in regard to the importance of the study of love. In his book *The Humanization of Man,* Ashley Montague states, "Scientists are today discovering that to live as if *life* and *love* were one is an indispensable condition—because this is the way of life which the innate nature of man demands."

When the late Dr. Smiley Blanton was Director of the American Foundation of Religion and Psychiatry, he defined love in a similar way:

True love is a continuing process, a basic way of life. It must pervade one's entire personality and infuse every action with its creative beneficence. It must well up from the depths of one's character or it will not flow at all. True love between two people, in its essence, is a free process of exchange. When people truly love they "give of themselves."

Love and life cannot be restricted to one marriage partner or one family; life-love reaches out to our friends, neighbors and strangers. Love alone enables us to make friends out of strangers. Love in diversity is as essential to human progress as is love in union.

Selfish people have a limited capacity for love, because they have so little gratitude in their hearts. Their attitude is one of negative acceptance of all that happens to them and of negative comparison between what they and others receive from life. They carry consistently a chip on their shoulders against fate and the universe.

To say that gratitude is the road to happiness may sound elemental, but for many it is not an easy road to travel. Even the strongest of us gets weary of the multitudinous problems of life; the ingratitude of others is discouraging and hard to take. I do not recommend a separation of heart and mind in the process of self-giving; the combination of both is essential in order to be kind without becoming a doormat. The proper giving of monetary help is difficult and it requires thoughtful consideration; helping others to help themselves is an art. But, when we make mistakes in these fields of human relationships, we cannot retire into seclusion and frustration, we must consider the many things we still possess, and thus restore our own equilibrium and revive our own gratitude for life in its ever-recurring possibilities for love and friendship. And so the energy, which is life, sustained by the radiance of love, creates happiness. Such happiness is not a gift; it is a reward for the proper pursuit of life, in which giving and gratitude are two of the essentials.

8

THE SEARCH FOR UTOPIAS

To the average individual, no search seems more futile than the search for Utopia. From the time of Plato to the present—when a group of idealistic Americans attempted to establish an ideal community on one of the Galapagos Islands in the Pacific Ocean—the failures of these enterprises have created the popular impression that Utopias and wishful thinking are practically synonymous.

Yet, none of us will ever understand the meaning of our lives until we have a clear concept of our own Utopia. I do not refer to any desire for an ideal existence on some far-off island, where tranquility and peace seem natural to the surroundings; I have in mind the Utopia that must be ours in the midst of the strains and stresses experienced in the bustle of modern, civilized life. This Utopia of ideals rather than places is best expressed in the old saying: "Tell me what a man believes in and I will tell you what kind of a man he is."

If a man believes in *nothing* but what "he can see for himself," we may recognize him as a thoroughgoing skeptic with no faith in his fellow man. If he believes only in what he knows, we may accept him at his own classification—as an agnostic. The man who makes no commitment at all is only half a man. The difference between an agnostic and a religious man is that the former stops when he has said, "I don't know"; while the religious man adds: ". . . but I believe." Certainly, no man can be wise if he refuses to base his beliefs on all the information that is available to him. In this sense, belief is man's commitment and response to the unknown. Without such commitment and response, we would still be savages today.

The basis of all Utopias is not the acceptance of the world as it is, but as we think it ought to be. While we must learn to accept ourselves and others as we are and to accept the world as it is, we must continue to strive for progress and never be satisfied with the *status quo.*

Most creators of Utopias, however, succumb to the paradox of divorcing ideals from actuality, subjectivity from objectivity, faith from reason, which gives a schizoid basis to modern culture.

Many Utopias have failed because they were not based upon experience; they were based on theories which were, in turn, predicated on abstract assumptions—some good, some bad.

Briefly, these are the Utopias I shall analyze:

1) The Utopia of the intellect, as shown in Ayn Rand's *Atlas Shrugged*;
2) The Utopia of Being, as given in J. Krishnamurti's *The First and Last Freedom*; and
3) The Utopia of "sane living," as presented in Aldous Huxley's *Island.*

From these samples, we may be able to build a synthesis that will help us understand the paradoxes of life and build our own Utopias.

THE UTOPIA OF THE INTELLECT

On first sight, the philosophy of reason is one which exerts a strong appeal to every thinking person. In *Atlas Shrugged,* Ayn Rand presents her philosophy of reason in a powerfully written novel.

Her literary craftsmanship enables her to inject intense emotion into her reasoning, which gives an illusion of reality to her supermen, her superwomen, and her own version of Utopia—the world as it *ought to be.*

When the hypnotic spell of her writing is broken, it becomes apparent that the strong appeal of her supermen arises almost entirely from the disgust she evokes in us for the weaklings who run our society. Miss Rand, who believes only in objective reality, is thoroughly monistic in all of her attitudes, and she accepts only absolute reason, complete self-interest, and 100 percent capitalism. In *Atlas Shrugged,* she does not fight the dual aspects of human life in this world as many of us see it, she fights what she considers the opposites of absolute reason: faith, mysticism, socialism, and altruism.

Miss Rand does not agree with the belief that life is a compromise between two opposing forces. To her, one is either objective or nonobjective; one either believes in reason or in faith, in intellect or in mysticism, in reality or in dreams, in atheism or in God, in capitalism or in socialism, in self-interest or in altruism. She does not believe that the "either-or" of Aristotle should be replaced by another concept. She believes only in objectivism and, to her, the opposites of capitalism, self-interest, and atheism are evil.

For example, no person may enter her fictitious Utopia without taking an oath: "I swear by my life and my love of

111

it that I will never live for the sake of another man, nor ask another man to live for mine." Miss Rand describes her philosophy as "consistency in essence . . . the concept of man as a heroic being, with his own happiness as the moral purpose of his life, with productive achievement as his noblest activity, and reason as his only absolute."

Her enthusiasm and keen intellect, expressed in sparkling statements and unusual situations, invoke a powerful hypnotic spell over the unsuspecting reader; he accepts her half-truths—unreal characters, a world hard to recognize as our own, and an unworkable philosophy—as the *final word of reason incarnate.*

We should always be wary of human absolutes in whatever form they may be presented. Although the apparent dualities of life will never be solved by any absolute, *Atlas Shrugged* is a significant book, because the philosophy it expounds has a tremendous impact on young minds and Miss Rand's skillful writing has a profound intellectual appeal.

It is unfortunate that the inexperienced react so positively to her ridiculous claim that life is only a matter of intellectual analysis. I do not wish to imply that Miss Rand does not score some excellent points. Her strong appeal for workers in the world, instead of loafers, is certainly a valid one, and her contention that productive achievements are man's noblest activities merits our serious consideration.

I cannot agree with her, however, when she insists that man's own happiness is the moral purpose of his life. Each of us has the right to *earn* his own happiness, but it is not a sin to show some concern for the happiness of others.

Altruism, like salt, is a relative thing. Too much salt spoils food; too much altruism may ruin a life. No salt leaves food with a flat taste; lack of altruism makes human life bare. Altruism should never be confused with sloppy sentimentality. There can be as much strength in an altruist as there is in Ayn Rand's supermen—and how much more humaneness!

Her supermen are gods—Greek gods, a special breed of men who believe only in *either-or,* black or white, good or bad. They share intellectual absolutism, an absolutely uncompromising attitude toward any concept other than their own. Somehow, her supermen are not believable, because Miss Rand's insistence on accepting the Aristotelian logic of either-or, holds no promise for modern life with its myriad complexities.

I do believe, though, in the superman—of the future. Men with godlike qualities may arise from our psychosocial evolution, which is accelerating at a greater speed than most of us realize. We will gain nothing by going back to an Aristotelian logic. Logic, being a tool, may be likened to a fine surgical instrument. Without it, an operation may not be successful, but since it is only the means to an end, *it has no answers of its own.*

THE UTOPIA OF A MYSTIC

The Utopia of Krishnamurti is an individual one: it is the search for Being or, since he might object to the term "search," we might say the acceptance of ultimate reality. This reality may also be expressed as an "eternal now," but it must not be thought of as a static condition or a changeless event. This timeless now is an ever-changing event, which is composed of knowledgeless understanding.

One who is not versed in mysticism may think that

"understanding everything without knowledge of any-thing" sounds like double-talk and may be tempted to push this concept aside. This purity of Being, however, as well as the purity of intellect, can teach us something.

The apparent simplicity of Krishnamurti's description of mystical union may be deceiving. When asked what simplicity is, he answers by saying: "Let us see what simplicity is not."

Let us apply Krishnamurti's technique by asking what he thinks we should not believe in.

He does not believe in a church or a creed. He does not believe that Buddha or Jesus saves. He does not believe in quoting any sacred book, for, if you quote, you repeat—and it cannot be the truth, for truth cannot be repeated. He does not believe in opinions, of the right or of the left, because they represent ideas—and ideas are not truth. He does not believe that men exist for society; and, if this sounds like Ayn Rand, he does not mean it in the sense in which she uses it. He does not believe in politicians and he has no faith in God.

Does this mean that Krishnamurti, a mystic, is denying the existence of God? No, he answers, it would be foolish to make such a denial: "Belief is a denial of truth, belief hinders truth; to believe in God is not to find God. Neither the believer nor the non-believer will find God; because reality is the unknown, and your belief or non-belief in the unknown is merely a self-projection and therefore not real."

Actually, it seems that Krishnamurti does not believe in anything. Why not? Because "all organized beliefs are based on separation, though they may preach brotherhood."

Is it a question of semantics? Would it be better if we

asked: What does Krishnamurti *think?* But, as he has as
little regard for thinking as he has for believing, communication between us and him seems nearly impossible.
Krishnamurti admits this readily, but he also states that
understanding comes "when we meet on the same level at
the same time." He points out that listening is an art and
that the only way we can truly listen is when we achieve a
truly receptive state of mind in which prejudices, worries,
and fears are entirely removed. Unfortunately, most of us
are not receptive, because we *use* our fears and prejudices
as a screen of resistance. All too often we "listen really to
our own noise, to our own sound, not to what is being
said."

When Krishnamurti asks "What are we seeking?" he
answers himself by saying that most of us are seeking
"some kind of happiness, some kind of peace" and that we
seek this as a refuge from war and chaos; that even if we
seek happiness, we cannot find it—we can find only
gratification. He asserts that "happiness is a derivative"—
a by-product of something else.

Krishnamurti adds that we cannot separate the searcher
from the search. In order to understand the one, we must
understand the other, which, of course, implies self-knowledge.

The three key words in Krishnamurti's philosophy are:

Reality—what is;
Separation—from reality;
Self-knowledge—leading back to reality, or allowing reality
    to come to us.

To understand Krishnamurti, we must know what he
means by these terms. To understand his reality, we must

begin with self-knowledge, which, he says, is something most of us do not want.

Self-knowledge is not an intellectual process of knowing, for knowledge depends on memory; memory implies choice; choice brings comparisons; comparisons require judgment and thus we are led to an irrevocable duality. Duality involves separation and *if we are to discover reality, which exists only in nonduality,* we must discard comparisons, judgments, and all intellectual efforts used to solve the world's problems. We can never solve the world's problems; we cannot change ourselves. To do so we must perceive truth directly; we can never analyze it, never repeat it. Reality always changes; it never stands still. We need an alert and pliable heart and mind to be aware of it. This awareness does not come by self-willing or through concentration, it comes only when one is in a state of "alert passivity" or of "choiceless awareness."

This concept is difficult for us to comprehend, because most of us in the Western world think of meditation in terms of dwelling on a special thought or subject. Krishnamurti tells us that in meditation we must "look" at each one of our thoughts passively, for we are not going to touch reality through self-discipline or any other method except that of allowing ourselves to stop the separation caused by all our thought processes, until our mind becomes completely stilled.

Before rejecting this concept as too naïve, we should note Krishnamurti's warning that it sounds simple but is extremely difficult. Not to think—and not to choose— involves the breaking of a lifetime's habit.

Unless we can achieve this state, we cannot know that tranquility of mind, that stillness in which we are no longer separated from reality.

116

Self-knowledge, according to Krishnamurti, comes only when we have succeeded in reviewing our thoughts and actions, our feelings and relationships in a detached manner. This self-knowledge has no end—reality comes to us in a never-ending flow, when our mind has become truly tranquil. Then we have creative action.

What is this reality? What is this creative event in which we live and move and have our being after we have stripped ourselves of all impurities? What happens when our "natural" minds are in a state of "choiceless awareness" and are at one with creative Reality (with a capital "R")?

Krishnamurti tells us that choiceless awareness will lead us to complete nonduality, and it will provide total understanding and perfect love. It must *not* be thought of, however, as a process of meditation in which one seeks or asks for anything. Such seeking or asking—praying, if you will—is as much a part of our conditioning as any other thought pattern and it may bring a response from our memories or from the unconscious, but it is not the voice of reality.

Since ideas are always conditional, we can be limited only by the action which follows. "Action," says Krishnamurti, "can never liberate men." He continues:

Can there be action without thought process? . . . Surely there is such action when the idea ceases, and the idea ceases only when there is love. Love is not memory. Love is not experience. Love is not thinking about the person that one loves, for then it is merely thought. You cannot *think* love. You can think of the person you love or are devoted to—your guru, your image, your wife, your husband, but the thought, the symbol, is not the real which is love. Therefore, love is not an experience.

117

After telling us what reality is not, what truth is not, what love is not, Krishnamurti states that love is the only action that is liberating, because there is no gap between love and action, no conflict between the ideal and the real.

In our search for reality (with a small "r") and for the ideal, must we choose between the absolute reason of Ayn Rand and the absolute Reality of Krishnamurti? Or, becoming weary, shall we summon forth the spirit of Shakespeare and exclaim: "A plague on both your houses"?

Life as we know it, life as we *must* live it, cannot exist at either extreme. Regardless of what we may think, believe, say, or do, we cannot escape from either our objective or subjective selves. We cannot accept the Utopia of pure intellect or of pure Being. Is there some middle way we might consider?

THE UTOPIA OF SANE LIVING

Our bodies have two legs, and little purpose seems to be served by arguing whether the right leg or the left is more valuable. As a balanced and useful life requires the use of two healthy legs; so must we use the resources of our objective and subjective selves in order to comprehend reality.

Erudite author Aldous Huxley was as much aware of this as any of us. In *Island,* he expressed a Utopia of "sane living" as a compromise between the philosophies of the eastern and the western worlds.

In *Brave New World,* Huxley gives the politicians full sway. Instead of creating supermen in order to bring them to their knees, as Ayn Rand does in *Atlas Shrugged,* Huxley has politicians use the scientists and, some six centuries hence, they create a modern world of controlled science, controlled economics, controlled eugenics, bottled babies, and a controlled press. In short, Mr. Huxley presents us with a Utopia of controlled and conditioned happiness in which everyone thinks his life is the best of all possible lives. Each person represented has been *chosen, created,* and *conditioned* according to a master plan. In this hedonistic society, sex is completely and exclusively a matter of pleasure; the thought of using sex for procreation makes people blush.

"The Savage," says Mr. Huxley, in his preface to a new edition of *Brave New World,* some dozen years later, "is offered only two alternatives, an insane life in Utopia, or the life of a primitive. . . . If I were now to rewrite the book, I would offer the Savage a third alternative. Between the Utopian and the primitive horns of his dilemma would lie the possibility of sanity. . . ."

Mr. Huxley appears to have presented this third Utopia in his novel, *Island.* The site of the novel is Pala, a forbidden island in the South Pacific. It is inhabited by Mahayana Buddhists, who are later joined by an English man of medicine whose scientific training puts him at odds with the prevailing philosophy. The local Rajah, a Tantrik Buddhist, soon recognizes the value of pure and applied science and, in turn, helps the doctor discover the value of pure and applied Mahayana. Together they decide to make the best of both their worlds.

Since their religion is respected and all they have to give up is "the old wive's science and the fairy tales," it is not difficult for the people of Pala to go along with the ideas of these two men. In time, they acquire the knowledge and technocracy of the Western world, both subordinated to

119

the theories of Buddhism and the psychological facts of applied metaphysics.

Tantrik Buddhists are Mahayanists who received their Buddhism from Bengal and Tibet, not from Ceylon. Tantriks, unlike the members of the Southern School, do not renounce the world. They do not attempt to escape into a Nirvana apart from life; they accept the world's values instead. They place great emphasis on Maithuna, the Yoga of love. This love is neither sacred nor profane, or else it is both, as the two are blended into one. Whether or not we agree with Mr. Huxley's use of Tantrik Buddhism, he does present us with interesting applications of the philosophy in the lives of the islanders.

For example, education of Palanese children begins almost at birth. While suckling their babies, mothers caress them, and repeat the word "good" over and over again—sometimes in the presence of some other person, or animal, or thing—which indoctrinates the baby in one of the basic philosophies of the island: "Food plus contact plus 'good' equals love. And love equals pleasure, love equals satisfaction."

The children are also taught to say grace at their meals in a very special way—they *chew* it. The first mouthful of each course is taken with full attention to its flavor, its temperature, and its texture. They are taught to isolate the sensations that are caused by the pressure against their teeth and the feeling of their jaw muscles as they chew. They give "thanks" for their food by noticing the fullness of it at the moment they eat it—by being totally aware of what is—or reality.

These same little children often go to the fields on scarecrow duty. They manipulate the wires that set beautifully carved, life-sized marionettes into motion. And what are these splendidly draped figures? They are gods—East Indian versions of God the Father and future Buddhas. The idea was that of the old Rajah, who wanted to make the children understand *"that all gods are homemade,* and that it is we who pull their strings and so give them the power to pull ours."

Palanese children are not subject to the compulsive discipline of one set of parents in one home; they have the option of adopting ten or twenty other families, as well. If a child feels resentment at home, he simply moves in with another couple for a while, until he feels different. This does not mean that he can escape discipline or responsibility easily; he simply exchanges one set of parents for another. Becoming a member of his adopted family, for however short a time, means sharing the responsibilities of that household.

Formal education in Pala adheres to the concept that the island's boys and girls are raised "for actualization, for being turned into full-blown human beings."

In order to achieve this exalted stage, each child is analyzed according to his anatomical structure, his talents and deficiencies, his temperament and all other such salient factors. Many questions about each child must be answered. The educators must know if the child is dominated by his gut, by his muscles, or by his nervous system. They must know if he is inclined to be sociable, or if he tends to retreat into his own inner world; they must know if he has a tendency to dominate others and if he is imaginative, or inclined to be prosaic and a follower of others.

After determining these factors as clearly as possible, the teacher faces the real problem of educating her pupils on a conceptual level without limiting their capacities for

121

intense nonverbal experience or for reconciling analysis with vision.

The children are separated into three groups: the introverts, the extroverts, and the little muscle people. These latter ones love power and have strong aggressive tendencies. Gradually, as the children learn to understand and tolerate all other levels of personality and ability, the groups are intermingled. Then their increased understanding and tolerance produces a society in which no great leaders arise. Pala does not want leaders.

Very early in every child's life, a specific examination is given to determine the potential small-scale tyrants—the incipient persecutors, the possible criminals and the budding sadists. Through work and social therapies, through medication, careful training in the use of awareness, and other techniques perfected by long practice, the Palanese children are cured of their undesirable tendencies.

In short, the Palanese educational system provides a training of the whole mind-body in its varying aspects—perception and imagination, physiology and psychology, practical ethics and religion, the exact use of language and, above all, self-knowledge. Mr. Huxley is careful to point out that the results of this educational concept could hardly be such as we find in our own world—scientific giants, for instance, with the emotional age and behavior of eleven-year-olds, or philosophic savants with compulsive eating problems.

It is made clear to the Palanese that their island is not a paradise. It is a pleasant place to live and it will remain so only as long as everyone works and behaves decently. For that, each individual must be detached and must "look at" everything receptively as well as conceptually. The educational system is geared to train the children in "receptivity as well as in analysis and symbol manipulation."

It is the islanders' belief that no good literature can be written without using the concept of dualism—and, contrarily, that no good life can exist with it. The "I am" of the religious-minded dualists is considered to be untrue. They may attempt to call "homemade spirits from the vasty deep; [a mystical concept of the inner core of reality] the nondualist calls the vasty deep into his spirit or, to be more accurate, he finds that the vasty deep is already there." It seems self-evident to them that wisdom and science neither see nor seek separation. They believe instead that our culture has been led astray by the Prophets, Pythagoras, Plato, and the early Buddhists, who created dualism between man and nature, between nature and God, between appearance and ideal reality. To the Tantriks, Mahayanists, and a few heretical Christians, this separation has not occurred. Dualism is a dirty word in Pala.

Similarly, the term monism is not used by the Mahayanists. To do so would imply the presence of dualism. Instead, they say the "not two," the "not me," and the "not this," "not that," etc. Of course, this method of negation must eventually lead to a final nothingness—a nothingness of the self which leads directly to the universal all. Buddha has said "I will show you sorrow," and he succeeded admirably in pointing out sickness and suffering; but he also said "I will show you the ending of sorrow." That was a more difficult feat, but it could be accomplished in one of two ways: 1) by *complete* detachment—a difficult feat even in his day; or 2) by dying, either naturally (physically) or by freeing the mind from the self so that "the vasty deep," which is already there, can take over and enjoy its natural, undisturbed reality.

123

To achieve this reality, or Buddha nature, the Palanese imbibe the "moksha medicine" made from the substance of toadstools. They call it the reality revealer, the truth and beauty pill. It apparently does something unusual to the silent areas of the brain—those which are not specifically concerned with perceiving, or moving, or feeling. The first reaction is a sensation of inexpressible joy which is often followed by moods of depression. (Mr. Huxley wrote this before the present notoriety and wide use of psychedelics.) The author explains that this sensation is not at all comparable to the elation of alcohol followed by hangover; it is a kind of heaven-hell episode—the brain does not respond to the moksha medicine with "visions or auditions, telepathy or clairvoyance," which Huxley feels are only amusing, premystical stuff, at best.

At the end of his book, Mr. Huxley allows outside materialistic interests to overwhelm his islanders. It seems that he did not intend to save them, for who ever heard of Utopia for a mystic? Rather, he seems determined that all things must have their ending in the "final end of man."

MUST WE CHOOSE?

Eventually, there must be an end to man just as there will be an end to this planet. The final chapter of man may well occur long before the end of the earth. Little of practical value may be derived from our concern about the extinction of the planet; but the end of man, as it is visualized in *this* book, is of the greatest importance for all humanity. My concept of the end of man is different from that of Rand, Krishnamurti, and Huxley, because, as we advance in our human evolution, our power to affect the end of man will increase.

In our psychosocial evolution there can be no Utopias as such, for Utopias are idealistic presentations of static concepts of perfection which have never existed in reality and are not likely to come into being. If this is so, what use can we make of the writings of Ayn Rand, Krishnamurti, and Aldous Huxley?

Miss Rand's intellectual and supra-individualistic concept of what life in the present ought to be presents an ideal based on absolute reason and complete self-centeredness. Many valuable elements are to be found in her various discourses, but her philosophy of life and her present-day use of the Aristotelian dictum of either-or is unsound, because life cannot be based on reason alone. Students, who are primarily occupied with intellectual pursuits and who have little experience in living, may find her appeal to a dominant reason sound and sensible. But a life based on reason alone will lead to irrationality as surely as does a life based only on emotion. The struggle we are all engaged in is the constant adjustment of the relationship between our hearts and our minds.

The perfect reason, complete objectivity and 100 percent capitalism of Ayn Rand hold no greater promise for our progressive psychosocial evolution than does the perfect detachment of Krishnamurti. Man cannot exist alone. For better or worse we must become involved in society. Our present democratic and so-called capitalistic society is far removed from being 100 percent in either category. The prevailing trends seem to push in the opposite direction of Miss Rand's formula for progress.

Krishnamurti wants to live in the present, and he maintains that we are forever in the present if we practice silence enough to experience it.

What does this mean? It means that the present always *is,* but we can never know it. To think about the present is impossible, because the present is always the past by the time we have conceptualized it. Not as thinking entities, therefore, but only as *being* entities can we experience the present. This means complete detachment from all ideas or attempts to think or act until we arrive at total stillness.

Unless we have had the mystical experience, which comes to one in total stillness, we cannot understand the beauty of the love Krishnamurti discusses when the self is lost in communion with the heart of the universe. But we can grasp such experiences of utter silence *only momentarily;* and afterward we return to this world, where there are always choices to be made. One cannot choose but choose.

Aldous Huxley has seen the problems in this dilemma clearly and, while remaining a confirmed mystic, he has amused himself by presenting an imaginary society on a secluded island where mysticism modifies the conduct of a rational group of people, producing what he calls a "reasonable irrationality." He claims that all societies created by men are irrational because men behave irrationally. According to Huxley, society can be made rational only by a complete surrender to the "vasty deep"; but, since such a surrender is not possible, Huxley shows us the best possible compromise. His imaginary society is destroyed at the close of the story, because, eventually, all societies must have their termination in the end of man.

If we have overdone our analysis and fear of dualism, we might do better by seeing it as polarity. Accepting the oneness of the universe and all it contains, we should be aware of the numerous polarities that are evidenced all through life. Let me use my simple illustration once more: Ice and steam are the extreme polarities of water. Steam and ice are equally real. Matter and spirit are the two extremes of the one psychic energy, which *is* the universe.

Since man is both matter and spirit, he must find his fulfillment in learning how the polarities of these two provide the best results. In order to do so, man must use his physical senses, his intellect and his imagination, as well as his mystical insights.

Life is a dynamic process. Any Utopia, any set of guiding ideals modern man can accept, must be an integral part of that process. Life demands a compromise between opposing principles. The Utopias of Ayn Rand and Krishnamurti are concepts of static perfection, allowing no compromise. Huxley compromises first and then destroys his compromise.

These three illustrations should suffice to show us that we must choose otherwise.

9

ARE WE MAKING PROGRESS?

Anyone reading the gloomy news in our daily newspapers may be inclined to answer this question with a resounding "No!"

Although we are living in an affluent society and are blessed with a high degree of scientific progress, one question persists: Why are we surrounded by so much unrest, dissatisfaction, and disillusionment?

Change is not new in the world. But the revolutionary changes in our era are new, for they are unusually rapid and far-reaching. We question everything from the authority of the pope and the moral standards of society to the economic concepts of our affluent capitalism and the political foundation on which it rests. To many people the "old" world seems to be crumbling all around them and there is no indication of a new and better structure to take its place.

THE TWILIGHT ZONE

In this period of national and international turmoil, we are in agonizing doubt as to whether civilization's new offspring will prove to be a hero or a monster.

128

Although it is impossible to go into all of the ramifications of our social unrest here, we should realize that such art forms as architecture, music, literature, painting, and sculpture all mirror the sensitivity and the thought patterns of our civilization, in many ways.

Modern fine art has experienced many and, in some cases, devastating revolutions. We have poetry that has lost its age-old identity in prose; music that seems primarily a protest against harmony and melodiousness; sculpture that borrows its "inspiration" from junkyard and tinsmith's shop; abstract painting that has lost all meaning for the viewer. Too much modern art has not been the result of the creative urge expressing itself in beauty, it has been a protest against the old order and a reflection of the vagueness and uncertainty of our times. There have been many exceptions, of course, but the general trend indicates that the era of the cold war has diffused its spirit of uncertainty, impersonality, and hostility into all the avenues of fine art.

In breaking away from tradition, many arguments have arisen between the modernists and the traditionalists about the nature of art and truth, and the traditionalists have had to struggle to defend the very foundation of their art. On the one hand, the result has been a brilliant individualism and, on the other, a chaotic conglomeration of both artlessness and meaninglessness.

The best of modern painting, whether in cubism, expressionism, or surrealism, most likely will survive the ravages of time. But if it be true, as has been stated so often, that the real artist is as much a truth seeker as the scientist, it should be evident that nonobjectivism in painting, which is based on the concept that art has no relation whatever to the existing forms and objects of the world as we see it, is a pure reflection of our present social state of uncertainty and philosophical relativism.

Whenever I see someone looking intently at an abstract painting, trying in vain to comprehend the incomprehensible and turning away with a look of distress mixed with guilt, I am reminded of the story of a legendary king. The court jester, coming before the king, bowed low and said: "Your Majesty, I hold here in my closed fist the most beautiful statue in the world. Only fools cannot see it. Shall I show it to you?"

At the king's assent, the jester held open his empty hand. The king, looking intently at empty space, admired the nonexistent statue for he did not wish to be considered a fool.

We can see the disruptive forces of our revolutionary century reflected in sculpture and painting. Sculpture is no longer restricted to the use of stone or clay; steel, iron, copper and brass are being shaped into wires, rods, bars, and sheets. Sculptors no longer use hammer and chisel; in their factory-like studios they work with tin nippers, welding torch, and soldering iron. We have seen the fantastic hybrid creations of their imagination, but we have not always understood or appreciated them.

Art students will find, as do those in the fields of law, knowledge, and philosophy, no definite standards for the guidance of the individual. Without such guidance, modern man feels lost and he is at war with himself and with society. Out of such conflicts have come bitter intellectuals, existentialists, and other nonconformists.

Without communication, civilization would be impossible. Participation and understanding are necessary for genuine communication. Youngsters complain about a communication gap with their parents. But grown-ups seem afraid to communicate—even with each other. This may be why the modern cocktail party is so popular. Here, we are not tied down to one person; we can flit hither and yon, talking without listening, and listening without hearing or bothering to comprehend.

Some see a reappraisal in art as the result of a trend away from chaos and back to order, which is reflected in a greater demand for representational art works that convey meaning to the ordinary viewer. It may be true that we are witnessing the early stages of a rebirth of aesthetic discrimination which, eventually, will separate the high grade from the second-rate in art.

Among many modern artists, beauty is considered a dirty word. I think, however, that the pendulum will swing back to an appreciation of beauty in art—whatever our deeper insights may contribute to a refinement of the concept of beauty.

The inevitable need for communication, meaning, and empathy on the part of the listener or viewer will have its effect on the true artist. In time, the bizarre, the meaningless, the shocking, and the inept will be relegated to the junk heap, which is their rightful depository.

My own feelings on the subject are best expressed by Lewis Mumford, who wrote:

If the artist is not to betray his art as well as his humanity, he must not think that nausea and vomit are the ultimate realities of our time. Those obscenities are indeed a part of the actual world we are conditioned to. But they do not belong to the possible world of the creator and the transvaluer who bring forth out of their own depths new forms and values that point to new destinations. The artist, too, has the responsibility to be sane and the duty to be whole and balanced. . . . the artist has the task of nourishing and developing every intuition of love and of finding images through which they become visible. If all he can say in his picture is: "This is the end," let it be the end and let him say no more about it. Let him be silent until he has recovered the capacity to conjure up once more, however timid at first, a world of fine perceptions and rich feelings, of values that sustain life and coherent forms that re-enforce the sense of human mastery.[9]

PROGRESS AND HUMANISM

Modern humanism is a liberal philosophy presenting a comprehensive system of ideas. Its liberalism flows from a lack of dogmatism and a scientific attitude toward life. Julian Huxley, in *The Humanist Frame,* defines humanism as an . . . "open system, capable of indefinite further development." [10] In this book he has collected the views of many scholars who present the modern humanist philosophy of life. This concept includes man's higher activities in science, art, and religion, which Huxley says do not appear "as independent entities but as interlocking functions of our evolving species." [11] Humanists look askance at supernaturalism and Lionel Elvin contends "that the leading concepts as to the nature of things handed down to us through religious dogmas do not afford us elements for a world view that we can regard as satisfactory for our own period of human history." [12] Elvin says the humanists believe that the "invocation of supernatural powers in all its varied forms, like the equally widespread former belief in witchcraft, belongs to an earlier stage of human development. It does not really explain anything and it darkens understanding more than it helps it." [13] The humanist, however, does not object to the free play of thought in the field of religion so long as that thought *is* kept free.

Aldous Huxley accepts the "free play of thought," and he is not concerned with supranaturalism any more than is his brother, Julian. Julian looks upon telepathy and clairvoyance as interesting phenomena of the human mind we need to learn more about; to Aldous, as we have noted in the previous chapter, these things are only "amusing premystical stuff." Aldous Huxley has no dogmas regarding this life; he believes in "the art of being irrational in a reasonable way." All gods are man-made and, if we are alert, we pull the strings. Aldous' antidualism is based on his concept of nonseparation—a monism which finds its unity in the absolute of the "vasty deep."

While some philosophers may argue that mysticism may produce a sharp dualism between the world of the senses and the world of the spirit, this charge cannot be leveled against Aldous Huxley, who has made it very clear in his presentation of the Palanese children's education that no such dualism exists in his concept of mind-body relationships. Humanists may find an even more scientific attitude toward life in the Utopia of the Palanese than in the so-called scientific civilization of our Western world. They certainly will not quarrel with his monism and his attitude toward a reasonably irrational development of human life as long as he supports them in the attempt to make it more reasonable. After all, there is no gainsaying the fact that much of human life *has been and still is irrational.*

No wonder then that Julian Huxley gives his brother the "last word" in *The Humanist Frame.* In this book's final chapter, "Human Potentialities," Aldoux Huxley repeats a great deal of what he has written in his novel *Island*.

In his introduction to Krishnamurti's *The First and Last Freedom*, Aldous quotes Krishnamurti as saying: "And what you are repeating is not the truth. It is a lie; for truth cannot be repeated." No doubt, as a mystic, Mr. Huxley agrees with this statement; nevertheless, in *Island* one of his characters says: "If we repeat it, it's because it happens to be true. If we didn't repeat it, we'd be ignoring the facts." Is this difference a question of semantics? Or is it Mr. Huxley's own contribution to being irrational in a reasonable way?

As to the final end of man, I think it may occur in one of four possible ways: 1) The voluntary cessation of human life by complete birth control (this method was highly recommended and explained by an anonymous Frenchman in a book entitled *Intelligence,* which he published privately in 1932); 2) As the result of total nuclear or chemical warfare, which will make this planet uninhabitable or destroy man's powers of reproduction; 3) The cooling of the sun, its explosion, or some other event in our galaxy which will make life on this planet impossible; 4) The evolution of man into a different or greater species.

The humanists might accept the first three as distinct possibilities, but they would place definite restrictions on the interpretation of the fourth, because they consider the advancement of man limited to life on this planet only. In contrast, my view of man's evolution is a continuous process expanding far beyond this earth. The mystic might answer by saying that the journey of life itself is of no great importance except the finish of it, when we return to or are united with the "vasty deep," and in so doing, they may

134

assert the "final end of man" does answer all questions. Julian Huxley writes:

> There have been two critical points in the past of evolution, points at which the process transcended itself by passing from an old state to a fresh one with quite new properties. The first was marked by the passage from the inorganic phase to the biological, the second by that from the biological to the psychosocial. Now we are on the threshold of a third. As the bubbles in a cauldron on the boil mark the onset of the critical passage of water from the liquid to the gaseous state, so the ebullition of humanist ideas in the cauldron of present-day thought marks the onset of the passage from the psychosocial to the consciously purposive phase of evolution.[14]

I find Julian Huxley's concept of the third transcendence a most encouraging statement of belief. I would add that my concept of the final end of man is the fourth passage of evolution, from the consciously purposive phase to the truly spiritual evolution of man. (Consciously purposive evolution means self-determining. Spiritual evolution means fully creative. See glossary.) But without this third phase, the fourth will never take place.

The aims and purposes of the humanists, though not strictly mine, *point in the same direction.* Therefore, we can work in harmony together in trying to bring about this third phase of human evolution.

Many important aims and purposes have been stated so far in our various searches. But what are the major goals on which we must concentrate to give full meaning to our lives?

I believe that we must start with the major assumption

135

that while each individual is responsible for his own progress, none can divorce himself from the evolutionary goal for the species to which he belongs. Since my philosophy includes the social as well as the individual aspects of life, I reject all Oriental and mystical attitudes that consider "civilized life" unimportant; at the same time, I remain aware of the need for the "within" and the "inner" development of man. As partners with nature, we must evaluate her controls and strengthen our own, realizing that, as evolution continues, control becomes more rather than less important; the *quality* of that control, however, must improve if we are to pass on to the next stage of evolution. As we advance on the evolutionary ladder, progress is no longer inevitable; it becomes a matter of choice and control.

Our consciously purposive phase of evolution will teach us how to command nature by first obeying her. We must not assume, however, that we can become masters of our fate overnight and that, because the body and brains of man are a so-called biochemical organism, we can treat man like a machine into which we pour gasoline and direct at will.

The only Utopia I believe in, is the one of *continuous* creativity. While our advancement in leisure time brings this possibility closer to realization, the problem of proper motivation remains.

Trying to make life effortless by taking drugs is as irrational as trying to accomplish miracles by wishful daydreaming. Whatever our definition of reality may be, let us remind ourselves that the universe *is an energy system* in which sloth and laziness pay no interest.

Unless we are able to increase our motivation for spiritual growth, the possibility exists that the future controls in

136

our complex technological society will pass more and more into the hands of politicians and demagogues, resulting in an eventual dictatorship.

My vision of evolution is that of an eternal process, in which man, as we know him, is still on one of the lower rungs of the ladder despite the fact that we may have been evolving for billions of years. I do not believe in the Buddhist doctrine of Nirvana; my vision is not of a closed universe but of an eternally expanding one. (Since there is no definite proof that the universe must contract after so many billions of years, I assume an expanding universe in which there is no end to the process of creativity.)

I believe that our graduation from "the school of man" is not a foregone conclusion, but it is a distinct possibility. I admit that the view is revolutionary and that it is based on reason and faith, pending future evidence. Of great importance is the fact that the concept of the evolutionary processes is based on a self-perpetuating purpose, which biologists observe in all organisms. This purpose, which I have expressed as my faith in my Utopia, is an eternal creative process in which we were conceived and in which we move and have our being. It will be my task to explain how we may live in it forever.

Part II

10

THE SEARCH FOR GOD

In December of 1961, the Gallup Poll stated that "Those persons who can be described as either 'atheists' or 'agnostics' account for only about 2 percent of the populace." If we were to accept this figure literally, we might conclude that the search for God in these United States was of the utmost importance to all of our citizens. I do not assume, however, that 98 percent of our population have all experienced what Francis Bacon put into words in his essay *Of Atheism*: "A little philosophy inclineth man's mind to atheism, but depth in philosophy bringeth man's mind about to religion." I think that the majority have not been touched by philosophy at all, and that large numbers of people believe in God in much the same way as they do in the Fourth of July—as part of their heritage.

God's name is on our money, signifying our trust in the spiritual as well as the material realm; in our pledge to the flag we state that we are "one nation under God." Both these statements sound like national commitments. Every president of the United States publicly speaks most respectfully of God and of our trust in Him. Do 98 percent of our people accept this trust and make these commitments? Or do they respond only to tradition and to conformity in "good taste"? Even Nikita Khrushchev referred to God occasionally, not, as he said, because he believed in God but because he recognized that God is an important symbol to a large proportion of the earth's population.

Universal belief in God does not prove His existence, nor does universal disbelief in God disprove it. If we remember the importance of asking the right questions, we shall not waste our time with the ancient and useless one: Does God exist? The important and right questions to ask are: What concepts of God will make sense to us as we view the world through the eyes of science? How do we exchange new concepts for old ones? From what sources do we derive our concepts of God?

RELIGIOUS CONCEPTS OF GOD

The sacred writings of the world's religions and the explanations of theologians have been the major sources of our concepts regarding God. In the Old Testament of the Bible, God the Creator of heaven and earth became the God of Israel; but, as such, He was still the Father of mankind, the Source of all life and the Ruler of all His creatures. The prophets of Israel, all of whom were mystical seers, visualized an infinite God whose Spirit filled the universe and whose attributes were love, truth, justice, and mercy.

Historically, however, the experience of the Jewish people did not conform in every aspect with this concept of God. Polytheism, as evidenced in idol worship, flourished for generations. An unusually long series of prophets and seers opposed polytheism by repeating the exhortation:

"Hear, O Israel, the Lord is our God, the Lord is One." Christianity and Islam owe their monotheism to Judaism, and they incorporated many of the attributes of the Judaic God, Jehovah, into their own religious concepts.

While mystics and prophets may have visualized God in terms of unity, eternity, and the infinite, the religious history of the Israelites has been developed in the experience of a small nation in which conquest, oppression, and suffering have played a dominant role. The persistent concept of a Saviour is readily understood. The God of Israel became the God of deliverance. In Chapter 5 we have observed the importance of the Search for Law. God, appearing in the burning bush, spoke to Moses and Moses became the lawgiver. Above all, Judaism is a religion of law, and the Talmud is its constitution.

Jesus, knowing the reverence for law among the Jews, said that He did not come to break the law, but to fulfill it. Jesus spoke of God as our Father, and Christianity accepted this concept literally for nearly 2,000 years, picturing God as a man in the sky. Christianity ignored other words of Jesus: "Believest thou not that I am in the Father, and the Father in me? . . . the Father that dwelleth in me, he doeth the works" (John 14:10) revealing the unmistakable mystical sense of his God concept.

The persistency of belief in old concepts is due, primarily, to literalism. Recently, I asked the minister of a church with one of the largest memberships in the country how many of his flock still think of God as a big man in the sky and he replied: "Too many!"

Paul Tillich has made a distinction between two stages of literalism. In primitive societies, which lack the scientific means of observations and experiment, individuals are not able to "separate the creations of symbolic imagination from the facts"; thus they operate in a natural stage of literalism "in which the mythical and the literal are indistinguishable." [15] Tillich believes that such a natural stage should not be disturbed until man's mind begins to question the literalness of mythological visions. Then, says Tillich, there are two ways open to him: one is "to replace the unbroken by the broken myth," the other is to accept the second stage of literalism in which the questions are repressed partly consciously, partly unconsciously.

Many people in the Western world are able still to accept the Bible literally. A literalist is one who, as H. J. Muller finds it ". . . far easier to compartmentalize his mind and admit evolution on the one hand but, on the other hand, to proceed wishfully in other spheres of thought and living." [16]

In February, 1961, the Right Reverend James A. Pike, Episcopal Bishop of San Francisco, created a heated discussion by stating that the Bible contained myths. The literalists attacked his statements; those who accept myths as the necessary language or symbols of faith agreed with the bishop.

In the Spring of 1963 another bishop, John A. T. Robinson from the Church of England, published a controversial book, *Honest to God.* The bishop, who wants to be honest to God and about God and who wishes to follow the argument wherever it leads, admits repeatedly that he is searching for something he cannot define.

The bishop should know that we can define only that which we know intellectually; what we *may* know mystically we cannot define nor describe. For us mortals, God is and remains the unknown. We cannot define the unknown but we can respond to it and the content of this response is the crux of all religions.

144

WHAT IS RELIGION?

In my student days, four decades ago, I defined religion as: man's response to the unknown. Only recently, I found a wholehearted acceptance of this definition by a number of clergymen. Like all definitions, however, it needs clarification.

What kind of a response can we make to the unknown? We divide the study of man into components, such as religious, philosophic, and scientific, but intrinsically man is a unit and as such he responds with his entire being. If we look at man from these different aspects, we may say that religiously man responds to the unknown in a sense of trust if he thinks of God as Father, or God as good; or he may respond in a sense of fear if he thinks of God as a revengeful God whose abiding joy it is to punish the wicked, as so many of the more primitive religions have pictured Him. Philosophically, man may respond to the unknown in a sense of awe and wonder and try to weave meaningful patterns between what he feels (religiously) and what he observes (scientifically). Science is the result of our observations and scientists who pursue the truth are first of all philosophers, though they may limit the philosophical method primarily to the subject in which they are interested. But the aim of philosophy, according to Whitehead, "is the attainment of some unifying concept which will set in assigned relationship within itself all that there is for knowledge, for feeling, and for emotion." [17]

In *The Road to Reason*, Lecomte du Noüy said that "science is essentially based on the strange need for unification that characterizes the human mind." This need for unification brings synthesis and analysis together and makes partners of philosophy and science.

Man is a searcher. Man has a compulsion to seek after truth, whether he be scientist or philosopher. If we wish to personify that spirit in man which searches for certainty in a world of uncertainty, we may call it God.

From Columbus who sailed the ocean, to Lindbergh who flew over it, from the first balloonist to go up in the air, to the first space traveler walking on the moon, man's innate compulsion to explore the unknown never ceases.

While we are in need of unifying concepts, we cannot ignore man's intellectual habit of departmentalization. For the sake of clarification, man's response to the unknown may be divided into two major categories: one religious, the other scientific.

The religious response is based on trust; it is a commitment of faith. But as Paul Tillich so clearly demonstrated, it is a faith that should not be confused with a belief that is based on things unseen, or a belief that is considered a type of knowledge with a low degree of evidence; it should be based on a faith defined as ultimate concern.

Ultimate concern in the Christian religion (perhaps not according to the creed, dogma, or theology of some sects, but according to Christ) is: ". . . Thou shalt love the Lord thy God with all thy heart, and with all thy soul and with all thy strength, and with all thy mind . . ." (Luke 10:27). Such a commitment to an absolute is subjective and involves trust and surrender of one's will. Out of this concept of trust and surrender comes the notion that God must come down to us; we can't go up to Him. The two avenues by which contact between man and God can be established are: 1) revelation from God direct; 2) a turning inward of man, in the mystical sense—letting God come in, as man opens the door.

Christianity expresses itself objectively, however, by a

146

series of beliefs: We trust in God because God is Love; God gives meaning to life because God cares for His children; the universe does have a purpose; this purpose is beneficent and is expressed in goodwill to men on earth. Christians believe in the commandment of Jesus: "Love thy neighbor as thyself," and this implies the development of a sense of social responsibility leading to the brotherhood of man. The Father-Son relationship is expressed in the belief that God loved us first and we, as children, must *learn* to love Him.

The scientific response to the unknown is also based on trust. But, unlike the religious trust in which the ultimate concern is the will of God, trust in science is the will of man, whose ultimate concern is truth; to find the reality— of whatever is—in the universe. The faith of the scientist is basically the same as the faith of the religionist, for both are equally concerned with the unknown. Truth and reality, as we observed in our chapter on wisdom, are but two aspects of what we call God. Any description of God must be a symbol for, as Tillich pointed out, only God can be a symbol of God.

Basically, science and religion share the same faith and ultimate concern we may designate by either the symbol Reality or the symbol God; the method of acquiring trust —of becoming more godlike—is quite different.

Religion places the emphasis on God reaching out to man; science places the emphasis on man reaching out to God. In religion, the unknown is feared by man (the fear of God) or he accepts it on trust in love (our Father in heaven); in science, the unknown is a challenge to man and he attempts to conquer it. In religion, man accepts the unknown (God) as part of himself and accepts himself as part of that unknown in which man has willfully separated himself from God, and God reaches out to return man unto Himself; in science, man, coming out of evolution—meaning something less than he is now—attempts to make bits of the unknown part of himself.

Scientists have succeeded in making many conquests, indicated in our knowledge explosion and exploration into space.

As Harry Emerson Fosdick stated long ago, the result of all this has been that religion has become less necessary as a part of our daily lives. For example, men used to pray before they crossed the ocean by ship; today, the safe arrival of a luxurious new ocean liner is taken for granted by most. When Lindbergh flew the ocean, millions of people prayed for the success of his attempt. I remember my first long and uncomfortable ocean crossing in a DC-4, but that fearful journey has been compensated for many times by crossings made later in modern jets. When John Glenn became America's first astronaut, the whole Western world sat glued to their television sets, praying that he might finish his journey safely and be fished out of the ocean in time. When our fourth astronaut, Gordon Cooper, circled the earth twenty-two times, Lieutenant Commander Benjamin C. Fairchild, stationed on board the U.S.S. Kearsarge, prayed:

We pray for Gordon Cooper because we are aware of his and our complete dependence upon Thee. We know that he will not travel alone. May he sense Thy presence during these hours of preparation and what will surely seem to be an eternity in the spacecraft. We don't know what lies ahead. Only Thou knowest. We commit him to Thy care and keeping.

148

Surely, the time will come when journeys taken by John Glenn and Gordon Cooper will be commonplace, and no longer will we fear what lies ahead. But, just as surely, some other accomplishment of man will challenge the unknown, one that will require our prayer and religious response of trust in the unknown. For our religious response has two aspects: 1) fear of the unknown; and 2) trust that there is a Knower who cares about us.

There is another way of looking at the conquest of the unknown. Instead of saying that we need God less, we may say that whenever a small portion of the unknown becomes part of our daily lives and thought we are becoming more godlike, in the sense of our growing knowledge and understanding of ourselves and of a universe that expresses the creativity of God. Our deeper awareness should not lead us to intellectual arrogance, however, nor to an attitude of independence from God; it should increase our concept of His majesty and power to sustain us. Therefore, our search for knowledge must include love as well as truth. Only in this way can we attain a more Christlike attitude and become wholly subservient to God's will, whose moral and loving force rules the universe. Without such an attitude, the conquest of the unknown can lead to the intellectual pride of Satan rather than to the love of God.

The scientist, although he may not state so publicly, makes also a commitment of trust in the unknown. He believes that there are laws in the universe and that man can discover some of these. These laws will affect both the just and the unjust and this explains the amoral attitude of scientists. Yet the deeper the scientist delves into the mysteries of the universe, the more he becomes convinced that a supreme intelligence rules the galaxies, until he exclaims with physicist George Davis: "If a universe could create itself, it would embody the powers of a creator, and we should be forced to conclude that the universe itself is a God."

Men like Einstein, whose vision exceeded his grasp, have sensed this religious or mystical quality in their concept of the universe. In his broader visions of the universe, Einstein believed that reality not only preceded man's intellect, it also stood outside of him. He defined his religion as follows:

> My religion consists of a humble admiration of the illimitable superior spirit who reveals himself in the slight details we are able to perceive with our frail and feeble minds. That deeply emotional conviction of the presence of a superior reasoning power, which is revealed in the incomprehensible universe, forms my idea of God.[18]

The question remains: How are modern Christians going to visualize God?

THE REVOLUTION WITHIN CHRISTIANITY

The revolt within the Christian faith, which is a movement for reform led by several theologians within the Protestant church, is more drastic than that led by Luther and Calvin. The fact that this revolution causes less consternation and heated discussion in our society than the Reformation did is due to the acceptance of the right to express our thoughts freely.

It seems natural that theologians with a strong philosophical bent should be the leaders of this revolt. Aware of the changing concepts regarding the universe presented by science, they have struggled thoughtfully to present new theological concepts that will carry the old Christian values without contradicting modern knowledge. One of the best known theologians in this group is Paul Tillich.

Accenting the traditional beliefs of His time, Jesus made no new statements regarding the structure of the universe and, as far as we know, He showed no interest whatever in metaphysics. The interpreters of Christianity did build a metaphysical structure, however, one in which the myths of the Old Testament blended or were added to the myths of the New Testament. These myths described the attributes of God, who created heaven and earth. God was presented in divine form—walking the earth in the person of Jesus—and also as a supranatural being "up there" or "out there" in the sky. Obviously, this gave Christianity a metaphysics based on dualism.

The difficulties philosophers have had with such concepts as monism, absolutism and dualism have been indicated earlier, as well as the attempt to escape dualism by such mystics as Krishnamurti and Aldous Huxley, and science's rejection of dualism.

It became the task of Tillich and others to reconstruct modern theology in such a way that dualism was removed from Christianity. The purpose was to supplant a supernaturalistic theology with a naturalistic one, without demolishing Christianity at the same time. This attempt to liberalize theology moved in two directions: the one objectified Christianity by secularizing it; the other subjectified Christianity by enshrouding it in mysticism.

Recalling the definition of religion as our response to the unknown and observing how science in our daily life has replaced more and more the trust, hope and fear of

151

our religious response, it seems clear that the attempt to secularize religion was a natural development. Our faith in the Christian values, however, our utmost concern—is not diminished in this secularization. For, in the words of Dietrich Bonhoeffer, the Christian life must be a life of "holy worldliness," of "sacred secularity." He described God as "the beyond" in the midst of our life, a depth of reality reached "not on the borders of life but at its center."

Here is a mystical trend at work, one strongly emphasized by Tillich:

> Our period has decided for a *secular* world. That was a great and much-needed decision. . . . It gave consecration and holiness to our daily life and work. Yet it excluded those deep things for which religion stands: the feeling for the inexhaustible mystery of life, the grip of an ultimate meaning of existence, and the invincible power of an unconditional devotion. These things *cannot* be excluded.[19]

Although these words may stir our emotions and enkindle our imagination, we may still ask: "What is the ultimate meaning of life?"

Tillich attempts to give us his answer by presenting two basic concepts: one of God; the other of faith. He defines God as the "ground of all being" and faith as "ultimate concern."

If we accept Tillich's definition of God as the ground of all being, it follows that our faith in *this* God may be expressed in many ways, from the scientist's in search of truth, (if truth is his ultimate concern) to the mystic's in search of reality, (if union with reality is his ultimate concern).

"The answer given by the mystics," says Tillich, "is that

there is a place where the ultimate is present within the finite world, namely, the depth of the human soul. This depth is the point of contact between the finite and the infinite." [20]

Tillich goes on to say that to reach this ultimate the mystic must overcome the division in himself between subject and object by "meditation, contemplation and ecstasy." [21]

As I observed in my analysis of *Island,* the mystic rarely reaches this exalted state and in order to do so he may even use "moksha medicine."

Tillich continues:

> Like sacramentalism, mysticism is a type of faith; and there is a mystical as well as a sacramental element in every type of faith.

> This is true even of the humanist kind of the ontological type of faith. A consideration of this kind of faith is especially important, because humanism is often identified with unbelief and contrasted with faith. . . . The difference is that the sacramental and mystical types transcend the limits of humanity and try to reach the ultimate itself beyond man and his world, while the humanist remains within these limits. For this reason the humanist faith is called "secular," in contrast to the two types of faith which are called "religious." [22]

In humanism, we place the emphasis on objectifying our subjective concern by not going beyond the meaning of life in its concrete expressions in science, politics and social relations; yet our subjective concern is for the ideal man, the ideal society, the truth in science. In an earlier work, Tillich included the deepest springs of our social and historical existence:

> The name of this infinite and inexhaustible ground of history is *God.* That is what the word means, and it is that to which the words *Kingdom of God* and *Divine Providence* point. And if these words do not have much meaning to you, translate them, and speak of the depth of history, of the ground and aim of our social life, and of what you take seriously without reservation in your moral and political activities. Perhaps you should call this depth *hope,* simply hope. For if you find hope in the ground of history, you are united with the great prophets who were able to look into the depth of their times, who tried to escape it, because they could not stand the horror of their visions, and who yet had the strength to look to an even deeper level and there to discover hope.[23]

By removing the supernatural Being from the skies and placing the emphasis on our symbol of God, as the Ground of all Being, pointing inward to the *depths* of our being, the *depths* of history, the *depths* of our souls, the "center of our whole being involved in the center of all being; and the center of all being resting in the center of our being," we can only conclude that modern Protestant theology now emphasizes the mystical approach to God. The immanence of God is firmly established in the center of our being, but what about the transcendence of God?

Tillich does not think that to prove the transcendence of God we need to believe in a *superworld of divine objects.* In *Systematic Theology* he states "that, within itself, the finite world points beyond itself. In other words, it is self-transcendent."

The philosophical subtleties of Tillich's theology are so stimulating that one is tempted to quote him endlessly. I believe in both immanence and transcendence, for without them the physical-spiritual evolution of man could not take place. The self-transcendence of the universe is an integral part of our theory of evolution. The chapter on consciousness deals with this interdependence of spirit and matter.

In considering religion as our response to the unknown, we can observe how theologians have tried to fill that unknown by giving us concepts suitable to our time and place. And this unknown stretches out psychologically as well as cosmologically. Theology is now less concerned with cosmology and more with the *depth* of the human soul, and "the *beyond* in the midst of our life," revealing a definite mystical trend.

Bishop Robinson believes that while the pagan world was concerned with metal images, we are troubled by mental images which do not endure. He said:

For the Christian gospel is in perpetual conflict with the images of God set up in the minds of men, even of Christian men, as they seek in each generation to encompass his meaning. These images fulfill an essential purpose, to focus the unknowable, to enclose the inexhaustible, so that ordinary men and women can get their minds round God and have something on which to fix their imagination and prayers.[24]

Old concepts are not replaced automatically by new ones—posing a problem for philosophers as well as for theologians. It is also a problem for fathers and mothers whose views of the universe have expanded in the light of science, but whose view of God is restricted to the primitive one of the Old Man in the sky. In old Sunday-school fashion they tell their children to be good, for God watches them and knows everything they are doing. Children, in turn, acquire a concept of God as a holy Santa Claus who rewards or punishes them.

The great challenge and hope of Christianity has been its profession of personal immortality. Take this away and Christianity disappears either into an ethical humanism or an ethical pantheistic philosophy like the intellectualized forms of Buddhism. The concept of Christianity must be so interpreted that it retains its belief in eternal life and still fits into our concept of *eternal* evolution.

PHILOSOPHICAL CONCEPTS OF GOD

We may define concepts by saying that all of them—philosophical, religious, or scientific—are mental structures or molds, in which liquid religious or philosophical notions and ideas are poured and later become cast into solid, recognizable and well-defined shapes. These serve as yard lines on the football fields of our mind, in which our fragmentary consciousness struggles to find the goal posts in order to register our scores.

Philosophically, one may conceive of God as: an entity that has existed eternally, without beginning or end; as a force pervading all nature, the entire cosmos, self-caused, self-willed, equally present everywhere. In short, everything is God and God is everything. There is no transcendence here, only immanence.

This second concept is that of Spinoza. A third concept regards God as an eternal entity, who, at *sometime,* created the universe and created us in His image, and He is both outside and inside the universe. As a Creator, He is outside of the Universe, and as a Father, He is a participant in it. This third concept is a development of the first and presents the theology of the traditional Christian religion.

A fourth concept does not consider God as an entity but equates Ultimate Reality as an Absolute Principle of existence. Being uncreated, it never created anything. It just *is*. It is never becoming, it is Being Eternal.

This concept forms the basis of Buddhism, which, in its lack of worship and its emphasis on depersonalization, is strictly a philosophy and not a religion as we define it in the Western world. True primarily of intellectual Buddhism such as Zen or the higher forms of Mahayana, this concept leaves out of consideration the large number of Buddhists who believe in Amida, the Saviour.

Amida is a legendary figure, not a historical one, who lived aeons ago in some long defunct universe. Although this monk had reached the stage where rebirth was no longer necessary, he made a solemn vow that he would never enter Nirvana until, by enduring rebirth after rebirth, aeon after aeon, and by continual perseverance in self-discipline, labor, and meditation, he had acquired so great a superfluity of merit it would make up for the deficiencies of all who could never have attained salvation by their own efforts. Buddhists, by believing in Amida and by calling upon his name in sincerity and faith, will, when they die, be received not into Nirvana itself but into the "Western Paradise" of Amida. The similarities to the Christian concept of heaven are obvious; the primary difference is in the concept of the "birth" of the Saviour.

Buddhism presents two ways of salvation: by faith and by works. Faith is stressed by the followers of Amida,

157

works by Zen. The "conversion" or psychological crisis which takes place in the disciples of Zen after long discipline in meditation, appertains to the intellectual side of the self rather than to the moral or emotional. Except a man be born again, intellectually, he cannot see Nirvana.

Although Buddhism shares these two phases of salvation, faith or works, with Christianity, its final goal is still Nirvana—the Ultimate Reality, nonentity, completely depersonalized Being Eternal. This is a complete antithesis of Christianity. Those who say that there are no major differences between Buddhism and Christianity may believe that religion is only a moral force in the world today. Buddha showed us how to escape from suffering; Jesus showed us how to accept and conquer it. If there is no difference between a negative and a positive response to the unknown, then, of course, Buddhism and Christianity are alike.

In *Buddha and Christ* Burnett Hillman Streeter has said that "Buddha was willing to live in order to show us how to die; Jesus was willing to die to show us how to live."

If religion is to be considered only a moral force, a fifth concept of God may present Him as an ideal—neither an entity nor a force pervading the cosmos. Its power is only the force of an ideal, created by man and so recognized. It presents the progressive goal of mankind in terms of moral traits and in triumph over nature, reaching out toward moral perfection as an ultimate, though never-to-be-reached, goal. In this concept, immortality becomes an ideal of each self contributing to the moral progress of the race.

The human aspiration described in such an ideal might be called the "religion" of humanism.

ASSUMPTIONS ABOUT THE UNKNOWN

Ancient Hindu philosophy conceived Brahma as the one universal mass-energy. In thus identifying mass and energy as a single entity, this ancient philosophy was nearly 5,000 years ahead of science. It was 1922 before Count Louis De Broglie formulated the wave-particle principle of matter-energy. Fritz Kahn, in his *Design of the Universe,* says it simply: "Mass is concentrated energy; energy is deconcentrated mass."

In its empirical approach to the universe, science sees an energy system without purpose. Such a view does not conflict with Buddhist philosophy, which holds that one universe succeeds another in endless succession but that Ultimate Reality has nothing whatever to do with it. In simple words, the universe has no meaning except what "foolish" people attribute to it; rather than the truth, it is the error of our desires and the sooner we surrender our desires and stop personalizing ourselves and others the sooner we will escape from illusion and return to Reality or Nirvana. How we separated ourselves from Ultimate Reality has never been clear to me.

To the scientist, however, there is no quarrel with this philosophy since the Buddhist concept of the universe is as far-flung and impersonal as his own.

The individual scientist with a mystical touch, or a philosophical sense of wonder, looks at the universe and sees the universe in the form of a creative intelligence or, as we quoted before, "the universe itself is a god."

In the former case of a depersonalized concept, Christianity is a completely alien philosophy; in the latter case, Christianity may be replaced by pantheism. In any case, Christian theology can no longer consider the universe in

159

terms of a closed-end heaven and earth. This is the problem faced by the theologians presented in previous sections. The question remains: What other concepts of the unknown can we present that will not destroy the main message of Christianity?

This message I consider as: 1) Love of God, which consists of a personal relationship between God and man; 2) the value and meaning of suffering in human life; 3) the survival of consciousness beyond the grave.

Love of God is expressed in eternal creativity, which moves in two directions; it contains the centrifugal and centripetal forces of the physico-spiritual evolution, and in its unfoldment expresses the polarity of the divine essence. (This polarity is discussed in a later chapter.)

Suffering is the pearl of great price; the initiation from the physical into the spiritual; the means to the one and *only* perfection in the universe—moral perfection. Moral perfection is essential for the safe transferral of consciousness from physical evolution to spiritual evolution. Even here, perhaps we should not use the word "perfection"; we should say that one should reach a stage of evolution where "goodness" becomes an integral part of consciousness. Intellect and wisdom may operate on two different levels; goodness and wisdom are on the same level.

The never-ceasing ascent of consciousness is the goal of creation; it is inherent in the physico-spiritual evolution, which comes out of consciousness and produces new consciousness, expanding the universe in all directions throughout eternity.

Our response to the unknown may now be stated in a new manner: God is consciousness—a consciousness far beyond our comprehension; a consciousness that extends itself beyond time and place and is expressed in creativity, conforming to the necessity of its own Being. Our image of this consciousness enables us to behold His Spirit, His Creativity, in the processes of evolution; the spiritual (consciousness) coming out of the physical and the physical out of the spiritual in never-ending cycles. Immanence and transcendance are their logical sequence.

A word here about changing our preoccupation with absolute terms in speaking of God: God, as creative activity, is a *living* God. To the human mind, absolutes, like eternity, infinity, and perfection, either are incomprehensible or they have a meaning of *lifelessness.*

The concept of God as a living Being, who has unfinished business, would indicate that the Ultimate Being is, in some ways, subject to the time process. The entire concept of evolution is in opposition to the idea of immutability. The concept of Perfection as something finished—complete and impossible of change—is equally in conflict with the processes of evolution, or with the concept of Ultimate Reality as the living God. Streeter says that

> . . . perfection is, as its derivation (i.e., completely finished) implies, a wholly static conception. A billiard ball may be (for practical purposes) a perfect sphere, the Venus de Milo may be a perfect work of art—but they are both dead. God is alive, and the essence of life is movement. Surely it would be a better analogy to liken God not to the perfect work of art, but to the perfect artist. But if we do that, at once we think of Him as One Who is always experiencing and always creating. "My Father worketh even until now, and I work." And I would urge that, although we may hold that in the eternal experience of God "death is swallowed up in victory," yet His experience of suffering must somehow be real. Were the attitude of God towards the

161

world's sorrow and the world's sin merely that of an unfeeling onlooker then the "perfection" which our theory saved would not be a moral one.[25]

Perfection must not be thought of as a static state of being, but as a dynamic relationship between the ideal and the actual. The moral "perfection" of Jesus consisted in His ability to blend perfectly (that is completely) the ideal and the real. His spiritual development had reached the point where He would do the will of the Father at any cost, including giving up physical life. Goodness does not depend on intellect and vice versa; goodness and wisdom cannot be separated. If a continuous cycle of spiritual and physical evolution is to endure, wisdom must take precedence over intellect in the universe.

Time and again, Jesus referred to Himself as the Son of Man. He knew, and admitted, His coming forth out of man's physical evolution. But spiritually, He had developed to a stage where wisdom was in full control over knowledge and as such He was truly a spiritual Son of God. Where this spiritual development took place is not for our present consideration; the fact that Jesus bore His cross and, by His suffering, showed that complete selflessness is neither impossible nor an idle gesture, is of the utmost importance. His ability to maintain the active relationship between the ideal and the real enabled Him, in the words of Emerson, "to speak from the within." His ability to maintain an attitude of complete concern for others without a slip presented, at least to Paul Tillich, the only reason for attributing divinity to Jesus.

Philosophers profess to seek wisdom; theologians seek pathways to God; scientists are the disciples of truth. But all of us carry within ourselves the collective unconscious of our human evolution. We are torn between the compulsions of our own subconscious and the light of reason. Inspired by our intuitive insights, we behold visions; frustrated, we bewail our realities. All of us are schizophrenic to a degree. But there is hope, even in the twilight zone of our spiritual evolution. Once we have risen to greater stature, we shall recognize this universe for what it is: a place of opportunity for unceasing creative effort. If we embrace the actual as well as the ideal, our search for God shall not be in vain.

11

THE SEARCH FOR IMMORTALITY

Since the search for immortality goes back to antiquity, we may assume that ancient peoples accepted belief in continued existence beyond the grave as part of their culture without questioning and demanding proof. In Western civilization, we have begun to question the *kind* of immortality we believe in, as well as the validity of a belief in immortality, which is a healthy sign.

The United States leads six European nations in a Gallup Poll of those who believe in life after death. Percentages given for the United States are: 74 percent believe, 14 percent do not, and 12 percent do not know; for Great Britain: 56 percent, 18 percent, and 36 percent; for Holland: 63 percent, 27 percent, and 10 percent; and for West Germany only 38 percent believe, 29 percent do not, and 33 percent do not know.

Unfortunately, neither belief nor disbelief will prove the fact of existence or nonexistence beyond the grave. In order to form a basis for judgment of knowledge in this field, we must consider the major pros and cons.

WHAT IS IMMORTALITY?

Unlike Catholics, Protestants do not seem to take their ideas of immortality from church creeds and doctrine, rather they appear to combine their religious heritage with scientific and pseudoscientific concepts of immortality regarding mind and matter.

The following concepts emerged from a course on comparative religion I attended: immortality means the continuance of one's life in the minds and memories of those we leave behind—especially in our children; immortality consists of contributions we have made to society; immortality means that the soul goes to God; immortality means that we will meet our loved ones after death and that they will know us. No one spoke of the "resurrection of the body" and no one wondered what he might *do* on the other side of the grave.

The Calvinist creed repeated by all good Presbyterians says: ". . . I believe in the resurrection of the body; and the life everlasting."

Today, some Presbyterian ministers tell their audiences that they must not interpret this literally. A body of thirty years of age resurrected may be all well and good, but at sixty or seventy, the resurrection of old bones and deteriorated bodies is not a joyful prospect. Although the ministers do not say this, modern science has made the process of countless millions of bodies being resurrected on this earth look more than slightly ridiculous. The ministers find their escape from this concept of resurrection, which, for a long time, *was interpreted literally,* by referring to the words of St. Paul who spoke of "the body incorruptible." This spiritual body, the ministers continue, will live in a spiritual world, doing very much what we are doing on earth.

In the chapter on the search for existence we touched on the problems that might arise should science succeed in prolonging man's life to a thousand years: Nobody would know the great-grandchildren of their own great-grand-children—and perhaps no one would care. A life of idleness, even a life with the same experiences over and over again, on earth or in heaven would be hell indeed, for nothing could be worse than continual boredom. Only one antidote to boredom and idleness exists: creative activity. The theme throughout this book remains: creativity is the glory of God and the meaning of life. Life and immortality must have meaning and that meaning can be found only in continuous creativity.

Of course, the notion of our continuance in the minds of others has nothing to do with our own existence beyond the grave.

Must we accept that notion that our souls go to God when He is already here? Should we accept a view of immortality that puts us in a heavenly straitjacket and condemns us to an eternal life of boredom? I think not.

My concept of immortality is one of continuous life processes, differentiated by a degree of consciousness; being worked on by creative consciousness (God) until the *unit* (that is, each of us, individually) reaches the level of development where it becomes creatively conscious. When a point is reached in which creative consciousness is self-sustaining and self-perpetuating, individually and in conjunction with a psychosocial-spiritual evolution, a new cycle of creative physical evolution may begin. This concept, which will be explained in more detail later, states in a very limited way the idea of the physical-spiritual evolution of man.

This concept of life beyond the grave includes the belief that individual consciousness continues to function in self-awareness; that it may progress or stand still as in this life; that its next phase of existence beyond the grave may also be limited in time, although time and space will not have the same meaning to a "disembodied spirit" as it has to us; and that new phases, new life processes, new opportunities to bring the individual to the desired goal of creative consciousness, will be part of our immortality.

THE PROOF FOR IMMORTALITY

Parapsychology, the science that investigates extrasensory perception, has become increasingly popular of late, even in lay circles. Special studies are being made of clairvoyance and telepathy, with the avowed purpose of proving that life continues after death—so far, however, none has succeeded in this endeavor.

Since its inception, the religion of spiritualism or "spiritism" as it is called in England, where it is generally recognized and "respectable," has tried to furnish "proof" of survival, at least to its members. With few exceptions, however, spiritualists do not attempt to prove immortality beyond a survival of the "spirit- or astral-body" after passing from the earth-life.

The theory of reincarnation, accepted by countless millions around the globe, assumes not one, but numerous lives on earth and possibly beyond. This continuous process, if followed to a logical conclusion, might lead to a proof of immortality.

Some years ago I joined a group of educators who discussed extrasensory perception informally. A professor of psychology at one of our largest universities told us that he did not believe in extrasensory perception. Luncheon was served and afterward this same professor told us that he had been asked by the editor of a scientific magazine to review three articles on extrasensory perception. Then, with a sudden look of concern in his eyes, he turned to us and added: "But I don't want you to think that I am prejudiced!" Our laughter was the only appropriate answer.

There is much we do not know about the human mind, but we do know that the moment we believe in a thing we are biased in its favor; the moment we disbelieve it we are prejudiced against it. To be truly uncommitted to a thing, one must be totally indifferent to it. As Tillich pointed out, only one who does not care, who is totally unconcerned, can be an atheist. But to live entirely without beliefs is impossible; we must decide about many things; making a choice is inevitable in thousands of little as well as important matters: How we build and organize our beliefs is most important as is awareness of the premises on which our beliefs are based.

Clairvoyance, the gift of seeing clearly, or second sight, manifests itself through various channels in persons thus endowed. Spontaneous visions, crystal balls, objects intimately connected with another individual, or even such crude means as coffee grounds, tea leaves, and playing cards, are able to connect the clairvoyant with the unseen aura, background, past, and—most inexplicable—future of that other person. Future events seem to appear in symbols or pictures, with the time of their occurrence usually hazy and hard to determine. While some of these predictions may not be fulfilled, too many people in all parts of the world have experienced proof of such predictions to doubt the validity of extrasensory perception.

The important question is whether disclosures of clairvoyance of the future are as clearly marked as those of the past. If all events were definitely delineated into the future, we would have to believe that they are forever "fixed" in the mind of God, depriving us of choice and decision. I reject such a view of life as being in direct opposition to my concept of its meaning.

Clairvoyants may "see" departed spirits, but since this appearance occurs in their *living* minds, it does not yet prove a life after death. The same is true of telepathy. The marvel of thought transference at a speed as yet undetermined, happens only in the living mind and explains nothing but its fantastic potentialities and ramifications. A person who has seen the form of a close friend or relative at the exact time of his death, may be convinced he has seen his friend's disembodied spirit. The parapsychologist will explain the phenomenon in terms of telepathy or strong emotional stimulus at the time of death, because the two individuals were intimately connected consciously as well as subconsciously.

While parapsychologists are interested primarily in clairvoyance, telepathy, and psychokinesis, spiritualists focus their attention mainly on spirit communication. This is based on the assumption—mostly erroneous—that departed spirits are wiser and in a better position to give advice than when they lived on earth; somehow they become sanctified by their death. The messages received prove to some spiritualists, beyond a shadow of a doubt, that survival after death is a certainty.

I have spent sufficient time researching this field to know that while many messages given by so-called mediums are utter nonsense, other experiences cannot be ridiculed.

Mrs. C. Thomas of Brooklyn, New York, a lifelong friend of Mrs. Piper, the "white crow" of William James, was a sincere person and an excellent "mediumistic instrument," who was highly thought of by such experts as Professor James Hyslop and Sir Oliver Lodge. Like Eileen Garrett, President of the Parapsychology Foundation, Mrs. Thomas was skeptical of her own mediumship. I visited her once a week for two years during which I had private "readings" that lasted from one to two hours. While she was in a deep trance, the answers that came from her lips were quite different from those I received from my college dean, to whose office I went three times a week to attend a private course in philosophy. It was during one of the readings with Mrs. Thomas that the germ of my idea concerning the physical-spiritual evolution was born.

In 1927, Mrs. Thomas died suddenly. She was a member of Dr. S. Parkes Cadman's church. Dr. Cadman knew of her work through some members of his family who had used her services. He demonstrated how deeply he respected her by leaving his own sickbed in order to conduct the funeral service for her.

My own "research" was left up in the air. Knowing how difficult it would be to find a medium as gifted as Mrs. Thomas, I solicited the opinion of Dr. Harry Emerson Fosdick. Dr. Fosdick, while believing in the importance of scientific investigation of psychic phenomena, warned me that there was no place "where cold-blooded, hardheaded objectivity is quite so much needed as there."

In my subsequent research, alone and together with the science editor of a New York city newspaper, I found Dr. Fosdick's warning of the utmost importance. The human mind resembles a mirror reflecting desires and fantasies as well as direct experiences; like a magnet it is drawing past and future events into the present; one's emotions determine largely what will appear on the mental screen. But emotion and scientific investigation do not mix.

Today, we have cameras which, in the dark of night, can photograph cars that were parked in a vacant lot during the day. Apparently these automobiles have left a physical vibration in the atmosphere, which can be recorded by the camera. It has been said that all of us have auras, although they may not be as prominent as the painted halos of the saints. Perhaps someday a camera may record them also.

If inanimate objects leave an aura of sufficient strength to be photographed, what about the consciousness of a once-living person? Conceivably, the consciousness may hover around the earth, visible to those with a clairvoyant eye. In cases of historic figures, such as Lincoln and Napoleon, the repeated thought processes of millions of people may explain in part why clairvoyants see or are in contact with the "thought forms" of such personages of the past, although they may have no actual contact with the real departed person.

Although some learned psychologists do not believe in extrasensory perception, parapsychology has become a generally respected field of investigation. How would psychologists explain the amazing revelations and accurate predictions made by Jeane Dixon of Washington, D.C.? The Russians were the first to establish a state-supported research laboratory in parapsychology at the Leningrad State University. In their experiments with subjects who were isolated in lead chambers immersed in mercury, they found that telepathy could still occur. The Russians concluded that electromagnetic radiation was not the basis for thought communication. Some Russian scientists call such experimental results impossible because no physical theory can explain them, and they consider the experiments a waste of time; but other scientists urge the continuance of studies in parapsychology.

Generally speaking, the major emphasis in parapsychological research seems to be on the investigation of how the mind functions in the human body rather than how the soul may survive after death.

REINCARNATION AND IMMORTALITY

If the existence of extrasensory perception does not prove personal survival after bodily death, would the proven fact of reincarnation do so? It would indeed. Such survival after bodily death, plus the reincarnation into a new human organism would not prove immortality in the sense of an individual existence throughout all eternity, but it would be the first step on the way.

The most important question is: What constitutes definite proof? Our belief or disbelief has nothing to do with its reality or nonexistence. The fact that hundreds of millions of Buddhists and Hindus believe in reincarnation is no more proof than is the naïve statement of the late Ernest Holmes, Founder of the Church of Religious Science, that he did not believe in reincarnation because he did not *want* to come back. Perhaps Dr. Holmes does not *have* to come back; but if reincarnation is a fact of life and he *needs* to come back, he will!

Who wants to live his life over again? I do not. Looking back over an interesting life filled with joys and sorrows, successes and failures, I would not want to repeat the *same* life. The old saying "If I had to live my life over again . . ." seems to indicate that many people would do things differently, if they were given a chance. In a hundred or more years from now, if the soul may look back on the experiences of its last life on earth, forgetting the pains and failures, it may feel challenged by the opportunity of a new and different life, in a better and more progressive environment to which the individual hopefully had contributed in his last life. In this way, we become the inheritors of our own past and participants in a progressive physical and spiritual evolution. The earth still seems to offer the best opportunity for our development, although the time may come when we may move on to new abodes.

Our belief or disbelief in reincarnation, however, may affect the evaluation of our own experiences and memories of what we may believe to be past lives as well as what we consider evidence for reincarnation in the experience of others. Dr. Ian Stevenson, Chairman, Department of Psychiatry, University of Virginia School of Medicine, has made a study of hundreds of cases in which children and adults claimed to remember their former lives. While admitting that these cases do not prove reincarnation, Dr. Stevenson believes that reincarnation offers the *most plausible hypothesis for understanding them.* I think that this statement by an outstanding psychiatrist, who has based his findings on hundreds of cases, has greater significance than the untold testimonies of spiritualists and their messages from so-called departed spirits. While I would not discourage the scientific investigation of psychic phenomena as they pertain to possible indications of personal survival after death, I have witnessed too many demonstrations of this nature not to sound a warning; most, if not all of these phenomena seem to be part of the still mys-

173

terious areas of the human mind. The majority of people who visit spiritualist mediums do so for emotional reasons and are hardly prepared for rational evaluations.

In a fairly recent anthology, Dr. Stevenson expresses clearly my own ideas on reincarnation.

> Expectations can harmfully influence perceptions. If we proceed in an investigation with the expectation of confirming a particular hypothesis, we may think we discover more evidence for it than we do. But the reverse type of misperception can also occur with equal harm. If we reject offhand, as most Westerners are inclined to do, the hypothesis of reincarnation, we may exclude from our investigation those conditions which could permit further relevant data to emerge.[26]

He goes on to suggest that further investigation of apparent recollections from former lives may reveal reincarnation as one of the most probable explanations for such experiences, and that we may ultimately obtain the most convincing form of evidence of human survival after physical death. It may be easier to prove that someone now living once died, than to show, as in mediumistic communications, that the spirit of someone dead still lives.

My own belief is that, if immortality is a fact, reincarnation seems a necessity. I base this deduction on my concept of the meaning of life. Who can be so naïve as to assume that anyone can learn enough in one earthly lifetime to become fit for eternal creativity? Even the Buddhists, whose concept of immortality is in direct opposition to mine, believe that reincarnation is a necessity in order to rid ourselves of our "personalities" and all of our desires. But the goal of attaining Nirvana does not appear to me to be our goal. Our view of heaven and earth, God and immortality, should not be one of eternal changelessness and eternal contemplation of perfection; but one of eternal change—new heavens and new earths—and of eternal creativity. Our goal should not be an escape from ourselves to find static being; our goal should be to become creative beings. Our goal should not be a return to God but a manifestation of God in ourselves as Jesus demonstrated. "My Father worketh hitherto, and I work," (John 5:17). Our goal should be to join the workers.

The separation and loneliness man feels so frequently derive from the instincts of the flesh warring with the intuitive promptings of the spirit. But this struggle is for a purpose. Furthermore, our intellect, focusing primarily on material things, tends to analyze *ad infinitum,* and acts as a separating force. All too frequently, it is a negative force. As Erich Fromm said: "Psychology can show us what man is *not.* It cannot tell us what man, each one of us, *is.*" Nevertheless, we would not wish to do away with psychology, for we need an analytical force in human life.

One may say that the intellect can also be used positively, as in synthesis. But, is it the intellect or is it the individual who uses imagination and other facets of his consciousness, to effect the synthesis? Einstein believed that serious scientific workers are the only profoundly religious people:

The most beautiful and most profound emotion we can experience is the sensation of the mystical. It is the sower of all true science. He to whom this emotion is a stranger, who can no longer wonder and stand rapt in awe, is as good as dead. To know that what is impenetrable to us really exists, manifesting itself as the highest wisdom and the most radi-

175

ant beauty which our dull faculties can comprehend only in their primitive forms—this knowledge, this feeling is at the center of true religiousness.[27]

I would like to see this quotation inscribed in a prominent place in every institution of higher learning. Or are we so low in our development of true religious feeling that only a mind like Einstein's can see the manifestation of wisdom and the most radiant beauty in our universe?

I am not a mystic, but neither am I an intellectualist. Neither Ayn Rand nor Krishnamurti provide me with the answer to the meaning of life. I do believe, however, that we should employ fully both our intellects and our mystical sense. Both are essential parts in the development of our understanding.

To those interested in reincarnation, extensive reading material on the subject is available. In addition to the anthology already mentioned, there is an interesting pamphlet by Leslie D. Weatherhead, retired Minister of the City Temple in London, *The Case for Reincarnation.* Dr. Weatherhead, in his conclusions, answers some of the objections to the theory of reincarnation. And, in a more recent book, *The Christian Agnostic,* Dr. Weatherhead includes a chapter on: "Reincarnation and Renewed Chances."

Not long ago, some people thought that hypnotism would be an infallible instrument in the search for proof of reincarnation. Through my wife's brief correspondence with Morey Bernstein, while he was working on the preparation of his book, *Bridey Murphy,* we became convinced of his utter sincerity. Yet, I must agree with Dr. J. B. Rhine that leading a person back through hypnotic regression is not a satisfactory course to follow. Extrasensory perception may take place in the process of hypnosis, which may lead to incalculable results.

In stating that my concept of immortality runs counter to that of the Buddhists, I do not wish to imply that their concept of reincarnation is of no consequence. Intellectual Buddhism has a wealth of theory, as is evidenced in the researches of Buddhist psychology known as the Abhidhamma Studies, which, unfortunately, are published only in Colombo. The concept of Karma as the law of action and reaction, or "what you sow, you shall reap," is refined into many groupings in intellectual Buddhism, such as regenerative, supportive, counteractive, and destructive Karma. In addition to the priority of these Karmas, we find weighty Karma, habitual Karma, and others. In turn, each group is divided into subgroups of well over a hundred subdivisions.

Considering such cumbersome reminders of the past mixed with warnings for the future, we may be fortunate that the Catholic Church, whether by design or accident, forbade or at least discouraged the theory of preexistence.

If we accept reincarnation as a fact, we may be interested in our past lives and in our goals for the future: but this should not keep us from centering our interest on *this* life. It will not do us any good to *know* (not to mention assume) that we were Napoleon or Washington in a previous life and a farmer or a dishwasher in the present unless we also know *why* we now live the life of a farmer or dishwasher and, instead of reliving our "past glory," know how to accept the lesson of simplicity and humility that appears to be the reason for our present incarnation.

In every period of history, many distinguished thinkers have believed or entertained the idea of reincarnation. I do not know how much their belief was due to "intuition," re-

177

call of previous existence, or to a need for a reasonable understanding of the universe in which they lived. The idea of preexistence, as David Hume said, is "the only system to which philosophy can hearken."

Throughout the ages, each great thinker has had to find the meaning of life, and he was rather lonely in his search. Psychosocially speaking, we are now ready for this search on a much larger scale. The time has also arrived for us to consider the meaning of immortality. The old heaven-and-earth must make way for the new.

Perhaps someday, science will prove existence beyond this life. But we must not count on it, for there is no assurance that such proof will be intelligible to our intellects.

THE MEANING OF IMMORTALITY

In spite of the universe's mystery, science has discovered essential unity throughout the cosmos, and this discovery is beginning to exert its influence upon the various divisions of the Christian church; both Protestants and Roman Catholics are emphasizing the need for unity.

As surely as we are moving toward one world-culture, in which a diversity of customs is tolerated, so we will move toward one universal world-religion in which various sacraments and interpretations will be allowed.

To bring about a new world-religion, the meaning of immortality is basic if we wish to keep religion from losing its main message and having it change into a mere cult of ethics. Henry T. Buckle once said: "If immortality be untrue, it matters little whether anything else be true or not."

Whatever variety of sacraments and worships the new world-religion may contain in its local divisions, it needs to express its unity in the direction of the psychosocial evolution and in the goal of our spiritual evolution. While man's spiritual evolvement takes place within our psycho-social evolution, the latter is so designated because its limits in time and space are inextricably interwoven with this planet. The spiritual evolution of man (in terms of consciousness) cannot be so limited for, as we know, the earth itself is not immortal.

The physicist looking at the universe observes various levels of energy. The psychosociologist observing man, individually and collectively, sees varying levels of consciousness. All life has a degree of consciousness, the different degrees of consciousness creating various kinds or levels of awareness.

The relationship of energy and consciousness is of the greatest importance. The universe is an energy system and, as Pierre Teilhard de Chardin has said: "We have seen and admitted that evolution is an ascent toward consciousness. That is no longer contested even by the most materialistic, or at all events by the most agnostic of humanitarians." [28]

Until science proves to us the nature of energy and consciousness, we must build our own hypothesis concerning them in the evolution and "involution" of the universe, subject to correction in the light of new data. Such a hypothesis will be presented in the chapter on consciousness.

Meanwhile, assuming the truth of immortality, we must now consider its meaning in terms acceptable to the highest intellect of man. A description of life after death as it is being presented by some Protestant ministers is simply a continuation of life as we know it on earth. Spiritualists presented such pictures many decades ago. Whether they are true as states of consciousness between births is of sec-

179

ondary importance. The important thing is that a continuous earthlike life would turn into insufferable boredom.

Such was the view of Paul Tillich. To him the Nirvana symbol for eternal life points to the life of absolute fullness rather than the death of absolute nothingness.

I can understand his dislike for endless *temporal* life after death, but I am unable to grasp his full meaning of Nirvana. Since he is no longer with us, it is too late to find out just how he visualized the Christian road to absolute fullness. Neither Christians nor Buddhists are able to conceptualize absolutes. Therefore, a "true" concept of Nirvana is as impossible as a "true" concept of infinity. A "true" concept of eternal life is likewise impossible. But we must not seek our solution by becoming lost in mysticism. If Tillich believes that eternal life will find its fulfillment only in a Nirvana symbol which points to the life of absolute fullness and in which the individual is preserved, but *only* in its reunion with the realm of essences, then I disagree with him.

First of all, I cannot conceive of any form of life as a punishment. (Suffering is essential and has a definite place and meaning in the scheme of evolution. An interpretation on the role of suffering in life will be found in the chapter on the Search for Self). Second, God as a creative agent must have a goal, and He must find *pleasure* in His creative activities as well as *disappointment.* Third, we are created not only as individuals; we develop throughout the ages a personality, which is not, in the Buddhist manner, to be obliterated but, in the Christian way, to be sanctified. Fourth, I wish to share in participation, but instead of the individual being preserved in the realm of essences (whatever that may mean) I believe in the continuous evolution of consciousness, both personally and collectively. Finally, instead of losing ourselves in the mysticism of absolutes we cannot comprehend, I suggest that we observe the processes of creation within the universe and within ourselves, thus studying the "ways of the Lord." In such a manner we may not know the ultimate "state" of immortality, but our vision, based on what we observe in the universe, can expand so it may present a picture or at least glimpses of a road ahead beyond the life of this planet and even beyond the life of this universe. Before that time is reached, our vision may be clearer and our pictures much brighter than the ones I shall attempt to give in later chapters regarding the possibilities of immortal life.

Rather than expend our efforts in a metaphysical attempt to find everything in nothing or to become an impersonal essence in everything, I accept "that evolution is an ascent towards consciousness." I believe that personal and collective consciousness coming out of so-called *physical* evolution is the other half of the spiritual consciousness which will create and direct the new physical evolution. We are living in an expanding universe, and growth is inherent in consciousness.

The purpose of eternal life is to create, to work increasingly for the joy of creating. Our philosophy regarding work on this earth must change. In many ways it has already changed. Push buttons are taking the place of the sweat of our brow, which removes the ancient curse and prepares us to operate on a higher level of consciousness. The scientific revolution is bringing us increasing possibilities for more enjoyable pursuits. Those who cannot find pleasure in work are not really living, for it is creative effort alone that gives permanent and increasing meaning to life. Einstein said: "The man who regards his own life and that of his fellow creatures as meaningless is not merely unfortunate but almost disqualified for life."

The meaning of life is expressed by each of us in our individualistic and special response to the known and the unknown. Creativity must not be thought of only as art expressed in sculpture, painting, or architecture, but as an act of love. Life without love is meaningless. The most menial task may express the "color" of personality, if it is performed with love. As we ascend in consciousness, our greater awareness should envelop our creative efforts with a deeper love. The wondrous thing is that on all levels of consciousness personal variation exists. Cooperation remains essential on all levels. Love is the cement that binds all things and all people together. To love our neighbors as ourselves is not to lose our own personalities; it is to respect and appreciate others who are different.

The cement of love is necessary in our psychosocial evolution. We will never travel alone throughout this universe. Even God has His associates. As the first chapter of Genesis puts it: "And God said, Let *us* make man in *our* image, after *our* likeness . . ." (1:26, Author's italics). Obviously this "likeness" or "image" was not a resemblance in physical form but a reflection of the divine consciousness. Man became a partner with God and nature in having dominion over life in the sea and on the land.

To sum up the meaning of immortality, let me repeat that I do not believe God was ever alone, or that one of us ever will be. Civilization has no meaning to an individual alone on an island; nor can love exist in a vacuum. We must find the meaning of immortality in an outlet for individual creativity, which cooperates with and is an indestructible part of our group consciousness, and of the still greater universal consciousness beyond.

If God had wanted all of us to be alike and to be absorbed within Himself, the purpose of creation would be nothing but playacting.

The continuity of immortality must be found in a two-fold process: spirit working on matter, matter working on spirit. Each is an essential part of the other. A clarification of this concept will be found in the last three chapters of this book.

The meaning of immortality includes the growing power of an individual in his creative expressions. Variety is essential to eternal creativity; eternal life is unthinkable without it. We will have reached the full awareness of our immortality, when we have reached that level of consciousness where our awareness blends our desire and ability to perform into a steady or self-perpetuating purpose. Until that time, our immortality may consist of a series of temporal existences. But, even if we are still in this transitional state, we need not be discouraged for we know that evolution is the ascent of consciousness. In the processes of time eternal, all of us have the opportunity to reach the ultimate fulfillment of our total being as conscious, personal and dynamically creative individuals.

12

THE SEARCH FOR CERTAINTY

In a world distressed by hot and cold wars, rumors of war and police actions, the danger of nuclear destruction ever present; race riots and rebelling youth all over the world; unrest and revolution in underdeveloped nations; millions facing starvation—who dares to speak of certainty? Are we nearing "the end of the world" and the approach of an Armageddon in which the world will be destroyed by nuclear fire? Or are we reaching the realization of the Great Society in which poverty, disease, and ignorance will be eradicated and modern science will enable us to live on a cultural and spiritual level undreamed of today?

Regardless of how we look at these matters, the search for certainty is still alive in the hearts of men, though it may be clouded over by thick layers of fear. What brought our fears and uncertainties into being—the pressures and dangers from outside or the change in our philosophical and religious concepts of life? How did we derive our ideas of certainty?

THE IDEA OF CERTAINTY

The Greeks, who gave us our philosophical conceptions concerning the nature of knowledge and reality, influenced also our ideas of values and certainty. But the world of ancient Greece was unlike ours. Plato and Aristotle looked at their world as fixed and solid. They regarded the earth and the cosmos in such a way that physics and metaphysics blended together without conflict. Modern science changed all that. Astronomy shows us a cosmos in which everything moves and the earth, instead of being its center, is only a speck of dust in the cosmic scheme of things. Physics reveals a microscopic universe within so-called solid matter and the atom is shown to have many subelements, all of which are in motion. Instead of stability, energy and motion have become two of the most important measuring sticks of physics.

Under Darwin, biology revealed evolution as a continuous life process in which change and motion are present everywhere.

Thus, the old metaphysics was no longer in accord with the new physics. But Western thought was slow to change; it clung to the old Greek ideas and modern philosophers, while accepting the conclusions of the new science, retained, as John Dewey pointed out:

> . . . three significant elements of ancient thought: the first, that certainty, security, can be found only in the fixed and unchanging; the second, that knowledge is the only road to that which is intrinsically stable and certain; the third, that practical activity is an inferior sort of thing; necessary simply because of man's animal nature and the necessity for winning subsistence from the environment.[29]

185

Even today, many religionists are affected strongly by elements one and three, while some philosophers still struggle with the idea that knowledge is the only road to that which is certain.

Again, Dewey disposes of the philosophic quest for certainty:

Philosophy has often entertained the idea of a complete integration of knowledge. But knowledge by its nature is analytic and discriminating. It attains large syntheses, sweeping generalizations. But these open up new problems for consideration, new fields for inquiry; they are transitions to more detailed and varied knowledge. Diversification of discoveries and the opening up of new points of view and new methods are inherent in the progress of knowledge. This fact defeats the idea of any complete synthesis of knowledge upon an intellectual basis. The sheer increase of specialized knowledge will never work the miracle of producing an intellectual whole. Nevertheless, the need for integration of specialized results of science remains, and philosophy should contribute to the satisfaction of the need.[30]

In philosophy, as elsewhere, we see a dynamic process in operation, in which growth replaces today's certainty with modifications of tomorrow, but each extension of knowledge is bridged to a larger body of knowledge and truth. In this sense, philosophers may be viewed as bridge builders in our knowledge expansion.

Finite man no longer seeks irrationally for an absolute certainty, he busies himself by seeking adjustments to the practical and changing problems of each day.

But what of our moral values? If they are not based on absolute authority, are we not confronted with a useless

186

scale of values that differs from person to person and from culture to culture? Some religionists see it this way and strive to retain their idea of the fixed and unchanging; in order to do this they require a separation between their absolute and the finitude of man. But twentieth-century man cannot accept the separation between the intellectual ideal of the absolute and the practical activities of everyday life. How can we resolve this paradox?

MORAL CERTAINTY

What is our highest authority? Is it found in the sayings of Confucius or Buddha, in the Natural Law or the Bible, in the Talmud or the Koran?

For Catholics the highest authority is the church and its doctrine; for many Protestants it is still the Bible or some particular ecclesiastic authority that interprets the Bible.

Churches, religious philosophies and theological ponderosities are all human creations, even though their authors or originators may have been deeply inspired and completely sincere in their devotion to the truth as they saw it. Bibles are documents produced by human beings who spoke and wrote in the language and meaning of their own time.

My reason for being a Christian is not because the Bible is my highest authority but because *I find in the words and life of Jesus my highest concept of moral certainty. His life and His words were one consistent whole, revealing His ultimate concern for God and His fellowmen.*

Jesus never built a church or wrote a line of Scripture. He taught and lived what He thought, and He died because the truth hurt most people too much. But that truth

187

is still hurting today! If Jesus returned to earth in the flesh, the greatest cathedrals built in His name would be the first to refuse Him their pulpits; the most prominent theological seminaries would laugh and belittle His efforts to speak with authority.

In spite of this, Jesus stands today as the greatest spiritual leader of all time. Unlike the Greeks, He did not propound a theory of the cosmos that is obsolete today. He recognized the concern of God as a Father-Creator for His children; He did not picture God as a big Man in the sky. He said that God was within and so was the Kingdom of Heaven. And because *He could see from within He also spoke from within.* His ultimate concern was within Himself (the Father and I are one) and the God within his fellowmen. The final authority of man, according to Tillich, is rooted in the truth of his ultimate concern. Thus, the highest and final authority of Jesus was rooted in God— but not an eternally changeless God, for this is one of life's contradictions. God's character may be changeless in its moral certainty and goodness, but God's creativity and action in behalf of man is undoubtedly dynamic rather than static.

One Eastern college has a song that hails its Alma Mater as "ever changing yet eternally the same." The small element of truth in this statement is overshadowed by the large sentiment of the alumni who wish to return to the college campus to find the same dear old college. But this once small college is now a large university, which has had so many changes that returning alumni hardly recognize the place. The *roots* of the old college's identity are still there but, for practical purposes, the *identity of the old is swallowed up in the identity of the new.*

Some religionists still think of God as *never* changing

and eternally the same. But God is life; life is action, motion, change. Life in God's terms is identical with love. It is in the fullness of God's love that we observe Jesus displaying His moral certainty.

He walked freely among sinners, without fear of contamination, knowing that God loved sinners as well as saints. When a self-righteous man rebuked Him for allowing a harlot to anoint His feet with oil, Jesus told him that indeed *love is greater than sin*. At the same time, He demonstrated that He knew the relativity of man's moral finitude and that what might be a waste of money in one case was a good investment in another. His moral certainty never missed fire because *He saw and understood what motivated each individual.* Being a master psychologist, He practiced semantics long before Alfred Korzybski was born. His inner life was uninhibited; He was free from guilt complexes and words had no emotional power over Him. He required no psychological tests to discover the personality complexes of individuals He contacted; He saw, He knew, He understood and He *forgave.* To forgive seems the most difficult thing in the world for us to do. "Forgive us our trespasses as we [*so seldom*] forgive those who trespass against us," is a prayer most of us could say more honestly than the one we normally use.

If our ultimate concern is in the Bible, then the Bible will be our highest authority. If it is in the church then the church will dominate our life. If it is in material wealth, then money will rule. The same will be true if our ultimate concern lies in power, social prestige, intellectual recognition or in a search for truth. Fortunate are those whose ultimate concern is in love, for they shall see God; they will see Him in the innocent face of a child and in the beauty of the lilies of the field; they will sense Him in the

189

stillness of the night and recognize His power in a tempest on the high seas; they will come close to Him in the ecstasy of joy even as they do in the depth of suffering; and He will speak to them through the cry of a newborn babe or the dying look of an old man. As the babe, emerging from the secure darkness of the womb, "died" before it was born into the light of day, so the old man in dying is being "born" into a new dimension of spirit.

Certainty is not to be found outside of ourselves; it is rooted within us. Our moral certainty can only be as strong as our inner light.

REMEDIES FOR UNCERTAINTIES

Do we really want certainty in the sense that everything is fixed and absolute? Wouldn't such a concept depict a static rather than a dynamic world?

Some years ago Joshua Liebman wrote a best seller, entitled *Peace of Mind,* but he dropped dead from a heart attack, at forty-one. Is peace of mind, as it is often visualized, such a desirable state of being?

On June 24th, 1962, at the Westwood Community Methodist Church of Los Angeles, Dr. Melvin Wheatley, Jr., gave his opinion in a delightful sermon, "Peace of Mind Is for the Birds":

A chief mark of being human is the possession of mind in that form of self-consciousness that makes peace of mind, as popularly interpreted, a contradiction in terms.

But the moment we begin to make responsible use of this power of self-consciousness where do we come out? And

190

the answer is exactly where the book of Genesis says we come out—out of the Garden. Out of the Garden of Eden characterized as it is by the security of irresponsibility, the innocence of ignorance and the perfection of impotence. And from that Garden of tranquility we emerge into the arena of tensions characterized by physical vulnerability, intellectual uncertainty and moral and ethical immaturity. . . .

. . . *the capacity for self-consciousness, which man developed,* God designed. . . . The human situation of being outside the garden, then, seems to me to be not exclusively or perhaps even primarily God's punishment of man for being disobedient. It seems, rather, to be much more elementally a part of the price man must apparently pay for becoming fully human.

It must be obvious from the various searches we have discussed so far, that God's spiritual laws could not function in a climate in which responsibility was not surrounded by hazards. It is the development of self-consciousness that raises man above the animals, otherwise we would still be in the Garden. But we have tasted the fruit of knowledge, we know the difference between good and evil and there can be no *reversal in the evolutionary process of consciousness.* We need to be courageous to meet the challenge of the choices to be made; our hunger for more knowledge spurs our efforts to greater creative endeavor; our loneliness, caused by the separation of our consciousness from the oneness with nature, makes us sense a higher reality, the shape of which is not yet clear to us. Such a state of mind is summed up in a statement by Dag Hammarskjöld:

191

Never let success hide its emptiness from you, achievement its nothingness, toil its desolation. And so keep alive the incentive to push on further, that pain in the soul which drives us beyond ourselves.

Whither? That I don't know. That I don't ask to know.

This pain in the soul which drives us beyond ourselves is the striving which is universal in the cosmos; it is the motivating force which leads to continuous change and creative effort; it is the mainstay of the dynamic process which we call life. Our lot is to accept and embrace it, not to bewail it.

If the nature of consciousness is connected inescapably with uncertainty, how do we meet the challenges this uncertainty brings us?

We are not as helpless as it may seem. We meet the practical problems of uncertainty in our everyday lives in many ways: We may carry insurance for airplane and automobile accidents, for theft, fire, flood, hail and many other calamities. Life insurance, especially against the risk of losing the breadwinner, runs into astronomical figures on a national scale. Social security and pension funds, Medicare and hospital insurance, provide for many of the uncertainties of old age. We are not able to forestall accidents or prevent the risks of living, but we are not entirely helpless in the face of these risks and accidents.

Are we complaining about crime and robberies? Considering the increase in our population, are robberies today more numerous percentagewise than they were four centuries ago? Of course, there were no statistics then and a man's identity had limited recognition. More than fifty miles away from home, a feudal baron—even a king— might be an unknown person.

There were no passport pictures, no newspapers or photographs to identify anyone. Any man alone on the highway was in danger of being robbed and perhaps losing his life. At night, city gates were closed against armed robbers.

Today, the darkness of night is dispelled by the bright electric lights. How fast news travels, how easily people are identified, how much safer as well as faster our journeys are. Earthquakes, floods, fires and dastardly crimes are front-page newspaper stories.

Because these unusual things clamor for our attention, our minds are hypnotized by uncertainties from morning paper to evening paper, with radio and television broadcasts in between.

We need to build up an immunity to such repetitions of unpleasant and frequently lopsided news, just as we need to learn to protect ourselves from wasting time on useless and negative information. The allocation of time for constructive endeavors should be a helpful part of everyone's education.

Do we actually have reason to complain about our uncertainties? Think how human suffering has been relieved by modern medicine. Miraculous operations are performed painlessly; doctors transplant eyes, kidneys—even hearts.

Nevertheless, people are high-strung and they get depressed by the great demands of modern living. The hippies and other nonconformists seek answers by ignoring society and by living in a world of their "own," though it seems more of an attempt to return to the happy, irresponsible life in the Garden. How do housewives, who have jobs and must take care of their families, solve their problems? Many of them do not; and complain to being worn-out by long hours of work. Usually, doctors do not find anything organically wrong with these people, but they know from experience that many such patients can meet the pressures of modern living more readily and function more efficiently if they increase their periods of sleep and rest each day. The irritability of many who follow this advice does cease, and stability (rather than peace) of mind results.

We are so caught up in daily trifling annoyances with small, but seemingly endless, uncertainties demanding decisions, that it is not always easy to maintain a sense of proportion. But would we accept the answer to this problem made by a young Nazi, as an alternative? This young man was glad to be free from freedom because this left him "free" to make no decisions at all. Such a concept of "static freedom" means retrogression to an animal status.

Freedom to make decisions does not mean, however, that we are free to obey or disobey law. Social control is as essential as self-control. The two need to be fused into one. Always, it is ignorance or willful disobedience to the law of living that gets us into trouble. The cure is to get right with the law.

Obedience to the law is essential to group living. Without such laws life would be chaotic, if not impossible. We are destined by the physical and spiritual laws of the cosmos to operate in groups, whether this be the grouping of a small town, a large nation, or the entire earth.

Affiliation with any group relieves man's "aloneness" and provides him with the opportunity to learn discipline and adaptation, the advantage of acquiring knowledge and enjoying companionship, and the chance to participate in innumerable other avenues for creative growth. Most of all, he must learn to cooperate with others and in this process to lose his innate tendency towards self-centeredness.

When nations and individuals decide to give up national as well as individual sovereignty for the common good, then "they shall beat their swords into plowshares" and the earth will produce better citizens.

CERTAINTY OF SURVIVAL

Recently, a social worker remarked that today's teenagers are lonely. "They're not sure who they are," she said, "or why they are on earth, or where they are going. They are searching for identity."

No purpose, no goal, no identity. Our lack of attachment makes us lonely; our lack of commitment prevents a sense of direction; our lack of self-understanding produces a loss of identity.

The search for identity is not new. Perhaps modern psychology has emphasized the problem. A minister, who read the preceding chapter on immortality in manuscript form, inserted the following notation: "A naïve question: How is true identity as well as continuity conserved in reincarnation concepts?"

I do not know if we can completely analyze the *true* identity of anyone, ourselves included. When Harry Emerson Fosdick was asked if he believed in his own immortality, he replied, "Yes, but not as Harry Emerson Fosdick." Precisely! A man of seventy bears little comparison to the boy of seven, even though the boy is father to the man. A million years, or even ten thousand years from now, no one who gives the matter any serious thought, would want to be the *same* as he is today. What our *true* identity will be then will bear as little or less resemblance to our present identity as does the man of seventy to the boy of seven.

The old man, looking back may try to visualize his true identity as a boy of seven, but his success will depend on accurate memory and emotional detachment. The boy of seven has a more difficult task looking ahead to seventy. When it comes to looking into the future, all of us are like the little boy of seven.

When we speak of the true identity of an individual, presumably we refer to his personality; his unique combination of elements and characteristics which spell *him!* (For our present discussion I leave aside the fact that *him* is a variable, existing primarily in the minds of relatives, friends, and acquaintances who form an opinion of *him* based on pleasant and/or unpleasant experiences with that individual.) Unconsciously, however, we tie his personality to his body.

God is a Spirit, a Spirit not only of love but also of law and order. Since we are created in His image, we must be spirits also; and the love, law, order, and creativity that is in God must be manifested in us more and more, until we attain godlike stature. Only then shall we be able and fit to leave these bodies and ascend from the evolution of man into the evolution of spirit. When we leave the physical man behind, our task will not be finished, for we shall work eternally with God.

My view on reincarnation is, of course, only a *belief* and not a *fact.* Until such a fact is established, any other belief of survival and spiritual growth may be as freely accepted as mine. I find nothing, however, in the teachings of Jesus that contradicts the theory of reincarnation; there is even some evidence in favor of a belief in reincarnation when Jesus asks his disciples: ". . . Whom do men say that I the Son of man am? And they said, Some say that thou art John the Baptist; some Elias; and others, Jeremias, or one of the prophets" (Matthew 16:13–14).

Jesus did not contradict the possibility of the reincarnation of Elias, Jeremias or any of the prophets and thus it seems reasonable to believe that the concept of reincarnation was by no means foreign or objectionable to him and his disciples. In testifying concerning John the Baptist, He said: "For all the prophets and the law prophesied until John. And if you will receive *it,* this is Elias, which was for to come" (Matthew 11:13–14).

While the Bible presents only a few evidences for a belief in reincarnation, *nowhere* is there a statement to contradict such a belief. Moreover, the theory of reincarnation answers more questions regarding man's spiritual development than any other theory with which I am acquainted. If anyone should present me with a more reasonable myth regarding the future destiny of man, however, I would accept it gratefully.

When we leave this earth, we take with us nothing but our personalities and our mental and spiritual assets or liabilities. Our spiritual progress depends entirely upon our ability, will, and attitude. The Great Presence can be felt only within.

Evolution is an eternal becoming. If the universe is one gigantic process, it is a process of becoming. If the universe exists by the will and consciousness of God, as we Christians believe, then God's eternal creativity must also be a process of becoming. While we may never see nor know God as He is in His totality, we can and do observe Him in the process of His becoming.

When we leave this plane of existence (we do not necessarily leave the earth) our personalities remain intact and

197

our friends and loved ones on the next plane can recognize us. But this is not the case when the soul is reincarnated into a new body on earth.

Why do we *die* on the next plane? Some die from utter boredom; others from "old age," as their mental processes or wills for creativity slow down. On the next plane greater creativity is required to keep on doing things. The reason is simple: there is no *compulsion* to work. There is no economic or physical necessity to maintain our bodies or to "stay alive." Therefore, the desire to work, the wish, imagination, and ability to think and create are absolutely essential, not only for progress but also for "survival." *In God's Garden, there are only voluntary workers.* The ambitionless individual becomes inert and must be reawakened by the *demands* of the flesh on the physical plane. In its own inner wisdom the soul may know that there are more lessons for it to learn on earth, or the spirit personality may develop a desire to revisit the planet in body form, thinking it may be able to do better than last time or wishing to make some contribution to humanity. Obviously, Jesus belonged to this latter group. Is it a revolting or inspiring thought that you, too, may wish to return to earth in your determination to boost our psychosocial, purposive and spiritual evolutions by helping to raise the level of human awareness in its various aspects?

If we would realize how little we learn in one lifetime and how much is required before we can make a journey not dependent on this planet, we would blush at our audacity to think we could graduate from the earth school in one lifetime. It is like the logic of a child in kindergarten who thinks he finishes his education with the first grade in grammar school.

If we trust the spiritual laws of God, which control all

phases of life in this universe, we can go to sleep just as confidently or pass through a coma in the reincarnation process, as we do when we go to bed at night. When I wake up in the morning, I am myself, you say, I recognize myself in the mirror; but not so when I am reborn as a little child.

God is not only just, He is kind. The veil is drawn over our memories, which enables us to have new experiences, to increase the positive elements of our personality and to eradicate our weaknesses. We become aware of previous lives gradually, and when we do the time for our journey of no return may be close at hand.

But what of our loved ones, our former relatives? Families are earthly concerns; in heaven there is neither marriage nor childbirth. People meet purely on the basis of attraction, love, and common interests. In a large measure, this is true of most adults on earth, but it is an unbroken law in spirit. If a relative on earth is also a close friend, however, most likely we will keep in touch with him through many incarnations—*as long as our "affinities" last.*

What do those who do not believe in reincarnation visualize? Further soul development on other planets? Or a spirit existence in which development is possible without the trials and necessities of the flesh? Such a possibility may exist, of course, and there can be no objection to such a belief. But, work and responsibility must be part of such a life; for Jesus made it abundantly clear that both He and God are unceasing workers.

Those in the Western world who believe in the theory of reincarnation are not as "peculiar" as many may think them to be. Numerous great thinkers in Western civilization have accepted the reincarnation theory. Apparently their personalities were sufficiently strong to face the loss of identity, and they may have considered the earth life a challenge and a blessing rather than a curse. Life today is better for many people than it was in the past, and life on earth can be still more beautiful in the future if we will it so. We are not only our own ancestors, we will inherit the future! Such a view of cosmic justice makes life a challenge worth fighting for.

How many complaining people run from doctor to doctor eagerly clinging to their illusory illnesses. Only the weak ones, in Buddhism or Christianity, want someone else to do their suffering for them. They want to be admitted into a golden, static, eternally secure heaven as a reward for their suffering on earth, or as their "just desserts" because they had faith. Faith in what? In the church? In Christ, in the Bible, in God's forgiveness of sin?

We all live in God's grace for there is no life without God. A certain Protestant theologian, in interpreting St. Paul's version of the relationship between man and God, states that the uniqueness of Christianity lies in the fact that it alone of all religions maintains that man can be accepted by God only through a Mediator—Jesus Christ—"whose blood was spilt for the sins of the world." The revengeful Jehovah of the Old Testament, and the equally angry God of today's literal-minded Christian, requires a blood sacrifice. Such a concept makes it appear that the Eternal Spirit, who rules this immense universe of which our earth is such a tiny part, must have His "pound of flesh" before He will be appeased. But why must God be appeased before He will accept man? Because, says this theologian, man has willfully separated himself from God. How did man do this? Through the act of disobedience by Adam and Eve to God's command: "Thou shalt not eat

200

the fruit of this tree." Thus "original" sin came into the world and mankind is forever cursed by this sin.

A close look at the beautiful myth of the Garden of Eden may present us with a different picture, if we do two things: 1) bear in mind the problem of semantics, i.e., we must look at words such as sin without the emotion of deep guilt that past generations have bestowed upon it; 2) we must remember that myths do not tell the *truth,* they only point toward it.

When man acquired self-awareness (symbolically represented through the act of eating an apple from the tree of knowledge of good and evil) he did indeed separate himself from nature and brought trouble (sin) into the world. I have stated many times that animals live *in* nature and that man's intellect and will repeatedly oppose nature instead of working harmoniously with it. Moreover, the intellect separates, it fragmentizes any unit into ever-smaller parts so that when the critical intellect looks at anything carefully, it vanishes. Therefore, if man depends only upon his critical intellect in evaluating his relationship with God, he will never find unity—he will rationalize it all into nothingness.

Our ascent in consciousness presents us with an ever-widening range of choices. In order to make proper decisions, we may need the assistance of the intellect, but we must always maintain our balance—our personal integrity and unity within ourselves—for we can never *live* in our intellect, it can serve us only as a tool. Intellectual analysis may not only destroy the unity we seek, intellectual pride may cause us to believe that we are God. Such an attitude produces Hitlers; it separates us from the power that controls the universe. We need genuine humility to realize that we are only a *feeble image* of the God who created us, that

201

we are still in the kindergarten stage of consciousness and that it is wisdom to obey the will of the Father, who, in the words of Jesus, *alone is good.*

By eating too much of the tree of knowledge of good and evil (which caused the fall of the unselfconsciousness of man) we all participate in the "original sin" of separation. Our pride, indeed, keeps us from relating to the Great Reality we call God. This is not to berate the intellect but to affirm that this intellectual power must remain subservient to our unity with God. The best way we can do this is to follow the example of Jesus, who in His bitterest hour of loneliness prayed: "Not my will but thine be done."

Jesus told us that God is the Father of us all, the Creator of all there is. So God in the act of creating has indeed accepted us, and, as a God of love, *He is ever ready to respond to our every move to find Him.*

In forgiving our sins again and again, God provides all of us with a new chance to do better and to overcome our mistakes and weaknesses. He has given us the *ability* to climb into ever-increasing awareness that enables us to make better decisions, but He is not going to make our decision or do the climbing for us!

The fine symbolism of the Lord's supper has been defiled by the more earthy and cruel concept of bloodletting. Two centuries ago William Cowper wrote a hymn about being saved by the blood that certainly few, if any, modern Christians can accept. Yet this hymn is still found in present-day hymnals:

> *There is a fountain filled with blood*
> *Drawn from Emmanuel's veins;*
> *And sinners, plunged beneath that flood*
> *Lose all their guilty stains.*

If Jesus were living today, I wonder what He would think of this verse. Jesus preached a God of love, not a barbaric concept of blood sacrifice to appease an angry God. We no longer live in the days of Abraham, and we need to think of sacrifice more in accord with our modern concept of law and justice.

Our belief that Jesus "saves" will work only when we accept His teachings: "Jesus saith unto him, I am the way, the truth, and the life: no man cometh unto the Father, but by me" (John 14:6).

I see no indication here of burnt offering and spilled blood, but clearly a command to accept His truth and way of life as the *only means* to *recognize* the Father within. The disciple Thomas was not the only doubter. Philip said, in effect, that they would believe what Jesus said about God if only He would *show* them the Father:

Believest thou not that I am in the Father, and the Father in me? the words that I speak unto you I speak not of myself; but the Father that dwelleth in me, he doeth the works. Believe me that I am in the Father, and the Father in me: or else believe me for the very works' sake (John 14:10–11).

Here Jesus pleads with His disciples that if they are too literal-minded to accept His concept of God, they should believe Him because of the things God has been able to manifest *through* Him. Then He shows His faith in His fellowmen by saying: "Verily, verily, I say unto you, He that believeth on me, the works that I do shall he do also; and greater works than these shall he do . . ." (John 14:12).

It would seem that there is very little room for the shirker and the literalist in the philosophy of Jesus.

If any earthling were to stand "face to face" with the Great Creative Source we call God, probably he would shrivel as rapidly as a fly in the center of the sun. Is it not time we abandoned that childlike version of an anthropomorphous being in the sky and raised our vision of the unknown God to heights in keeping with His colossal power and spirit?

To the Christian, a chain of reincarnations should not be a call to stoicism; it should present a vision of a glorious future, in which each of us will play a realistic part. The amazing psychology expressed in Jesus' interpretation of life was based not on make-believe or wish-fulfillment, but on the essence of reality.

The Christian should realize that in the Christian concept of eternal life, we do not strive to depersonalize our personality, we try to increase its force, mentally, spiritually and morally. The unselfishness of Jesus, sometimes called meekness, did not diminish the power and radiance of the Christ. God did not create us, in all our diversity, in order to amuse Himself for a while and then throw us back into the pot to melt us all together. Creativity means diversity. As distinctive individuals we create in different ways. The universe must continue in infinite diversity. If it were not so, I, for one, would not desire eternal life. Life means change; immortality without change would be an eternal bore. Such a concept is not one of heaven but of hell.

Fortunately, Jesus gave us an entirely different concept of God as a Being eternally at work. What an exciting thought: we, too, may join in the search eternal!

13

THE SEARCH FOR SELF

Throughout the history of philosophy and religion the search for being has been paramount. ". . . in him we live, and move, and have our being . . ." (Acts 17:28). According to Martin Heidegger, the search for being is the only genuine philosophical question. Theologian Paul Tillich considers God as the ground of all being, but the question remains: "What is man that thou art mindful of him?"

Libraries are filled with the opinions of philosophers and psychologists as to what man is or is not. Man needs understanding of himself, for all thought and experience return to our subjective selves.

In the search for self, what are the possibilities for knowing one's self? Dr. Arthur Jersild, psychologist at Columbia University, discovered that an individual at any age may be able to alleviate his psychological troubles by self-examination. Contrary to the theory held by some psychologists, that we stop growing emotionally after adolescence, psychological research now has proved that emotional growth never stops. Another misconception is that only intensive therapy can remove flaws built into a person's character during the early years of his life. Actually, many personalities are capable of straightening themselves out in later years.

Dr. Jersild is not the only one who has disagreed with current theories of psychology. In *Man for Himself*, Erich Fromm states that

> . . . while psychoanalysis has increased our knowledge of man, it has not increased our knowledge of how man ought to live and what he ought to do. Its main function has been that of "debunking," of demonstrating that value judgments and ethical norms are the rationalized expressions of irrational—and often unconscious—desires and fears, and that they therefore have no claim to objective validity. While this debunking was exceedingly valuable in itself, it became increasingly sterile when it failed to go beyond mere criticism." [31]

Fromm believes that psychoanalysis, in its attempt to establish psychology as a natural science, made the mistake of divorcing psychology from philosophy and ethics. He also feels that human personality cannot be understood unless we look at man in his totality, which includes his need to find an answer to the question of the meaning of his existence and to discover norms according to which he ought to live.

I agree with Fromm, but only on the basis that back of man's rationality and meaning stand cosmic order and meaning, which man discovers as he matures.

TWO ASPECTS OF MAN'S EVOLUTION

The meaning of life, as we now know it, is directly related to both the physical and spiritual aspects of evolution. Although much of life remains a mystery, we do know a great deal about the first phase of evolution—a theory which is now accepted freely in all areas of the civilized world. Someone once said, however, that even scientists speak of evolution as if they were standing outside of it. Man is not only an integral part of evolution, he stands at the peak of the first aspect of evolution, which is history, and at the beginning of the second aspect, which is a highly speculative view of what he may become. While "it is not yet known what we shall be," there are definite indications of the directions in which man may travel.

Man has insight and foresight, as well as sight. The "vision" of man—his ability to see in the manner that Pierre Teilhard de Chardin saw life—will grow in significance as man reaches a higher level of knowledge and understanding.

What is the basis of evolution? Of all life? According to science, it is energy, which is deconcentrated mass or matter. One modern view of science is that matter is being created continuously in an expanding universe, or, matter is constantly coming into being.

Energy, which has been called the new god of science, is the most primitive stuff of the universe. The scientist, probing into the interior of the atom may feel like a voyager on a mystical journey, as he wanders off into the infinity of microscopic time and space. The scientist looking into the "heart" of the atom approaches the mystic who searches for the depth of the human soul. Therefore, the question asked by Father Teilhard: "Has science ever troubled to look at the world other than from *without?*" can be answered: the trend in science is changing. Science has no choice other than to become more and more concerned about the within of things, for the synchrotron proves how much energy can be produced from the within of matter.

The evolution and involution of consciousness present not a duality but a polarity, which is eternally in motion or at work. It is difficult, even for scientists, to visualize the evolution of the myriad forms of energy—from physico-chemical to biological and from the biological surface to the within (consciousness) of man—as being only one phase of the great polarity. Our understanding of this polarity will enable us to see the meaning of life, the purpose of creation.

Consciousness, instead of being an epiphenomenon as Jean Paul Sartre tries to explain, is *the* phenomenon out of which all things move and have their being. Involuted consciousness forms the second aspect of man's evolution. We cannot understand the meaning of man's present consciousness until we understand the meaning of the second phase of the great polarity toward which man is moving.

At present, man may be likened to the chick which, although it has succeeded in making a small opening in the shell, is still embedded in the egg. Standing in the dawn of his own awareness, man's perplexity is understandable. He is still in the process of emerging from one phase of evolution, and he has not come fully into the second phase. He stands, as it were, with one foot in either dimension and he is in the unhappy position of being half caterpillar and half butterfly. Man is not at home in either world, but he will value his importance when he realizes that he is the link between the two aspects of evolution.

Man has emerged from co-consciousness to consciousness and from consciousness to self-consciousness. His self-awareness has made him a partner with nature and while he is still in the first phase of evolution, he will learn to govern nature. Then, he will enter into the second phase of evolution in which, through the power of his own consciousness, he will create at will. The universe is a collector of consciousness, said Father Teilhard. I agree and I would add that the universe exists by and for consciousness which, since it functions on many levels, is exceedingly complex. The polarity of consciousness—from the lowest to the highest—contains all of life, all of energy, all of knowledge, all of creativity, and all of love. The second phase of evolution, which beckons man, is unbelievably majestic and beautiful.

THE SEARCH FOR MEANING

A purely anthropocentric view of life may cause us to experience the existential anguish of Sartre, or to embrace a stoicism of the kind suggested by Professor Walter Kaufmann—a stoicism without hope.

Without hope there can be no vision; without hope motivation ceases and darkness creeps into the heart of man. This book, however, is based on the assumption that although we may be inclined to take an anthropocentric view of life, there is a reality, a power, a consciousness, and a purpose outside of us—a force which includes all the forms of energy known and unknown to man, a force which directs the universe, and which operates both phases of evolution: matter and spirit.

This great creative force, still largely unknown to us, we call God. Once we understand the purpose of this tremendous creativity, meaning will enhance every moment of our existence.

The time seems near when we must decide whether to

accept Sartre's idea that man's ideals are nothing but his own inventions and that he designs his own "essence," or Viktor Frankl's belief that instead of inventing the meaning of our existence we "detect" such meaning.

The reason for urgency in taking a stand for the *greater* meaning is that the electronic revolution is upon us. The effects of the industrial revolution will pale in comparison with the changes that will be caused by the electronic revolution. As we enter this new era, the extension of our mental faculties by intellectronics will demand clearer delineations of purpose, together with a deeper sense of responsibility for all life. The interrelatedness of man with man will become so intensified that it will surpass the expectations of those who believe in the brotherhood of man.

What is the meaning of life? First of all, this question contains the answer to the mystery of creation; and, in a more relative sense, it would seek answers to the changing needs and developments of the human species. As to the questions regarding the meaning of our earthly existence, the answers are many and varied, and it is impossible to provide an abstract meaning for each individual life. All human action is determined by attitude. While attitudes may be swayed by mass hypnosis, usually individual choice determines individual attitude. How life "treats" us depends on our attitude. President John F. Kennedy said: "Ask not what your country can do for you but what you can do for your country." We may add: Ask not what life owes you but what you owe life! Is your attitude one of love and responsibility? Are you willing to perform even the smallest task in love? Then you *know truth and you live in reality.*

This task would not seem so difficult, if we lived in the

conviction that we *are* life and that life *is* love; that love is a flame which dispels the darkness of fear, of self-pity, and of anger.

What do we long for in the depths of our being? Whether we know it or not, we want to love and be loved. Unfortunately, we do not always know how to love. Yet without love our lives can have no meaning. As our love expands, life unfolds its meaning to us.

Psychologists do not observe, however, the phenomenon of the need or will to meaning with a single eye. Many still trace back all of man's frustrations to unconscious roots and sources. In dealing with man's neuroses in strictly instinctual terms, they strip man of his human values, his meanings and his aspirations, reducing him to his primitive aspect.

In his primitive state, man is primarily instinctual. In early civilization, man was pushed up the evolutionary ladder; as he toiled in the sweat of his brow, necessity pushed him on but, as he progressed, he was more and more pulled up by his values. These values represented his meanings for life and these values were not merely "defense mechanisms" and "sublimations." This type of "debunking," as Fromm said, is not enough to give man the courage and the will to meaning that is essential to healthy and progressive living.

Why do such an increasing number of people suffer from boredom? Viktor E. Frankl explains why the existential vacuum is a widespread phenomenon of the twentieth century. Having lost the safety of Paradise (his basic animal instinct) and the security of traditional behavior, man must make and depend upon his own choices. Unfortunately, as Dr. Frankl says, "No instinct tells him what he

211

has to do, and no tradition tells him what he ought to do; soon he will not know what he wants to do."[32]

Boredom, says Dr. Frankl, creates more problems for psychiatrists to solve than does distress. People seem to vacillate between the distress created by the tensions of modern life and the boredom of "Sunday neurosis," when, after the rush of the busy week, they discover the void within themselves.

Boredom can be eliminated only when the individual has inner resources, when he is motivated by his aspirations to make a creative response to life.

The tensions of life are part of human existence and frequently they are aids in human development. Tension is what differentiates a man from an ox—a genius from a dullard. "Mental health," says Dr. Frankl, "is based on a certain degree of tension, the tension between what one has already achieved and what one still ought to accomplish, or the gap between what one is and what one should become. Such a tension is inherent in the human being and therefore is indispensable to well-being." [33]

The meaning of immortal life is beyond the meaning of earthly life. In Frankl's logotherapy, this ultimate meaning is spoken of as a "suprameaning."

What is demanded of man is not, as some existential philosophers teach, to endure the meaninglessness of life; but rather to bear his incapacity to grasp its unconditional meaningfulness in rational terms.[34]

This is the point of view accepted by many Christians, as they place their trust in an unseen Knower who cares. This phase of religion is still effective but, as we grow in scientific knowledge, we will become aware that the search

212

eternal promises to bring the revelation of that suprameaning.

Since the universe exists by and for consciousness, we must seek the answer to the suprameaning in consciousness.

THE MEANING OF SUFFERING

Sooner or later every human being must face suffering. The reality of physical and mental suffering is clearly evident in our homes as well as in hospitals. Even our civil courts are occupied in establishing the cause of mental suffering (incompatibility), which is the basis for so many divorces.

In addition, a devastating kind of suffering is brought about by war, pestilence, acts of God in which nature goes on the rampage, horrible accidents in which young people are killed or maimed for life.

We experience the deepest agony when we can find no reason for its cause. Modern man can no longer accept the "blind" faith of our ancestors who ascribed all causes of suffering to the will of God; an angry God, who took revenge on a sinning people. Nor can we, as Christians, accept that theory of karma which holds that whatever happens to us is our karmic due. Such a determinism is not in accord with our concept of freedom. Nor is it in accord with the teaching of Jesus, who, when his disciples asked him: ". . . who did sin, this man, or his parents, that he was born blind?" answered, ". . . neither has this man sinned, nor his parents; but that the works of God should be made manifest in him" (John 9:2,3).

In broad terms, we may classify the causes of suffering

as: 1) those that come about through our own mistakes or evil intent; 2) those that are brought upon us through the wrong action or evil intent of others; 3) those that come upon us or our loved ones by chance or accident, and through acts of God.

From infancy we are taught to avoid mistakes. Nature, as well as parents, forces us to develop "correct" attitudes. Nature, however, restricts her guidance to events on the physical plane. Fingers burned on a hot stove do not teach children that stealing is wrong. Parents and teachers must carry the responsibility for their mental and spiritual development. The current growth of juvenile delinquency has nothing to do with nature. It is the result of moral breakdown and lack of responsibility in parents and teachers, who tell the child not to cheat in school and, by example, show how to cheat in life.

In school, the student can cheat by looking up the answers to his lessons in the back of the textbook; all the problems contained in the lessons have already been solved. In human life it is different, for there are no solutions in the back of any book, and the only realistic and profitable attitude is to face willingly and courageously all the problems of life and such suffering as may come one's way.

Difficult as it is to maintain the correct attitude toward our own mistakes, guilt and misdeeds, it is even harder to keep our equilibrium when we suffer through the actions of others; especially when evil intent is added to the wrong action. Turning the other cheek, and to "bless them that curse you" is a practice reserved for the saints. Yet all victories of great men in their "finest hour" have been moral victories. The wonder and mystery of the Western world for twenty centuries has been the willingness of Jesus to

214

suffer all the iniquities heaped upon Him and to retain a constructive attitude in the midst of His suffering. As Dr. Ralph Sockman remarked: ". . . *the mystery of goodness is even greater than the mystery of suffering.*" In spite of His unblemished character, Jesus did not take any credit for His saintly behavior and maintained that only God was good.

From the Biblical days of Job to the present, we have been shown how difficult it is to preserve a positive attitude in the presence of "innocent" suffering. What loving God can let babies die, allow pestilence, earthquakes, floods, and fires? There are two important aspects we must consider, when we shape our attitudes toward this devastating type of suffering.

The first concerns freedom. We consider our human freedom priceless, even if it presents us with difficult decisions. This freedom entails wrong choices, wrong action, evil, and sorrow. Rather than bewail our fate we should be grateful that God considers us worthy of developing our character, our consciousness, and our progress through the discipline inherent in freedom. Would not a universe without law presuppose chaos? Only a child would insist that laws be broken for his personal benefit. The underdeveloped nations show clearly that freedom must be earned through the acceptance of responsibility. The two cannot be separated.

The second aspect is our own shortsightedness. If we had to analyze man as he is today without the aid of history, without the aid of science and our knowledge of evolution, he would be a total mystery. We look at our suffering in the light of the moment rather than "that the works of God may be made manifest" in us. Or, as Paul put it:

". . . tribulation worketh patience; And patience, experience; and experience, hope" (Romans 5:3–4).

These words of St. Paul must have been realized by Katherine Mansfield when she wrote, near the end of her long and fatal illness:

> I do not want to die without leaving a record of my belief that suffering can be overcome. For I do believe it. What must one do? There is no question of what is called "passing beyond it." This is false.

> One must submit. Take it. Be overwhelmed. Accept it fully. Make it part of life. Everything that we really accept undergoes a change. So suffering must become Love . . . I must put my agony into something. Change it.[35]

In accepting suffering, we steel our spirits and rise in God's consciousness, which is Love. Katherine Mansfield could not change her pain, but she could, and did, change her *attitude toward* suffering. By accepting the inevitable—not by rejecting the realities of life—she achieved a moral victory over suffering in the spirit of Jesus who said: "I have overcome the world."

None of us who are concerned about the progress of civilization can escape mental and spiritual suffering. Such sorrow, says Dr. Frankl, ". . . may well be a human achievement. . . . A man's concern, even his despair, over the worthwhileness of life is a *spiritual distress* but by no means a mental disease."[36]

Moral victory, such as Jesus displayed in overcoming evil, seems to require superhuman courage and endurance; but the very acceptance of such suffering seems to generate its own strength. Such acceptance must always be based on *inevitable* suffering; a person who refuses to be cured of a curable pain or disease is not accepting the inevitable, he is foolish. To seek suffering for its own sake would be immoral.

Life and suffering consist of innumerable threads; one's attitude may weave these threads into either beautiful or ugly patterns of meaning.

The pathway of human evolution leads inevitably upwards; we may linger on the road or take side excursions but all of us must climb that mountain eventually.

SELF-TRANSCENDENCE

"You have only yourself" is an admonition that is frequently negated by our recognition of the elusiveness of the self. Millions of people are eagerly searching for self-fulfillment without an adequate idea of what they are searching for.

The need for self-actualization emerges usually after the other basic needs are satisfied (although these various needs are not mutually exclusive). But our basic need for self-actualization cannot be realized by concentrating only on personal needs outside of the self, nor by finding the meaning of life completely within ourselves; rather we must find a meaning for our efforts within the psychosocial progress of our world, our society, our family, our friends, and our community. Only in extending himself outwardly does man become enriched inwardly; in this process he finds self-transcendence.

To repeat: the more we abandon our subjectivity and the more we embrace objectivity, the greater becomes our freedom and the greater grows our capacity to accept truth

217

within ourselves. This may seem paradoxical, but we must look at the self not as a static identity or as a vessel with a limited capacity we can readily fill, but as a consciousness in the process of continuous growth.

Paul Tillich said that ". . . within itself, the finite world points beyond itself. In other words, it is self-transcendent." This pointing beyond itself implies a goal. "The goal of evolution," said Pierre Teilhard, "is the ascent towards consciousness." In the next chapter we will analyze the important question: What is the goal of consciousness as it is now in man and beyond?

Meanwhile we may note that only by "pointing beyond himself" does man gain his self-transcendence and find his self-fulfillment. In the dynamic process of life, however, both self-transcendence and self-fulfillment are but resting places on the long road all of us travel. Nevertheless, it is in our self-transcendence that we become truly free.

Jesus, as the son of man, suffered all the disappointments, temptations, and physical difficulties of the flesh. Perhaps the hardest thing He had to bear was the anguish of His great loneliness, for, even in the midst of His disciples, He had to face the reality of His mission alone. When He said that He had overcome the world, He did not mean it as a denial of the world; in accepting the world as it is, Jesus rose in His consciousness above it.

I became deeply aware of human self-transcendence during my last meeting with Helen Keller, deaf and blind since infancy. Her companion, Polly Thompson, served as our translator. But when Miss Keller and I exchanged memories of our previous meeting, she became too excited to wait for the translation. In her enthusiasm, the words poured forth from her throat. As she was leaving, her radiant joy transformed her blind countenance with indescribable beauty—a sight I shall never forget. I was filled with profound humility, overwhelmed by the realization of her magnificent victory over blindness and soundlessness. Miss Keller had conquered the void of darkness and utter loneliness and achieved glorious self-transcendence. It might be said that she became blind, not because either she or her parents had sinned "but that the works of God might be made manifest" in her.

In true Christianity there is no acceptance of escapism; there is an acceptance of heavy labor and great effort to conquer obstacles of whatever nature: Those in the moral realm, which we call evil, and all those that stand in the way of human progress.

The scientist's response to the unknown is a truly religious one, as Einstein indicated. Jesus said: "Greater things than these, ye shall do." Science has already given us an affirmative demonstration of the truth of this prophecy.

The search eternal is a continuous effort to increase our own creativity. Can we provide a logical foundation for the assumption of our own immortal creativity? Can we divine the spiritual (supraconscious) laws upon which our assumptions must rest, even as the scientists base their assumptions on the physical laws of the universe, which they have formulated?

I believe in an affirmative answer to these two basic questions. Once this answer is accepted as satisfactory, Christianity will be able to provide us with a tremendous incentive to develop our own inner resources.

We need a concept of immortality that will enable religion to walk arm in arm with science. We should welcome any new scientific discoveries that will enlarge our understanding. We need not fear changes in our religious concepts as long as we are secure in our belief that the truth of God goes on forever. I agree wholeheartedly with Julian Huxley that "Man's religious aim must therefore be to achieve not a static but a dynamic spiritual equilibrium. And his emergent religion must therefore learn how to be an open and self-correcting system, like that of his science." [37]

In this attitude, let us examine the search for consciousness.

14

THE SEARCH FOR CONSCIOUSNESS

So far I have emphasized scientific thought and method, but now I must go beyond scientific explanation. There will be places where my primary purpose will be to appeal to the reader's vision. Vision, as an extension of scientific thought, may lead us beyond the known world of reality. In other words, our vision need not be divorced from scientific knowledge; we must learn to see beyond our physical realities. It may well be that in future generations "seeing" will acquire a deeper significance in the process of understanding life.

In *The Phenomenon of Man,* Pierre Teilhard de Chardin stated that his aim was to see, rather than to explain. Nevertheless, his vision rested on a solid scientific background. Dr. William G. Pollard, who is also both a scientist and a man of the church, is convinced that a renaissance of discovering supernatural reality has already begun. He says:

> Like every renaissance, it will be a slow process of historic growth. One does not revolutionize patterns of thought and the pervasive convictions of a whole culture overnight. The very existence of this renaissance will remain undetectable to the vast majority of people for several decades more.[38]

Perhaps so. On the other hand, there is nothing more powerful than an idea whose time has come. Forty years ago, I wrote that we were living in a period of transition unequalled in the history of the world. This proved to be so, but now we see that the next forty years will bring an even greater revolution in the minds of men.

THE ASCENT TOWARDS CONSCIOUSNESS

In the theory of evolution there is no room for duality: from subatomic units to atoms, from atoms to both organic and inorganic molecules, from these subcellular living units to cells, from multicellular metazoa to Zinjanthropus (Zinjanthropus, the most primitive man we have knowledge of now, was discovered recently by archeologist Louis S. B. Leaky and his wife), and from this primitive creature, who lived 1,750,000 years ago, to the proud man of today—all these are composed of the same basic stuff.

Pierre Teilhard, who played an important part in the discovery of the Peking man, also clarified our concept of evolution and the development of consciousness in man. Being a strong visualizer, Teilhard emphasized synthesis and vision rather than overdependence on analysis, which, however important and necessary it may be to science, can, in its exclusive use, lead us to illusion rather than to vision. He stated that there can be no mind without synthesis:

> . . . modern thought is at last getting acclimatised once more to the idea of the creative value of synthesis in the evolutionary sense. It is beginning to see that there is defin-

itely *more* in the molecule than in the atom, *more* in the cell than in the molecule, *more* in society than in the individual, and *more* in mathematical construction than in calculations and theorems. We are now inclined to admit that at each further degree of combination *something* which is irreducible to isolated elements *emerges* in a new order." [39]

What we are witnessing in the process of evolution is the definite and persistent trend towards ever-increasing complexity, and yet unification. The material synthesis of both the inorganic and organic layers of the earth is a process which Pierre Teilhard called "complexification." (See glossary.) To him the process of evolution can be understood only by involution, the tendency throughout the cosmos for all of its parts to "roll up" or to "fold in" upon themselves. This process of self-complexification causes an increase in the energetic tension within each corpuscular organization from molecule to man.

Pierre Teilhard assumed that mental or mindlike properties must exist throughout the universe, in inorganic as well as biological units of organization. He struggled, as all of us do, with the concept of energy, the basic "stuff" of the universe. While he recognized the scientific view of energy as the stuff from "which all emerges and into which all falls back as into an ocean," he believed that science was too severe in thus depersonalizing the world. "Physics," he claimed, "is no longer sure whether what is left in its hands is pure energy, or, on the contrary, thought." [40] So he postulated a "within" as well as a "without" of matter, i.e. he "interiorized" matter in which the *without* was determined and the *within* "free," although the *within* assumed the same granulation as matter itself. In fact, he

223

claimed that, *"Atomicity is a common property of the Within and the Without of things."* [41]

In addition to the energy that is measurable in the physicist's sense, Teilhard postulated a second energy, which he named psychic energy. Of course, he did not propose a duality of energies, but two definitely different "forms" of energy, which are not readily, if at all, interchangeable, for how can we measure the energy of thought? He saw no hope to direct the transformation of psychic energy into mechanical energy, since we cannot discover a "mechanical equivalent" for will or thought. He was fully aware of the reason why physicists have not been searching for psychic or spiritual energy, stating that ". . . the nature of this inner power is so intangible that the whole description of the universe in mechanical terms has had no need to take account of it, but has been successfully completed in deliberate disregard of its reality." [42]

Although until now science may have made no attempt to connect these two energies of the body and the mind in a coherent manner, Teilhard remained steadfast in his belief that "Without the slightest doubt *there is something* through which material and spiritual energy hold together and are complementary. In last analysis, *somehow or other,* there must be a single energy operating in the world." [43]

He points out, however, that while the two energies of mind and matter are associated constantly and in some way pass into each other, there is no "direct transformation of one of these energies into the other"; for instance, in thinking, "only a minute fraction of 'physical' energy is used up in the highest exercise of spiritual energy." Therefore, he abandoned "all hope of discovering a 'mechanical equivalent' for will or thought. Between the within and the without of things, the interdependence of energy is incontestable. But it can in all probability only be expressed by a complex symbolism in which terms of a different order are employed." [44]

As a scientist, Teilhard could not accept a fundamental dualism and he assumed therefore that essentially all energy is psychic in nature. This concept is a basic part of my own belief and I will return to it in the discussion of cosmic polarity.

In rejecting a purely mechanistic evolution and in accepting the theory of emergent evolution, Pierre Teilhard combined it also with teleological evolution. He firmly believed in "the prime mover ahead"; thus he visualized a universe in which direction pointed to a face and a heart—not in an anthropological sense but symbolically. To him the universe is distinctly a personalizing universe in which personality is definitely *more* than individuality. Grains of sand share individuality with man, but only in reflective centers do we find personality. Another most important factor of self-consciousness he pointed out is that "Once formed, a reflective center can no longer change except by involution upon itself." [45] Thus, in human life progress takes the place of degeneration in the lower or less complex units of matter.

Not all scientists will agree with Teilhard's concept that complexification is the *cause* of evolution and that, as Julian Huxley points out, it may be better to say that complexity of a sort is a necessary prerequisite for mental evolution. Nevertheless, no one will quarrel with Pierre Teilhard's statement that "The degree of concentration of a consciousness varies in inverse ratio to the simplicity of the material compound lined by it. Or again: a consciousness is that much more perfected according as it lines a richer and better organized material edifice." [46]

225

Evolution equals rise of consciousness and rise of consciousness equals effect of union, Teilhard believes. "We have seen and admitted that evolution is an ascent toward consciousness. . . . Therefore it should culminate forwards in some sort of supreme consciousness." [47]

EVOLVING SUPRACONSCIOUSNESS

States of consciousness are familiar to all of us. We recognize our dreams as being not states of consciousness but of subconsciousness. Modern psychiatry has made us familiar with states of deep unconsciousness: the reservoir of our race mind or Jung's collective unconscious. Supraconsciousness, however, is not within man's general experience, and thus the question arises: Are we justified in assuming that there are higher levels of consciousness beyond those within our present knowledge?

Assuming a dog could answer the question: "Do you think that human consciousness is on a higher level than yours?" we know that the animal could not answer in the affirmative unless he were able to visualize what human consciousness might be. Are we in the same position as the dog, in regard to our understanding of a consciousness higher than that of the human race?

No! We are not, because humans have the ability and the power of imagination to see beyond the here and now. Studying the direction of events, we can forecast certain future happenings.

The limitations of human consciousness have been apparent to me for so long that I too need Teilhard's reminder that such concepts as supraconsciousness may

226

seem highly improbable to the common sense of the man in the street and even to those scientists whose philosophy of the world presumes nothing possible save what has always been. To Teilhard, however, it is quite credible ". . . that the stuff of the universe, by becoming thinking, has not yet completed its evolutionary cycle, and that we are therefore moving forward towards some new critical point that lies ahead." [48]

Realism demands our admission that this "critical point" lies so far ahead that most of us cannot see it. Our present difficulty lies in the fact that, as of now, our human awareness is still on the lowest rung of the long ladder which represents conscious evolution, and that our psychosocial evolution must progress a long way before society has a firm grip on that ladder.

Mind is still being studied in its lower forms. Much modern analytical psychology is still based upon the Freudian concept:

Mental processes are essentially unconscious . . . and those that are conscious are merely isolated acts and parts of the whole psychic entity. . . . The psychoanalytical definition of the mind is that it comprises processes of the nature of feeling, thinking and wishing, and it maintains that there are such things as unconscious thinking and unconscious wishing." [49]

Realism demands our admission that this Freudian concept is basically correct in respect to the majority of the human race. The point is: it should not be so. We must cease living within our subconscious, stop being dominated by it; we must learn to operate this computer machine we call the subconscious mind for our benefit, making it our servant, not our master. A proper method of understanding and operating the subconscious mind would lift us out of the animalistic state, in which we are controlled by our emotions and have only occasional conscious moments of "isolated acts."

Animals not only have emotions, they *live* in and *are* their emotions. Human consciousness should not be controlled by emotion, nor should intellect. In self-consciousness, emotion and intellect should serve as tools. Consciousness, freed from the subconscious and the physical, is immortal being, unobstructed by time and space; its will is the focus of its eternal creativity. Consciousness does not move with the speed of light, consciousness *is present always and everywhere at the focus of its will.*

Consciousness is awareness. A sudden expansion of mind, in a flash of cosmic consciousness or by means of using LSD, may reveal the possibility of extending our awareness. The dangerous extension of our awareness by LSD is not necessarily desirable, but there are other ways for increasing consciousness.

As stated before, cybernetics and intellectronics will undoubtedly be the means to force the psychosocial evolution rapidly ahead. While this will be a great boon to the intensification of the "noosphere" (a word coined by Pierre Teilhard, meaning the layer of human thought surrounding the surface of the globe; see Glossary.), cybernetics can also teach us how our individual centers of reflection can increase their powers of creativity, by liberating the consciousness from its "false" personalities with their irrational unconscious convictions. These "false" personalities are being created by the wrong information and judgments we have fed our subconscious minds. If we can see the folly of feeding wrong information into our ma-

228

chines and, if we realize the necessity of preparing the right programming for our physical computers, we may eventually recognize the importance of feeding the right information to our own mental computers. If we want our true selves to rise to the surface, we must be masters not slaves of our subconscious minds.

Once we have full control of our mental equipment, so that our subconscious no longer compels us to irrationality, our full development into integrated personalities is assured. Cybernetics and intellectronics can become useful instruments in the development of our individual as well as collective awareness. Meanwhile proper diet and modern eugenics will play their parts in the development of a superior race.

Where will all this lead us? While there is no doubt that our psychosocial evolution, or the "spirit of the earth," is primarily dependent upon this planet, the very nature of consciousness signifies more than that. We are bound by the curvature of the earth, but our vision must be directed beyond our present environment and we must recognize that anthropogenesis is only a part of cosmogenesis.

The irreversibility of self-conscious units implies the involution of consciousness to the nth degree. This will result in increasing degrees or levels of supraconsciousness.

Self-conscious man is a rather recent arrival in the history of evolution. In the more than million years between Zinjanthropus and the Peking man, the increase in consciousness was minute compared to the advancement in consciousness made during the less than ten thousand years of recorded history. The multiplication of men on earth and the convergence of mind have led to unification and increasing tension within the noosphere, thus producing ever more consciousness. But, while it is true that all of us benefit by the inventions and contributions made to civilization *by a few,* and that our opportunities for self-development are increased manifoldly by the advance of our psychosocial evolution, each of us faces the task of evolving our own supraconsciousness. Others may teach us how to develop our "mental muscles," but no one graduates to a higher consciousness without individual effort and concentration.

In the lower forms of life, evolution appears to be automatic. But nature allows us to play our part in the collaboration for progress as we become increasingly the conscious agents of our own evolution. The inevitable freedom of the "within" demands our voluntary cooperation, or in the words of Teilhard, "Taken individually, each human will can repudiate the task of ascending higher towards union." [50]

POLARITY

Every human being has had experiences with polarities —hot and cold; light and dark; east and west; and innumerable others. The negative and positive aspects of the physical world, such as the two opposite currents of electricity, do not present too great a problem for the human mind, as the use of electricity can be practically applied everywhere, and it is unaffected by the inability to explain its nature. However, in such polarities as freedom—destiny, body—mind, or good—evil, the inability to explain the nature of the polarity creates a difficulty for our intellects.

In civilization, man must have reasons for his conduct and he tries to find his answers by searching for a unified reality, which he strives to understand through theories or myths of polarity.

The subject of polarity is a difficult one, because polar entities are never single and pure. The representation of their characteristics is a question of degree, for in each polar character we may find some traces of its opposite. Chinese, Indian, Buddhist and Hindu myths present images in which the principle of polarity, the inner unity of opposites, is recognized explicitly.

In *The Dialogues of Plato,* Aristophanes, in the "Symposium," tells how the sexes were three in number originally, consisting of man, woman, and the union of the two. The body was round and had four hands, four feet, with back and sides forming a circle, one head with two faces, four ears and two private members. Then Zeus decided to cut their bodies in two, and men and women were divided: they walked on two legs, had two hands and appeared as men and women do now. But they had a great desire to be reunited because they remembered—not consciously but instinctively—that human nature was originally one and that man was a whole. Plato reasoned that the desire for and the pursuit of the whole is called love.

This concept describing the polarity between separation and unity appears repeatedly in various forms and disguises in numerous myths of the ancient world.

Modern scientists and philosophers are not the only ones to face the problem of dualism, according to history, so have all nations, races and religions of man.

Is Christianity dualistic? Probably, most Christian theologians would reject dualism and might point also to the theoretical opposition of monotheism to dualism. I agree with this view only if we assume that God *and* the universe represent a polarity, not an irrevocable separation. Yet or-

231

thodox Christianity presents an ultimate good—evil dualism, in its pictorialization of the sharp conflict between God and Satan, heaven and hell, the body and the soul.

The polarity between Adam and Jesus is that of the disobedience of the first man (the faint image) to the Will of God, and that of the first Son (the vivid image) refusing Satan's temptations. The first man initiated separation and original sin, and the Son of God, through obedience to the will of the Father, even unto death, brought atonement—at-one-ment or unity. Yet Jesus, when told that he was good, replied that only God was good.

The problem of evil, which for centuries has occupied the minds of the most profound philosophers and theologians will not be resolved here. Perhaps Alan Watts points to a way out:

> Good and evil are abstract categories like up and down, and categories do not perform their function unless they are kept distinct. It is thus perfectly proper that the *concepts* of good and evil be distinct, dualistic, and irreconcilable, that they be as firm and clear as any other measure. The "problem of duality" arises only when the abstract is confused with the concrete, when it is thought that there are as clearly distinguishable entities in the natural universe.[51]

Our difficulty with the problem of evil is that we are as unable to evolve a concept of absolute goodness as we are to develop a concept of absolute evil. This does not prevent us from dealing with the problem of evil in concrete terms, however, nor from working towards relative good.

What is polarity exactly? Says Alan Watts:

> It is something much more, than simple duality or opposition. For to say that opposites are *polar* is to say much more

than that they are far apart: it is to say that they are related and joined—that they are the terms, ends, or extremities of a single whole. Polar opposites are therefore *inseparable* opposites, like the poles of the earth or of a magnet, or the ends of a stick or the faces of a coin. Though what lies between the poles is more substantial than the poles themselves—since they are the abstract "terms" rather than the concrete body—nevertheless man thinks in terms and therefore divides in thought what is undivided in nature.[52]

In essence, polarity combines both separation and unity. To try to encompass the immense diversity of polarities is to attempt to achieve the ultimate synthesis—an ultimate synthesis that is beyond our grasp. The factual language of our logic can dissipate the evidence only through analysis; the poetic language of our myths cannot define the truth of ultimate synthesis; it can only point towards it.

We can define and describe only that which we know. We do not know the exact nature of God so how can we attempt to describe the Great Creative Source? We can present only a "vision" of it. For lack of a definition, we may clothe our vision in the garment of a new myth which I have called "Cosmic Polarity." Such a myth, in the form of a picture, gives a view of reality from our present perspective, but this view need not be in conflict with modern science. When future scientific knowledge presents facts that disprove such a vision, the vision will have to be modified in the same manner that the "facts" of today are changed by the "facts" of tomorrow. Our mythical vision therefore is an *aid* to our understanding and not an *irrevocable* truth.

The principle of polarity may be observed in all life.

Electricity is only one of the better known examples that combine a positive and a negative force. Repulsion and attraction, push and pull are present everywhere.

Some exponents of mysticism have classified the polarities existing between men and women as follows: On the physical level, man exerts the positive push and woman the negative pull. On the next level—of emotion—polarity shifts, with woman in the positive dominant role of the leader and man in the negative role of responding. On the third and mental plane, polarity shifts again, with man resuming the positive aspect and woman functioning as the receiver, the follower and the adjuster. On the fourth—the spiritual level—polarity shifts once more, with woman in the positive and man in the negative position.

In observing universal polarity, we see that the negative principle is not less desirable than the positive one, but that it is a *necessary complementary element on every level of existence.* True polarity results in union on every level and produces energy as in electricity.

COSMIC POLARITY

One of the attempts to explain the physical cosmos is to assume that it came forth from a single giant atom, which, for reasons unknown, exploded. Considering the immensity of the universe, this atom must have been an "egg" of unbelievable size, or the physical energy condensed within it must have been an energy raised to the nth power.

The physicist's approach to the explanation of the origin of the physical universe is inclined to be in terms of the mechanical processes he observes to be in existence now. The energy surrounding us must have originated somewhere; energy is gradually running down; entropy will eventually put the physical universe out of existence. But no physicist can explain how the universe originated, nor what will happen when it ends. His observation leads us only to the conclusion that we live "between the miracle of our origin and the mystery of our destiny."

Our increasing understanding of the power of human consciousness and its unrealized potentialities allows us to make "respectable" speculations, concerning the nature and the direction of the cosmos, as Pierre Teilhard did.

"The universe," he said, "goes on building itself above our heads in the inverse direction of matter which vanishes. The universe is a collector and conservator, not of mechanical energy, as we supposed, but of persons." [53]

Even for scientists and philosophers, it is presumptuous to attempt to explain in words the "nature" of that Great Creative Source which brought us into being. "Matter and spirit," said Teilhard, "do not present themselves as 'things' or 'natures' but as simple related *variables,* of which it behooves us to determine not the secret essence but the curve in function of space and time." [54] The best we can do is to make reasonable assumptions concerning the manifestations of their beingness.

Instead of using the analogy of an "egg-like atom" to explain the existence of the physical universe, let us assume the existence of a nucleus of supreme consciousness —in full awareness that the "last word" about the nature and origin of energy may not be forthcoming in many centuries of research. Considering the presence of polarity everywhere, it seems reasonable to assume that polarity exists within as well as without the Great Creative Consciousness.

We may visualize the inner polarity as consisting of a female principle or awareness, which gathers within itself all that the male principle, or conscious-will, accumulates. Awareness is wordless, it is the womb of creation. Conscious-will is the force that moves; the logos which initiates meaning; the word that creates a multitude of abstractions; and, above all, a psychic energy that makes the word become flesh.

Furthermore, we must assume the power of the involuted consciousness of the divine Being to be so intense that psychic energy is continuously being created. Life-energy flows from the Great Cosmic Center in an unending stream. Universes may come and go—no matter. What matters to us is our own part in this eternally creative process; important as the polarity within the Great Being may be, of even greater importance to us is the great Cosmic Polarity which binds us to this Creative Center.

In the process of extending its own divine seed or psychic energy, Cosmic Consciousness creates space and time. Psychic energy—in spite of Pierre Teilhard's assumption that *all* energy is psychic energy—is still a vague term to many people. Yet I believe that psychic energy presents the only reasonable explanation of creation. The within and the without of matter reflects the within and the without of God: Awareness as the wordless being within; conscious creative activity as the without of Being.

When man became a reflective center—in the image of God—the purpose of life in the universe became dimly realized on this planet. We know now that evolution is the ascent towards consciousness; that love-energy or psychic energy is found not only in man, but that it is present in all of life and even pre-life down to the molecule. We know that the *direction of progress places matter more and more to the service of mind,* as is evidenced by our great computers.

236

Since psychic energy, in all its elements, expresses a powerful affinity, we can be assured that the "love of God" must be a strong and binding reality throughout the universe. But, if this affinity pulls us forward to higher levels of consciousness, what is the future of man? Our future is as integral a part of Cosmic Polarity as is our past.

The involuted consciousness of the Great Spirit unrolls itself in a continuous stream of thought, love, and energy produced by the principle of its own polarity. We are part of this cosmic unfoldment, which we now recognize as evolution—the process of energy or matter "folding back" upon itself. In this process, individuality emerges and consciousness ascends to the level of man.

The pole extending between the Cosmic Center and the basic stuff from which evolution emerges may be visualized as being divided into two halves. The upper half represents pure self-consciousness or spirit; the lower half consists of physical substance, non-self-conscious energy or matter.

We must remember, however, that such a division is only an aid to our visualization. In polarity there is no complete cleavage at a definite point. Moreover, both the lower and the upper part of cosmic polarity are interdependent.

While still in the lower half (the physical aspect) of cosmic consciousness, man partakes increasingly of the higher vibrations—forms of rarefied psychic energy—expressed by the inner forces of will, love and consciousness.

Struggling upward on the pole of cosmic consciousness, man is only dimly aware of his high potential, yet he has already evolved to the point where he can demonstrate that spirit works on matter, that matter serves for increased mind, which, in turn, serves for increased being. While we know that the lower half evolves at the expense of energy, we are only dimly aware that *the upper half provides new energy.*

Man's consciousness, we have agreed, is irreversible. Eventually, all of us must reach the level attained by Jesus, whose spirit ruled His emotional life. When we have evolved to the point where we can function without the compulsive needs of material bodies and our creative reflective centers have reached self-motivation for spiritual development, then we will graduate into the upper half. We *ascend,* so to speak. And, as we ascend higher and higher, our power of creativity rises and, eventually, *we add to the conscious upper half of the polarity what is lost in the unconscious lower half.*

Thus cosmic polarity remains in equilibrium.

15

THE SEARCH FOR REALITY

From the beginning man has searched for reality—especially philosophers, scientists, and theologians.

Throughout the history of the Christian church, theologians debated reality in terms of the "truth" as revealed in sacred writings. Currently, theologians emphasize the philosophical-historical approach in demythologizing the myths of the Bible. They are attempting to discover the enduring meanings which have vital applications to life.

Philosophers have sought reality by spinning theories about ultimate truth based on concepts of physical monism, mental monism, and dualism. Modern science has rejected them all. Therefore, modern philosophers no longer accept the "idealism" of Bradley and Berkeley, which, by some magical polarization, is now called "realism." Instead, they embrace nominalism and call themselves logical positivists, which means that man can have no knowledge of anything but phenomena and that such knowledge is merely relative. Obviously, such thinkers have given up the search for absolutes.

Scientists accept neutral monism, which means that they base their faith on an ultimate oneness which must contain both physical and mental elements. (Cosmic Polarity, de-

scribed in the previous chapter, is based on this concept.)
In their search for this ultimate, they have probed into the
microscopic world of energy and revealed an "inner" universe so refined, so infinitesimally minute and yet so unbelievably powerful that it staggers our imagination. Science
follows the path of energy because that is measurable. The
ultimate concept of energy, however, may well be a reality
lost in such "pure" or absolute abstraction in terms of
mathematical symbology that it will have no meaning for
the human mind.

No one can be sure how future scientific discoveries will
change our philosophy and concepts of life. All we can say
now is that science is primarily concerned with the manifestations of life. In this practical pursuit, science has
helped man improve his environment and his knowledge
of the physical elements surrounding him. Although
science has learned a great deal about man, it cannot yet
explain his basic nature.

I have frequently used the expression: Whatever is, is;
meaning that the ultimate reality cannot be changed by
philosophical, religious, or scientific argumentations and
concepts. But how do we discover this ultimate reality? It
cannot be found in the ever-changing components of
physical substance. Ultimate reality must be found in
spirit, for God—*the ultimate—is* spirit. But what is spirit
and how do we discern it?

First we must differentiate between spirit and matter.
Matter operates only in time and space; spirit is timeless
and spaceless. Spirit may manipulate matter; it expresses
itself through consciousness. Matter cannot comprehend
spirit, but spirit may understand matter. The Great Consciousness, in creating the universe, also created time and

space. Consciousness itself, however, can be anywhere, because it is not obstructed by time and space.

On earth, all that is created by man has been achieved through his growing self-awareness. But, while we advance along the pole of Cosmic Polarity, man is still bound by a body operating in a dense physical atmosphere. Our vision is blurred, and we are limited by our physical needs. Our spiritual needs demand that we look inward to find real freedom. But we must recognize that we are in a stage of cosmic evolution where a balance between our physical and spiritual needs is necessary. At some future point, when our bodies become more refined, the balance will shift to the more spiritual phase. Therefore, the modern Christian can neither afford to live the Krishnamurti philosophy we discussed in chapter Eight nor can he ignore its implications of the reality to be found within.

Pierre Teilhard complained that science has looked only at the *outside* of things and ignored the *within*. In delving within the atom, science may give the impression that it has begun to look at the within of matter, but this is not so. The atom contains other elements within itself; also, the atom is *filled with space*. The atom, as a miniature solar system, proves that even the smallest physical substance can exist only in time and space.

In making our spiritual prognosis we are closer to the medical diagnostician, who must frequently limit himself to the best "educated guess," than to the scientist who looks only at the outside of things. The doctor must consider both the inside and outside of man and a good doctor frequently performs like a good artist—he adds his creative insight to his medical knowledge.

We too must look at physical and spiritual man "through a glass darkly" and, using our best educated guess, we must try to see him as he really is in his relative state of development. Because we are still living in the lower part of the Cosmic Polarity, it is difficult to tell by looking at a man what he is like inside. Usually, we must wait until he acts, before we can decide whether he is foe or friend, thief and liar, or a well-intentioned, honest man. When we are more spiritually developed, as Jesus was, we will be able to separate a man's looks and words from what he really is.

Practically all people on this earth are concerned with their existence in our three-dimensional plane only. There is no denying that science is preeminent in its research and development at this level of our existence. Science presents us with a host of temporary realities. So let us give to the physical that which the physical requires, and to the spirit that which is its essence: eternal creativity.

The concept of Cosmic Polarity is a difficult one; it may be useful in our research for Reality to place the *being* of philosophy, the *Sonship* of religion, and the *energy* of science together in a triangle to suggest a new trinity. It will be difficult to describe the creative process contained within this triangle, but I hope that some illustrations will help abstract such truths and realities as we are able to visualize.

THE TRINITY AND THE CREATIVE PROCESS

The concept of the Holy Trinity has caused a great deal of difficulty and confusion in the Christian church. Some modern theologians wish to discard the concept completely and, considering that science rejects duality and has even less sympathy for trinities, this may not seem an altogether unreasonable proposal.

Nevertheless, the concepts of duality and of the trinity may be useful to the human mind. A few simple geometric illustrations may help us to visualize the highly abstract concepts of cosmic polarity, the trinity, and the creative process. These graphic explanations, however, will not *prove reality;* they are only a feeble attempt to *enlarge* our concept of the Great Reality we call God.

Let us begin by drawing a straight line representing our Cosmic Polarity, God, male and female being. (According to Genesis, God made Eve from a rib he took from Adam. This is just another symbolic representation of the male-female unity, which is described in a different way by Plato.)

A line is a series of dots that can be extended into infinity. Next, let us take any two points on this line and draw two more lines, each at an angle of 45 degrees. The two lines will meet at a 90-degree angle, forming a rectangular triangle with two equal sides. The sum of the squares of these two equal sides (as in any rectangular triangle) will equal the square of the hypotenuse. The hypotenuse represents the Cosmic Polarity, the Creative Source, God, or Being. Or, in our older and more familiar concept, we may call it: Father. The Father desires a Son. It takes energy to produce a Son. So here we have a rectangular triangle with two equal sides, representing Father, Son, and Holy Spirit.

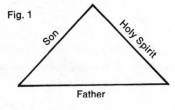
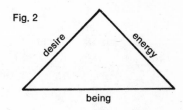

Fig. 1 — Son, Holy Spirit, Father

Fig. 2 — desire, energy, being

But, we may also rename the three sides, using modern terminology as in figure 2. In other words, God extends His Being through desire and energy. This energy may also be called psychic or life energy. The desire of God is His creativity, which can be expressed as the *Word* which "was made flesh." As God thinks, so it is. The Word, or the Son, is thus the expression of God's creative thought. (Even the thought of man is more powerful than we realize.)

We may designate God's creative process as a trinity: Being, desire, and energy. Jesus was very insistent that God worked not only in the past, but that "he is working today."

It requires spiritual insight to weave a logical pattern between the parables in the Bible and the mystical message of Jesus within and beyond these words. When His disciples asked Him why He spoke in parables, Jesus replied: ". . . Because it is given unto you to know the mysteries of the kingdom of heaven, but to them it is not given" (Matthew 13:11).

Is there any justification for identifying physical and psychic energy with the Holy Ghost or Holy Spirit? There is indeed. In Romans 15:19, St. Paul says: "Through mighty signs and wonders, by the power of the Spirit of God. . . ." Science is revealing power, signs, and wonders in increasing numbers.

But, let us consider the words of Jesus as reported in Matthew 12:32: "And whosoever speaketh a word against the Son of man, it shall be forgiven him: but whosoever speaketh against the Holy Ghost, it shall not be forgiven him, neither in this world, neither in the world to come."

Here we have that famous problem: the unpardonable sin against the Holy Ghost; the "bugaboo" of theology and the fear of many sincere Christians. What if you commit an unpardonable sin and you do not know what that sin is?

Jesus said: Look, as an individual being I can forgive your trespasses against Me, but if you use power wrongly, no one can either help or forgive you. In the parable of the good and the corrupt tree, He describes the thought, the word, the use of physical and psychic power. He shows that the tree is known by its fruit and He points out the difference between good and evil thoughts in the heart of man.

Atomic power can be used constructively or destructively, but, once it is used, the result can no longer be changed. The Holy Spirit of God on earth is manifested as condensed energy in matter and as psychic energy in man's mind. The word of the mind, bathed in its psychic energy, goes forth for good or ill in both this world and the next.

In these words and parables Jesus was enunciating, for those who "have ears to hear and eyes to see," the basic spiritual law by which our universe is operated.

For the strong visualizers we interpose another concept here:

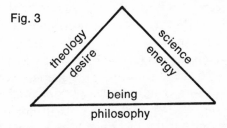

Fig. 3

theology
desire

science
energy

being
philosophy

Philosophy looks at ontology: the reality of being. Theology looks at the offspring of God: the only begotten Son, the desire or extension of the Father. Science is concerned primarily with the various manifestations of energy: from the motion and power within the atom to the motion and gravity within the galaxies.

The three are separate as they observe the universe from their own viewpoints. But they are restless, especially theology and philosophy. Theology looks through its side of the triangle and speaks of the God of history. It becomes more and more interested in existentialism. Tillich says that God is the ground of all being. He has fused philosophy with theology and is considered a philosophic theologian.

Against the blank wall of the unprovable ultimate being, philosophy has turned its eye toward existentialism. Of course, many philosophers have become unconcerned with "ultimate being," and they have satisfied themselves with other tasks, such as the philosophy of science or logical analysis.

Once sure of its own foundation based on the solidity of matter, science has lost that *solid* substance in the almost pure abstraction of mathematical symbols and in a substance so refined and "unsolid" it disappears into metaphysics—the former enemy of physics.

Just as the Son and Holy Spirit are the extensions of God, so desire and energy are the extensions of His Being. We have reached the stage where science, philosophy, and religion must join hands in order to obtain a unified concept of man and the cosmos.

One may, of course, hold to the unity of these three disciplines and their perspective on experience without accepting the theory of the dynamic Trinity. But, if one accepts the *vision* of the Trinity as outlined, then the unification of these disciplinary perspectives would follow as desirable and indeed necessary.

Let us return to our triangle and observe that God's creative process produces *inner* space. Naturally, there is always room for more space *outside* of the triangle regardless of how much we enlarge the triangle of the creative process, even *ad infinitum.*

The inner space of the preceding triangles is obvious. But how can we visualize the inner space—the *within* of man and of all matter assumed by Pierre Teilhard?

Everything in the universe is multiplied by division, so let us divide our triangle:

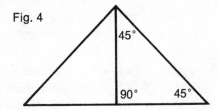

Fig. 4

Now, we have two rectangular triangles, each having equal sides with 45-degree angles and joining each other at an angle of 90 degrees. The theorem of Pythagoras that the square of the hypotenuse is equal to the sum of the squares of the two opposite sides is just as true for both triangles. Furthermore, we may continue to divide each rectangular triangle—theoretically without limit.

The illustration in figure 5 may help us to visualize the

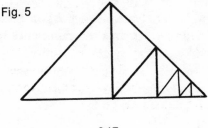

Fig. 5

division of the macrocosm into the microcosm. Although science is still searching for the minute particles within the atom, we may assume that there must be a microscopic space within the smallest of the triangles. Does this not substantiate—at least theoretically—the view of Teilhard that there is a *within* in matter as well as in man? Thus the atom is a microcosmic reflection of the universe, man is a microcosmic reflection of God's creative spirit, each with a within as well as a without.

Our image of the divine is weak because it is still small. Since the inherent characteristic of life is growth, however, in time our image will expand. A triangle divided into the microcosmic and unseen triangles, representing atoms, does *not* expand, since atoms are fixed in nature and law. The triangles, *symbolically* representing human souls, do not only divide and multiply, as living entities they expand. This expansion in man, not in terms of his physical structure but in terms of his "true nature," i.e. his divine consciousness, is likewise subject to—spiritual—law and order. Because man has choice, he can will to deny his ascension to unity and, in so doing, create disorder. The Son *must* do the will of the Father; it is the only way the universe and the creative process of spirit and matter can operate. Jesus obeyed this law and the First Commandment: ". . . thou shalt love the Lord thy God with all thy heart, and with all thy soul, and with all thy mind, and with all thy strength . . ." (Mark 12:30). Thus He could state: "I am the way and the [creative] life." He made it clear that if we wish to obtain our sonship, we must obey the same law.

Man may willfully attempt to change the shape of his divine triangle by extending the line of his desire without at the same time extending the line of energy. But if he does, he is aiming at false growth, which results in extending the line of his being—creating a false being and a false personality. In doing so, he destroys the 90-degree rectangle of his own triangle and interferes with the creative process essential to the equilibrium of his own trinity.

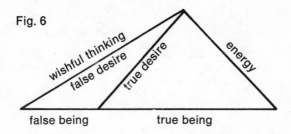

Fig. 6

wishful thinking
false desire
true desire
energy

false being   true being

Man carries the center of his own universe (Kingdom) within him. He must be true to himself in order to find the Kingdom of Heaven within. If we are to reach our evolutionary spiritual goal, we must recognize and develop our inner power and *keep it in balance.*

Referring to the Cosmic Polarity briefly described in the preceding chapter, we may visualize it by extending the Cosmic Polarity into space, not in one direction, but in two, as in figure 7.

Fig. 7

45°   45°
45°   45°

If we draw the four angles thus formed, each at 45 degrees, and extend the lines, we will obtain two rectangular triangles, which together form a square. The square has been called the building block of the universe.

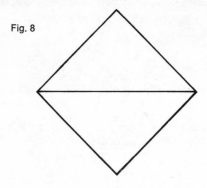

Fig. 8

These upper and lower triangles may be indicated as follows:

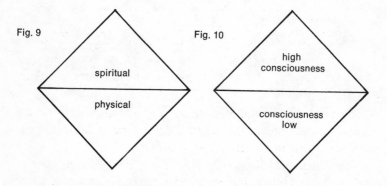

Fig. 9

spiritual

physical

Fig. 10

high consciousness

consciousness low

There are those who say that the physical is only a reflection of the spiritual. Others contend that the reverse is true. It might be better to say that each triangle reflects the other. They are inseparably bound together, as we can observe in the two triangles above.

A line may be drawn from the top of the spiritual to the bottom of the physical and another line from the high point of consciousness to the low point of consciousness to indicate their respective polarities.

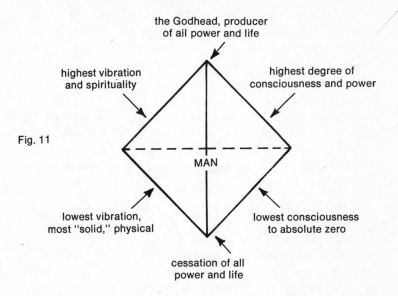

Fig. 11

the Godhead, producer
of all power and life

highest vibration
and spirituality

highest degree of
consciousness and power

MAN

lowest vibration,
most "solid," physical

lowest consciousness
to absolute zero

cessation of all
power and life

Through the center of our square we may draw innumerable lines, each representing one of the various polarities we know, including good and evil.

The allegorical Lucifer had achieved high consciousness before he fell. Because of his disobedience to the will of the Father (the morality inherent in high spiritual development), Satan lost his place in "Heaven" and was thrown back into the lower consciousness of man, there to tempt us by providing us with a choice. The Christ, however, descending voluntarily, came down to dwell among us as the Son of Man, in order to show us how to rise in consciousness and to "ascend into heaven," by obeying the law of God. The *ascension into heaven* is identical with the *rise in consciousness* and thus, according to the very words of Jesus, "the Kingdom of Heaven is within" us. All of the refinements and complexities of theology and the speculations of philosophy will not change this basic and all-inclusive concept of Christ's mission on earth. Therefore, all human beings are committed to the mental, social, and spiritual evolution of man. *There is no other way.*

Lest the reader criticize these analogies as too farfetched, let me emphasize once more that we can never *prove the ultimate reality.* In the last analysis, our lives and actions must be based on faith. This faith may range from the simple but hopeful expectation that we will have another tomorrow on this earth, to my basic belief that we originated in the creative consciousness of the Ruler of the Universe and that we are living now and forever more in His divine Grace.

While our poor blueprints of His Being, belying an infinitely more complex structure of the universe, will not prove the unprovable, they may aid us in our visualization of a profound abstraction. More important than our theories of the cosmos is the love of God, His psychic love energy which flows throughout the universe, binding all things together.

We should always be aware that love creates unity in diversity. To feel this love we must experience it. Perhaps someday we may also "hear" it, when we are able to listen to the "music of the spheres." What is music but harmonious vibrations creatively organized? When we are touched by great music are we not "lifted up" in consciousness and feeling?

Our radios can contact the astronauts flying to the moon. Few of us have the technical know-how to understand the mathematical computations involved in such a project, but certainly our imaginations are adequate to visualize the wonders of this universe.

Recently, scientists of the Bell Telephone Laboratories have discovered Laser pulses that last only a trillionth of a second. Previously, scientists thought that Laser pulses were of much longer duration, and they were not aware of the tremendous power inherent in these pulses. Moreover, the Bell scientists have introduced a technique which proves that these tiny light pulses are capable of carrying billions of watts of power. The benefits of this discovery for science and human existence will become apparent in future years.

This new event should prove a great help in grasping the creative process in our perpetual searching. Our minds find it difficult to conceive of life in a universe extending over billions of light years in space. How much more effort is required to visualize events that have reality (proven existence) but for a trillionth of a second. Now, scientists can actually measure these "realities." Considering how much our concepts of time and reality have changed, why should we be dogmatic about our present concepts? It seems foolish indeed to refuse to change them in light of new discoveries which also may enhance the insights of our religious and philosophical concepts. These elevated insights will replace our old crutches and provide us with new hope to make our lives more meaningful.

THE SECRET OF CREATION

Einstein said that the universe is finite but unbounded. In principle, the universe can grow eternally but, even if the present cosmos were extended a trillion times into space, there would still be the limitless void beyond it. In other words, our cosmos is an open-end universe, the expansion of which is limited only by the sum total of the creative power within it.

Long before Western civilization began, the Hindu thinkers were as bold as our modern scientists in speculating about the origin of the cosmos and the principles underlying its structure. The Vedic thinkers not only evolved an ether theory, they classified mind as a more rarefied ether. They did not stop there, they looked beyond that for a still more rarefied ether. Then as now, the question remained: Can any knowledge of the external world reveal "ultimate reality"? Scientists hope it may some day; we need not disagree, although our basic difficulty may lie in our uncertainty as to what to search for. We should realize that the secret of creation cannot be found in either dualism or monism, its mystery is hidden in a polarism that contains both of them. And further discovery in this area depends on our openness for exploring the *within* of things.

The two halves of Cosmic Polarity may be visualized in another way: the lower half consisting of condensed mass with a low conscious vibration, but clearly visible to the human eye; the upper half "purified" psychic energy of such high vibration that it cannot be detected by man— similar to the high-pitched tones human ears cannot detect.

If the extension of conscious power is the purpose of

creation, then the universe must extend indefinitely. Before our galaxy was born there was a void. Taking all the galaxies together in our one universe, there must still be a void outside of it. Simply put, there is endless room for expansion.

If *the void* was in the beginning, why did God extend his Being into it? Because He is a creative God. In creating the heavens and all that is therein, He projected His spirit seed into the universe. If we are the individualized offspring of the Great Spirit and our natures are free, pure, and immortal, why was it necessary for us to take on physical form? Because, in the friction between spirit and matter, our souls gained and will continue to gain a long, varied, and *individualized* experience that sets us apart as personalities and prepares us to become useful and fully creative entities. It provides each of us an opportunity to "overcome the world" in our own personal unique way, even though we follow in the footsteps of the Man who first uttered those famous words.

We need not return to the Great Spirit to be "all in all," as Western thought frequently interprets the meaning of the Eastern religions and philosophies. God is within us *now,* experiencing the joys and sorrows, successes and failures of our individual growths.

Our spirits are created equal, but God in His wondrous wisdom allows us free choice in setting our own pace and rate of progress; He permits mistakes and retrogressions. This freedom is an essential part of our spiritual evolution. In God's "democracy," concern for others and responsibility for self are kept in balance. The highly developed, spiritual individual must assist the less advanced. In our present stage of evolution, we have left the careless days of childhood and entered the troublesome period of spiritual puberty. Slowly and uncertainly, we are awakening to God's creative urge within us. After puberty there will still be years—perhaps millions of them—for the development of our future manhood when, allegorically speaking, God may say to us: "Son, you are now a man; go forth in wisdom and love, and create joyfully—even as I do."

Surely we have advanced far enough to stop our childish depiction of God as a physical person whom we can see and touch with our physical senses. It seems time to concentrate more on finding Him within us, by using our spiritual awareness.

Jesus was the Christ revealed; the true Son of God who had found God within Himself. Jesus *is* the Way and we can be "saved"; not, literally, by the blood He shed, but by our unconditional acceptance of the Christ revealed and by our commitment to follow in His steps whatever the cost, until we also find the Father within us.

THE NECESSITY OF CREATION

From the ancient mysteries of the Egyptian temples to the Masonic rites of today, men have been interested in "secret" wisdom. Occult history is nothing but a recital of mysteries, kept and perpetuated by various mystic brotherhoods.

Modern science has taken a considerable edge off these ancient mysteries. Science reveals its "secrets" frankly—about nature and the cosmos—to everyone who pays the price of admission: a lecture or book and some mental effort. But the mysteries discovered by science reveal an ever-increasing number of difficult questions concerning the cosmos.

We should consider the process of creation as a necessity, rather than as a secret. We need to rid ourselves of the ancient religious concept that one day God sat down to think and then He proceeded to create a universe.

That the Great Creative Source, *by the necessity of its own Being, must reproduce* is the fact, rather than the secret, of creation. For, if it is the nature of God to love, there must be *someone to be loved.*

Matter-energy is constantly coming into being; self-consciousness is continuously increased. The "immortality" of the worm—its ceaseless self-reproduction on the physical plane—is repeated on the spiritual plane in the irreversibility, and therefore immortality, of self-conscious centers.

The never-ceasing love-energy of the Great Creative Source leads to an expanding universe (or universes), in which increasing numbers are matched by increasing consciousness, maintaining forever the Cosmic Polarity between Creator and created.

Science and religion should combine their efforts in discovering the spiritual laws that sustain the physical and the spiritual cosmos.

Does the concept of the necessity of creative reproduction make the universe impersonal in nature? I do not think so. We need, of course, to change some of our concepts regarding the personal and impersonal.

A child's world is more personal and circumscribed than is an adult's. To an "ascended" consciousness, awareness is less personal in a restricted and self-centered sense than is that of a present-day adult. An adult would not give up his extended awareness in order to live in the more personal world of his child. Likewise, an "ascended" consciousness has an extended awareness that more than

257

makes up for the loss of what seemed at one time more intensely personal.

Greater awareness does not imply, however, the loss of personal reactions and personal feelings. The "personal" simply moves on to a higher plateau in correlation with the higher consciousness.

This process can readily be discerned at work in our own experience. A baby has an awareness limited to a few things; it cannot comprehend a beautiful sunset. An adult, however, may react to a sunset with an intense feeling of awe or enjoyment; his reaction, even if he stands in the midst of a multitude, will also be completely personal. Each individual, among thousands listening to music played by a symphony orchestra, has a deeply personal reaction to what he hears.

Life is full of such personal reactions to stimulating events shared by many. We may therefore assume that, as we ascend into higher consciousness, our individual reactions to whatever we are, do, or see, will remain personal.

The continuation of our personal responses to life not only remains with us, it causes each reflective center to become ever more personalized—in the sense that we overcome our limitations and, as individual centers, reflect more and more, each in its own unique way, the reality of the cosmos. I agree with Pierre Teilhard that the universe is a personalizing one and that personality is more than individuality.

Our real concern should be not for man but for his consciousness, which, some day—in its inevitable progress—will leave man behind. Yet, as man alone is nothing, we need to think of a collection of consciousness rather than of a single consciousness, which leads us to a consideration of the end of man.

258

THE END OF MAN

As we have previously observed, man may come to an end by means of a sidereal cataclysm or the cooling of the sun; as the result of total nuclear or chemical warfare; by voluntary cessation of human life by complete birth control or by destruction of man's power of reproduction; or, finally, by the evolution of man into something greater than man.

All scientists—whether Christians, agnostics, or atheists—probably can agree on these various possibilities regarding the end of man. But, for the Christian, something more has to be said about the future of man than is necessary in discussing the destiny of the race on this planet.

Although the development of man is an integral part of the earth's evolution, we make a mistake if we limit our future existence to the fate of this planet. If we, as reflective centers, are immortal, then the destruction of the earth should not affect our immortality. This concept does not imply, however, that our continued and progressive existence on earth is not important.

The whole tenor and subject matter of this book has pointed to the necessity of improving the quality of the human race. The possibilities for such progress in the light of modern research are enormous. Whether or not this progress is to take place depends on the readiness of man to accept his own responsibility.

The crux of the matter lies in the will of man. God's Will leads us, but does not compel us. Evil is all around us and wicked ones remain free to "repudiate the task of ascending higher towards union."

A depraved individual does not affect the destiny of the

race noticeably, but evildoers acting in groups may change the course of history. Communism as a theory of providing "plenty for everybody" may be a harmless Utopia. But communism in terms of a group of determined individuals, who use deceit, perversion, lies, cruelty, murder, dictatorship, and tyranny in order to gain control over all the people in the world, is a malignant cancer that may destroy our culture.

A realistic appraisal of this fact demands our acceptance of the possibility of failure for our own civilization. A return to the Dark Ages—if not worse—is possible. Freedom of choice comprises decline as well as progress. Our faith in ultimate victory of good over evil cannot be based on the history of civilizations on earth, it must be rooted in our acceptance of a cosmic love, which again and again rebuilds on the ashes of the old. Without such a concept, life is devoid of meaning. The strengthening of the immortal soul—not in spite of, but *by means of repeated failures*—will finally make us worthy sons of God. The recurring victories of life, notwithstanding the failures, are ample cause for a valid faith in ultimate victory. The statement of Jesus: "I have overcome the world," (i.e. the selfishness of the lower human instincts) must some day be uttered by all of His followers.

Important as individual victory may be, however, the need for social success is even more urgent. We are never going to be, nor are we ever going to operate, alone in this universe. We will always be part of and acting in groups. Therefore, we need not only to "save ourselves," but our brothers and neighbors as well—for our own sake as well as theirs. *Concern for others* seems to be a cosmic affinity and urge for unity, counteracting the push away from others caused by individualization or the involution of matter and mind upon itself.

Individual consciousness, in cooperation with other individual consciousnesses, contributes to progressive psychosocial evolution on earth, as well as to spiritual evolution. It is in spiritual evolution that we—immortal souls—must express the search eternal.

Those earthlings who come after us may well be of a higher breed than we. Civilizations far superior to ours may arise—ten, fifty or a hundred million years hence. Many, if not most of us, should have learned the lessons of earth life before then, so that we should have graduated from the school of man to something higher.

Our knowledge of the cosmos has advanced sufficiently for us to realize that schooling—by which I mean the gaining of knowledge and experience—is an integral part in the scheme of cosmogenesis as well as anthropogenesis. In order for us to earn self-conscious immortality and to move forward into spiritual evolution, we must *ascend* and break the bonds of man. The dual aspects of man, in which he is both animal and spirit, must be resolved in favor of spirit—incorruptible.

If we accept this premise as a necessity—and how can we be Christians if we do not accept the ascension into higher consciousness—what challenge does a spiritual life hold for us? The answer can be found only in the search eternal: the joy of creating (as our creativity advances we *do* create) carries its own reward and fulfillment. In an eternally expanding universe, (eternity and infinity can never reach an ending) there remains abundant opportunity for creativity.

In our present undeveloped stage, someone may ques-

261

tion if the victory of the incorruptible over the corruptible is worth the struggle. The evidence points toward an affirmative answer, if we are willing to adapt our traditional Christian concepts to the modern knowledge of today.

16

THE SEARCH ETERNAL

If the assumptions made in the previous chapters regarding immortality are correct, what significance does such immortality have for Christians? Let me define first what I mean by Christianity.

Christianity, stripped of its theological accessories, speaks plainly and is understood readily. At the center of the universe it sees the Great Creative Source as a self-conscious God, a Knower who cares about us. Christ, the perfect example of divine Sonship, revealed the moral and spiritual laws of the Father-Universe. Steeped in true spirituality, His concern for others never faltered. ". . . Before Abraham was, I am . . ." (John 8:58), He said, secure in the knowledge of His immortality. Love for God, and love for man are God's two great commandments, on which all other laws are based. When Jesus said: ". . . My Father worketh hitherto, and I work" (5:17), He revealed His knowledge of how the universe operates. Energy, work, love, and concern for others are the spiritual and physical cores around which the universe revolves.

Is not such an assertion in conflict with other religions? In a sense, Christianity has become a world religion, but

the same can be said of Buddhism. On what do we base
the superiority of Christianity as a world religion?

WHICH WORLD RELIGION?

Both Christianity and Islam owe many of their beliefs to
Judaism. Buddhism evolved from Hinduism. It has been
said that Buddhism is Hinduism stripped for export. Hinduism is a way of life that cannot be transported.

China had Confucianism—an ethical philosophy rather
than a religion—until Zen Buddhism, modified by Taoism,
took over. Zen reached its highest development in China
between A.D. 700 and A.D. 1100.

Buddhism in India and Burma split into a high form
and a low form. Mahayana Buddhism (the high form) is
an intellectual philosophy, and its psychological dueling is
a match for Western psychiatry. The great variety of karmas it has devised and the fear of disturbing the conse-
quences of these karmas place the emphasis on present action in a negative rather than a positive aspect. Such
cumbersome karmas, complicating the interpretation of
reincarnation, are usually sufficient to induce a dislike and
disbelief in Christians regarding the theory of reincarnation.

Zen Buddhism, it may be said, is Buddhism stripped of
intellectual pride and dominion. Zen Buddhism has faded
in China; it is fading in Japan, but it is *arising in the West.*

At first glance, Zen may seem an antiintellectual movement. It is not. It aims at complete spontaneity. It attempts
to cut out all mental blocking, anxiety, and nervousness.
To think spontaneously, however, requires training. In approaching the Zen master, the pupil may be disturbed by

264

the apparent nonsense uttered by the teacher in response to his questions. What is the purpose of the Zen master? His purpose is to aggravate and irritate the student to the point that the student can see the immensity of the small, the complexity of the simple; thus the student gains the vision and understanding of the wordless and is able to act in response to any situation spontaneously. When the student understands that the important goal lies in the living of life, not in the intellectual description of life, he no longer needs a teacher. Living life means going with the flow of the tide; meeting nature with nonresistance rather than seeking its conquest.

Obviously, these are important concepts of life, which are ignored by the West all too frequently. It is also a condition—an attitude towards life—not readily acquired. The Zen method is one of negation: it shocks, it creates surprise, it talks nonsense so the disciple will stop using his intellect and become conscious of an awareness which accepts that whatever is, *is,* and goes along with it.

This cursory review of Zen may give the Westerner the impression that Zen's techniques of relaxation and conditioning for surprises is nothing but a return of man to his animalistic state in which he is one with nature. But such a view is shortsighted and wrong. During this process, the student is led by the teacher to become aware of what is his intellect and what he himself is in reality, and as an individual, he gains a great deal of knowledge about himself. But, are not those Westerners who become interested in Zen, the ones who have tasted Christianity on the outside only? Have they experienced the essence and inner power of the Christ?

What has Zen that Christianity does not have? Jesus preached only *what He lived.* The real and the ideal (a combination fervently sought by many philosophers) were one in the life of Christ. He never sacrificed principle for gain. He gave all and sought nothing in return.

The objectives of Zen and the Christ are the same, but their methods vary. Zen uses shock or surprise to gain spontaneity in life. In Christianity love achieves this aim. God so loved the world and Christ so loved humanity that He was willing to bear the cross.

In Zen, man worships neither God nor teacher. Man must awaken to his own Godhood. In Christianity we worship God and awaken to our own sonship. But only God is good, said Jesus, and in our faith that God rules the universe, we stand in awe before Him and worship the Lord. Our feeling of awe in what we see of this wondrous universe, our faith in what there is still to discover, and our hope of participating in the creative processes of the cosmos under the direction of One who knows and cares, has a positive influence on our lives and actions. To the Chinese, God is not in control of all there is, but the universe is orderly of and by itself. This is the same as saying that the universe itself is God.

To the Christian the universe is the expression of God's creativity. If we take this thesis out of Christianity we reduce Christianity to an ethical philosophy.

The impersonal universe of the Hindu is drawn in black and white; the Christian's universe is painted in vivid color. For it is God's love that colors life and the entire cosmos. A recognition of color is one of the later developments in man's evolution; the power of love is one of the more recent developments in civilization. Only an understanding, acceptance, and practice of universal love can prevent our civilization from destroying itself. As Arnold Toynbee said: "Civilizations will not be destroyed from

Aids to Radiological
Differential Diagnosis

Aids to Radiological Differential Diagnosis

3rd Edition

Stephen Chapman

MB, BS, MRCP, FRCR

Consultant Paediatric Radiologist
The Children's Hospital, Birmingham;
Honorary Senior Clinical Lecturer
University of Birmingham.

Richard Nakielny

MA, BM, BCh, FRCR

Consultant Radiologist
CT Body Scan Department
Central Sheffield University Hospitals;
Honorary Clinical Lecturer
University of Sheffield.

WB Saunders Company Ltd
London   Philadelphia   Toronto   Sydney   Tokyo

W.B. Saunders Company Ltd   24–28 Oval Road
London NW1 7DX, UK

The Curtis Center
Independence Square West
Philadelphia, PA 19106-3399, USA

Harcourt Brace & Company
55 Horner Avenue
Toronto, Ontario M8Z 4X6, Canada

Harcourt Brace & Company, Australia
30-52 Smidmore Street
Marrickville, NSW 2204, Australia

Harcourt Brace & Company, Japan
Ichibancho Central Building, 22-1 Ichibancho
Chiyoda-ku, Tokyo 102, Japan

A catalogue record for this book is available from the British Library

ISBN 0-7020-1895-3

First published 1984
Second Edition 1990
Reprinted with corrections 1992
First edition translated into French, Japanese and Spanish
Second edition translated into French, German and Spanish

Typeset by Photo·graphics, Honiton, Devon
Printed in Great Britain by MacKays of Chatham PLC, Chatham, Kent

Contributors

Michael Collins
FRCR

Consultant Radiologist Royal Hallamshire Hospital, Sheffield; Honorary Clinical Lecturer University of Sheffield.

Mark Davies
FRCR

Consultant Radiologist, The Royal Orthopaedic Hospital, Birmingham; Honorary Senior Clinical Lecturer University of Birmingham.

Keith Harding
BSc, MB, FRCP, FRCR

Consultant in Nuclear Medicine City Hospital NHS Trust, Birmingham; Senior Clinical Lecturer in Medicine University of Birmingham.

Josephine McHugo
MBBS, MRCP, FRCR

Consultant Radiologist Birmingham Maternity Hospital; Honorary Senior Clinical Lecturer University of Birmingham.

Tom Powell
FRCP, FRCR

Consultant Neuro-Radiologist Royal Hallamshire Hospital, Sheffield; Honorary Clinical Lecturer University of Sheffield.

Contents

PART 1

7   Gallbladder, Liver, Spleen, Pancreas and Adrenals   257

* 6.47 and 6.48 have been placed out of sequence for display reasons.

12 Skull and Brain *with contributions by Tom Powell* 379

13 Nuclear Medicine / *Keith Harding* 456

PART 2

Preface to the First Edition

During the period of study prior to taking the final Fellowship of the Royal College of Radiologists, or other similar radiological examinations, many specialist textbooks and the wealth of radiological papers are carefully scoured for lists of differential diagnoses of radiological signs. These will supplement the information already learned and enable that information to be used logically when analysing a radiograph. All this takes precious time when effort is best spent trying to memorize these lists rather than trying to find them within the massive texts or, even worse, trying to construct them oneself.

Consequently we decided to write a book which contains as many useful lists as one might reasonably be expected to know for a postgraduate examination. To make it manageable, we have omitted those lists and conditions which have limited relevance to routine radiological practice. In addition, many of the lists are constructed in terms of a 'surgical sieve' and by using this method we would hope that the lists are easier to remember. We have tried to present the conditions in some order of importance, although we realize that local patient selection and the geographical distribution of diseases will have a great influence in modifying the lists. The lists will, almost certainly, not be acceptable to all radiologists. However, the basic lists are supplemented with useful facts and discriminating features about each condition and these should enable the trainee to give a considered opinion of the radiograph. So that this added information can be kept concise and to avoid unnecessary repetition we have summarized the radiological signs of many important conditions separately in Part 2 of the book.

The book has no radiographs. We have assumed a basic knowledge of radiology in the reader and expect him or her to already be able to recognize the abnormal signs. A limited number of line drawings have been used to emphasize radiographic abnormalities.

The aim of the book is to assist with logical interpretation of the radiograph. It is not intended for use on its own because it is not a complete radiological textbook. Recourse will need to be made to the larger general and specialist texts and journals and the reading of them is still a prerequisite to passing the postgraduate examinations.

More exhaustive lists are to be found in Felson & Reeder's *Gamuts in Radiology* (Pergamon Press, Oxford, 1975) and Kreel's *Outline of Radiology* (Heinemann, London, 1971) and these books are to be commended.

Stephen Chapman
Richard Nakielny

Preface to the Second Edition

In the five years since the publication of the first edition we have seen it accepted not only by radiologists in training but also by those who are more experienced. However, in preparing a second edition we have tried to keep to our premise to produce a book with relatively short lists, aimed primarily at those taking postgraduate examinations. The lists have been revised since the first edition by adding in information from the last five years of radiological literature.

Now that a knowledge of other methods of imaging is necessary for postgraduate examinations we decided that the scope of the book should be broadened. Further lists of CT differential diagnoses have been included and we are grateful for the co-operation of three of our specialist colleagues who have written new chapters on topics which are outside our own fields of expertise. Michael Collins, Keith Harding and Josephine McHugo have expertly accomplished the production of chapters on mammography, nuclear medicine and obstetric and gynaecological ultrasonography, respectively. The few general ultrasonography lists are, we admit, little more than a token gesture but to have included an extensive input in this field would have increased the size of the book beyond what will fit comfortably in a white coat pocket.

It is inevitable that our knowledgeable readers will not agree with the arrangement of all our lists. We hope that such differences of opinion will be made known to us so that we can make any appropriate changes to future editions.

Stephen Chapman
Richard Nakielny

Preface to the Third Edition

The prime role of this book has been always to assist the junior radiologist with basic radiological interpretation rather than to be a miniaturized complete textbook of imaging or a bench book during reporting sessions. This third edition has continued the tradition of the first two so that, the CT, ultrasound, and now MRI, lists continue to be limited in their depth and breadth. The success of the earlier editions and the foreign language translations has demonstrated that this style of presentation is universally acceptable to those who have used the book. We have endeavoured to maintain the original style in the present edition although some of the new 'lists' are longer and contain more discussion than has been the norm to date.

The specialist contributors to the second edition, Mike Collins, Keith Harding and Josephine McHugo, have remained with us and we are grateful to them for their continued support. For this edition we also welcome Mark Davies who has helped revise the musculoskeletal entries and Tom Powell who has brought the skull and central nervous system topics up to date by improving our previous endeavours and adding much information on MRI with which all radiologists surely must have some degree of contact.

Stephen Chapman
Richard Nakielny

Explanatory Notes

The 'surgical sieve' classification used in the longer lists is presented in order of commonness, e.g. when 'neoplastic' is listed first then this is the commonest cause as a group. Within the group of neoplastic conditions, number 1 is more common or as common as number 2. However, it does not necessarily follow that all the conditions in the first group are more common than those in subsequent groups, e.g. infective, metabolic, etc.

The groups entitled 'idiopathic' or 'others' are usually listed last even though the disease or diseases within them may be common. This has been done for the sake of neatness only.

In order that the supplementary notes are not unnecessarily repeated in several lists, those conditions which appear in several lists are denoted by an asterisk (*) and a summary of their radiological signs is to be found in Part 2 of the book. In this section conditions are listed alphabetically.

Abbreviations

ACTH	Adrenocorticotrophic hormone
AD	Autosomal dominant
AFP	Alphafeto protein
AP	Anteroposterior
AR	Autosomal recessive
ASD	Atrial septal defect
AV	Atrioventricular
AVM	Arteriovenous malformation
CMCJ	Carpometacarpal joint
CMV	Cytomegalovirus
CNS	Central nervous system
CSF	Cerebrospinal fluid
CT	Computerized tomography
CXR	Chest X-ray
DIC	Disseminated intravascular coagulopathy
DIPJ	Distal interphalangeal joint
HCG	Human chorionic gonadotrophin
HOA	Hypertrophic osteoarthropathy
HOCM	Hypertrophic obstructive cardiomyopathy
HU	Hounsfield units
IAM	Internal auditory meatus
IUCD	Intrauterine contraceptive device
IVC	Inferior vena cava
IVU	Intravenous urogram
LAT	Lateral
MCPJ	Metacarpophalangeal joint
MPS	Mucopolysaccharidosis
MRI	Magnetic resonance imaging
NEC	Necrotizing enterocolitis
NFT	Neurofibromatosis
PA	Postero-anterior
PAS	Perodic acid-Schiff (stain)
PDA	Patent ductus arteriosus
PIPJ	Proximal interphalangeal joint
PMF	Progressive massive fibrosis
PPH	Post-partum haemorrhage

SIJ	Sacroiliac joint
SLE	Systemic lupus erythematosus
SMA	Superior mesenteric artery
SOL	Space occupying lesion
SXR	Skull X-ray
TAPVD	Total anomalous pulmonary venous drainage
TB	Tuberculosis
TE	Echo time or time to echo
TGA	Transposition of the great arteries
TOF	Tracheo-oesophageal fistula
TR	Repetition time
T_1W	T_1 weighted
T_2W	T_2 weighted
US	Ultrasound
VMA	Vanillylmandelic acid
VSD	Ventricular septal defect

PART 1

1
Bones

with contributions by Mark Davies

1.1 Retarded Skeletal Maturation

Chronic Ill Health
1. Congenital heart disease – particularly cyanotic.
2. Renal failure.
3. Inflammatory bowel disease.
4. Malnutrition.
5. Rickets*.
6. Maternal deprivation.
7. Any other chronic illness.

Endocrine Disorders
1. Hypothyroidism* – with granular, fragmented epiphyses. This causes severe retardation (five or more standard deviations below the mean).
2. Steroid therapy and Cushing's disease – see Cushing's syndrome*.
3. Hypogonadism – including older patients with Turner's syndrome.
4. Hypopituitarism – panhypopituitarism, growth hormone deficiency and Laron dwarfism.

Chromosome Disorders
1. Trisomy 21.
2. Most other chromosome disorders – severely depressed in trisomy 18.

Other Congenital Disorders
1. Most bone dysplasias.
2. Most malformation syndromes.

Further Reading
Poznanski A.K. (1984) *The Hand in Radiological Diagnosis*, Chapter 3, pp. 67–96. Philadelphia: Saunders.

1.2   Generalized Accelerated Skeletal Maturation

Endocrine Disorders
1. Idiopathic sexual precocity.
2. Intracranial masses in the region of the hypothalamus (hamartoma, astrocytoma and optic chiasm glioma), hydrocephalus and encephalitis.
3. Adrenal and gonadal tumours.
4. Hyperthyroidism.

Congenital Disorders
1. McCune–Albright syndrome – polyostotic fibrous dysplasia with precocious puberty.
2. Cerebral gigantism (Soto's syndrome).
3. Lipodystrophy.
4. Pseudohypoparathyroidism.
5. Acrodysostosis.
6. Weaver (Weaver–Smith) syndrome.
7. Marshall (Marshall–Smith) syndrome.

Others
1. Large or obese children.

Further Reading
Poznanski A.K. (1984) *The Hand in Radiological Diagnosis*, Chapter 3, pp. 67–96. Philadelphia: Saunders.
Rieth K.G., Comite F., Dwyer A.J., Nelson M.J., Pescovitz O., Shawker T.H., Cutler G.B. & Loriaux D.I. (1987) CT of cerebral abnormalities in precocious puberty. *Am. J. Roentgenol.*, 148: 1231–8.

1.3 Premature Closure of a Growth Plate

1. **Local hyperaemia** – juvenile chronic arthritides, infection, haemophilia or arteriovenous malformation.
2. **Trauma.**
3. **Vascular occlusion** – infarcts and sickle-cell anaemia.
4. **Radiotherapy.**
5. **Thermal injury** – burns, frostbite.
6. **Multiple exostoses** and **enchondromatosis** (Ollier's disease).

1.4 Asymmetrical Maturation

1. **Normal children** – minor differences only.

Hemihypertrophy or Localized Gigantism
1. **Vascular anomalies**
   (a) haemangioma and AVM.
   (b) Klippel–Trenaunay–Weber syndrome – hypertrophy of the skeleton and soft tissues of one limb or one side of the body in association with an angiomatous malformation.
   (c) Maffucci's syndrome – enchondromas + haemangiomas.
2. **Chronic hyperaemia** – e.g. chronic arthritides (juvenile chronic arthritis or haemophilia).
3. **Hemihypertrophy** – M > F. R > L. May be a presenting feature of Beckwith–Wiedemann syndrome (hemihypertrophy, macroglossia and umbilical hernia). Increased incidence of Wilms' tumour.
4. **Neurofibromatosis*.**
5. **Macrodystrophia lipomatosa.**
6. **Russell–Silver dwarfism** – evident from birth. Triangular face with down-turned corners of the mouth, frontal bossing, asymmetrical growth and skeletal maturation.

Hemiatrophy or Localized Atrophy
1. **Paralysis** – with osteopenia and overtubulation of long bones.
2. **Radiation treatment in childhood.**

1.5   Short Limb Skeletal Dysplasias

Rhizomelic (Proximal Limb Shortening)
1. Hypochondroplasia – resembles a mild form of achondroplasia.
2. Achondroplasia*.
3. Chondrodysplasia punctata – see 1.45.
4. Pseudoachondroplasia – see 1.6.

Mesomelic (Middle Segment Limb Shortening)
1. Dyschondrosteosis (Leri–Weil disease) – limb shortening with a Madelung deformity.
2. Mesomelic dysplasia
   (a) Type Langer.
   (b) Type Reinhardt–Pfeiffer.

Acromesomelic (Middle and Distal Segment Limb Shortening)
1. Chondroectodermal dysplasia (Ellis–van Creveld syndrome) – similar to asphyxiating thoracic dysplasia but (a) hexadactyly is a constant finding, (b) there is severe hypoplasia of the fingers and nails, (c) congenital heart disease is common and (d) hypoplastic lateral tibial plateau is characteristic in childhood.
2. Acromesomelic dysplasia.
3. Mesomelic dysplasia
   (a) Type Nievergelt.
   (b) Type Robinow.
   (c) Type Werner.

Acromelic (Distal Segment Shortening)
1. Asphyxiating thoracic dysplasia (Jeune's syndrome) – narrow thorax with short ribs leading to respiratory distress. Spur-like projections of the acetabular roof. Premature ossification of the femoral capital epiphyses. Occasional post-axial hexadactyly. Cone-shaped epiphyses in childhood.
2. Peripheral dysostosis.

1.6 Short Spine Skeletal Dysplasias

1. **Pseudoachondroplasia** – short limb and short spine
   dwarfism, marked joint laxity, platyspondyly with exaggerated grooves for the ring apophyses, C1/2 dislocation.
2. **Spondyloepiphyseal dysplasia** – ovoid or 'pear-shaped' vertebral bodies in infancy ⟶ severe platyspondyly in later
   life; normal metaphyses; retarded development of the symphysis pubis and femoral heads; coxa vara, which may be
   severe; ± odontoid hypoplasia and C1/2 instability.
3. **Spondylometaphyseal dysplasias**
   (a) Type Kozlowski.
   (b) Other types.
4. **Diastrophic dwarfism** – progressive kyphoscoliosis, hitch-
   hiker thumb, delta-shaped epiphyses, interpedicular narrowing of the lumbar spine.
5. **Metatropic dwarfism** – short limbed dwarfism in infancy
   ⟶ short spine dwarfism in later childhood, severe progressive scoliosis, dumbbell shaped long bones, hypoplastic odontoid.
6. **Kniest syndrome** – dumbbell shaped long bones, irregular
   epiphyses, kyphoscoliosis, platyspondyly, interpedicular
   narrowing of the lumbar spine, limited and painful joint
   movements.

1.7   Lethal Neonatal Dysplasia

1. **Osteogenesis imperfecta*** – usually type II.
2. **Thanatophoric dwarfism** – small thorax, severe platyspon-dyly with 'H'-shaped or 'inverted U'-shaped vertebral bod-ies, 'telephone handle' shaped long bones ± 'clover-leaf' skull deformity.
3. **Chondrodysplasia punctata** – rhizomelic form. See 1.45.
4. **Asphyxiating thoracic dysplasia (Jeune's syndrome)** – see 1.5.
5. **Campomelic dwarfism** – bowed long bones.
6. **Achondrogenesis** – types I and II.
7. **Short rib syndromes ± polydactyly**
   (a) Type I (Saldino–Noonan).
   (b) Type II (Majewski).
   (c) Type III (lethal thoracic dysplasia).
8. **Homozygous achondroplasia***.
9. **Hypophosphatasia*** – lethal type.

1.8   Dumbbell Shaped Long Bones

Short narrow diaphyses with marked metaphyseal widening.

1. **Metatropic dwarfism** – see 1.6.
2. **Pseudoachondroplasia** – see 1.6.
3. **Kniest syndrome** – see 1.6.
4. **Diastrophic dwarfism** – see 1.6.
5. **Osteogenesis imperfecta (type III)***.
6. **Chondroectodermal dysplasia (Ellis–van Creveld syn-drome)** – see 1.5.

1.9 Conditions Exhibiting Dysostosis Multiplex

Dysostosis multiplex is a constellation of radiological signs which are exhibited, in total or in part, by a number of conditions due to defects of complex carbohydrate metabolism. These signs include (a) abnormal bone texture, (b) widening of diaphyses, (c) tilting of distal radius and ulna towards each other, (d) pointing of the proximal ends of the metacarpals, (e) large skull vault with calvarial thickening, (f) anterior beak of upper lumbar vertebrae and (g) 'J-shaped' sella.

Mucopolysaccharidoses

Type	Eponym	Inheri-tance	Onset	Osseous and visceral abnormalities	Neurological features
IH	Hurler*	AR	By 1–2 yrs	Marked. Severe dwarfism. Skeletal abnormalities ++. Corneal clouding	Severe
IS (V)	Scheie	AR	Child-hood	Carpal tunnel syndrome	Mild
II	Hunter	XR	2–4 yrs	Marked. Severe dwarfism. Dysostosis multiplex similar to Hurler but less severe. No corneal clouding	Mild to moderate
III	Sanfilippo	AR	Child-hood	Mild	Severe
IV	Morquio*	AR	1–3 yrs	Severe skeletal abnormalities	Absent (but may be neurological complications of spinal abnormalities)

cont.

Type	Eponym	Inheritance	Onset	Osseous and visceral abnormalities	Neurological features
VI	Maroteaux–Lamy	AR	Childhood	Severe dwarfism and skeletal abnormalities	Absent (except as a complication of meningeal involvement)
VII	Sly	AR		Mild to severe	Absent to severe

Mucolipidoses
1. MLS I (neuraminidase deficiency).
2. MLS II (I–Cell disease).
3. MLS III (pseudopolydystrophy of Maroteaux).

Oligosaccharidoses
1. Fucosidosis I.
2. Fucosidosis II.
3. GM_1 gangliosidosis.
4. Mannosidosis.
5. Aspartylglucosaminuria.

1.10 Generalized Increased Bone Density – Children

NB. Infants in the first few months of life can exhibit 'physiological' bone sclerosis which regresses spontaneously.

Dysplasias
1. **Osteopetrosis***.
2. **Pycnodysostosis** – short stature, hypoplastic lateral ends of clavicles, hypoplastic terminal phalanges, bulging cranium and delayed closure of the anterior fontanelle. AR.
3. **The craniotubular dysplasias** – abnormal skeletal modelling ± increased bone density.
   (a) Metaphyseal dysplasia (Pyle).
   (b) Craniometaphyseal dysplasia.
   (c) Craniodiaphyseal dysplasia.
   (d) Frontometaphyseal dysplasia.
   (e) Osteodysplasty (Melnick–Needles).
4. **The craniotubular hyperostoses** – overgrowth of bone with alteration of contours and increased bone density.
   (a) Endosteal hyperostosis, Van Buchem type.
   (b) Endosteal hyperostosis, Worth type.
   (c) Sclerosteosis.
   (d) Diaphyseal dysplasia (Camurati–Engelmann).

Metabolic
1. **Renal osteodystrophy*** – rickets + osteosclerosis.

Poisoning
1. **Lead** – dense metaphyseal bands. Cortex and flat bones may also be slightly dense. Modelling deformities later, e.g. flask-shaped femora.
2. **Fluorosis** – more common in adults. Usually asymptomatic but may present in children with crippling stiffness and pain. Thickened cortex at the expense of the medulla. Periosteal reaction. Ossification of ligaments, tendons and interosseous membranes.

(continued)

3. **Hypervitaminosis D** – slightly increased density of skull and vertebrae early, followed later by osteoporosis. Soft-tissue calcification. Dense metaphyseal bands and widened zone of provisional calcification.
4. **Chronic hypervitaminosis A** – not before 1 yr of age. Failure to thrive, hepatosplenomegaly, jaundice, alopecia and haemoptysis. Cortical thickening of long and tubular bones, especially in the feet. Subperiosteal new bone. Normal epiphyses and reduced metaphyseal density. The mandible is not affected (cf. Caffey's disease).

Idiopathic
1. **Caffey's disease (infantile cortical hyperostosis)** – see 1.14.
2. **Idiopathic hypercalcaemia of infancy** – probably a manifestation of hypervitaminosis D. Elfin facies, failure to thrive and mental retardation. Generalized increased density or transverse dense metaphyseal bands. Increased density of the skull base.

Further Reading
Beighton P. & Cremin B.J. (1980) *Sclerosing Bone Dysplasias*. Berlin: Springer-Verlag.

1.11 Generalized Increased Bone Density – Adults

Myeloproliferative
1. Myelosclerosis – marrow cavity is narrowed by endosteal new bone. Patchy lucencies due to persistence of fibrous tissue. (Generalized osteopenia in the early stages due to myelofibrosis). Hepatosplenomegaly.

Metabolic
1. Renal osteodystrophy*.

Poisoning
1. Fluorosis – with periosteal reaction, prominent muscle attachments and calcification of ligaments and interosseous membranes. Changes are most marked in the innominate bones and lumbar spine.

Neoplastic (more commonly multifocal than generalized)
1. Osteoblastic metastases – most commonly prostate and breast. See 1.17.
2. Lymphoma*.
3. Mastocytosis – sclerosis of marrow containing skeleton with patchy areas of radiolucency. Urticaria pigmentosa. Can have symptoms and signs of carcinoid syndrome.

Idiopathic (more commonly multifocal than generalized)
1. Paget's disease* – coarsened trabeculae, bony expansion and thickened cortex.

Those Conditions with Onset in the Paediatric Age Group (see 1.10)

1.12 Solitary Sclerotic Bone Lesion

Developmental
1. Bone island.
2. Fibrous dysplasia*.

Neoplastic
1. Metastasis – most commonly prostate or breast.
2. Lymphoma*.
3. Osteoma/osteoid osteoma/osteoblastoma*.
4. Healed or healing benign or malignant bone lesion – e.g. lytic metastasis following radiotherapy or chemotherapy, bone cyst, fibrous cortical defect, eosinophilic granuloma or brown tumour.
5. Primary bone sarcoma.

Vascular
1. Bone infarct (see 1.17).

Traumatic
1. Callus – especially a transverse density around a healing stress fracture.

Infective
1. Sclerosing osteomyelitis of Garré.

Idiopathic
1. Paget's disease*.

1.13 Multiple Sclerotic Bone Lesions

Developmental
1. Bone islands.
2. Fibrous dysplasia.*
3. Osteopoikilosis – asymptomatic. 1–10 mm, round or oval densities in the appendicular skeleton and pelvis. Ribs, skull and spine are usually exempt. Tend to be parallel to the long axis of the affected bones and are especially numerous near the ends of bones.
4. Osteopathia striata (Voorhoeve's disease) – asymptomatic. Linear bands of dense bone parallel with the long axis of the bone. The appendicular skeleton and pelvis are most frequently affected; skull and clavicles are spared.
5. Tuberous sclerosis*.

Neoplastic
1. Metastases (see 1.17) – most commonly prostate or breast.
2. Lymphoma*.
3. Mastocytosis.
4. Multiple healed or healing benign or malignant bone lesions – e.g. lytic metastases following radiotherapy or chemotherapy, eosinophilic granuloma and brown tumours.
5. Multiple myeloma* – sclerosis in up to 3% of cases.
6. Osteomata – e.g. Gardner's syndrome.
7. Multifocal osteosarcoma*.

Idiopathic
1. Paget's disease*.

Vascular
1. Bone infarcts (see 1.17).

Traumatic
1. Callus – around numerous fractures.

1.14   Bone Sclerosis with a Periosteal Reaction

Traumatic
1. Healing fracture with callus.

Neoplastic
1. Metastasis.
2. Lymphoma*.
3. Osteoid osteoma/osteoblastoma*.
4. Osteosarcoma*.
5. Ewing's sarcoma.
6. Chondrosarcoma*.

Infective
1. Osteomyelitis – including Garré's sclerosing osteomyelitis and Brodie's abscess.
2. Syphilis – congenital or acquired.

Idiopathic
1. Infantile cortical hyperostosis (Caffey's disease) – in infants up to 6 months of age. Multiple bones involved at different times, most frequently mandible, ribs and clavicles; long bones less commonly; spine, hands and feet are spared. Increased density of bones is due to massive periosteal new bone. In the long bones the epiphyses and metaphyses are spared.
2. Melorheostosis – cortical and periosteal new bone giving the appearance of molten wax flowing down a burning candle. The hyperostosis tends to extend from one bone to the next. Usually affects one limb but both limbs on one side may be affected. Sometimes it is bilateral but asymmetrical. Skull, spine and ribs are seldom affected.

1.15 Solitary Sclerotic Bone Lesion with a Lucent Centre

Neoplastic
1. Osteoid osteoma*.
2. Osteoblastoma*.

Infective
1. Brodie's abscess.
2. Syphilis, yaws and tuberculosis.

1.16 Coarse Trabecular Pattern

1. **Paget's disease*** – an enlarged bone with a thickened cortex. If only part of the bone is affected the demarcation between normal and pagetoid bone is clear cut.
2. **Osteoporosis** (see 1.32) } Resorption of secondary trabeculae accentuates the remaining primary trabeculae.
3. **Osteomalacia***
4. **Haemoglobinopathies** – especially thalassaemia*.
5. **Haemangioma** – especially in a vertebral body.
6. **Gaucher's disease.**

1.17   Skeletal Metastases – Most Common Radiological Appearances

Lung
1. Carcinoma   lytic
2. Carcinoid   sclerotic

Breast   lytic or mixed

Genito-urinary
1. Renal cell carcinoma   lytic, expansile
2. Wilms' tumour   lytic
3. Bladder (transitional cell) lytic, occasionally sclerotic
4. Prostate   sclerotic

Reproductive Organs
1. Cervix   lytic or mixed
2. Uterus   lytic
3. Ovary   lytic
4. Testis   lytic; occasionally sclerotic

Thyroid   lytic expansile

Gastrointestinal Tract
1. Stomach   sclerotic or mixed
2. Colon   lytic; occasionally sclerotic
3. Rectum   lytic

Adrenal
1. Phaeochromocytoma   lytic, expansile
2. Carcinoma   lytic
3. Neuroblastoma   lytic; occasionally sclerotic

Skin
1. Squamous cell carcinoma   lytic
2. Melanoma   lytic, expansile

1.18 Paediatric Tumours that Metastasize to Bone

1. Neuroblastoma.
2. Leukaemia – although not truly metastases.
3. Lymphoma*.
4. Clear cell sarcoma (Wilms' variant).
5. Rhabdomyosarcoma.
6. Retinoblastoma.
7. Ewing's sarcoma – lung metastases much more common.
8. Osteosarcoma* – lung metastases much more common.

Further Reading

Kagan R.A., Steckel R.J., Bassett L.W. & Gold R.H. (1986) Radiologic contributions to cancer management. Bone metastases. *Am. J. Roentgenol.*, 147: 305–12.
Pagani J.J. & Libshitz H.I. (1982) Imaging bone metastases. *Radiol. Clin. North Am.*, 20 (3): 545–60.
Thrall J.H. & Ellis B.I. (1987) Skeletal metastases. *Radiol. Clin. North Am.*, 25 (6): 1155–70.

1.19   Sites of Origin of Primary Bone Neoplasms

(A composite diagram modified from Madewell *et al.*, 1981).

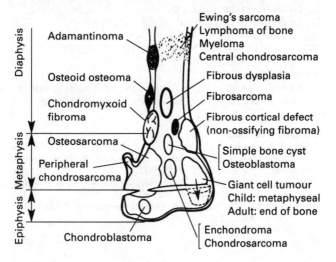

Further Reading

Madewell J.E., Ragsdale B.D. & Sweet D.E. (1981) Radiologica and pathologic analysis of solitary bone lesions. *Radiol. Clin. North Am.*, 19: 715–48.

1.20 Peak Age Incidence of Primary Bone Neoplasms

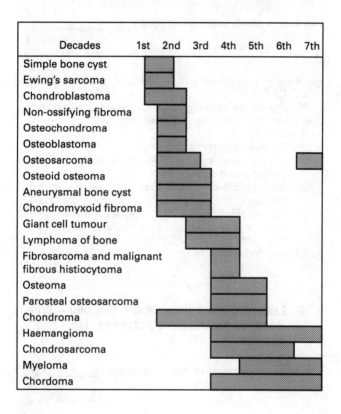

1.21 Lucent Bone Lesion in the Medulla – Well-defined, Marginal Sclerosis, No Expansion

Indicates a slowly progressing lesion.

1. **Geode** – a subarticular cyst. Other signs of an arthritis. See 1.26.
2. **Healing benign or malignant bone lesion** – e.g. metastasis, eosinophilic granuloma or brown tumour.
3. **Brodie's abscess.**
4. **Benign bone neoplasms**
   (a) Simple bone cyst* – 75% arise in the proximal humerus and femur.
   (b) Enchondroma* – more than 50% are found in the tubular bones of the hands. ± internal calcification.
   (c) Chondroblastoma* – in an epiphysis. Most common sites are proximal humerus, distal femur and proximal tibia. Internal hazy calcification.
5. **Fibrous dysplasia***.

1.22 Lucent Bone Lesion in the Medulla – Well-defined, No Marginal Sclerosis, No Expansion

The absence of reactive bone formation implies a fast growth rate.

1. **Metastasis** – especially from breast, bronchus, kidney or thyroid.
2. **Multiple myeloma***.
3. **Eosinophilic granuloma***.
4. **Brown tumour of hyperparathyroidism***.
5. **Benign bone neoplasms**
   (a) Enchondroma*.
   (b) Chondroblastoma*.

1.23 Lucent Bone Lesion in the Medulla – Ill-defined

An aggressive pattern of destruction.

1. Metastatis.
2. Multiple myeloma*.
3. Osteomyelitis.
4. Lymphoma of bone.
5. Long bone sarcomas
   (a) Osteosarcoma*.
   (b) Ewing's sarcoma*.
   (c) Central chondrosarcoma*.
   (d) Fibrosarcoma and malignant fibrous histiocytoma.

1.24 Lucent Bone Lesion in the Medulla – Well-defined, Eccentric Expansion

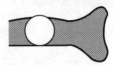

1. **Giant cell tumour*** – typically subarticular after epiphyseal fusion (3% are metaphyseal prior to fusion). Ill-defined endosteal margins. Septa. ± soft-tissue extension and destroyed cortex. Mostly long bones.
2. **Aneurysmal bone cyst*** – in the unfused metaphysis or metaphysis and epiphysis following fusion of the growth plate. Intact but thin cortex. Well-defined endosteal margin. ± thin internal strands of bone. Fluid levels on CT and MRI.
3. **Enchondroma*** – diaphyseal. Over 50% occur in the tubular bones of the hands and feet. Internal ground glass appearance ± calcification within it. May be multilocular in long bones.
4. **Non-ossifying fibroma (fibrous cortical defect)*** – frequently in the distal tibia or femur and produces an eccentric expanded cortex. (In a thin bone such as the fibula central expansion is observed.) Metaphyseal. Smooth, sharp margins with a thin rim of surrounding sclerosis.
5. **Chondromyxoid fibroma*** – 75% in the lower limbs (50% in the proximal tibia). Metaphyseal and may extend into the epiphysis. Frequently has marginal sclerosis.

1.25 Lucent Bone Lesion – Grossly Expansile

Malignant Bone Neoplasms
1. **Metastases** – renal cell carcinoma and thyroid; less commonly melanoma, bronchus, breast and phaeochromocytoma.
2. **Plasmacytoma*** – ± soft tissue extension. ± internal septa.
3. **Central chondrosarcoma/lymphoma of bone/ fibrosarcoma** — when slow growing may have this appearance.
4. **Telangiectatic osteosarcoma*** – rare, poor prognosis.

Benign Bone Neoplasms
1. **Aneurysmal bone cyst*** – in the unfused metaphysis or metaphysis and epiphysis following fusion of the growth plate. ± internal septa. Fluid level on CT.
2. **Giant cell tumour*** – typically subarticular after epiphyseal fusion. Ill-defined endosteal margin. ± soft-tissue extension and destroyed cortex.
3. **Enchondroma*** – ground-glass appearance ± internal calcifications.

Non-neoplastic
1. **Fibrous dysplasia*** – ground-glass appearance ± internal calcification. Modelling deformities of affected bone.
2. **Haemophilic pseudotumour** (see Haemophilia*) – especially in the iliac wing and lower limb bones. Soft-tissue swelling. ± haemophilic arthropathy.
3. **Brown tumour of hyperparathyroidism*** – the solitary skeletal sign of hyperparathyroidism in 3% of patients. Most commonly in the mandible, followed by pelvis, ribs and femora. Usually unilocular.
4. **Hydatid.**

1.26 Subarticular Lucent Bone Lesion

Arthritides

1. **Osteoarthritis** – may be multiple 'cysts' in the load-bearing areas of multiple joints. Surrounding sclerotic margin. Joint-space narrowing, subchondral sclerosis and osteophytes.
2. **Rheumatoid arthritis*** – no sclerotic margin. Begin periarticularly near the insertion of the joint capsule. Joint-space narrowing and juxta-articular osteoporosis.
3. **Calcium pyrophosphate arthropathy** (see Calcium pyrophosphate dihydrate deposition disease*) – similar to osteoarthritis but frequently larger and with more collapse and fragmentation of the articular surface.
4. **Gout** – ± erosions with overhanging edges and adjacent soft-tissue masses.
5. **Haemophilia***.

Neoplastic

1. **Metastases/multiple myeloma*** – single or multiple. Variable appearance.
2. **Aneurysmal bone cyst*** – solitary. Expansile. Narrow zone of transition.
3. **Giant cell tumour*** – solitary. Eccentric. Ill-defined endosteal margin.
4. **Chondroblastoma*** – solitary. Predilection for the proximal ends of the humerus, femur and tibia. Contains amorphous or spotty calcification in 50%.
5. **Pigmented villonodular synovitis** – mainly the lower limb, especially the knee. Soft-tissue mass. Cyst-like defects with sharp sclerotic margins. May progress to joint destruction.

Others

1. **Post-traumatic** – particularly in the carpal bones. Well-defined.
2. **Osteonecrosis** – with bone sclerosis, collapse and fragmentation. Preservation of joint space.
3. **Tuberculosis** – wholly epiphyseal or partly metaphyseal. Well-defined or ill-defined. No surrounding sclerosis.

Further Reading

Bullough P.G. & Bansal M. (1988) The differential diagnosis of geodes. *Radiol. Clin. North Am.*, 26: 1165–84.
Resnick D. Niwayama G. & Coutts R.D. (1977) Subchondral cysts (geodes) in arthritic disorders: Pathologic and radiographic appearance of the hip joint. *Am. J. Roentgenol.*, 128: 799–806.

1.27 Lucent Bone Lesion – Containing Calcium or Bone

Neoplastic
1. Metastases – especially from breast.
2. **Cartilage neoplasms**
   (a) Benign – enchondroma, chondroblastoma and chondromyxoid fibroma.
   (b) Malignant – chondrosarcoma.
3. **Bone (osteoid) neoplasms**
   (a) Benign – osteoid osteoma and osteoblastoma.
   (b) Malignant – osteosarcoma.
4. **Fibrous-tissue neoplasms**
   (a) Malignant – fibrosarcoma and malignant fibrous histiocytoma.

Others
1. Fibrous dysplasia*.
2. Osteoporosis circumscripta (Paget's disease*)
3. Avascular necrosis and bone infarction
4. Osteomyelitis – with sequestrum.
5. Eosinophilic granuloma*.
6. Intraosseous lipoma.

1.28 'Moth-eaten Bone'

Multiple scattered lucencies of variable size with no major central lesion. Coalescence may occur later. Cancellous and/or cortical bone is involved.

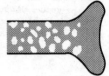

Neoplastic
1. Metastases – including neuroblastoma in a child.
2. Multiple myeloma*.
3. Leukaemia*.
4. Long-bone sarcomas
    (a) Ewing's sarcoma*.
    (b) Lymphoma of bone.
    (c) Osteosarcoma*.
    (d) Chondrosarcoma*.
    (e) Fibrosarcoma and malignant fibrous histocytoma.
5. Langerhans cell histiocytosis*.

Infective
1. Osteomyelitis.

1.29 Regional Osteopenia

Decreased bone density confined to a region or segment of the appendicular skeleton.

1. **Disuse** – during the immobilization of fractures, in paralysed segments and in bone and joint infections. Usually appears after 8 weeks of immobilization. The patterns of bone loss may be uniform (commonest), spotty (mostly periarticular), band-like (subchondral or metaphyseal) or endosteal cortical scalloping and linear cortical lucencies.
2. **Sudeck's atrophy (reflex sympathetic dystrophy syndrome)** – is mediated via a neurovascular mechanism and associated with post-traumatic and post-infective states, myocardial infarction, calcific tendinitis and cervical spondylosis. It most commonly affects the shoulder and hand and develops rapidly. Pain and soft-tissue swelling are clinical findings. In addition to the radiological signs of disuse there may be subperiosteal bone resorption and small periarticular erosions.
3. **Transient osteoporosis of the hip** – a severe, progressive osteoporosis of the femoral head and, to a lesser degree, of the femoral neck and acetabulum. Full recovery is seen in 6 months.
4. **Regional migratory osteoporosis** – pain, swelling and osteoporosis affect the joints of the lower limbs in particular. The migratory nature differentiates it from other causes. Marrow oedema in affected areas is seen as low signal on T_1W and high signal on T_2W MRI.

1.30   Generalized Osteopenia

1. **Osteoporosis** – diminished quantity of normal bone.
2. **Osteomalacia*** – normal quantity of bone but it has an excess of uncalcified osteoid.
3. **Hyperparathyroidism*** – increased bone resorption by osteoclasts.
4. **Diffuse infiltrative bone disease** – e.g. multiple myeloma and leukaemia.

1.31   Osteoporosis

1. Decreased bone density.
2. Cortical thinning with a relative increase in density of the cortex and vertebral end-plates. Skull sutures are relatively sclerotic.
3. Relative accentuation of trabecular stress lines because of resorption of secondary trabeculae.
4. Brittle bones with an increased incidence of fractures, especially compression fractures of vertebral bodies, femoral neck and wrist fractures.

Endocrine
1. **Hypogonadism.**
   (a) Ovarian – menopausal, Turner's syndrome*.
   (b) Testicular – eunuchoidism.
2. **Cushing's syndrome***.
3. **Diabetes mellitus.**
4. **Acromegaly***.
5. **Addison's disease.**
6. **Hyperthyroidism.**
7. **Mastocytosis** – mast cells produce heparin.

Disuse

Iatrogenic
1. Steroids*.
2. Heparin.

Deficiency States
1. Vitamin C (scurvy*).
2. Protein.

Idiopathic
1. In young people – a rare self-limiting condition occurring in children of 8–12 years. Spontaneous improvement is seen.

Congenital
1. Osteogenesis imperfecta*.
2. Turner's syndrome*.
3. Homocystinuria*.
4. Neuromuscular diseases.
5. Mucopolysaccharidoses.
6. Trisomy 13 and 18.
7. Pseudo- and pseudopseudohypoparathyroidism*.
8. Glycogen storage diseases.
9. Progeria.

1.32   Osteomalacia and Rickets*

Vitamin D Deficiency
1. Dietary.
2. Malabsorption.

Renal Disease
1. Glomerular disease (renal osteodystrophy*).
2. Tubular disease
   - (a) Renal tubular acidosis
     - (i) Primary – sporadic or hereditary.
     - (ii) Secondary
       Inborn errors of metabolism, e.g. cystinosis, galactosaemia, Wilson's disease, tyrosinosis, hereditary fructose intolerance.
       Poisoning, e.g. lead, cadmium, beryllium.
       Drugs, e.g. amphotericin B, lithium salts, outdated tetracycline, ifosfamide.
       Renal transplantation.
   - (b) Fanconi syndrome – osteomalacia or rickets, growth retardation, renal tubular acidosis (RTA), glycosuria, phosphaturia, aminoaciduria and proteinuria. It is most commonly idiopathic in aetiology but may be secondary to those causes of RTA given above.
   - (c) Vitamin D resistant rickets (familial hypophosphataemia, X-linked hypophosphataemia) – short stature developing after the first 6 months of life, genu varum or valgum, coxa vara, waddling gait. Radiographic changes are more severe in the legs than the arms.

Hepatic Disease
1. Parenchymal failure.
2. Obstructive jaundice – especially biliary atresia.

Vitamin D Dependent Rickets – see below

Anticonvulsants
1. Phenytoin and phenobarbitone.

Tumour Associated
1. **Soft tissues** – haemangiopericytoma.
2. **Bone** – non-ossifying fibroma, giant cell tumour, osteoblastoma (and fibrous dysplasia, neurofibromatosis and melorheostosis).

Conditions which Mimic Rickets/Osteomalacia
1. **Hypophosphatasia*** – low serum alkaline phosphatase.
2. **Metaphyseal chondrodysplasia (type Schmid)** – normal serum phosphate, calcium and alkaline phosphatase differentiate it from other rachitic syndromes.

If the patient is less than 6 months of age then consider:
1. **Biliary atresia.**
2. **Metabolic bone disease of prematurity** – combined dietary deficiency and hepatic hydroxylation of vitamin D.
3. **Hypophosphatasia*.**
4. **Vitamin D dependent rickets** – rachitic changes are associated with a severe myopathy in spite of adequate dietary intake of vitamin D.

1.33   Periosteal Reactions – Types

(Modified from Ragsdale *et al.*, 1981.)

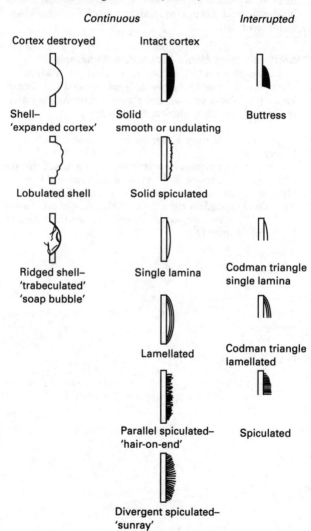

Continuous		*Interrupted*
Cortex destroyed	Intact cortex	
Shell– 'expanded cortex'	Solid smooth or undulating	Buttress
Lobulated shell	Solid spiculated	
Ridged shell– 'trabeculated' 'soap bubble'	Single lamina	Codman triangle single lamina
	Lamellated	Codman triangle lamellated
	Parallel spiculated– 'hair-on-end'	Spiculated
	Divergent spiculated– 'sunray'	

The different types are, in general, non-specific, having multiple aetiologies. However, the following comments can be made.

Continuous with Destroyed Cortex
This the result of an expanding lesion. See 1.24 and 1.25.

Parallel Spiculated ('Hair-on-end')
1. Ewing's sarcoma*.
2. Syphilis.
3. Infantile cortical hyperostosis (Caffey's disease).

See 12.13 for causes in the skull vault.

Divergent Spiculated ('Sunray')
1. Osteosarcoma*
2. Metastases – especially from sigmoid colon and rectum.
3. Ewing's sarcoma*
4. Haemangioma*.
5. Meningioma.
6. Tuberculosis.
7. Tropical ulcer.

Codman Triangle (Single Lamina or Lamellated)
1. Aggressive malignant tissue extending into the soft tissues.
2. Infection – occasionally.

Further Reading
Ragsdale B.D., Madewell J.E. & Sweet D.E. (1981) Radiologic and pathologic analysis of solitary bone lesions. Part II: Periosteal reactions. *Radiol. Clin. North Am.*, 19: 749–83.

1.34 Periosteal Reaction – Solitary and Localized

1. Traumatic.
2. Inflammatory.
3. Neoplastic
   (a) Malignant
      primary.
      secondary.
   (b) Benign – an expanding shell or complicated by a fracture.

1.35 Periosteal Reactions – Bilaterally Symmetrical in Adults

1. **Hypertrophic osteoarthropathy (HOA)** – clinically there is clubbing of the fingers and painful swelling of knees, ankles, wrists, elbows and metacarpophalangeal joints. The periosteal reaction occurs in the metaphysis and diaphysis of the radius, ulna, tibia, fibula and, less commonly, the humerus, femur and tubular bones of the hands and feet. It can be a single lamina, lamellated or solid and undulating. The thickness of the periosteal reaction correlates with the duration of disease activity. Periarticular osteoporosis, soft-tissue swelling and joint effusions are other features. The condition can be caused by the conditions in section 1.36 (q.v.).
2. **Pachydermoperiostosis** – a rare, self-limiting and familial condition, usually affecting boys at puberty and with a predilection for blacks. Clinically there is an insidious onset of thickening of the skin of the extremities (including the face), hyperhidrosis and clubbing. Compared with HOA it is relatively pain free. The bones most commonly affected are the tibia, fibula, radius and ulna (less commonly the carpus, tarsus and tubular bones of the hands and feet). The periosteal reaction is similar to HOA but is more solid and spiculated and also involves the epiphysis to produce outgrowths around joints. The concavity of the diaphysis may be filled in. ± ligamentous calcification.

3. **Vascular insufficiency (venous, lymphatic or arterial)** – the legs are almost exclusively affected with involvement of tibia, fibula, metatarsals and phalanges. There is a solid undulating periosteal reaction, which is, initially, separated from the cortex but later merges with it. No definite relationship to soft-tissue ulceration. Phleboliths may be associated with venous stasis. Soft-tissue swelling is a feature whatever the aetiology. Arterial insufficiency due to polyarteritis nodosa or other arteritides may also be associated with a mild periostitis and is also usually confined to the lower limbs.

4. **Thyroid acropachy** – in 0.5–10% of patients following thyroidectomy for thyrotoxicosis and who may now be euthyroid, hypothyroid or hyperthyroid. Clinically there is soft-tissue swelling, clubbing, exophthalmos and pretibial myxoedema. A solid, spiculated, almost lace-like periosteal reaction affects the diaphysis of the metacarpals and phalanges of the hands, especially the radial side of the thumbs and index fingers. Less commonly the feet, lower legs and forearms are involved.

5. **Fluorosis** – solid, undulating periosteal reaction with osteosclerosis. The long bones and tubular bones are most frequently affected. Ligamentous calcification.

Further Reading

Pineda C.J., Sartoris D.J., Clopton P. & Resnick D. (1987) Periostitis in hypertrophic osteoarthropathy: relationship to disease duration. *Am. J. Roentgenol.*, 148: 773–78.

1.36   Periosteal Reactions – Bilaterally Asymmetrical

1. Metastases.
2. Osteomyelitis.
3. Arthritides – especially Reiter's syndrome* and psoriatic arthropathy*.
4. Osteoporosis (q.v.) } because of the increased
5. Osteomalacia (q.v.) } liability to fractures.
6. Non-accidental injury*.
7. Bleeding diatheses.
8. Hand–foot syndrome (sickle-cell dactylitis) – see Sickle-cell anaemia*.

1.37 Hypertrophic Osteoarthropathy

Pulmonary
1. Carcinoma of bronchus.
2. Lymphoma*.
3. Abscess.
4. Bronchiectasis – frequently due to cystic fibrosis*.
5. Metastases.

Pleural
1. Pleural fibroma – has the highest incidence of accompanying HOA, although it is itself a rare cause.
2. Mesothelioma.

Cardiovascular
1. Cyanotic congenital heart disease – produces clubbing but only rarely a periosteal reaction.

Gastrointestinal
1. Ulcerative colitis*.
2. Crohn's disease*.
3. Dysentery – amoebic or bacillary.
4. Lymphoma*.
5. Whipple's disease.
6. Coeliac disease.
7. Cirrhosis – especially primary biliary cirrhosis.
8. Nasopharyngeal carcinomas (Schmincke's tumour).
9. Juvenile polyposis.

1.38 Periosteal Reactions – Bilaterally Symmetrical in Children

1. **Normal infants** – diaphyseal, not extending to the growth plate, bilaterally symmetrical and a single lamina.
2. **Juvenile chronic arthritis*** – in approx. 25% of cases. Most common in the periarticular regions of the phalanges, metacarpals and metatarsals. When it extends into the diaphysis it will eventually result in enlarged, rectangular tubular bones.
3. **Acute leukaemia** – associated with prominent metaphyseal bone resorption ± a dense zone of provisional calcification. Osteopenia. Periosteal reaction is due to cortical involvement by tumour cells. Metastatic neuroblastoma can look identical.
4. **Rickets*** – the presence of uncalcified subperiosteal osteoid *mimics* a periosteal reaction because the periosteum and ossified cortex are separated.
5. **Caffey's disease** – first evident before 5 months of age. Mandible, clavicles and ribs show cortical hyperostosis and a diffuse periosteal reaction. The scapulae and tubular bones are less often affected and tend to be involved asymmetrically.
6. **Scurvy*** – subperiosteal haemorrhage is most frequent in the femur, tibia and humerus. Periosteal reaction is particularly evident during the healing phase. Age 6 months or older.
7. **Prostaglandin E_1 therapy** – in infants with ductus dependent congenital heart disease. Severity is related to duration of therapy. Other features include fever, flushing, diarrhoea, skin oedema, pseudowidening of cranial sutures and bone-in-bone appearance.
8. **Congenital syphilis** – an exuberant periosteal reaction can be due to infiltration by syphilitic granulation tissue or the healing (with callus formation) of osteochondritis. The former is essentially diaphyseal and the latter around the metaphyseal/epiphyseal junction.

Further Reading
Matzinger M.A., Briggs V.A., Dunlap H.J., Udjus K., Martin D.J. & McDonald P. (1992) Plain film and CT observations in prosta-glandin-induced bone changes. *Pediatr. Radiol.*, 22: 264–6.
Shopfner C.E. (1966) Periosteal bone growth in normal infants. *Am. J. Roentgenol.*, 97: 154–63.
Swischuk L.E. (1984) *Differential Diagnosis in Pediatric Radiology*. Baltimore: Williams and Wilkins.

1.39 Differential Diagnosis of Skeletal Lesions in Non-accidental Injury*

Disease	Shaft fractures	Abnormal Meta-physis	Osteo-penia	Periosteal reaction	Comments
Non-accidental injury*	+	+	−	+	
Accidental trauma	+	−	−	callus	
Birth trauma	+	±	−	±	Clavicle, humerus and femur are most frequent fractures
Osteogenesis imperfecta*	+	±	+	−	Highly unlikely in the absence of osteopenia, Wormian bones dentinogenesis imperfecta and a relevant family history
Osteomyelitis	−	+	localized	+	May be multifocal
Rickets*	+	+	+	+	↑ Alkaline phosphatase
Scurvy*	−	+	+	+	Not before 6 months age
Congenital syphilis	−	+	−	+	
Congenital insensitivity to pain	+	+	−	+	

Disease	Shaft fractures	Abnormal Meta-physis	Osteo-penia	Periosteal reaction	Comments
Paraplegia	+	+	+	with fractures	Lower limb changes only
Prostaglandin E_1 therapy	–	–	–	+	
Menke's syndrome	–	+	+	+	Males only. Abnormal hair. Retardation. Wormian bones
Copper deficiency	+	+	+	±	See note 1

[1] *Copper deficiency.* Rare. Unlikely in the absence of at least one risk factor – prematurity, total parenteral nutrition, malabsorption or a low copper diet. Unlikely in full term infants less than 6 months age. Microcytic, hypochromic anaemia. Leukopenia. Normal serum copper and caeruloplasmin does not exclude the diagnosis.
Skull fracture never recorded in copper deficiency. Rib fractures only recorded in premature infants.

Further Reading

Kleinman P. (1987) *Diagnostic Imaging of Child Abuse.* Baltimore: Williams & Wilkins.
Shaw J.C.L. (1988) Copper deficiency and non-accidental injury. *Arch. Dis. Childhood*, 63: 448–55.

1.40 Syndromes and Bone Dysplasias with Multiple Fractures as a Feature

With Reduced Bone Density
1. Osteogenesis imperfecta*.
2. Achondrogenesis.
3. Hypophosphatasia.
4. Mucolipidosis II (I-cell disease).
5. Cushing's syndrome.

With Normal Bone Density
1. Cleidocranial dysplasia.
2. Enchondromatosis (Ollier's disease).
3. Fibrous dysplasia.

With Increased Bone Density
1. Osteopetrosis*.
2. Pycnodysostosis – see 1.9.

1.41 Excessive Callus Formation

1. Steroid therapy and Cushing's syndrome*.
2. Neuropathic arthropathy* – including congenital insensitivity to pain.
3. Osteogenesis imperfecta*.
4. Non-accidental injury*.
5. Paralytic states.
6. Renal osteodystrophy*.
7. Multiple myeloma*.

1.42 Stress Fractures – Sites and Causations

(Modified from Daffner, 1978).

Site	*Activity*
Lower cervical/upper thoracic spinous processes	Clay shovelling
Pars interarticularis	Ballet; heavy lifting; scrubbing floors
Obturator ring	Stooping; bowling; gymnastics
Ribs	Carrying heavy pack; coughing; golf
Coracoid process of scapula	Trap shooting
Humerus – distal shaft	Throwing a ball
Hamate	Golf; tennis; baseball
Ulna – coronoid	Pitching a ball
– shaft	Pitchfork worker; propelling a wheelchair
Femur – neck	Ballet; marching; long-distance running; gymnastics
– shaft	Ballet; long distance running
Patella	Hurdling
Fibula – proximal shaft	Jumping; parachuting
– distal shaft	Long distance running
Tibia – proximal shaft	Running
– mid and distal shaft	Ballet; long distance running
Calcaneus	Jumping; parachuting; prolonged standing
Navicular	Marching; long distance running
Metatarsal – shaft	Marching; prolonged standing; ballet
Sesamoids of metatarsals	Prolonged standing

Further Reading
Daffner R.H. (1978) Stress fractures: current concepts. *Skeletal Radiol.*, 2: 221–9.

1.43   Pseudarthrosis

1. **Non-union of a fracture** – including pathological fracture.
2. **Congenital** – in the middle to lower third of the tibia ± fibula. 50% present in the first year. Later there may be cupping of the proximal bone end and pointing of the distal bone end.
3. **Neurofibromatosis***.
4. **Osteogenesis imperfecta***.
5. **Cleidocranial dysplasia*** – congenitally in the femur.
6. **Fibrous dysplasia***.
7. **Ankylosing spondylitis*** – in the fused bamboo spine.

Further Reading

Boyd H.B. & Sage F.P. (1958) Congenital pseudarthrosis of the tibia. *J. Bone Joint Surg.*, 40A; 1245–70.
Park W.M., Spencer D.G., McCall I.W., Ward D.J., Watson Buchanan W. & Stephens W.H. (1981) The detection of spinal pseudarthrosis in ankylosing spondylitis. *Br. J. Radiol.*, 54: 467–72.

1.44   'Bone Within a Bone' Appearance

1. **Normal neonate** – especially in the spine.
2. **Growth arrest/recovery lines.**
3. **Paget's disease***.
4. **Osteopetrosis***.
5. **Acromegaly***.
6. **Heavy metal poisoning.**
7. **Prostaglandin E$_1$ therapy** – see 1.38.

Further Reading

Brill P.W., Baker D.H. & Ewing M.L. (1973) Bone within bone in the neonatal spine. *Radiology*, 108: 363–6.
Frager D.H. & Subbarao K. (1983) The 'bone within a bone'. *JAMA*, 249: 77–9.
Matzinger M.A., Briggs V.A., Dunlap H.J., Udjus K., Martin D.J. & McDonald P. (1992) Plain film and CT observations in prostaglandin-induced bone changes. *Pediatr. Radiol.*, 22: 264–6.
O'Brien J.P. (1969) The manifestations of arrested bone growth: The appearance of a vertebra within a vertebra. *J. Bone Jt Surg.* 51A: 1376–8.

1.45 Irregular or Stippled Epiphyses

1. **Normal** – particularly in the distal femur.
2. **Avascular necrosis** (q.v.) – single, e.g. Perthes' disease (although 10% are bilateral), or multiple, e.g. sickle-cell anaemia.
3. **Cretinism*** – not present at birth. Delayed appearance and growth of ossification centres. Appearance varies from slightly granular to fragmentation. The femoral capital epiphysis may be divided into inner and outer halves.
4. **Morquio's syndrome*** – irregular ossification of the femoral capital epiphyses results in flattening.
5. **Multiple epiphyseal dysplasia** – onset 5–14 years. May be familial. Delayed appearance and growth of epiphyses but the time of fusion is normal. ± metaphyseal irregularity. Carpal and tarsal bones, hips, knees and ankles are most commonly affected. Tibio-talar slant. Short, stubby digits and metacarpals. Spine usually, but not always, normal. Early and severe osteoarthritis.
6. **Meyer dysplasia** – an epiphyseal dysplasia resembling MED but confined to the femoral heads.
7. **Chondrodysplasia punctata** – autosomal dominant and (rarer) autosomal recessive types are recognized.
   (a) Autosomal dominant type (Conradi–Hünerman) – in the newborn the stippling is evident in the long bone epiphyses, spine and larynx. ± malsegmentation of vertebral bodies. Stippling disappears by 2 years of age. Asymmetrical shortening of limbs. Usually survive to adulthood.
   (b) Autosomal recessive (severe rhizomelic) type – marked symmetrical rhizomelia with humeri more severely affected than femora. Spinal stippling is mild. Stillborn or perinatal death.
8. **Trisomy 18 and 21.**
9. **Prenatal infections.**
10. **Warfarin embryopathy** – stippling of uncalcified epiphyses, particularly of the axial skeleton, proximal femura and calcanei. Disappears after 1st year.
11. **Zellweger syndrome** (cerebro-hepato-renal syndrome).
12. **Fetal alcohol syndrome** – mostly calcaneum and lower extremities.

1.46   Avascular Necrosis

Toxic

1. **Steroids*** – probably does not occur with less than 2 years of treatment.
2. **Anti-inflammatory drugs** – indomethacin and phenylbutazone.
3. **Alcohol** – possibly because of fat emboli in chronic alcoholic pancreatitis.
4. **Immunosuppressives.**

Traumatic

1. **Idiopathic** – e.g. Perthes' disease and other osteochondritides.
2. **Fractures** – especially femoral neck, talus and scaphoid.
3. **Radiotherapy.**
4. **Heat** – burns.
5. **Fat embolism.**

Inflammatory

1. **Rheumatoid arthritis*** ⎫ in the absence of drugs
2. **Systemic lupus** ⎬ probably due to a
   erythematosus* ⎭ vasculitis
3. **Scleroderma*.**
4. **Infection** – e.g. following a pyogenic arthritis.
5. **Pancreatitis.**

Metabolic and Endocrine

1. **Pregnancy.**
2. **Diabetes.**
3. **Cushing's syndrome*.**
4. **Hyperlipidaemias.**
5. **Gout*.**

Haemopoietic Disorders

1. **Haemoglobinopathies** – especially sickle-cell anaemia*.
2. **Polycythaemia rubra vera.**
3. **Gaucher's disease.**
4. **Haemophilia*.**

Thrombotic and Embolic
1. Dysbaric osteonecrosis.
2. Arteritis.

MRI detects changes earlier than CT or radionuclide scanning. These are:

	T_1W	T_2W	Comment
Margin	↓	↓	Well-delineated dark band
Central region			
Grade 1	↑ (= fat)	↑ (= fat)	Viable marrow fat due to revascularization Haemorrhage
Grade 2	↑ or ↓	↑ or ↓	Oedema
Grade 3	↓	↑	Established sclerotic bone
Grade 4	↓	↓	

1.47 Solitary Radiolucent Metaphyseal Band

Apart from **3**, this is a non-specific sign which represents a period of poor endochondral bone formation.

1. Normal neonate.
2. Any severe illness.
3. Metaphyseal fracture – especially in non-accidental injury*. Depending on the radiographic projection there may be the additional appearance of a 'corner' or 'bucket-handle' fracture.
4. Healing rickets.
5. Leukaemia, lymphoma* or metastatic neuroblastoma.
6. Congenital infections.
7. Intrauterine perforation.
8. Scurvy*.

Further Reading

Kleinman P.K., Marks S.C. & Blackbourne B. (1986) The metaphyseal lesion in abused infants: A radiologic-histopathologic study. *Am. J. Roentgenol.*, 146: 895–905.
Wolfson J.J. & Engel R.R. (1969) Anticipating meconium peritonitis from metaphyseal bands. *Radiology*, 92: 1055–60.

1.48 Alternating Radiolucent and Dense Metaphyseal Bands

1. Growth arrest or Park's lines.
2. Rickets* – especially those types that require prolonged treatment such as vitamin D dependent rickets.
3. Osteopetrosis*.
4. Chemotherapy.
5. Chronic anaemias – sickle-cell and thalassaemia.
6. Treated leukaemia.

Further Reading

Follis R.H. & Park E.A. (1952) Some observations on bone growth, with particular respect to zones and transverse lines of increased density in the metaphysis. *Am. J. Roentgenol.*, 68: 709–24.

1.49 Solitary Dense Metaphyseal Band

1. Normal infants.
2. Lead poisoning – dense line in the proximal fibula is said to differentiate from normal. Other poisons include bismuth, arsenic, phosphorus, mercury fluoride and radium.
3. Radiation.
4. Cretinism*.
5. Osteopetrosis*.
6. Hypervitaminosis D.

1.50   Dense Vertical Metaphyseal Lines

1. **Congenital rubella** – celery stalk appearance. Less commonly in congenital CMV.
2. **Osteopathia striata** – ± exostoses.
3. **Hypophosphatasia***.
4. **Localized metaphyseal injury.**

1.51   Fraying of Metaphyses

1. **Rickets***.
2. **Hypophosphatasia***.
3. **Chronic stress (in the wrists of young gymnasts)** – with wide, irregular, asymmetrical widening of the distal radial growth plate and metaphyseal sclerosis.
4. **Copper deficiency.**

Further Reading

Carter S.R., Aldridge M.J., Fitzgerald R. & Davies A.M. (1988) Stress changes of the wrist in adolescent gymnasts. *Br. J. Radiol.*, 61: 109–12.

Grünebaum M., Horodniceanu C. & Steinherz R. (1980) The radiographic manifestations of bone changes in copper deficiency. *Paed. Radiol.*, 9: 101–4.

1.52   Cupping of Metaphyses

Often associated with fraying.

1. **Normal** – especially of the distal ulna and proximal fibula of young children. No fraying.
2. **Rickets*** – with widening of the growth plate and fraying.
3. **Trauma** – to the growth plate and/or metaphysis. Asymmetrical and localized changes.
4. **Bone dysplasias** – a sign in a large number, e.g. achondroplasia*, pseudoachondroplasia, metatropic dwarfism, diastrophic dwarfism, the metaphyseal chondrodysplasias and hypophosphatasia*.
5. **Scurvy*** – usually after fracture.

1.53 Erlenmeyer Flask Deformity

An Erlenmeyer flask is a wide-necked glass container used in chemical laboratories and named after the German chemist Richard August Carl Emil Erlenmeyer (1825–1907). The shape of the flask is also used to describe the distal expansion of the long bones, particularly the femora, that is observed in a number of the sclerosing skeletal dysplasias and in other affections of bone.

1. **Pyle's disease (metaphyseal dysplasia)** – rare. AR. Individuals have good health and normal life span. Genu valgum is associated with limited elbow extension. Cranial nerve compression and impairment of marrow function are not features of this sclerosing dysplasia. Radiologically there is sclerosis of the skull vault and base. widening of the medial ends of the clavicles and expansion of the pubic and ischial bones. The long bone metaphyses are grossly expanded, this expansion being most marked in the distal femora but also present in the proximal humeri, distal radii and ulnae and proximal tibiae and fibulae. The expanded portions are relatively lucent and the mid-diaphyses show endosteal sclerosis.
2. **Craniometaphyseal dysplasia** – AD (common) or AR (rare). It is confused with Pyle's disease but unlike that condition Vth and VIIIth cranial nerve palsies do occur. The long bone modelling abnormalities are not as severe as Pyle's disease and although the distal femora are flask-shaped in childhood they are more club-shaped in adulthood.
3. **Osteodysplasty (Melnick–Needles syndrome)** – nearly all the reported cases have been females. Clinically these patients having bulging eyes, prominent cheeks, high forehead, malaligned teeth and micrognathia. Radiologically, the ribs are distorted and irregular and the clavicles are sigmoid shaped. In addition to the metaphyseal flaring, the long bones show cortical irregularity, patchy sclerosis and an S-shape or bowing of the longitudinal axis. 'Osteodysplasty' means 'bones which are badly formed'.
4. **Osteopetrosis***.

(continued)

5. **Thalassaemia** – coarse trabecular pattern, thickened calvarium with a spiculated or 'hair-on-end' appearance.
6. **Gaucher's disease** – three forms recognized and all due to a defect in the activity of the enzyme beta-glucosidase. AR. Infantile and juvenile types are lethal, due to accumulation of cerebrosides in the brain; the adult type is compatible with a normal life span. This form has its maximal prevalence in Ashkenazi Jews with an incidence as high as 1 in 2500. Presentation is usually with splenomegaly but orthopaedic problems and bone pain are important features. Skeletal involvement is evident by late childhood and includes patchy sclerosis and lysis, pathological fractures and avascular necrosis of femoral heads.
7. **Niemann–Pick Disease** – a rare disorder characterized by the accumulation of lipid in the body. Because the pathogenesis of this and Gaucher's disease are similar the skeletal manifestations are also similar but unlike the latter condition there is no epiphyseal osteonecrosis.
8. **Lead poisoning** – thick transverse dense metaphyseal bands are the classic manifestation of chronic infantile and juvenile lead poisoning. Additionally there may be flask-shaped femora which may persist for years before resolving.

Further Reading

Beighton P. & Cremin B.J. (1980) *Sclerosing Bone Dysplasias*. Berlin: Springer-Verlag.

Goldblatt J., Sacks S. & Beighton P. (1978) Orthopaedic aspects of Gaucher disease. *Clin. Orthop. Rel. Res.* 137: 208–14.

Myer H.S., Cremin B.J., Beighton P. & Sacks S. (1975) Chronic Gaucher's disease: radiological findings in 17 South African cases. *Br. J. Radiol.*, 48: 465–9.

Pease C.N. & Newton G.G. (1962) Metaphyseal dysplasia due to lead poisoning in children. *Radiology*, 79: 233.

1.54 Erosions of the Medial Metaphysis of the Proximal Humerus

1. Normal variant.
2. Leukaemia.
3. Metastatic neuroblastoma.
4. Gaucher's disease.
5. Hurler's syndrome*.
6. Glycogen storage disease.
7. Niemann–Pick disease.
8. Hyperparathyroidism.
9. Rheumatoid arthritis.

Further Reading
Li J.K.W., Birch P.D. & Davies A.M. (1988) Proximal humerus defects in Gaucher's disease. *Br. J. Radiol.*, 61: 579–83.

1.55 Erosion or Absence of the Outer End of the Clavicle

1. Rheumatoid arthritis*.
2. Hyperparathyroidism*.
3. Multiple myeloma*.
4. Metastasis.
5. Post-traumatic osteolysis.
6. Cleidocranial dysplasia*.
7. Pyknodysostosis.

1.56   Focal Rib Lesion (Solitary or Multiple)

Neoplastic

Secondary more common than primary. Primary malignant more common than benign.

1. Metastases
   (a) **Adult male** – bronchus, kidney or prostate most commonly.
   (b) **Adult female** – breast.
   (c) **Child** – neuroblastoma.
2. Primary malignant
   (a) **Multiple myeloma/plasmacytoma***.
   (b) **Chondrosarcoma***.
   (c) **Ewing's sarcoma*** – in a child.
   (d) **Askin tumour** – uncommon tumour of an intercostal nerve causing rib destruction.
3. Benign
   (a) **Osteochondroma***.
   (b) **Enchondroma***.
   (c) **Langerhans cell histiocytosis***.

Non-neoplastic

1. Healed rib fracture.
2. Fibrous dysplasia.
3. Paget's disease*.
4. Brown tumour of hyperparathyroidism*.
5. Osteomyelitis – bacterial, tuberculous or fungal.

Further Reading

Omell G.H., Anderson L.S. & Bramson R.T. (1973) Chest wall tumours. *Radiol. Clin. North Am.*, 11: 197–214.

1.57   Rib Notching – Inferior Surface

Arterial
1. **Coarctation of the aorta** – rib signs are unusual before 10 years of age. Affects 4–8th ribs bilaterally; not the upper two if conventional. Unilateral and right-sided if the coarctation is proximal to the left subclavian artery. Unilateral and left-sided if associated with an anomalous right subclavian artery distal to the coarctation. Other signs include a prominent ascending aorta and a small descending aorta with an intervening notch, left ventricular enlargement and possibly signs of heart failure.
2. **Aortic thrombosis** – usually the lower ribs bilaterally.
3. **Subclavian obstruction** – most commonly post Blalock operation (either subclavian-to-pulmonary artery anastomosis) for Fallot's tetralogy. Unilateral rib notching of the upper three or four ribs on the operation side.
4. **Pulmonary oligaemia** – any cause of decreased pulmonary blood supply.

Venous
1. Superior vena caval obstruction.

Arteriovenous
1. Pulmonary arteriovenous malformation.
2. Chest wall arteriovenous malformation.

Neurogenic
1. Neurofibromatosis* – 'ribbon ribs' may also be a feature.

Further Reading
Boone M.L., Swenson B.E. & Felson B. (1964) Rib notching: its many causes. *Am. J. Roentgenol.*, 91: 1075–88.

1.58   Rib Notching – Superior Surface

Connective Tissue Diseases
1. Rheumatoid arthritis*.
2. Systemic lupus erythematosus*.
3. Scleroderma*.
4. Sjögren's syndrome.

Metabolic
1. Hyperparathyroidism*.

Miscellaneous
1. Neurofibromatosis*.
2. Restrictive lung disease.
3. Poliomyelitis.
4. Marfan's syndrome*.
5. Osteogenesis imperfecta*.
6. Progeria.

Further Reading
Boone M.L., Swenson B.E. & Felson B. (1964) Rib notching: its many
    causes. *Am. J. Roentgenol.*, 91: 1075–88.

1.59   Wide or Thick Ribs

1. Chronic anaemias – due to marrow hyperplasia.
2. Fibrous dysplasia*.
3. Paget's disease*.
4. Healed fractures with callus.
5. Achondroplasia*.
6. Mucopolysaccharidoses.

1.60 Madelung Deformity

1. Isolated – bilateral > unilateral. Asymmetrical. Predominantly adolescent or young adult women.
2. Dyschondrosteosis (Leri–Weil disease) – bilateral with mesomelic limb shortening. AD. Predominantly men.
3. Diaphyseal aclasis.
4. Turner syndrome*.
5. Post-traumatic.
6. Post-infective.

1.61 Carpal Fusion

Isolated
Tends to involve bones in the same carpal row (proximal or distal). More common in Afro-Caribbeans than Caucasians.
1. Triquetral–lunate – the most common site. Affects 1% of the population.
2. Capitate–hamate.
3. Trapezium–trapezoid.

Syndrome-related
Tends to exhibit massive carpal fusion affecting bones in different rows (proximal and distal).
1. Acrocephalosyndactyly (Apert's syndrome).
2. Arthrogryposis multiplex congenita.
3. Ellis–van Creveld syndrome.
4. Holt–Oram syndrome.
5. Turner's syndrome*.
6. Symphalangism.

Acquired
1. Inflammatory arthritides – especially juvenile chronic arthritis* and rheumatoid arthritis*.
2. Pyogenic arthritis.
3. Post-traumatic.
4. Post-surgical.

Further Reading
Cope J.R. (1974) Carpal coalition. *Clin. Radiol.*, 25: 261–6.

1.62   Short Metacarpal(s) or Metatarsal(s)

1. Idiopathic.
2. Post-traumatic – iatrogenic, fracture, growth plate injury, thermal or electrical.
3. Post-infarction – e.g. sickle-cell anaemia*.
4. Turner's syndrome* – 4th ± 3rd and 5th metacarpals.
5. Pseudo- and pseudopseudohypoparathyroidism* – 4th and 5th metacarpals.

Further Reading

Bell J. (1951) On brachydactyly and symphalangism. In: Penrose L.S. (ed.) *The Treasury of Human Inheritance*, Vol. 5, Part 1, pp. 1–31. Cambridge: University Press.

Poznanski A.K. (1984) *The Hand in Radiologic Diagnosis*, 2nd edn, Vol. 1, Chapter 9, pp. 209–62. Philadelphia: Saunders.

1.63 Arachnodactyly

Elongated and slender tubular bones of the hands and feet. The metacarpal index is an aid to diagnosis and is estimated by measuring the lengths of the 2nd, 3rd, 4th and 5th metacarpals and dividing by their breadths taken at the exact mid-points. These four figures are then added together and divided by 4.
Normal range 5.4–7.9.
Arachnodactyly range 8.4–10.4.

The metacarpal index is a poor discriminator between Marfan's syndrome and constitutional tall stature.

1. **Marfan's syndrome*** – although arachnodactyly is not necessary for the diagnosis.
2. **Homocystinuria*** – morphologically resembles Marfan's syndrome but 60% are mentally handicapped, they have a predisposition to arterial and venous thromboses and the lens of the eye dislocates downward rather than upward.

Further Reading
Eldridge R. (1964) The metacarpal index: a useful aid in the diagnosis of the Marfan syndrome. *Arch. Intern. Med.*, 113: 14–16.
Nelle M, Tröger J., Rupprath G. & Bettendorf M. (1994) Metacarpal index in Marfan's syndrome and in constitutional tall stature. *Arch. Dis. Child.*, 70: 149–50.
Sinclair R.J.G., Kitchin A.H. & Turner R.W.D. (1960) The Marfan syndrome. *Q. J. Med.*, 29: 19–46.

1.64   Abnormal Thumbs – Congenital

Broad

1. **Acrocephalopolysyndactyly (Carpenter type)** – two ossification centres for the proximal phalanx in childhood → duplication in adulthood.
2. **Acrocephalosyndactyly (Apert type)** – partial or complete duplication of the proximal phalanx. Complete syndactyly of digits II–V – 'mitten hand' and 'sock foot'.
3. **Diastrophic dysplasia** – short, ovoid thumb metacarpal with proximally located thumb.
4. **Rubinstein–Taybi syndrome** – terminal phalanx + 'hitch-hiker thumb'.
5. **Oto-palato-digital syndrome** – large cone epiphysis of the dital phalanx.

Large

1. **Klippel–Trenaunay–Weber syndrome.**
2. **Macrodystrophia lipomatosa.**
3. **Maffucci syndrome.**
4. **Neurofibromatosis*.**

Short or Small

1. **Fanconi anaemia** – ± other radial ray abnormalities. Onset of pancytopenia at 5–10 years of age.
2. **Holt–Oram syndrome** – finger-like, absent, hypoplastic or triphalangeal thumb + congenital heart disease (ASD, VSD).
3. **Brachydactyly C or D.**
4. **Cornelia de Lange syndrome** – hypoplastic metacarpal.
5. **Fetal hydantoin** – finger-like thumb with hypoplasia of all the distal phalanges.

Absent

1. **Fanconi anaemia.**
2. **Poland syndrome** – partial or complete absence of pectoralis muscles + abnormalities of the ipsilateral upper limb.
3. **Thalidomide.**
4. **Trisomy chromosome 18.**

Triphalangeal
1. Fanconi anaemia.
2. Holt–Oram syndrome.
3. Blackfan–Diamond syndrome – pure red cell aplasia. Musculoskeletal abnormalities in 30%.
4. Poland syndrome.
5. Trisomy chromosome 13 and 21.
6. Thalidomide.

Abnormally Positioned
1. Cornelia de Lange syndrome – proximally placed.
2. Diastrophic dysplasia – 'hitch-hiker thumb'.
3. Rubinstein–Taybi syndrome – 'hitch-hiker thumb' + broad terminal phalanx.

Further Reading
Jones K.L. (1988) *Smith's Recognizable Patterns of Human Malformation*, 4th edn. Philadelphia: W.B. Saunders Company.
Taybi H. & Lachman R.S. (1990) *Radiology of Syndromes, Metabolic Disorders and Skeletal Dysplasias*, 3rd edn, pp. 877–8. Chicago: Year Book Medical Publishers.

1.65 Distal Phalangeal Destruction

| Normal | Resorption of the tuft | Resorption of the mid portion | Periarticular |

NB. Because of reinforced Sharpey's fibres periosteal reaction is rare at this site.

Resorption of the Tuft

1. **Scleroderma***.
2. **Raynaud's disease.**
3. **Psoriatic arthropathy*** – can precede the skin changes
4. **Neuropathic diseases** – diabetes mellitus, leprosy, myelomeningocele, syringomyelia and congenital indifference to pain.
5. **Thermal injuries** – burns, frostbite and electrical.
6. **Trauma.**
7. **Hyperparathyroidism***.
8. **Epidermolysis bullosa.**
9. **Porphyria** – due to cutaneous photosensitivity leading to blistering and scarring.
10. **Phenytoin toxicity** – congenitally in infants of epileptic mothers.
11. **Subungual exostosis.**
12. **Snake and scorpion venom** – due to tissue breakdown by proteinases.

Resorption of the Mid Portion

1. **Polyvinyl chloride tank cleaners.**
2. **Acro-osteolysis of Hajdu and Cheney.**
3. **Hyperparathyroidism***.

Periarticular – i.e. erosion of the distal interphalangeal joints.
1. Psoriatic arthropathy*.
2. Erosive osteoarthritis.
3. Hyperparathyroidism*.
4. Thermal injuries.
5. Scleroderma*.
6. Multicentric reticulohistiocytosis.

Poorly Defined Lytic Lesions
1. **Osteomyelitis** – mostly staphylococcal with diabetics at particular risk. Periosteal reaction is infrequent.
2. **Metastases** – bronchus is most common primary site. Bone metastases to the hand are commonest in the terminal phalanx and may be the only metastasis to bone. The subarticular cortex is usually the last to be destroyed.
3. **Multiple myeloma***.
4. **Aneurysmal bone cyst*** – rare at this site. Marked thinning and expansion of cortex.
5. **Giant cell tumour*** – usually involving the base of the phalanx.
6. **Leprosy** – at any age, but 30% present before 15 years of age.

Well Defined Lytic Lesions
1. **Implantation dermoid/epidermoid cyst** – an expanding lesion. 1–20 mm, with minimal sclerosis ± soft-tissue swelling.
2. **Enchondroma***.
3. **Sarcoidosis*** – associated 'lace-like' destruction of phalangeal shaft, subperiosteal erosion leading to resorption of terminal tufts and endosteal sclerosis.
4. **Glomus tumour** – soft-tissue swelling with disuse osteoporosis because of pain. Bone involvement is uncommon but there may be pressure erosion or a well-defined lytic lesion.
5. **Osteoid osteoma***.
6. **Fibrous dysplasia***.

Further Reading

Jones S.N. & Stoker D.J. (1988) Radiology at your fingertips; lesions of the terminal phalanx. *Clin. Radiol.*, 39: 478–85.

Qteishat W.A., Whitehouse G.H. & Hawass N-E-D. (1985) Acro-osteolysis following snake and scorpion envenomation. *Br. J. Radiol.*, 58: 1035–9.

1.66   Fluid Levels in Bone Lesions on CT and MRI

Benign

1. Aneurysmal bone cyst*.
2. Chondroblastoma*.
3. Giant cell tumour*.
4. Simple bone cyst*.
5. Fibrous dysplasia*.

Malignant

1. Telangiectatic osteosarcoma*.
2. Malignant fibrous histiocytoma.
3. Synovial sarcoma.
4. Any necrotic bone tumour.

1.67 MRI of Normal Bone Marrow

	T_1W	T_2W	Comment
Red marrow (haemopoietic)	↓	↑	Usually symmetrical in distribution but can mimic metastases in metaphyses of long bones. Reconversion to red marrow can occur due to increased demand (e.g. chronic anaemia, cardiac failure) or malignant infiltrate elsewhere in the skeleton.
Yellow marrow (fat)	↑	↑	Variable quantity, increases with age, can be focal in spine. Radiotherapy causes marked increase in fat.
Trabecular bone	↓	↓	Produces an inhomogeneous ripple in the applied magnetic field which produces a susceptibility artefact (signal loss due to dephasing). This is most marked on gradient echo images as there is no 180 degree rephasing pulse.
Epiphyseal plate	↓	↓	If the plate is at an angle to the scan plane it can appear as a patchy signal loss on T_1W and mimic a metastasis.

NB. Chemical shift artefact can interfere with visualization of the vertebral end-plates (particularly at high field strength). It occurs along the frequency encoded direction which is usually along the axis of the spine because the phase encoded axis is along the short axis of the image in order to decrease the time of the examination.

Further Reading

Hosten N., Schorner W., Neuman K., Huhn D. & Felix R. (1993) MR imaging of bone marrow – review of the literature and possible indications for contrast nehanced studies. *Adv. MR Contrast*, 1: 84–98.

1.68   MRI of Abnormal Bone Marrow

NB. Fat suppression/saturation techniques may be required to highlight the T2 component of the lesion.

	T_1W	T_2W	Comments
Metastases			
– lytic	↓	±↑	
– sclerotic	↓	↓	Discs appear higher in signal intensity than adjacent vertebra on T_1W – normally they appear lower in signal intensity.
Myeloma	↓	±↑ (↓ after treatment)	
Lymphoma	↓	iso	
Osteoporotic vertebral collapse	±↓ due to oedema	±↑	Osteoporotic collapse is said not to have an associated epidural soft-tissue mass. However, discrimination from metastatic collapse is only possible if there is no oedema and the normal marrow signal is preserved. Osteoporotic and metastatic collapse can both show gadolinium enhancement.
Radiotherapy	↑++	±↑	The striking increase in signal on T_1W is due to fat deposition. There is a sharp cut off at the edge of the radiotherapy field. The increase in signal can be observed from 3 weeks after the radiotherapy.

	T_1W	T_2W	*Comments*
Haemangioma	↑+	↑	Rounded in shape, relatively common.
Discitis	↓	↑	Vertebral end-plates destroyed.
Vertebral end-plate reaction to a degenerative disc:			
Type 1	↓	↑	Vascularized fibrous tissue. Intact vertebral end plate distinguishes it from discitis.
Type 2	↑	↑	Conversion of red to yellow marrow.
Gaucher's disease	↓	iso	
Bone marrow transplantation	↑ in centre with bands of ↓ around this due to regeneration of red marrow		

Further Reading

Hosten N., Schorner W., Neumann K., Huhn D. & Felix R. (1993) MR imaging of bone marrow – review of literature and possible indication for contrast enhanced studies. *Adv. MR Contrast*, 1: 84–98.

2
The Spine

with contributions by Tom Powell

2.1 Imaging of Spinal Abnormalities

1. **Plain Radiography (with tomography)** – still valuable for acute trauma and for long-term sequelae, congenital and other causes of spinal deformity, suspected spondylolisthesis, spinal (as opposed to radicular) pain, and survey views for metastases. Limited role in degenerative diseases (rarely contributes to management), and suspected spinal tumours (may show remodelling in slow growing tumours such as neurofibroma and ependymoma).

2. **Myelography** – a largely obsolescent method, but widely used in the absence of sufficient availability of MRI. Certain attributes remain of considerable diagnostic value:
   (a) Suspected disc herniation: sensitive and specific, limited only by inability to show very laterally placed intraforaminal disc fragments.
   (b) Suspected spinal vascular malformation. More sensitive and more specific than MRI, which is sometimes equivocal due to flow related artefacts.
   (c) Intraspinal mass lesions: sensitive, and specific in terms of the compartment involved by the tumour. In most cases it is possible to predict tumour type on the basis of the myelogram.

3. **CT** – of less overall usefulness compared with MRI, but having advantages in its better definition of bone and joint abnormalities.
   (a) Suspected disc herniation: of little value in the cervical region, but still regarded as sensitive on the detection of prolapsed lumbar disc. Sensitivity further enhanced by postmyelogram–CT. Time and dose considerations usually confine the examination to three levels, and this can be a problem in atypical presentations. In the

thoracic region, the lack of level specific clinical information prevents the effective use of CT, other than as a post-myelographic method, and where further assessment of previously detected calcification is required.

(b) Suspected fractures and dislocations: CT has great advantages in its potential for detailed study without additional trauma to the patient, and in its excellent definition of bone abnormalities. However, transversely oriented fractures and mild wedge compression fractures are difficult to visualize.

(c) Facet joint disease: technique of choice in most cases, though MRI is not without usefulness in this area.

(d) Congenital abnormalities: spondylolisthesis, dysraphism, diastematomyelia, and foramen magnum anomalies require CT for full assessment.

(e) Bone tumours of the spine require CT for full assessment, particularly to identify and quantify any calcific components. Intraspinal tumours are not well shown, though calcific components may be shown in meningiomas, and fatty elements in dermoid and teratomatous lesions.

(f) Spinal infection: CT is sensitive in the demonstration of epidural and subdural abscess, though a high volume of intravenous contrast may be required. The extraspinal components are also well known.

4. MRI – the high soft-tissue contrast, the better tissue characterization, and the freedom from artefact make MRI the optimal technique in many types of spinal pathology. The lack of bone signal is an occasional disadvantage.

(a) Suspected disc herniation: sensitive and specific in the detection of disc herniation in cervical, thoracic, and lumbar regions. Partial volume averaging, and soft-tissue contrast problems sometimes limit the demonstration of laterally placed cervical disc fragments. Sagittal scanning allows for multilevel demonstrations, thereby avoiding errors due to over-reliance on clinical findings: this is particularly important in suspected thoracic disc.

(b) Spinal stenosis: sagittal sections allow for multilevel displays, which are invaluable in the detection of cervical and lumbar canal stenosis.

(continued)

(c) Spinal tumours: the sensitivity of tumour detection is very high, and the good tissue characterization allows confident histological diagnosis in many cases. Gadolinium enhancement often useful: almost all tumours enhance; other expanding lesions such as infarcts, and acute plaques may not. The non-invasive nature of MR avoids disturbance of CSF flow dynamics in the potentially unstable situation of total or near total spinal block. By contrast, myelography may precipitate the need for surgery.

(d) Vascular malformations: MR will show the distended veins characteristic of spinal (usually dural) vascular malformations as flow voids, best shown on spin-echo T_2W sections. Sensitivity probably a little inferior to myelography.

(d) Arachnoiditis: adhesion of the nerves of the cauda equina to the theca and to themselves is best shown by MRI. Given that since myelography has a causal role in many cases, it is undesirable to use myelography for its demonstration.

(e) Trauma: MRI will show ligamentous injury, particularly oedema and haemorrhage, whereas CT may appear normal or equivocal. Bone marrow oedema secondary to incremental fractures is also shown. Intraspinal complications of trauma (haemorrhage into the epidural or subdural space, or into the cord) are optimally shown by MRI.

(f) Spinal infection: MRI is rather more sensitive than CT for showing both the intraspinal and extraspinal components, and will demonstrate the rare intramedullary abscess, which CT is unlikely to show.

(g) Vascular and inflammatory lesions including MS: MRI will show spinal cord infarction and haemorrhage, and also acute and chronic plaques in demyelinating disease.

2.2 Scoliosis

Idiopathic
2% prevalence for curves > 10°.
1. **Infantile** – diagnosed before the age of 4 years. 90% are thoracic and concave to the right. More common in boys. 90% resolve spontaneously.
2. **Juvenile** – diagnosed between 4 and 10 years. More common in girls. Almost always progressive.
3. **Adolescent** – diagnosed between 10 years and maturity. More common in females. Majority are concave to the left in the thoracic region.

Congenital
Prognosis is dependent on the anatomical abnormality and a classification (see figure) is, therefore, important.

Failure of Formation. A. Incarcerated hemivertebra. A straight spine with little tendency to progression. **B.** Free hemivertebra. May be progressive. **C.** Wedge vertebra. Better prognosis than a free hemivertebra. **D.** Multiple hemivertebrae. Failure of formation on the same side results in a severe curve. Hemivertebrae on opposite sides may compensate each other. **E.** Central defect. Butterfly vertebra.
Failure of Segmentation. A. Bilateral → block vertebra and a short spine, e.g. Klippel–Feil. **B.** Unilateral unsegmented bar. Severely progressive curve with varying degrees of kyphosis or lordosis depending on the position of the bar.
Mixed defects. A. Unilateral unsegmented bar and a hemivertebra. Severely progressive. **B.** Partially segmented incarcerated hemivertebra. **C.** Bilateral failure of segmentation incorporating a hemivertebra.

Indicators of serious progression are:
  (a)   Deformity present at birth.
  (b)   Severe deformity of the chest wall.
  (c)   Unilateral unsegmented bars.
  (d)   Thoracic abnormality.
Associated abnormalities may occur – urinary tract (18%), congenital heart disease (7%), undescended scapulae (6%) and diastematomyelia (5%).

FAILURE OF FORMATION

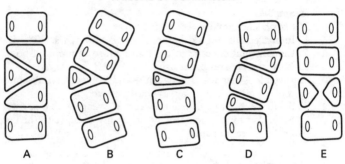

A   B   C   D   E

FAILURE OF SEGMENTATION

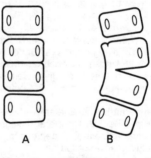

A   B

MIXED
e.g.

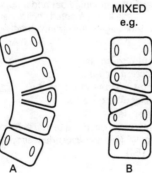

A   B

C

Neuromuscular Diseases
1. Myelomeningocele.
2. Spinal muscular atrophy.
3. Friedreich's ataxia.
4. Poliomyelitis.
5. Cerebral palsy.
6. Muscular dystrophy.

Mesodermal and Neuroectodermal Diseases
1. **Neurofibromatosis*** – in up to 40% of patients. Classically a sharply angled short segment scoliosis with a severe kyphosis. The apical vertebrae are irregular and wedged with adjacent dysplastic ribs. 25% have a congenital vertebral anomaly.
2. **Marfan's syndrome*** – scoliosis in 40–60%. Double structural curves are typical.
3. **Homocystinuria*** – similar to Marfan's syndrome.

Post Radiotherapy
Wedged and hypoplastic vertebrae ± unilateral pelvic or rib hypoplasia.

Leg Length Discrepancy
A flexible lumbar curve, convex to the side of the shorter leg. Disparity of iliac crest level.

Painful Scoliosis
1. **Osteoid osteoma*** – 10% occur in the spine. A lamina or pedicle at the apex of the curve will be sclerotic or overgrown.
2. **Osteoblastoma***.
3. **Intraspinal tumour** (see 2.21).
4. **Infection.**

Further Reading
Winter R.B. (1983) *Congenital Deformities of the Spine*. New York: Thieme-Stratton.

2.3   Solitary Collapsed Vertebra

1. Neoplastic disease
   (a) Metastasis – breast, bronchus, prostate, kidney and thyroid account for the majority of patients with a solitary spinal metastasis. The disc spaces are preserved until late. The bone may be lytic, sclerotic or mixed. ± destruction of a pedicle.
   (b) Multiple myeloma/plasmacytoma* – a common site, especially for plasmacytoma. May mimic an osteolytic metastasis or be expansile and resemble an aneurysmal bone cyst.
   (c) Lymphoma*.
2. Osteoporosis (q.v.) – generalized osteopenia. Coarsened trabecular pattern in adjacent vertebrae due to resorption of secondary trabeculae.
3. Trauma.
4. Infection – with destruction of vertebral end-plates and adjacent disc spaces.
5. Langerhans cell histiocytosis* – eosinophil granuloma is the most frequent cause of a solitary vertebra plana in childhood. The posterior elements are usually spared.
6. Benign tumours – haemangioma, giant cell tumour and aneursymal bone cyst.
7. Paget's disease* – diagnosis is difficult when a solitary vertebra is involved. Neural arch is affected in most cases. Sclerosis and expansion. If other non-collapsed vertebrae are affected then diagnosis becomes much easier.

2.4 Multiple Collapsed Vertebrae

1. **Osteoporosis** (q.v.) – reduced bone density. Vertebral bodies may be wedged or biconcave (fish-shaped).
2. **Neoplastic disease** – wedge fractures are particularly related to osteolytic metastases and osteolytic marrow tumours, e.g. multiple myeloma, leukaemia and lymphoma. Altered or obliterated normal trabeculae. Disc spaces are usually preserved until late. Paravertebral soft-tissue mass is more common in myeloma than metastases.
3. **Trauma** – discontinuity of trabeculae, sclerosis of the fracture line due to compressed and overlapped trabeculae. Disc space usually preserved. The lower cervical, lower dorsal and upper lumbar spine are most commonly affected. Usually no soft-tissue mass.
4. **Scheuermann's disease** – irregular end-plates and numerous Schmorl's nodes in the thoracic spine of children and young adults. Disc space narrowing. Often progresses to a severe kyphosis. Secondary degenerative changes later.
5. **Infection** – destruction of end-plates adjacent to a destroyed disc. Although it is usually not possible to differentiate radiologically between pyogenic and tuberculous spondylitis in white patients the following signs are said to be helpful.

Pyogenic	*Tuberculous*
Rapidly progressive	Slower progression
Marked osteoblastic response	Less sclerosis
Less collapse	Marked collapse
Small or no paravertebral abscess	Large paravertebral
Early bridging of affected vertebrae	abscess

6. **Langerhans cell histiocytosis*** – the spine is more frequently involved in eosinophilic granuloma and Hand–Schüller–Christian disease than in Letterer–Siwe disease. Most common in young people. The thoracic and lumbosacral spine are the usual sites of disease. Disc spaces are preserved.
7. **Sickle-cell anaemia*** – characteristic step-like depression in the central part of the end-plate.

Further Reading (for 2.4)
Allen E.H., Cosgrove D. & Millard F.J.C. (1978) The radiological changes in infections of the spine and their diagnostic value. *Clin. Radiol.*, 29: 31–40.
Goldman A.B. & Freiberger R.H. (1978) Localised infections and neuropathic disease. *Semin. Roentgenol.*, 14: 19–32.

2.5   Platyspondyly in Childhood

This sign describes a decrease in the distance between the upper and lower vertebral end-plates and should be differentiated from wedge shaped vertebrae. Platyspondyly may be *generalized*, affecting all the vertebral bodies, *multiple*, affecting some of the vertebral bodies or *localized*, involving one vertebral body (also termed vertebra plana).

Congenital Platyspondyly
1. Thanatophoric dwarfism – inverted 'U' or H-shaped vertebrae with a markedly increased disc space: body height ratio. Telephone handle shaped long bones.
2. Metatropic dwarfism.
3. Osteogenesis imperfecta* – type IIA.

Platyspondyly in Later Childhood
1. Morquio's disease*.
2. Spondyloepiphyseal dysplasia congenita.
3. Spondyloepiphyseal dysplasia tarda.
4. Kniest syndrome.

Acquired Platyspondyly – see 2.4.

Further Reading
Kozlowski K. (1974) Platyspondyly in childhood. *Paed. Radiol.*, 2: 81–8.

2.6 Erosion, Destruction or Absence of a Pedicle

1. **Metastasis**

2. **Multiple myeloma***

   metastatic carcinoma involves the pedicle relatively early and contrasts with the late preservation of the pedicle in multiple myeloma.

3. **Neurofibroma** – often causes erosion of adjacent pedicle or pedicles. Chronic intramedullary tumours, typically ependymoma, cause flattening of both pedicles at affected levels, with a widened interpedicular distance.
4. **Tuberculosis** – uncommonly. With a large paravertebral abscess.
5. **Benign bone tumour** – aneurysmal bone cyst or giant cell tumour.
6. **Congenital absence** – ± sclerosis of the contralateral pedicle.

Further Reading

Bell D. & Cockshott W.P. (1971) Tuberculosis of the vertebral pedicle. *Radiology*, 99: 43–8.

2.7 Solitary Dense Pedicle

1. **Osteoblastic metastasis** – no change in size.
2. **Osteoid osteoma*** – some enlargement of the pedicle ± radiolucent nidus.
3. **Osteoblastoma*** – larger than osteoid osteoma and more frequently a lucency with a sclerotic margin rather than a purely sclerotic pedicle.
4. **Secondary to spondylolysis** – ipsilateral or contralateral.
5. **Secondary to congenitally absent or hypoplastic contralateral posterior elements.**

Further Reading

Pettine K. & Klassen R. (1986) Osteoid osteoma and osteoblastoma of the spine. *J. Bone Joint Surg.*, 68A: 354–61.
Wilkinson R.H. & Hall J.E. (1974) The sclerotic pedicle: tumour or pseudotumour? *Radiology*, 111: 683–8.

2.8   Enlarged Vertebral Body

Generalized
1. Gigantism.
2. Acromegaly*.

Local (Single or Multiple)
1. Paget's disease*.
2. Benign bone tumour
   (a) Aneurysmal bone cyst* – typically purely lytic and expansile. Involves the anterior and posterior elements more commonly than the anterior or posterior elements alone. Rapid growth.
   (b) Haemangioma* – with a prominent vertical trabecular pattern.
   (c) Giant cell tumour* – involvement of the body alone is most common. Expansion is minimal.
3. Hydatid – over 40% of cases of hydatid disease in bone occur in vertebrae.

Further Reading
Beabout J.W., McLeod R.A. & Dahlin D.C. (1979) Benign tumours. *Semin. Roentgenol.*, 14: 33–43.
Dahlin D.C. (1977) Giant cell tumour of vertebrae above the sacrum. A review of 31 cases. *Cancer*, 39: 1350–6.
Mohan V., Gupta S.K., Tuli S.M. & Sanyal B. (1980) Symptomatic vertebral haemangiomas. *Clin. Radiol.*, 31: 575–9.

2.9   Squaring of One or More Vertebral Bodies

1. Ankylosing spondylitis*.
2. Paget's disease*.
3. Psoriatic arthropathy*.
4. Reiter's syndrome*.
5. Rheumatoid arthritis*.

2.10 Block Vertebrae

1. **Klippel–Feil syndrome** – segmentation defects in the cervical spine, short neck, low hairline and limited cervical movement, especially rotation. The radiological appearance of the cervical spine resembles (1) above. C2–C3 and C5–C6 are most commonly affected. Other anomalies are frequently associated, the most important being
   (a) Scoliosis > 20° in more than 50% of patients.
   (b) Sprengel's shoulder in 30%, ± an omovertebral body.
   (c) Cervical ribs.
   (d) Genito–urinary abnormalities in 66%; renal agenesis in 33%.
   (e) Deafness in 33%.
2. **Isolated congenital** – a failure of segmentation. Most common in the lumbar spine but also occurs in the cervical and thoracic regions. The ring epiphyses of adjacent vertebrae do not develop and thus the AP diameter of the vertebrae at the site of the segmentation defect is decreased. The articular facets, neural arches or spinous processes may also be involved. A faint lucency representing a vestigial disc may be observed.
3. **Rheumatoid arthritis*** – especially juvenile onset rheumatoid arthritis and juvenile chronic arthritis with polyarticular onset. There may be angulation at the fusion site and this is not a feature of the congenital variety. The spinous processes do not fuse.
4. **Ankylosing spondylitis*** – squaring of anterior vertebral margins and calcification in the invertebral discs and anterior and posterior longitudinal ligaments.
5. **Tuberculosis** – vertebral body collapse and destruction of the disc space, paraspinal calcification. There may be angulation of the spine.
6. **Operative fusion.**
7. **Post-traumatic.**

2.11   Ivory Vertebral Body

Single or multiple very dense vertebrae. The list excludes those causes where increased density is due to compaction of bone following collapse. If there is generalized involvement of the spine see 1.11.

1. **Metastases** – sclerotic metastases or an initially lytic metastasis which, after treatment, has become sclerotic. Usually no alteration in vertebral body size. Disc spaces preserved until late.
2. **Paget's disease*** – usually a single vertebral body is affected. Expanded body with a thickened cortex and coarsened trabeculation. Disc space involvement is uncommon.
3. **Lymphoma*** – more frequent in Hodgkin's disease than the other reticuloses. Normal size vertebral body. Disc spaces intact.
4. **Low-grade infection** – with end-plate destruction, disc space narrowing and a paraspinal soft-tissue mass.
5. **Haemangioma** – sclerosis is accompanied by a coarsened trabecular pattern, predominantly vertical in orientation. ± expansion.

2.12 Atlanto-axial Subluxation

When the distance between the posterior aspect of the anterior arch of the atlas and the anterior aspect of the odontoid process exceeds 3 mm in adults and older children or 5 mm in younger children, or an interosseous distance that changes considerably between flexion and extension.

Trauma

Arthritides
1. **Rheumatoid arthritis*** – in 20–25% of patients with severe disease. Associated erosion of the odontoid may be severe enough to reduce it to a small spicule of bone.
2. **Psoriatic arthropathy*** – in 45% of patients with spondylitis.
3. **Juvenile chronic arthritis*** – most commonly in seropositive juvenile onset adult rheumatoid arthritis.
4. **Systemic lupus erythematosus***.
5. **Ankylosing spondylitis*** – in 2% of cases. Usually a late feature.

Congenital
1. **Down's syndrome*** – in 20% of cases. ± odontoid hypoplasia. May, rarely, have atlanto-occipital instability.
2. **Morquio's syndrome***.
3. **Spondyloepiphyseal dysplasia.**
4. **Congenital absence/hypoplasia of the odontoid process** – many have a history of previous trauma (NB In children < 9 years it is normal for the tip of the odontoid to fall well below the top of the anterior arch of the atlas.

Infection
1. **Retropharyngeal abscess in a child.**

Further Reading
Elliott S. (1988) The odontoid process in children – is it hypoplastic? *Clin. Radiol.*, 39: 391–3.
Martel W. (1961) The occipito-atlanto-axial joints in rheumatoid

arthritis and ankylosing spondylitis. *Am. J. Roentgenol.*, 86: 223–40.

Rosenbaum D.M., Blumhagen J.D. & King H.A. (1986) Atlanto-occipital instability in Down syndrome. *Am. J. Roentgenol.*, 146: 1269–72.

2.13 Intervertebral Disc Calcification

1. **Degenerative spondylosis** – in the nucleus pulposus. Usually confined to the dorsal region. With other signs of degenerative spondylosis – disc-space narrowing, osteophytosis and vacuum sign in the disc. A frequent finding in the elderly.

2. **Alkaptonuria*** – symptoms of arthropathy first appear in the 4th decade. Widespread disc calcification, osteoporosis, disc-space narrowing and osteophytosis. The disc calcification is predominantly in the inner fibres of the annulus fibrosus but may be diffusely throughout the disc. Severe changes progress to ankylosis and may mimic ankylosing spondylitis.

3. **Calcium pyrophosphate dihydrate deposition disease*** – predominantly in the outer fibres of the annulus fibrous.

4. **Ankylosing spondylitis*** – in the nucleus pulposus. Ankylosis, square vertebral bodies and syndesmophytes.

5. **Juvenile chronic arthritis*** – may mimic ankylosing spondylitis.

6. **Haemochromatosis*** – in the outer fibres of the annulus fibrosus.

7. **Diffuse idiopathic skeletal hyperostosis (DISH)** – may mimic ankylosing spondylitis.

8. **Gout*.**

9. **Idiopathic** – a transient phenomenon in children. The cervical spine is most often affected. Clinically associated with neck pain and fever but may be asymptomatic. Persistent in adults.

10. **Following spinal fusion.**

Further Reading

Weinberger A. & Myers A.R. (1978) Intervertebral disc calcification in adults: a review. *Semin. Arthritis Rheum.*, 18: 69–75.

2.14 Bony Outgrowths of the Spine

Syndesmophytes
Ossification of the annulus fibrosus. Thin, vertical and symmetrical. When extreme results in the 'bamboo spine'.
1. Ankylosing spondylitis*.
2. Alkaptonuria.

AP

Paravertebral Ossification
Ossification of paravertebral connective tissue which is separated from the edge of the vertebral body and disc. Large, coarse and asymmetrical.
1. Reiter's syndrome*.
2. Psoriatic arthropathy*.

AP

Claw Osteophytes
Arising from the vertebral margin with no gap and having an obvious claw appearance.
1. Stress response – but in the absence of disc-space narrowing does not indicate disc degeneration.

Lateral

Traction Spurs
Osteophytes with a gap between the end-plate and the base of the osteophyte and with the tip not protruding beyond the horizontal plane of the vertebral end-plate.
1. Shear stresses across the disc – more likely to be associated with a degenerative disc.

Lateral

Undulating Anterior Ossification
Undulating ossification of the anterior longitudinal ligament, intervertebral disc and paravertebral connective tissue.
1. Diffuse idiopathic skeletal hyperostosis (DISH).

Lateral

Further Reading
Jones M.D., Pais M.J. & Omiya B. (1988) Bony overgrowths and abnormal calcifications about the spine. *Radiol. Clin. North Am.*, 26: 1213–34.

2.15   Coronal Cleft Vertebral Bodies

Normal Variant

Fusion of the anterior and posterior ossification centres of the vertebral body normally occurs before the 16th week of intrauterine life. Persisting notochordal remnants in the lower thoracic and lumbar region may prevent fusion but the condition usually resolves without sequelae in the first few months of life.

As a Feature of Bone Dysplasias

1. **Chondrodysplasia punctata** – rhizomelic type.
2. **Kniest syndrome**.
3. **Metatropic dwarfism**.

Acquired

As a result of herniation of a normal intervertebral disc into an osteoporotic vertebral body or secondary to trauma.

Further Reading

Fielden P. & Russell J.G.B. (1970) Coronally cleft vertebrae. *Radiology*, 21: 327–8.
Wilson A.R.M., Wastie M.L., Preston B.J., Cassar-Pullicino V., Worthington B.S. & McKim-Thomas H. (1989) Acquired coronal cleft vertebra. *Clin. Radiol.*, 40: 167–73.

2.16 Anterior Vertebral Body Beaks

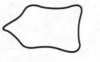

Central

Lower third

Involves 1–3 vertebral bodies at the thoracolumbar junction and usually associated with a kyphosis. Hypotonia is probably the common denominator which leads to an exaggerated thoracolumbar kyphosis, anterior herniation of the nucleus pulposus and subsequently an anterior vertebral body defect.

Central
1. Morquio's syndrome*.

Lower Third
1. Hurler's syndrome*.
2. Achondroplasia*.
3. Pseudoachondroplasia.
4. Cretinism*.
5. Down's syndrome*.
6. Neuromuscular diseases.

Further Reading
Swischuk L.E. (1970) The beaked, notched or hooked vertebra. Its significance in infants and young children. *Radiology*, 95: 661–4.

2.17   Posterior Scalloping of Vertebral Bodies

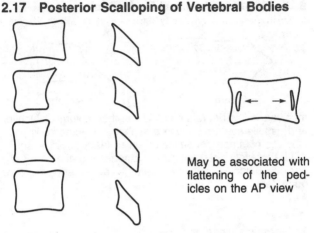

May be associated with flattening of the pedicles on the AP view

Scalloping is most prominent (a) at either end of the spinal canal, (b) with large and slow growing lesions and (c) with those lesions which originate during the period of active growth and bone modelling.

1. **Tumours in the spinal canal** – ependymoma (especially of the filum terminale and conus), dermoid, lipoma, neurofibroma and less commonly meningioma. Chronic raised intraspinal pressure distal to a tumour producing spinal block also causes extensive vertebral scalloping.
2. **Neurofibromatosis*** – scalloping is due to a mesodermal dysplasia and is associated with dural ectasia. Localized scalloping can also result from pressure resorption by a neurofibroma, in which case there may also be enlargement of an intervertebral foramen and flattening of one pedicle ('dumbbell tumour'). However, multiple wide thoracic intervertebral foramina are more likely due to lateral meningoceles than to local tumours.
3. **Acromegaly*** – other spinal changes include increased AP and transverse diameters of the vertebral bodies giving a spurious impression of decreased vertebral height, osteoporosis, spur formation and calcified discs.
4. **Achondroplasia*** – with spinal stenosis and anterior vertebral body beaks.

5. **Communicating hydrocephalus** – if severe and untreated.
6. **Syringomyelia** – especially if the onset is before 30 years of age.
7. **Other congenital syndromes**
   (a) Ehlers–Danlos ⎫ both associated
   (b) Marfan's*. ⎬ with dural ectasia.
   (c) Hurler's*.
   (d) Morquio's*.
   (e) Osteogenesis imperfecta*.

Further Reading

Mitchell G.E., Lourie H. & Berne A.S. (1967) The various causes of scalloped vertebrae and notes on their pathogenesis. *Radiology*, 89: 67–74.

2.18 Anterior Scalloping of Vertebral Bodies

1. **Aortic aneurysm** – intervertebral discs remain intact. Well-defined anterior vertebral margin. ± calcification in the wall of the aorta.
2. **Tuberculous spondylitis** – with marginal erosions of the affected vertebral bodies. Disc-space destruction. Widening of the paraspinal soft tissues.
3. **Lymphadenopathy** – pressure resorption of bone results in a well-defined anterior vertebral body margin unless there is malignant infiltration of the bone.
4. **Delayed motor development** – e.g. Down's syndrome.

2.19 Syndromes with a Narrow Spinal Canal

1. Achondroplasia*.
2. Hypochondroplasia – AD. Large calvarium, short stature and long fibula.
3. Pseudohypoparathyroidism* and pseudopseudohypoparathyroidism*.
4. Diastrophic dwarfism.
5. Kniest syndrome.
6. Acrodysostosis.

2.20 Widened Interpedicular Distance

Most easily appreciated by comparison with adjacent vertebrae. ± flattening of the inner side of the pedicles.

1. **Meningomyelocele** – fusiform distribution of widened interpedicular distances with the greatest separation at the midpoint of the involved segment. Disc spaces are narrowed and bodies appear to be widened. Spinous processes and laminae are not identifiable. Facets may be fused into a continuous mass. Scoliosis (congenital or developmental) in 50–70% of cases ± kyphosis.
2. **Intraspinal mass** (q.v.) – especially ependymoma.
3. **Diastematomyelia** – 50% occur between L1 and L3; 25% between T7 and T12. Widened interpedicular distances are common but not necessarily at the same level as the spur. The spur is visible in 33% of cases and extends from the neural arch forward. Laminar fusion associated with a neural arch defect at the same or adjacent level are important signs in predicting the presence of diastematomyelia. ± associated meningocele, neurenteric cyst or dermoid.

2.21 Intraspinal Masses

Mass lesions in the spinal canal are classified as extradural, intradural, and intramedullary in situation. Techniques for demonstration include plain radiography (to show secondary bony changes), myelography (obsolescent but much used in areas of inadequate MRI provision), CT (of limited value but may show bone changes, calcification, and contrast uptake), and MRI which is the definitive method at the present time.

The nature of an intraspinal mass may be partly elucidated by myelography, which allows the above subclassification to be made:

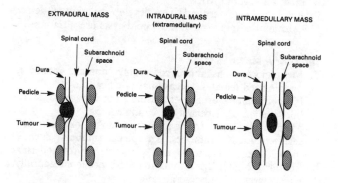

Extradural Mass

1. **Prolapsed or sequestrated intervertebral disc** – occurs at all levels. Usually extradural, but occasionally penetrates dura, especially in thoracic region. May calcify, especially thoracic disc prolapse.
2. **Metastases**, myeloma and lymphoma deposits – common; look for associated vertebral infiltration, destruction in body or neural arch, collapse, paravertebral mass, other bone lesions, evidence of primary tumour.
3. **Neurofibroma** – solitary, or multiple in neurofibromatosis. Lateral indentation of theca at the level of the intervertebral foramen.

(continued)

4. **Neuroblastoma and ganglioneuroma** – tumours of childhood arising in adrenal or sympathetic chain, close to spine: direct invasion of spinal canal may occur.
5. **Meningioma** – may be extradural, but most are largely intradural (see below). Commonest site is thoracic, middle aged females predominate.
6. **Haematoma** – may be due to trauma, dural AVM, anticoagulant therapy, some spontaneous. Long segment extradural mass on myelography, postmyelogram – CT, or MRI, which may show signal characteristics of blood.
7. **Abscess** – usually secondary to disc or vertebral sepsis. Long segment extradural mass, with marginal enhancement on CT and MRI.
8. **Arachnoid cyst** – secondary to developmental dural defect. Uncommon, most spinal arachnoid cysts are intradural.

Intradural Mass
1. **Meningioma** – as above commonly thoracic, mainly in middle-aged females. Occasional calcification.
2. **Neurofibroma** – usually extradural, but intradural neurofibromas occur, especially in cauda equina.
3. **Metastases** – from remote primary tumours, or due to CSF seeding in CNS tumours, e.g. pineal tumours, ependymoma, medulloblastoma and primitive neuroectodermal tumour (PNET). Lymphoma may also occur intradurally, particularly in lumbosacral canal.
4. **Subdural empyema.**

Intramedullary Mass
1. **Ependymoma** – can occur anywhere in spinal canal, but commonest at conus and in lumbar canal (from filum terminale). Very slow growing, and bone remodelling is often seen with expansion of the spinal canal. Best shown on MRI: high signal mass on T_2W images, low on T_1W, but with enhancement. Associated cord cavitation may occur.
2. **Astrocytoma** – commonest intramedullary tumour. Appearances similar to ependymoma, but faster growing, and bone changes not a feature.

3. **Dermoid** (including lipoma, teratoma) – most commonly seen in conus medullaris. Different tissue elements include lipomatous tissue: low attenuation on CT, bright on T_1W MRI, cystic spaces (low attenuation on CT, low signal on T_1W, high on T_2W MRI), and soft tissue (intermediate density on CT, and intermediate signal on T_1W MRI, enhancing after gadolinium).
4. **Infarct** – expanding in acute phase.
5. **Haematoma** – cord swelling only on CT, but features of blood on MRI.

3
Joints

with contributions by Mark Davies

3.1 Monoarthritis

1. **Trauma** – pointers to the diagnosis are (a) the history, (b) the presence of a fracture and (c) a joint effusion, especially a lipohaemarthrosis.
2. **Osteoarthritis** – including the late complication of avascular necrosis.
3. **Crystal induced arthritis**
   (a) Gout*.
   (b) Calcium pyrophosphate dihydrate deposition disease*.
   (c) Calcium hydroxyapatite deposition disease.
4. **Rheumatoid arthritis*** – occasionally. Also juvenile chronic arthritis.
5. **Pyogenic arthritis** – commonest joints affected are the hip, knee and small joints of the hands and feet. 15% of those due to *Staphylococcus aureus* and 80% of those of gonococcal aetiology involve two or more joints. The joint may be radiologically normal at first clinical examination. Initially there is soft-tissue swelling due to effusion and synovial enlargement. Periarticular erosions progress to involve all of the articular cartilage and subchondral bone. Periosteal reaction. Osteoporosis follows the destructive changes.
6. **Tuberculous arthritis** – sometimes associated with pulmonary or renal tuberculosis. Similar sites of predilection to pyogenic arthritis. Insidious onset with radiological changes present at the time of first examination. Slowly developing osteoporosis precedes the destructive changes. Erosions first develop at peripheral non-contact points of the joint.
7. **Pigmented villonodular synovitis** – most commonly at the knee.

8. Sympathetic – a joint effusion can occur as a response to a tumour in the adjacent bone.
9. Neuropathic arthropathy*.

3.2 The Major Polyarthritides

Inflammatory		Chondropathic		Depositional
Periarticular (synovial) erosions Osteoporosis Tendon-related erosions Periosteal reaction Syndesmophytes Malalignment		Subchondral erosions Subchondral sclerosis Osteophytes Chondrocalcinosis Normal bone density		Soft-tissue masses Extra-articular erosions – well defined – roofed – mass-related Normal bone density
Rheumatoid and its variants	*Seronegative*	*Degenerative*	*Metabolic*	
Symmetrical Small joints – esp. MCPJ and PIPJ Osteoporosis	Asymmetrical Large joints – SIJs, spine and DIPJs of hand Osteoporosis less marked Periosteal reaction Syndesmophytes	Weight bearing joints, DIPJs and first CMCJs Localized cartilage loss Marginal calcification	Atypical distribution Uniform cartilage loss Diffuse chondrocalcinosis Large subchondral cysts Greater destruction	
Rheumatoid arthritis Systemic lupus erythematosus Scleroderma Dermatomyositis	Ankylosing spondylitis Reiter's syndrome Psoriatic arthropathy Enteropathic arthritis Juvenile chronic arthritis	Osteoarthritis Neuropathic Haemophilic	Calcium pyrophosphate Haemochromatosis Alkaptonuria Hyperparathyroidism Wilson's disease	Gout Hypercholesterolaemia Reticulohistiocytosis Amyloidosis

3.3 Arthritis with Osteoporosis

1. Rheumatoid arthritis*.
2. Juvenile chronic arthritis.
3. Systemic lupus erythematosus*.
4. Pyogenic arthritis.
5. Reiter's syndrome* – in the acute phase.
6. Scleroderma*.
7. Haemophilia*.

3.4 Arthritis with Preservation of Bone Density

1. Osteoarthritis.
2. Calcium pyrophosphate arthropathy – see Calcium pyro-phosphate dihydrate deposition disease*.
3. Gout*.
4. Psoriatic arthropathy*.
5. Ankylosing spondylitis.
6. Reiter's syndrome* – in chronic or recurrent disease.
7. Neuropathic arthropathy* – especially in the spine and lower extremities.
8. Pigmented villonodular synovitis.

3.5 Arthritis with a Periosteal Reaction

1. Juvenile chronic arthritis*.
2. Reiter's syndrome*.
3. Pyogenic arthritis.
4. Psoriatic arthropathy*.
5. Rheumatoid arthritis* – in less than 5% of patients.
6. Hypertrophic osteoarthropathy.
7. Haemophilia*.
8. AIDS associated arthritis.

3.6   Arthritis with Preserved or Widened Joint Space

1. **Early infective or inflammatory arthritis** – because of joint effusion.
2. **Psoriatic arthropathy*** – due to deposition of fibrous tissue.
3. **Acromegaly*** – due to cartilage overgrowth.
4. **Gout*.**
5. **Pigmented villonodular synovitis.**

3.7   Arthritis with Soft-tissue Nodules

1. **Gout*.**
2. **Rheumatoid arthritis*.**
3. **Pigmented villonodular synovitis.**
4. **Multicentric reticulohistocytosis.**
5. **Amyloidosis.**
6. **Sarcoidosis*.**

3.8   Arthritis Mutilans

A destructive arthritis of the hands and feet with resorption of bone ends and telescoping joints (main-en-lorgnette).

1. **Rheumatoid arthritis*.**
2. **Juvenile chronic arthritis*.**
3. **Psoriatic arthropathy*.**
4. **Diabetes.**
5. **Leprosy.**
6. **Neuropathic arthropathy*.**
7. **Reiter's syndrome*** – in the feet.

3.9 Diffuse Terminal Phalangeal Sclerosis

1. **Normal variant** – in 10% of normal individuals.
2. **Rheumatoid arthritis*** – most commonly in association with erosive arthropathy but may occur in its absence.
3. **Scleroderma***.
4. **Systemic lupus erythematosus***.
5. **Sarcoidosis***.

Further Reading
Goodman N. (1967) The significance of terminal phalangeal osteo-sclerosis. *Radiology*, 89: 709–12.
Williams M. & Barton E. (1984) Terminal phalangeal sclerosis in rheumatoid arthritis. *Clin. Radiol.*, 35: 237–8.

3.10 Erosion (Enlargement) of the Intercondylar Notch of the Distal Femur

1. **Juvenile chronic arthritis***.
2. **Haemophilia***.
3. **Psoriatic arthropathy***.
4. **Tuberculous arthritis**.
5. **Rhematoid arthritis***.

3.11 Plantar Calcaneal Spur

1. **Idiopathic**.
2. **Diffuse idiopathic skeletal hyperostosis (DISH)**.
3. **Ankylosing spondylitis***.
4. **Psoriatic arthropathy***.
5. **Reiter's syndrome***.
6. **Rheumatoid arthritis***.

3.12 Calcified Loose Body (Single or Multiple) in a Joint

1. **Detached osteophyte** – larger and more variable in size than synovial osteochondromata. Other signs of degenerative arthritis.
2. **Osteochondral fracture.**
3. **Osteochondritis dissecans** – most commonly the knee, talus and elbow. A corresponding defect in the parent bone may be visible.
4. **Neuropathic arthropathy*** – joint disorganization.
5. **Synovial osteochondromatosis** – knee most commonly; hip, ankle, wrist and shoulder less commonly. Multiple small nodules of fairly uniform size. Faintly calcified initially; later ossified. Secondary erosion of intracapsular bone, joint-space narrowing and osteophyte formation may occur later in the disease.

3.13 Calcification of Articular (Hyaline) Cartilage (Chondrocalcinosis)

1. **Calcium pyrophosphate dihydrate deposition disease***.
2. **Hyperparathyroidism***.
3. **Haemochromatosis***.
4. **Acromegaly***.
5. **Gout***.
6. **Wilson's disease.**

Further Reading
Jensen P. (1988) Chondrocalcinosis and other calcifications. *Radiol. Clin. North Am.*, 26: 1315–25.

3.14 Sacroiliitis

1. Changes initially in the lower and middle thirds of the joint and the iliac side is more severely affected than the sacral side.
2. Periarticular osteoporosis, superficial erosions and sclerosis of subchondral bone.
3. Further erosion leads to widening of the joint space.
4. Subchondral sclerosis progresses to bony ankylosis.
5. Eventual return of the bones to normal density.

The most typical patterns of distribution are:

Bilateral Symmetrical

1. **Ankylosing spondylitis*** – may be asymmetrical early in the disease. Radiological signs as above.
2. **Inflammatory bowel disease** – ulcerative colitis, Crohn's disease and Whipple's disease. Identical appearances to ankylosing spondylitis.
3. **Psoriatic arthropathy*** – ankylosis is less frequent than in ankylosing spondylitis. Occurs in 30–50% of patients with arthropathy. Less commonly is asymmetrical or unilateral.
4. **Osteitis condensans ilii** – predominantly in young, multiparous women. A triangular segment of bone sclerosis on the inferior aspect of the iliac side of the joint is associated with a well-defined joint margin and a normal joint space.
5. **Hyperparathyroidism*** – subchondral bone resorption and joint-space widening only.
6. **Paraplegia** – joint-space narrowing and osteoporosis.

Bilateral Asymmetrical

1. **Reiter's syndrome***.
2. **Psoriatic arthropathy*** – this pattern in 40% of cases.
3. **Rheumatoid arthritis*** – rare. Minimal sclerosis and no significant bony ankylosis.
4. **Gouty arthritis** (see Gout*) – large well-defined erosions with surrounding sclerosis.
5. **Osteoarthritis** – the articular margins are smooth and well defined. Joint-space narrowing, subchondral sclerosis and anterior osteophytes are observed.

Unilateral

1. **Infection.**

3.15   Protrusio Acetabuli

1. **Rheumatoid arthritis*** – including juvenile chronic arthritis.
2. **Osteoporosis** (q.v.).
3. **Osteomalacia and rickets** (q.v.)*.
4. **Paget's disease***.
5. **Ankylosing spondylitis***.
6. **Osteoarthritis** – occasionally.
7. **Trauma** – acetabular fractures.
8. **Familial or idiopathic.**
9. **Marfan's syndrome*** – 45% show evidence of protrusio acetabuli. Of these, 50% are unilateral and 90% have an associated scoliosis.

Further Reading

Kuhlman J.E., Scott W.W., Fishman E.K., Pyeritz R.E. & Siegelman S.S. (1987) Acetabular protrusion in the Marfan Syndrome. *Radiology*, 164: 415–17.

3.16 Widening of the Symphysis Pubis

> 10 mm in the newborn.
> 9 mm at age 3 years.
> 8 mm 7 years and over.

Acquired

1. **Pregnancy** – resolves by the 3rd post-partum month.
2. **Trauma.**
3. **Osteitis pubis** – one or more months following parturition or pelvic surgery, especially prostatic surgery. It may also be observed as a chronic stress reaction in athletes. Symmetrical bone resorption with subchondral bony irregularity and sclerosis. Ankylosis may be a late finding.
4. **Osteolytic metastases.**
5. **Infection** – low-grade osteomyelitis shows similar radiological features to osteitis pubis.
6. **Ankylosing spondylitis* and rheumatoid arthritis*** – early in the disease.
7. **Hyperparathyroidism*** – due to subperiosteal bone resorption.

Congenital

WITH NORMAL OSSIFICATION
1. **Exstrophy of the bladder.**
2. **Epispadias** – the degree of widening correlates well with the severity of the epispadias.
3. **Hypospadias.**
4. **Imperforate anus with recto-vaginal fistula.**
5. **Urethral duplication.**
6. **Prune belly syndrome.**
7. **Sjögren–Larsson syndrome.**
8. **Goltz syndrome.**

POORLY OSSIFIED CARTILAGE
1. **Achondrogenesis.**
2. **Campomelic dysplasia.**
3. **Chondrodysplasia punctata** (Conradi–Hünermann syndrome).

(*continued*)

POORLY OSSIFIED CARTILAGE (*continued*)
4. Chromosome 4p– syndrome (Wolf's syndrome).
5. Chromosome 9(p+) trisomy syndrome.
6. Cleidocranial dysplasia*.
7. Hypochondrogenesis.
8. Hypophosphatasia.
9. Hypothyroidism*.
10. Larsen syndrome.
11. Pycnodysostosis.
12. Spondyloepimetaphyseal dysplasia.
13. Spondyloepiphyseal dysplasia congenita.

Further Reading

Abramson D., Roberts S.M. & Wilson P.D. (1934) Relaxation of pelvic joints in pregnancy. *Surg. Gynecol. Obstet.*, 58: 595–613.

Cortina H., Vallcanera A., Andres V., Gracia A., Aparici R. & Mari A (1979) The non-ossified pubis. *Pediatr. Radiol.*, 8: 87–92.

Muecke E.C. & Currarino G. (1968) Congenital widening of the symphysis pubis. Associated clinical disorders and roentgen anatomy of affected bony pelves. *Am. J. Roentgenol.*, 103: 179–85.

Patel K. & Chapman S. (1993) Normal symphysis pubis width in children. *Clin. Radiol.*, 47: 56–7.

Taybi H. & Lachman R.S. (1990) *Radiology of Syndromes, Metabolic Disorders, and Skeletal Dysplasias*, 3rd edn, p. 879. Chicago: Year Book Medical Publishers.

Vix V.A. & Ryu C.Y. (1971) The adult symphysis pubis: normal and abnormal. *Am. J. Roentgenol.*, 112: 517–25.

3.17   Fusion or Bridging of the Symphysis Pubis

1. Post-traumatic.
2. Post-infective.
3. Osteitis pubis – see 3.16.
4. Osteoarthritis.
5. Ankylosing spondylitis*.
6. Alkaptonuria*.
7. Fluorosis.

3.18 MRI Signal Intensities in Musculoskeletal Imaging

Tissue	T_1W	Proton density	T_2W	T_2^*
Cortical bone	↓	↓	↓	↓
Bone marrow	↑	↑	Intermediate	↓
Articular cartilage	Intermediate	Intermediate	↓	↑
Fibrocartilage	↓	↓	↓	↓
Ligament/tendon	↓	↓	↓	↓
Fat	↑	↑	Intermediate	↓
Nerve	↓	↓	↓	↓
Muscle	Intermediate	Intermediate	↓	↓
CSF	↓	Intermediate	↑	↑
Annulus fibrosus	↓	↓	↓	↓
Nucleus pulposus	Intermediate	Intermediate	↑	↑

3.19 Intrameniscal Signal Changes on Knee MRI

1. Myxoid degeneration.
2. Meniscal tear.
3. Postoperative scar tissue.

Pitfalls

1. Popliteus tendon sheath.
2. Posterior ligaments of Humphry and Wrisberg.
3. Transverse ligaments.
4. Truncation artefact.

4
Respiratory Tract

4.1 Acute Upper Airway Obstruction

Most commonly in infants, because of the small calibre of the airways. Small or normal volume lungs with distension of the upper airway proximal to the obstruction during inspiration.

1. **Choanal atresia** – bilateral (33%) or unilateral, bony (90%) or membranous, complete or incomplete. When bilateral and complete presentation is with severe respiratory distress at birth. Incomplete obstruction is associated with respiratory difficulty during feeding. Diagnosis is by failure to pass a catheter through the nose and nasopharyngography or CT.
2. **Laryngo-tracheobronchitis** – narrowing of the glottic and subglottic regions. Indistinct tracheal margin because of oedema.
3. **Acute epiglottitis** – the epiglottis is swollen and may be shortened. Other components of the supraglottic region – aryepiglottic folds, arytenoids, uvula and prevertebral soft tissues – are also swollen. The hypopharynx and pyriform sinuses are distended with air.
4. **Retropharyngeal abscess** – enlargement of the prevertebral soft tissues which may contain gas or an air fluid level.
5. **Oedema** – due to angio-oedema (allergic, anaphylactic or hereditary), inhalation of noxious gases or trauma. Predominantly laryngeal oedema.
6. **Foreign body** – more commonly produces a major bronchial occlusion rather than upper airway obstruction.
7. **Retropharyngeal haemorrhage** – due to trauma, neck surgery, direct carotid arteriography and bleeding disorders. Widening of the retropharyngeal soft-tissue space.

4.2 Chronic Upper Airway Obstruction in a Child

May be associated with overinflation of the lungs.

Nasal

1. **Choanal atresia** – bilateral (33%) or unilateral, bony (90%) or membranous, complete or incomplete. When bilateral and complete presentation is with severe respiratory distress at birth. Incomplete obstruction is associated with respiratory difficulty during feeding. Diagnosis is by failure to pass a catheter through the nose and nasopharyngography or CT.
2. **Nasal angiofibroma** – adolescent males. Symptoms of nasal obstruction and/or epistaxis. Plain films may show (1) anterior bowing of the posterior wall of the maxillary antrum, (2) deviation of the nasal septum and (3) a nasopharyngeal soft-tissue mass with erosion of contiguous bony structures.
3. **Antrochoanal polyp.**

Supraglottic

1. **Grossly enlarged tonsils and adenoids.**
2. **Laryngomalacia** – presents at or shortly after birth, persists for several months and usually resolves by 2 years. Diagnosis is confirmed by direct laryngoscopy but fluoroscopy reveals anterior motion of the aryepiglottic folds and distenion of the hypopharynx.
3. **Micrognathia** – in the Pierre Robin syndrome.
4. **Cysts** – of the epiglottis or aryepiglottic folds. The degree of obstruction depends on the size and location.

Glottic

1. **Laryngeal polyp, papilloma or cyst.**

(*continued*)

Subglottic and Tracheal

1. **Tracheomalacia** – weakness of tracheal wall which may be primary or secondary:

   PRIMARY   Premature infants – probably related to intubation.

   Normal infants.

   SECONDARY With innominate artery compression – persistent narrowing of the anterior tracheal wall at the level of the thoracic inlet.

   With tracheo-oesophageal fistula/oesophageal atresia.

   With vascular ring – most commonly a double aortic arch.

   With external compression by tumour etc.

2. **Subglottic hemangioma** – the most common subglottic soft-tissue mass in infancy. Occurs before 6 months. 50% have associated cutaneous haemangiomas. Characteristically it produces an asymmetrical narrowing of the subglottic airway.

3. **Following prolonged tracheal intubation** – see 4.3.

4. **External compression from other mediastinal structures** – e.g. lymphadenopathy or thymic enlargement.

5. **Respiratory papillomatosis** – occurs anywhere from the nose to the lungs. Irregular soft-tissue masses around the glottis or in the trachea mostly. (Papillomata in adults are usually single.)

Further Reading

Kushner, D.C. & Clifton Harris, G.B. (1978) Obstructing lesions of the larynx and trachea in infants and children. *Radiol. Clin. North Am.*, 16: 181–94.

Strife, J.L. (1988) Upper airway and tracheal obstruction in infants and children. *Radiol. Clin. North Am.*, 26: 309–22.

4.3 Chronic Upper Airway Obstruction in an Adult

May be associated with overinflation of the lungs.

Supraglottic
1. **Supraglottic carcinoma of the larynx** – involving the posterior surface of the epiglottis, the ventricle or the superolateral part of the vestibule. Dyspnoea is a late feature.

Glottic
1. **Vocal cord paralysis** – airway obstruction is most likely with bilateral recurrent nerve paresis and this most commonly occurs as a result of a thyroidectomy or malignant disease in the neck.
2. **Carcinoma of the glottis** – accounts for more than two-thirds of laryngeal carcinomas. Occurs mostly in the anterior two-thirds of the cords. Morphologically it can be proliferative or infiltrative.

Subglottic and Tracheal
1. **Extrinsic compression** – due to lymph nodes or local invasion from carcinomas of the bronchus, thyroid or oesophagus.
2. **Following prolonged tracheal intubation** – occurs in 5% of cases. The stenosis occurs most commonly at the level of the stoma. Less common sites are at the level of the inflatable cuff and where the tip impinged on the mucosa.
3. **Infraglottic carcinoma of the larynx** – either arising *de novo* at this site or as an extension from a glottic growth.
4. **Tracheal malignancy** – squamous cell carcinoma is the commonest tracheal primary.

Further Reading
Weber A.L. (ed.) (1978) The larynx and trachea. *Radiol. Clin. North Am.*, 16 (2).

4.4 Unequal Lung Size, Lucency and Vascularity. Which is the Abnormal Side?

If Vascularity is Decreased, the Lung is Abnormal

If Vascularity is Normal or Increased, the Lung is Probably Normal

A Small Completely Opaque Hemithorax is Abnormal
When the small hemithorax is *completely* opaque the diagnosis is total collapse or agenesis. Furthermore the atelectasis can be presumed to be resorptive (i.e. secondary to obstruction) rather than compressive (i.e. from an overdistended contralateral lung) because *on the fully inspired film* an overexpanded lung will never compress the other lung to the extent of obliterating the costophrenic angle.

With Inspiration – Expiration, the Lung Changing Least or Not at All, is Abnormal

Further Reading
Swischuk L.E. (1984) *Differential Diagnosis in Paediatric Radiology*, pp. 7–12. Baltimore: Williams & Wilkins.

4.5 Unilateral Hypertransradiant Hemithorax

Exclude *contralateral* increased density, e.g. pleural effusion in a supine patient or pleural thickening.

Rotation
1. Poor technique } the hypertransradiant hemithorax is the
2. Scoliosis } side to which the patient is turned.

Chest Wall
1. **Mastectomy** – absent breast ± absent pectoral muscle shadows.
2. **Poliomyelitis** – atrophy of pectoral muscles ± atrophic changes in the shoulder girdle and humerus.
3. **Poland's syndrome** – unilateral congenital absence of pectoral muscles ± rib defects. Occurs in 10% of patients with syndactyly.

Pleura
1. **Pneumothorax** – note the lung edge and absent vessels peripherally.

Lung
1. **Compensatory emphysema** – following lobectomy (rib defects and opaque bronchial sutures indicate previous surgery) or lobar collapse.
2. **Obstructive emphysema** – due to bronchial stenosis or occlusion (q.v.). Air trapping on expiration results in increased lung volume and shift of the mediastinum to the contralateral side.
3. **Unilateral bullae** – vessels are absent rather than attenuated. May mimic pneumothorax.
4. **Macleod's syndrome** – the late sequela of childhood bronchiolitis. Small lung with small main and peripheral arteries. Air trapping occurs on expiration. Decreased number of bronchial divisions (5–10).
5. **Congenital lobar emphysema** – one-third present at birth. Marked overinflation of a lobe, most commonly the left upper lobe, right upper lobe or right middle lobe. The ipsilateral lobes are compressed and there is mediastinal displacement to the contralateral side.

Pulmonary Vessels
1. **Pulmonary embolus** (see Pulmonary embolic disease*) – to a major pulmonary artery (at least lobar in size). The pulmonary artery is dilated proximally and the affected lung shows moderate loss of volume.

4.6 Bilateral Hyertransradiant Hemithoraces

With Overexpansion of the Lungs

1. **Chronic obstructive emphysema** – with large central pulmonary arteries and peripheral arterial pruning. ± bullae.
2. **Asthma** – overinflation is secondary to bronchial constriction and mucus plugs.
3. **Acute bronchiolitis** – particularly affects children in the first year of life. Overexpansion is due to bronchial obstruction, secondary to mucosal swelling and this produces bronchial wall thickening on the radiograph. Collapse or consolidation are not a primary feature of the condition but are frequent complications of it.
4. **Tracheal, laryngeal or bilateral bronchial stenoses** (see 4.7).

With Normal or Small Lungs

1. **Congenital heart disease producing oligaemia** – includes those conditions with right heart obstruction and right-to-left shunts. The hila are usually small except when there is post-stenotic dilatation of the pulmonary artery.
2. **Pulmonary artery stenosis** – if due to valvar stenosis there will be post-stenotic dilatation. 60% of congenital lesions have other associated cardiovascular abnormalities.
3. **Multiple pulmonary emboli**
4. **Primary pulmonary hypertension (PPH)**
5. **Schistosomiasis**
6. **Metastatic trophoblastic tumour**

{ identical radiological picture of big hilar vessels with peripheral pruning. History is most important. PPH occurs predominantly in young females and may be familial. Schistosomiasis more usually presents as a diffuse reticulonodular pattern.

Further Reading

Hodson M.E., Simon G. & Batten J.C. (1974) Radiology of uncomplicated asthma. *Thorax*, 29: 296–303.
Thurlbeck W.M. & Simon G. (1978) Radiographic appearance of the chest in emphysema. *Am. J. Roentgenol.*, 130: 427–40.

4.7 Bronchial Stenosis or Occlusion

In the Lumen
1. **Foreign body** – air trapping is more common than atelectasis. The lower lobe is most frequently affected. The foreign body may be opaque.
2. **Mucus plug** – in asthma or cystic fibrosis.
3. **Misplaced endotracheal tube.**
4. **Aspergillosis** – with thickened bronchial walls.

In the Wall
1. **Carcinoma of the bronchus** – tapered narrowing ± irregularity.
2. **Bronchial adenoma** – usually a smooth, rounded filling defect, convex toward the hilum.
3. **Sarcoid granuloma.**
4. **Fibrosis** – e.g. tuberculosis and fungi. Can mimic carcinoma but usually produces a longer constriction.
5. **Bronchial atresia** – most commonly the apico-posterior segment of the left upper lobe.
6. **Fractured bronchus.**

Outside the Wall
1. **Lymph nodes**
2. **Mediastinal tumour**
3. **Enlarged left atrium** } smooth, eccentric narrowing.
4. **Aortic aneurysm**
5. **Anomalous origin of left pulmonary artery from right pulmonary artery** – producing compression of the right main bronchus as it passes over it, between the trachea and oesophagus to reach the left hilum. PA chest X-ray shows the right side of the trachea to be indented and the vessel is seen end-on between the trachea and oesophagus on the lateral view.

4.8   Increased Density of a Hemithorax

With Central Mediastinum

1. **Consolidation** – ± air bronchogram. Includes pneumonia, unilateral oedema (see 4.18), aspiration pneumonia and radiation pneumonitis.
2. **Pleural effusion** – when the patient is supine a small or moderate effusion gravitates posteriorly producing a generalized increased density with an apical cap of fluid. Erect or decubitus films confirm the diagnosis.
3. **Mesothelioma** – often associated with a pleural effusion which obscures the tumour. Encasement of the lung limits mediastinal shift. ± pleural calcification.

With Mediastinal Displacement away from the Dense Hemithorax

1. **Pleural effusion** (q.v.) – NB a large effusion with no mediastinal shift implies underlying collapse which, in an older person, is often secondary to a bronchial carcinoma.
2. **Diaphragmatic hernia** – on the right side with herniated liver; on the left side the hemithorax is not usually opaque because of air within the herniated bowel. The left hemithorax may be opaque in the early neonatal period when air has not yet had time to reach the herniated bowel.

With Mediastinal Displacement towards the Dense Hemithorax

1. **Collapse.**
2. **Post-pneumonectomy** – rib resection ± opaque bronchial sutures.
3. **Lymphangitis carcinomatosa** – unilateral disease is uncommon. Linear and nodular opacities ± ipsilateral hilar and mediastinal lymphadenopathy. Septal lines.
4. **Pulmonary agenesis and hypoplasia** – usually asymptomatic. Absent or hypoplastic pulmonary artery.

NB   70% of unilateral diffuse *lung* opacities involve the right lung. Pneumonia, aspiration, pulmonary oedema, lymphangitis carcinomatosa and radiotherapy account for 90% (Youngberg, 1977).

Further Reading
Youngberg A.S. (1977) Unilateral diffuse lung opacity. *Radiology*,
    123: 277–82.

4.9 Pneumatoceles

One or more air-filled, thin-walled 'cysts'. They are usually
infective in origin and are thought to result from a check
valve obstruction of a communication between a cavity and
a bronchus. They appear during the first 2 weeks of the
pneumonia and resolve within several months. They may
contain fluid levels.

Infections
1. *Staphylococcus aureus* – a characteristic feature of child-
    hood staphylococcal pneumonia, developing in 40–60%
    of cases.
2. *Streptococcus pneumoniae.*
3. *Escherichia coli.*
4. *Klebsiella pneumoniae.*
5. *Haemophilus influenzae.*
6. *Pneumocystis carinii* – usually multiple and in the upper
    parts of the lungs. Patients with cysts are more likely to
    suffer pneumothorax.
7. *Legionella pneumophila* (Legionnaire's disease).

Traumatic
1. **Interstitial emphysema** – may be followed by thin-walled,
    air-containing cysts.

Neoplastic
1. **Following treatment of pulmonary metastases** – bladder
    cancer and germ cell tumours. May be visible only on CT.

Further Reading
Charig M.J. & Williams M.P. (1990) Pulmonary lacunae: sequelae
    of metastases following chemotherapy. *Clin. Radiol.*, 42: 93–6.
Chow C., Templeton P.A. & White C.S. (1993) Lung cysts associated
    with *Pneumocystis carinii* pneumonia. *Am. J. Roentgenol.*,
    161: 527–31.

4.10   Slowly Resolving or Recurrent Pneumonia

1. **Bronchial obstruction** – especially neoplasm or foreign body.
2. **Inappropriate chemotherapy** – especially for tuberculosis, *Klebsiella* and mycoses.
3. **Repeated aspiration**
   (a) Pharyngeal pouch.
   (b) Achalasia.
   (c) Scleroderma*.
   (d) Hiatus hernia.
   (e) 'H'-type tracheo-oesophageal fistula.
   (f) Paralytic or neuromuscular disorders.
   (g) Chronic sinusitis.
4. **Underlying lung pathology**
   (a) Abscess.
   (b) Bronchiectasis – see 4.14.
   (c) Cystic fibrosis*.
5. **Immunological incompetence**
   (a) Cachexia.
   (b) Steroids and immunosuppressives.
   (c) Diabetes.
   (d) White-cell and immunoglobulin deficiency states.
6. **Pneumonias that resolve by fibrosis**
   (a) Tuberculosis.
   (b) Fungi.

4.11   Pneumonia with an Enlarged Hilum

Hilar lymph-node enlargement may be secondary to the pneumonia or pneumonia may be secondary to bronchial obstruction by a hilar mass. Signs suggestive of a secondary pneumonia are:
  (a) Segmental or lobar consolidation which is better defined than a primary pneumonia.
  (b) Slow resolution.
  (c) Recurrent consolidation in the same part of the lung.
  (d) Associated collapse.

Secondary Pneumonias
See 4.7, but note particularly 'Carcinoma of the bronchus'.

Primary Pneumonias
1. **Primary tuberculosis** – lymph-node enlargement is unilateral in 80% and involves the hilar (60%), or combined hilar and paratracheal (40%) nodes.
2. **Viral pneumonias.**
3. **Mycoplasma** – lymph-node enlargement is common in children but rare in adults. May be uni- or bilateral.
4. **Primary histoplasmosis** – in endemic areas. Hilar lymphadenopathy is common, particularly in children. During healing the lymph nodes calcify and may cause bronchial obstruction thereby initiating distal infection.
5. **Coccidioidomycosis** – in endemic areas. The pneumonic type consists of predominantly lower lobe consolidation which is frequently associated with hilar lymph-node enlargement.

See also 4.30.

4.12   Lobar Pneumonia

Consolidation involving the air spaces of an anatomically recognizable lobe. The entire lobe may not be involved and there may be a degree of associated collapse.

1. *Streptococcus pneumoniae* – the commonest cause. Usually unilobar. Cavitation rare. Pleural effusion is uncommon. Little or no collapse.
2. *Klebsiella pneumoniae* – often multilobar involvement. Great propensity for cavitation and lobar enlargement.
3. *Staphylococcus aureus* – especially in children. 40–60% of children develop pneumatoceles. Effusion (empyema) and pneumothorax are also common. Bronchopleural fistula may develop. No lobar predilection.
4. **Tuberculosis** – in primary or post-primary tuberculosis, but more common in the former. Associated collapse is common. The right lung is affected twice as often as the left and primary tuberculosis predilects the anterior segment of the upper lobe or the medial segment of the middle lobe.
5. *Streptococcus pyogenes* – affects the lower lobes predominantly. Often associated with pleural effusion.

4.13   Consolidation with Bulging of Fissures

Homogeneous or inhomogeneous air-space opacification with bulging of the bounding fissures.

1. **Infection with abundant exudates** – *Klebsiella pneumoniae* (Friedländer's pneumonia), *Streptococcus pneumoniae*, *Mycobacterium tuberculosis* and *Yersinia pestis* (plague pneumonia).
2. **Abscess** – when an area of consolidation breaks down. Organisms which commonly produce abscesses are *Staphylococcus aureus*, *Klebsiella* spp. and other Gram-negative organisms.
3. **Carcinoma of the bronchus** – this can fill and expand a lobe.

4.14 Bronchiectasis

1. Peribronchial thickening and retained secretions.
2. Crowded vessels, i.e. loss of volume.
3. Compensatory emphysema.
4. Cystic spaces ± air fluid levels.
5. Coarse honeycomb pattern in very severe disease.
6. Normal radiograph in 7%.

1. **Secondary to childhood infections** – especially measles and pertussis.
2. **Secondary to bronchial obstruction** – foreign body, neoplasm, mucus plugs (cystic fibrosis and asthma) and aspergillosis.
3. **Chronic aspiration.**
4. **Congenital structural defects.**
   (a) Kartagener's syndrome – bronchiectasis with immobile cilia, dextrocardia and absent frontal sinuses. 5% of patients with dextrocardia will eventually develop bronchiectasis.
   (b) Williams–Campbell syndrome – bronchial cartilage deficiency.
5. **Immune deficiency states** – e.g. hypogammaglobulinaemia, chronic granulomatous disease and Chédiak–Higashi syndrome.

4.15 Widespread Air-space (Acinar) Disease

This is commonly referred to as alveolar shadowing but the term is incorrect because the lung densities are due to the anatomically larger acinus. The general term 'air-space' shadow, nodule or disease is recommended. The signs of air-space disease are:

1. Acinar nodules, 4–10 mm diameter.
2. Ill-defined margins.
3. Coalescence.
4. Mostly non-segmental.
5. Air bronchogram. NB This sign may also be a feature of relaxation atelectasis (e.g. collapsed lung behind a large pneumothorax), cicatrization atelectasis (e.g. bronchiectasis and radiation fibrosis) and adhesive atelectasis (e.g. acute radiation pneumonitis and hyaline membrane disease).
6. Air bronchiologram and alveologram – lucencies due to residual air in bronchioles and alveoli.

1. **Oedema** (see 4.17).
2. **Pneumonia** – most often the unusual types
   (a) Tuberculosis.
   (b) Histoplasmosis.
   (c) *Pneumocystis carinii*.
   (d) Influenza – particularly in patients with mitral stenosis or who are pregnant.
   (e) Chicken pox – may be confluent in the central areas of the lungs. ± hilar lymph-node enlargement.
   (f) Other viral pneumonias.
3. **Haemorrhage**
   (a) Trauma (contusion).
   (b) Anticoagulants, haemophilia, leukaemia and disseminated intravascular coagulopathy.
   (c) Goodpasture's syndrome.
   (d) Idiopathic pulmonary haemosiderosis – in the acute stage.
4. **Fat emboli** – 1–2 days post-trauma. Predominantly peripheral. Resolves in 1–4 weeks.
5. **Alveolar cell carcinoma** – effusions are common. Mediastinal lymph nodes are uncommon. Diagnosis by sputum cytology or lung biopsy.

6. **Haematogenous metastases** – especially chorioncarcinoma. Others are rare.
7. **Lymphoma*** – usually with hilar or mediastinal lymphadenopathy.
8. **Sarcoidosis*** – often associated with a reticulonodular pattern elsewhere.
9. **Löffler's** – peripheral ('reversed bat's wing'), often in the upper zones.

Further Reading

Fraser R.G., Peter Paré J.A., Paré P.D., Fraser R.S. & Genereux G.P. (1988) *Diagnosis of Diseases of the Chest*, pp. 459–72. Philadelphia: Saunders.

4.16 Localized Air-space Disease

See 4.15.

1. **Pneumonia.**
2. **Infarction** (see Pulmonary embolic disease*) – usually in the lower lobes. Often indistinguishable from pneumonia.
3. **Contusion** – ± rib fractures or other signs of trauma.
4. **Oedema** (see 4.17).
5. **Radiation** – several weeks following radiotherapy. May have a straight margin, corresponding to the field of treatment.
6. **Alveolar cell carcinoma.**
7. **Lymphoma*.**

4.17 Pulmonary Oedema

1. **Heart failure.**
2. **Fluid overload** – excess i.v. fluids, renal failure and excess hypertonic fluids, e.g. contrast media.
3. **Cerebral disease** – cerebrovascular accident, head injury or raised intracranial pressure.
4. **Near drowning** – radiologically no significant differences between fresh-water and sea-water drowning.
5. **Aspiration (Mendelson's syndrome).**
6. **Radiotherapy** – several weeks following treatment. May have a characteristic straight edge.
7. **Rapid re-expansion of lung following thoracentesis.**
8. **Liver disease and other causes of hypoproteinaemia.**
9. **Transfusion reaction.**
10. **Drugs**
    (a) Those which induce cardiac arrhythmias or depress myocardial contractility.
    (b) Those which alter pulmonary capillary wall permeability, e.g. overdoses of heroin, morphine, methadone, dextropropoxyphene and aspirin. Hydrochlorothiazide, phenylbutazone, aspirin and nitrofurantoin can cause oedema as an idiosyncratic response.

    NB Contrast media can induce arrhythmias, alter capillary wall permeability and produce a hyperosmolar load.
11. **Poisons**
    (a) Inhaled – NO_2, SO_2, CO, Phosgene, hydrocarbons and smoke.
    (b) Circulating – paraquat and snake venom.
12. **Mediastinal tumours** – producing venous or lymphatic obstruction.
13. **Shock lung (adult respiratory distress syndrome)** – 24–72 hours post insult.

Further Reading

Milne E.N.C., Pistolesi M., Miniati M. & Giuntini C. (1985) The radiological distinction of cardiogenic and noncardiogenic edema. *Am. J. Roentgenol.*, 144: 879–94.

4.18   Unilateral Pulmonary Oedema

Pulmonary Oedema on the Same Side as a Pre-existing Abnormality
1. Prolonged lateral decubitus position.
2. Unilateral aspiration.
3. Pulmonary contusion.
4. Rapid thoracentesis of air or fluid.
5. Bronchial obstruction.
6. Systemic artery to pulmonary artery shunts – e.g. Waterston (on the right side). Blalock–Taussig (left or right side) and Pott's procedure (on the left side).

Pulmonary Oedema on the Opposite Side to a Pre-existing Abnormality
Oedema on the side opposite a lung with a perfusion defect.
1. Congenital absence or hypoplasia of a pulmonary artery.
2. Macleod's syndrome.
3. Thromboembolism.
4. Unilateral emphysema.
5. Lobectomy.
6. Pleural disease.

Further Reading
Calenoff L., Kruglik G.D. & Woodruff A. (1978) Unilateral pulmonary oedema. *Radiology*, 126: 19–24.

4.19   Septal Lines (Kerley B Lines)

1. Due to visible interlobular lymphatics and their surrounding connective tissue.
2. 1–3 cm long, less than 1 mm thick, extending from and perpendicular to the pleural surface.
3. Best seen in the costophrenic angles.

Pulmonary Venous Hypertension
1. Left ventricular failure.
2. Mitral stenosis.

Lymphatic Obstruction
1. Pneumoconioses – surrounding tissues may contain a heavy metal, e.g. tin, which contributes to the density.
2. Lymphangitis carcinomatosa.
3. Sarcoidosis* – septal lines are uncommon.

4.20 'Honeycomb Lung'

1. A generalized reticular pattern or miliary mottling which when summated produces the appearance of air containing 'cysts' 0.5–2.0 cm in diameter.
2. Obscured pulmonary vasculature.
3. Late appearance of radiological signs after the onset of symptoms.
4. Complications
   (a) pneumothorax is frequent;
   (b) cor pulmonale later in the course of the disease.

1. **Collagen disorders**
   (a) Rheumatoid lung – most pronounced at the bases and may be preceded by basal infiltrates. ± small effusions.
   (b) Scleroderma* – predominantly basal. Less regular 'honeycomb' pattern, which is preceded by fine, linear, basal streaks. Cor pulmonale is unusual.
2. **Extrinsic allergic alveolitis*** – predominantly in the upper zones.
3. **Sarcoidosis*** – sparing of extreme apices. Hilar lymphadenopathy usually resolved by this stage but if present it is a useful sign.
4. **Pneumoconiosis** – particularly frequent in asbestosis*, but also in other reactive dusts.
5. **Cystic bronchiectasis** (see 4.14) – in lower and middle lobes especially. Bronchial-wall thickening. ± localized areas of consolidation.
6. **Cystic fibrosis***.
7. **Drugs** – nitrofurantoin, busulphan, cyclophosphamide, bleomycin and melphalan.
8. **Langerhans cell histiocytosis*** – 'honeycomb' pattern probably always preceded by disseminated nodules. May be predominantly in the mid and upper zones. Cor pulmonale is uncommon.
9. **Tuberous sclerosis*** – lung involvement in 5% of patients. Symptoms first in adult life. Differentiated clinically.
10. **Idiopathic interstitial fibrosis (cryptogenic fibrosing alveolitis)** – no specific differentiating features. More marked in the lower half of the lungs initially and progresses to involve the whole of the lungs.
11. **Neurofibromatosis*** – ± rib notching, 'ribbon' ribs and/or scoliosis. In 10%, but not before adulthood.

4.21 Pneumoconioses

Inorganic Dusts

WITHOUT FIBROSIS
1. **Ferric oxide** – siderosis.
2. **Ferric oxide + silver** – argyrosiderosis.
3. **Tin oxide** – stannosis.
4. **Barium** – barytosis.
5. **Calcium.**

WITH FIBROSIS
1. **Free silica** – silicosis*.
2. **Coal dust** – coal miner's pneumoconiosis*.
3. **Silicates** – asbestosis*, china clay, talc and mica.

WITH CHEMICAL PNEUMONITIS
1. **Beryllium.**
2. **Manganese.**
3. **Vanadium.**
4. **Osmium.**
5. **Cadmium.**

CARCINOGENIC DUSTS
1. **Radioactive dusts** – e.g. uranium.
2. **Asbestos** – see Asbestos inhalation*.
3. **Arsenic.**

Organic Dusts (Extrinsic Allergic Alveolitis)*
1. **Mouldy hay** – farmers' lung.
2. **Bagasse (sugar cane dust)** – bagassosis.
3. **Cotton or linen dust** – byssinosis.
4. **Mouldy vegetable compost** – mushroom workers' lung.
5. **Pigeon and budgerigar excreta** – pigeon breeder's and budgerigar fancier's lung.

Further Reading
Felson B (ed.) (1967) The pneumoconioses. *Semin. Roentgenol.*, 2 (3).
Fraser R.G. & Pare J.A.P. (1975)Extrinsic allergic alveolitis. *Semin. Roentgenol.*, 10: 31–42.
McLoud T.C. (ed.) (1992) Occupational lung disease. *Radiol. Clin. North Am.*, 30 (6).

4.22 Multiple Pin-point Opacities

Must be of very high atomic number to be rendered visible.

1. **Post lymphogram** – iodized oil emboli. Contrast medium may be visible at the site of termination of the thoracic duct.
2. **Silicosis*** – usually larger than pin-point but can be very dense, especially in goldminers.
3. **Stannosis** – inhalation of tin oxide. Even distribution throughout the lungs. With Kerley A and B lines.
4. **Barytosis** – inhalation of barytes. Very dense, discrete opacities. Generalized distribution but bases and apices usually spared.
5. **Limestone and marble workers** – inhalation of calcium.
6. **Alveolar microlithiasis** – familial. Lung detail obscured by miliary calcifications. Few symptoms but may progrss to cor pulmonale eventually. Pleura, heart and diaphragm may be seen as negative shadows.

4.23   Multiple Opacities (0.5–2 mm)

Soft-tissue Density

1. **Miliary tuberculosis** – widespread. Uniform size. Indistinct margins but discrete. No septal lines. Normal hila unless superimposed on primary tuberculosis.
2. **Fungal diseases** – miliary histoplasmosis, coccidioidomycosis, blastomycosis and cryptococcosis (torulosis). Similar appearance to miliary tuberculosis.
3. **Coal miner's pneumoconiosis*** – predominantly mid zones with sparing of the extreme bases and apices. Ill defined and may be arranged in a circle or rosette. Septal lines.
4. **Sarcoidosis*** – predominantly mid zones. Ill defined. Often with enlarged hila.
5. **Acute extrinsic allergic alveolitis*** – micronodulation in all zones, but predominantly basal.
6. **Fibrosing alveolitis** – initially most prominent in the lower halves of the lungs and later spreads upwards. Poorly defined. Obliteration of vascular markings.

Greater than Soft-tissue Density

1. **Haemosiderosis** – secondary to chronic raised venous pressure (seen in 10–15% of patients with mitral stenosis), repeated pulmonary haemorrhage (e.g. Goodpasture's disease) or idiopathic. Septal lines. Smaller than miliary TB.
2. **Silicosis*** – relative sparing of bases and apices. Very well defined and dense when due to pure silica: ill defined and of lower density when due to mixed dusts. Septal lines.
3. **Siderosis** – lower density than silica. Widely disseminated. Asymptomatic.
4. **Stannosis** ⎫
5. **Barytosis** ⎭   see 4.22.

4.24 Multiple Opacities (2–5 mm)

Remaining Discrete

1. **Carcinomatosis** – breast, thyroid, sarcoma, melanoma, prostate, pancreas or bronchus (eroding a pulmonary artery). Variable sizes and progressive increase in size. ± lymphatic obstruction.
2. **Lymphoma*** – nearly always with hilar or mediastinal lymphadenopathy.
3. **Sarcoidosis*** – predominantly mid zones. Often with enlarged hila.

Tending to Confluence and Varying Rapidly

1. **Multifocal pneumonia** – including aspiration pneumonia and tuberculosis.
2. **Pulmonary oedema** (q.v.).
3. **Extrinsic allergic alveolitis*** – predominantly basal.
4. **Fat emboli** – predominantly peripheral.

4.25   Solitary Pulmonary Nodule

Granulomas

1. **Tuberculoma** – more common in the upper lobes and on the right side. Well defined. 0.5–4 cm. 25% are lobulated. Calcification frequent. 80% have satellite lesions. Cavitation is uncommon and when present is small and eccentric. Usually persist unchanged for years.

2. **Histoplasmoma** – in endemic areas (Mississippi and the Atlantic coast of USA). More frequent in the lower lobes. Well-defined. Seldom larger than 3 cm. Calcification is common and may be central producing a target appearance. Cavitation is rare. Satellite lesions are common.

Malignant Neoplasms

1. **Carcinoma of the bronchus** – usually greater than 2 cm. Accounts for less than 15% of all solitary nodules at 40 years: almost 100% at 80 years. Appearances suggesting malignancy are
   (a) Recent appearance or rapid growth (previous CXRs are very helpful here).
   (b) Size greater than 4 cm.
   (c) The lesion crosses a fissure (although some fungus diseases also do so).
   (d) Ill-defined margins.
   (e) Umbilicated or notched margin (if present it indicates malignancy in 80%).
   (f) Corona radiata (spiculation). (But also seen in PMF and granulomas.)
   (g) Peripheral line shadows.
   (h) Calcification is very rare, except in scar carcinomas.

2. **Metastasis** – accounts for 3–5% of asymptomatic nodules. 25% of pulmonary metastases are solitary. Most likely primaries are breast, sarcoma, seminoma and renal cell carcinoma. Predilection for the lung periphery. Calcification is rare but occurs with metastatic osteosarcoma, chondrosarcoma and some other rarer metastases. When considering the diagnosis of pulmonary metastases in children the following points must be borne in mind:
   (a) Unlike adults, it is highly unlikely that there will be an incidental finding of pulmonary metastatic disease.

   (b) The majority of single lung nodules are benign and even in a child with known malignancy one-third of new lung nodules may be benign.

   (c) Multiple lung nodules are more likely to be malignant than a single nodule.

   (d) Therapy usually results in complete resolution of a metastatic nodule but occasionally there may be a residual scar.

3. **Alveolar cell carcinoma** – when localized, a mass is the most common presentation. More commonly ill-defined. Air bronchogram is common. No calcification. Pleural effusion in 5%. Mediastinal lymphadenopathy is much less common than with carcinoma of the bronchus.

Benign Neoplasms

1. **Adenoma** – 90% occur around the hilum: 10% are peripheral. Round or oval and well-defined. 25% present as a solitary nodule; 75% present with the effects of bronchial stenosis. Calcification and cavitation are rare. Histologically, 80–90% are carcinoids and 10–20% are cylindromas. The former may metastasize to bone (sclerotic secondaries) or to liver and may produce the carcinoid syndrome.

2. **Hamartoma** – 96% occur over 40 years. 90% are intrapulmonary and usually within 2 cm of the pleura. 10% produce bronchial stenosis. Usually less than 4 cm diameter. Well-defined. Lobulated rather than smooth. Calcification in 30%, although the incidence increases with the size of the lesion (in 75% when greater than 5 cm). Calcification is 'popcorn', craggy or punctate.

Infections

1. **Pneumonia** – simple consolidation, especially pneumococcal. Air bronchogram.

2. **Hydatid** – in endemic areas. Most common in the lower lobes and more frequent on the right side. Well-defined. 1–10 cm. Solitary in 70%. May have a bizarre shape. Rupture results in the 'water lily' sign.

(continued)

Congenital

1. **Sequestration** – usually more than 6 cm. Two-thirds occur in the left lower lobe, one-third in the right lower lobe and contiguous to the diaphragm. Well-defined, round or oval. Diagnosis confirmed by aortography and venous drainage is via the pulmonary veins (intralobar type) or bronchial veins (extralobar type).
2. **Bronchogenic cyst** – peak incidence in the 2nd and 3rd decades. Two-thirds are intrapulmonary and occur in the medial one-third of the lower lobes. Round or oval. Smooth-walled and well-defined.

Vascular

1. **Pulmonary infarction** (see Pulmonary embolic disease*) – most frequent in the lower lobes. With a pleural effusion and elevation of the hemidiaphragm.
2. **Haematoma** – peripheral, smooth and well-defined. 2–6 cm. Slow resolution over several weeks.
3. **Arteriovenous malformation** – 66% are single. Well-defined, lobulated ('bag of worms'). Tomography may show feeding or draining vessels. Calcification is rare.

4.26 Multiple Pulmonary Nodules (> 5 mm)

Neoplastic

1. **Metastases** – most commonly from breast, thyroid, kidney, gastrointestinal tract and testes. In children, Wilms' tumour, Ewing's sarcoma, neuroblastoma and osteosarcoma. Predilection for lower lobes and more common peripherally. Range of sizes. Well-defined. Ill-definition suggests prostate, breast or stomach. Hilar lymphadenopathy and effusions are uncommon.

Infections

1. **Abscesses** – widespread distribution but asymmetrical. Commonly *Staphylococcus aureus*. Cavitation common. No calcification.
2. **Coccidioidomycosis** – in endemic areas. Well-defined with a predilection for the upper lobes. 0.5–3 cm. Calcification and cavitation may be present.
3. **Histoplasmosis** – in endemic areas. Round, well-defined and few in number. Sometimes calcify. Usually unchanged for many years.
4. **Hydatid** – more common on the right side and in the lower zones. Well defined unless there is surrounding pneumonia. Often 10 cm or more. May rupture and show the 'water lily' sign.

Immunological

1. **Wegener's granulomatosis** – widespread distribution. 0.5–10 cm. Round and well defined. No calcification. Cavitation in 30–50% of cases. ± focal pneumonitis.
2. **Rheumatoid nodules** – peripheral and more common in the lower zones. Round and well-defined. No calcification. Cavitation common.
3. **Caplan's syndrome** – well-defined. Develop rapidly in crops. Calcification and cavitation occur. Background stippling of pneumoconiosis.

(*continued*)

Inhalational

1. **Progressive massive fibrosis** – mid and upper zones. Begin peripherally and move centrally. Peripheral emphysema. Oval in shape. Calcification and cavitation occur. Background nodularity of pneumoconiosis.

Vascular

1. **Arteriovenous malformations** – 33% are multiple. Well-defined. Lobulated. Tomography may show feeding or draining vessels. Calcification is rare.

4.27 Lung Cavities

Infective, i.e. Abscesses

1. *Staphylococcus aureus* – thick-walled with a ragged inner lining. No lobar predilection. Associated with effusion and empyema ± pyopneumothorax – almost invariable in children, not so common in adults. Pneumatoceles (q.v.). Multiple.
2. *Klebsiella pneumoniae* – thick-walled with a ragged inner lining. More common in the upper lobes. Usually single but may be multilocular ± effusion.
3. **Tuberculosis** – thick-walled and smooth. Upper lobes and apical segment of lower lobes mainly. Usually surrounded by consolidation. ± fibrosis.
4. **Aspiration** – look for foreign body, e.g. tooth.
5. **Others** – Gram-negative organisms, actinomycosis, nocardiosis, histoplasmosis, coccidioidomycosis, aspergillosis, hydatid and amoebiasis.

Neoplastic

1. **Carcinoma of the bronchus** – thick-walled with an eccentric cavity. Predilection for the upper lobes. Found in 2–10% of carcinomas and especially if peripheral. More common in squamous cell carcinomas and may then be thin-walled.
2. **Metastases** – thin- or thick-walled. May only involve a few of the nodules. Seen especially in squamous cell, colon and sarcoma metastases.
3. **Hodgkin's disease** – thin- or thick-walled and typically in an area of infiltration. With hilar or mediastinal lymphadenopathy.

Vascular

1. **Infarction** – three situations may be encountered. *Primary* infection due to a septic embolus almost invariably results in cavitation. There may be *secondary* infection of an initially sterile infarct. An aseptic cavitating infarct may

(*continued*)

subsequently become infected – *tertiary infection*. Aseptic cavitation is usually solitary and arises in a large area of consolidation after about 2 weeks. If localized to a segment the commonest sites are apical or posterior segment of an upper lobe or apical segment of lower lobe (cf. lower lobe predominance with non-cavitating infarction). Majority have scalloped inner margins and cross cavity band shadows. ± effusion.

Abnormal Lung

1. **Cystic bronchiectasis** (see 4.14) – thin-walled. More common in the lower lobes.
2. **Infected emphysematous bulla** – thin-walled. ± air fluid level.
3. **Sequestrated segment** – thick- or thin-walled. 66% in the left lower lobe, 33% in the right lower lobe. ± air fluid level. ± surrounding pneumonia.
4. **Bronchogenic cyst** – in medial third of lower lobes. Thin-walled. ± air fluid level. ± surrounding pneumonia.

Granulomas

1. **Wegener's granulomatosis** – widespread. Cavitation in some of the nodules. Thick-walled, becoming thinner with time. Can be transient.
2. **Rheumatoid nodules** – thick-walled with a smooth inner lining. Especially in the lower lobes and peripherally. Well-defined. Become thin-walled with time.
3. **Progressive massive fibrosis** – predominantly in the mid and upper zones. Thick-walled and irregular. Background nodularity.
4. **Sarcoidosis*** – thin-walled. In early disease due to a combination of central necrosis of areas of coalescent granulomas and a check-valve mechanism beyond partial obstruction of airways by endobronchial sarcoidosis.

Traumatic

1. **Haematoma** – peripheral. Air fluid level if it communicates with a bronchus.
2. **Traumatic lung cyst** – thin-walled and peripheral. Single or multiple. Uni- or multilocular. Distinguished from cavitating haematomas as they present early, within hours of the injury.

Further Reading

John P.R., Beasley S.W. & Mayne V. (1989). Pulmonary sequestration and related congenital disorders. A clinico–radiological review of 41 cases. *Pediatr. Radiol.*, 20: 4–9.

Jones D.K., Dent R.G., Rimmer M.J. & Flower C.D.R. (1984) Thin-walled ring shadows in early pulmonary sarcoidosis. *Clin. Radiol.*, 35: 307–10.

Wilson A.G., Joseph A.E.A. & Butland R.J.A. (1986) The radiology of aseptic cavitation in pulmonary infarction. *Clin. Radiol.*, 37: 327–33.

4.28 Opacity with an Air Bronchogram

Infective

1. Pneumonia.

Inflammatory

1. Radiation pneumonitis.
2. Progressive massive fibrosis.

Neoplastic

1. Alveolar cell carcinoma.
2. Lymphoma*.
3. Lymphosarcoma.

4.29 Pulmonary Calcification or Ossification

Localized Calcification

1. **Tuberculosis** – demonstrable in 10% of those with a positive tuberculin test. Small central nidus of calcification. Calcification ≠ healed.
2. **Histoplasmosis** – in endemic areas, calcification due to histoplasmosis is demonstrable in 30% of those with a positive histoplasmin test. Calcification may be laminated producing a target lesion. ± multiple punctate calcifications in the spleen.
3. **Coccidioidomycosis**.
4. **Blastomycosis** – rare.

Calcification Within a Solitary Nodule

Calcification within a nodule equates with a benign lesion. The exceptions are:

  (a) Carcinoma engulfing a pre-existing calcified granuloma (eccentric calcification).
  (b) Solitary calcifying/ossifying metastasis – osteosarcoma, chondrosarcoma, mucinous adenocarcinoma of the colon or breast, papillary carcinoma of the thyroid, cystadenocarcinoma of the ovary and carcinoid.
  (c) 1° peripheral squamous cell or papillary adenocarcinoma.

Diffuse or Multiple Calcifications

1. **Infections**.
   (a) Tuberculosis – healed miliary.
   (b) Histoplasmosis.
   (c) Varicella – following chicken pox pneumonia in adulthood. 1–3 mm. Numbered in 10s.
2. **Chronic pulmonary venous hypertension** – especially mitral stenosis. Up to 8 mm. Most prominent in mid and lower zones. ± ossification.
3. **Silicosis** – in up to 20% of those showing nodular opacities.
4. **Metastases** – as above.
5. **Alveolar microlithiasis** – often familial. Myriad minute calcifications in alveoli which obscure all lung detail. Because

of the lung's increased density, the heart, pleura and diaphragm may be evident as negative shadows.
6. **Metastatic due to hypercalcaemia** – chronic renal failure, 2° hyperparathyroidism and multiple myeloma*. Predominantly in the upper zones.
7. **Lymphoma following radiotherapy.**

Interstitial Ossification

Branching calcific densities extending along the bronchovascular distribution of the interstitial space.
1. **Fibrosing alveolitis.**
2. **Long-term busulphan therapy.**
3. **Chronic pulmonary venous hypertension.**
4. **Idiopathic.**

Further Reading

Jacobs A.N., Neitzschman H.R. & Nice C.M. Jr. (1973) Metaplastic bone formation in the lung. *Am. J. Roentgenol.*, 118: 344–6.

Kuplic J.B., Higley C.S. & Niewoehner D.E. (1972) Pulmonary ossification associated with long-term busulfan therapy in chronic myeloid leukaemia. Case report. *Am. Rev. Resp. Dis.*, 106: 759.

Maile C.W., Rodan B.A., Godwin J.D., Chen J.T.T. & Ravin C.E. (1982) Calcification in pulmonary metastases. *Br. J. Radiol.*, 55: 108–13.

Mendeloff J. (1971) Disseminated nodular pulmonary ossification in the Hamman–Rich lung. *Am. Rev. Resp. Dis.*, 103: 269.

4.30 Unilateral Hilar Enlargement

Lymph Nodes
1. **Carcinoma of the bronchus** – the hilar enlargement may be due to the tumour itself or involved lymph nodes.
2. **Lymphoma*** – unilateral is very unusual; involvement is usually bilateral and asymmetrical.
3. **Infective**
   (a) Primary tuberculosis.
   (b) Histoplasmosis.
   (c) Coccidioidomycosis.
   (d) Mycoplasma.
   (e) Pertussis.
4. **Sarcoidosis*** – unilateral disease in only 1–5%.

Pulmonary Artery
1. **Post-stenotic dilatation** – on the left side.
2. **Pulmonary embolus** (see Pulmonary embolic disease*) – massive to one lung. Peripheral oligaemia.
3. **Aneurysm** – in chronic pulmonary arterial hypertension. ± egg-shell calcification.

Others
1. **Mediastinal mass** – superimposed on a hilum.
2. **Perihilar pneumonia** – ill-defined, ± air bronchogram.

See also 4.11.

4.31 Bilateral Hilar Enlargement

Due to lymph-node enlargement or pulmonary artery enlargement.

Idiopathic
1. Sarcoidosis* – symmetrical and lobulated. Bronchopulmonary ± unilateral or bilateral paratracheal lymphadenopathy.

Neoplastic
1. Lymphoma* – asymmetrical.
2. Lymphangitis carcinomatosa.

Infective
1. Viruses – most common in children.
2. Primary tuberculosis – rarely bilateral and symmetrical.
3. Histoplasmosis.
4. Coccidioidomycosis.

Vascular
1. Pulmonary arterial hypertension – see section 5.16.

Immunological
1. Extrinsic allergic alveolitis* – in mushroom workers.

Inhalational
1. Silicosis* – symmetrical.
2. Chronic berylliosis – only in a minority of cases. Symmetrical.

4.32 'Eggshell' Calcification of Lymph Nodes

The criteria for diagnosis were listed by Gross *et al.* and Jacobsen *et al.* as:

1. Shell-like calcifications up to 2 mm thick in the periphery of at least two lymph nodes.
2. Calcifications may be solid or broken.
3. In at least one of the lymph nodes the ring of calcification must be complete.
4. The central part of the lymph node may show additional calcifications.
5. One of the affected lymph nodes must be at least 1 cm in its greatest diameter.

1. **Silicosis*** – seen in approximately 5% of silicotics. Predominantly hilar lymph nodes but may also be observed in the anterior and posterior mediastinal lymph nodes, cervical lymph nodes and intraperitoneal lymph nodes. More frequently seen in complicated pneumoconiosis. Lungs show multiple small nodular shadows or areas of massive fibrosis.
2. **Coal miner's pneumoconiosis*** – occurs in only 1% of cases. Associated pulmonary changes include miliary shadowing or massive shadows.
3. **Sarcoidosis*** – calcification of lymph nodes occurs in approximately 5% of patients and is occasionally 'eggshell' in appearance. There may be extensive lymph-node involvement throughout the mediastinum. Calcification appears about 6 years after the onset of the disease and is almost invariably associated with advanced pulmonary disease and in some cases with steroid therapy. The pulmonary manifestations include reticulonodular, acinar or fibrotic changes in the mid to upper zones.
4. **Lymphoma following radiotherapy** – appears 1–9 years post radiotherapy.

Differential Diagnosis

1. **Pulmonary artery calcification** – a rare feature of pulmonary arterial hypertension.
2. **Aortic calcification** – especially in the wall of a saccular aneurysm.
3. **Anterior mediastinal tumours** – teratodermoids and thymomas may occasionally exhibit rim calcification.

Further Reading
Gross B.H., Schneider H.J. & Proto A.V. (1980) Eggshell calcification
    of lymph nodes: an update. *Am. J. Roentgenol.*, 135: 1265.
Jacobsen G., Felson B., Pendergrass E.P., Flinn R.H. & Lainhart W.S.
    (1967) Eggshell calcification in coal and metal miners. *Semin.
    Roentgenol.*, 2: 276–82.

4.33 Upper Zone Fibrosis

1. **Tuberculosis** – calcification frequent.
2. **Radiotherapy** – no calcification. ± evidence of the cause,
   e.g. mastectomy for carcinoma, or radiation osteonecrosis
   of ribs or clavicle.
3. **Sarcoidosis*** – no calcification. ± 'eggshell' calcification of
   lymph nodes.
4. **Chronic extrinsic allergic alveolitis***.
5. **Histoplasmosis** – similar to tuberculosis.
6. **Progressive massive fibrosis** – conglomerate infiltrates with
   peripheral emphysema. Background nodularity. ± 'egg-
   shell' calcification of lymph nodes.
7. **Ankylosing spondylitis*** – resembles tuberculosis. Cavitation frequent with mycetoma. Disease is almost
   invariably bilateral and associated with severe spondylitis.

Further Reading
Howarth F.H., Kendall M.J., Lawrence D.S. & Whitfield A.G.W.
    (1975) Chest radiograph in ankylosing spondylitis. *Clin.
    Radiol.*, 26: 455–60.

4.34 Pleural Effusion

Transudate (protein < 30 g l^{-1})
1. Cardiac failure.
2. Hepatic failure.
3. Nephrotic syndrome.
4. Meigs syndrome.

Exudate (protein > 30 g l^{-1})
1. Infection.
2. Malignancy.
3. Pulmonary infarction – see Pulmonary embolic disease*.
4. Collagen vascular diseases.
5. Subphrenic abscess.
6. Pancreatitis.

Haemorrhagic
1. Carcinoma of the bronchus.
2. Trauma.
3. Pulmonary infarction – see Pulmonary embolic disease*.
4. Bleeding disorders.

Chylous
1. Obstructed thoracic duct – due to trauma, malignant invasion or filariasis.

4.35 Pleural Effusion due to Extrathoracic Disease

1. **Pancreatitis** – acute, chronic or relapsing. Effusions are predominantly left-sided. Elevated amylase content.
2. **Subphrenic abscess** – with elevation and restriction of movement of the ipsilateral diaphragm and basal atelectasis or consolidation.
3. **Following abdominal surgery** – most often seen on the side of the surgery and larger after upper abdominal surgery. Disappears after 2 weeks.
4. **Meigs syndrome** – pleural effusion + ascites + benign pelvic tumour (most commonly an ovarian fibroma, thecoma, granulosa cell tumour or cystadenoma).
5. **Nephrotic syndrome.**
6. **Fluid overload** – e.g. due to renal disease.
7. **Cirrhosis.**

4.36 Pleural Effusion with an Otherwise Normal Chest X-ray

Effusion may be the only abnormality or other signs may be obscured by the effusion.

Infective

1. **Primary tuberculosis** – more common in adults (40%) than children (10%). Rarely bilateral.
2. **Viruses and mycoplasma** – effusions occur in 10–20% of cases but are usually small.

Neoplastic

1. **Carcinoma of the bronchus** – effusion occurs in 10% of patients and a peripheral carcinoma may be hidden by the effusion.
2. **Metastases** – most commonly from breast; less commonly pancreas, stomach, ovary and kidney.
3. **Mesothelioma** – effusion in 90%; often massive and obscures the underlying pleural disease.
4. **Lymphoma*** – effusion occurs in 30% but is usually associated with lymphadenopathy or pulmonary infiltrates.

Immunological

1. **Systemic lupus erythematosus*** – effusion is the sole manifestation in 10% of cases. Usually small but may be massive. Bilateral in 50%. 35–50% of those with an effusion have associated cardiomegaly.
2. **Rheumatoid disease** (see Rheumatoid arthritis*) – observed in 3% of patients. Almost exclusively males. Usually unilateral and may antedate joint disease. Tendency to remain unchanged for a long time.

Extrathoracic Diseases
See 4.35.

Others

1. **Pulmonary embolus** (see Pulmonary embolic disease*) – effusion is a common sign and it may obscure an underlying area of infarction.

2. **Closed chest trauma** – effusion may contain blood, chyle or food (due to oesophageal rupture). The latter is almost always left-sided.
3. **Asbestosis*** – mesothelioma and carcinoma of the bronchus should be excluded but an effusion may be present without these complications. Effusion is frequently recurrent and usually bilateral. Usually associated with pulmonary disease.

4.37 Pneumothorax

1. **Spontaneous** – M:F, 8:1. Especially those of tall thin stature. ? due to ruptured blebs or bullae. 20% are associated with a small pleural effusion.
2. **Iatrogenic** – e.g. postoperative, after chest aspiration, during artificial ventilation, after lung biopsy or following attempted insertion of a subclavian venous line.
3. **Traumatic** – ± rib fractures, haemothorax, surgical emphysema or mediastinal emphysema.
4. **Secondary to mediastinal emphysema** (see 4.38).
5. **Secondary to lung disease**
   (a) Emphysema.
   (b) 'Honeycomb lung' (q.v.).
   (c) Cystic fibrosis*.
   (d) Pneumonia.
   (e) Bronchopleural fistula, e.g. due to lung abscess or carcinoma.
   (f) Lung neoplasms – especially metastases from osteogenic sarcomas and other sarcomas.
6. **Pneumoperitoneum** – air passes through a pleuroperitoneal foramen.

4.38 Pneumomediastinum

May be associated with pneumothorax and subcutaneous emphysema.

1. **Lung tear** – a sudden rise in intra-alveolar pressure, often with airway narrowing, causes air to dissect through the interstitium to the hilum and then to the mediastinum.
   (a) Spontaneous – the most common cause and may following coughing or strenuous exercise.
   (b) Asthma – but usually not < 2 years of age.
   (c) Diabetic ketoacidosis related to severe and protracted vomiting.
   (d) Childbirth – because of repeated Valsalva manoeuvres.
   (e) Artificial ventilation.
   (f) Chest trauma.
   (g) Foreign body aspiration – especially if < 2 years.
2. **Perforation of oesophagus, trachea or bronchus** – ruptured oesophagus is often associated with a hydrothorax or hydropneumothorax, usually on the left side.
3. **Perforation of a hollow abdominal viscus** – with extension of gas via the retroperitoneal space.

Further Reading

Burton E.M., Riggs Jr W., Kaufman R.A. & Houston C.S. (1989) Pneumomediastinum caused by foreign body aspiration in children. *Pediatr. Radiol.*, 20: 45–7.

Fraser R.G., Paré J.A.P., Paré P.D., Fraser R.S. & Genereux G.P. (1991) Pneumomediastinum. In: *Diagnosis of Diseases of the Chest*, 3rd edn, Vol. 4, Ch. 19, pp. 2801–13. Philadelphia: Saunders.

4.39 Right Sided Diaphragmatic Humps

At Any Site
1. Collapse/consolidation of adjacent lung.
2. Localized eventration.
3. Loculated effusion.
4. Subphrenic abscess.
5. Hepatic abscess.
6. Hydatid cyst.
7. Hepatic metastasis.

Medially
1. Pericardial fat pad.
2. Aortic aneurysm.
3. Pleuro-pericardial (spring water cyst).
4. Sequestrated segment.

Anteriorly
1. Morgagni hernia.

Posteriorly
1. Bochdalek hernia.

Further Reading
Baron R.L., Lee J.K.T. & Melson G.L. (1980) Sonographic evaluation of right juxtadiaphragmatic masses in children using transhepatic approach. *J. Clin. Ultrasound*, 8: 156–8.

Kangerloo H., Sukov R., Sample F., Lipson M. & Smith L. (1977) Ultrasonic evaluation of juxtadiaphragmatic masses in children. *Radiology*, 125: 785–7.

Khan A.N. & Gould D.A. (1984) The primary role of ultrasound in evaluating right sided diaphragmatic humps and juxtadiaphragmatic masses: a review of 22 cases. *Clin. Radiol.*, 35: 413–18.

4.40   Unilateral Elevated Hemidiaphragm

Causes Above the Diaphragm

1. **Phrenic nerve palsy** – smooth hemidiaphragm. No movement on respiration. Paradoxical movement on sniffing.
   The mediastinum is usually central. The cause, e.g. bronchial carcinoma or mediastinal nodes, may be evident on
   the X-ray.
2. **Pulmonary collapse.**
3. **Pulmonary infarction** – see Pulmonary embolic disease*.
4. **Pleural disease** – especially old pleural disease, e.g. haemothorax, empyema or thoracotomy.
5. **Splinting of the diaphragm** – associated with rib fractures
   or pleurisy.
6. **Hemiplegia** – an upper motor neuron lesion.

Diaphragmatic Causes

1. **Eventration** – more common on the left side. The heart
   is frequently displaced to the contralateral side. Limited
   movement on normal respiration and paradoxical movement on sniffing. Stomach may show a partial volvulus.

Causes Below the Diaphragm

1. **Gaseous distension of the stomach or splenic flexure** – left
   hemidiaphragm only.
2. **Subphrenic inflammatory disease** – subphrenic abscess,
   hepatic or splenic abscess and pancreatitis.

Scoliosis

The raised hemidiaphragm is on the side of the concavity.

Decubitus Film

The raised hemidiaphragm is on the dependent side.

Differential Diagnosis

1. **Subpulmonary effusion** – movement of fluid is demonstrable on a decubitus film. On the left side there is
   increased distance between the lung and stomach fundal
   gas.
2. **Ruptured diaphragm** – more common on the left. Barium
   meal confirms the diagnosis.

4.41 Bilateral Elevated Hemidiaphragms

Poor Inspiratory Effort

Obesity

Causes Above the Diaphragms
1. Bilateral basal pulmonary collapse – which may be secondary to infarction of subphrenic abscesses.
2. Small lungs – fibrotic lung disease, e.g. fibrosing alveolitis.

Causes Below the Diaphragms
1. Ascites.
2. Pregnancy.
3. Pneumoperitoneum.
4. Hepatosplenomegaly.
5. Large intra-abdominal tumour.
6. Bilateral subphrenic abscesses.

Differential Diagnosis
1. Bilateral subpulmonary effusions.

4.42 Pleural Calcification

1. Old empyema
2. Old haemothorax
} amorphous bizarre, plaques, often with a vacuolated appearance near the inner surface of greatly thickened pleura. Usually unilateral.
3. Asbestos inhalation* – small curvilinear plaques in the parietal pleura. More delicate than (1) and (2). Often multiple and bilateral and found over the domes of the diaphragms and immediately deep to the ribs. Observed in 50% of people exposed to asbestos but not before 20 years have elapsed. Not necessarily associated with asbestosis, i.e. pulmonary disease.
4. Silicosis*
5. Talc exposure.
} similar appearances to asbestos exposure.

4.43 Local Pleural Masses

1. **Loculated pleural effusion.**
2. **Metastases** – from bronchus or breast. Often multiple.
3. **Malignant mesothelioma** – nearly always due to asbestos exposure. Extensive thickening of the pleura which may be partly obscured by an effusion. Little mediastinal shift. Adjacent bone destruction in 12%.
4. **Pleural fibroma (local benign mesothelioma)** – a smooth lobular mass, 2–15 cm diameter, arising more frequently from the visceral pleura than the parietal pleura. Tendency to change position with respiration as 30–50% are pedunculated. They form an obtuse angle with the chest wall which indicates their extrapulmonary location. Usually found in patients over 40 years of age and usually asymptomatic. However, it causes hypertrophic osteoarthropathy in a greater proportion of cases than any other disease.
5. **Fibrin balls** – develop in a serofibrinous pleural effusion and become visible following absorption of the fluid. They are small and tend to be situated near the lung base. They may disappear spontaneously or remain unchanged for many years.

Differential Diagnosis

1. **Extrapleural masses** – see 4.44.
2. **Plombage** – the insertion of foreign material into the extrapleural space as a treatment for tuberculosis. The commonest materials used were solid Lucite spheres, hollow 'ping-pong' balls (which may have fluid levels in them) or crumpled cellophane. They produce a well-defined, smooth pleural surface, convex inferiorly and medially and displacing the lung apex. The pleura makes an acute angle with the chest wall.

4.44 Rib Lesion with an Adjacent Soft-tissue Mass

Neoplastic
1. **Bronchogenic carcinoma** – solitary site unless metastatic.
2. **Metastases** – solitary or multiple.
3. **Multiple myeloma*** – classically multiple sites and bilateral.
4. **Mesothelioma** – rib destruction occurs in 12%.
5. **Lymphoma***.
6. **Fibrosarcoma** – similar appearances to mesothelioma.
7. **Neurofibroma** – rib notching.

Infective
1. **Tuberculosis osteitis** – commonest inflammatory lesion of a rib. Second only to malignancy as a cause of rib destruction. Clearly defined margins ± abscess.
2. **Actinomycosis** ⎫ usually a single rib. Adjacent con-
3. **Nocardiosis** ⎭ solidation.
4. **Blastomycosis** – adjacent patchy or massive consolidation ± hilar lymphadenopathy.

Inflammatory
1. **Radiation osteitis**.

Metabolic
1. **Renal osteodystrophy** ⎫ rib fractures and osteopenia
2. **Cushing's syndrome** ⎭ associated with a subpleural haematoma.

Further Reading
Steiner R.M., Cooper M.W. & Brodovsky H. (1982) Rib destruction: a neglected finding in malignant mesothelioma. *Clin. Radiol.*, 33: 61–5.

4.45 The Chest Radiograph Following Chest Trauma

Soft Tissues
1. Foreign bodies.
2. Surgical emphysema.

Ribs

1. Simple fracture
2. Flail chest
} may be associated with surgical emphysema, pneumothorax, extrapleural haematoma or haemothorax. First rib fractures have a high incidence of other associated injuries.

Sternum
1. Fracture – may be associated with a clinically unsuspected dorsal spine fracture.
2. Sternoclavicular dislocation.

Clavicles and Scapulae
1. Fracture – scapular fractures are usually associated with other bony or intrathoracic injuries.

Spine
1. Fracture – when present, are multiple in 10% and non-contiguous in 80% of these. Thoracic spine injuries have a much higher incidence of neurological deficit than cervical or lumbar spine injuries.
2. Cord trauma.
3. Nerve root trauma – especially to the brachial plexus.

Pleura
1. Pneumothorax – simple (in 20–40% of patients with blunt chest trauma and 20% of patients with penetrating injuries) or tension. Signs of a small pneumothorax on a supine chest radiograph include a deep costophrenic sulcus, basal hyperlucency, a 'double' diaphragm, unusually

clear definition of the right cardiophrenic angle or left cardiac apex and visualization of apical pericardial fat tags.
CT is more sensitive than plain film radiography.
2. **Haemothorax** – in 25–50% of patients with blunt chest
trauma and 60–80% of patients with penetrating wounds.

Lung

1. **Contusion** – non-segmental alveolar opacities which
resolve in a few days.
2. **Haematoma** – usually appears following resolution of contusion. Round, well-defined nodule. Resolution in several
weeks.
3. **Aspiration pneumonia.**
4. **Foreign body.**
5. **Pulmonary oedema** – following blast injuries or head
injury (neurogenic oedema).
6. **Adult respiratory distress syndrome** – widespread air-space
shadowing appearing 24–72 hours after injury.
7. **Fat embolism.**

Trachea and Bronchi

1. **Laceration or fracture** – initially surgical emphysema and
pneumomediastinum followed by collapse of the affected
lung or lobe.

Diaphragm

1. **Rupture** – in 3–7% of patients with blunt and 6–46% of
patients with penetrating thoraco-abdominal trauma.
Diagnosis may be delayed months or years. Plain film findings include herniated stomach or bowel above the diaphragm, pleural effusion, a supra-diaphragmatic mass or
a poorly visualized or abnormally contoured diaphragm.
Probable equal incidence on both sides but rupture of the
right hemidiaphragm is not so easily diagnosed.

Mediastinum

1. **Aortic injury** – 90% of aortic ruptures occur just distal to
the origin of the left subclavian artery. The majority of

(*continued*)

patients with this complication die before radiological evaluation, especially when rupture involves the ascending aorta. Plain film radiographic abnormalities of aortic rupture are:

(a) Widening of the mediastinum (sensitivity 53–100%; specificity 1–60%).

(b) Abnormal aortic contour (sensitivity 53–100%; specificity 21–42%).

(c) Tracheal displacement to the right (sensitivity 12–100%; specificity 80–95%).

(d) Nasogastric tube displacement to the right of the T4 spinous process (sensitivity 9–71%; specificity 90–96%).

(e) Thickening of the right paraspinal stripe (sensitivity 12–83%; specificity 89–97%).

(f) Depression of the left mainstem bronchus > 40° below the horizontal (sensitivity 3–80%; specificity 80–100%).

(g) Loss of definition of the aortopulmonary window (sensitivity 0–100%; specificity 56–83%).

A normal chest radiograph has a 98% negative predictive value for traumatic aortic rupture.

2. **Mediastinal haematoma** – blurring of the mediastinal outline.

3. **Mediastinal emphysema** (see 4.38).

4. **Haemopericardium.**

5. **Oesophageal rupture.**

Further Reading

Groskin S.A. (1992) Selected topics in chest trauma. *Radiology*, 183: 605–17.

Marnocha K. & Maglinte D. (1985) Plain-film criteria for excluding aortic rupture in blunt chest trauma. *Am. J. Roentgenol.*, 144: 19–21.

Mirvis S., Bidwell J., Buddemeyer E. *et al.* (1987) Value of chest radiography in excluding traumatic aortic rupture. *Radiology*, 163: 487–93.

Reynolds J. & Davis J.T. (1966) Thoracic injuries. The radiology of trauma. *Radiol. Clin. North Am.*, 4: 383–402.

4.46 Neonatal Respiratory Distress

Pulmonary Causes

A. WITH NO MEDIASTINAL SHIFT

1. **Hyaline membrane disease** – in premature infants. Fine granular pattern throughout both lungs, air bronchograms and, later, obscured heart and diaphragmatic outlines. Often cardiomegaly. May progress to a complete 'white-out'. Interstitial emphysema, pneumomediastinum and pneumothorax are frequent complications of ventilator therapy.
2. **Transient tachypnoea of the newborn** – prominent interstitial markings and vessels, thickened septa, small effusions and mild cardiomegaly. Resolves within 24 hours.
3. **Meconium aspiration syndrome** – predominantly postmature infants. Coarse linear and irregular opacities of uneven size, generalized hyperinflation and focal areas of collapse and emphysema. Spontaneous pneumothorax and effusions in 20%. No air bronchograms.
4. **Pneumonia** – segmental or lobal consolidation. May resemble hyaline membrane disease or meconium aspiration syndrome, but should be suspected if unevenly distributed.
5. **Pulmonary haemorrhage** – 75% are less than 2.5 kg. Onset at birth or delayed several days. Resembles meconium aspiration syndrome or hyaline membrane disease.
6. **Upper airway obstruction** – e.g. choanal atresia and micrognathia.
7. **Mikity–Wilson syndrome (pulmonary dysmaturity)** – always premature infants and usually less than 1.5 kg. Initially well but there is an insidious onset of respiratory distress between 1 and 6 weeks. Streaky opacities radiating from both hila with small bubbly areas of focal hyperaeration throughout both lungs. Moderate hyperinflation. Severe disease leads to death but infants may recover fully. Resolution over a period of 12 months. Bases clear before apices and hyperinflation is the last feature to disappear.
8. **Abnormal thoracic cage** – e.g. osteogenesis imperfecta and Jeune's thoracic dysplasia.

(continued)

B. WITH MEDIASTINAL SHIFT AWAY FROM THE ABNORMAL SIDE

1. **Diaphragmatic hernia** – 6 × more common on the left side. Multiple lucencies due to gas containing bowel in the chest. Herniated bowel may appear solid if X-rayed too early but there will still be a paucity of gas in the abdomen.
2. **Congenital lobar emphysema** – involves the left upper, right upper and right middle lobes (in decreasing order of frequency) with compression of the lung base (cf. pneumothorax which produces symmetrical lung compression).
3. **Cystic adenomatoid malformation** – translucencies of various shapes and sizes scattered throughout an area of opaque lung with well-defined margins.
4. **Pleural effusion (empyema, chylothorax)** – rare.

C. WITH MEDIASTINAL SHIFT TOWARDS THE ABNORMAL SIDE

1. **Atelectasis** – most commonly due to incorrect placement of an endotracheal tube down a major bronchus. Much less commonly primary atelectasis may occur without any other abnormality.
2. **Agenesis** – rare. May be difficult to differentiate from collapse but other congenital defects especially hemivertebrae are commonly associated.

Cardiac Causes (q.v.)

Cerebral Causes
Haemorrhage, oedema and drugs. After cardiopulmonary causes these account for 50% of the remainder.

Metabolic Causes
Metabolis acidosis, hypoglycaemia and hypothermia.

Abdominal Causes
Massive organomegaly, e.g. polycystic kidneys, elevating the diaphragms.

4.47 Ring Shadows in a Child

Neonate
1. **Diaphragmatic hernia** – unilateral.
2. **Interstitial emphysema** – secondary to ventilator therapy. Bilateral.
3. **Cystic adenomatoid malformation** – unilateral.
4. **Mikity–Wilson syndrome** – bilateral.

Older Child
1. **Cystic bronchiectasis** (q.v.).
2. **Cystic fibrosis***.
3. **Pneumatoceles** (q.v.).
4. **Langerhans cell histiocytosis***
5. **Neurofibromatosis*** } see 4.20.

See also 4.46.

4.48   Drug-induced Lung Disease

Lung Parenchyma

1. **Diffuse pneumonitis** – methotrexate, procarbazine, azathioprine, amiodarone.
2. **Diffuse pneumonitis progressing to fibrosis** – nitrofurantoin, melphalan, busulphan, cyclophosphamide and bleomycin.
3. **Pneumonitis associated with drug-induced systemic lupus erythematosus** – procainamide, hydralazine and isoniazid.
4. **Pulmonary haemorrhage** – anticoagulants and those drugs which produce an idiosyncratic thrombocytopenia.
5. **Pulmonary eosinophilia** – sulphonamides, chlorpropamide, sulphasalazine and imipramine.
6. **Allergic alveolitis** – pituitary snuff.

Pulmonary Vasculature

1. **Pulmonary oedema**
   (a) Excess intravenous fluids.
   (b) Altered capillary wall permeability – heroin, dextropropoxyphene, methyldopa, hydrochlorothiazide, aspirin, nitrofurantoin and contrast media.
   (c) Drug-induced cardiac arrhythmias or impaired myocardial contractility.
2. **Pulmonary emboli** – high oestrogen oral contraceptives causing thromboemboli and oily emboli following lymphangiography.

Bronchospasm

1. **β-blockers.**
2. **Histamine liberators** – iodine containing contrast media and morphine.
3. **Drugs as antigens** – antisera, penicillins and cephalosporins.
4. **Others** – aspirin, anti-inflammatory agents, paracetamol.

Hilar Enlargement or Mediastinal Widening

Phenytoin and steroids.

Increased Opportunistic Infections

1. Antimitotics.
2. Steroids.
3. Actinomycin C.
4. **Drug-induced neutropenia or aplastic anaemia** – idiosyncratic or dose-related.

Further Reading

Millar J.W. (1982) Drugs and the lungs. *Medicine International*, 1 (20): 944–7.

Morrison D.A. & Goldman A.L. (1979) Radiographic patterns of drugs induced lung disease. *Radiology*, 131: 299–304.

4.49 High Resolution CT – Patterns of Parenchymal Disease Processes

Normal vessels are only visualized up to a distance of 1 cm from the pleura. Any linear opacity distal to this is abnormal. Although HRCT is sensitive in detecting interstitial opacification, there is an overlap of appearances for different disease processes which can cause difficulty in making a specific diagnosis. Scans must be done prone to avoid the gravitational effect obscuring early interstitial fibrosis.

Peripheral, Base
1. **Crytogenic fibrosing alveolitis**
   (a) Early – ground-glass opacities, subpleural reticulation at lung base.
   (b) Later – reticulation extends centrally.
   (c) Chronic – small cyst formation commencing at subpleural site.
2. **Asbestos related lung disease**
   (a) Earliest changes are at the lung bases posteriorly.
   (b) Thickened curvilinear subpleural lines.

   (c) Thickened subpleural septal (interlobular) lines.

   (d) Coarse parenchymal lines extending centrally separate from pulmonary vessels.

   (e) 'Honeycombing'.

   (f) ± rounded atelectasis – wedge shaped contiguous with pleural, thickening 'comet tail' vessels.

Central, Upper/mid Zone
1. **Sarcoidosis:**
   Thickened bronchovascular sheath ± 'beading' centrally.
   ± patchy alveolar opacification.
   Nodules – subpleural and peri-bronchovascular.

Peripheral and Central
1. **Lymphangitis** – can mimic sarcoidosis, but rarely has alveolar opacification. Approx. 50% cases are focal – CT can be used to guide optimum biopsy site.

Widespread
1. **Lymphangioleiomyomatosis** – characteristic widespread uniformly distributed cysts with normal lung parenchyma surrounding them. Tuberous sclerosis is identical.

Further Reading
Engeler C.E., Tashjion J.H., Trenkner S.S. & Walsh J.W. (1993) Ground glass opacity of the lung parenchyma: a guide to analysis with High Resolution C.T. *Am. J. Roentgenol.*, 160: 249–51.

Muller N. (ed.) (1991) Imaging of diffuse lung disease. *Radiol. Clin. North Am.*, 29 (5).

4.50 The Thymus

The normal thymus is a bilobed anterosuperior mediastinal structure. It is only visible on plain films of infants and young children and is inconstantly visible after 2–3 years of age. On plain films three radiological signs aid diagnosis – the 'sail' sign (a triangular projection to one or both sides of the mediastinum), the 'wave' sign (a rippled thymic contour due to indentations by the anterior rib ends) or the 'notch' sign (an indentation at the junction of thymus with heart). A large normal thymus may be seen in:

(a) Well nourished children.
(b) Following recovery from illness (rebound overgrowth in 25% following previous involution).
(c) Hyperthyroidism and euthyroid children following treatment for hypothyroidism.

It has the following CT characteristics:

1. **Incidence** – identifiable in 100% < 30 years of age, decreasing to 17% > 49 years. However, < 10 years of age the distinction from great vessels is very difficult without the use of contrast enhancement.
2. **Shape** – quadrilateral shape in childhood with, usually, convex, undulating margins. After puberty two separate lobes (ovoid, elliptical, triangular or semilunar) or an arrowhead (triangle). The normal thymus is never multilobular.
3. **Size** – progressive enlargement during childhood. Maximum absolute size is in the 12–19 year age group but relative to body size it is largest in infancy. Left lobe nearly always > right lobe. Becomes narrower with increasing age. Maximum thickness (the perpendicular to the long axis) of one lobe > 20 years is 1.3 cm. > 40 years there may be linear or oval soft-tissue densities but they are never > 7 mm in size and never alter the lateral contour of the mediastinal fat.
4. **Density** – homogeneous, isodense or hyperdense when related to chest wall musculature in childhood. After puberty becoming inhomogeneous and progressively lower in attenuation due to fatty infiltration. > 40 years the majority will have total fatty involution.

On MRI the normal thymus is:

1. Larger than is seen by CT (probably because the study is undertaken during quiet respiration rather than with suspended full inspiration).
2. Homogeneous in childhood (T_1W slightly greater than muscle, T_2W similar to fat).
3. Heterogeneous in adults (T_1W and T_2W similar to fat).

Further Reading

Baron R.L., Lee J.K.T., Sagel S.S. & Peterson R.R. (1982) Computed tomography of the normal thymus. *Radiology*, 142: 121–5.

Baron R.L., Lee J.K.T., Sagel S.S., Peterson R.R. & Levitt R.G. (1982) Computed tomography of the abnormal thymus. *Radiology*, 142: 127–34.

de Geer G., Webb W.R. & Gamsu G. (1986) Normal thymus: Assessment with MR and CT. *Radiology*, 158: 313–17.

Francis I.R., Glazer G.M., Bookstein F.L. & Gross B.H. (1985) The thymus: re-examination of age-related changes in size and shape. *Am. J. Roentgenol.*, 145: 249–54.

Han B., Babcock D. & Oestreich A. (1989) Normal thymus in infancy: sonographic characteristics. *Radiology*, 170: 471–4.

Siegal M.J., Glazer H.S., Wiener J.I. *et al.* (1989) Normal and abnormal thymus in childhood: MR imaging. *Radiology*, 172: 367–71.

Williams M.P. (1989) Problems in radiology: CT assessment of the thymus. *Clin. Radiol.*, 40: 113–14.

4.51   Anterior Mediastinal Masses in Children

The anterior mediastinum is bounded by the clavicles (superiorly), the diaphragm (inferiorly), the sternum (anteriorly) and the anterior surfaces of the heart and great vessels (posteriorly). 45% of paediatric mediastinal masses occur at this site.

Congenital

1. **Normal thymus** – see 4.50.
2. **Cystic hygroma** – 5% of anterior mediastinal masses but the majority are extensions from the neck with only 1% being purely mediastinal.
3. **Morgagni hernia.**

Neoplastic

1. **Hodgkin's disease (HD), non-Hodgkin's lymphoma (NHL) and leukaemia** – majority of neoplastic anterior mediastinal masses are due to Hodgkin's disease. At presentation, mediastinal lymph nodes are seen in 23% of HD, 14% of NHL and 5–10% of leukaemics. Comparing mediastinal involvement in HD with NHL:

Hodgkin's disease	Non-Hodgkin's lymphoma
Usually > 10 yrs old	Any age in children
Mostly localized. Mediastinal lympadenopathy (LN) in 85% of those with cervical LN	Disseminated disease in > 75% at presentation
Histology usually nodular sclerosing	Histology usually lymphoblastic
Displacement of other mediastinal structures rather than compression	Tracheal compression is more likely
Paratracheal > hilar > subcarinal LN. Hilar LN without mediastinal LN is rare	

Hodgkin's disease	Non-Hodgkin's lymphoma
Lung involvement in 10% at diagnosis – direct spread from LNs	Pulmonary involvement is higher
	Pleural effusion is more common but may be 2° to ascites or lymphatic obstruction.

After treatment for lymphoma a residual anterior mediastinal mass may present a diagnostic difficulty. If CT shows this to be homogeneous and there is no other lymphadenopathy then tumour is unlikely to be present but only the lack of deterioration on follow-up imaging studies will provide confirmation.

2. **Germ cell tumours** – 5–10% of germ cell tumours arise in the mediastinum. Two age peaks – at 2 years and during adolescence. Majority (80%) are teratomas and benign. Endodermal sinus (yolk sac) tumours are more aggressive. Seminomas are rare. All tumours are moderate to large in size and may contain calcification (including teeth), fat and cystic/necrotic areas. Radiological appearance does not accurately correlate with histology but large size, marked mass effect and local infiltration suggest an aggressive lesion.

3. **Thymoma** – 5–8% of mediastinal tumours in childhood. Most occur after 10 yrs of age. 50% discovered incidentally. Calcification in 10% – linear. Only rarely associated with myasthenia gravis.

Inflammatory

1. **Lymphadenopathy** – inflammatory lymph node masses are less common than neoplasia. Most frequent causes are tuberculosis and histoplasmosis.

Further Reading

Cohen M.D. (1992) *Imaging of Children With Cancer*, Ch. 4, pp. 89–133. St Louis: Mosby Year Book.

Merten D.F. (1992) Diagnostic imaging of mediastinal masses in children. *Am. J. Roentgenol.*, 158: 825–32.

Meza M.P., Benson M. & Slovis T. (1993) Imaging of mediastinal masses in children. *Radiol. Clin. North Am.*, 31: 583–604.

4.52   Middle Mediastinal Masses in Children

The middle mediastinum is bordered by the anterior and posterior mediastinum. 20% of paediatric mediastinal masses occur at this site.

Neoplastic
1. Most middle mediastinal tumours are extensions of those which arise primarily in the anterior mediastinum. (See 4.51.)

Inflammatory
1. **Lymphadenopathy** – tuberculosis, histoplasmosis and sarcoidosis.

Congenital
1. **Foregut duplication cysts** – account for 10–20% of paediatric mediastinal masses. The spectrum of abnormalities includes bronchogenic cysts, oesophageal duplication cysts and neurenteric cysts.
   Bronchogenic cyst – round or oval, unilocular, homogeneous, water-density mass (usually 0–20 HU, but up to 100 HU due to mucus or milk of calcium contents) with well-defined borders. There may be airway obstruction and secondary infection, both within the cyst and in the surrounding lung. Communication with the tracheobronchial tree, resulting in a cavity, is rare. Four groups may be defined according to location:
   (a) Paratracheal cysts are attached to the tracheal wall above the carina.
   (b) Carinal cysts are the most common and are attached to the carina ± anterior oesophageal wall.
   (c) Hilar cysts are attached to a lobar bronchus and appear to be intrapulmonary.
   (d) Paraoesophageal cysts may be attached or communicate with the oesophagus but have no communication with the bronchial tree.
   Oesophageal Duplication Cyst – 10–15% of intestinal duplications. Less common than bronchogenic cysts, usually larger and usually situated to the right of the midline

extending into the posterior mediastinum. May be an incidental finding or produce symptoms related to oesophageal or tracheobronchial tree compression. May contain ectopic gastric mucosa (positive ^{99m}Tc-pertechnetate scan) which causes ulceration, haemorrhage or perforation. Communication with the oesophageal lumen is rare.

Neurenteric Cyst – located in the middle or posterior mediastinum, contain neural tissue and maintain a connection with the spinal canal. More commonly right sided. Vertebral body anomalies (hemivertebra, butterfly vertebra and scoliosis) are usually superior to the cyst.

2. **Cystic hygroma** – 5% of cystic hygromas extend into the mediastinum from the neck. Most present at birth. Cystic with some solid components on all imaging modalities.
3. **Hiatus hernia.**
4. **Achalasia.**
5. **Cardiomegaly or vena caval enlargement** – see Chapter 5.

Further Reading

Merten D.F. (1992) Diagnostic imaging of mediastinal masses in children. *Am. J. Roentgenol.*, 158: 825–32.

Meza M.P., Benson M. & Slovis T. (1993) Imaging of mediastinal masses in children. *Radiol. Clin. North Am.*, 31: 583–604.

4.53   Posterior Mediastinal Masses in Children

The posterior mediastinum is bounded by the thoracic inlet (superiorly), the diaphragm (inferiorly), the bodies of the thoracic vertebrae and paravertebral gutters (posteriorly) and the pericardium (anteriorly). In children 30–40% of mediastinal masses lie in the posterior mediastinum and 95% of these are of neurogenic origin.

Neoplastic

1. **Ganglion cell tumours** – neuroblastoma (most malignant, usually < 5 years), ganglioneuroblastoma (age 5–10 years) and ganglioneuroma (benign, usually > 10 years). Imaging features of all three types are similar but metastases do not occur with ganglioneuroma. Plain films show a paravertebral soft-tissue mass with calcification in 30%. Thinning of posterior ribs, separation of ribs and enlargement of intervertebral foramina. CT shows calcification in 90%. Both CT and MRI may show extradural extension.

Congenital

1. **Bochdalek hernia** – most present at, or shortly after, birth with respiratory distress but 5% present after the neonatal period. Rarely it may complicate Group B streptococcal infection. Bochdalek hernias include:
   (a) Persistence of the pleuroperitoneal canal with a posterior lip of diaphragm.
   (b) Larger defects with no diaphragm.
   (c) Herniation through the costo-lumbar triangles.
   The appearance of herniated liver may provoke thoracentesis and herniated bowel may mimic pneumothorax, pneumatoceles or cystic adenomatoid malformation.

Further Reading

Berman L., Stringer D.A., Ein S. & Shandling B. (1988) Childhood diaphragmatic hernias presenting after the neonatal period. *Clin. Radiol.*, 39: 237–44.

4.54 Anterior Mediastinal Masses in Adults

Anterior to the pericardium and trachea. Superiorly the retrosternal air space is obliterated. For ease of discussion it can be divided into three regions:

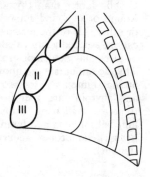

Region I

1. **Retrosternal goitre** – goitre extends into the mediastinum in 1–3% of cases. On a PA chest X-ray it appears as an inverted truncated cone with its base uppermost. It is well defined, smooth or lobulated. The trachea may be displaced posteriorly and laterally and may be narrowed. Calcification is common. Uptake by ^{131}I is diagnostic when positive but they are seldom functioning.
2. **Tortuous innominate artery** – a common finding in the elderly.
3. **Lymph nodes** – due to reticuloses, metastases or granulomas.
4. **Thymic tumours** – are uncommon but occur in 15% of adult patients with myasthenia gravis. They are round or oval and smooth or lobulated. They may contain nodular or rim calcification. If it contains a large amount of fat (thymolipoma) then it may be very large and soft and reach the diaphragm, leaving the superior mediastinum clear.
5. **Aneurysm of the ascending aorta.**

Region II

1. **Germinal cell neoplasms** – including dermoids, teratomas, seminomas, choriocarcinomas, embryonal carcinomas and endodermal sinus tumours. More than 80% are benign

(*continued*)

and they occur with equal incidence to thymic tumours. Usually larger than thymomas (but not thymolipomas). Round or oval and smooth. They usually project to one or other side of the mediastinum on the PA view. Calcification, especially rim calcification, and fragments of bone or teeth may be demonstrable, the latter being diagnostic.

2. **Thymic tumours** – see above.

3. **Sternal tumours** – metastases (breast, bronchus, kidney and thyroid) are the most common. Of the primary tumours, malignant (chondrosarcoma, myeloma, reticulum cell sarcoma and lymphoma) are more common than benign (chondroma, aneurysmal bone cyst and giant cell tumour).

Region III (Anterior Cardiophrenic Angle Masses)

1. **Pericardiac fat pad** – especially in obese people. A triangular opacity in the cardiophrenic angle on the PA view. It appears less dense than expected because of the fat content. CT is diagnostic. Excessive mediastinal fat can be due to steroid therapy.

2. **Diaphragmatic hump** – or localized eventration. Commonest on the anteromedial portion of the right hemidiaphragm. A portion of liver extends into it and this can be confirmed by ultrasound or isotope examination of the liver.

3. **Morgagni hernia** – through the defect between the septum transversum and the costal portion of the diaphragm. It is almost invariably on the right side but is occasionally bilateral. It usually contains a knuckle of colon or, less commonly, colon and stomach. Appears solid if it contains omentum and/or liver. US and/or barium studies will confirm the diagnosis.

4. **Pericardial cysts** – either a true pericardial cyst ('spring water' cyst) or a pericardial diverticulum. The cyst is usually situated in the right cardiophrenic angle and is oval or spherical. CT confirms the liquid nature of the mass.

4.55 Middle Mediastinal Masses in Adults

Between the anterior and posterior mediastinum and containing the heart, great vessels and pulmonary roots. Causes of cardiac enlargement are excluded.

1. **Lymph nodes** – the paratracheal, tracheobronchial, bronchopulmonary and/or subcarinal nodes may be enlarged. This may be due to neoplasm (most frequently metastatic bronchial carcinoma), reticuloses (most frequently Hodgkin's disease), infection (most commonly tuberculosis, histoplasmosis or coccidioidomycosis) or sarcoidosis.
2. **Carcinoma of the bronchus** – arising from a major bronchus.
3. **Aneurysm of the aorta** – CT scanning after i.v. contrast medium or, if this is not available, aortography is diagnostic. Peripheral rim calcification is a useful sign if present.
4. **Bronchogenic cyst** – see 4.52.

4.56   Posterior Mediastinal Masses in Adults

For ease of discussion it can
be divided into three regions:

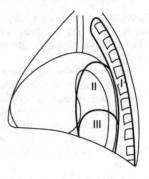

Region I (Paravertebral)
1. **Reticuloses, myeloma and metastases** – bone destruction
   with preserved discs.
2. **Extramedullary haemopoiesis** – with splenomegaly ± bone
   changes of specific disease entities, e.g. haemolytic anaemias.
3. **Abscess** – with disc space and vertebral body destruction.
4. **Ganglioneuroma** – see 4.53.

Region II
1. **Dilated oesophagus** – especially achalasia. Contains
   mottled gas shadows ± an air fluid level. Diagnosis is confirmed by barium swallow.
2. **Aorta** – unfolded, dilated or ruptured.

Region III
1. **Hiatus hernia** – often contains an air fluid level which is
   projected through the cardiac shadow on a penetrated
   PA view.

4.57 CT Mediastinal Mass Containing Fat

1. **Teratodermoid** – well-defined soft-tissue mass containing fat and calcification.
2. **Diaphragmatic hernia** – bowel, liver, kidney or stomach may also be present. Anterior (Morgagni) hernias are usually on the right, and posterior (Bochdalek) hernias usually on the left. Linear soft-tissue densities representing omental vessels help to distinguish hernias which only contain omental fat from pericardial fat pads.
3. **Lipoma** – relatively rare. Can occur anywhere in mediastinum.
4. **Liposarcoma** – can contain calcification, and may also appear as a soft-tissue mass with no visible fat, due to excess soft-tissue component of the sarcoma.
5. **Thymolipoma** – occurs in children and young adults. Accounts for 2–9% of thymic tumours. Usually asymptomatic.
6. **Mediastinal lipomatosis** – associated with Cushing's, steroid treatment and obesity.
7. **Hamartoma.**
8. **Chylolymphatic cyst** – fat/fluid level in cyst.
9. **Neurofibroma** – can have a negative CT attenuation due to myelin content.

Further Reading

Phillips G.W.L., Serapati A. & Young A.E. (1988) Chylolymphatic-mesenteric cyst: a diagnostic appearance on computed tomography. *Br. J. Radiol.*, 61: 413–14.

Reed D.H. (1988) The changing mediastinum. *Br. J. Radiol.*, 61: 695–6.

Shirkhoda A., Chasen M.H., Eftekhari F., Goldman A.M. & Decaro L.F. (1987) M.R. imaging of mediastinal thymolipoma. *J. Comput. Assist. Tomogr.*, 11: 364–5.

4.58 CT Mediastinal Cysts

1. **Congenital**
   (a) Bronchogenic cyst – usually subcarinal or right para-tracheal site. 50% homogeneous water density, 50% soft-tissue density due to mucus or milk of calcium content. Occasional calcification in cyst wall, and air in cyst if communicates with airway.
   (b) Enteric cyst – paraoesophageal site.
   (c) Neuroenteric cyst – associated anomaly of spine.
2. **Pericardial cyst** – usually cardiophrenic angle.
3. **Thymic cyst** – can develop following radiotherapy for Hodgkin's.
4. **Cystic tumours**
   (a) Lymphangioma.
   (b) Teratoma.
   (c) Teratodermoid.
5. **Pancreatic pseudocyst** – can track up into mediastinum.
6. **Meningocele** – 75% association with neurofibromatosis.
7. **Chronic abscess.**
8. **Old haematoma.**

Further Reading

DuMontier C., Graviss E.R., Silberstein M.J. & McAlister W.H. (1985) Bronchogenic cysts in children. *Clin. Radiol.*, 36: 431–6.

Nakata H, Sato Y., Nakayama T., Yoshimatsu H. & Kobayashi T. (1986) Bronchogenic cyst with high C.T. numbers: analysis of contents. *J. Comput. Assist. Tomogr.*, 10 (2): 360–2.

4.59 CT Thymic Mass

Normal shape of thymus is an arrowhead with maximum length less than 2 cm and maximum width less than 1.8 cm if age less than 20 years, and 1.3 cm if age greater than 20 years. However measurements are misleading, and a multi-lobular appearance or focal alteration in shape is abnormal at any age. Fatty involution occurs after the age of 30.

1. **Thymoma** – occurs in 15% of myasthenia gravis (usually occurring in the 4th decade) and 40% of these will be malignant. If malignant it is usually locally invasive and can extend along pleura to involve diaphragm and even spread into abdomen. Can contain calcification.
2. **Thymic hyperplasia**
   (a) Lymphoid – occurs in 65% of myasthenia gravis. Only medulla enlarges and this is not sufficient to be visible on CT.
   (b) True hyperplasia – occurs in myasthenia gravis, post chemotherapy rebound, Graves thyrotoxicosis, Addison's and acromegaly. Thymus increases in size but is normal in shape.
3. **Germ cell tumour** – teratodermoid, benign and malignant teratomas.
4. **Lymphoma** – thymus is infiltrated in 35% of Hodgkin's disease but there is always associated lymphadenopathy.
5. **Thymolipoma** – usually children or young adults. Asymptomatic.

Further Reading

Heron C.W., Husband, J.E. & Williams M.P. (1988) Hodgkin's disease: C.T. of the thymus. *Radiology*, 167: 647–51.

Moore N.R. (1989) Imaging in myasthenia gravis. *Clin. Radiol.* , 40: 115–16.

Williams M.P. (1989) Problems in radiology: C.T. assessment of the thymus. *Clin. Radiol.*, 40: 113–14.

5
Cardiovascular System

5.1 Situs and Cardiac Malpositions

Assess the positions of the cardiac apex, aortic arch, left and right main bronchi, stomach bubble, liver and spleen. (Isolated right sided aortic arch is not considered a malposition.)

1. **Situs solitus** – normal. All structures are concordant.
2. **Situs inversus** – cardiac apex, aortic arch and stomach are on the right; visceral organs are on the opposite side to normal. Slight increase in the incidence of congenital heart disease. Patients have sinusitis and bronchiectasis (Kartagener's syndrome).
3. **Situs solitus with dextrocardia** – cardiac apex on right with stomach bubble on left. Due to failure of rotation of the embryonic cardiac loop and > 90% of cases are associated with congenital heart disease, usually cyanotic (corrected TGA, VSD and pulmonary stenosis). Scimitar syndrome is dextrocardia, hypoplastic right lung and partial anomalous pulmonary venous drainage into the inferior cava.
4. **Levoversion with abdominal situs inversus** – incidence of congenital heart disease 100%.
5. **Situs ambiguous with bilateral 'right-sidedness': asplenia syndrome** – absent spleen, bilateral trilobed lungs, right and left lobes of liver are similar size. Cardiac apex left, right or midline. Complex cardiac anomalies ± small bowel malrotation.
6. **Situs ambiguous with bilateral 'left-sidedness': polysplenia syndrome** – bilateral bilobed lungs, absent hepatic segment of IVC and enlarged azygos and hemiazygos veins. Intra-cardiac anomalies, but less complex than in bilateral 'right-sidedness'.

5.2 Gross Cardiac Enlargement

1. **Multiple valvular disease** – aortic and mitral valve disease, particularly with regurgitation.
2. **Pericardial effusion** – no recognizable chamber enlargement. Flask-shaped heart on the erect film which becomes globular on the supine film. Acute angle between right heart border and right hemidiaphragm. The effusion masks ventricular wall movement; therefore, unusually sharp cardiac outline on the chest radiograph and poor pulsation on the fluoroscopy. Rapid change in size on serial films. Diagnosis best made by echocardiography.
3. **ASD** – with pulmonary pleonaemia or an Eisenmenger situation.
4. **Cardiomyopathy** – including ischaemia.
5. **Ebstein's anomaly** – the posterior or septal cusp of the tricuspid valve arises distally from the wall of the right ventricle. Marked tricuspid incompetence. Marked right atrioventricular enlargement. Small aorta. Oligaemic lungs. Sharp cardiac outline.

5.3 Small Heart

1. **Normal variant.**
2. **Emphysema.**
3. **Addison's disease.**
4. **Dehydration/malnutrition.**
5. **Constrictive pericarditis.**

5.4   Enlarged Right Atrium

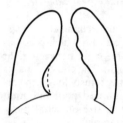

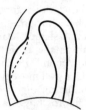

PA	Lateral
Prominent right heart border	Prominent anterosuperior part of cardiac shadow

Volume Overload
1. **ASD.**
2. **AV canal.**
3. **Tricuspid incompetence** – including Ebstein's anomaly, endocardial fibroelastosis and endomyocardial fibrosis. In 9% of patients following mitral valve replacement. In Uhl's disease there is a thin-walled, dilated right ventricle due to focal or complete absence of right ventricular myocardium.
4. **Anomalous pulmonary venous drainage.**

Pressure Overload
1. **Tricuspid stenosis** – NB in tricuspid atresia a shunt must exist to preserve life. This decompresses the right atrium, so that it is not large (typically a straight right heart border).
2. **Myxoma of the right atrium** – may cause tricuspid obstruction.

Secondary to Right Ventricular Failure
See 5.5.

Further Reading
Rubin S.A., Hightower C.W. & Flicker S. (1987) Giant right atrium after mitral valve replacement: plain film findings in 15 patients. *Am. J. Roentgenol.*, 149: 257–60.

5.5 Enlarged Right Ventricle

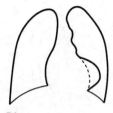

PA
Prominent left heart
border
Elevated apex

Lateral
Prominent anterior part
of cardiac shadow

Secondary to Left Heart Failure/Mitral Valve Disease
See 5.7.

Pulmonary Arterial Hypertension
1. **Diffuse lung disease** – e.g. chronic obstructive airways disease, interstitial fibrosis, cystic fibrosis etc.
2. **Pulmonary emboli** – see Pulmonary embolic disease*.
3. **Chronic left to right shunt** – with pulmonary hypertension and right ventricular failure.
4. **Vasculitis** – e.g. polyarteritis nodosa.
5. **Idiopathic** – mostly young females.

Pressure Overload
1. Pulmonary stenosis.

Volume Overload
1. ASD.
2. VSD.

5.6   Enlarged Left Atrium

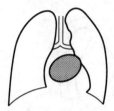

PA
1 Prominent left atrial appendage
2 'Double' right heart border
3 Increased density due to left atrium
4 Splaying of carina and elevated
   left main bronchus

Lateral
1 Prominent
   posterosuperior
   part of cardiac
   shadow
2 Prominent left
   atrial impression
   on oesophagus
   during barium
   swallow

Volume Overload
1. Mitral incompetence.
2. VSD.
3. PDA.
4. ASD with shunt reversal – Eisenmenger's complex or tri-cuspid atresia.

Pressure Overload
1. Mitral stenosis.
2. Myxoma of the left atrium.

Secondary to Left Ventricular Failure

5.7 Enlarged Left Ventricle

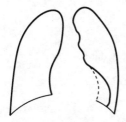

PA
1 Prominent left heart border
2 Rounding of left heart border
3 Apex displaced inferiorly

Lateral
Prominent posteroinferior
part of cardiac shadow

Myocardial
1. Ischaemia.
2. Cardiomyopathy/myocarditis.

Volume Overload
1. Aortic incompetence.
2. Mitral incompetence.
3. VSD.
4. PDA.

High Output States
1. Anaemia.
2. Hyperthyroidism.
3. Paget's disease*.
4. AV fistula.

Pressure Overload (dilatation is end stage)
1. Aortic stenosis.
2. Hypertension.
3. Coarctation of the aorta.

5.8 Bulge on the Left Heart Border

1. Enlarged left atrial appendage.
2. Ventricular aneurysm.
3. Pericardial cyst.
4. Pericardial sac defect.
5. Myocardial mass – e.g. neoplasm, hydatid.
6. Coronary artery aneurysm.

5.9 Cardiac Calcification

Pericardial
Primarily located over the right sided chambers and in the atrioventricular grooves; less frequently over the base of the left ventricle and rarely over the apex of the left ventricle. When the left ventricle is involved there is always more extensive calcification elsewhere in the pericardium.
1. **Post-pericarditis** – TB, rheumatic fever, pyogenic, viral.
2. **Post-traumatic/postoperative.**
3. **Uraemia.**
4. **Asbestosis***   } may appear to be
5. **Coronary artery**   } 'pericardial'.

Myocardial
Predominantly in the apex of the left ventricle or, uncommonly, in the posterior wall of the left ventricle.
1. **Calcified infarct.**
2. **Aneurysm.**
3. **Post-myocarditis** – especially rheumatic fever.
4. **Hydatid.**

Intracardiac
1. **Calcified valve** – see 5.10.
2. **Calcified thrombus** – overlying an infarct or in an aneurysm.
3. **Atrial myxoma** – larger, more mobile and lobulated than a calcified thrombus.

Further Reading
MacGregor J.H., Chen J.T.T., Chiles C., Kier R., Godwin J.D. & Ravi C.E. (1987) The radiographic distinction between pericardial and myocardial calcifications. *Am. J. Roentgenol.*, 148: 675–7.
Shawdon H.H. & Dinsmore R.E. (1967) Pericardial calcification: radiological features and clinical significance in twenty-six patients. *Clin. Radiol.*, 18: 205–14.

5.10 Valve Calcification

Aortic Valve
1. Bicuspid aortic valve.
2. Rheumatic heart disease.
3. Ageing.
4. Syphilis.
5. Ankylosing spondylitis*.

Mitral Valve
1. Rheumatic heart disease.

Pulmonary Valve
1. Pulmonary valve stenosis } in middle age.
2. Fallot's tetralogy
3. Pulmonary hypertension.
4. Homograft – for severe Fallot's tetralogy or pulmonary atresia.

Tricuspid Valve
1. Pulmonary valve stenosis (with high systolic pressures).
2. ASD.
3. Isolated tricuspid regurgitation.

5.11 Large Aortic Arch

1. **Unfolded (atherosclerotic) aorta** – parallel walls ± calcification.
2. **Hypertension** – on its own only leads to slight unfolding with left ventricular enlargement.
3. **Aortic incompetence** – prominent ascending aorta.
4. **Aortic stenosis** – post-stenotic dilation. ± aortic valve calcification.
5. **Aneurysm** – loss of parallelism of walls. Aetiologies include
   (a) Atherosclerosis – calcification prominent.
   (b) Trauma.
   (c) Infection – e.g. syphilis, subacute bacterial endocarditis.
   (d) Intrinsic abnormality – e.g. Marfan's syndrome.
   Macroscopically the aneurysm may be
   (a) Fusiform.
   (b) Saccular.
   (c) Dissecting – signs on the plain chest X-ray include
      (i) Ill-defined aortic outline (because of mediastinal haematoma).
      (ii) Tracheal shift.
      (iii) Left pleural effusion (haemothorax).
      (iv) Left apical cap (also due to effusion).
      (v) Sudden increase in size of the aorta when compared with a previous film.
6. **PDA.**

Further Reading
Dow J., Roebuck E.J. & Cole F. (1970) Dissecting aneurysms of the aorta. *Br. J. Radiol.*, 39: 915–27.

5.12 Small Aortic Arch

1. **Decreased cardiac output** – e.g. mitral stenosis, HOCM.
2. **Intracardiac left to right shunt.**
3. **Coarctation** – long segment 'infantile' type.
4. **(Transposition of great arteries** – rotated but not small.)

5.13   Right Sided Aortic Arch

1. Aortic knuckle on right side.
2. Absent left sided aortic knuckle.
3. Trachea central or slightly to the left side.
4. In 0.1% of normal adults and 6% of neonates with significant congenital heart disease.

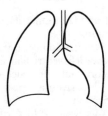

Type 1: Mirror Image Branching
98% incidence of congenital heart disease – nearly all of which will be tetralogy of Fallot. However, because of the relative incidence of different cardiac defects the incidence of right sided aortic arch in different congenital heart defects is:
1. **Dextrocardia with situs inversus** – a feature in 30% of cases.
2. **Fallot's tetralogy** – 25%.
3. **Pulmonary atresia + VSD** – 25%.
4. **Double outlet right ventricle** – 15%.
5. **Truncus arteriosus** – 15–50%.
6. **Corrected transposition of the great vessels** – 20%.
7. **Uncomplicated VSD** – 3%.

Type 2 (rare)

Type 3: Right Sided Aortic Arch with Aberrant Left Subclavian Artery
12% incidence of congenital heart disease – Fallot's tetralogy (70%), VSD (20%), Coarctation (10%).

Further Reading
Glew D. & Hartnell G.G. (1991) The right aortic arch revisited. *Clin. Radiol.*, 43: 305–7.
Knight L. & Edwards J.E. (1974) Right aortic arch. Types and associated anomalies. *Circulation*, 50: 1047–51.

5.14 Enlarged Superior Vena Cava

Volume Overload
1. Tricuspid incompetence.
2. **TAPVD** – if supracardiac. 'Cottage loaf' cardiac configuration, with pulmonary pleonaemia.

Obstruction
1. Carcinoma of the bronchus.
2. Mediastinal mass.
3. Mediastinal fibrosis – radiotherapy, idiopathic.
4. Constrictive pericarditis.

5.15 Enlarged Azygos Vein

If greater than 1 cm in diameter. (A normal or abnormal azygos vein will decrease in size in the erect position, on deep inspiration, and during a Valsalva manoeuvre.)

1. Heart failure.
2. Portal hypertension.
3. Superior or inferior vena cava obstruction.
4. Pregnancy.
5. Constrictive pericarditis/pericardial effusion.

Differential Diagnosis
1. Sinus venosus defect – right upper and middle lobe pulmonary veins drain into the superior vena cava (+ ASD).

5.16   Enlarged Pulmonary Arteries

Volume Overload (enlarged central and peripheral vessels)
1. **Left-to-right shunt** – the sign is apparent when the shunt reaches 3:1.
2. **Hyperdynamic circulation** – e.g. thyrotoxicosis, severe anaemia, beri-beri and Paget's disease.

Peripheral Arterial Vasoconstriction (enlarged central vessels only)
1. **Hypoxia** – e.g. due to chronic obstructive airways disease or cystic fibrosis.
2. **Secondary to pulmonary venous hypertension** – e.g. mitral stenosis or left ventricular failure.
3. **Secondary to left-to-right shunts.**

Peripheral Arterial Obliteration (enlarged central vessels only)
1. **Secondary to left-to-right shunts.**
2. **Thromboembolic disease** (see Pulmonary embolic disease*).
3. **Tumour emboli.**
4. **Schistosomiasis.**
5. **Vasculitides** – e.g. polyarteritis nodosa.
6. **Idiopathic pulmonary arterial hypertension** – typically in young females.

5.17   Enlarged Pulmonary Veins

Left Ventricular Failure

Obstruction at Mitral or Atrial Level
1. **Mitral stenosis.**
2. **Left atrial myxoma.**
3. **Ball-valve thrombus.**
4. **Cor triatriatum.**

Obstruction Proximal to the Atrium
1. TAPVD.
2. Constrictive pericarditis – rarely.
3. Mediastinal fibrosis.

5.18 Neonatal Pulmonary Venous Congestion

1. Prominent interstitial markings.
2. Indistinct vessels.
3. Perihilar haze.
4. Pleural effusions.
5. Cardiomegaly – in all except the infradiaphragmatic type of TAPVD.

1st Week
1. **Overhydration** – delayed clamping of the cord and twin–twin transfusion.
2. **Asphyxia** – the most common cause of cardiomegaly on the first day.
3. **Hypoplastic left heart.**
4. **Critical aortic stenosis.**
5. TAPVD (obstructed).

2nd–3rd Weeks
1. Coarctation of the aorta.
2. Interrupted aortic arch.
3. Critical aortic stenosis.

4th–6th Weeks
1. Coarctation.
2. Critical aortic stenosis.
3. Endocardial fibroelastosis.
4. Anomalous left coronary artery.

NB Left-to-right shunts are usually asymptomatic during the neonatal period because of the high pulmonary vascular resistance. However, pulmonary vascular resistance in premature infants is lower, so shunts may present earlier in this particular group. Patent ductus arteriosus is the commonest shunt to cause heart failure in premature infants.

5.19   Neonatal Cyanosis

With Pleonaemia
Cyanosis and congestive cardiac failure – either may predominate.
1. Transposition.
2. Truncus arteriosus.
3. TAPVD.
4. Single ventricle.
5. Hypoplastic left ventricle } predominantly congestive
6. Interrupted aortic arch } cardiac failure, but may be cyanosed.

With Oligaemia and Cardiomegaly
All have an ASD.
1. Pulmonary stenosis.
2. Ebstein's anomaly.
3. Pulmonary atresia with an intact ventricular septum.
4. Tricuspid atresia.

With Oligaemia but no Cardiomegaly
Signs appear towards the end of the first week due to closure of the ductus arteriosus.

1. Fallot's tetralogy.
2. Pulmonary atresia with a VSD.
3. Tricuspid atresia.

See also 'Neonatal respiratory distress' (4.46).

5.20 Cardiovascular Involvement in Syndromes

Cri-du-chat	Variable.
Down's*	AV canal, VSD, PDA, ASD, and aberrant right subclavian artery.
Ehlers–Danlos	Mitral valve prolapse, aortic root dilatation, dissecting aortic aneurysm and intracranial aneurysm.
Ellis–Van Creveld	ASD and common atrium.
Friedreich's ataxia	Hypertrophic cardiomyopathy.
Holt–Oram	ASD and VSD.
Homocystinuria*	Medial degeneration of the aorta and pulmonary artery causing dilatation. Arterial and venous thromboses.
Hurler's/Hunter's*	Intimal thickening of coronary arteries and valves.
Kartagener's	Situs inversus ± septal defects.
Marfan's	Cystic medial necrosis of the wall of the aorta, and less commonly the pulmonary artery, leading to dilatation and predisposing to dissection. Aortic and mitral regurgitation.
Morquio's*	Late onset of aortic regurgitation.
Noonan's	Pulmonary valve stenosis, and branch stenosis of pulmonary arteries septal defects.
Osteogenesis imperfecta*	Aortic and mitral regurgitation. Ruptured chordae.
Rubella	Septal defects, PDA, pulmonary artery branch stenoses and myocardial disease.
Trisomy 13	VSD, ASD, PDA and dextroposition.
Trisomy 18	VSD, ASD and PDA.
Tuberous sclerosis*	Cardiomyopathy and rhabdomyoma of the heart.
Turner's	Coarctation, aortic and bicuspid aortic valve stenosis.

5.21 Complications of Subclavian Vein Catheterization

(After Gibson *et al.*)

Major
1. **Pneumothorax** – in up to 6% of cases and 30% of all major complications.
2. **Vascular injury** – haemomediastinum, haemothorax, arteriovenous fistula.
3. **Extravascular infusion** – intrapleural, mediastinal.
4. **Thrombosis.**
5. **Air embolism.**
6. **Catheter embolism.**
7. **Nerve injury** – e.g. brachial plexus.
8. **Cardiac** – arrhythmias, myocardial perforation, tamponade.

Minor
1. **Failed catheterization.**
2. **Catheter malposition.** } potentially major complications.
3. **Subclavian artery puncture.** } complications.
4. **Local haematoma.**
5. **Subcutaneous infusion.**
6. **Occluded catheter.**
7. **Dislodged catheter.**

Further Reading
Gibson R.N., Hennessy O.F., Collier N. & Hemingway A.P. (1985) Major complications of central venous catheterization: a report of five cases and a brief review of the literature. *Clin. Radiol.*, 36: 205–8.

Mitchell S.E. & Clark R.A. (1979) Complications of central venous catheterization. *Am. J. Roentgenol.*, 138: 467–76.

6
Abdomen and Gastrointestinal Tract

6.1 Extraluminal Intra-abdominal Gas

1. **Pneumoperitoneum** – see 6.2.
2. **Gas in bowel wall**
   (a) Pneumatosis coli.
   (b) Linear pneumatosis intestinalis – infarction (e.g. due to vascular disease, volvulus, necrotizing enterocolitis).
3. **Biliary tree gas** (q.v.) – see 7.3.
4. **Portal vein gas** (q.v.) – see 7.4.
5. **Urinary tract gas** (q.v.) – see 8.4.
6. **Abscess** – mottled gas which may mimic gas within colonic faeces. A homogeneous gas distribution (less common) may mimic gas in normal bowel. Lack of mucosal pattern helps to differentiate it.
7. **Necrotic tumour** – especially following chemotherapy, radiotherapy and therapeutic embolization.
8. **Retroperitoneal gas** – small 'bubbles' or linear translucencies. Secondary to perforation or post-nephrectomy.

Further Reading
Rice R.P., Thompson W.M. & Gedgandas R.K. (1982) The diagnosis and significance of extraluminal gas in the abdomen. *Radiol. Clin. North Am.*, 20: 819–37.

6.2 Pneumoperitoneum

1. Erect – free gas under diaphragm or liver. Can detect 10 ml of air. Can take 10 min for all gas to rise.
2. Supine – gas outlines both sides of bowel wall, which then appears as a white line. In infants a large volume of gas will collect centrally producing a rounded, relative translucency over the central abdomen. The falciform ligament may also be outlined by free gas. This is seen as a characteristic curvilinear white line in the right upper abdomen.

1. **Perforation**
   (a) Peptic ulcer – 30% do not have free air visible.
   (b) Inflammation – diverticulitis, appendicitis, toxic megacolon, necrotizing enterocolitis.
   (c) Infarction.
   (d) Malignant neoplasms.
   (e) Obstruction.
   (f) Pneumatosis coli – the cysts may rupture.
2. **Iatrogenic (surgery: peritoneal dialysis)** – may take 3 weeks to reabsorb (faster in obese and children), but serial views will show progressive diminution in volume of free air.
3. **Pneumomediastinum** – see 4.38.
4. **Introduction per vaginam** – e.g. douching.
5. **Pneumothorax** – due to a congenital pleuroperitoneal fistula.
6. **Idiopathic.**

6.3 Gasless Abdomen

Adult

1. **High obstruction.**
2. **Ascites** – see 6.4.
3. **Pancreatitis** (acute) – due to excess vomiting.
4. **Fluid-filled bowel** – closed-loop obstruction, total active colitis, mesenteric infarction (early), bowel wash-out.
5. **Large abdominal mass** – pushes bowel laterally.
6. **Normal.**

Child

1. **High obstruction**
   (a) Oesophageal atresia, without a fistula distally.
   (b) Duodenal atresia.
   (c) Annular pancreas.
   (d) Volvulus (secondary to malrotation).
   (e) Hypertrophic pyloric stenosis.
   (f) Choledochal cyst.
2. **Vomiting** – including excess nasogastric aspiration.
3. **Fluid-filled bowel** – see above.
4. **Congenital diaphragmatic hernia** – bowel in the chest.

6.4 Ascites

1. Hazy appearance of entire abdomen.
2. Bowel gas 'floats' centrally on supine film.
3. Bulging flank lines.

1. **Cirrhosis.**
2. **Tumours.**
   (a) Malignant – peritoneal metastases, primary carcinoma (particularly ovary and gastrointestinal tract).
   (b) Benign – fibroma of ovary (Meigs' syndrome).
3. **Hypoalbuminaemia** – e.g. nephrotic syndrome.
4. **Peritonitis** – particularly TB.
5. **Increased pressure in vascular system distal to liver** – congestive cardiac failure, constrictive pericarditis, thrombosis of inferior vena cava.
6. **Lymphatic obstruction** – chylous ascites, lymphoma, radiation, trauma or filariasis.

6.5 Abdominal Mass in a Neonate

(After Kirks *et al.*, 1981).

Renal (55%) (q.v.)

1. **Hydronephrosis** (25%) – e.g. pelviureteric junction obstruction, posterior urethral valves, ectopic ureterocele, prune-belly and ureterovesical junction obstruction.
2. **Multicystic kidney** (15%).
3. **Infantile polycystic kidneys** (see Polycystic disease*) – ± hepatic fibrosis.
4. **Mesoblastic nephroma** – benign hamartoma.
5. **Renal vein thrombosis** – complication of dehydration/ sepsis.
6. **Renal ectopia.**
7. **Wilms' tumour.**

Genital (15%)

1. **Hydrometrocolpos** – dilated fluid-filled vagina and/or uterus, due to vaginal stenosis. ± Associated with imperforate anus or gastrointestinal fistula.
2. **Ovarian cyst.**

Gastrointestinal (15%) – commonly associated with obstruction

1. **Duplication** – commonest bowel mass in neonate. Commonly in right lower quadrant.
2. **Mesenteric cyst.**

Non-renal Retroperitoneal (10%)

1. **Adrenal haemorrhage** – relatively common. Due to neonatal stress. ± asymptomatic.
2. **Neuroblastoma.**
3. **Teratoma.**

Hepato/spleno/biliary (5%)

1. **Hepatoblastoma** – see 7.7.
2. **Hepatic cyst.**

3. **Splenic haematoma.**
4. **Choledochal cyst** – see 7.10.

Further Reading
Kirks D.R., Merten D.F., Grossman H. & Bowie J.D. (1981) Diagnostic imaging of paediatric abdominal masses: an overview. *Radiol. Clin. North Am.*, 19: 527–45.
See also 'Renal mass in the newborn and young infant', section (8.18).

6.6 Abdominal Mass in a Child

(After Kirks *et al.*, 1981.)

Renal (55%)
1. **Wilms' tumour** – second commonest primary abdominal neoplasm in childhood (just behind neuroblastoma). See 8.13.
2. **Hydronephrosis** (20%) – see 8.19.
3. **Cysts** – see 8.16.

Non-renal Retroperitoneal (23%)
1. Neuroblastoma (21%)
   Age: 75% < 5 years; 15–30% < 1 year. Accounts for 50% of all neonatal tumours.
   Site: adrenal (40%), abdominal sympathetic chain (25%), posterior mediastinal sympathetic chain (15%), neck (5%), pelvis (5%), unknown (10%).
   Staging: In addition to staging along conventional lines, stage IVS (or 4S) is defined as localized primary tumour not crossing the midline and with remote disease confined to liver, subcutaneous tissues and bone marrow but without evidence of cortical bone involvement. This group invariably presents in the first year of life and has an excellent prognosis.
   Clinical presentation: 70% have metastases at presentation and a similar percentage have systemic symptoms. There may be local effects – pain, mass, spinal cord compression, dyspnoea or dysphagia, the effects of metastases – scalp masses, pain, weight loss, anaemia, fatigue etc., or other effects due to hormone secretion – opsomyoclonus (cerebellar ataxia and jerky eye movements; 50% have neuroblastoma), hypertension, diarrhoea (due to vasoactive intestinal peptide, VIP), flushing and sweating.
   Plain films: calcification in 2/3, loss of psoas outline, bony metastases, enlargement of intervertebral foramina and, in the chest, abnormal posterior ends of ribs.
   Ultrasound: heterogeneous, echogenic mass.
   CT: soft-tissue mass with calcification in nearly all. Encasement rather than displacement of major vessels.
   MRI: Prolonged T_1 and T_2 relaxation times. Calcification

is not as readily recognized as on CT but MRI is superior for lymph node metastases, liver metastases and extradural spread of tumour.

Radionuclide scanning: bone scanning and MIBG scanning are complementary techniques for the demonstration of skeletal metastases. MIBG is superior for follow-up of disease.

Gastrointestinal (18%)

1. **Appendix abscess** (10%) – particularly spreads to pouch anterior to rectum.
2. **Hepatoblastoma** – more commonly in right lobe, but 40% in both lobes. 40% calcify. See 7.7.
3. **Haemangioma** – commonly multiple, involving entire liver. Rarely calcify. ± associated with congestive heart failure, and cutaneous haemangiomas.
4. **Choledochal cyst** – the classical triad of mass, pain and jaundice is only present in 10%. Dynamic radionuclide scintigraphy with ^{99}Tc-TBIDA is diagnostic. See 7.10.

Genital (4%)

1. **Ovarian cysts or teratoma.**

Further Reading

Cohen M.D. (1992) *Imaging of Children with Cancer*, Ch. 6, pp. 134–76. St Louis: Mosby Year Book.

Kirks D.R., Merten D.F., Grossman H. & Bowie J.D. (1981) Diagnostic imaging of paediatric abdominal masses: an overview. *Radiol. Clin. North Am.*, 19: 527–45.

6.7 Intestinal Obstruction in a Neonate

Duodenal – most common
1. **Stenosis/atresia** – 'double bubble' sign, which may also be seen by ultrasound of fetus (+ hydramnios). Associated with annular pancreas (20%), mongolism (30%) and other abnormalities of gastrointestinal tract (60%).
2. **Annular pancreas** – if not associated with duodenal atresia it may not present until adulthood.
3. **Congenital fibrous band (of Ladd)** – connects caecum to posterolateral abdominal wall and commonly crosses the duodenum. May be complicated by malrotation and midgut volvulus.
4. **Congenital web.**
5. **Choledochal cyst.**
6. **Preduodenal portal vein.**

Jejunal
1. **Malrotation and volvulus.**
2. **Atresia** – 50% associated with atretic sites distally (ileum > colon).

Ileal
1. **Meconium ileus** – mottled lucencies due to gas trapped in meconium but only few fluid levels (since it is very viscous). Bowel loops of variable calibre. Rapid appearance of fluid levels suggests volvulus. Peritoneal calcification due to perforation occurring *in utero* is seen in 30%. Secondary microcolon.
2. **Atresia.**
3. **Inguinal hernia.**
4. **Inspissated milk** – presents 3 days to 6 weeks of age. Dense, amorphous intraluminal masses frequently surrounded by a rim of air, ± mottled lucencies within them. Usually resolves spontaneously.
5. **Paralytic ileus** – e.g. due to drugs administered during labour.

Colonic
1. **Hirschsprung's disease.**
2. **Functional immaturity** – including meconium plug syndrome and small left colon syndrome.

3. **Imperforate anus**
   (a) High – ± sacral agenesis and gas in the bladder (due to a recto–vesical fistula).
   (b) Low – ± perineal or urethral fistula.
4. **Atresia.**

Further Reading

Carty H. & Brereton R.J. (1983) The distended neonate. *Clin. Radiol.*, 34: 367–80.

LeQuesne G.W. & Reilly B.J. (1975) Functional immaturity of the large bowel. *Radiol. Clin. North Am.*, 13: 331–42.

Martin D.J. (1975) Experiences with acute surgical conditions. *Radiol. Clin. North Am.*, 13: 297–329.

Rathaus V., Grunebaum M., Ziv N., Kornreich L. & Horev G. (1992) The bubble sign in the gasless abdomen of the newborn. *Pediatr. Radiol.*, 22: 106–9.

6.8 Abnormalities of Bowel Rotation

1. **Exomphalos** – total failure of the bowel to return to the abdomen from the umbilical cord. Bowel is contained within a sac. To be differentiated from gastroschisis in which bowel protrudes through a defect in the abdominal wall.

2. **Non-rotation** – usually an asymptomatic condition with the small bowel on the right side of the abdomen and the colon on the left side. Small and large bowel lie on either side of the superior mesenteric artery (SMA) with a common mesentery. CT or transverse US scans show the superior mesenteric vein (SMV) lying to the left of the SMA cf the normal arrangement in which the SMV lies to the right of the SMA.

3. **Malrotation** – the duodeno-jejunal flexure lies to the right and caudad to its usual position which is to the left of the midline and approximately in the same axial plane as the 1st part of the duodenum. The caecum is usually more cephalad than normal but is normally sited in 5%. Malrotation nearly always complicates left sided diaphragmatic hernia. US or CT shows the SMV immediately anterior to the SMA. *This sign is not reliable when SMA lies to the left of the aorta, e.g. in association with hepatomegaly, aortic aneurysm or scoliosis and a normal US does not exclude malrotation (3% false negative rate).*

4. **Reverse rotation** – rare. Colon lies dorsal to the SMA with jejunum and duodenum anterior to it.

5. **Paraduodenal hernia** – rare.

6. **Extroversion of the cloaca** – rare. No rotation of the bowel and the ileum and colon open separately onto the extroverted area in the midline below the umbilical cord.

Further Reading

Dufour D., Delaet M.H., Dassonville M., Cadranel S. & Perlmutter N. (1992) Midgut malrotation, the reliability of sonographic diagnosis. *Pediatr. Radiol.*, 22: 21–3.

Gaines P.A., Saunders A.J.S. & Drake D. (1987) Midgut malrotation diagnosed by ultrasound. *Clin. Radiol.*, 38: 51–3.

Houston C.S. & Wittenborg M.H. (1965) Roentgen evaluation of anomalies of rotation and fixation of the bowel in children. *Radiology*, 84: 1–17.

Nichols D.M. & Li D.K. (1983) Superior mesenteric vein rotation: a CT sign of midgut malrotation. *Am. J. Roentgenol.*, 141: 707–8.

6.9 Intra-abdominal Calcifications in the Newborn

Extraluminal

1. Fetal perforation and meconium peritonitis

Intraluminal

1. Non-hereditary intestinal obstructions – imperforate anus, small bowel atresia and Hirschsprung's disease.
2. Multiple gastrointestinal atresias with AR inheritance.
3. Without obstruction.

See 7.8.

Further Reading

Beasley S.W. & de Campo M. (1986) Intraluminal calcification in the newborn: diagnostic and surgical implications. *Pediatr. Surg.*, 1: 249.

Berdon W.E., Baker D.H., Wigger H.J. *et al.* (1975) Calcified intraluminal meconium in newborn males with imperforate anus. *Am. J. Roentgenol.*, 125: 449–55.

Miller J.P., Smith S.D. & Sukarochana K. (1988) Neonatal abdominal calcification: is it always meconium peritonitis? *J. Pediatr. Surg.*, 23: 555.

Yousefzadeh D.K., Jackson Jr J.H., Smith W.L. & Lu Ch. H. (1984) Intraluminal meconium calcification without distal obstruction. *Pediatr. Radiol.*, 14: 23–27.

6.10 Haematemesis

Oesophagus
1. **Hiatus hernia.**
2. **Varices** – 20% of cases are bleeding from a coexisting peptic ulcer.
3. **Neoplasms.**
4. **Mallory–Weiss tears.**

Stomach
1. **Ulcer**
2. **Erosions** – may be associated with steroids, analgesics or alcohol.
3. **Carcinoma.**

Duodenum
1. **Ulcer.**

Others
1. **Blood dyscrasias.**
2. **Osler–Weber–Rendu (hereditary telangiectasia)** – autosomal dominant. Telangiectasis not prominent until age 20. Epistaxis is often the first symptom.
3. **Connective tissue disorders** – Ehlers–Danlos syndrome, pseudoxanthoma elasticum.

6.11 Dysphagia – Adult

Intrinsic
1. **Reflux stricture.**
2. **Tumours** – carcinoma, lymphoma, leiomyoma.
3. **Ingestion** – corrosive, lye, foreign body.
4. **Iatrogenic** – radiotherapy, prolonged nasogastric intubation.

5. **Plummer–Vinson web** – narrow anterior indentation. Can occur from C4 to T1. Females with iron deficiency anaemia; males post-gastrectomy. Premalignant, but tumour can occur at different site.
6. **Schatzki ring** – marks the squamo-columnar junction lying above the diaphragm. Acute obstruction may occur if internal diameter is less than 6 mm.
7. **Monilia** – painful dysphagia. Can involve entire oesophagus – 'shaggy', ulcerated. Immunosuppression, long-term antibiotics, hypoparathyroidism and debilitation all predispose. Herpes simplex and CMV may cause identical changes.
8. **Skin disorders** – epidermolysis bullosa and pemphigus can produce strictures.

Extrinsic

1. **Tumours** – lymph nodes, mediastinal tumours.
2. **Vascular** – aortic aneurysm; aberrant right subclavian artery (posterior indentation); aberrant left pulmonary artery (anterior indentation); right sided aortic arch (right lateral and posterior indentation).
3. **Pharyngeal pouch** – ± air/fluid level in neck. Can cause superior mediastinal mass. Signs of aspiration on chest X-ray.
4. **Goitre**.
5. **Enterogenous cyst** – adjacent to, but rarely communicates with, the oesophagus. Hemivertebra and anterior meningocele may be associated (neuro-enteric cyst).
6. **Prevertebral abscess/haematoma**.

Neuromuscular

1. **Achalasia**.
2. **Scleroderma***.
3. **Chagas' disease**.
4. **Myasthenia gravis***.
5. **Bulbar/pseudobulbar palsy**.

Psychiatric

1. **Globus hystericus**.

6.12   Dysphagia – Neonate

1. Cleft palate.
2. **Macroglossia/glossoptosis** – e.g. Beckwith–Wiedemann syndrome and Pierre Robin syndrome.
3. **Osteophageal atresia.**
4. **Vascular rings.**

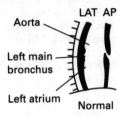

Normal

Aberrant right subclavian artery

Right-sided aortic arch

Aberrant left pulmonary artery

5. **Choanal atresia.**
6. **Neuromuscular defects** – e.g. delayed maturation, prematurity and mental subnormality.

Further Reading

Illingworth R.S. (1969) Sucking and swallowing difficulties in infancy. Diagnostic problems of dysphagia. *Arch. Dis. Child.*, 44: 655–65.

6.13   Pharyngeal/Oesophageal 'Diverticula'

Upper Third

1. **Pouch (Zenker's)** – posteriorly, usually on left side, between the fibres of the inferior constrictor and cricopharyngeus. Can cause dysphagia, regurgitation, aspiration and hoarseness ± an air/fluid level. If large, can appear as a superior mediastinal mass. Food residue with it seen as 'mobile' filling defects.
2. **Lateral pharyngocele**
   (a) Congenital – remnant of the second branchial arch. Wide mouth (may not retain barium and so may only be seen in recumbent position).
   (b) Acquired – glassblower, trumpeter, etc.

Middle third

1. **Traction** – at level of carina. May be related to fibrosis after treatment for TB. Asymptomatic.
2. **Developmental** – failure to complete closure of tracheo-oesophageal communication.
3. **Intramural** – very rare. Multiple, tiny flask-shaped outpouchings. 90% have associated strictures, mainly in the upper third of the oesophagus.

Lower Third

1. **Epiphrenic.**
2. **Ulcer** – peptic or related to steroids, immunosuppression and radiotherapy.
3. **Mucosal tears** – Mallory–Weiss syndrome, post-oesophagoscopy.
4. **Post-Heller's operation.**

Further Reading

Levine M.S., Moolten D.N., Herlinger H. & Laufer I. (1986) Esophageal intramural pseudodiverticulosis: a reevaluation. *Am. J. Roentgenol.*, 147: 1165–70.

Schwartz E.E., Tucker J. & Holt G.P. (1981) Cervical dysphagia: pharyngeal protrusions and achalasia. *Clin. Radiol.*, 32: 643–50.

6.14 Oesophageal Ulceration

In addition to ulceration there may be non-specific signs of oesophagitis:

1. Thickening of longitudinal folds (> 2 mm), which may be slightly scalloped.
2. Thickening of tranverse folds resembling small bowel mucosal folds.
3. Reduced or absent peristalsis.

Inflammatory

1. **Reflux oesophagitis** – ± hiatus hernia. Signs characteristic of reflux oesophagitis are
   (a) a gastric fundal fold crossing the gastro-oesophageal junction and ending as a polypoid protuberance in the distal oesophagus,
   (b) erosions – dots or linear streaks of barium in the distal oesophagus,
   (c) ulcers which may be round or, more commonly, linear or serpiginous.
2. **Barrett's oesophagus** – to be considered in any patient with oesophageal ulceration or stricture but especially if the abnormality is in the body of the oesophagus.
3. **Moniliasis** – predominantly in immunosuppressed patients. Sudden onset of pain and dysphagia, not relieved by antacids. Early – small, plaque-like filling defects, often orientated in the long axis of the oesophagus. Advanced – cobblestone mucosal surface ± luminal narrowing. Ulceration is uncommon.

   Patients with mucocutaneous candidiasis or oesophageal stasis due to achalasia, scleroderma etc., may develop chronic infection which is characterized by a lacy or reticular appearance of the mucosa ± nodular filling defects.
4. **Viral** – herpes and CMV occurring mostly in immunocompromised patients. May manifest as discrete ulcers, ulcerated plaques or mimic monilial oesophagitis. Discrete ulcers on an otherwise normal background mucosa are strongly suggestive of a viral aetiology.
5. **Caustic ingestion** – ulceration is most marked at the sites of anatomical hold-up and progress to a long, smooth stricture.

6. **Radiotherapy** – ulceration is rare. Altered oesophageal motility is frequently the only abnormality.
7. **Crohn's disease*** – aphthous ulcers and, in advanced cases, undermining ulcers, intramural tracking and fistulae.
8. **Drug induced** – due to prolonged contact with tetracyline, quinidine and potassium supplements.
9. **Behçet's disease.**
10. **Intramural diverticulosis.**

Neoplastic

1. **Carcinoma.**
2. **Leiomyosarcoma and leiomyoma.**
3. **Lymphoma*.**
4. **Melanoma.**

Further Reading

Cynn W.S., Chon H.K., Gureghian P.A. & Levin B.L. (1975) Crohn's disease of the esophagus. *Am. J. Roentgenol.*, 125: 359–64.

Goldstein H.M., Rogers L.F. & Fletcher G.H. (1975) Radiological manifestations of radiation induced injury to the normal upper gastrointestinal tract. *Radiology*, 117: 135–40.

Heading R.C. (1987) Barrett's oesophagus. *Br. Med. J.*, 294: 461–2.

Laufer I. (1982) Radiology of esophagitis. *Radiol. Clin. North Am.*, 20 (4): 687–99.

Levine M.S., Laufer I., Kressel H.Y. & Friedman H.M. (1981) Herpes esophagitis. *Am. J. Roentgenol.*, 136: 863–6.

Lewicki A.M. & Moore J.P. (1975) Eosophageal moniliasis. A review of common and less frequent characteristics. *Am. J. Roentgenol.*, 125: 218–25.

Shortsleeve M.J., Gauvin G.P. & Gardner R.C. (1981) Herpetic esophagitis. *Radiology*, 141: 611–17.

6.15   Oesophageal Strictures – Smooth

Inflammatory

1. **Peptic** – the stricture develops relatively late. Most frequently at the oesophagogastric junction and associated with reflux and a hiatus hernia. Less commonly, more proximal in the oesophagus and associated with heterotopic gastric mucosa (Barrett's oesophagus). ± ulceration.

2. **Scleroderma*** – reflux through a wide open cardia may produce stricture. Oesophagus is the commonest internal organ to be affected. Peristalsis is poor, cardia wide open and the oesophagus dilated (contains air in the resting state).

3. **Corrosives** – acute – oedema, spasm, ulceration and loss of mucosal pattern at 'hold-up' points (aortic arch and oesophago-gastric junction). Strictures are typically long and symmetrical, may take several years to develop and are more likely to be produced by alkalis than acid.

4. **Iatrogenic** – prolonged use of a nasogastric tube. Stricture in distal oesophagus probably secondary to reflux.

Neoplastic

1. **Carcinoma** – squamous carcinoma may infiltrate submucosally. The absence of a hiatus hernia and the presence of an extrinsic soft-tissue mass should differentiate it from a peptic stricture but a carcinoma arising around the cardia may predispose to reflux.

2. **Mediastinal tumours** – carcinoma of the bronchus and lymph nodes. Localized obstruction ± ulceration and an extrinsic soft-tissue mass.

3. **Leiomyoma** – narrowing due to a smooth, eccentric, polypoid mass. ± central ulceration.

Others

1. **Achalasia** – 'rat-tail' tapering may mimic a stricture; this occurs below the diaphragm. Considerable oesophageal dilatation with food in the lumen.

2. **Skin disorders** – epidermolysis bullosa, pemphigus.

6.16 Oesophageal Strictures – Irregular

Neoplastic

1. **Carcinoma** – increased incidence in achalasia, Plummer–Vinson syndrome, Barrett's oesophagus, coeliac disease, asbestosis, lye ingestion and tylosis. Mostly squamous carcinomas; adenocarcinoma is rare. Appearances include
   (a) Irregular filling defect – annular or eccentric.
   (b) Extraluminal soft-tissue mass.
   (c) Re-entrant angles at its margins (shouldering).
   (d) Ulceration.
   (e) Proximal dilatation.
2. **Leiomyosarcoma.**
3. **Carcinosarcoma** – big polypoid tumour ± pedunculated. Better prognosis than squamous carcinoma.
4. **Lymphoma*** – usually extension from gastric involvement.

Inflammatory

1. **Reflux** – rarely irregular.
2. **Crohn's disease*** – rare.

Iatrogenic

1. **Radiotherapy** – rare, unless treating an oesophageal carcinoma. Dysphagia post radiotherapy is usually due to a motility disorder. Acute oesophagitis may occur with a dose of 50–60 Gy (5000–6000 rad).
2. **Fundoplication.**

Further Reading

Levine M.S., Dillon E.C., Saul S.H. & Laufer I. (1986) Early esophageal cancer. *Am. J. Roentgenol.*, 146: 507–12.

6.17 Tertiary Contractions in the Oesophagus

Uncoordinated, non-propulsive contractions.

1. **Reflux oesophagitis.**
2. **Presbyoesophagus** – impaired motor function due to muscle atrophy in the elderly. Occurs in 25% of people over 60 years.
3. **Obstruction at the cardia** – from any cause.
4. **Neuropathy**
   (a) Early achalasia – before dilatation occurs.
   (b) Diabetes.
   (c) Alcoholism.
   (d) Malignant infiltration.
   (e) Chagas' disease.

6.18 Stomach Masses and Filling Defects

Primary Malignant Neoplasms
1. **Carcinoma** – most polypoidal carcinomas are 1–4 cm in diameter. (Any polyp greater than 2 cm in diameter must be considered to be malignant.) Granular/lobulated surface pattern is suggestive of carcinoma. Asbestosis, adenomatous polyps and Peutz–Jeghers syndrome predispose. Metastases may calcify and sclerotic or lytic bone metastases may occur.
2. **Lymphoma*** – primary gastric lymphoma is usually non-Hodgkin's. It can be ulcerative and infiltrative as well as polypoid. Often cannot distinguish it from carcinoma, but extension across the pylorus is suggestive of a lymphoma.

Polyps
1. **Hyperplastic** – accounts for most polyps. Usually multiple, small (less than 1 cm in diameter) and occur randomly throughout stomach but predominantly affect body and fundus. Associated with chronic gastritis.

2. **Adenomatous** – usually solitary, 1–4 cm in diameter, sessile and occur in antrum. High incidence of malignant transformation (particularly if greater than 2 cm in size) and carcinomas elsewhere in stomach (because of dysplastic epithelium). Associated with pernicious anaemia.
3. **Hamartomatous** – characteristically multiple, small and relatively spare the antrum. Occur in 30% of Peutz– Jeghers syndrome, 40% of familiar polyposis coli and Gardner's syndrome.

Submucosal Neoplasms
Smooth, well-defined filling defect, with a re-entry angle.
1. **Leiomyoma** – commonest by far. Can be very large with a substantial exogastric component. Central ulceration and massive haematemesis may occur.
2. **Lipoma** – can change shape with position of patient and may be relatively mobile on palpation.
3. **Neurofibroma** – NB Leiomyomas and lipomas are more common, even in patients with generalized neurofibromatosis.
4. **Metastases** – Frequently ulcerate – 'bull's eye' lesion (q.v.). Usually melanoma, but bronchus, breast, lymphoma, Kaposi's sarcoma and any adenocarcinoma may metastasize to stomach. Breast primary often produces a scirrhous reaction in the distal part of the stomach which is indistinguishable from linitis plastica (q.v.).

Extrinsic Indentation
1. **Pancreatic tumour/pseudocyst.**
2. **Splenomegaly/hepatomegaly.**
3. **Retroperitoneal tumours.**

Others
1. **Nissen fundoplication** – may mimic a distorted mass in the fundus.
2. **Bezoar** – 'mass' is mobile. Tricho- (hair) or phyto (vegetable matter).
3. **Pancreatic 'rest'** – ectopic pancreatic tissue causes a small filling defect, usually on the inferior wall of the antrum, and resembles a submucosal tumour. Central 'blob' of barium ('bull's eye' or target lesion) in 50%.

6.19   Thick Stomach Folds

Thickness greater than 1 cm.

Inflammatory

1. **Gastritis** – associated with peptic ulceration.
2. **Zollinger–Ellison syndrome** – suspect if post-bulbar ulcers. Ulceration in both 1st and 2nd parts of duodenum is suggestive, but ulceration distal to this is virtually diagnostic. Thick folds and small bowel dilatation may occur in response to excess acidity.

   Due to gastrinoma of non-beta cells of pancreas (no calcification, moderately vascular). 50% malignant – metastases to liver. (10% of gastrinomas may be ectopic – usually in medial wall of the duodenum.)
3. **Pancreatitis (acute).**
4. **Crohn's disease*** – mild thickening of folds with aphthous ulceration may occur in up to 40% of Crohn's. However, these signs are subtle, and more obvious disease (i.e. deformity and narrowing of the antrum) only occurs in 2% of these.

Infiltrative/Neoplastic

1. **Lymphoma*** – usually non-Hodgkin's lymphoma and may be primary or secondary. Accounts for half of all gastrointestinal lymphomas. The predominant features of early disease are shallow ulceration or uneven mucosa with enlarged, radiating folds. Features which may suggest the diagnosis of advanced disease are: multiple masses or ulcerations, diffuse thickening of folds, extensive submucosal infiltration, extension across the pylorus or the gastro-oesophageal junction, large tumours over 10 cm in diameter and preservation of wall pliability.
2. **Carcinoma** – irregular folds with rigid wall.
3. **Pseudolymphoma** – benign reactive lymphoid hyperplasia. 70% have an ulcer near the centre of the area affected.
4. **Eosinophilic gastroenteritis.**

Others

1. **Ménétrier's disease** – smooth folds predominantly on greater curve. Rarely extend into antrum. No rigidity or

ulcers. 'Weep' protein sufficient to cause hypoproteinaemia (effusion, oedema, thick folds in small bowel). Commonly achlorhydric – cf. Zollinger–Ellison syndrome. In adults it pursues a chronic and unremitting course but in children resolution should be expected after weeks or months. In children the aetiology is likely to be cytomegalovirus infection.
2. **Varices** – occur in fundus and usually associated with oesophageal varices.

Further Reading

Coad N.A.G. & Shah K.J. (1986) Ménétrier's disease in childhood associated with cytomegalovirus infection: a case report and review of the literature. *Br. J. Radiol.*, 59: 615–20.

Hricak H., Thoeni R.F., Margulis A.R., Eyler W.R. & Francis I.R. (1980) Extension of gastric lymphoma into the esophagus and duodenum. *Radiology*, 135: 309–12.

Sato T., Sakai Y., Ishiguro S. & Furukawa H. (1986) Radiologic manifestations of early gastric lymphoma. *Am. J. Roentgenol.*, 146: 513–17.

6.20   Linitis Plastica

Neoplastic
1. Gastric carcinoma.
2. Lymphoma*.
3. Metastases – particularly breast.
4. Local invasion – pancreatic carcinoma.

Inflammatory
1. **Corrosives** – can cause rigid stricture of antrum extending up to the pylorus.
2. **Radiotherapy** – can cause rigid stricture of antrum with some deformity. Mucosal folds may be thickened or effaced. Large antral ulcers can also occur.
3. **Granulomata** – Crohn's disease, TB.
4. **Eosinophilic enteritis** – commonly involves gastric antrum (causing narrowing and nodules) in addition to small bowel. Blood eosinophilia. Occasionally spares the mucosa, so needs full thickness biopsy for confirmation.

6.21   Gastrocolic Fistula

Inflammatory
1. Peptic ulcer.
2. Crohn's disease*.
3. Pancreatitis (chronic).
4. Infections – tuberculosis, actinomycosis.

Neoplastic
1. Carcinoma – of stomach, colon or pancreas.
2. Metastases.

6.22   Gastric Dilatation

Gas- or food-filled stomach. Mottled translucencies (due to gas trapped in food residue) may be seen in gastric dilatation secondary to chronic obstruction. Resembles heavy faecal loading of the colon.

Mechanical Obstruction

1. **Fibrosis secondary to ulceration** – long history of dyspepsia.
2. **Malignancy** – shorter history, therefore dilatation is usually less marked. Often no abdominal pain.
3. **Volvulus** – 'organo-axial', associated with hiatus hernia. 'Vertical axis', not associated with hiatus hernia.
4. **Infantile hypertrophic pyloric stenosis** – the radiological signs on a barium meal are

   (a) 'String sign' – barium in the narrowed pyloric canal.
   (b) 'Shoulder sign', the pyloric 'tumour' indenting the barium-filled antrum.
   (c) 'Beak sign' – incomplete extension of the barium into the narrowed pyloric channel.
   (d) 'Double track sign' – parallel mucosal folds in the pyloric channel.

   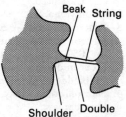

   US has now largely replaced the barium meal for diagnosis.
5. **Proximal small bowel obstruction** – gastric and small bowel dilatation.
6. **Bezoar.**

Paralytic Ileus

1. **Postoperative.**
2. **Post-vagotomy.**
3. **Drugs** – e.g. anticholinergics.
4. **Metabolic** – uraemia, hypokalaemia, etc.
5. **Acute gastric dilatation** – see 7.4.

6.23 'Bull's Eye' (Target) Lesion in the Stomach

Ulcer on apex of a nodule.

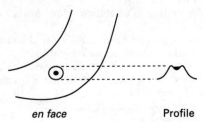

en face   Profile

1. **Submucosal metastases** – may be multiple
   (a) Melanoma – commonest.
   (b) Lymphoma*.
   (c) Carcinoma – breast, bronchus, pancreas.
   (d) Carcinoid.
2. **Leiomyoma.**
3. **Pancreatic 'rest'** – ectopic pancreatic tissue. Usually on inferior wall of antrum. A central 'blob' of barium is seen in 50% – collects in primitive duct remnant. Can also occur in duodenum, jejunum, Meckel's diverticulum, liver, gallbladder and spleen.
4. **Neurofibroma** – may be multiple. Other stigmata of neurofibromatosis.

6.24 Gas in the Stomach Wall

Interstitial Gastric Emphysema
Linear or curvilinear gas shadows in the wall of the stomach ± extension into the duodenum.
1. **Raised intragastric pressure** – obstruction and gastric distension.
2. **Post-gastroscopy.**
3. **Peptic ulceration** – with submucosal gas.
4. **Necrotizing enterocolitis.**

Emphysematous Gastritis
Due to gas-forming organisms in the stomach wall. Severe epigastric pain, haematemesis, prostration and toxaemic shock. Contracted stomach with mottled lucencies resembling interstitial emphysema.
1. **Diabetes.**
2. **Alcohol abuse.**
3. **Corrosive ingestion.**

Cystic Pneumatosis
Mild symptoms; usually in elderly patients and often associated with chronic obstructive airways disease.

Further Reading
Colquhoun J. (1965) Intramural gas in hollow viscera. *Clin. Radiol.*, 16: 71–86.
Tuck J.S. & Boobis L.H. (1987) Case report: interstitial emphysema of the stomach due to perforated appendicitis. *Clin. Radiol.*, 38: 315–17.

6.25   Cobblestone Duodenal Cap

Big 'Polypoid'

1. **Oedema** – associated with an ulcer.
2. **Hypertrophied Brunner's glands** – can extend from pylorus to ampulla of Vater. Uniform in size. May occur in 25% of patients with end-stage renal failure.
3. **Crohn's disease*** – involved in 2% and may rarely present here. Usually signs present in gastric antrum also.
4. **Varices** – base of cap. Decrease in size in erect position. Invariably associated with oesophageal varices.
5. **Lymphoma***.
6. **Carcinoma**.

Small

1. **Duodenitis** – ± central flecks of barium.
2. **Nodular lymphoid hyperplasia** – pinpoint (1–3 mm) nodules involving the entire duodenal loop. (Duodenum > jejunum.)
3. **Food residue/effervescent granules** – move around.
4. **Heterotopic gastric mucosa** – base of cap adjacent to pylorus.

Further Reading

Cassar-Pullicino V.N., Davies A.M., Hubscher S. & Burrows F. (1990) The nodular duodenum in chronic renal failure. *Clin. Radiol.*, 41: 326–30.

Schulman A. (1970) The cobblestone appearance of the duodenal cap, duodenitis and hyperplasia of Brunner's glands. *Br. J. Radiol.*, 43: 787–95.

6.26 Decreased/Absent Duodenal Folds

1. Scleroderma*.
2. Crohn's disease*.
3. Strongyloides.
4. Cystic fibrosis*.
5. Amyloidosis.

6.27   Thickened Duodenal Folds

Inflammatory
1. Duodenitis.
2. Pancreatitis.
3. Crohn's disease* – occurs before aphthous ulcers. Mild signs occur in duodenum in up to 40%, but severe involvement only occurs in 2%. Cap and proximal half of second part of duodenum predominantly affected.
4. Zollinger–Ellison syndrome – response to excess acidity.

Neoplastic
1. Lymphoma*.
2. Metastases – particularly melanoma, breast, ovary, gastrointestinal tract (lung, kidney are rare).

Infiltrative
1. Amyloidosis – bowel commonly involved (primary generalized thickening; secondary – segmental thickening).
2. Eosinophilic enteritis – gastric antrum commonly involved. Blood eosinophilia.
3. Mastocytosis – dense bones. ± gastric polyps.
4. Whipple's disease.

Vascular
1. Intramural haematoma – due to trauma. Common in the duodenum because it is fixed to the posterior abdominal wall. 'Stacked coins' appearance. An extensive haematoma may occur in bleeding diatheses.
2. Ischaemia – widespread changes can occur in vasculitis secondary to radiotherapy, collagen diseases and Henoch–Schönlein purpura.

Oedema
1. Hypoproteinaemia – nephrotic syndrome, cirrhosis or protein-losing enteropathy.
2. Venous obstruction – cirrhosis, Budd–Chiari syndrome or constrictive pericarditis.
3. Lymphatic obstruction.
4. Angioneurotic oedema.

Infestations

1. **Worms**
   (a) Hookworm (*Ankylostoma duodenale*) – the head of the worm produces an inflammatory reaction.
   (b) Tapeworm (*Taenia saginata* or *T. solium*) – has a similar effect on the duodenum. The worm may be visible as a filling defect during a barium study.
   (c) Strongyloides – similar appearance to giardiasis (see below). Strictures in chronic cases.
2. **Giardiasis** – predominantly affects the duodenum and proximal jejunum. Thickened, blunted and distorted mucosal folds. Hypermotility leads to rapid transit. Spasm produces narrowing. May be associated with nodular lymphoid hyperplasia or hypogammaglobulinaemia.

See also 6.31 and 6.32.

Further Reading

Clements R., Evans K.T. & Rhodes J. (1990) Coarse mucosal folds in the duodenum: a twenty-year follow-up. *Clin. Radiol.*, 41: 421–4.

Gelfand D.W., Dale W.J., Ott D.J., Wu W.C., Kerr R.M., Munitz H.A. *et al.* (1985) Duodenitis: endoscopic–radiologic correlation in 272 patients. *Radiology*, 157: 577–81.

6.28   Dilated Duodenum

Mechanical Obstruction

1. **Bands** – most frequent cause of neonatal duodenal obstruction. Associated with malrotation and midgut volvulus.
2. **Atresia, webs, stenosis** – often associated with Down's syndrome. 'Double bubble' sign in neonate due to dilated stomach and duodenum. Webs have a high incidence of incomplete rotation.
3. **Annular pancreas.**
4. **Superior mesenteric artery syndrome** – hold up of barium in third part of duodenum with some proximal dilatation and vigorous peristalsis (prior to muscle relaxant). Postprandial pain relieved by lying on left side. Associated with a plaster of Paris body cast. 20% have associated duodenal ulcer. Never occurs in obese people.

Paralytic Ileus
– particularly due to pancreatitis.

Scleroderma*

Further Reading
Anderson J.R., Earnshaw P.M. & Fraser G.M. (1982) Extrinsic compression of the third part of the duodenum. *Clin. Radiol.*, 33: 75–81.

6.29 Dilated Small Bowel

Calibre: proximal jejunum > 3.5 cm (4.5 cm if small bowel enema)
mid-small bowel > 3.0 cm (4.0 cm if small bowel enema)
ileum > 2.5 cm (3.0 cm if small bowel enema).

Normal Folds
1. **Mechanical obstruction** – ± dilated large bowel, depending on level of obstruction.
2. **Paralytic ileus** – dilated small and large bowel.
3. **Coeliac disease, tropical sprue, dermatitis herpetiformis** – can produce identical signs. Dilatation is the hallmark, and correlates well with severity, but it is relatively uncommon. ± dilution and flocculation of barium. See 6.34.
4. **Scleroderma**.
5. **Iatrogenic** – post-vagotomy and gastrectomy may produce dilatation due to rapid emptying of stomach contents. Dilatation may also occur proximal to a small bowel loop.

Thick Folds
1. **Ischaemia**.
2. **Crohn's disease*** – combination of obstructive and inflammatory changes.
3. **Radiotherapy**.
4. **Lymphoma***.
5. **Zollinger–Ellison syndrome** – ileus due to excess acidity.
6. **Extensive small bowel resection** – compensatory dilatation and thickening of folds.
7. **Amyloidosis**.

6.30   Strictures in the Small Bowel

1. **Adhesions** – angulation of bowel which is constant in site. Normal mucosal folds.
2. **Crohn's disease*** – ± ulcers and altered mucosal pattern.
3. **Ischaemia** – ulcers are rare. Evolution is more rapid than Crohn's ± long strictures.
4. **Radiation enteritis** – see 6.31.
5. **Tumours**
   (a) Lymphoma – usually secondary to contiguous spread from lymph nodes. Primary disease may occur and is nearly always due to non-Hodgkin's lymphoma.
   (b) Carcinoid – although the appendix is the commonest site, these never metastasize. Of those occurring in small bowel, 90% are in ileum (mostly distal 2 feet), and 30% are multifocal. A fibroblastic response to infiltration produces a stricture, ± mass. It is the commonest primary malignancy of small bowel, but only 30% metastasize (more likely if > 2 cm diam.) or invade. Carcinoid syndrome only develops with liver metastases – see 6.36.
   (c) Carcinoma – if duodenal lesions are included this is the most common primary malignancy of the small bowel and the duodenum is the most frequent site. Ileal lesions are rare (unless associated with Crohn's disease). Short segment stricture with mucosal destruction, ulcerating or polypoidal lesion. High incidence of second primary tumours.
   (d) Sarcoma – lymphoma- or leiomyo-. Thick folds with an eccentric lumen. Leiomyosarcomas may present as a large mass displacing bowel loops with a large barium-filled cavity.
   (e) Metastases – usual sites of origin are malignant melanoma, ovary, pancreas, stomach, colon, breast, lung and uterus. Rounded deformities of the bowel wall with flattened mucosal folds. In patients with gynaecological malignancies duodenal or jejunal obstruction are most likely due to metastases; most radiation induced strictures are in the ileum.
6. **Enteric coated potassium tablets.**

Further Reading

Papadopoulos V.D. & Nolan D.J. (1985) Carcinoma of the small intestine. *Clin. Radiol.*, 36: 409–13.

Yuhasz M., Laufer I., Sutton G., Herlinger H. & Caroline D.F. (1985) Radiography of the small bowel in patients with gynaecological malignancies. *Am. J. Roentgenol.*, 144: 303–7.

6.31 Thickened Folds in Non-dilated Small Bowel – Smooth and Regular

Fold thickness: jejunum > 2.5 mm
                   ileum   > 2.0 mm

Vascular

1. **Intramural haematoma**
   (a) Trauma – commonest in duodenum, since fixed to posterior abdominal wall ('stacked coin' appearance).
   (b) Bleeding diathesis – commonly localized to a few loops.
2. **Ischaemia**
   (a) Acute – embolus, Henoch–Schönlein purpura. Can produce ileus. May perforate. Ulcers rare.
   (b) Chronic – vasculitis (collagen, radiotherapy), atheroma, fibromuscular dysplasia. Present with postprandial pain, and malabsorption.

Radiotherapy

Infrequently seen with tumour doses < 45 Gy. Underlying pathological process is endarteritis obliterans and concomitant arterial disease will exacerbate the damage. Majority of cases are secondary to treatment of female genital tract malignancy. Acute symptoms during radiotherapy do not correlate with the development of chronic radiation enteritis which may have a latent period of up to 25 years. Distal jejunum and ileum are the commonest sites.

1. **Acute** – thickening of valvulae conniventes and poor peristalsis. Ulceration is rare.
2. **Chronic** – most common signs are submucosal thickening of valvulae conniventes and/or mural thickening. Stenoses, adhesions, sinuses and fistulae may also occur. (The absence of ulceration, cobblestoning and asymmetry differentiate it from Crohn's disease.)

Oedema

1. **Adjacent inflammation** – focal.
2. **Hypoproteinaemia** – e.g. nephrotic, cirrhosis, protein losing enteropathy. Generalized.

3. **Venous obstruction** – e.g. cirrhosis, Budd–Chiari syndrome, constrictive pericarditis.
4. **Lymphatic obstruction** – e.g. lymphoma, retroperitoneal fibrosis, primary lymphangiectasia (child with leg oedema).
5. **Angioneurotic.**

Early Infiltration
1. **Amyloidosis** – gastrointestinal tract commonly involved. Primary amyloid tends to produce generalized thickening, whereas secondary amyloid produces focal lesions. Malabsorption is unusual.
2. **Eosinophilic enteritis** – focal or generalized. Gastric antrum frequently involved. No ulcers. Blood eosinophilia. Occasionally spare mucosa – therefore need full thickness biopsy for diagnosis.

Coeliac Disease
Thickening of folds is not common, and is probably a functional abnormality rather than true fold thickening. ± jejunal dilatation.

Abetalipoproteinaemia
Rare, inherited. Malabsorption, acanthocytosis, and CNS abnormality. ± dilated bowel.

Further Reading
Mendelson R.M. & Nolan D.J. (1985) The radiological features of chronic radiation enteritis. *Clin. Radiol.*, 36: 141–8.
Taylor P.M., Johnson R.J., Eddleston B. & Hunter R.D. (1990) Radiological changes in the gastrointestinal and genitourinary tract following radiotherapy for carcinoma of the cervix. *Clin. Radiol.*, 41: 165–9.

6.32   Thickened Folds in Non-dilated Small Bowel – Irregular and Distorted

Fold thickness: jejunum < 2.5 mm
ileum   < 2.0 mm

Localized

Inflammatory
1. **Crohn's disease*** – occurs before aphthous ulcers.
2. **Zollinger–Ellison syndrome** – predominantly proximal small bowel. Dilatation may occur.

Neoplastic
1. **Lymphoma***.
2. **Metastases** – particularly melanoma, breast, ovary and gastrointestinal tract.
3. **Carcinoid** – commonest primary malignant small bowel tumour. 90% in the ileum and mostly in the distal 60 cm. It is more common in the appendix, where it is a benign tumour.

Infective
1. **Tuberculosis** – can look identical to Crohn's disease, but predominant caecal involvement may help to distinguish it. Less than 50% have pulmonary tuberculosis.

Widespread

Infiltrative
1. **Amyloidosis.**
2. **Eosinophilic enteritis.**
3. **Mastocytosis** – may have superimposed small nodules, urticaria pigmentosa and sclerotic bone lesions.
4. **Whipple's disease** – flitting arthralgia, lymphadenopathy and sacroiliitis.

Inflammatory
1. Crohn's disease*.

Infestations
1. **Giardiasis** – associates with hypogammaglobulinaemia and nodular lymphoid hyperplasia.
2. **Strongyloides** – ± absent folds in chronic cases.

Stomach Abnormality with Thickened Small Bowel Mucosal Folds
1. Lymphoma/metastases.
2. Zollinger–Ellison syndrome.
3. Ménétrier's disease.
4. Amyloidosis.
5. Eosinophilic enteritis.

Further Reading
Goldberg H.I. & Sheft D.J. (1976) Abnormalities in small intestine contour and calibre. *Radiol. Clin. North Am.*, 14: 461–75.

6.33 Multiple Nodules in the Small Bowel

Inflammatory

1. **Nodular lymphoid hyperplasia** – nodules 2–4 mm with normal fold thickness. Associated with hypogammaglobulinaemia (IgA and IgM). Produces malabsorption, and there is a high incidence of intestinal infections (particularly giardiasis, but strongyloides and monilia may also occur). Can also affect the colon, where in children it may be a normal variant, but in adults it may be an early sign of Crohn's disease.
2. **Crohn's disease*** – 'cobblestone' mucosa but other characteristic signs present.

Infiltrative

1. **Whipple's disease** – ± myriad of tiny (< 1 mm) nodules superimposed on thick folds.
2. **Waldenström's macroglobulinaemia** – ± myriad of tiny (< 1 mm) nodules. Folds usually normal, but may occasionally be thick.
3. **Mastocytosis** – nodules a little larger and folds usually thick.

Neoplastic

1. **Lymphoma*** – can produce diffuse nodules (2–4 mm) of varying sizes. Ulceration in the nodules is not uncommon.
2. **Polyposis**
   (a) Peutz–Jeghers' syndrome – autosomal dominant. Buccal pigmentation. Multiple hamartomas (± intussuscept) 'carpeting' the small bowel. Can also involve the colon (30%) and stomach (25%). Not in themselves premalignant, but associated with carcinoma of stomach, duodenum and ovary.
   (b) Gardner's syndrome – predominantly in the colon. Occasionally has adenomas in small bowel.
   (c) Canada–Cronkhite syndrome – predominantly stomach and colon, but may affect the small bowel.
3. **Metastases** – on antimesenteric border. Particularly melanoma, breast, gastrointestinal tract and ovary. (Rarely bronchus and kidney.) ± ascites.

Infective
1. **Typhoid** – hypertrophy of 'Peyer's patches'.
2. **Yersinia** – ± nodules in terminal ileum.

Further Reading
Marshak R.H., Lindner A.E. & Maklansky D. (1976) Immunoglobulin disorders of the small bowel. *Radiol. Clin. North Am.*, 14: 477–91.

6.34 Malabsorption

Mucosal
1. **Coeliac disease** – commonest cause of malabsorption. Not all have steatorrhoea – can present with iron of folate deficiency. Jejunal biopsy shows subtotal villous atrophy (this can also occur in Whipple's disease, primary lymphoma and chronic ulcerative enteritis). Jejunal dilatation is the hallmark, but is relatively uncommon. It correlates well with severity. Fold thickness is normal in uncomplicated coeliac disease. An increase in ileal fold pattern ± a decrease of jejunal folds, i.e. a reversal of the normal fold pattern indicates long-standing disease and should heighten awareness to potential malignant complications. Other signs, which are occasionally demonstrable on a barium follow through examination, are
   (a) Dilution of barium, because of hypersecretion of fluid by the bowel.
   (b) Segmentation of the column of barium. This is most marked in the ileum.
   (c) Moulage sign. The appearance of barium in a featureless tube due to the complete effacement of mucosal folds.
   If bowel calibre increases while on a gluten free diet suspect a complication, i.e. lymphoma, carcinoma or intussusception (rare and non-obstructive). Tropical sprue and dermatitis herpetiformis can present with identical appearances.
2. **Inflammation**
   (a) Crohn's disease*.
   (b) Radiotherapy – if there is widespread involvement.
   (c) Scleroderma* – due to hypomotility.
3. **Ischaemia** – can cause mild malabsorption if chronic and widespread.
4. **Infiltration**
   (a) Whipple's disease.
   (b) Mastocytosis.
   (c) Amyloidosis – particularly in primary amyloidosis, since generalized bowel involvement is more common.
   (d) Eosinophilic enteritis – blood eosinophilia is common.
5. **Lymphangiectasia** – child. Blocked lymphatics interfere

with the transport of fat. Hypoproteinaemia due to protein loss into the gut is common.
6. **Parasites** – particularly *Giardia* and *Strongyloides* spp.

Digestive
1. **Gastrectomy.**
2. **Biliary obstruction.**
3. **Pancreatic dysfunction** – pancreatitis, cystic fibrosis, carcinoma and pancreatectomy.
4. **Disaccharidase deficiency** – lactase deficiency is the commonest.

Anatomical
1. **Fistula** – even a small one to the colon allows bacterial colonization.
2. **Resection.**
3. **Stagnant loop/stricture.**
4. **Jejunal diverticulosis** – in the erect view may resemble obstruction with multiple fluid levels. However, the diverticula have smooth walls, i.e. no mucosal folds. Produces folate deficiency.

Further Reading

Bova J.G., Friedman A.C., Weser E., Hopens T.A. & Wytock D.H. (1985) Adaptation of the ileum in nontropical sprue: reversal of the jejunoileal fold pattern. *Am. J. Roentgenol.*, 144: 299–302.
Laws J.W. & Pitman R.G. (1960) The radiological investigation of the malabsorption syndromes. *Br. J. Radiol.*, 33: 211–22.

6.35   Protein-losing Enteropathy

Oedema in small bowel will occur if plasma albumin $< 20 \text{ g l}^{-1}$.

'Mucosal'
1. Coeliac disease.
2. Ménétrier's disease.
3. Sprue.

Inflammatory
1. Crohn's disease*.
2. Ulcerative colitis*.
3. Radiotherapy.

Ulceration
1. Carcinoma stomach/colon.
2. Villous adenoma.

Venous Obstruction
1. Cirrhosis.
2. Inferior vena cava thrombosis.
3. Constrictive pericarditis.

Chronic Arterial Obstruction

Lymphatic Obstruction
1. Lymphangiectasia.
2. Lymphoma*.
3. Retroperitoneal fibrosis – see 8.28.

Infiltrative
1. Whipple's disease.
2. Eosinophilic enteritis.

Further Reading
Marshak R.H., Wolf B.S., Cohen N. & Janowitz H.D. (1961) Protein-losing disorders of the gastrointestinal tract: Roentgen features. *Radiology*, 77: 893–905.

6.36 Lesions in the Terminal Ileum

Inflammatory
1. **Crohn's disease***.
2. **Ulcerative colitis*** – 10% of those with total colitis have 'backwash' ileitis for up to 25 cm causing granular mucosa, ± dilatation. No ulcers.
3. **Radiation enteritis** – submucosal thickening of mucosal folds, mural thickening, symmetrical stenoses, adhesions, sinuses and fistulae. Ulceration and cobblestoning are not seen.

Infective
1. **Tuberculosis** – can look identical to Crohn's disease. Continuity of involvement with caecum and ascending colon can occur. Longitudinal ulcers are uncommon. Less than 50% have pulmonary TB. Caecum is predominantly involved – progressive contraction of caecal wall opposite the ileocaecal valve, and cephalad retraction of the caecum with straightening of the ileocaecal angle.
2. **Yersinia** – 'cobblestone' appearance and aphthous ulcers. No deep ulcers and spontaneous resolution, usually within 10 weeks, distinguishes it from Crohn's disease.
3. **Actinomycosis** – very rare. Predominantly caecum. ± associated bone destruction with periosteal reaction.
4. **Histoplasmosis** – very rare.

Neoplastic
1. **Lymphoma*** – may look like Crohn's disease.
2. **Carcinoid** – appendiceal carcinoid tumours are the most common and usually benign. Most ileal carcinoids originate in the distal ileum and are invariably malignant if > 2 cm. Radiological signs reflect the primary lesion (annular fibrotic stricture (± obstruction); intraluminal filling defect(s)), the mesenteric secondary mass (stretching of loops; rigidity and fixation), interference with the blood supply to the ileum by the secondary mass (thickening of mucosal folds) or the effects of fibrosis (sharp angulation of a loop; stellate arrangement of loops). The caecum may be involved and strictures may be multifocal.

(continued)

3. Metastases – no ulcers.

Ischaemia
Rare site. Thickened folds, 'cobblestone' appearance and 'thumb printing', but rapid progression of changes helps to discriminate it from Crohn's disease.

Further Reading
Calenoff I. (1970) Rare ileocaecal lesions. *Am. J. Roentgenol.*, 110: 343–51.

Jeffree M.A., Barter S.J., Hemingway A.P. & Nolan D.J. (1984) Primary carcinoid tumours of the ileum: the radiological appearances. *Clin. Radiol.*, 35: 451–5.

Mendelson R.M. & Nolan D.J. (1985) The radiological features of chronic radiation enteritis. *Clin. Radiol.*, 36: 141–8.

6.37 Colonic Polyps

Adenomatous

1. **Simple tubular adenoma – tubulovillous adenoma – villous adenoma** – these three form a spectrum both in size and degree of dysplasia. Villous adenoma is the largest, shows the most severe dysplasia and has the highest incidence of malignancy. Signs suggestive of malignancy are
   (a)

Size –	< 5 mm	– 0% malignant
	5 mm–1 cm	– 1% malignant
	1–2 cm	– 10% malignant
	> 2 cm	– 50% malignant.

   (b) Sessile – base greater than height.
   (c) 'Puckering' of colonic wall at base of polyp.
   (d) Irregular surface.

   Villous adenomas are typically fronded, sessile and are poorly coated by barium because of their mucous secretion. May cause a protein-losing enteropathy or hypokalaemia.

2. **Familial polyposis coli and Gardner's syndrome** – AD. Both conditions may represent a spectrum of the same disease. Multiple adenomas of the colon which are more numerous in the distal colon and rectum. Colonic carcinoma develops in early adulthood (in 30% by 10 years after diagnosis and in 100% by 20 years). 60% of those who present with colonic symptoms already have a carcinoma. The carcinoma is multifocal in 50%. Extracolonic abnormalities may occur:
   (a) Hamartomas of the stomach (40%).
   (b) Gastric adenomas (more common in the Japanese).
   (c) Adenomas of the duodenum (25%).
   (d) Periampullary carcinoma (12%).
   (e) Jejunal and ileal polyps (in 60% of patients in the Japanese literature).
   (f) Mesenteric fibromatosis – a non-calcified soft-tissue mass which may displace bowel loops and produce mucosal irregularity from local invasion. Ultrasound reveals a hypo- or hyperechoic mass and CT a homogeneous mass of muscle density.

   (continued)

(g) Multiple osteomas, most frequently in the outer table of the skull, the angle of the mandible and frontal sinuses.

(h) Dental abnormalities – hypercementomas, odontomas, dentigerous cysts, supernumerary teeth and multiple caries.

(i) Multiple epidermoid cysts – usually on the legs, face, scalp and arms.

(j) Pigmented lesions of the ocular fundus – in 90% of patients with Gardner syndrome and other extracolonic manifestations.

(k) Thyroid carcinoma in 0.6%.

Hyperplastic

1. **Solitary/multiple** – most frequently found in rectum.
2. **Nodular lymphoid hyperplasia** – usually children. Filling defects are smaller than familial polyposis coli.

Hamartomatous

1. **Juvenile polyposis** – ± familial. Children under 10. Commonly solitary in rectum.
2. **Peutz–Jeghers syndrome** – autosomal dominant. 'Carpets' small-bowel, but also affects colon and stomach in 30%. Increased incidence of carcinoma of stomach, duodenum and ovary.

Inflammatory

1. **Ulcerative colitis*** – polyps can be seen at all stages of activity of the colitis (no malignant potential): acute – pseudo-polyps (i.e. mucosal hyperplasia); chronic – sessile polyp (resembles villous adenoma); quiescent – tubular/filiform ('wormlike') and can show a branching pattern.

   Dysplasia in colitic colons is usually not radiologically visible. When visible it appears as a solitary nodule, several separate nodules (both non-specific) or as a close grouping of multiple adjacent nodules with apposed, flattened edges (the latter appearance being associated with dysplasia in 50% of cases).

2. **Crohn's disease*** – polyps less common than in ulcerative colitis.

Infective

1. **Schistosomiasis** – predominantly involves rectum. ± strictures.
2. **Amoebiasis.**

Others

1. **Canada–Cronkhite syndrome** – not hereditary. Predominantly affects stomach and colon, but can occur anywhere in bowel. Increased incidence of carcinoma of colon. Other features are alopecia, nail atrophy and skin pigmentation.
2. **Turcot's syndrome** – autosomal recessive. Increased incidence of CNS malignancy.

Further Reading

Bresnihan E.R. & Simpkins K.C. (1975) Villous adenoma of the large bowel: Benign and malignant. *Br. J. Radiol.*, 48: 801–6.

Dodds W.J. (1976) Clinical and roentgen features of the intestinal polyposis syndromes. *Gastrointest. Radiol.*, 1: 127–42.

Dolan K.D., Seibert J. & Siebart R.W. (1973) Gardner's syndrome. *Am. J. Roentgenol.*, 119: 359–64.

Harned R.K., Buck J.L., Olmsted W.W., Moser R.P. & Ros P.R. (1991) Extracolonic manifestations of the familial adenomatous polyposis syndromes. *Am. J. Roentgenol.*, 156: 481–5.

Hooyman J.R., MacCarty R.L., Carpenter H.A., Schroeder K.W. & Carlison H.C. (1987) Radiographic appearance of mucosal dysplasia associated with ulcerative colitis. *Am. J. Roentgenol.*, 149: 47–51.

Morson B.C. (1974) The polyp cancer sequence in the large bowel. *Proc. Roy. Soc. Med.*, 67: 451–7.

Morson B.C. (1984) The evolution of colorectal carcinoma. *Clin. Radiol.*, 35: 425–31.

6.38 Colonic Strictures

Neoplastic
1. **Carcinoma** – mucosal destruction and 'shouldering'. Often shorter than 6 cm.
2. **Lymphoma***.

Inflammatory
Tend to be symmetrical, smooth and tapered.
1. **Ulcerative colitis*** – usually requires extensive involvement for longer than 5 years. Commonest in sigmoid colon. May be multiple. Beware malignant complications – these are commonly irregular, annular strictures (30% are multiple). Risk factors are: total colitis, length of history (risk starts at 10 years and increases by 10% per decade), epithelial dysplasia on biopsy.
2. **Crohn's disease*** – strictures occur in 25% of colonic Crohn's disease, and 50% of these are multiple.
3. **Pericolic abscess** – can look malignant, but relative lack of mucosal destruction.
4. **Radiotherapy** – occurs several years after treatment. Commonest site is rectosigmoid colon, which appears smooth and narrow and rises vertically out of pelvis due to thickening of surrounding tissue.

Ischaemia
Infarction heals by stricture formation relatively rapidly. Commonest site is splenic flexure, but 20% occur in other sites. It can be extensive and has tapering ends.

Infective
1. **Tuberculosis** – commonest in ileocaecal region. Short, 'hourglass' stricture.
2. **Amoeboma** – more common in descending colon. Occurs in 2–8% of amoebiasis and is multiple in 50%. Rapid improvement after treatment with metronidazole.
3. **Schistosomiasis** – commonly rectosigmoid region. Granulation tissue forming after the acute stage (oedema, fold-thickening and polyps) may cause a stricture.

4. **Lymphogranuloma venereum** – sexually transmitted chlamydia. Late complications are strictures which are characteristically long and tubular and affect the rectosigmoid region. Fistulae may occur.

Extrinsic masses – inflammatory, tumours (primary and secondary), and endometriosis.

Cathartic colon – pseudostrictures which alter their configuration during the barium enema. The colon may be atonic and dilated. Changes are initially in the ascending colon, but can progress to involve all of the colon.

Further Reading

Simpkins K.C. and Young A.C. (1971) The differential diagnoses of large bowel strictures. *Clin. Radiol.*, 22: 449–57.

Taal B.G., Steinmetz R. & Den Hartog Jager F.C.A. (1990) Rectosigmoid obstruction caused by ovarian cancer. *Clin. Radiol.*, 41: 170–4.

6.39   Pneumatosis Intestinalis (Gas in the Bowel Wall)

Primary (15%)

1. **Pneumatosis coli** – cystic blebs of air. Can produce 'polypoid' filling defects on a barium enema. Some are associated with chronic obstructive airways disease.

Secondary (85%)

1. **Necrotizing enterocolitis** – in the neonate.
2. **Steroid and other immunosuppressive therapy.**
3. **Collagen disorders** – mainly scleroderma but also dermatomyositis and juvenile chronic arthritis.
4. **Leukaemia.**
5. **Colitis and enteritis** – ulcerative colitis (including toxic megacolon – see 6.40), Crohn's disease, ischaemia, severe gastroenteritis (particularly rotavirus) and CMV colitis and cryptosporidiosis in HIV infection.

Further Reading

Bornes P.F. & Johnston T.A. (1973) Indolent pneumatosis of the bowel wall associated with suppressive therapy. *Ann. Radiol.*, 16: 163–6.

Jamart J. (1979) Pneumatosis cystoides intestinalis. A statistical study of 919 cases. *Acta Hepat. Gastroenterol.*, 26: 419–22.

Keats T.E. & Smith T.H. (1974) Benign pneumatosis intestinalis in childhood leukaemia. *Am. J. Roentgenol.*, 122: 150–2.

Meyers M.A., Ghahremani G.G., Clements J.L. & Goodman G. (1977) Pneumatosis intestinalis. *Gastrointest. Radiol.*, 2: 91–105.

Mueller C.F., Morehead R., Alter A.J. & Michener W. (1972) Pneumatosis intestinalis in collagen disorders. *Am. J. Roentgenol.*, 115: 300–5.

6.40 Megacolon in an Adult

Colonic calibre greater than 5.5 cm.

Non-toxic (without mucosal abnormalities)
1. **Distal obstruction** – e.g. carcinoma.
2. **Ileus** – paralytic or secondary to electrolyte imbalance.
3. **Pseudo-obstruction** – symptoms and signs of large bowel obstruction but with no organic lesion identifiable by barium enema. A continuous, gas-filled colon with sharp, thin bowel wall, few fluid levels and gas or faeces in the rectum may differentiate from organic obstruction. Mortality is 25–30% and the risk of caecal necrosis and perforation is up to 15%.
4. **Purgative abuse.**

Toxic (with severe mucosal abnormalities)
Deep ulceration and inflammation produce a neuromuscular degeneration. Thick oedematous folds and extensive sloughing of the mucosa leaves mucosal islands. The underlying causes produce similar plain film changes. The presence of intramural gas indicates that perforation is imminent.
1. **Inflammatory**
    (a) Ulcerative colitis*.
    (b) Crohn's disease*.
    (c) Pseudomembranous colitis.
2. **Ischaemic colitis.**
3. **Dysentery**
    (a) Amoebiasis.
    (b) Salmonella.

Further Reading
Gilchrist A.M., Mills J.O.M. & Russell C.F.J. (1985) Acute large-bowel pseudo-obstruction. *Clin. Radiol.*, 36: 401–4.

6.41   Thumbprinting' in the Colon

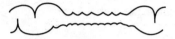

Colitides

1. Ulcerative colitis*.
2. Crohn's disease*.
3. Ischaemic colitis – commonest at the splenic flexure, but anywhere possible. Air insufflation may obliterate the 'thumbprinting'.
4. Pseudomembranous colitis.
5. Amoebic colitis.
6. Schistosomiasis.

Neoplastic

1. Lymphoma*.
2. Metastases.

Differential Diagnosis

1. Pneumatosis coli – cysts may indent the mucosa, giving a similar appearance, but gas is seen in the wall.

6.42 Aphthoid Ulcers

Barium in a central ulcer
surrounded by a halo of
oedematous mucosa.

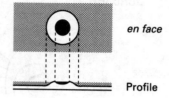

en face

Profile

In Colon
1. **Crohn's disease*** – the earliest sign in the terminal ileum and colon. Observed in 50% of patients.
2. **Yersinia enterocolitis.**
3. **Amoebic colitis.**
4. **Ischaemic colitis.**
5. **Behçet's disease** – mostly resembles Crohn's disease, but can occasionally simulate an idiopathic ulcerative proctocolitis.

In Small Bowel
1. **Crohn's disease*.**
2. **Yersinia enterocolitis.**
3. **Polyarteritis nodosa.**

Further Reading
Simpkins K.C. (1977) Aphthoid ulcers in Crohn's colitis. *Clin. Radiol.*, 28: 601–8.

6.43 Anterior Indentation of the Rectosigmoid Junction

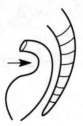

1. **Tumours**
   (a) Peritoneal metastases – common site. Particularly stomach, colon, pancreas and ovary.
   (b) Primary pelvic tumour.
2. **Abscess.**
3. **Haematoma.**
4. **Ascites** – if in erect position.
5. **Endometriosis** – common site.
6. **Hydatid** – metastatic cyst from rupture of a peripheral hepatic cyst.
7. **Surgical** – sling repair for rectal prolapse.

Further Reading

Schulman A. & Fataar S. (1979) Extrinsic stretching, narrowing, and anterior indentation of the rectosigmoid junction. *Clin. Radiol.*, 30: 463–9.

6.44 Widening of the Retrorectal Space

The post-rectal soft-tissue space at
S3–S5 is greater than 1.5 cm.

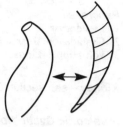

Normal Variation
40% of cases and these are mostly large or obese individuals.

Inflammatory
1. **Ulcerative colitis*** – seen in 50% of these patients and the
   width increases as the disease progresses.
2. **Crohn's disease*** – the widening may diminish during the
   course of the disease.
3. **Radiotherapy**.
4. **Diverticulitis**.
5. **Abscess**.

Neoplastic
1. **Carcinoma of the rectum**.
2. **Metastases to the rectum** – especially from prostate, ovary
   and bladder.
3. **Sacral tumours** – metastases, plasmacytoma, chordoma
   and, in children, sacrococcygeal teratoma.

Others
1. **Anterior sacral meningocele** – a sac containing CSF protrudes through a round or oval defect in the anterior wall
   of the sacrum. The diagnosis is confirmed by CT myelography or MRI.
2. **Pelvic lipomatosis**.
3. **Enteric duplication cysts**.

Further Reading
Teplick S.K., Stark P., Clark R.E., Metz J.R. and Shapiro J.H. (1978)
The retrorectal space. *Clin. Radiol.*, 29: 177–84.

6.45   CT Retroperitoneal Cystic Mass

Pancreas
1. Pseudocyst.
2. Cystadenoma/carcinoma.
3. von Hippel–Lindau.

Kidney – see section 8.

Para-aortic Cystic Nodes
1. Testicular teratoma.
2. Carcinoma cervix.

Retroperitoneal Cystic Tumour
1. Lymphangioma.
2. Leiomyosarcoma.
3. Haemangiopericytoma.

NB Any tumour with a fatty content can appear cystic due to density averaging, e.g. neurofibroma.

Others
1. Haematoma – late stage.
2. Abscess.
3. Lymphocele.
4. Meningocele.

Further Reading
Alpern M.B., Thorsen M.K., Kellman G.M., Pojunas K. & Lawson T.L. (1986) C.T. appearances of haemangiopericytoma. *J. Comput. Assist. Tomogr.*, 10 (2): 264–7.
Munechika H., Honda M., Kushihashi T., Koizumi K. & Gokan T. (1986) Computed tomography of retroperitoneal cystic lymphangiomas. *J. Comput. Assist. Tomogr.*, 11 (1): 116–19.

6.46 CT Mesenteric Cystic Lesion

Cyst
1. Pancreatic pseudocyst.
2. Enteric duplication cyst.
3. Mesothelial cyst.

Tumour
1. Teratoma.
2. Cystic leiomyoma/sarcoma.
3. Cystic mesothelioma.
4. Lymphangioma.

Further Reading
Ros P., Olmsted W., Moser R., Dachman A., Hjermstad B. & Sobin
    L. (1987) Mesenteric and omental cysts: histology classifi-
    cation with imaging correlation. *Radiology*, 164: 327–32.

6.47 MRI of Post-radiation Changes in the Pelvis

Due to lay-out requirements for 6.48, 6.47 is positioned after
6.48 on p. 256.

6.48 MRI of Female Pelvic Pathology (*note*: this precedes 6.47).

	T_1W	T_2W	Comments
Carcinoma of cervix	Isointense	↑	15–20% not visible (presumably superficial).
Endometrial carcinoma	↓ (↑ if haemorrhage or retained fluid)	Variable, but usually ↑ compared to myometrium and junctional zone. (If ↓, looks like fibroid)	Haemorrhage, metastases, leiomyosarcoma and endometrial hyperplasia can mimic
Gestational trophoblastic disease	Isointense (↑ if haemorrhage)	Usually ↑	May have signal voids +, due to marked vascularity. 30–50% have associated theca lutein cysts due to hormonal stimulation
Uterine fibroid non-degenerative	iso (↓ if Ca²⁺)	↓	
degenerative	iso, ↑	↑	
Uterine adenomyosis diffuse	±↑	±↑	Thickened junctional zone like fibroid
focal	iso	↓	

Ovarian carcinoma			Cannot distinguish benign from malignant
solid	Isointense	→	
cystic		→	
Ovarian dermoid	↑ (fat)	↑ (fat) →	± fluid/fluid levels
Ovarian fibroma	→	→	
Endometrioma	↑ (blood)	↓ (inhomogeneous) →	Haemorrhage into ovarian carcinoma can mimic
Vaginal carcinoma	Isointense	Isointense, ↑	Only seen if vaginal outline is distorted. The rich peri-vaginal venous plexus can mask the tumour
Post-radiation change			
fibrous	→	→	No gadolinium enhancement
granulation	→	↑	Gadolinium enhancement can persist for several years and mimic tumour

Further Reading

Outwater E. & Kressel H.Y. (1992) Evaluation of gynaecologic malignancy by magnetic resonance imaging. *Radiol. Clin. North Am.*, 30: 789–806.

6.47 MRI of Post-radiation Changes in the Pelvis (*note*: this follows 6.48).

	T_1W	T_2W	Comments
Bone marrow in sacrum	↑	↑	Due to fat deposition
Fibrous tissue	↓	↑	No gadolinium enhancement
Granulation tissue	↓	↑	Enhances with gadolinium Mimics tumour recurrence Can persist for several years
Bladder, rectum, muscle	Isointense	± ↑	Thickened, oedematous neovascularity
Ovary/uterus	Isointense	↓	Atrophy
Fascial planes	↓	Variable	Thickened

Further Reading
Outwater E. & Kressel H.Y. (1992) Evaluation of gynaecologic malignancy by magnetic resonance imaging. *Radiol. Clin. North Am.*, 30: 789–806.

7
Gallbladder, Liver, Spleen, Pancreas and Adrenals

7.1 Non-visualization of the Gallbladder

During Oral Cholecystography
1. Technical failures
   (a) No fatty meal prior to taking of contrast medium.
   (b) Tablets not taken or taken at the wrong time.
   (c) Vomiting or diarrhoea.
   (d) Failure to fast after taking contrast medium.
   (e) Films taken too early or too late.
   (f) Bilirubin greater than 34 mmol l⁻¹.
2. Previous cholecystectomy.
3. Ectopic gallbladder – confirmed by taking a film of the entire abdomen.
4. Cholecystitis.
5. Cystic duct obstruction.

During Intravenous Cholangiography
1. Technical failures
   (a) Contrast medium given too rapidly – renal excretion is seen.
   (b) Bilirubin greater than 50 mmol l⁻¹.
2. Previous cholecystectomy.
3. Ectopic gallbladder.
4. Cystic duct obstruction.
5. Cholecystitis.

7.2 Filling Defect in the Gallbladder

Multiple

1. **Calculi** – 30% are radio-opaque. Freely mobile.
2. **Cholesterosis ('strawberry' gallbladder)** – characteristically multiple fixed mural filling defects.

Single and Small

1. **Calculus.**
2. **Adenomyomatosis** – three characteristic signs
   (a) Fundal nodular filling defect.
   (b) Stricture – anywhere in the gallbladder. Sharply localized or a diffuse narrowing. More prominent following contraction after a fatty meal.
   (c) Rokitansky–Aschoff sinuses – may only be visible after gallbladder contraction.

Single and Large

1. **Calculus.**
2. **Carcinoma** – difficult to diagnose as the radiological presentation is usually with a non-functioning gallbladder. Nearly always associated with gallstones and, therefore, if filling does occur it is indistinguishable from them.

7.3   Gas in the Biliary Tract

Irregularly branching gas shadows
which do not reach to the liver edge,
probably because of the direction of
bile flow. The gallbladder may also
be outlined.

Within the Bile Ducts

INCOMPETENCE OF THE SPHINCTER OF ODDI
1. Following sphincterotomy.
2. Following passage of a gallstone.
3. Patulous sphincter in the elderly.

POSTOPERATIVE
1. Cholecystoenterostomy.
2. Choledochoenterostomy.

SPONTANEOUS BILIARY FISTULA
1. **Passage of a gallstone directly from an inflamed
   gallbladder into the bowel** – 90% of spontaneous fistulae.
   57% erode into the duodenum and 18% into the colon.
   May result in a gallstone ileus.
2. **Duodenal ulcer perforating into the common bile duct** –
   6% of spontaneous fistulae.
3. **Malignancy or trauma** – 4% of spontaneous fistulae.

Within the Gallbladder
1. All of the above.
2. **Emphysematous cholecystitis** –
   due to gas-forming organisms and
   associated with diabetes in 20%
   of cases. There is intramural and
   intraluminal gas but, because
   there is usually cystic duct
   obstruction, gas is present in the
   bile ducts in only 20%. The erect
   film may show an air/bile interface.

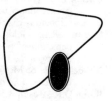

7.4   Gas in the Portal Veins

Gas shadows which extend to within 2 cm of the liver capsule because of the direction of blood flow in the portal veins. Gas may also be present in the portal and mesenteric veins and the bowel wall.

Children

1. **Necrotizing enterocolitis** – 10% develop gas in the portal vein. Necrotic bowel wall allows gas or gas-forming organisms into the portal circulation. The finding of portal vein gas is of serious significance.
2. **Umbilical vein catheterization** – with the inadvertent injection of air.
3. **Erythroblastosis fetalis.**

Adults

1. **Mesenteric infarction** – the majority of patients die soon after gas is seen in the portal veins.
2. **Air embolus during double contrast barium enema** – this has been observed during the examination of severely ulcerated colons and is not associated with a fatal outcome.
3. **Acute gastric dilatation** – in bedridden young people. May recover following decompression with a nasogastric tube.

Further Reading

Benson M.B. (1985) Adult survival with intrahepatic portal venous gas secondary to acute gastric dilatation with a review of portal venous gas. *Clin. Radiol.*, 36: 441–3.

Meritt C.R.B., Goldsmith J.P. & Shary M.J. (1984) Sonographic detection of portal venous gas in infants with NEC. *Am. J. Roentgenol.*, 143: 1059.

Mindelzun R. & McCort J.J. (1980) Hepatic and perihepatic radiolucencies. *Radiol. Clin. North Am.*, 18: 221–38.

Radin D.R., Roson R.S. & Halls J.M. (1987) Acute gastric dilatation: a rare cause of portal venous gas. *Am. J. Roentgenol.*, 148: 279–80.

Sisk P.B. (1961) Gas in the portal venous system. *Radiology*, 77: 103–6.

Wiot J.F. & Felson B. (1961) Gas in the portal venous system. *Am. J. Roentgenol.*, 86: 920–9.

7.5 Segmental Anatomy of the Liver

25% of colorectal carcinomas have liver secondaries at presentation. Of these 10% have surgically resectable disease. Surgeons need to know the number, size, location and proximity to vessels.

The liver is divided into segments in the horizontal plane by the right and left main portal veins, and in the vertical plane by the right, middle, and left hepatic veins.

Upper Segments: above the level of the right and left portal veins.

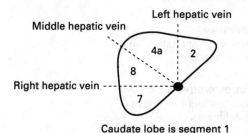

Caudate lobe is segment 1

Lower Segments: below the level of the right and left portal veins.

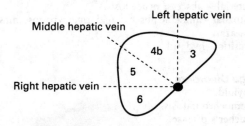

Further Reading

Nelson R.C., Chezmer J.L., Sugarbaker P.H., Murray D.R. & Bernardino M.E. (1990) Preoperative localisation of focal liver lesions to specific liver segments. *Radiology*, 176: 86–94.

7.6 Hepatomegaly

Neoplastic
1. Metastases.
2. Hepatoma.
3. Lymphoma*.

Raised Venous Pressure
1. Congestive cardiac failure.
2. Constrictive pericarditis.
3. Tricuspid stenosis.
4. Budd–Chiari syndrome.

Degenerative
1. Cirrhosis – especially alcoholic.
2. Fatty infiltration.

Myeloproliferative Disorders
1. Polycythaemia rubra vera.
2. Myelofibrosis.

Infective
1. **Viral** – infectious and serum hepatitis; infectious mononucleosis.
2. **Bacterial** – abscess; brucellosis.
3. **Protozoal** – amoebic abscess, malaria, trypanosomiasis and kala-azar.
4. **Parasitic** – hydatid.

Storage Disorders
1. Amyloid.
2. Haemochromatosis.
3. Gaucher's disease.
4. Niemann–Pick disease.

Congenital
1. Riedel's lobe.
2. Polycystic disease*.

7.7 Hepatic Tumours in Children

Feature	Hepatoblastoma	Hepatocellular carcinoma
Age	Usually < 5 years old	Usually > 5 years old
Sex	M >> F	M > F
Associated liver disease	No	↑ incidence (cirrhosis, glycogen storage disease I, tyrosinaemia, biliary atresia and chronic hepatitis)
Presentation	Mass ± pain. Hormone production may lead to male sexual precocity, polycythaemia, hypoglycaemia, hyperlipidaemia or hypercalcaemia. ± signs of chronic liver disease	
↑ serum alphafeto protein	Almost all	Most
Multifocal	Less likely	More likely
Location	Right lobe >> left lobe	Right lobe > left lobe, but in most both lobes are involved
Resectability at diagnosis	More likely	Less likely
Relative prognosis	Better	Worse
Ultrasound	Very variable; usually non-homogeneous increased echoes	
CT	Non-homogeneous low attenuation with some enhancement	
MRI	↓ signal on T_1W and ↑ signal on T_2W. Tumour invasion of vessels is seen best by this modality	
Metastases	Lungs (in 10% at diagnosis), abdominal lymph nodes and skeleton	

Modified from Cohen (1992).

1. **Hepatoblatoma**   there are no major imaging
2. **Hepatocellular**   differences between these two
   carcinoma   tumours but clinical differences,
                          particularly age, may enable pre-
                          biopsy differentiation. (see above
                          table).
3. **Haemangioendothelioma** – often present in the newborn
   period with hepatomegaly and congestive cardiac failure.
   ± skin haemangiomas. Uni- or multifocal, well-defined or
   diffuse. Typical pattern of enhancement on CT with early
   rim enhancement and delayed 'filling-in' of the centre of
   the tumour over next 30 minutes. ^{99m}Tc-labelled red cells
   will accumulate in this tumour. In the neonate, this and
   cavernous haemangioma may be considered together.
4. **Stage IV-S neuroblastoma** – diffuse and infiltrating.
   Lesions in bone and bone marrow, ↑ urinary VMAs and
   positive MIBG scan.
5. **Adenoma** – usually solitary, occurring spontaneously or
   complicating glycogen storage disease and Fanconi's anaemia treated with anabolic steroids.

Differential Diagnosis
1. Focal nodular hyperplasia.
2. Simple cyst.
3. Choledochal cyst.
4. Abscess.

Further Reading
Cohen M.D. (1992) *Imaging of Children with Cancer*, Chapter 3,
   pp. 20–42. St Louis: Mosby Year Book.

7.8 Hepatic Calcification

Multiple and Small
1. **Healed granulomas** – tuberculosis, histoplasmosis and, less commonly, brucellosis and coccidioidomycosis.

Curvilinear
1. **Hydatid** – liver is the commonest site of hydatid disease. Most cysts are in the right lobe and are clinically silent but may cause pain, a palpable mass or a thrill. Calcification in 20–30% and although calcification does not necessarily indicate death of the parasite extensive calcification favours an inactive cyst. Calcification of daughter cysts produces several rings of calcification.
2. **Abscess** – especially amoebic abscess when the right lobe is most frequently affected.
3. **Calcified (porcelain) gallbladder** – strong association with gallbladder carcinoma.

Localized in Mass
1. **Metastases** – calcification is uncommon but colloid carcinoma of the rectum, colon or stomach calcify most frequently. It may be amorphous, flaky, stippled or granular and solitary or multiple. Calcification may follow radiotherapy or chemotherapy.
2. **Hepatoma** – rare. Calcifications are punctate, stippled or granular.

Sunray Spiculation
1. **Haemangioma** – phleboliths may also occur but are uncommon.
2. **Metastases** – infrequently in metastases from colloid carcinomas.
3. **Hepatoma**.

(*continued*)

Diffuse Increased Density

1. Haemochromatosis*.
2. **Thorotrast** – lacy, bubbly increased density ± opacification of the liver capsule. Adjacent lymph nodes and spleen also show increased density, although the latter is more granular.

Further Reading

Ashur H., Siegal B., Oland Y. and Adam Y.G. (1978) Calcified gall bladder (porcelain gall bladder). *Arch. Surg.*, 113: 594–6.

Beggs I. (1985) The radiology of hydatid disease. *Am. J. Roentgenol.*, 145: 639–48.

Darlak J.J., Moskowitz M. & Katten K.R. (1980) Calcifications in the liver. *Radiol. Clin. North Am.*, 18: 209–19.

Gondos B. (1973) Late clinical roentgen observations following Thorotrast administration. *Clin. Radiol.*, 24: 195–203.

Levy D.W., Rindsberg S., Friedman A.C., Fishman E.K., Ros P.R., Radecki P.D., Siegelman S.S., Goodman Z.D., Pyatt R.S. & Grumbach K. (1986) Thorotrast-induced hepatosplenic neoplasia: CT identification. *Am. J. Roentgenol.*, 148: 997–1004.

7.9 Fetal or Neonatal Liver Calcification

Peritoneal

1. **Meconium peritonitis** – the commonest cause of neonatal abdominal calcification. US reveals intra-abdominal solid or cystic masses with calcified walls.
2. **Plastic peritonitis due to ruptured hydrometrocolpos** – similar appearance to meconium peritonitis but US may demonstrate a dilated, fluid-filled uterus and vagina.

Parenchymal

1. **Congenital infections** – TORCH complex (toxoplasmosis, rubella, cytomegalovirus, herpes simplex) and varicella. Randomly scattered nodular calcification. Often calcification elsewhere and other congenital abnormalities.
2. **Tumours** – haemangioma, hamartoma, hepatoblastoma, teratoma and metastatic neuroblastoma. Complex mass on US.

Vascular

1. **Portal vein thromboemboli** – subcapsular branching calcification.
2. **Ischaemic infarcts** – branching calcifications but distributed throughout the liver.

Further Reading

Brugman S.M., Bjelland J.J., Thomason J.E., Anderson S.F. & Giles H.R. (1979) Sonographic findings with radiologic correlation in meconium peritonitis. *J. Clin. Ultrasound*, 7: 305–6.

Friedman A.P., Haller J.O., Boyer B. & Cooper R. (1981) Calcified portal vein thromboemboli in infants: radiography and ultrasonography. *Radiology*, 140: 381–2.

Nguyen D.L. & Leonard J.C. (1986) Ischaemic hepatic necrosis: a cause of fetal liver calcification. *Am. J. Roentgenol.*, 147: 596–7.

Schackelford G.D. & Kirks D.R. (1977) Neonatal hepatic calcification secondary to transplacental infection. *Radiology*, 122: 753–7.

7.10   Jaundice in Infancy

Anatomical Abnormalities

1. **Biliary atresia** – 1 in 15 000 live births. A 'correctible' type
   in 15% of cases in which the proximal extrahepatic bile
   ducts are patent and the distal ducts occluded and a 'non-
   correctible' type, in which the proximal extrahepatic ducts
   are occluded.

   U/S:
   (a) A normal sized gallbladder that contracts following a
       fatty meal excludes the diagnosis.
   (b) Absence of or a small gallbladder favours the diag-
       nosis but a normal gallbladder may be seen in 10%
       of cases.
   (c) Liver echogenicity is normal or increased.

   TBIDA scan:
   (a) Normal uptake by hepatocytes but no excretion into
       the bowel suggests the diagnosis but is not diagnostic
       since alpha-1-antitrypsin may show similar appear-
       ances. Operative cholangiography is indicated.

2. **Choledochal cyst** – may present in the neonatal period or
   at a later age. Classification is:
   I   (80–90%) Fusiform or focal dilatation of the common
         bile duct ± common hepatic duct.
   II   (2%) Diverticulum of the common bile duct.
   III   (2–5%) Outpouching of the common bile duct in the
         wall of the 2nd part of the duodenum – a choledocho-
         cele.
   IVa   Dilatation of the common bile duct and focal dila-
         tations of the intrahepatic ducts.
   IVb   Focal dilatations of the common bile duct.
   V   Focal dilatations of the intrahepatic bile ducts
         (Caroli's disease).

   U/S:
   (a) Anechoic structure which communicates with the bili-
       ary tree and is separate from the gallbladder.

   TBIDA scan:
   (a) Photopenic area which accumulates tracer on
       delayed images.

   Complications:
   (a) Calculi.
   (b) Pancreatitis.

(c) Intrahepatic abscesses.
(d) Biliary cirrhosis.
(e) Portal hypertension.
(f) Malignancy – 4–28%; in the cyst in 3%.
3. **Alagille syndrome** – AD with variable expressivity. Dysmorphic facies, eye abnormalities, cardiovascular abnormalities, especially peripheral pulmonary stenosis or hypoplasia, hypoplasia of intrahepatic bile ducts, butterfly vertebrae, radioulnar synostosis.

Metabolic Defects
e.g. Alpha-1-antitrypsin deficiency, galactosaemia, tyrosinaemia.

Infections
1. **Neonatal hepatitis** – possibly secondary to reovirus.
   U/S:
   (a) Liver echogenicity and size normal or increased.
   TBIDA scan:
   (a) May have delayed uptake by hepatocytes.
   (b) Normal excretion into bowel but may be little, if any, if hepatocyte function is severely impaired.

Further Reading
Crittenden S.L. & McKinley M.J. (1985) Choledochal cyst – clinical features and classification. *Am. J. Gastroenterol.*, 80: 643–7.
Savader S.J., Benenati J.F. & Venbrux A.C. (1991) Choledochal cysts: classification and cholangiographic appearance. *Am. J. Roentgenol.*, 156: 327–31.

7.11   Ultrasound Liver – Generalized Hypoechoic

1. **Acute hepatitis** – mild hepatitis has normal echo pattern.
2. **Diffuse malignant infiltration.**

7.12   Ultrasound Liver – Generalized Hyperechoic (Bright Liver)

1. **Fatty infiltration.**
2. **Cirrhosis.**
3. **Hepatitis** – particularly chronic.
4. **Infiltration/deposition** – malignant, granulomata (e.g. TB, brucellosis, sarcoid), glycogen storage disease.

Further Reading

Barnett E. & Morley P. (eds) (1985) *Clinical Diagnostic Ultrasound.* D.O. Cosgrove, Liver and biliary tree. pp. 365–86. Chapter 22. Oxford: Blackwell Scientific Publications.

7.13   Ultrasound Liver – Focal Hyperechoic

1. **Metastases** – gastrointestinal tract, ovary, pancreas, urogenital tract.
2. **Capillary haemangioma.**
3. **Adenoma** – particularly if associated haemorrhage.
4. **Focal nodular hyperplasia** – may be hyperechoic.
5. **Focal fatty infiltration.**
6. **Debris within lesion** – e.g. abscess, haematoma.
7. **Hepatoma** – can be hyper or hypoechoic.

7.14 Ultrasound Liver – Focal Hypoechoic

1. **Metastasis** – including cystic metastases (e.g. ovary, pancreas, stomach, colon).
2. **Lymphoma.**
3. **Hepatoma** – can be hypo- or hyperechoic.
4. **Cysts** – benign, hydatid.
5. **Abscess** – ± hyperechoic wall due to fibrosis, ± surrounding hypoechoic rim due to oedema. Gas produces areas of very bright echoes.
6. **Haematoma** – acute stage.
7. **Cavernous haemangioma.**

7.15 Ultrasound Liver – Periportal Hyperechoic

1. **Air in biliary tree.**
2. **Schistosomiasis.**
3. **Cholecystitis.**
4. **Recurrent pyogenic cholangitis (oriental).**

Further Reading

Chau E.M.T., Leong L.L.Y. & Chan F.L. (1987) Recurrent pyogenic cholangitis: ultrasound evaluation compared with endoscopic retrograde cholangiopancreatography. *Clin. Radiol.*, 38: 79–85.

7.16 Periportal Hypoechogenicity (Collar Sign) on Ultrasound/Periportal Low Attenuation on CT

1. **Orthoptic liver transplant rejection** – particularly when the peripheral and central parts of the liver are affected. May also be observed in non-rejecting liver transplants and then severed lymphatic channels and tracking of extrahepatic fluid contribute to the sign.
2. **Congestive hepatomegaly.**
3. **Malignant lymphatic obstruction.**
4. **Blunt abdominal trauma** – localized or widespread but many with this sign may have no other evidence of hepatic injury or even any intra-abdominal injury and is probably due to distended periportal lymphatics and lymphoedema associated with elevated central venous pressure following vigorous i.v. fluid replacement. Related to the severity of injury and associated with a higher mortality.
5. **Cholangitis.**
6. **Viral hepatitis.**

Further Reading

Fataar S., Bassiony H., Satyanath S. *et al.* (1985) CT of hepatic Schistosomiasis mansoni. *Am. J. Roentgenol.*, 145: 63–6.

Kaplan S.B., Sumkin J.H., Campbell W.L., Zajko A.B. & Demetris A.J. (1989) Periportal low-attenuation areas on CT: value as evidence of liver transplant rejection. *Am. J. Roentgenol.*, 152: 285–7.

Patrick L.E., Ball T.I., Atkinson G.O. and Winn K.J. (1992) Pediatric blunt abdominal trauma: periportal tracking at CT. *Radiology*, 183: 689–91.

Shanmuganathan K., Mirvis S.E. & Amoroso M. (1993) Periportal low density on CT in patients with blunt trauma: association with elevated venous pressure. *Am. J. Roentgenol.*, 160: 279–83.

Siegel M.J. & Herman T.E. (1992) Periportal low attenuation at CT in childhood. *Radiology*, 183: 685–8.

Sivit C.J., Taylor G.A., Eichelberger M.R., Bulas D.I., Gotschall C.S. & Kushner D.C. (1993) Significance of periportal low-attenuation zones following blunt trauma in children. *Pediatr. Radiol.*, 23: 388–90.

Wechsler R.J., Munoz S.J., Needleman L. *et al.* (1987) The periportal collar: a CT sign of liver transplant rejection. *Radiology*, 165: 57–60.

7.17 Thickened Gallbladder Wall

> 3 mm – excluding the physiological, contracted (empty) gallbladder.

1. Cholecystitis.
2. Hepatitis.
3. Hypoalbuminaemia.
4. Cirrhosis.
5. Congestive heart failure.
6. Renal failure.

In infants also consider bright echoes around the gallbladder due to NEC.

Further Reading

Avni E.F., Rypens F., Cohen E. & Pardou A. (1991) Pericholecystic hyperechogenicities in necrotizing enterocolitis: a specific sonographic sign? *Pediatr. Radiol.*, 21: 179–81.

Patriquin H.B., DiPietro M., Barber F.E. & Teele R.L. (1983) Sonography of thickened gallbladder wall: causes in children. *Am. J. Roentgenol.*, 141: 57–60.

7.18   CT Liver – Focal Hypodense Lesion Pre Intravenous Contrast

Appearances post intravenous contrast

1. **Malignant tumours** – e.g. hepatoma, metastases, lymphoma, haemangiosarcoma intrahepatic cholangiocarcinoma

   ± irregular patchy enhancement

2. **Benign tumours**

   (a) Haemangioma – usually well defined, in right lobe of liver, ±multiple. Technetium 99^M-labelled red blood cells may help make diagnosis

   75% peripheral enhancement
   10% central enhancement
   74% progressively isodense on delayed scan
   24% partially isodense on delayed scan
   2% remain hypodense on delayed scan

   (b) Adenoma – often young woman, related to use of oral contraceptive. Usually only slightly hypodense, and can be hyperdense due to predisposition to acute haemorrhage. Very rarely transforms to hepatoma

   85% hyperdense during arterial phase but rapidly (45 s–1 min) becomes iso or hypodense

3. **Cyst** – benign hepatic, polycystic, hydatid, von Hippel–Lindau. Water density if large enough. Small cysts can have higher density and apparently ill defined walls due to partial volume effect

   margins more clearly demarcated

4. **Abscess**

(a) Pyogenic	± peripheral enhancement
(b) Fungal – immunosuppressed, multiple small lesions, can effect spleen	may not show any peripheral enhancement
(c) Amoebic – ± crescent of low attenuation just peripheral to wall of abscess	± peripheral enhancement

5 **Focal nodular hyperplasia** – usually only slightly hypodense. Often young female, asymptomatic unless large when pressure effects produce pain. Can contain sufficient functioning Kupffer cells to be normal or even increased in uptake on technetium 99^M sulphur colloid scan which can help to discriminate it from other lesions, such as adenomas

most hyperdense during arterial phase but rapidly (45 s–1 min) becomes iso or hypodense, ± stellate central low density due to scar, but this is not specific and occurs in adenomas, haemangiomas and fibrolamellar hepatomas

6. **Focal fatty infiltration** – occasionally rounded in appearance, but usually diffuse or 'geographical' in distribution

no change

7. **Vascular** – infarction, laceration, old haematoma

no change

8. **Biliary tree dilatation** – Caroli's, choledochal cyst

no change

Further Reading

Farman J., Javors B., Chao P., Fagelman D., Collins R. & Glanz S. (1987) C.T. demonstration of giant choledochal cysts in adults. *J. Comput. Assist. Tomogr.*, 11 (5): 771–4.

Freeny P.C. & Marks W.M. (1986) Hepatic haemangioma: dynamic bolus C.T. *Am. J. Roentgenol.*, 147: 711–19.

Mathieu D., Bruneton J.N., Drouillard J., Pointreau C.C. & Vasile N. (1986) Hepatic adenomas and focal nodular hyperplasia: dynamic C.T. study. *Radiology*, 160: 53–8.

Maxwell A.J. & Mamtora H. (1988) Fungal liver abscesses in acute leukaemia – a report of two cases. *Clin. Radiol.*, 39: 197–201.

Yates C.K. & Streight R.A. (1986) Focal fatty infiltration of the liver simulating metastatic disease. *Radiology* 159: 83–4.

7.19   CT Liver – Focal Hyperdense Lesion

Pre Intravenous Contrast

1. **Calcification in:**
   (a) Metastasis – usually colorectal, but ovary, stomach, islet cell pancreas also possible.
   (b) Primary tumour – hepatoma, hepatoblastoma, haemangioendothelioma.
   (c) Infective lesion – hydatid, tuberculous granuloma.
2. **Acute haemorrhage** – post traumatic or bleed into a vascular tumour, e.g. adenoma.

Post Intravenous Contrast

1. **Hypervascular masses**
   (a) Metastases – carcinoid, renal cell carcinoma, islet cell pancreas, and phaeochromocytoma.
   (b) Adenoma ⎤ enhancement only seen during
            ⎟ arterial phase, i.e. within 1
            ⎟ minute of injection. After this
   (c) Focal modular ⎟ they may appear hypodense.
       hyperplasia ⎦
2. **Vascular abnormalities** – e.g. arterio portal shunts which may occur in hepatoma.

Further Reading

Bressler E.L., Alpern M.B., Glazer G.M., Francis I.R. & Ensminger W.D. (1987) Hypervascular hepatic metastases: C.T. Evaluation. *Radiology*, 162: 49–51.

Scatarige J.C., Fishman E.K., Saksouk F.A. & Siegelman S.S. (1983) Computed tomography of calcified liver masses. *J. Comput. Assist. Tomogr.*, 7: 83–9.

7.20 CT Liver – Generalized Low Density Pre Intravenous Contrast

Assess by comparing liver with spleen. Also intrahepatic vessels stand out as 'high' density against low density background of liver, but aorta shows normal soft-tissue density indicating the apparent high density of the intrahepatic vessels is not due to intravenous contrast.

1. **Fatty infiltration** – early cirrhosis, obesity, parenteral feeding, bypass surgery, malnourishment, cystic fibrosis, steroids, Cushing's, late pregnancy, carbon tetrachloride exposure, chemotherapy, high dose tetracycline, and glycogen storage disease.
2. **Malignant infiltration.**
3. **Budd–Chiari**
   (a) Acute – big low density liver with ascites. After intravenous contrast there is patchy enhancement of the hilum of the liver due to multiple collaterals, and non-visualization of the hepatic veins and/or inferior vena cava.
   (b) Chronic – atrophied patchy low density liver with sparing and hypertrophy of caudate lobe. Post intravenous contrast scans show similar signs as the acute stage.
4. **Amyloid** – no change after intravenous contrast.

Further Reading

Halversen R.A., Korobkin M., Ram P.C. & Thomson W.M. (1982) C.T. appearance of focal fatty infiltration of the liver. *Am. J. Roentgenol.*, 139: 277–81.

Mathieu D., Vasile N., Menu Y., Van Beers B., Lorphelin J.M. & Pringot J. (1987) Budd Chiari syndrome: Dynamic C.T. *Radiology*, 165: 409–13.

Suzuki S., Takizawa K., Nakajima Y., Katayama M. & Sagawa F. (1986) C.T. findings in hepatic and splenic amyloidosis. *J. Comput. Assist. Tomogr.*, 10 (2): 332–4.

Vogelzang R.L., Anscheutz S.L. & Gore R.M. (1987) Budd Chiari syndrome: C.T. observations. *Radiology* 163: 329–33.

Yates C.K. & Streight R.A. (1986) Focal fatty infiltration of the liver simulating metastatic disease. *Radiology*, 159: 83–4.

7.21   CT Liver – Generalized Increase in Density Pre Intravenous Contrast

Assess by comparing liver with spleen. Also intrahepatic vessels stand out as low density against high density background of liver.

1. **Haemochromatosis** – may be an associated hepatoma present.
2. **Haemosiderosis.**
3. **Iron overload** – e.g. from large number of blood transfusions.
4. **Glycogen storage disease** – liver may be increased or decreased in density.
5. **Amiodarone treatment** – contains iodine. Can also cause pulmonary interstitial and alveolar infiltrates.

Further Reading
Butler S. & Smathers R.L. (1985) Computed tomography of Amiodarone pulmonary toxicity. *J. Comput. Assist. Tomogr.*, 9 (2): 375–6.

7.22   CT Liver – Patchy Areas of Low Density Post Intravenous Contrast

1. Cirrhosis.
2. Hepatitis.
3. Portal vein thrombosis.
4. Budd–Chiari – chronic.
5. Lymphoma infiltration*.
6. Sarcoidosis*.

7.23 MRI Liver

	T_1W	T_2W	Gadolinium
Hepatocellular carcinoma	↓, iso or ↑ (due to fat degeneration)	↑	↑
Metastases	↓	↑	±↑
Haemangioma	↓	↑++ = to CSF at long TE	↑ (like CT)
Adenoma	↑	↓	
Focal nodular hyperplasia central scar margins	↓ isointense	↑+ ↑	↑ ±↑
Regenerating nodule	↓, isointense	↓	
Haemochromatosis/Iron deposition	↓	↓++	

Further Reading

Choi B.I., Takayasu K. & Han M.C. (1993) Small hepatocellular carcinomas and associated nodular lesions of the liver: pathology, pathogenesis and imaging findings. *Am. J. Roentgenol.*, 160: 1177–87.

Vilgrain V., Flejou J.-F. & Arrive L. (1992) Focal nodular hyperplasia of the liver: MR imaging and pathologic correlation in 37 patients. *Radiology*, 184: 699–703.

7.24 MRI Liver – Focal Hyperintense Lesion on T₁W

NB   Most lesions are hypointense on T_1W.

1. **Fat** – lipomas, angiomyolipomas, focal fatty deposits, surgical defect packed with omental fat, occasionally hepatomas undergo fatty degeneration.
2. **Blood** – in the acute stage due to methaemoglobin (which is paramagnetic)
3. **Proteinaceous material** – occurs in dependent layer of fluid/fluid levels in abscesses and haematomas due to increased concentration of hydrated protein molecules.
4. **Melanoma metastases** – ? due to paramagnetic effect of melanin or associated haemorrhage.
5. **Chemical** – gadolinium, lipiodol (contains fat).
6. **'Relative'** – i.e. normal signal intensity liver surrounded by low signal intensity liver which may occur with iron deposition (haemochromatosis, i.v. ferrite particles), cirrhosis (unclear aetiology, but a regenerating nodule within a cirrhotic area may appear artefactually hyperintense), oedema.
7. **Artefact** – pulsation artefact from abdominal aorta can produce a periodic 'ghost' artefact along the phase encoded direction which can be hypo- or hyperintense depending on the phase.

Further Reading

Lee M.J., Hahn P.F., Saini S. & Mueller P.R. (1992) Differential diagnosis of hyperintense liver lesions on T_1W MR images. *Am. J. Roentgenol.*, 159: 1017–20.

7.25 MRI Liver – Ringed Hepatic Lesions

One or several layers which may be a component of the lesion itself or a response of the liver to the presence of the adjacent lesion.

1. **Capsules of 1° liver tumours** – a low signal ring (because of collagen and best seen on T_1) may be seen in 25–40% but does not differentiate between benign and malignant. A peritumoural halo of high signal on T_2 is seen in 30% of 1° tumours and more closely correlates with malignancy.
2. **Metastases** – halo of high signal on T_2 or, with central liquefaction to give an even higher centre and a 'target' lesion. A peritumoural halo or a target on T_2 distinguishes metastasis from cavernous haemangioma.
3. **Subacute haematoma** – low signal rim on T_1 and T_2 (because of iron) with an inner bright ring on T_1 (because of methaemoglobin).
4. **Hydatid cyst** – T_2 high signal cyst contents with a low signal capsule. The capsule is not well seen on T_1.
5. **Amoebic abscess** – prior to treatment incomplete concentric rings of variable intensity, better seen on T_2 than T_1. During antibiotic treatment, T_1 and T_2 images show the development of four concentric zones because of central liquefaction and resolution of hepatic oedema.

Further Reading

Elizondo G., Weissleder R., Stark D.D. *et al.* (1987) Amebic liver abscess – diagnosis and treatment evaluation with MR imaging. *Radiology*, 165: 795–800.

Hahn P.F., Stark D.D., Saini S. *et al.* (1990) The differential diagnosis of ringed hepatic lesions in MR imaging. *Am. J. Roentgenol.*, 154: 287–90.

Hoff F.L., Aisen A.M., Walden M.E., Glazer G.M. (1987) MR imaging in hydatid disease of the liver. *Gastrointest. Radiol.*, 12: 39–42.

Ralls P.W., Henley D.S., Colletti P.M. *et al.* (1987) Amebic liver abscess: MR imaging. *Radiology*, 165: 801–4.

Rummeny E., Weissleder R., Stark D.D. *et al.* (1989) Primary liver tumours: diagnosis by MR imaging. *Am. J. Roentgenol.*, 152: 63–72.

Wittenberg J., Stark D.D., Forman B.H. *et al.* (1988) Differentiation of hepatic metastases from hepatic hemangiomas and cysts by using MR imaging. *Am. J. Roentgenol.*, 151: 79–84.

7.26 Splenomegaly

Huge Spleen
1. Chronic myeloid leukaemia.
2. Myelofibrosis.
3. Malaria.
4. Kala-azar.
5. Gaucher's disease.
6. Lymphoma*.

Moderately Large Spleen
1. All of the above.
2. Storage diseases.
3. Haemolytic anaemias.
4. Portal hypertension.
5. Leukaemias.

Slightly Large Spleen
1. All of the above.
2. Infections.
   (a) Viral – infectious hepatitis, infectious mononucleosis.
   (b) Bacterial – septicaemia, brucellosis, typhoid and tuberculosis.
   (c) Rickettsial – typhus.
   (d) Fungal – histoplasmosis.
3. Sarcoidosis*.
4. Amyloidosis.
5. Rheumatoid arthritis (Felty's syndrome)*.
6. Systemic lupus erythematosus*.

7.27 Splenic Calcification

Curvilinear
1. Splenic artery atherosclerosis – including splenic artery aneurysm.
2. Cyst – hydatid or post-traumatic.

Multiple Small Nodular
1. Phleboliths – may have small central lucencies.
2. Haemangioma – phleboliths.
3. Tuberculosis.
4. Histoplasmosis.
5. Brucellosis.
6. Sickle-cell anaemia*.

Diffuse Homogeneous or Finely Granular
1. Sickle-cell anaemia*.
2. Thorotrast – densities also in the liver and upper abdominal lymph nodes.
3. Pneumocystis carinii.

Solitary Greater than 1 cm
1. Healed infarct or haematoma.
2. Healed abscess.
3. Tuberculosis.

Further Reading
McCall I.W., Vaidya S. & Serjeant G.R. (1981) Splenic opacification in homozygous sickle cell disease. *Clin. Radiol.*, 32: 611–15.

7.28 CT Spleen – Focal Low Density Lesion

1. Lymphoma*.
2. Metastases.
3. Haemangioma.
4. Abscess – fungal abscesses are small and multifocal.

7.29 Pancreatic Calcification

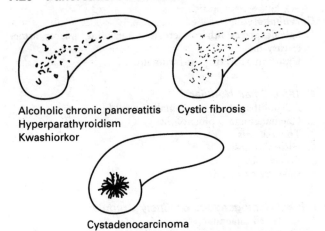

Alcoholic chronic pancreatitis   Cystic fibrosis
Hyperparathyroidism
Kwashiorkor

Cystadenocarcinoma

1. **Alcoholic pancreatitis** – calcification, which is almost exclusively due to intraductal calculi is seen in 20–40% (compared with 2% of gallstone pancreatitis). Usually after 5–10 years of pain. Limited to head or tail in 25%. Rarely solitary. Calculi are numerous, irregular and generally small.
2. **Pseudocyst** – 12–20% exhibit calcification which is usually similar to that seen in chronic pancreatitis but may be curvilinear rim calcification.
3. **Carcinoma of the pancreas** – although for all practical purposes adenocarcinoma does not calcify there is an increased incidence of pancreatic cancer in chronic pancreatitis and the two will be found concurrently in about 2% of cases.
4. **Hyperparathyroidism*** – pancreatitis occurs as a complication of HPT in 10% of cases and 30% of these show calcification which is similar to that observed in chronic pancreatitis. 70% have nephrocalcinosis or urolithiasis and this should suggest the diagnosis.
5. **Cystic fibrosis*** – calcification occurs late in the disease when there is advanced pancreatic fibrosis associated with diabetes mellitus. Calcification is typically finely granular.
6. **Kwashiorkor** – pancreatic lithiasis is a frequent finding and

appears before adulthood. Its pattern is similar to chronic alcoholic pancreatitis.

7. **Hereditary pancreatitis** – autosomal dominant 60% show calcification which is typically rounded and often larger than in other pancreatic diseases. 20% die from pancreatic malignancy. The diagnosis should be considered in young, non-alcoholic patients.

8. **Tumours** – calcification is observed in 10% of cystadenomas and cystadenocarcinomas. It is non-specific but occasionally 'sunburst'. The rare cavernous lymphangioma contains phleboliths in and adjacent to it.

9. **Idiopathic.**

Further Reading

Ring E.J., Eaton S.B., Ferrucci J.T. & Short W.F. (1973) Differential diagnosis of pancreatic calcification. *Am. J. Roentgenol.*, 117: 446–52.

7.30 CT Pancreas – Focal Mass

1. **Adenocarcinoma** – 60% head, 10% body, 5% tail, 20% diffuse. 40% are isodense on pre-contrast scan, but most of these show reduced density on a post-contrast scan. Virtually never contain calcification. The presence of metastases (nodes, liver) or invasion around vascular structures (SMA, coeliac axis, portal and splenic vein) helps to distinguish this from focal pancreatitis.
2. **Focal pancreatitis** – usually in head of pancreas. Can contain calcification, but if not may be difficult to distinguish from carcinoma.
3. **Metastasis** – e.g. breast, lung, stomach, kidney, thyroid.
4. **Islet cell tumour** – equal incidence in head, body and tail. 80% are functioning and so will present at a relatively small size. 20% are non-functioning and so are larger and more frequently contain calcification at presentation. In general functioning islet cell tumours, other than insulinomas, are often malignant, whereas 75% of non-functioning tumours are benign.
   (a) Beta cell:

insulinoma –	90% benign, 10% multiple, 80% less than 2 cm in diameter. Usually isodense with marked contrast enhancement. Can calcify.

   (b) Non beta cell:

gastrinoma –	60% malignant, 30% benign adenoma, 10% hyperplasia. 90% located in pancreas, 5% duodenum, occasionally stomach and splenic hilum. Shows marked contrast enhancement. Multiple adenomas seen as part of Multiple endocrine adenopathy I syndrome (pituitary, parathyroid and pancreatic adenomas).
glucagonoma –	usually greater than 4 cm, since endocrine disturbance is often less marked.

5. **Mucinous cystadenoma** – multiple small (less than 2 cm) cysts usually in head. Frequently calcified. Usually female aged over 60.

6. **Mucinous cystadenocarcinoma** – multiple thick-walled big (greater than 5 cm) cysts usually in body or tail. The thick walls may help to distinguish from pseudocysts. 15% calcify.

7. **Pancreatic abscess** – infected phlegmon/pseudocyst. Occurs in 3% of pancreatitis.

Further Reading

Breatnach E.S., Han S.Y., Rahatzad M.T. & Stanley R.J. (1985) C.T. evaluation of glucagonomas. *J. Comput. Assist. Tomogr.*, 9 (1): 25–9.

Clark L.R., Jaffe M.H., Choyke P.L., Grant E.G. & Zaman R.K. (1985) Pancreatic imaging. *Radiol. Clin. North Am.*, 23 (3): 489–501.

7.31   Adrenal Calcification

Child

1. **Cystic disease** – usually the result of haemorrhage which may be secondary to birth trauma, infection, haemorrhagic disorders of arterial or venous thromboses. Partial or complete ring-like calcification is observed initially but this later becomes compact as the cyst collapses. Frequently asymptomatic.

2. **Neuroblastoma** – in 50% of cases on plain films; 90% on CT. Ill-defined, stippled and non-homogeneous. Lymphnode and liver metastases can also calcify.

3. **Ganglioneuroma** – similar appearance to neuroblastoma, but only 20% are within the adrenal.

4. **Wolman's disease** – a rare autosomal recessive lipoidosis. Hepatomegaly, splenomegaly and adrenomegaly with punctate cortical adrenal calcification is pathognomonic.

Adult

1. **Cystic disease** – similar to that seen in the child. Bilateral in 15% of cases.

2. **Carcinoma** – irregular punctate calcifications. Average size of tumour is 14 cm and there is frequently displacement of the ipsilateral kidney.

3. **Addison's disease** – now most commonly due to autoimmune disease or metastasis. In the past when tuberculosis was a frequent cause calcification was a common finding.

4. **Ganglioneuroma** – 40% occur over the age of 20 years. Slightly flocculent calcifications in a mass which is usually asymptomatic. If the tumour is large enough there will be displacement of the adjacent kidney and/or ureter.

5. **Inflammatory** – primary tuberculosis and histoplasmosis.

6. **Phaeochromocytoma** – calcification is rare but when present is usually an 'eggshell' pattern.

Further Reading

Queloz J.M., Capitanio M.A. & Kirkpatrick I.A. (1972) Wolman's disease. Roentgen observations in three siblings. *Radiology*, 104: 357–9.

Computed Tomography

Haaga J.R. & Alfidi R.J. (1983) *Computed Tomography of the Whole Body*. Toronto: The C.V. Mosby Company.
Moss A.A., Gamsu G. & Gerant H.K. (1983) *Computed Tomography of the Body*. Philadelphia: W.B. Saunders Company.

7.32   CT Adrenal Masses

Length of limbs is variable: can be up to 4 cm. Width of limb
is normally less than 1 cm. The right adrenal lies behind
inferior vena cava and above right kidney, i.e. not on same
slice as the kidney. The left adrenal lies in front of upper pole
of left kidney, i.e. on same slice as the kidney – do not mistake
upper pole of left kidney for an adrenal mass.

Structures Mimicking Left Adrenal Mass
1. **Upper pole of left kidney.**
2. **Gastric diverticulum** – give oral contrast.
3. **Splenic lobulation/accessory spleen** – give intravenous contrast, should enhance to the same level as the body of
   the spleen.
4. **Large mass in tail of pancreas** – give intravenous contrast,
   pancreatic mass usually displaces splenic vein posteriorly
   whereas adrenal mass displaces it anteriorly.

Functioning Tumours
1. **Conn's adenoma** – accounts for 70% of Conn's syndrome.
   Usually small, 0.5–1.5 cm. Homogeneous, relatively low
   density due to build up of cholesterol. 30% of Conn's syndrome due to hyperplasia which can occasionally be nodular and mimic an adenoma.
2. **Phaeochromocytoma** – usually large, 3–5 cm, with marked
   contrast enhancement (beware hypertensive crisis with
   intravenous contrast). 10% malignant, 10% bilateral,
   10% ectopic (of these 50% are located around the kidney,
   particularly renal hilum. If CT does not detect, MIBG isotope scan may be helpful). 10% multiple (usually part of
   multiple endocrine adenopathy II (MEA II) syndrome).
   Associated with neurofibromatosis, von Hippel–Lindau,
   and MEA II.
3. **Cushing's adenoma** – accounts for 10% of Cushing's syndrome. Usually over 2 cm. 40% show slight reduction in
   density. 80% of Cushing's syndrome due to excess ACTH
   from pituitary tumour or ectopic source (oat cell carcinoma, pancreatic islet cell, carcinoid, medullary carcinoma
   thyroid, thymoma) which causes adrenal hyperplasia not
   visible on CT scan. Other 10% of Cushing's syndrome due

to adrenal carcinoma. The possibilities for adrenal mass in Cushing's syndrome are:
(a) Functioning adenoma/carcinoma.
(b) Coincidental non-functioning adenoma.
(c) Metastasis from oat cell primary.
(d) Nodular hyperplasia, which occurs in 20% of Cushing's syndrome due to pituitary adenoma.
4. **Adrenal carcinoma** – 50% present as functioning tumours (Cushing's 35%, Cushing's with virilization 20%, virilization 20%, feminization 5%).

Malignant Tumours

1. **Metastases** – may be bilateral, usually greater than 2–3 cm, irregular outline with patchy contrast enhancement. Recent haemorrhage into a vascular metastasis (e.g. melanoma) can give a patchy high density on pre contrast scan.
2. **Carcinoma** – usually greater than 5 cm, mixed density, may calcify, and metastatic nodes or liver secondaries may be seen.
3. **Lymphoma** – 25% also involve kidneys at autopsy. Lymphadenopathy will be seen elsewhere.
4. **Neuroblastoma** – greater than 5 cm. Calcification in 90%. Extends across midline. Nodes commonly surround and displace the aorta and inferior vena cava.

Benign

1. **Non-functioning adenoma** – occurs in 5% at autopsy. Usually relatively small (50% less than 2 cm), homogeneous, and well-defined.
2. **Angiomyolipoma** – occurs in 0.2% at autopsy. Usually 1–2 cm. May contain fat density.
3. **Cyst** – well-defined, water density.
4. **Post-traumatic haemorrhage** – homogeneous, hyperdense. Occurs in 25% of severe trauma, 20% bilateral, 85% in right. Adrenal haemorrhage can also occur in vascular metastases, anticoagulant treatment, and severe stress (e.g. surgery, sepsis, burns, hypotension).

(continued)

Further Reading

Falke T.H.M., te Strake L. & van Peters A.P. (1984) C.T. of the adrenal glands: adenoma or hyperplasia? *Radiology*, 153: 358.

Peretz G.S. & Lam A.H. (1985) Distinguishing neuroblastoma from Wilms' tumour by computed tomography. *J. Comput. Assist. Tomogr.*, 9 (5): 889–93.

Wilms G., Marchal G., Baert A., Adisoejoso B. & Mangkuwerdojo (1987) C.T. and ultrasound features of post traumatic adrenal haemorrhage. *J. Comput. Assist. Tomogr.*, 11 (1): 112–15.

8
Urinary Tract

8.1 Loss of a Renal Outline on the Plain Film

Not necessarily associated with a non-visualized kidney after intravenous contrast medium.

1. **Technical factors** – e.g. poor radiography, overlying faeces, etc.
2. **Congenital absence** – 1 : 1000 live births. Increased incidence of extrarenal abnormalities (ventricular septal defect, meningomyelocele, intestinal tract strictures, imperforate anus, skeletal abnormalities and unicornuate uterus). The normal solitary kidney may approach twice normal size.
3. **Displaced or ectopic kidney** – presacral, crossed ectopia or intrathoracic.
4. **Perinephric haematoma** – obliteration of the perirenal fat. ± other signs of trauma, e.g. fractured transverse processes.
5. **Perinephric abscess** – scoliosis concave to the affected side. May be associated with gas in the perirenal tissues. ± localized ileus.
6. **Tumour** – when perinephric fat is replaced by tumour.
7. **Post-nephrectomy** – rare because residual perinephric fat preserves an apparent renal outline. Surgical resection of 12th rib is usually evident.

8.2   Renal Calcification

Calculi (see 8.3)

Dystrophic Calcification Due to Localized Disease
Usually one kidney or part of one kidney.
1. **Infections**
    (a)   Tuberculosis – variable appearance of nodular, curvilinear or amorphous calcification. Typically multifocal with calcification elsewhere in the urinary tract.
    (b)   Hydatid – the cyst is usually polar and calcification is curvilinear or heterogeneous.
    (c)   Xanthogranulomatous pyelonephritis.
    (d)   Abscess.
2. **Carcinoma** – in 6% of carcinomas. Usually amorphous or irregular, but occasionally curvilinear.
3. **Aneurysm** – of the renal artery. Curvilinear.

Nephrocalcinosis
Parenchymal calcification associated with a diffuse renal lesion (i.e. dystrophic calcification) or metabolic abnormality, e.g. hypercalcaemia (metabolic or metastatic calcification). May be medullary or cortical.

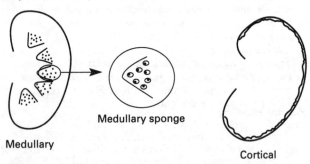

Medullary sponge

Medullary

Cortical

MEDULLARY (PYRAMIDAL)
The first three causes account for 70% of cases.
1. **Hyperparathyroidism***.
2. **Renal tubular acidosis** – may be associated with osteomalacia or rickets. Calcification tends to be more severe than

that due to other causes. It is the commonest cause in children. Almost always a distal tubular defect.

3. **Medullary sponge kidney** – a variable portion of one of both kidneys contains numerous small medullary cysts which communicate with tubules and therefore opacify during excretion urography. The cysts contain small calculi giving a 'bunch of grapes' appearance. Big kidneys. ± multiple cysts or large medullary cystic cavities which may be > 2 cm diameter. (Although not strictly a cause of nephrocalcinosis, because it comprises calculi in ectatic ducts, it is included here because of the plain film findings which simulate nephrocalcinosis.)

4. **Renal papillary necrosis** – calcification of necrotic papillae. See 8.21.

5. **Causes of hypercalcaemia or hypercalciuria**
   (a) Milk-alkali syndrome.
   (b) Idiopathic hypercalciuria.
   (c) Sarcoidosis*.
   (d) Hypervitaminosis D.

6. **Primary hyperoxaluria** – rare. AR 65% present below 5 years of age (younger than the other causes). Radiologically – nephrocalcinosis (generally diffuse and homogeneous but may be patchy), recurrent nephrolithiasis, dense vascular calcification, osteopenia or renal osteodystrophy and abnormal metaphyses (dense and/or lucent bands).

CORTICAL

1. **Acute cortical necrosis** – classically 'tramline' calcification.
2. **Chronic glomerulonephritis** – rarely.
3. **Chronic transplant rejection.**

Further Reading

Daniel W.W., Hartman G.W., Witten D.M., Farrow G.M. & Kelalis P.P. (1972) Calcified renal masses. *Radiology*, 103: 503–8.

Day D.L., Scheinman J.I. & Mahan I. (1986) Radiological aspects of primary hyperoxaluria. *Am. J. Roentgenol.*, 146: 395–401.

Gedroyc W.M.W. & Saxton H.M. (1988) More medullary sponge variants. *Clin. Radiol.*, 39: 423–5.

Lalli A.F. (1982) Renal parenchyma calcifications. *Semin. Roentgenol.*, 17 (2): 101–12.

Wrong O.M. & Feest T.G. (1976) Nephrocalcinosis. *Adv. Med.*, 12: 394–406.

8.3   Renal Calculi

Opaque
Calcium phosphate/calcium oxalate, calcium oxalate, calcium phosphate/magnesium ammonium phosphate and calcium phosphate. Calcium oxalate stones are more opaque than triple phosphate stones.

Poorly Opaque
Cystine (in cystinuria).

Non-opaque
Uric acid, xanthine and matrix (mucoprotein).

Calcium Containing
1. **With normocalcaemia** – obstruction, urinary tract infection, prolonged bedrest, 'horseshoe' kidney, vesical diverticulum, renal tubular acidosis, medullary sponge kidney and idiopathic hypercalciuria.
2. **With hypercalcaemia** – hyperparathyroidism, milk-alkali syndrome, excess vitamin D, idiopathic hypercalcaemia of infancy and sarcoidosis.

Pure Calcium Oxalate due to Hyperoxaluria
1. **Primary hyperoxaluria** – rare. AR 65% present below 5 years of age. Radiologically – nephrocalcinosis (generally diffuse and homogeneous but may be patchy), recurrent nephrolithiasis, dense vascular calcification, osteopenia or renal osteodystrophy and abnormal metaphyses (dense and/or lucent bands).
2. **Enteric hyperoxaluria** – due to a disturbance of bile acid metabolism. Mainly in patients with small bowel disease, either Crohn's disease or surgical resection.

Uric Acid
1. **With hyperuricaemia** – gout, myeloproliferative disorders and during the treatment of tumours with antimitotic agents.
2. **With normouricaemia** – idiopathic or associated with acid,

concentrated urine (in hot climate and in ileostomy patients).

Xanthine
Due to a failure of normal oxidation of purines.

Matrix
Rare. In poorly functioning, infected urinary tracts.

Further Reading

Banner M.P. & Pollack H.M. (1982) Urolithiasis in the lower urinary tract. *Semin. Roentgenol.*, 17 (2): 140–8.

Day D.L., Scheinman J.I. & Mahan J. (1986) Radiological aspects of primary hyperoxaluria. *Am. J. Roentgenol.*, 146: 395–401.

Elkin M. (1983) Calcification in the urinary tract. In: Baker S.R. & Elkin M. *Plain Film Approach to Abdominal Calcifications*, pp. 39–46. Philadelphia: Saunders.

Singh E.O. & Malek R.S. (1982) Calculus disease in the upper urinary tract. *Semin. Roentgenol.*, 17 (2): 113–32.

Thornbury J.R. & Parker T.W. (1982) Ureteral calculi. *Semin. Roentgenol.*, 17 (2): 133–9.

8.4 Gas in the Urinary Tract

Gas shadows which conform to the position and shape of the bladder, ureters or pelvicalyceal systems.

Gas Inside the Bladder
1. **Vesico-intestinal fistula** –diverticular disease, carcinoma of the colon or rectum and Crohn's disease.
2. **Cystitis** – due to gas-forming organisms and fermentation, especially in diabetics. Usually *Escherichia coli*. Clostridial infections are rare and usually secondary to septicaemia.
3. **Following instrumentation.**
4. **Penetrating wounds.**

Gas in the Bladder Wall
1. **Emphysematous cystitis** – usually in diabetics.

Gas in the Ureters and Pelvicalyceal Systems
1. **Any cause of gas in the bladder.**
2. **Ureteric diversion** – into the colon or bladder.
3. **Fistula** – Crohn's disease or perforated duodenal ulcer.
4. **Infection** – usually in diabetics. Gas may also be present in the renal parenchyma and retroperitoneal tissues.

8.5 Non-visualization of One Kidney During Excretion Urography

1. **Absent kidney** – congenital absence or post-nephrectomy.
2. **Ectopic kidney.**
3. **Chronic obstructive uropathy.**
4. **Infection** – pyonephrosis, xanthogranulomatous pyelonephritis or tuberculosis.
5. **Tumour** – an avascular tumour completely replacing the kidney or preventing normal function of residual renal tissue by occluding the renal vein or pelvis.
6. **Renal artery occlusion** – including trauma.
7. **Renal vein occlusion** – see 8.23.
8. **Multicystic kidney** – see 8.18.

8.6 Unilateral Scarred Kidney

NORMAL
Cortex parallel to
interpapillary line

FETAL LOBULATION
Normal size.
Cortical depressions
between papillae

DUPLEX KIDNEY
Renal size usually
larger than normal

SPLEEN IMPRESSION
Right kidney may
show hepatic
impression

OVERLYING BOWEL
Spurious
loss of cortex

**REFLUX
NEPHROPATHY**
Focal scars over
dilated calyces. Most
prominent at upper
and lower poles. May
be bilateral

LOBAR INFARCTION
Broad depression
over a normal calyx

Redrawn from Taylor C.M. & Chapman S. (1989) *Handbook of
Renal Investigations in Children*. London: Wright. By kind permission of the publisher.

(*continued*)

1. **Reflux nephropathy** – a focal scar over a dilated calyx. Usually multifocal and may be bilateral. Scarring is most prominent in the upper and lower poles. Minimal scarring, especially at a pole, may produce decreased cortical thickness with a normal papilla and is then indistinguishable from lobar infarction.
2. **Tuberculosis** – calcification differentiates it from the other members of this section.
3. **Lobar infarction** – a broad contour depression over a normal calyx. Normal interpapillary line.
4. **Renal dysplasia** – a forme fruste multicystic kidney. Dilated calyces. Indistinguishable from chronic pyelonephritis. Arteriography outlines a small thread-like renal artery.

Differential Diagnosis
1. **Persistent fetal lobulation** – lobules overlie calyces with interlobular septa between the calyces. **Normal-size kidney.**

Further Reading
Davidson A.J. (1977) *Radiological Diagnosis of Renal Parenchymal Disease*, Chap. 4, pp. 47–68. Philadelphia: Saunders.

8.7 Unilateral Small Smooth Kidney

In all these conditions chronic unilateral disease is associated with compensatory hypertrophy of the contralateral kidney.

With a Dilated Collecting System
1. **Post-obstructive atrophy** – ± thinning of the renal cortex and if there is impaired renal function this will be revealed by poor contrast medium density in the collecting system.

With a Small-volume Collecting System
This is a sign of diminished urinary volume and together with global cortical thinning, delayed opacification of the calyces, increased density of the opacified collecting system and delayed wash-out following oral fluids or diuretics, indicates ischaemia.
1. **Ischaemia due to renal artery stenosis** – ureteric notching is due to enlarged collateral vessels and differentiates this from the other causes in this group. See 8.22.
2. **Radiation nephritis** – at least 23 Gy (2300 rad) over 5 weeks. The collecting system may be normal or small. Depending on the size of the radiation field both, one or just part of one kidney may be affected. There may be other sequelae of radiotherapy, e.g. scoliosis following radiotherapy in childhood.
3. **End result of renal infarction** – due to previous severe trauma involving the renal artery or renal vein thrombosis. The collecting system does not usually opacify during excretion urography.

With Five or Less Calyces
1. **Congenital hypoplasia** – the pelvicalyceal system is otherwise normal.

Further Reading
Davidson A.J. (1977) *Radiological Diagnosis of Renal Parenchymal Disease*, Chap. 5, pp. 69–95. Philadelphia: Saunders.

8.8   Bilateral Small Smooth Kidneys

1. **Generalized arteriosclerosis** – normal calyces.
2. **Chronic glomerulonephritis** – normal calyces. Reduced nephrogram density and poor calyceal opacification.
3. **Chronic papillary necrosis** (see 8.21) – with other signs of necrotic papillae.
4. **Arterial hypotension** – distinguished by the time relationship to the contrast medium injection and its transient nature.
5. **Cause of unilateral small smooth kidneys occurring bilaterally** – e.g. obstructive uropathy or renal artery stenosis.

Further Reading

Davidson A.J. (1977) *Radiological Diagnosis of Renal Parenchymal Disease*, Chap. 6, pp. 96–131. Philadelphia: Saunders.

8.9 Unilateral Large Smooth Kidney

1. **Compensatory hypertrophy.**
2. **Obstructed kidney** ⎫
3. **Pyonephrosis** ⎬ dilated calyces.
4. **Duplex kidney** – female : male, 2 : 1. Equal incidence on both sides and 20% are bilateral. Incomplete more common than complete. Only 50% are bigger than the contralateral kidney; 40% are the same size; 10% are smaller (Privet *et al.*, 1976).
5. **Tumour** – see 8.12 and 8.13.
6. **Crossed fused ectopia** – may be associated with anorectal anomalies and renal dysplasia. No kidney on the contralateral side and ureter crosses the midline.
7. **Multicystic kidney** – see 8.18.
8. **Acute pyelonephritis** – impaired excretion of contrast medium. ± increasingly dense nephrogram. Attenuated calyces but may have non-obstructive pelvicalyceal or ureteric dilatation. Completely reversible within a few weeks of clinical recovery.
9. **Trauma** – haematoma or urinoma.
10. **Renal vein thrombosis** – see 8.23.
11. **Acute arterial infarction.**
12. **Adult polycystic disease*** – asymmetrical bilateral enlargement, but 8% of cases are unilateral. Lobulated rather than completely smooth.

Further Reading

Davidson A.J. (1977) *Radiological Diagnosis of Renal Parenchymal Disease*, chap. 8, pp. 162–92. Philadelphia: Saunders.

Privett J.T.J., Jeans W.D. & Roylance J. (1976) The incidence and importance of renal duplication. *Clin. Radiol.*, 27: 521–30.

8.10 Bilateral Large Smooth Kidneys

It is often difficult to distinguish, radiologically, the members of this group from one another. The appearance of the nephrogram may be helpful – see 8.20. Associated clinical and radiological abnormalities elsewhere are often more useful, e.g. in sickle-cell anaemia, Goodpasture's disease and acromegaly.

Proliferative and Necrotizing Disorders
1. Acute glomerulonephritis.
2. Polyarteritis nodosa.
3. Wegener's granulomatosis.
4. Goodpasture's disease.
5. Systemic lupus erythematosus*.

Deposition of Abnormal Proteins
1. Amyloid – renal involvement in 80% of secondary and 35% of primary amyloid. Chronic deposition results in small kidneys.
2. Multiple myeloma*.

Abnormal Fluid Accumulation
1. Acute tubular necrosis.
2. Acute cortical necrosis – may show an opacified medulla and outer rim with non-opacified cortex. Cortical calcification is a late finding.

Neoplastic Infiltration
1. Leukaemia and lymphoma.

Inflammatory Cell Infiltration
1. Acute interstitial nephritis.

Miscellaneous
1. Renal vein thrombosis (see 8.23).
2. Acute renal papillary necrosis (see 8.21).
3. Polycystic disease* – infantile form has smooth outlines.

4. Acute urate nephropathy.
5. Sickle-cell anaemia*.
6. Bilateral hydronephrosis.
7. Medullary sponge kidneys – with 'bunch of grapes' calcification.
8. Acromegaly* and gigantism – as part of the generalized visceromegaly.

Further Reading

Davidson A.J. (1977) *Radiological Diagnosis of Renal Parenchymal Disease*, chap. 7, pp. 132–61. Philadelphia: Saunders.

8.11 Localized Bulge of the Renal Outline

RENAL CYST
US confirms typical
echo-free cyst

**MULTIPLE RENAL
CYSTS**
e.g. adult type
polycystic disease.
Spider leg deformity
of calyces

TUMOUR
Replacement of much
or all of normal renal
tissue

DROMEDARY HUMP
Left sided variant

**PROMINENT SEPTUM
OF BERTIN**
Increased activity on
Tc-DMSA scanning

HILAR LIP
Hyperplasia of
parenchyma adjacent
to the renal hilum.
Normal on Tc-DMSA scan

**PSEUDOTUMOUR IN
REFLUX
NEPHROPATHY**
Hypertrophy of
unscarred renal
parenchyma

**DUPLEX KIDNEY WITH
HYDRONEPHROTIC
UPPER MOIETY**
Drooping flower
appearance

**DILATATION OF A
SINGLE CALYX**
Most commonly due
to extrinsic
compression by an
intrarenal artery
(Fraley syndrome)

Redrawn from Taylor C.M. & Chapman S. (1989) *Handbook of Renal Investigations in Children*. London: Wright. By kind permission of the publisher.

1. **Cyst** – well-defined nephrographic defect with a thin wall on the outer margin. Beak sign. Displacement and distortion of smooth-walled calyces without obliteration.
2. **Tumour** – mostly renal cell carcinoma in adults and Wilms' tumour in children. See 8.12 and 8.13.
3. **Fetal lobulation** – the lobule directly overlies a normal calyx. Normal interpapillary line. See 8.6.
4. **Dromedary hump** – on the mid portion of the lateral border of the kidney. The arc of the interpapillary line parallels the renal contour.
5. **Splenic impression** – on the left side only. This produces an apparent bulge inferiorly.
6. **Enlarged septum of Bertin** – overgrowth of renal cortex from two adjacent renal lobules. EU (Excretion urography) shows a pseudomass with calyceal splaying and associated short calyx ± attempted duplication. Tc-DMSA (Technetium-Dimercapto succinic acid) accumulates normally or in excess. On US echogenicity is usually similar to normal renal cortex but may be of increased echogenicity.
7. **Localized hypertrophy** – e.g. adjacent to an area of pyelonephritic scarring.
8. **Abscess** – loss of renal outline and psoas margin on the control film. Scoliosis concave to the involved side. Initially there is no nephrographic defect but following central necrosis there will be a central defect surrounded by a thick irregular wall. Adjacent calyces are displaced or effaced.
9. **Non-functioning moiety of a duplex** – usually a hydronephrotic upper moiety. Delayed films may show contrast medium in the upper moiety calyces. Lower moiety calyces have 'drooping flowers' appearance.

Further Reading

Felson B. & Moskowitz M. (1969) Renal pseudotumours. The regenerated nodule and other lumps, bumps and dromedary humps. *Am. J. Roentgenol.*, 107: 720–9.

Hardwick D. & Hendry G.M.A. (1984) The ultrasonic appearances of the septa of Bertin in children. *Clin. Radiol.*, 34: 107–12.

Maklad N.F., Chuang V.P., Doust B.D., Cho K.T. & Curran J.E. (1977) Ultrasound characteristics of solid renal lesions. Echographic, urographic and pathological correlation. *Radiology*, 123: 733.

8.12 Renal Neoplasms in an Adult

Malignant

1. **Renal cell carcinoma** – 90% of adult malignant tumours. Bilateral in 10% and an increased incidence of bilaterality in polycystic kidneys and von Hippel–Lindau disease. A mass lesion (showing irregular or amorphous calcification in 10% of cases). Calyces are obliterated, distorted and/or displaced. Half-shadow filling defect in a calyx or pelvis. Arteriography shows a typical pathological circulation in the majority.

2. **Transitional cell carcinoma** – usually papilliferous. May obstruct or obliterate a calyx or obstruct a whole kidney. Seeding may produce a second lesion further down the urinary tract. Bilateral tumours are rare. Calcification in 2%.

3. **Squamous cell carcinoma** – ulcerated plaque or stricture. 50% are associated with calculi. There is usually a large parenchymal mass before there is any sizeable intrapelvic mass. No calcification. Avascular at arteriography.

4. **Leukaemia/lymphoma** – bilateral large smooth kidneys. Thickened parenchyma with compression of the pelvicalyceal systems.

5. **Metastases** – not uncommon. Usually multiple. Bronchus, breast and stomach.

Benign

1. **Hamartoma** – usually solitary but often multiple and bilateral in tuberous sclerosis. Diagnostic appearance on the plain film of radiolucent fat (but only observed in 9%). Other signs are of any mass lesion and angiography does not differentiate from renal cell carcinoma.

2. **Adenoma** – usually small and frequently multiple. Majority are found at autopsy. Hypovascular at arteriography.

3. **Others** – myoma, lipoma, haemangioma and fibroma are all rare.

8.13 Primary Renal Neoplasms in Childhood

1. **Wilms' tumour** – $8/10^6$ children. 80% present in the first 3 years. Bilateral in 5%. Associated abnormalities: cryptorchidism (3%), hypospadias (2%), hemihypertrophy (2%), sporadic aniridia (1%) [30% of those with aniridia and 10% of those with Beckwith syndrome (macroglossia, organomegaly, exomphalos ± hemihypertrophy) develop Wilms' tumour]. 90% have favourable histology. $2° \rightarrow$ lungs and liver. 5% have tumour thrombus in the IVC or right atrium.

   Plain film: bulging flank (75%), loss of renal outline (66%), enlargement of renal outline (33%), displacement of bowel gas (50%), loss of psoas outline (33%), calcification (10%).

   Ultrasound: large well-defined mass, greater echogenicity than liver. Solid with haemorrhage/necrosis. Lack of IVC narrowing on inspiration suggests occlusion.

   CT: well-defined, low attenuation; foci of even lower attenuation due to necrosis.

   MRI: inhomogeneous, low signal on T1, high signal on T2.

2. **Nephroblastomatosis** – nephrogenic rests which maintain the potential for malignant induction to Wilms' tumour. Nephrogenic tests in 40% of unilateral and 99% of bilateral Wilms' tumours. May be: *perilobar*: most common; at the lobar surface, *intralobar*: anywhere in the cortex or medulla, or *combined*.

   Ultrasound: hypoechoic.

   CT: low attenuation.

3. **Congenital mesoblastic nephroma** – most common solid renal tumour in the newborn. Mean age at diagnosis – $3\frac{1}{2}$ months. No recurrence when diagnosed in first 3 months. Indistinguishable from Wilms' tumour but some demonstrate function.

4. **Clear cell sarcoma** – 4–6% of childhood renal tumours. Presentation at 3–5 years. Poor prognosis with early $2°$ (to bone (usually lytic but may be sclerotic)). Never bilateral.

5. **Rhabdoid tumour of kidney** – 2% of childhood renal tumours. Presentation at 3 months to $4\frac{1}{2}$ years (50% in first year). Most malignant renal tumour with extrarenal extension or haematogenous $2°$ (to brain or bone) often

(*continued*)

present at diagnosis. Association with midline posterior fossa tumours. Hypercalcaemia sometimes present. Imaging of the primary tumour is similar to Wilms' tumour.

6. **Multilocular cystic nephroma** – presents 3 months to 4 years. Multiple cysts of varying size. Thin septae. Thick septae, nodules or a large solid component suggest Wilms' tumour with cystic degeneration. Resection is curative and local recurrence is rare. Differential diagnosis is a multicystic dysplastic kidney but this affects the entire kidney.
   Ultrasound and CT: cystic with thin septae.
   MRI: round collections of variable signal intensity suggesting haemorrhage or proteinaceous material.

7. **Renal cell carcinoma** – rare. Differentiating features from Wilms' tumour are: older age at presentation (mean 11–12 years), calcification is more common (25%) and more homogeneous, it is smaller at the time of diagnosis and haematuria is more common. Poorer prognosis compared with Wilms' tumour.

8. **Angiomyolipoma** in 50–80% of patients with tuberous sclerosis*. 50% of patients with angiomyolipomas have tuberous sclerosis. Multiple bilateral tumours which are usually small.
   Ultrasound, CT and MRI: fat densities within the tumours. NB fat may occasionally be identified within Wilms' tumour.

Further Reading
Cohen M.D. (1992) Genitourinary tumors. In *Imaging of Children with Cancer*, Chap. 4, pp. 52–88. St Louis: Mosby Year Book.
White K.S. & Grossman H. (1991) Wilms' and associated renal tumours of childhood. *Pediatr. Radiol.*, 21: 81–8.

8.14 MRI of Renal Masses

MRI is not tissue specific and it is usually not possible to differentiate benign from malignant lesions.

	T_1W	T_2W	Comments
Simple cysts	↓	↑	Wall not visible. If haemorrhage, infection or debris present the cyst may appear to be 'solid'
Abscess	Variable ↓ ± areas of ↑	↑	
Renal cell carcinoma	Iso or ↓ ± ↑ in areas containing clear cells	↑, iso	Can miss lesions < 3 cm but vascular anatomy well shown
Lymphoma	↓ homogeneous	slightly ↑	
Angiomyolipoma	↑ (fat content)	↑ (fat content)	

8.15   CT Kidney – Focal Hypodense Lesion

Tumours
1. **Malignant**
   - (a) Renal cell carcinoma – usually inhomogeneous and irregular if large.
   - (b) Metastases.
   - (c) Lymphoma – usually late stage Non-Hodgkin's lymphoma; only 5% at initial staging. 70% multiple and bilateral. Usually rounded in appearance.
   - (d) Transitional cell carcinoma – can infiltrate and mimic renal cell carcinoma.
   - (e) Wilms' – see 8.13.
2. **Benign**
   - (a) Oncocytoma – adenoma arising from proximal tubular cells. Round, well-defined, homogeneous (usually high density pre contrast, low density post contrast), ± central stellate low density scar if tumour bigger than 3 cm.
   - (b) Angiomyoplipoma – well-defined containing fat densities. Association with tuberous sclerosis.

Inflammation
1. **Abscess** – thick irregular walls ± perirenal fascial thickening, but this can occur in malignancy.
2. **Xanthogranulomatous pyelonephritis** – obstructing calculus seen in 80% cases leading to chronic sepsis, perinephric fluid collections and fistula formation.
3. **Acute focal bacterial nephritis** – wedge-shaped low density ± radiating striations after intravenous contrast.

Vascular
1. **Infarcts** – well defined, peripheral, wedge shaped.

Cyst – see 8.16 and 8.17.

Further Reading
Ishikawa I., Saito Y., Onouchi Z., Matsuura H., Saito T., Suzuki M. & Futyu Y. (1985) Delayed contrast enhancement in acute

focal bacterial nephritis: C.T. features. *J. Comput. Assist. Tomogr.*, 9 (5): 894–7.

Neirius D., Braedel H.U., Schindler E., Hoene E. & Sch. Alloussi (1988) Computed tomographic and angiographic findings in renal oncocytoma. *Br. J. Radiol.*, 61: 1019–25.

Quinn M.J., Hartman D.S., Friedman A.C., Sherman J.L., Lautin E.M., Pyatt R.S., Ho C.K., Csere R. & Fromowitz F.B. (1984) Renal oncocytoma: new observations. *Radiology*, 153: 49–53.

8.16   Classification of Renal Cysts

(After Elkin & Bernstein, 1969).

Renal Dysplasia
1. Multicystic kidney – see 8.18.
2. Focal and segmental cystic dysplasia.
3. Multiple cysts associated with lower urinary tract obstruction – usually posterior urethral valves in males.

Polycystic Disease*
1. Childhood polycystic disease – AR.
2. Adult polycystic disease – AD.

Cortical Cysts
1. Simple cyst – unilocular. Increase in size and number with age.
2. Multilocular cystic nephroma – see 8.13.
3. Syndromes associated with cysts – Zellweger's syndrome, tuberous sclerosis, Turner's syndrome, von Hippel–Lindau disease, trisomy 13 and 18.
4. Haemodialysis.

Medullary Cysts
1. Calyceal cyst (diverticulum) – small, usually solitary cyst communicating via an isthmus with the fornix of a calyx.
2. medullary sponge kidney – bilateral in 60–80%. Multiple, small, mainly pyramidal cysts which opacify during excretion urography and contain calculi.
3. Papillary necrosis – see 8.21.
4. Juvenile nephronophthisis (medullary cystic disease) – usually presents with polyuria and progressive renal failure. Positive family history. Normal or small kidneys. US shows a few medullary or corticomedullary cysts, loss of corticomedullary differentiation and increased parenchymal echogenicity.

Miscellaneous Intrarenal Cysts
1. Inflammatory
   (a) Tuberculosis.

(b) Calculus disease.
(c) Hydatid.
2. **Neoplastic** – cystic degeneration of a carcinoma.
3. **Traumatic** – intrarenal haematoma.

Extraparenchymal Renal Cysts

1. **Parapelvic cyst** – located in or near the hilum, but does not communicate with the renal pelvis and therefore does not opacify during urography. Simple or multilocular; single or multiple, unilateral or bilateral. It compresses the renal pelvis and may cause hydronephrosis.
2. **Perinephric cyst** – beneath the capsule or between the capsule and perinephric fat. Secondary to trauma, obstruction or replacement of haematoma. It may compress the kidney, pelvis or ureter, leading to hydronephrosis or causing displacement of the kidney.

Further Reading

Banner M.P., Pollack H.M., Chatten J. & Witzleben C. (1981) Multilocular renal cysts: radiologic pathologic correlation. *Am. J. Roentgenol.*, 136: 239–47.

Elkin M. & Bernstein J. (1969) Cystic diseases of the kidney – radiological and pathological considerations. *Clin. Radiol.*, 20: 65–82.

Hartmann D.S., Davies C.J., Sanders R.C., Johns T., Smirniotopoulos J. & Goldman S.M. (1984) The multiloculated renal mass: proposed classifications and differential features (Abstract). *Radiology*, 153: 18.

Levine E., Slusher S.L., Grantham J.J. & Wetzel L.H. (1991) Natural history of acquired renal cystic disease in dialysis patients: a prospective longitudinal CT study. *Am. J. Roentgenol.*, 156: 501–6.

Madewell J.E., Hartman D.S. & Lichtenstein J.E. (1979) Radiologic–pathologic correlations in cystic disease of the kidney. *Radiol. Clin. North Am.*, 17: 261–79.

Manns R.A., Burrows F.G.O., Adu D. & Michael J. (1990) Acquired cystic disease of the kidney: ultrasound as the primary screening procedure. *Clin. Radiol.*, 41: 248–9.

8.17 CT Renal Cysts – see 8.16

1. **Simple** – thin-walled, no enhancement. Occasionally haemorrhage can occur within one producing a round hyperdense lesion.
2. **Malignant** – 5% renal cell carcinomas are cystic. Suspect if thick walls or separations but this may just indicate previous infection/haemorrhage in cyst.
3. **Polycystic** – associated with hepatic cysts in approximately 60% of cases. Haemorrhage into cysts relatively common, so may be of varying density. Associated with increased incidence of renal cell carcinoma.
4. **Haemodialysis related cysts** – cysts develop in approximately 50% of long-term haemodialysis, but can involute after a successful renal transplant. 7% incidence of associated renal cell carcinoma.
5. **von Hippel–Lindau** – associated pancreatic, hepatic cysts and renal cell carcinoma and phaeochromocytoma.
6. **Hydatid** – affected in 10% cases. ± curvilinear calcification in wall.
7. **Multicystic** – usually detected in infancy.
8. **Cystic hamartoma** – usually large with thick capsule and septations.

Further Reading

Beggs I (1985) The radiology of hydatid disease. *Am. J. Roentegenol.*, 145: 639–48.

Cho C., Friedland G.W. & Swenson R.S. (1984) Acquired renal cystic disease and renal neoplasms in haemodialysis patients. *Urol. Radiol.*, 6: 153–7.

Jennings C.M. & Games P.A. (1988) The abdominal manifestation of von Hippel–Lindau disease and a radiological screening protocol for an affected family. *Clin. Radiol.*, 39: 363–7.

8.18 Renal Mass in the Newborn and Young Infant

1. **Hydronephrosis** (q.v.) – uni- or bilateral.
2. **Multicystic kidney** – unilateral, but 30% have an abnormal contralateral kidney (mostly pelviureteric junction obstruction). Non-functioning, multilobulated kidney. Rarely, nephrographic crescents and late pooling of contrast medium in cysts is observed. Curvilinear calcification is characteristic but only seen occasionally. Ultrasound reveals multiple cysts of unequal size. The commonest renal mass in the first year of life.
3. **Polycystic kidneys** (see Polycystic disease*) – bilateral. Poor renal excretion. Striated nephrogram with no visualization of calyces. Highly echogenic on US.
4. **Renal vein thrombosis** (q.v.) – uni- or bilateral.
5. **Nephroblastomatosis or mesoblastic nephroma** – see 8.13.
6. **Renal ectopia.**

Further Reading

Merten D.F. & Kirks D.R. (1985) Diagnostic imaging of paediatric abdominal masses. *Pediatr. Clin. North Am.*, 32: 1397–425.

8.19   Hydronephrosis in a Child

1. **Pelviureteric junction obstruction** – more common on the left side. 20% bilateral. Due to stricture, neuromuscular incoordination or aberrant vessels. Contralateral kidney is dysplastic in 25% of cases and absent in 12%.
2. **Bladder outflow obstruction** (q.v.) – bilateral upper tract dilatation.
3. **Ureterovesical obstruction** – more common in males and more common on the left side. May be bilateral.
4. **Reflux without obstruction.**
5. **Associated with urinary tract infection** – but no obstruction or reflux. ? represents atony.
6. **Neurogenic.**

Further Reading
Lebowitz R.L. & Griscom N.T. (1977) Neonatal hydronephrosis: 146 cases. *Radiol. Clin. North Am.*, 15: 49–59.

8.20   Nephrographic Patterns

Immediate Faint Persistent Nephrogram
1. **Proliferative/necrotizing disorders** – e.g. acute glomerulonephritis. See 8.10.
2. **Renal vein thrombosis.**
3. **Chronic severe ischaemia.**

Immediate Distinct Persistent Nephrogram
1. **Acute tubular necrosis** – in 60% of cases.
2. **Other causes of acute renal failure.**
3. **Acute-on-chronic renal failure.**
4. **Acute hypotension** – uncommonly.

Increasingly Dense Nephrogram
1. **Acute obstruction** – including urate nephropathy.
2. **Acute hypotension.**
3. **Acute tubular necrosis** – in 30% of cases.

4. Acute pyelonephritis.
5. Multiple myeloma.
6. Renal vein thrombosis.
7. Acute glomerulonephritis.
8. Amyloid.
9. Acute papillary necrosis – and rarely chronic papillary necrosis.

Rim Nephrogram
1. Severe hydronephrosis – scalloped nephrogram with a negative pyelogram.
2. Acute complete arterial occlusion – smooth nephrogram from cortical perfusion by capsular arteries.

Striated Nephrogram
1. Acute ureteric obstruction.
2. Infantile polycystic disease – contrast medium in dilated tubules.
3. Medullary sponge kidney – in the medulla only. Parallel or fan-shaped streaks radiating from the papilla to the periphery of the kidney.
4. Acute pyelonephritis.

Further Reading
Newhouse J.H. & Pfister R.C. (1979) The nephrogram. *Radiol. Clin. North Am.*, 17: 213–26.

8.21   Renal Papillary Necrosis

1. Normal – small kidneys with smooth outlines.
2. Bilateral in 85% with multiple papillae affected.
3. Papillae may show
    (a) Enlargement (early).
    (b) Partial sloughing – a fissure forms and may communicate with a central irregular cavity.
    (c) Total sloughing – the sloughed papillary tissue may (i) fragment and be passed in the urine, (ii) cause ureteric obstruction, (iii) remain free in a calyx, or (iv) remain in the pelvis and form a ball calculus.
    (d) Necrosis-in-situ – the papilla is shrunken and necrotic but has not separated.
4. Calyces will appear dilated following total sloughing of a papilla.
5. Calcification and occasionally ossification of a shrunken, necrotic papilla. If marginal, it appears as a calculus with a radiolucent centre.

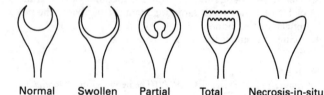

Normal   Swollen   Partial papillary necrosis   Total papillary necrosis   Necrosis-in-situ

A useful mnemonic is *ADIPOSE* –
A   Analgesics – phenacetin and aspirin.
D   Diabetes.
I   Infants in shock.
P   Pyelonephritis.
O   Obstruction.
S   Sickle-cell disease.
E   Ethanol.

However, diabetes, analgesics and sickle-cell anaemia are the most important, with diabetes the most frequent cause.

Further Reading
Hare W.S.C. and Poynter J.D. (1974) The radiology of renal papillary necrosis as seen in analgesic nephropathy. *Clin. Radiol.*, 25: 423–43.

8.22 Renal Induced Hypertension

Signs of Unilateral Renal Artery Stenosis on IVU
1. Unilateral delay of 1 minute or more in the appearance of opacified calyces.
2. Small, smooth kidney
   – left more than 1.5 cm shorter than the right
   – right more than 2 cm shorter than the left.
3. Increased density of opacified calyces.
4. Ureteric notching by collateral vessels.

Renal Artery
1. **Arteriosclerosis** – 66% of renovascular causes. Stenosis of the proximal 2 cm of the renal artery; less frequently the distal artery or early branches at bifurcations. More common in males.
2. **Fibromuscular dysplasia** – 33% of renovascular causes. Stenoses ± dilatations which may give the characteristic 'string of beads' appearance. Mainly females less than 40 years. Bilateral in 60% of cases.
3. **Thrombosis/embolism.**
4. **Arteritis** – polyarteritis nodosa, thromboangiitis obliterans. Takayasu's disease, syphilis, congenital rubella or idiopathic.
5. **Neurofibromatosis*** – coarctation of the aorta. ± stenoses of other arteries. ± intrarenal arterial abnormalities.
6. **Trauma.**
7. **Aneurysm** – of the aorta or the renal artery.
8. **Arteriovenous fistula** – traumatic, congenital or a stump fistula following nephrectomy.
9. **Extrinsic compression** – neoplasm, aneurysm or lymph nodes.

Chronic Bilateral Parenchymal Disease
1. **Chronic glomerulonephritis.**
2. **Reflux nephropathy.**
3. **Adult polycystic disease*.**
4. **Diabetic glomerulosclerosis.**
5. **Connective tissue disorders** – systemic lupus erythematosus, scleroderma and polyarthritis nodosa.
6. **Radiotherapy.**

7. Hydronephrosis.
8. Analgesic nephropathy.
9. Renal vein thrombosis.

Unilateral Parenchymal Disease
Much less common as a cause of hypertension.
1. Reflux nephropathy.
2. Hydronephrosis.
3. Tumours – hypertension is more common with Wilms' tumour than with renal cell carcinoma. The rare juxtaglomerular cell tumour secretes renin.
4. Tuberculosis.
5. Xanthogranulomatous pyelonephritis.
6. Radiotherapy.
7. Renal vein thrombosis.

Further Reading
Webb J.A.W. & Talner L.B. (1979) The role of intravenous urography in hypertension. *Radiol. Clin. North Am.*, 17: 187–95.

8.23   Renal Vein Thrombosis

Unilateral or bilateral.
The ultrasound findings (after Cremin *et al.*, 1991) are:
1st Week
1. Globular renal enlargement.
2. Increase in echogenicity which may be more prominent in the cortex.
3. Loss of cortico-medullary differentiation.
4. Echogenic streaks in the direction of the interlobular vessels.
5. Loss of definition of normal renal sinus echoes.
2nd Week
1. Diffuse renal enlargement is more obvious.
2. Diffuse 'snow storm' appearance of increased echogenicity.
3. Loss of cortico-medullary differentiation.
4. Mixed hyperechoic areas (haemorrhage) and hypoechoic areas (oedema and/or resolving haemorrhage).
5. Thrombus in main renal vein or IVC.
Late
1. Kidney returns to normal size or becomes small and atrophic.
2. Calcification may occur in kidney or IVC.

Conventional radiography findings are:
Sudden occlusion
1. Large non-functioning kidney which over a period of several months becomes small and atrophic.
2. Retrograde pyelography reveals thickened parenchyma (due to oedema) with elongation and compression of the major calyces.
3. Arteriography shows stretching and separation of arterial branches with decreased flow and a poor persistent nephrogram. No opacification of the renal vein.
Gradual occlusion
1. Large kidney
2. Nephrogram may be normal, poor persistent or increasingly dense.
3. Thickened parenchyma with elongation of major calyces.
4. Ureteric notching due to venous collaterals.

Children
1. **Dehydration and shock** – especially in infants delivered of diabetic mothers.
2. **Nephrotic syndrome.**
3. **Cyanotic heart disease.**

Adults
1. **Extension of renal cell carcinoma into the renal vein.**
2. **Local compression by tumour or retroperitoneal nodes.**
3. **Extension of thrombus from the IVC.**
4. **Trauma.**
5. **Secondary to renal disease** – especially amyloid and chronic glomerulonephritis with nephrotic syndrome.

Further Reading
Cremin B.J., Davey H. & Oleszczuk-Raszke K. (1991) Neonatal renal venous thrombosis: sequential ultrasonic appearances. *Clin. Radiol.*, 44: 52–55.

8.24 Non-visualization of a Calyx

1. **Technical factors** – incomplete filling during excretion urography.
2. **Tumour** – most commonly a renal cell carcinoma (adult) or Wilms' tumour (child).
3. **Obstructed infundibulum** – due to tumour, calculus or tuberculosis.
4. **Duplex kidney** – with a non-functioning upper or lower moiety. Signs suggesting a non-functioning upper moiety are
   (a) Fewer calyces than the contralateral kidney. This sign is only reliable in unilateral duplication (Calyceal distribution is symmetrical in 80% of normal individuals).
   (b) A shortened upper calyx which does not reach into the upper pole.
   (c) The upper calyx of the lower moiety may be deformed by a dilated upper pole pelvis.
   (d) The kidney may be displaced downward by a dilated upper moiety pelvis. The appearances mimic a space occupying lesion in the upper pole.
   (e) The upper pole may be rotated laterally and downward by a dilated upper moiety pelvis and the lower pole calyces adopt a 'drooping flower' appearance.
   (f) Lateral displacement of the entire kidney by a dilated upper moiety ureter.
   (g) The lower moiety ureter may be displaced or compressed by the upper pole ureter, resulting in a series of scalloped curves.
   (h) The lower moiety renal pelvis may be displaced laterally and its ureter then takes a direct oblique course to the lumbosacral junction.
5. **Infection** – abscess or tuberculosis.
6. **Partial nephrectomy** – with a surgical defect in the 12th rib.

8.25 Radiolucent Filling Defect in the Renal Pelvis or a Calyx

Technical Factors
1. Incomplete filling during excretion urography.
2. Overlying gas shadows.

Extrinsic with a Smooth Margin
1. **Cyst** (see 8.16).
2. **Vascular impression** – an intrarenal artery producing linear transverse or oblique compression lines and most commonly indenting an upper pole calyx, especially on the right side.
3. **Renal sinus lipomatosis** – most commonly in older patients with a wasting disease of the kidney. Fat in the renal hilum produces a relative lucency and narrows and elongates the major calyces.
4. **Collateral vessels** – most commonly ureteric artery collaterals in renal artery stenosis. Multiple small irregularities in the pelvic wall.

Inseparable from the Wall and with Smooth Margins
1. **Blood clot** – due to trauma, tumour or bleeding diathesis. May be adherent to the wall or free in the lumen. Change in size or shape over several days.
2. **Papilloma** – solitary or multiple.
3. **Pyeloureteritis cystica** – due to chronic infection. Multiple well-defined submucosal cysts project into the lumen of the pelvis and/or ureter.

Arising from the Wall with an Irregular Margin
1. **Transitional cell carcinoma**
2. **Squamous cell carcinoma** } see 8.12.
3. **Renal cell carcinoma**
4. **Squamous metaplasia (cholesteatoma)** – occurs rarely in association with chronic irritation from a calculus. Indistinguishable from tumour and may be premalignant.

(continued)

In the Lumen
1. Blood clot.
2. Lucent calculus (see 8.3).
3. Sloughed papilla.
4. Air (see 8.4).

Further Reading
Brown R.C., Jones M.C., Boldus R. & Flocks R.H. (1973) Lesions causing radiolucent defects in the renal pelvis. *Am. J. Roentgenol.*, 119: 770–8.

8.26   Dilated Calyx

With a Narrow Infundibulum
1. **Stricture** – tumour, calculus or tuberculosis.
2. **Extrinsic impression by an artery** – most commonly a right upper pole calyx (Fraley syndrome).
3. **Hydrocalycosis** – may be a congenital anomaly. Can only be safely diagnosed in childhood when calculus, tumour and tuberculosis are uncommon.

With a Wide Infundibulum
1. **Post-obstructive atrophy** – generally all the calyces are affected and associated with parenchymal thinning.
2. **Megacalyces** – dilated calyces ± a slightly dilated pelvis. ± stones. Increased number of calyces – 20–25 (normal 8–12). Because of the large volume collecting system full visualization during urography is delayed. Normal cortical thickness and good renal function differentiate it from post-obstructive atrophy.
3. **Polycalycosis** – rare. ± ureteric abnormalities.

Further Reading
Talner L.B. & Gittes R.F. (1974) Megacalyces, further observations and differentiation from obstructive renal disease. *Am. J. Roentgenol.*, 121: 473–86.

8.27 Dilated Ureter

Obstruction

WITHIN THE LUMEN
1. **Calculus** (see 8.3).
2. **Blood clot.**
3. **Sloughed papilla.**

IN THE WALL
1. **Oedema or stricture due to calculus.**
2. **Tumour** – carcinoma or papilloma.
3. **Tuberculous stricture** – a particular hazard during the early weeks of treatment.
4. **Schistosomiasis** – especially the distal ureter. ± calcification in the ureter or bladder.
5. **Post-surgical trauma** – e.g. a misplaced ligature.
6. **Ureterocele.**
7. **Megaureter** – symmetrical tapered narrowing above the uretero–vesical junction.

OUTSIDE THE WALL
1. **Retroperitoneal fibrosis** (q.v.).
2. **Carcinoma of cervix, bladder or prostate.**
3. **Retrocaval ureter** – right side only. Distal ureter lies medial to the dilated proximal portion.

Vesico–ureteric Reflux

No Obstruction or Reflux
1. **Post-partum** – more common on the right side.
2. **Following relief of obstruction** – most commonly calculus of prostatectomy.
3. **Urinary tract infection** – due to the effect of P fimbriated *E. coli* on the urothelium.
4. **Primary non-obstructive megaureter** – children > adults. The juxtavesical segment of ureter is of normal calibre but fails to transmit an effective peristaltic wave.

Further Reading
Hamilton S. & Fitzpatrick J.M. (1987) Primary non-obstructive megaureter in adults. *Clin. Radiol.*, 38: 181–5.

8.28 Retroperitoneal Fibrosis

1. Ureteric obstruction of variable severity. 75% bilateral.
2. Tapering lumen or complete obstruction – usually at L4–5 level and never the extreme lower end.
3. Medial deviation of the ureters – more significant if there is a right-angled step in the course of the ureter rather than a gentle drift. The position of the ureters is frequently normal.
4. Easy retrograde catheterization of ureter(s).
5. Retroperitoneal, periaortic mass – demonstrable by CT or US.
6. Clinically – back pain, high ESR and elevated creatinine.

1. **Retroperitoneal malignancy** – lymphoma and metastases from colon and breast especially. The tumour initiates a fibrotic reaction around itself.
2. **Inflammatory conditions** – Crohn's disease, diverticular disease, actinomycosis, pancreatitis and extravasation of urine from the pelvicalyceal system.
3. **Aortic aneurysm** ⎫ fibrosis occurs secondary to
4. **Trauma** ⎬ blood in the retroperi-
5. **Surgery** ⎭ toneal tissues.
6. **Drugs** – methysergide.
7. **Idiopathic** – > 50% all cases. May be due to an immune reaction to atheromatous material in the ureter aorta.

Differential Diagnosis of Medially Placed Ureters

1. **Normal variant** – 15% of individuals. Commoner in blacks, in whom bilateral displacement is also commoner.
2. **Pelvic lipomatosis** – other signs suggesting the diagnosis are (a) elevation and elongation of the bladder, (b) elongation of the rectum and sigmoid with widening of the rectorectal space, and (c) increased lucency of the pelvic wall.
3. **Following abdomino–perineal resection** – the ureters are medially placed inferiorly.
4. **Retrocaval ureter** – the right ureter passes behind the inferior vena cava at the level of LV4. The distal ureter lies medial to the dilated proximal portion.

Further Reading

Brooks A.P. (1990) Computed tomography of idiopathic retroperi-
    toneal fibrosis ('periaortitis'): variants, variations, patterns and
    pitfalls. *Clin. Radiol.*, 42: 75–9.
Brooks A.P., Reznek R.H., Webb J.A.W. & Baker R.I. (1987) Com-
    puted tomography in the follow-up of retroperitoneal fibrosis.
    Clin. Radiol., 38: 597–601.
Dixon A.K., Mitchinson M.J. & Sherwood T. (1984) Computed
    tomographic observations in peri-aortitis: a hypothesis. *Clin.
    Radiol.*, 35: 39–42.
Minford J.E. & Davies P. (1984) The urographic appearances in acute
    and chronic retroperitoneal fibrosis. *Clin. Radiol.*, 35: 51–7.

8.29 Filling Defect in the Bladder (in the Wall or in the Lumen)

1. **Prostate.**
2. **Neoplasm** – especially transitional cell carcinoma in an adult and rhabdomyosarcoma in a child.
3. **Blood clot.**
4. **Instrument** – urethral or suprapubic catheter.
5. **Calculus.**
6. **Ureterocele.**
7. **Schistosomiasis.**
8. **Endometriosis.**

8.30   Bladder Calcification

In the Lumen
1. **Calculus.**
2. **Foreign body** – encrustation of the balloon of a Foley catheter.

In the Wall
1. **Transitional and squamous cell carcinoma** – radiographic incidence about 0.5%. Usually surface calcification which may be linear, curvilinear or stippled. Punctate calcification of a villous tumour may suggest chronicity. No extravesical calcification.
2. **Schistosomiasis** – an infrequent cause in the Western hemisphere but the commonest cause of mural calcification worldwide. Thin curvilinear calcification outlines a bladder of normal size and shape. Calcification spreads proximally to involve the distal ureters (appearing as two parallel lines) in 15%.
3. **Tuberculosis** – rare and usually accompanied by calcification elsewhere in the urogenital tract. Unlike schistosomiasis the disease begins in the kidney and spreads distally. Contracted bladder.
4. **Cyclophosphamide-induced cystitis.**

Further Reading
Pollack H.M., Banner M.P., Martinez L.O. & Hodson C.J. (1986) Diagnostic considerations in urinary bladder wall calcification. *Am. J. Roentgenol.*, 136: 791–7.

8.31 Bladder Fistula

Congenital
1. Ectopia vesicae.
2. Imperforate anus – high type.
3. Patent urachus.

Inflammatory
1. Diverticular disease.
2. Crohn's disease*.
3. Appendix abscess – and other pelvic sepsis.

Neoplastic
1. Carcinoma of the colon, bladder or reproductive organs.
2. Radiotherapy.

Trauma
1. Accidental.
2. Iatrogenic – particularly in obstetrics and gynaecology.

8.32 Bladder Outflow Obstruction in a Child

1. Distended bladder with incomplete emptying.
2. ± bilateral upper tract dilatation.
3. ± upper tract cystic disease.

Causes (from proximal to distal)

1. **Vesical diverticulum** – posteriorly behind the bladder base. It fills during micturition and compresses the bladder neck and proximal urethra. More common in males.
2. (**Bladder neck obstruction** – probably not a distinct entity and only occurs as part of other problems such as ectopic ureterocele and rhabdomyosarcoma.)
3. **Ectopic ureterocele** – 80% are associated with the upper moiety of a duplex kidney. 15% are bilateral. More common in females. Opens into the urethra, bladder neck or vestibule. May be largely outside the bladder and the bladder base may be elevated. 'Drooping flower' appearance of lower moiety. May prolapse into the urethra.
4. **Posterior urethral valves** – posterior urethra is dilated and the distal urethra is small. Almost exclusively males.
5. **Urethral stricture** – post-traumatic strictures are most commonly at the peno-scrotal junction and follow previous instrumentation or catheterization.
6. **Anterior urethral diverticulum** – a saccular wide-necked, ventral expansion of the anterior urethra, usually at the peno–scrotal junction. The proximal lip of the diverticulum may show as an arcuate filling defect and during micturition the diverticulum expands with urine and obstructs the urethra.
7. **Prune-belly syndrome** – almost exclusively males. High mortality. Bilateral hydronephrosis and hydroureters with a distended bladder are associated with undescended testes, hypoplasia of the anterior abdominal wall and urethral obstruction.
8. **Calculus or foreign body.**
9. **Meatal stenosis** ⎫
10. **Phimosis** ⎬ clinical diagnosis.

NB The commonest cause in males is posterior urethral valves and in females is ectopic ureterocele.

8.33 Calcification of the Seminal Vesicles or Vas Deferens

1. **Diabetes mellitus** – the cause in the vast majority of cases.
2. **Chronic infection** – tuberculosis, schistosomiasis, chronic urinary tract infection and syphilis.
3. **Idiopathic.**

Further Reading
King J.C. & Rosenbaum H.D. (1971) Calcification of the vasa deferentia in non-diabetes. *Radiology*, 100: 603–6.

8.34   Ultrasound of the Testes and Scrotum

Testicular

Neoplastic

Colour Doppler does not accurately differentiate neoplasm from acute inflammation or benign from malignant tumours.

1. **Germ cell tumours** – 95% of primary testicular tumours. 40% are of mixed histology. 8% are bilateral.

    (a) *Seminoma* – most common testicular tumour in the adult – 40–50% of testicular germ cell tumours. 25% have metastases at presentation. Most common tumour in the undescended testis. A solid, homogeneous, hypoechoic, round or oval mass which is sharply delineated from normal testicular tissue.

    (b) *Embryonal carcinoma* – 20–25% of germ cell tumours. More aggressive than seminoma and more heterogeneous because of necrosis, haemorrhage, cysts and calcification.

    (c) *Choriocarcinoma* – rare.

    (d) *Teratoma* – 5–10% and most common in infants and children. Heterogeneous echo texture because of the different tissue elements present.

2. **Non-germ cell tumours** – usually benign. May secrete oestrogens (Sertoli cell) or testosterone (Leydig cell). Nonspecific appearance but usually solid hypoechoic mass ± cystic areas.

3. **Metastases** – kidney, prostate, bronchus, pancreas. More common than germ cell tumours in the over 50 year age group. Patients with leukaemia or lymphoma may relapse in the testis and present as focal or diffuse decreased echogenicity in an enlarged testis.

Vascular

1. **Testicular torsion**

    (a) *Acute* – presentation within 24 hours.
        Enlarged hypoechoic or heterogeneous testis ± hydrocele and enlargement of the epididymis. Colour Doppler: absent testicular flow; normal peritesticular flow.

    (b) *Subacute or missed* – presentation at 1–10 days.

Colour Doppler: absent testicular flow; increased peri-testicular flow.
(c) *Spontaneous detorsion*
Colour Doppler: normal or increased testicular flow; increased peritesticular flow.

Inflammatory

1. **Orchitis** – usually secondary to spread from epididymitis. Focal hypoechoic, hypervascular, testicular abnormality adjacent to an enlarged, hypervascular epididymis.
2. **Abscess** – complicating epididymo-orchitis, often in a diabetic patient or those with mumps. Hypoechoic or mixed echogenic mass.

Extratesticular

Inflammatory

1. **Epididymitis** – enlarged, hypoechoic, hypervascular epididymis with a hydrocele and skin thickening. Normal testis in the absence of orchitis but coexisting orchitis in 20%.

Idiopathic

1. **Hydrocele** – fluid collection anterolaterally in the scrotum.
   (a) *Congenital* – due to persistence of the processus vaginalis.
   (b) *Infantile* – accumulation of fluid along the processus vaginalis but with no communication with the abdominal cavity.
   (c) *Secondary to trauma, infection, torsion or neoplasm.*

Vascular

1. **Varicocele** – dilated pampiniform plexus of veins posterior to the testis. In 15% of adult males and virtually always on the left side. Important to exclude a compressive retroperitoneal aetiology if the varicocele is right sided or does not decompress in the erect position or with a Valsalva manoeuvre.

(*continued*)

Neoplastic
1. **Adenomatoid tumour of the epididymis** – a benign tumour
   which accounts for 30% of extratesticular tumours. Other
   tumours are varied and uncommon.

Further Reading
Feld R. & Middleton W.D. (1992) Recent advances in sonography of
     the testis and scrotum. *Radiol. Clin. North Am.*, 30: 1033–51.
Krone K.D. & Carroll B.A. (1985) Scrotal ultrasound. *Radiol. Clin.
     North Am.*, 23: 121–39.

9
Soft Tissues

9.1 Gynaecomastia

Physiological
1. **Neonatal** – due to high placental oestrogens.
2. **Pubertal** – due to an excess of oestradiol over testosterone.
3. **Senile** – due to falling androgen and rising oestrogen levels with age.

Pharmacological
1. **Oestrogen** – especially in the treatment of carcinoma of the prostate.
2. **Digitalis** – binds to oestrogen receptors.
3. **Anti-cancer drugs** – producing testicular damage.
4. **Anti-androgens** – spironolactone.
5. **Reserpine.**
6. **Phenothiazines.**
7. **Tricyclic antidepressants.**
8. **Methyldopa.**

Pathological
1. **Carcinoma of the bronchus** } secreting human chorionic gonadotrophin.
2. **Teratoma of the testis**
3. **Cirrhosis** – due to increased conversion of androgens to oestrogens.
4. **Hypogonadism** – e.g. Klinefelter's syndrome and castration.
5. **Hypopituitarism** – including acromegaly.
6. **Testicular feminization** – androgen insensitivity.
7. **Adrenal tumours** } secreting oestrogens.
8. **Leydig cell tumours**

9.2   Linear and Curvilinear Calcification in Soft Tissues

Arterial
1. **Atheroma/aneurysm.**
2. **Diabetes.**
3. **Hyperparathyroidism*** – more common in secondary than primary.
4. **Werner's syndrome** – premature ageing in a Jewish diabetic (male or female).

Nerve
1. **Leprosy.**
2. **Neurofibromatosis*.**

Ligament
1. **Tendinitis** – Pellegrini–Stieda syndrome, supraspinatus.
2. **Ankylosing spondylitis*.**
3. **Fluorosis.**
4. **Diabetes.**
5. **Alkaptonuria.**

Bismuth Injection
In the buttocks. ± neuropathic joints.

Parasites
1. Cysticerci – oval with lucent centre. Often arranged in the direction of muscle fibres.

2. Guinea worm – irregular coiled appearance.

3. Loa loa – thread-like coil. Particularly in the web spaces of the hand.

4. Armillifer – 'comma' shaped. Only in trunk muscles.

See also 9.4.

9.3   Conglomerate Calcification in Soft Tissues

Collagenoses
1. **Scleroderma*** – acrolysis and flexion contractures in the hands.
2. **Dermatomyositis.**
3. **Ehlers–Danlos syndrome.**

Metabolic
1. **Hyperparathyroidism*** – more common in secondary hyperparathyroidism. Vascular calcification is common.
2. **Gout*** – calcified tophus.

Traumatic
1. **Haematoma.**
2. **Burns.**
3. **Myositis ossificans** – outer part is more densely calcified than the centre.

Infective
1. **Tuberculous abscess/mode.**

Neoplastic
1. **Benign**
   (a) Parosteal lipoma – lucent. ± pressure erosion of adjacent bone.
   (b) Haemangioma – Suspect if phleboliths present in an unusual site. ± soft-tissue mass with adjacent bone destruction.
2. **Malignant**
   (a) Parosteal osteosarcoma – age 20–40. Lobulated calcification around a metaphysis. Inner part is more densely calcified than the periphery. Early – a thin lucent line may separate it from underlying bone.
   (b) Juxta-cortical chondrosarcoma – particularly pelvis.
   (c) Liposarcoma.

9.4 'Sheets' of Calcification/Ossification in Soft Tissues

1. **Congenital myositis ossificans progressiva** – manifest in childhood. Initially neck and trunk muscles involved. Short first metacarpal and metatarsal.
2. **Dermatomyositis.**

9.5 Periarticular Soft-tissue Calcification

Inflammatory
1. Scleroderma* – ± acro-osteolysis.
2. Dermatomyositis.
3. Gout* – calcified tophi. Punched-out erosions.
4. Bursitis – can be dense and lobulated.

Degenerative
1. Calcific periarthritis (calcium hydroxyapatite deposition disease).
2. Calcium pyrophosphate deposition disease*.

Renal Failure
1. Secondary hyperparathyroidism – ± vascular calcification.
2. Treatment with 1-α-OHD$_3$ – particularly shoulder, hip and metacarpophalangeal joints.

Hypercalcaemia
1. Sarcoidosis* – rare. Affects hands and feet. ± lace-like trabecular pattern in tubular bones.
2. Hypervitaminosis D.
3. Milk–alkali syndrome.

Neoplastic
1. Synovial osteochondromatosis – age 20–50 years. Most commonly affects a large joint. Multiple calcified loose bodies. ± secondary degenerative changes or pressure erosion of bone.
2. Synovioma – age 20–50 years. Soft-tissue mass with amorphous calcification, irregular bone destruction and osteoporosis.

Idiopathic
1. Tumoral calcinosis – age 20–30 years. Adjacent to a major joint. Firm, non-tender, moveable mass which is well-defined, lobulated and calcified on X-ray. Osseous involvement is rare. ± calcium fluid level.

9.6 Soft-tissue Ossification

Traumatic
1. **Myositis ossificans.**
2. **Burns.**
3. **Paraplegia** – ossification adjacent to the ischium – may be related to pressure sores.

Neoplastic
1. **Parosteal osteosarcoma.**
2. **Liposarcoma.**

Congenital Myositis Ossificans Progressiva

9.7   Increased Heel Pad Thickness

Males: if 'x' is > 23 mm.
Females: if 'x' is > 21.5 mm.

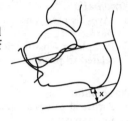

1. **Acromegaly*** – but heel pad thickness is a poor predictor of biochemical remission.
2. **Obesity.**
3. **Peripheral oedema.**
4. **Infection/injury.**
5. **Myxoedema.**
6. **Epanutin therapy.**

Further Reading

Kattan K.R. (1975) Thickening of the heel pad associated with long-term Dilantin therapy. *Am. J. Roentgenol.*, 124: 52–6.

Kho K.M., Wright A.D. & Doyle F.H. (1970) Heel pad thickness in acromegaly. *Br. J. Radiol.*, 43: 119–22.

MacSweeney J.E., Baxter M.A. & Joplin G.F. (1990) Heel pad thickness is an insensitive index of biochemical remission in acromegaly. *Clin. Radiol.*, 42: 348–50.

9.8   CT of Swollen Legs

1. **Normal** – homogeneous subcutaneous fat containing superficial veins. Interstitial tissue not visible.
2. **Venous thrombosis and insufficiency** – increased cross-sectional areas of muscle and subcutaneous fat. Prominent interstitial tissues in the subcutaneous fat.
3. **Lymphoedema** – increased subcutaneous fat with visible interstitial tissue and skin thickening. When secondary to malignant pelvic lymphadenopathy, pelvic CT may give additional positive findings.
4. **Haematoma** – variable high attenuation dependent on the age of the haematoma.
5. **Popliteal cyst** – water density fluid collection between the medial head of gastrocnemius and soleus muscles.

Further Reading

Vaughan B.F. (1990) CT of swollen legs. *Clin. Radiol.*, 41: 24–30.

10
Breast Disease and Mammography

Michael Collins

10.1 Introduction

Modern mammography demands meticulously high standards in all its aspects. These include X-ray equipment, radiographic technique, film–screen combinations, processing, viewing conditions and interpretation. Shortcomings in any of these factors will lead to serious errors. Other factors that lead to difficulty include dense parenchymal background that may obscure malignancy, benign conditions that mimic malignancy and malignant tumours with 'benign' appearances on mammography. The radiologist now has a central role in the management of breast disease and should have use of all facilities to ensure accurate diagnosis including mammography, ultrasound and biopsy/localization techniques.

Close cooperation between radiologists, radiographers, surgeons and pathologists is essential.

10.2 The Normal Breast

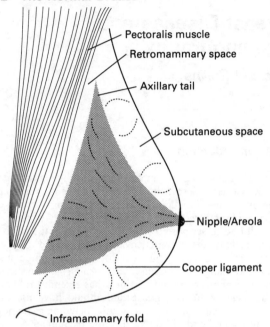

Normal lateral oblique projection

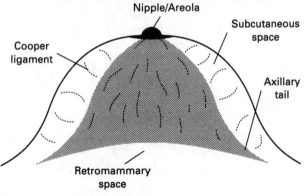

Normal craniocaudal projection

10.3   Benign *v.* Malignant

	Benign	Malignant
1. **Opacity**	Smooth margin	Ill-defined margin – stellate, spiculated, comet tail.
	Low density Homogeneous Thin 'halo'	High density Inhomogeneous Wide 'halo'
2. **Calcification**		see 10.4
3. **Surrounding parenchyma**	Normal	Disrupted
4. **Nipple/areola**	± Retracted	± Retracted
5. **Skin**	Normal	Thickened
6. **Cooper ligaments**	Normal	Thickened, increased number
7. **Ducts**	Normal	Focal dilatation
8. **Subcutaneous/ retromammary space**	Normal	Obliterated

Note: The above distinguishing features are not invariable and may be found in 'classical cases' only.

10.4 Calcification

1. Microcalcification is defined as individual calcific opacities measuring < 0.5 mm diameter.
2. Macrocalcification: opacities > 0.5 mm diameter.
3. Microcalcification is not specific to carcinoma.
4. Microcalcification is seen in 30–40% of carcinomas on mammography.
5. Macrocalcification may be found in carcinoma.

Definitely Benign (see figure)
1. Arterial – tortuous, tramline.
2. Smooth, widely separated, some with radiolucent centre.
3. Linear thick, rod-like, widespread, some with radiolucent centre.
4. 'Egg-shell' curvilinear: margin of cyst, fat necrosis.
5. 'Pop-corn' in fibroadenoma.
6. Large individual calcific opacity > 2 mm, e.g. involutional fibroadenoma.
7. 'Floating' calcification – seen as calcific/fluid level seen on lateral oblique projection in 'milk of calcium' cysts.

Probably Benign
1. Widespread – all one/both breasts.
2. Macrocalcification of one size.
3. Symmetrical distribution.
4. Widely separated opacities.
5. Superficial distribution.
6. Normal parenchyma.

Possibly Malignant – Biopsy indicated – see microcalcification figure

1. Microcalcification – particularly segmental, cluster distribution (> 5 particles in 1.0 cm^3 space; of these 30% will be malignant).
2. Mixture of sizes and shapes – linear, branching, punctate.
3. Associated suspicious soft-tissue opacity.
4. Microcalcification eccentrically located in soft-tissue mass.
5. Deterioration on serial mammography.

Examples of definitely benign calcification

1. Arterial

2. Smooth ± lucent centre
widely separated

3. Linear, thick, rod-like
± lucent centres

4 'Egg-shell'

5. 'Pop-corn'

6. Large calcific opacity

7. Floating calcification

Microcalcification; mixture of sizes,
shapes, cluster, haphazard arrangement,
linear branching patterns

(*continued*)

Further Reading
Sickles E.A. (1986) Breast calcification: mammographic evaluation. *Radiology*, 160: 289–93.

10.5 Disappearance of Calcification

1. Surgery.
2. Radiotherapy.
3. Chemotherapy.
4. Spontaneous.

10.6 Benign Lesions with Typical Appearances

1. **Lipoma** – large, rounded, radiolucent, well-defined with compression of adjacent parenchyma.
2. **Fibroadenoma** – rounded, lobulated, well-defined homogeneously dense soft-tissue opacity with eccentrically sited 'pop-corn' calcification.
3. **Intramammary lymph node** – well-defined, usually 1.0 cm approx. in diameter soft-tissue opacity often with an eccentric radiolucency situated in the upper outer quadrant of the breast.
4. **Lipid cyst** – well-defined, multiple, lucent, 'egg-shell' calcification.

10.7 Single Well-defined Soft-tissue Opacity

Benign
1. Cyst.
2. Fibroadenoma.
3. Intramammary lymph node.
4. Skin lesion.
5. Papilloma.
6. Nipple not in profile.
7. Galactocoele.
8. Hamartoma.

Malignant
1. Cystosarcoma Phylloides – usually large, may be benign but have malignant potential.
2. Carcinoma – a small group of carcinomas look 'benign' on mammography, medullary, encephaloid, mucoid, papillary.

Note: Any well defined opacity > 1.0 cm in diameter should be subjected to ultrasound; if solid, biopsy should be performed.

10.8 Multiple Well-defined Soft-tissue Opacities

1. Cysts.
2. Fibroadenomas – 10/20% are multiple.
3. Skin lesions – e.g. neurofibromas.
4. Silicone injections – usually dense.
5. Intramammary lymph nodes.
6. Metastases – lymphoma, lung, ovarian carcinoma and melanoma are common primary lesions.

10.9 Large (> 5 cm) Well-defined Opacity

1. Giant cyst.
2. Giant fibroadenoma.
3. Lipoma.
4. Sebaceous cyst.
5. Cystosarcoma phylloides.

10.10   Benign Conditions that Mimic Malignancy

1. **Microcalcification**
   (a) Sclerosing adenosis: one/both breasts, widely separated opacities.
2. **Suspicious soft-tissue opacity**
   (a) Fibroadenoma – when one margin ill-defined.
   (b) Fat necrosis – ill-defined, sometimes with radiolucent centre.
   (c) Post biopsy scar.
   (d) Radial scar.
   (e) Plasma cell mastitis.
   (f) Haematoma.
   (g) Summation of normal tissues.
   (h) Irregular skin lesion, e.g. wart.

10.11   Carcinoma

Primary Features
1. **Opacity** – ill-defined, spiculated outline, comet tail. Usually dense.
2. **Microcalcification** – mixture of sizes, shapes; linear, branching, punctate cluster arrangement. Eccentric to and/or outside soft-tissue opacity.

Secondary Features
1. **Distortion** – adjacent tissues, obliteration subcutaneous, retromammary spaces.
2. **Skin, nipple retraction.**
3. **Oedema** – all or part of breast.
4. **Halo** – wide around primary opacity.
5. **Duct dilatation.**
6. **Venous engorgement.**

Note: Approximately 10% of palpable carcinomas in premenopausal women are not diagnosable on mammography.

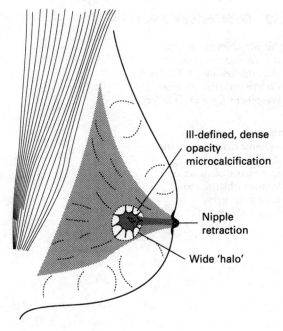

Ill-defined, dense
opacity
microcalcification

Nipple
retraction

Wide 'halo'

Typical carcinoma

10.12 Oedematous Breast

Signs on Mammography
1. Diffuse increased density.
2. Skin thickening (> 1.5 mm).
3. Coarse reticular pattern.
4. Prominent Cooper ligaments.

Causes
1. Inflammatory carcinoma.
2. Radiotherapy.
3. Lymphatic obstruction.
4. Venous obstruction.
5. Recent surgery.
6. Breast abscess.

10.13 Ultrasound in Breast Disease

Uses and Indications
1. Dense parenchyma in young women.
2. Breast tenderness (compression for mammography not possible).
3. Breast implant (mammography not useful).
4. Equivocal mammography, biopsy.
5. Biopsy, localization guidance.

Typical Appearances of Carcinoma
1. Poorly reflective mass.
2. Ill-defined mass.
3. Heterogeneous internal echo pattern.
4. Absent 'far wall' echoes.
5. Posterior acoustic shadowing.

Typical Appearances of Simple Cysts
1. Round, oval in shape.
2. Well defined.
3. Anechoic (echo free).
4. Post wall enhancement.
5. Posterior acoustic enhancement.

Typical Appearances of Fibroadenoma
1. Rounded or oval (may be lobulated).
2. Poorly reflective.
3. Homogeneous echo pattern.
4. Variable posterior echo pattern.

10.14   Breast Cancer Screening – Forrest Report

Summary

1. Screening by mammography alone.
2. 50–64 year age group.
3. Screening at 3 yearly intervals.
4. Lateral oblique projection recommended (but cranio–caudal projections in addition ideal).
5. Said to lead to 30% reduction in mortality.

Other Points

1. Basic screening unit – population of 41 150 women.
2. Minimal acceptable acceptance rate (attendance) – 70%.
3. Expected referral to Assessment Clinics – maximum of 10% of screening attendances.
4. Expected biopsy rate – 1.5% of screening attendances.
5. Incidence of carcinoma in screened population – 0.55%.

Further Reading

Feig S.A. (1992) *Diagnostic Radiology: A Textbook of Organ Imaging*, 2nd edition. *The Breast*, Vol. 3, Ch. 89, pp. 1871–1900. Edinburgh: Churchill Livingstone.

Forrest Report (1986) *Breast Cancer Screening*. London: HMSO.

Sickles F.A. (1986) Breast calcification: mammographic evaluation. *Radiology*, 160: 289–93.

11
Face and Neck

11.1 Orbital Mass Lesions

Classify by site in relation to the muscle cone. Axial sections suffice in most cases, but coronal sections are useful for muscle cone lesions and abscesses. Most orbital lesions enhance following the administration of contrast medium so this is not a useful means of discrimination.

Within or Involving the Globe
1. **Retinoblastoma** – the most important ocular tumour of childhood. Incidence of 1 : 20 000 live births. Four types have been recognized:
   (a) Those that are non-inheritable.
   (b) Those that are inherited as an autosomal dominant trait.
   (c) Those that are associated with a partial deletion of chromosome 13.
   (d) Bilateral retinoblastoma and pineal tumour – so-called trilateral retinoblastoma.
   Most children present with leukokoria or white pupillary reflex. 20–40% of patients have bilateral tumours and this is most often the autosomal dominant type. 5–10% of patients have a family history of retinoblastoma.
   Over 90% of tumours show calcification by CT which may be small, large, single or multiple. Intraocular calcification in children under 3 years of age is highly suggestive of retinoblastoma. The non-calcified component of the tumour is moderately dense, enhances poorly or not at all and may be difficult to differentiate from the associated retinal detachment and subretinal effusion. The presence of enhancement does exclude subretinal exudate and haemorrhage while marked enhancement suggests persistent hyperplastic primary vitreous (PHPV) (see 11.3).

Children with the hereditary form are at risk of developing second non-ocular malignancies, either within or out of the radiation field. Osteosarcoma is the commonest tumour.

2. **Melanoma** – increases in frequency after middle age. Lentiform mass related to the choroid. Contrast enhancing. High signal on T_1W MRI if melanotic. May invade outside the globe.
3. **Detachment and choroidal effusion** – may mimic melanoma.

Within the Muscle Cone (Intraconal)

1. **Optic nerve glioma** – see 11.2 and 11.4. Visual loss and painless with preservation of eye movements because the lesion is intraconal. There may also be other soft-tissue neurofibromas visible on the images. It should be remembered that patients with NFT may have other causes of proptosis such as sphenoid wing dysplasia.
2. **Optic nerve meningioma** – see 11.4.
3. **Haemangioma (usually cavernous) and arteriovenous malformation** – an enhancing mass but usually not seen on angiography, except for the relatively rare AVM.
4. **Inflammatory orbital pseudotumour** – an enhancing soft-tissue mass which may involve the muscle cone or optic nerve.
5. **Lymphoma and metastases.**
6. **Haematoma** – most are intraconal.
7. **Neurofibroma** – rare.

Arising from the Muscle Cone

1. **Inflammatory orbital pseudotumour.**
2. **Dysthyroid ophthalmopathy** – muscle tendons are spared.
3. **Rhabdomyosarcoma** – 10% arise in the orbit. The single most important cause of primary *orbital* malignancy in children. 50% are less than 7 years of age. Rapid onset of proptosis, usually with lateral deviation of the eye, as anteromedial or superomedial points of origin are most common. Vision is preserved. The tumour is closely related to the paranasal sinuses and though extension out of the orbit anteriorly and medially is not uncommon, most tumours lie preseptally or extraconally and extension backwards into the brain is not common. It is important

(*continued*)

to differentiate between a primary orbital location and a parameningeal location (defined as a tumour close enough to the meninges to permit intracranial spread of tumour) because therapy differs.

Outside the Muscle Cone (Extraconal)
1. **Orbital cellulitis and abscess** – contrast enhanced study may show the abscess cavity outlined by an enhancing wall; do coronal sections if possible.
2. **Lymphoma and metastases.**
3. **Dermoid and teratoma** – mixed tissue densities on CT.
4. **Lymphangioma, lympho-haemangioma** – tumours of childhood. See 11.2.
5. **Spread from lacrimal gland tumours.**

Arising from the Orbital Wall
1. **Metastases and lymphoma.**
2. **Langerhans cell histiocytosis*.**
3. **Invasion by ethmoidal or maxillary antral tumours.**
4. **Ethmoidal mucocele.**
5. **Spread of ethmoidal or antral infection.**

Further Reading

Azar-Kia B., Naheedy M.H., Elias D.A., Mafee M.F. & Fine M. (1987) Optic nerve tumours: role of magnetic resonance imaging and computed tomography. *Radiol. Clin. North Am.*, 25 (3): 561–81.

Curtin H.D. (1987) Pseudotumour. *Radiol. Clin. North Am.*, 25 (3): 583–99.

Flanders A.E., Espinosa G.A., Markiewicz D.A. & Howell D.D. (1987) Orbital lymphoma. Role of CT and MRI. *Radiol. Clin. North Am.*, 25 (3): 601–13.

Forbes G. (1992) An algorithm for imaging the orbit. In: *ARRS Neuroradiology Categorical Course Syllabus* (ed. M.S. Huckman), pp. 159–67.Reston: American Roentgen Ray Society.

Mafee M.F., Goldberg M.F., Greenwald M.J., Schulman J., Malmed A. & Flanders A.E. (1987) Retinoblastoma and simulating lesions: Role of CT and MR imaging. *Radiol. Clin. North Am.*, 25: 667–82.

Price H. & Danziger A. (1979) The computerised tomographic findings in paediatric orbital tumours. *Clin. Radiol.*, 30: 435–40.

Vade E. & Armstrong D. (1987) Orbital rhabdomyosarcoma in childhood. *Radiol. Clin. North Am.*, 25: 701–14.

11.2 Features of Orbital Masses in Children
CT Characteristics of Orbital Masses in Children

	Clinical features	Age	Preseptal	Extraconal	Intraconal	Muscle only	Orbital expansion	Bone destruction	Calcification	Intracranial	Facial	Attenuation	Enhancement	T_1W	T_2W
			Location					Extension				CT		MRI signal intensities	
Optic nerve glioma	Visual loss; painless proptosis; occasionally bilateral, especially in neurofibromatosis	<10 y; (50% <5 y)	-	-	‡	-	+	-	-	+	-	Isodense ± central lucencies	‡	↓	↑
Rhabdomyosarcoma	Rapid unilateral proptosis ± lid swelling; vision is preserved; may be parameningeal spread	90% <16 y	‡	‡	+	+	-	‡	-	‡	‡	Isodense or increased	‡	↓	↑
2° Neuroblastoma	Proptosis and orbital ecchymosis. Diagnosis known in 90%	<4 y	+	‡	-	-	-	‡	‡	+	+	Isodense or increased	‡	↓	↑
Leukaemia	Proptosis, lid oedema, pain, chemosis. May be bilateral.	>10 y	‡	‡	‡	‡	-	+	+	+	-	Increased	‡	↓	↑

Tumour	Features	Age								Density	Homogeneity
Lymphoma	± haemorrhage. Chloroma describes focal tumour deposits, usually in AML. Usually Burkitt type and bilateral	> 10 y	++	++	+	-	-	+	+	Increased	Homogeneous↓ Homogeneous↓
Haemangioma	Increase in size followed by regression. 30% have cutaneous naevus	0–3 m	++	‡	-	-	+	+	+	Mixed	Heterogeneous↓ Heterogeneous↓
Lymphangioma	Variable proptosis. Lids and conjunctiva. No spontaneous resolution. May haemorrhage	0–10 y	++	+	‡	-	+	-	+	Mixed low	Heterogeneous↓ Heterogeneous↓
Dermoid	Usually upper, outer orbital margin but may be deep	Newborn	++	+	-	+	-	+	-	Low	↑
Cellulitis	Pain; fever; sinus disease	Any age	++	+	-	-	+	+	‡	Isodense or low	↑
Pseudotumour	Painful proptosis; malaise; lid swelling; chemosis; may be recurrent	Any age	++	‡	-	-	+	-	++	Isodense	↓

Modified from Lallemand *et al.*
– not present; + uncommon; ++ common; ↑ increased; ↓ decreased.

Further Reading

Lallemand D.P., Brasch R.C., Char D.H. & Norman D. (1984) Orbital tumours in children. Characterisation by computed tomography *Radiology*, 151: 85–8.

11.3 Differential Diagnosis of Retinoblastoma

> 50% of children presenting with a clinical diagnosis of retinoblastoma may have another diagnosis. Ocular toxocariasis, PHPV and Coat's disease are the three commonest conditions confused with retinoblastoma. Under the age of 3 years, which is when retinoblastoma usually presents, none of the conditions shown in the table show calcification, but above that age some – retinal astrocytoma, retrolental fibroplasia and toxocariasis – may do so.

	Clinical features	*Age*	*Radiology*
Persistent hyperplastic primary vitreous	Unilateral leukokoria	At or soon after birth	Microphthalmia. Small irregular lens; shallow anterior chamber. No calcification. Increased attenuation of the vitreous. Enhancement of abnormal intravitreal tissue. Triangular retrolental density with its apex on the posterior lens and base on the posterior globe. Fluid level on decubitus scanning
Coat's disease	A vascular anomaly of telangiectatic vessels which leak proteinaceous material into the subretinal space. Usually boys; unilateral. Present at birth but usually asymptomatic until the retina detaches and vision deteriorates	4–8 y	Appearances of retinal detachment. Indistinguishable from non-calcified retinoblastoma on CT. High signal subretinal effusion on T_1W and T_2W MRI

(*continued*)

	Clinical features	Age	Radiology
Retinopathy of prematurity	Uni- or bilateral leukokoria. Appropriate previous medical history of oxygen therapy and prematurity	7–10 weeks	No calcification (but may calcify in the older child). Microphthalmia
Toxocariasis	Close contact with dogs. No systemic symptoms. Positive ELISA test	Mean 6 y	Opaque vitreous or a localized, irregular retinal mass. No contrast enhancement
Chronic retinal detachment	Rare. Presentation late. More common in developmentally abnormal eyes and dysmorphic syndromes		No enhancement or calcification
Retinal astrocytoma (astrocytic hamartoma)	In 40% of patients with tuberous sclerosis or, less commonly, neurofibromatosis, retinitis pigmentosa or as an isolated abnormality		May be bilateral. Multiple, small retinal masses. May calcify in the older child
Retinal dysplasia	Bilateral leukokoria	At or soon after birth	Bilateral retrolental masses. No calcification

(*continued*)

Further Reading
Howard G.M. & Ellsworth R.M. (1965) Differential diagnosis of retinoblastoma. A statistical survey of 500 children. I. Relative
frequency of the lesions which simulate retinoblastoma. *Am.
J. Ophthalmol.*, 60: 610–18.

Mafee M.F., Goldberg M.F., Greenwald M.J., Schulman J., Malmed
A. & Flanders A.E. (1987) Retinoblastoma and simulating
lesions: Role of CT and MR imaging. *Radiol. Clin. North Am.*,
25: 667–82.

Shields J.A. & Augsberger J.J. 1981. Current approaches to the diagnosis and management of retinoblastoma. *Survey Ophthalmol.*, 25: 347–71.

11.4 Optic Nerve Glioma *v.* Orbital Meningioma. Clinical and CT Differentiation

Optic nerve glioma	Meningioma
50% less than 5 years of age ± bilateral	Usually middle-aged women ± bilateral
Well-defined margins	More infiltrative Tubular thickening in 66% Fusiform enlargement in 25%
Calcification rare without prior radiotherapy	Calcification more common
No orbital hyperostosis	Hyperostosis
Enhancement, but with mottled lucencies due to mucinous degeneration	Diffuse homogeneous enhancement
Kinking and buckling of the optic nerve is common. Smooth outline	Straight optic nerve Negative image of optic nerve within tumour (tram-track sign)
Widened optic canal in 90% but intracranial extension is unusual	Widened optical canal in 10%
25% have neurofibromatosis * NF1; 15% of NF1 have optic nerve glioma; bilateral disease strongly suggests neurofibromatosis	Less frequently associated with neurofibromatosis

Further Reading

Azar-Kia B., Naheedy M.H., Elias D.A., Mafee M.F. & Fine M. (1987) Optic nerve tumours: role of magnetic resonance imaging and computed tomography. *Radiol. Clin. North Am.*, 25 (3): 561–81.

Linder B., Campos M. & Schafer M. (1987) CT and MRI of orbital abnormalities in neurofibromatosis and selected craniofacial anomalies. *Radiol. Clin. North Am.*, 25 (4): 787–802.

11.5   Enlarged Orbit

Exclude small contralateral orbit, e.g. enucleation as a child.
1. **Neurofibromatosis*** – ± 'bare' orbit due to elevation of the lesser wing of the sphenoid and associated dysplasia.
2. **Congenital glaucoma (buphthalmos)** – asymmetrical enlargement.
3. **Any space-occupying lesion** – if present long enough. The enlargement in children occurs much faster. (See 11.1.)

11.6   'Bare' Orbit

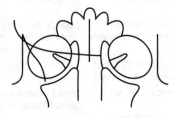

1. **Neurofibromatosis*** – dysplasia of the sphenoid.
2. **Metastasis** – bone destruction.
3. **Meningioma** – adjacent bone sclerosis.

Further Reading
Burrows E.H. (1963) Bone changes in orbital neurofibromatosis. *Br. J. Radiol.*, 36: 549–61.

11.7 Enlarged Optic Foramen

Diameter greater than 7 mm (normal range of 4.4–6 mm is reached by the age of four). However, the final arbiter is always comparison with the asymptomatic side. A difference in diameter of 1 mm is abnormal.

Concentric Enlargement
1. **Optic nerve glioma** – child/young adult. 25% associated with neurofibromatosis. Bone margins intact.
2. **Neurofibroma** – may occur without any associated glioma.
3. **Extension of retinoblastoma.**
4. **Vascular** – ophthalmic artery aneurysm, arteriovenous malformation.
5. **Granuloma** – very rarely in sarcoid or pseudotumour.

Local Defect

ROOF
1. **Adjacent neoplasm** – meningioma, metastases, glioma.
2. **Raised intracranial pressure** – due to thinning of the floor of the anterior and cranial fossa.

MEDIAL WALL
1. **Adjacent neoplasm** – carcinoma of the ethmoid/sphenoid.
2. **Sphenoid mucocele.**

INFEROLATERAL WALL
1. **Same conditions as cause enlarged superior orbital fissure** (q.v.).

Further Reading
Lloyd G.A.S. (1975) *Radiology of the Orbit*, pp. 26–9. Philadelphia: Saunders.

11.8 Enlarged Superior Orbital Fissure

1. Normal variant.
2. Neurofibromatosis*.
3. Extension of intracranial lesion
   (a) Meningioma – adjacent sclerosis.
   (b) Infraclinoid aneurysm – occurs in 75%. Usually accompanied by erosion of the inferior surface of the anterior clinoid.
   (c) Parasellar chordoma.
4. Metastasis to wing of sphenoid.
5. Extension of orbital lesion (anterior clinoids not eroded)
   (a) Arteriovenous malformation.
   (b) Haemangioma.
   (c) Orbital meningioma.
   (d) Lymphoma.

11.9 Intraorbital Calcification

In the Globe
1. Cataract.
2. Retinoblastoma – see 11.1 and 11.3.
3. Old trauma/infection – of the vitreous humour.

Outside the Globe
1. Phleboliths
   (a) Arteriovenous malformation – enlarged orbit and proptosis. ± prominent vascular markings. Can also occur in an arteriovenous shunt (e.g. secondary to a traumatic carotico-cavernous fistula).
   (b) Haemangioma – only rarely have calcified phleboliths.
2. Orbital meningioma – 12% calcify (more common in extradural location). 10% show enlargement of the optic foramen. Sclerosis of the orbital apex may be present if extradural in location.
3. Others – rarely in neurofibroma, intraorbital dermoid and adenocarcinoma of the lacrimal gland.

11.10 Hyperostosis in the Orbit

1. **Meningioma.**
2. **Sclerotic metastases.**
3. **Fibrous dysplasia*** – bone expansion may cause some reduction in size of the orbit.
4. **Paget's disease*** – usually widespread changes in the calvarium.
5. **Osteopetrosis*** – and other sclerosing bone dysplasias, see 12.5.
6. **Chronic osteomyelitis** – adjacent to a chronically infected frontal sinus.
7. **Lacrimal gland malignancy.**
8. **Langerhans cell histiocytosis*.**
9. **Radiotherapy.**

11.11 Small or Absent Sinuses

Congenital
1. **Congenital absence** – absence of the frontal sinuses occur in 5% of the normal population.
2. **Cretinism*.**
3. **Down's syndrome*** – 90% have absent frontal sinuses.
4. **Kartagener's syndrome** – dextrocardia, bronchiectasis and absent frontal sinuses.

Overgrowth of Bony Wall
1. **Paget's disease*.**
2. **Fibrous dysplasia*.**
3. **Haemolytic anaemia*.**
4. **Post Caldwell–Luc operation.**

11.12 Opaque Maxillary Antrum

Traumatic
1. Fracture – blood in the antrum.
2. Overlying soft-tissue swelling – gives apparent opacification of the antrum.
3. Postoperative – washout/Caldwell–Luc.
4. Epistaxis.
5. Barotrauma.

Inflammatory/Infective
1. Infection.
2. Allergy.
3. Pyocele – infected mucocele (rare in the antrum). Severe systemic symptoms.

Neoplastic
1. Carcinoma – ± bone destruction and extension of the soft-tissue mass.
2. Lymphoma*.

Others
1. Fibrous dysplasia* – ± bone expansion.
2. Cysts – dentigerous and mucous retention cysts may be large enough to fill the antrum.
3. Wegener's granulomatosis.
4. Technical – overtilted view.
5. Anatomical – thick skull vault, sloping antral wall.

11.13 Mass in the Maxillary Antrum

1. **Cysts**
   (a) Mucous retention cyst – complication of sinusitis. Maxillary antrum is a common site, and it often arises from the floor. Commoner than a polyp, but hard to differentiate between them.
   (b) Dentigerous cyst – expands upwards into the floor of the antrum. The involved tooth may be displaced into the antrum.
2. **Trauma** – due to 'tear-drop' of prolapsed muscle through the roof of the antrum in an orbital blow-out fracture.
3. **Neoplasms**
   (a) Polyp – complication of sinusitis.
   (b) Carcinoma – ± bone destruction and soft-tissue mass extending beyond the boundary of the antrum.
4. **Wegener's granulomatosis** – age usually 40–50. Early mucosal thickening progresses to a mass with bone destruction.

11.14   Cystic Lesions in the Jaw

Dental

1. **Periodontal/radicular/periapical cyst** – develops in a carious tooth, often in an asymptomatic patient. Well-defined lucency with a thin sclerotic margin at the apex of a tooth. If large may erode the inner cortex of the mandible, displace adjacent teeth and/or extend into the maxillary antrum.

2. **Dentigerous cyst** – adjacent to the crown of an unerupted tooth (usually a wisdom tooth or canine). Well-defined, uni- or multilocular. If large, may displace adjacent teeth. Maxillary cysts may extend into the maxillary antra or nose. Multiple cysts occur in Gorlin's syndrome (multiple basal cell naevi, rib anomalies and lamellar falx calcification; AD).

Non-dental

1. **Developmental/fissural cysts**
   (a) Nasopalatine duct cyst/incisive canal cyst – usually 4–6th decade. A small asymptomatic cyst near the anterior palatine papilla.
   (b) Globulomaxillary cyst – between the lateral incisor and canine.
   (c) Nasolabial cyst – in the soft tissues between the nose and the upper lip. There may be resorption of the adjacent maxilla.

2. **Hyperparathyroidism** – a common site for a brown tumour.

3. **Neoplasms**
   (a) Ameloblastoma – 80% in mandible, 20% in maxilla. Most mandibular lesions are near the angle. Slow growing, painless mass which can reach a considerable size. Uni- or multilocular, well-defined, bony expansion ± extension through the cortex to form an extra-bony soft-tissue mass.
   (b) Langerhans cell histiocytosis*.
   (c) Aneurysmal bone cyst*.
   (d) Giant cell tumour*.

   (e) Haemangioma.
   (f) Metastases.
4. **Fibrous dysplasia*** – rare site.
5. **Bone cyst** – possibly following an injury. Usually second decade of life. Asymptomatic. Unilocular, indistinct borders and most commonly in the marrow space of the mandibular body.

Further Reading
Weber A.L. (1993) Imaging of cysts and odontogenic tumours of the jaw. *Radiol. Clin. North Am.*, 31 (1): 101–20.

11.15   'Floating' Teeth

No obvious supporting bone for the teeth.

1. Severe periodontal disease.
2. Langerhans cell histiocytosis*.
3. Hyperparathyroidism*.
4. Metastases.
5. Multiple myeloma*.

11.16   Loss of Lamina Dura of Teeth

Generalized
1. Endocrine/metabolic
   (a) Osteoporosis (q.v.).
   (b) Hyperparathyroidism*.
   (c) Cushing's syndrome*.
   (d) Osteomalacia (q.v.).
2. Paget's disease*.
3. Scleroderma* – thickened periodontal membrane.

Localized
1. Infection.
2. Neoplasms – leukaemia, multiple myeloma, metastases, Burkitt's lymphoma, Langerhans cell histiocytosis.

11.17 Mass in the Nasopharynx

1. **Adenoids** – enlargement is normal between 1 and 7 years of age.
2. **Trauma** – fracture of the base of the skull or upper cervical spine with associated haematoma.
3. **Infection** – abscess may be confined above C2 by strong attachment of the prevertebral fascia. ± speckled gas in the mass.
4. **Neoplasms, benign**
   (a) Adolescent angiofibroma – very vascular. Young male – ± spontaneous regression after adolescence. Can cause pressure erosion of the sphenoid and opacification of the antra.
   (b) Antro–choanal polyp.
5. **Neoplasms, malignant**
   (a) Nasopharyngeal carcinoma.
   (b) Lymphoma*.
   (c) Rhabdomyosarcoma.
   (d) Plasmacytoma*.
   (e) Extension – carcinoma of the sphenoid/ethmoid, and chordoma.
6. **Encephalocele** – midline defect in the base of the skull.

11.18   Prevertebral Soft-tissue Mass in the Cervical Region

Child

NB   Anterior buckling of the trachea with an increase in the thickness of the retropharyngeal tissues may occur as a normal phenomenon in expiration during the first 2 years of life and is due to laxity of the retropharyngeal tissues. These soft tissues may contain a small collection of air, trapped in the inferior recess of the laryngeal pharynx above the contracted upper oesophageal sphincter. An ear lobe may also mimic a prevertebral mass.

1. **Trauma/haematoma** – ± an associated fracture.
2. **Abscess** – ± gas lucencies within it. Unlike the normal variant described above these lucencies are constant and persist during deep inspiration.
3. **Neoplasms**
   (a) Cystic hygroma.
   (b) Lymphoma*.
   (c) Nasopharyngeal rhabdomyosarcoma.
   (d) Neuroblastoma.

Adult

1. **Trauma**
2. **Abscess.**
3. **Neoplasms**
   (a) Post-cricoid carcinoma.
   (b) Lymphoma*.
   (c) Chordoma.
4. **Pharyngeal pouch** – ± air/fluid level within it.
5. **Retropharyngeal goitre.**

See also 11.17.

Further Reading

Brenner G.H. (1964) Variations in the depth of the cervical prevertebral tissues in normal infants studied by cine fluorography. *Am. J. Roentgenol.*, 91: 573–7.

Currarino G. & Williams B. (1993) Air collection in the retropharyngeal soft tissues observed in lateral expiratory films of the neck in 9 infants. *Pediatr. Radiol.*, 23: 186–8.

12
Skull and Brain

with contributions by Tom Powell

12.1 Lucency in the Skull Vault, with no Surrounding Sclerosis – Adult

Neoplastic

1. **Multiple myeloma*** – involves cancellous and both tables of cortical bone, hence punched out appearance. It can affect the mandible (metastases rarely do). Lesions are cold on radioisotope bone-scan. The skull may be normal even with widespread lesions elsewhere.
2. **Metastases** – usually irregular and ill-defined. Breast, kidney and thyroid are common primary tumours.
3. **Haemangioma** – may have 'soap bubble' appearance, and can cause 'hair-on-end' appearance (see 12.13).
4. **Neurofibroma** – may cause a lucent defect in the occipital bone (usually adjacent to the left lambdoid suture).
5. **Adjacent malignancy** – e.g. rodent ulcer, carcinoma of the ear.
6. **Paget's sarcoma.**

Traumatic

1. **Burr hole** – very well-defined when recent.
2. **Leptomeningeal cyst.**

Idiopathic

1. **Osteoporosis circumscripta** – occurs in the active lytic phase of Paget's disease*. It starts in the lower part of the frontal and occipital regions (i.e. rare in the vertex) and can cross suture lines to involve large areas of the calvarium.

Metabolic

1. **Hyperparathyroidism*** – 'pepper pot skull'. Rarely severe enough to cause overt lytic lesions. The calvarium is affected in approximately 20% of primary hyperparathyroidism causing 'pepper pot' appearance. The mandible is a common site for 'brown' tumours and there may be loss of the lamina dura around the teeth. Basilar invagination may occur.

Infective

1. **Tuberculosis** – tuberculous osteomyelitis is much less common than tuberculous arthritis and the skull is a rare site (the spine being the most common). It can produce a punched out lytic lesion.
2. **Hydatid.**
3. **Syphilis** – 'moth-eaten' appearance.
4. **Pyogenic osteomyelitis** – rarely haematogenous, usually direct infection from adjacent frontal sinus, or secondary to compound fracture, and to surgery.

12.2 Lucency in the Skull Vault, with no Surrounding Sclerosis – Child

Neoplastic

1. **Metastases** – especially neuroblastoma and leukaemia. ± wide sutures.
2. **Langerhans cell histiocytosis*** – eosinophilic granuloma usually produces a solitary lesion which only causes local pain. It can have bevelled edges, due to differential destruction of the inner and outer tables, and can grow several centimetres in size in a few weeks. There is no sclerosis unless the lesion is healing. A sequestrum may be seen.

   Hand–Schüller–Christian syndrome produces the 'geographical' skull, with associated systemic symptoms. Exophthalmos and diabetes insipidus accompany it in less than 10% of cases. Chronic otitis media, and loose teeth due to surrounding lucencies ('floating' teeth), commonly occur. 'Honeycomb lung' occurs in 10% of cases and worsens the prognosis.

Traumatic

1. **Leptomeningeal cyst** – if the dura is torn, the arachnoid membrane can prolapse, and the pulsations of the CSF can cause progressive widening and scalloping of the fracture line. The bone changes take several weeks to appear and may persist into adult life.
2. **Burr hole.**

NB   Normal variants such as parietal foramina and venous lakes, apart from having characteristic configurations, will also be 'cold' on a radioisotope bone-scan.

12.3   Lucency in the Skull Vault, with Surrounding Sclerosis

*Fibrous Dysplasia**

Developmental
1. **Epidermoid** – scalloped appearance with thin sclerotic margins. It is intramedullary in origin and so can expand both inner and outer tables. Although any site is possible, it is commonly in the squamous portion of the occipital or temporal bones.
2. **Meningocele** – this is a mid-line defect and has a smooth sclerotic margin with an overlying soft-tissue mass. It usually occurs in the occipital bone, but may occur in the frontal, parietal or basal bones.

Neoplastic
1. **Haemangioma** – only rarely has a sclerotic margin. Radiating spicules of bone within it are a helpful discriminatory sign.
2. **Langerhans cell histiocytosis** * – only has a sclerotic margin if it is in the healing phase.

Infective
1. **Chronic osteomyelitis** – sclerosis dominates, with only a few lytic areas.
2. **Frontal sinus mucocele** – secondary to sinusitis.

Further Reading
Lane B. (1974) Erosions of the Skull. *Radiol. Clin. North Am.*, 12: 257–82.

12.4 Generalized Thickening of the Skull Vault in Children

With Homogeneous Increased Density
1. Normal variant.
2. Sclerosing bone dysplasias.
3. Chronic decreased intracranial pressure – in cerebral atrophy or following successful shunting of hydrocephalus.
4. Phenytoin therapy.

With Non-homogeneous Sclerosis or No Sclerosis
1. Chronic haemolytic anaemias.
2. Renal osteodystrophy.
3. Fibrous dysplasia*.

Further Reading
Anderson R., Kieffer S.A., Wolfson J.J. & Peterson H.O. (1970) Thickening of the skull in surgically treated hydrocephalus. *Am. J. Roentgenol.*, 110: 96–101.

Griscom N.T. & Kook Sang O. (1970) The contracting skull; inward growth of the inner table as a physiologic response to diminution of intracranial content in children. *Am. J. Roentgenol.*, 110: 106–10.

12.5 Generalized Increase in Density of the Skull Vault

1. **Paget's disease*** – multiple islands of dense bone. Later the differentiation between the inner and outer tables is lost and the skull vault is thickened (2–5 times normal). Basilar invagination may occur. The sinuses may be involved giving an appearance similar to leontiasis ossea. Loss of lamina dura may occur.
2. **Sclerotic metastases** (see 1.17).
3. **Fibrous dysplasia*** – if the lesions are widespread throughout the skeleton, then the skull always has a lesion. However, if only the facial bones and base of skull are involved (leontiasis ossea), the rest of the skeleton is rarely affected. Younger age group than Paget's disease.
4. **Myelosclerosis** – there is endosteal thickening which causes narrowing of the diploë. The spleen is greatly enlarged.
5. **Renal osteodystrophy*** – osteosclerosis occurs in 25%. The skull and spine are commonly involved and can look similar to Paget's disease. ± vascular calcification.
6. **Fluorosis** – mottling of the tooth enamel is a pronounced feature. The calvarium is a rare site for changes to be seen, the axial skeleton being the most frequent. Calcification of muscle attachments.
7. **Acromegaly*** – enlarged frontal sinuses, prognathism, enlarged sella, thick vault.
8. **Phenytoin therapy.**
9. **Chronic haemolytic anaemias.**
10. **Congenital** and see 1.9 – 1.53.
    (a) Osteopetrosis* – 'bone in bone' appearance in the spine. The mandible is not affected. Flask-shaped femora.
    (b) Pyknodysostosis – particularly involves the skull base. Wormian bones. Wide sutures.
    (c) Pyle's disease – associated with metaphyseal splaying of the long bones.

12.6 Localized Increase in Density of the Skull Vault

In Bone

1. Neoplasms
   (a) Sclerotic metastases (q.v.).
   (b) Osteoma (ivory).
   (c) Treated lytic metastases – especially breast primary.
   (d) Treated 'brown' tumour.
2. Paget's disease*.
3. Fibrous dysplasia*.
4. Depressed fracture – due to overlapping bone fragments.
5. Benign hyperostosis – commonly seen in post-menopausal females (rare in men). Mainly involves the frontal region and is characteristically bilateral and symmetrical. Thickening of inner table – 'choppy sea' appearance.

Adjacent to Bone

1. Meningioma – mainly involves the inner table, but if it breaks through the outer table it may cause a 'hair-on-end' appearance. About 15% show calcification in the tumour itself. There may be an abnormal increase in the vascular channels and also signs of raised intracranial pressure. The characteristic sites are parasagittal, olfactory groove, sphenoid ridge and tentorium.
2. Calcified sebaceous cyst.
3. Old cephalhaematoma – it is usually in the parietal region, and may be bilateral.
4. Soft-tissue tumours – e.g. neurofibroma, sebaceous cyst.
5. Hair bunch.

12.7   Increase in Density of the Skull Base

Localized
1. Fibrous dysplasia*.
2. Meningioma – particularly sphenoid wings.
3. Sclerotic metastases (q.v.).
4. Sclerosis of mastoid in chronic mastoiditis.

Generalized
1. Paget's disease*.
2. Fibrous dysplasia*.
3. Other causes of generalized increase in bone density (q.v.).

12.8   Destruction of Petrous Bone – Apex

1. **Acoustic neuroma** – eighth nerve. Increase in size of IAM (greater than 1 cm in diameter or more than 2 mm asymmetry between the sides). Erosion of the crista transversalis and apparent 'shortening' of the IAM may occur. Bilateral in neurofibromatosis 2 (NF2)*.
2. **Congenital cholesteatoma** – lytic defect with no sclerosis. Petrous ridge may be elevated. Seventh nerve may be involved (this is rare in acoustic neuroma).
3. **Cholesterol granuloma** – appearances similar to congenital cholesteatoma. Non-enhancing, well demarcated lytic lesion in petrous apex. Bilateral in 30% of cases. Cholesterol granuloma also occurs in the middle ear.
4. **Meningioma** – hyperostosis rarely seen at this site.
5. **Metastases** – particularly breast, kidney and lung. Irregular lytic defect. Pain and nerve palsies are common.
6. **Fifth nerve neuroma.**
7. **Nasopharyngeal carcinoma** – usually large area of destruction in the floor of the middle cranial fossa also.
8. **Chordoma.**
9. **Apical petrositis.**

Further Reading
Livingstone P.A. (1974) Differential diagnosis of radiolucent lesions of the temporal bone. *Radiol. Clin. North Am.*, 12: 571–83.

12.9 Destruction of Petrous Bone – Middle Ear

Adult

1. **Acquired cholesteatoma** – usually diagnosed by auroscopy. Bony destruction extending from the epitympanic recess, with clear cut but not sclerotic margins. Earliest sign is destruction of the spur (80%). Ossicles may be destroyed. The mastoid is often sclerotic due to the associated chronic infection.
2. **Carcinoma of the external auditory meatus** – 30% associated with chronic otitis media. Pain and bleeding are late.
3. **Metastases.**
4. **Glomus jugulare** – the jugular foramen is enlarged and destroyed, with minimal or no sclerosis. Very vascular on angiography. Glomus tympanicum tumours present earlier but may also show similar destructive changes. See 12.10.
5. **Intra-temporal carotid aneurysm.**
6. **Tuberculosis** – rare. Destruction with no sclerosis. May be no evidence of TB elsewhere.

Child

1. **Rhabdomyosarcoma** – commonest primary malignancy of ear in childhood. Pain is rare.

Further Reading

Livingstone P.A. (1974) Differential diagnosis of radiolucent lesions of the temporal bone. *Radiol. Clin. North Am.*, 12: 571–83.

Phelps P.D. & Lloyd G.A.S. (1981) The radiology of carcinoma of the ear. *Br. J. Radiol.*, 54: 103–9.

Phelps P.D. & Lloyd G.A.S. (1980) The radiology of cholesteatoma. *Clin. Radiol.*, 31: 501–12.

Phelps P.D. & Wright A. (1990) Imaging cholesteatoma. *Clin. Radiol.*, 41: 156–62.

12.10   Vascular Masses in the Ear

1. **Glomus tumour** – commonest type is a chemodectoma (paraganglioma) of the glomus jugulare. Peak incidence after middle age, females predominating. The tumour arises in the jugular fossa and invades the middle ear, giving rise to the clinical presence of a dusky red swelling in the posterior middle ear on otoscopy. Patients complain of pulsatile tinnitus, variable jugular fossa syndrome (see 12.11), deafness and pain.
   Diagnosis: a soft-tissue mass arising from the jugular fossa, intensely enhancing ('salt and pepper' pattern on MRI due to small intratumoral vessels). Both CT and MRI are suitable for diagnosis. Permeative bone invasion looking like a malignant tumour, though true malignancy is rare. Vascular tumour blush on angiography: venous phase may show filling defect or obstruction in the jugular bulb.
2. **Glomus tympanicum** – generally similar to glomus jugulare, but causes such intense tinnitus that it presents very early, and is therefore smaller at presentation. Situated more anteriorly in the middle ear over the cochlear promontory. MRI is the best diagnostic tool, though CT is also sensitive, particularly with dynamic studies for display of contrast accumulation.
3. **Dehiscence of the jugular bulb** – the bony septum between the jugular fossa and the middle ear is deficient, leading to herniation of the bulb, with a soft-tissue mass lying posteriorly, strongly resembling a glomus jugulare tumour. These patients also present with pulsatile tinnitus.
4. **Deshiscence of the carotid canal** – carotid artery takes a more lateral and posterior course than normal, with a defect in the wall between the canal and the mesotympanum. The artery bulges into the cavity and is visible anteriorly on otoscopy, again with pulsatile tinnitus.

Further Reading

Phelps P.D. (1990) Glomus tumours of the ear. *Clin. Radiol.*, 41: 301–5.

12.11 Metastases in the Skull Base

1. Breast
2. Bronchus
3. Prostate

} metastatic disease is best shown by CT.

Patients may present with one of four clinical syndromes:

Orbital syndrome – pain, diplopia, proptosis and external ophthalmoplegia.

Parasellar and middle fossa syndrome – headache, ocular paresis without proptosis and facial numbness caused by invasion of the maxillary and mandibular divisions of the fifth cranial nerve. Radiological changes occur late.

Jugular foramen syndrome – hoarseness and dysphagia. Radiological features often absent.

Occipital condyle syndrome – stiffness and pain in the neck, worse on flexion.

The differential diagnosis of these clinical syndromes includes:

1. Carotid or vertebrobasilar aneurysm.
2. Tolosa–Hunt syndrome.
3. Primary neoplasms of the skull base.

Further Reading

Kagan R.A., Steckel R.J., Bassett L.W. & Gold R.H. (1986) Radiologic contributions to cancer management. Bone metastases. *Am. J. Roentgenol.*, 147: 305–12.

12.12 Basilar Invagination

McGregor's line (posterior end of hard palate to the base of the occiput). The tip of the odontoid peg is normally less than 0.5 cm above this line. If basilar invagination is severe obstructive hydrocephalus may occur.

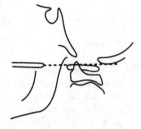

Primary Anomalies of the Occiput, Atlas and Axis

Generalized Bone Disease
1. Rickets*/osteomalacia (q.v.).
2. Paget's disease*.
3. Fibrous dysplasia*.

Delayed or Defective Cranial Ossification
1. Osteogenesis imperfecta*.
2. Achondroplasia*.
3. Cleidocranial dysplasia*.
4. Hypophosphatasia.
5. Progeria.
6. Craniolacunia (lacunar skull) – NB this is a mesenchymal skull dysplasia, which is not the same as the generally thinned skull of chronic hydrocephalus.
7. Hydrocephalus.
NB
1. Platybasia – does not always accompany basilar invagination, but occurs in similar circumstances. The index of this is the basal angle, normal < 140°. By itself it is symptomless, but if associated with basilar invagination, then obstructive hydrocephalus may occur.

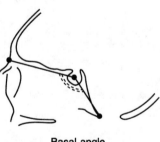

Basal angle

2. **Basilar invagination** – elevation of the floor of the posterior cranial fossa. This may be associated with anomalies of the cervical spine such as atlanto-occipital fusion or Klippel–Feil syndrome.

Further Reading

Dolan K.D. (1977) Cervicobasilar relationships. *Radiol. Clin. North Am.*, 15: 155–66.

12.13   'Hair-on-end' Skull Vault

Haemolytic Anaemias

1. **Sickle-cell anaemia*** – occurs in 5%. Begins in the frontal region and can affect all the calvarium except that which is below the internal occipital protuberance, since there is no marrow in this area. The diploic space is widened due to marrow hyperplasia.
2. **Thalassaemia*** – marrow hyperplasia in thalassaemia major is more marked than in any other anaemia. May be severe enough to cause marrow hyperplasia of the facial bones, resulting in obliteration of the maxillary antra. (This does not occur in sickle-cell anaemia.)
3. **Others** – hereditary spherocytosis, elliptocytosis, pyruvate kinase deficiency and glucose-6-phosphate dehydrogenase deficiency.

Neoplastic

1. **Haemangioma.**
2. **Meningioma** – only rarely, when it breaks through the outer table.
3. **Metastases.**
4. **Osteosarcoma** – very rare.

Others

1. **Cyanotic heart disease** – due to erythroid hyperplasia. Hypertrophic pulmonary osteoarthropathy may occur.
2. **Iron-deficiency anaemia** – severe childhood cases.

12.14 Craniostenosis

Simple Primary

1. **Scaphocephaly** – long, narrow, 'boat-shaped' skull. Commonest type. Premature fusion of the sagittal suture. Usually uncomplicated and relatively benign but may be part of a complex craniofacial malformation.
2. **Trigonocephaly** – premature fusion of the metopic suture. Wedge-shaped frontal region with a narrow forehead and hypotelorism.
3. **Turricephaly, oxycephaly and acrocephaly** – high forehead with a 'tower-' or 'turret-shaped' head. Premature fusion of the coronal and sphenofrontal sutures. This type of skull deformity is present in the acrocephalosyndactyly syndromes (Apert, Carpenter, Pfeiffer and Saethre–Chotzen).
4. **Plagiocephaly** – asymmetry of the skull due to asymmetrical sutural fusion.
5. **Triphyllocephaly** – 'cloverleaf skull' or *Kleeblattschädel*. Trilobular skull with temporal and frontal bulges.

Complex Primary

1. **Apert syndrome (acrocephalosyndactyly, type 1)**
   (a) Acrocephaly with shallow orbits.
   (b) Mental retardation.
   (c) Severe osseous and cutaneous syndactyly (mitten hands and feet).
   (d) Abnormal thumb and hallux.
2. **Carpenter syndrome (acrocephalopolysyndactyly)** – similar to Apert syndrome but distinguished from it by
   (a) Duplication of the proximal phalanx of the thumb and hallux.
   (b) Cardiac abnormalities, obesity and hypogonadism may also be present.
3. Crouzon syndrome (craniofacial dysotosis)
   (a) Craniostenosis of the sagittal, coronal and lambdoid sutures.
   (b) Midface hypoplasia with relative mandibular prognathism.
   (c) Hypertelorism and proptosis.

(*continued*)

(d) Normal intelligence.
(e) Normal hands.

Secondary

1. **Microcephaly** – failure of brain growth in the first few years of life.
2. **Treatment of severe hydrocephalus** – by low pressure ventricular shunting.

Metabolic Disorders Sometimes Complicated by Craniostenosis

1. **Rickets.**
2. **Hyperthyroidism.**
3. **Polycythaemia.**
4. **Thalassaemia*.**

Further Reading

David D.J., Poswillo D. & Simpson D. (1982) *The Craniosynostoses.* Berlin: Springer-Verlag.

12.15 Multiple Wormian Bones

Common in infancy but only considered significant when 6 × 4 mm, or larger, in size, > 10 in number and with a tendency to be arranged in a mosaic pattern (Cremin *et al.*, 1982).

1. **Osteogenesis imperfecta***.
2. **Cleidocranial dysplasia*** – autosomal dominant. Brachycephaly with open sutures and anterior fontanelle. The teeth are always poorly formed/delayed and multiple supernumerary teeth may be present. Small facial bones.
3. **Pyknodysostosis** – autosomal recessive. Short-limbed dwarf, with some features of osteopetrosis and cleidocranial dysplasia.
4. **Hypophosphatasia*** – autosomal recessive. Low alkaline phosphatase, and excessive phosphoethanolamine in the urine. Premature fusion of the sutures.
5. **Cretinism*** – delayed, fragmented epiphyses. There is usually a hypoplastic 'bullet-shaped' vertebra at L1 or L2 level.
6. **Acro-osteolysis** – particularly Hajdu–Cheney syndrome.
7. **Chromosomal disorders** – particularly trisomy 21.
8. **Pachydermoperiostosis.**
9. **Menkes kinky hair syndrome.**
10. **Increased frequency in mentally retarded individuals.**

Further Reading

Cremin B., Goodman H., Spranger J. & Beighton P. (1982) Wormian bones in osteogenesis imperfecta and other disorders. *Skel. Radiol.*, 8: 35–8.

Pryles C.V. & Khan A.J. (1979) Wormian bones. *Am. J. Dis. Child.*, 133: 380–2.

12.16 Large Head in Infancy

1. Hydrocephalus – see 12.17.
2. Hydranencephaly.
3. Chronic subdural haematoma.
4. Megalencephaly.
5. Storage diseases – MPS etc.
6. Neurofibromatosis*.

Further Reading
DeMeyer W. (1972) Megalencephaly in children. *Neurology*, 22: 634–43.
Harwood-Nash D.C. & Fitz C.R. (1975) Large heads and ventricles in infants. *Radiol. Clin. North Am.*, 13: 119–224.
Holt J.F. & Kuhns L.R. (1976) Macrocranium and macrocephaly in neurofibromatosis. *Skeletal Radiol.*, 1: 25–8.

12.17 Hydrocephalus

Dilatation of the ventricular system, usually due to obstruction to CSF flow or absorption, rarely to overproduction in a choroid plexus papilloma or carcinoma.

Obstructive Hydrocephalus
May be of non-communicating type (obstruction at or proximal to the outlets of the 4th ventricle), or communicating (obstructed CSF flow in the subarachnoid space or arachnoid granulations).

NON-COMMUNICATING OBSTRUCTIVE HYDROCEPHALUS
Radiological features: ventricular dilatation proximal to an obstructing lesion, with flattening of cortical sulci and fissures. Periventricular radiolucency on CT (periventricular high signal on T_2W MRI), particularly when the rise in pressure is acute.
1. **Intraventricular 'mass'** – papilloma, ependymoma, intraventricular meningioma or glioma, subependymal nodules

in tuberous sclerosis*. At the foramen of Monro obstruction may result from a colloid cyst of the 3rd ventricle. The 3rd ventricle may be obstructed by pituitary tumours and craniopharyngioma, hypothalamic glioma, basilar artery ectasia and aneurysm.

2. **Aqueductal obstruction** – developmental stenosis, midbrain tumour or haemorrhage, tentorial meningioma, pineal region tumour, vein of Galen aneurysm.

3. **Fourth ventricular obstruction** – cerebellopontine angle tumours and arachnoid cysts, intrinsic tumours (including astrocytoma, ependymoma and medulloblastoma), congenital outlet obstruction or Dandy Walker syndrome, acquired outlet obstruction due to old haemorrhage or infection.

COMMUNICATING, OBSTRUCTIVE HYDROCEPHALUS

Radiological features: ventricular dilatation as above, but with widened extracerebral CSF spaces, particularly in the lower half of the cranial cavity, with relatively inconspicuous sulci over the high convexities. Intrathecal radionuclide tracer (^{131}In-DTPA or equivalent) persists up to 48 hours in the ventricles with delayed ascent over the convexities.

1. **Meningitis** – active or old, particularly tuberculous meningitis.

2. **Meningeal carcinomatosis** – including meningeal lymphoma and leukaemia and spread of CNS tumours such as ependymoma, medulloblastoma, pineal germinoma.

3. **Cerebral dural sinus thrombosis.**

4. **Idiopathic form in elderly patients** – 'intermittent' or 'normal pressure hydrocephalus', presenting with dementia, incontinence and gait apraxia.

Congenital Hydrocephalus

A complex condition incorporating one or more of the above factors. Obstruction is at aqueductal level in up to 40% of cases and may be associated with Chiari malformation. May be associated with various neural tube closure defects including meningocele, meningomyelocele and encephalocele.

Numerous genetic defects are associated with hydrocephalus (see 12.18).

12.18   Congenital Syndromes Associated with Enlarged Ventricles

Common
1. Achondroplasia*.
2. X-linked hydrocephalus syndrome.
3. Soto's syndrome – cerebral gigantism.
4. Acrocephalosyndactyly – types Apert and Pfeiffer.
5. Crouzon's syndrome.
6. Fetal alcohol syndrome.
7. Lissencephaly.
8. Osteopetrosis* – AR.

Uncommon
1. Metachromatic leukodystrophy.
2. Mucopolysaccharidoses IH and VI.
3. Thanatophoric dysplasia.

Further Reading
Jones K.L. (1988) *Smith's Recognizable Patterns of Human Malformation*, 4th edn., p. 710. Philadelphia: W.B. Saunders Company.
Taybi H. & Lachman R.S. (1990) *Radiology of Syndromes, Metabolic Disorders and Skeletal Dysplasias*. 3rd edn., p. 861. Chicago: Year Book Medical Publishers.

12.19 Wide Sutures

1. Birth to 1 month – suture width greater than 1 cm.
2. Over 3 months – suture width greater than 3 mm.
Beware the normal prominent coronal suture in infancy. If the sagittal suture is normal the appearance of the coronal suture is probably physiological.

Raised Intracranial Pressure
Suture diastasis only if onset before 10 years of age. May take only a few days to appear.
1. Space-occupying lesion.
2. Hydrocephalus.
3. Deprivational dwarfism – when children are removed from their deprived environment rebound growth of brain and skull occurs. Rapid brain growth results in raised intracranial pressure and separation of sutures.

Infiltration of the Sutures
1. Neuroblastoma – ± lucencies in skull vault and 'sunray' spiculation (a reaction to subpericranial deposits).
2. Leukaemia ⎫ in children.
3. Lymphoma* ⎭

Defective Ossification
1. Rickets*.
2. Renal osteodystrophy*.
3. Bone dysplasias with defective skull mineralization.

Further Reading
Capitanio M.A. & Kirkpatrick J.A. (1969) Widening of the cranial sutures, a roentgen observation during periods of accelerated growth in patients treated for deprivation dwarfism. *Radiology*, 92: 53–9.
Swischuk L.E. (1974) The growing skull. *Semin. Roentgenol.*, 9: 115–24.
Swischuk L.E. (1984) *Differential Diagnosis in Paediatric Radiology*, pp. 347–9. Baltimore: Williams and Wilkins.

12.20 Pneumocephalus

1. **Trauma** – major compound fractures of the skull vault allow entry of air. Fractures involving the frontal, ethmoidal or sphenoidal sinuses may allow air to enter the cranial cavity and fluid to collect in the sinuses (horizontal ray film essential for detection). CSF rhinorrhoea may occur (fluid tests positive for glucose).
2. **Iatrogenic** – postoperative or following pneumoencephalography.
3. **Osteoma of ethmoid sinus** – may erode the ethmoid roof, penetrating the dura to allow air to enter the cranial cavity.
4. **Tumours eroding the skull base arising in sinuses or nasopharynx.**
5. **Empty sella** – occasionally empty sella is complicated by the development of a spontaneous communication between the sella and the sphenoid sinus.

12.21 Small Pituitary Fossa

1. **Normal variant.**
2. **Dystrophia myotonica** – hereditary. Usually starts in early adult life. Cataracts, frontal baldness, testicular atrophy, thick skull and large frontal sinus.
3. **Radiotherapy as child.**
4. **Hypopituitarism.**

12.22 Expanded Pituitary Fossa

1. **Size** – normal range is: height 6.5–11 mm
                                    length 9–16 mm
                                    breadth 9–19 mm
2. **Double floor** – can be a normal variant (asymmetrical development) but a tumour should be suspected.
3. **Elevation/destruction of clinoid processes**.
4. **Loss of lamina dura**.

1. **Para/intrasellar mass**
   (a) Pituitary adenoma
       (i)   Null cell (non-functioning); commonest cause of expansion and commonest adenoma to produce suprasellar extension. 10% do not expand the sella.
       (ii) Eosinophilic (acromegaly); only slight expansion.
       (iii) Basophilic (Cushing's syndrome); virtually never expands.
   (b) Craniopharyngioma – 50% cause expansion – usually slight.
   (c) Prolactinoma – typically a blister on the antero-inferior wall. SXR abnormal in 20%. Tomography detects abnormality in 50%. CT useful for detecting superasellar extension.
       NB Other causes of hyperprolactinaemia are:
       (i)   Physiological – pregnancy.
       (ii) Drugs – phenothiazines, tricyclics, methyldopa, metoclopramide and oral contraceptives.
       (iii) Hypothalamic and stalk lesions – encephalitis, tumours, trauma and histiocytosis.
       (iv) Severe hypothyroidism.
       (v)   Renal failure.
   (d) Meningioma – usually produces sclerosis, but may cause erosion and expansion of the sella.
   (e) Aneurysm – well-defined pressure resorption of bone ± curvilinear calcification.
2. **Raised intracranial pressure** – due to dilated third ventricle.

(continued)

3. **Empty sella**
   (a) Primary – defect in diaphragma sellae allows pulsating CSF to expand the sella. Typically obese with hypertension. Headache common. Visual and endocrine defects uncommon. Associated with benign intracranial hypertension. SXR abnormal in 85% – symmetrical expansion with no erosion.
   (b) Secondary – pituitary tumour or treatment of a pituitary lesion may distort the diaphragma sellae.
4. **Nelson's syndrome** – post adrenalectomy for Cushing's syndrome.

Further Reading

Doyle F.H. (1979) Radiology of the pituitary fossa. In: Lodge T. & Steiner R.E. (eds) *Recent Advances in Radiology*, Vol. 6, pp. 121–43. Edinburgh, Churchill Livingstone.

Sage M.R., Chan E.S.H. & Reilly P.L. (1980) The clinical and radiological features of the empty sella syndrome. *Clin. Radiol.*, 31: 513–19.

Teasdale E., Macpherson P. & Teasdale G. (1981) The reliability of radiology in detecting prolactin-secreting pituitary microadenomas. *Br. J. Radiol.*, 54: 556–71.

12.23   J-shaped Sella

Flattened tuberculum sellae with a prominent sulcus chiasmaticus. Rare in adults.

1. **Normal variant** – 5% of normal children.
2. **Optic chiasm glioma** – if the chiasmatic sulcus is markedly depressed (W- or omega-shaped sella), the tumour may be bilateral.
3. **Chronic hydrocephalus** – due to downward pressure of an enlarged third ventricle.
4. **Mucopolysaccharidoses.**
5. **Achondroplasia*.**
6. **Neurofibromatosis*** – sphenoid dysplasia.

12.24 Erosion and Osteoporosis of the Sella, with no Expansion

1. **Erosion** – the earliest sign is interruption of the lamina dura at the base of the dorsum sellae. The line of the lamina dura should normally be complete, even in the elderly, and any defect is significant.
2. **Osteoporosis** (q.v.) – the cortex may become blurred.

Raised Intracranial Pressure (ICP) – commonest cause of erosion. (In children, suture diastasis is a more prominent sign.) 30% show this if raised ICP has been present more than 5–6 weeks. In 20% of those with X-ray changes papilloedema is not present.

Parasellar Masses
1. Craniopharyngioma.
2. Meningioma.
3. Pituitary adenoma.
4. Aneurysm.
5. Chordoma.
6. Metastases – kidney, bronchus, breast, prostate, malignant melanoma.
7. Local invasion – (e.g. carcinoma of the sphenoid or nasopharynx).

Generalized Decrease in Bone Density
1. Osteoporosis (q.v.).
2. Osteomalacia (q.v.).
3. Hyperparathyroidism.

Malignant Hypertension

12.25 Pituitary Mass Lesions

Indications for Pituitary Imaging
1. Hormonal abnormalities (75%)
   (a) Hyperprolactinaemia.
   (b) Acromegaly, pituitary gigantism.
   (c) Pituitary Cushing's disease.
   (d) Pituitary hyperthyroidism.
   (e) Infertility and menstrual disorders due to high FSH secretion.
2. Effects of a mass lesion (25%)
   (a) Visual failure.
   (b) Headache.
   (c) Cranial nerve palsies.
   (d) CSF rhinorrhoea.

Pituitary adenomas (macroadenoma > 10 mm; microadenoma < 10 mm)
1. Prolactin secreting (27%).
2. Growth hormone (GH) secreting (13%).
3. Mixed GH and prolactin (8%).
4. ACTH secreting (small) (10%).
5. FSH secreting (9%).
6. TSH secreting (1%).
7. Null cell and invasive types (34%).

Radiological Features of Pituitary Adenomas
1. Plain radiographs
   (a) Enlargement (ballooning) of the sella.
   (b) Erosion of the clinoids and dorsum sellae.
   (c) Calcification (rare).
2. In microadenomas
   (a) Mass in gland, hypo-attenuating (CT) and hypointense (T_1W, MRI) relative to normal gland.
   (b) Mass shows less enhancement than normal gland (CT and MRI).
   (c) Displacement of infundibulum (stalk) (CT and MRI).
   (d) Bulging upper surface of gland.
3. In macroadenomas
   (a) Sellar erosion (on CT).
   (b) Enlargement of gland into sphenoidal air sinus.

   (c)   Mass arising out of sella, hyperdense on CT, isointense on T_1W MRI. Areas of cystic change due to necrosis are commonly seen.

   (d)   Contrast enhancement, often heterogeneous, on CT and MRI.

   (e)   Displacement/compression of optic chiasm (better seen on MRI than CT).

   (f)   Compression of anterior end of 3rd ventricle, sometimes with hydrocephalus.

   (g)   Cavernous sinus invasion (CT, MRI and angiography). Difficult to recognize in some cases; best evidence of non-invasion is preservation of normal pituitary tissue between gland and cavernous sinus.

   (h)   Haemorrhage in tumour (seen as hyperintense areas on MRI) in up to 25% of cases and in up to 50% after bromocriptine therapy.

4. **Additional information required from imaging to help plan surgery**
    (a) Anatomy of the sphenoid sinus.
    (b) Anatomy of the optic and carotid canals.
    (c) Detection of cavernous and intradural aneurysms.
    (d) Position of the optic chiasm relative to the microadenoma.
    (e) Anatomy of the carotid arteries.

5. **Complications**
    (a) Invasion (hypothalamus, cavernous sinus, sphenoid sinus).
    (b) Infarction (spontaneous; pituitary apoplexy); also haemorrhage and infarction following bromocriptine.
    (c) Metastasis (subarachnoid and haematogenous; both rare).

6. **Other pituitary and related diseases**
    (a) Pituitary hyperplasia – in infancy, adolescence and pregnancy. May be drug induced, due to tumours, idiopathic or secondary to hypothyroidism.
    (b) Craniopharyngioma.
    (c) Rathke cleft cysts.
    (d) Parasellar meningioma.
    (e) Diabetes insipidus.

(*continued*)

(f) Pituitary dwarfism.
(g) Other rare pituitary disorders:

Aplasia and hypoplasia	Abscess
Duplication	Cysticercosis
Melanoma	Sarcoidosis*
Germinoma	Erdheim–Chester disease
Choristoma	Langerhans cell histiocytosis*
Glioma	Blastomycosis
Familial amenorrhoea/ galactorrhoea	Tuberculosis
MEN Type I (Werner syndrome)*	Wegener's granulomatosis
Tolosa–Hunt syndrome	Amyloidosis
Lymphocytic adeno- hypophysitis	Hurler's syndrome*
Haemochromatosis	Aneurysm
Carotico-cavernous fistula	Orbital granuloma

Further Reading

Elster A.D. (1993) Modern imaging of the pituitary. *Radiology*, 187: 1–14.

Kucharczyk W. (1992) The pituitary gland: 'bright spots' and 'dark spots'. In: *ARRS Neuroradiology Categorical Course Syllabus* (ed. M.S. Huckman). Reston: American Roentgen Ray Society, pp. 47–56.

12.26 Cerebral Calcification

Tumours

1. **Meningioma** – vary from small granular calcifications to dense involvement of the whole mass.
2. **Craniopharyngioma** – largely confined to childhood cases.
3. **Oligodendroglioma** – coarse amorphous masses.
4. **Astrocytoma** – occasional granular deposits in the more malignant variants.
5. **Choroid plexus papilloma** – commonly calcify.
6. **Ganglioglioma and ependymoma** – occasional slight calcification.
7. **Pineal tumours** – all types calcify, particularly teratoma.
8. **Chordoma** – usually calcifies.
9. **Lipoma of corpus callosum** – coarse marginal calcifications which are a feature on plain films and CT.
10. **Metastases** – particularly adenocarcinoma and osteosarcoma.

Vascular Lesions

1. **Atheroma** – seen in larger vessels (carotid, middle cerebral, vertebral and basilar arteries).
2. **Aneurysms** – curvilinear calcification is a feature, especially in giant aneurysms.
3. **Arteriovenous malformations** – nodular calcifications often seen.
4. **Venous malformations** – small nodular and linear calcifications.
5. **Cavernous malformations** – nodular calcifications.
6. **Sturge–Weber syndrome** – gyral pattern of calcification, especially in the occipital lobe. (Gyral calcification may also be observed in tuberous sclerosis*, following cerebral infarction, purulent meningitis and viral encephalitis, following craniospinal irradiation and intrathecal methotrexate therapy of leukaemia.)

Infections

1. **Cysticercosis** – cystic lesions particularly at the grey/white matter interface. Calcification (about 5 mm diameter) follows death of the scolex.
2. **Toxoplasmosis** – the congenital form causes calcifications in subependymal, basal ganglion and peripheral locations.

(continued)

The opportunistic form (in AIDS, lymphoma, immunosuppression) rarely calcifies.
3. **CMV** – the congenital form causes multifocal calcification. The opportunistic form does not calcify.
4. **Tuberculosis** – intracerebral granulomas and meningeal deposits calcify, particularly after therapy.
5. **Fungal infections** – cryptococcus, aspergillus, nocardia and mucormycosis rarely calcify.

Miscellaneous
1. **Methotrexate encephalopathy (subacute necrotizing encephalopathy)** – a complication seen particularly when radiation has also been used, especially in childhood leukaemia.
2. **Infarction** – occasionally leads to dystrophic calcification.
3. **Tuberous sclerosis*** – causes calcifications in subependymal nodules and in tubers which may lie anywhere in the brain, most commonly frontal.
4. **Basal ganglion calcification** – includes many of the above together with hypo-, pseudohypo- and pseudopseudohypoparathyroidism, Cockayne's syndrome (microcephaly, truncal dwarfism and progeria), Wilson's disease, Fahr's disease (presentation in childhood with choreoathetoid movements and progressive mental retardation), anoxia, lead poisoning and carbon monoxide poisoning. Idiopathic calcification increases in incidence with age and is asymptomatic.

Further Reading

Kapila A. (1984) Calcification in cerebral infarction. *Radiology*, 153: 685.
Kendall B. & Cavanagh N. (1986) Intracranial calcifications in paediatric computed tomography. *Neuroradiology*, 28: 324–30.
Ketonen L. & Koskiniemi M.-L. (1983) Gyriform calcification after herpes simplex virus encephalitis. *J. Comp. Assist. Tomogr.*, 7: 1070–72.
Reyes P.F., Gonzalez C.F., Zalewska M.K. & Besarab A. (1986) Intracranial calcification in adults with chronic lead exposure. *Am. J. Roentgenol.*, 146: 267–70.
Wilms G., Van Wijck E., Demaerel Ph., Smet M.-H., Plets C. & Brucher J.M. (1992) Gyriform calcifications in tuberous sclerosis simulating the appearance of Sturge–Weber disease. *Am. J. Neuroradiol.*, 13: 295.

12.27 Differences between MR Imaging and CT

Computed tomography	*Magnetic resonance imaging*
Radiation exposure to patient	No radiation exposure
Hazard small but measurable	No known hazard to patient
Few contraindications other than considerations of radiation exposure in the young, and in pregnancy	Contraindicated in those with a cardiac pacemaker, cochlear implant, ferrous intraocular foreign body, some aneurysm clips and prosthetic heart valves
Most patients tolerate procedure without any problem	About 10% of patients claustrophic to some degree
Single factor influences image formation (linear attenuation coefficient of tissues)	Image formation influenced by many factors including: T1 relaxation rate T2 relaxation rate Proton density Blood and CSF flow Pulse sequence
Easy to use for patients in a critical condition and on life support	Difficult to use in emergency situations
Excellent bone images	Bone imaging limited: compact bone generates no MR signal
Soft-tissue contrast limited in some organs	Excellent soft-tissue contrast in most organs
Artefacts due to motion, and to radio-dense structures, including cortical bone and metal	Artefacts due to motion, blood flow, CSF flow, metal and other high magnetic susceptibility materials, aliasing, truncation and many other effects

(continued)

Fast imaging readily available (slice acquisition time of less than 2 seconds)	Fast scanning not available on most scanners in current use
Data acquired slice by slice (except for latest spiral scanners)	Data acquired as blocks of tissue by simultaneous multislice methods
Primary section plane axial. Coronal possible in cranium	Any section plane possible, but field of view must exceed dimensions of scanned volume in phase encoding direction to avoid aliasing
Still relatively inexpensive but top of the range scanners are now very costly with increasing clinical demands for speed and versatility	Still relatively expensive, but lower cost scanners of limited performance are available

12.28   CT Attenuation of Cerebral Masses

(Relative to normal brain)

Hyperdense
1. **Neoplasms**
   (a) Meningioma 95%.
   (b) Microglioma (primary lymphoma).
   (c) Metastases 30%.
   (d) Glioma 10% (most glioblastomas show mixed attenuation).
   (e) Ependymoma.
   (f) Papilloma.
   (g) Medulloblastoma 80%.
   (h) Pituitary adenoma 25%.
   (i) Craniopharyngioma (if solid).
   (j) Acoustic neuroma 5%.
2. **Haematoma** – if ≤ 2 weeks old.
3. **Giant aneurysm.**
4. **Colloid cyst** – 50%.

Isodense
1. **Neoplasms**
   (a) Acoustic neuroma 95%.
   (b) Pituitary adenoma 65%.
   (c) Glioma 10%.
   (d) Metastases 10%.
   (e) Chordoma.
   (f) Pinealoma.
2. **Haematoma** – if 2–4 weeks old.
3. **Tuberculoma.**
4. **Colloid cyst** – 50%.

Hypodense
1. **Tumours**
   (a) Craniopharyngioma.
   (b) Glioma (95% of astrocytomas).
   (c) Metastases.
   (d) Prolactinoma.
   (e) Haemangioblastoma.   (*continued*)

Hypodense

   Tumours (*continued*)
   (f)   Lipoma.
   (g)   Epidermoid.
   (h)   Dermoid.
2. **Haematoma** – ± if > 4 weeks old.
3. **Abscess** – pyogenic.
4. **Tuberculoma.**
5. **Cyst**
   (a)   Arachnoid.
   (b)   Porencephalic.
   (c)   Hydatid.

12.29 CT Appearances of Cerebral Masses

A

Tumours	Attenuation (μ)	Surrounding oedema	Contrast enhancement
Glioma	Increased or decreased (if cystic/necrotic)	Yes	95% if high grade; relatively infrequent in low grade; often *irregular ring*, but may be homogeneous or patchy
Metastases	Increased or decreased; often multifocal	Yes, extensive	Marked; may be *irregular ring*, homogeneous or patchy
Meningioma	Increased; multifocal in 5%	Minimal, perifocal (moderate in 20%)	Marked, homogeneous
Microglioma (i.e. primary lymphoma)	Increased (occasionally decreased, infiltrating); multifocal 50%	Yes	Marked, homogeneous
Pituitary adenoma	Isodense 65%; increased 25%	No	Marked, homogeneous
Prolactinoma	Hypodense	No	No
Craniopharyngioma	Decreased if cystic; increased if solid	No	± moderate homogeneous (solid), or *ring* (cystic)
Pinealoma	Isodense	No	Marked, homogeneous
Acoustic neuroma	Isodense 95%; increased 5%	No	Marked, homogeneous

Tumours	Attenuation (μ)	Surrounding oedema	Contrast enhancement
Epidermoid (cholesteatoma)	Decreased	No	No
Medulloblastoma	Increased	Minimal, perifocal	Moderate, homogeneous
Haemangioblastoma	Decreased	Minimal	Moderate, homogeneous
Dermoid	Decreased	No	No
Chordoma	Isodense, poorly defined	No	Variable
Lipoma	Decreased	No	No
Papilloma	Increased	No	Marked, homogeneous
Ependymoma	Increased	May occur	± patchy
Glomus jugulare	Isodense	No	Moderate

B

Infections	Attenuation (μ)	Surrounding oedema	Contrast enhancement
Pyogenic abscess	Decreased	Yes	*Regular ring* (thin-walled)
Tuberculoma	Decreased or isodense; often multifocal	Yes	*Regular* or *irregular ring*; ± central ('target') enhancement characteristic
Hydatid	Decreased	No	No

C

Vascular	Attenuation (μ)	Surrounding oedema	Contrast enhancement
Giant aneurysm	Increased	No	*Ring* or homogeneous
Arteriovenous malformation	± patchy increased	± patchy low attenuation due to surrounding infarcts	± marked, sinuous
Haematoma	Increased if fresh (isodense at 2 weeks; ± decreased at 4 weeks)	No	No (some peripheral enhancement may occur during the resorption phase)

D

Cysts	Attenuation (μ)	Surrounding oedema	Contrast enhancement
Colloid	Increased 50%; isodense 50%	No	No
Arachnoid	Decreased (CSF)	No	No
Porencephalic	Decreased (CSF)	No	No

Further Reading

Lange S., Grumme T. & Meese W. (1980) *Computerized Tomography of the Brain*. Berlin: Schering A.G. Medico-scientific book series.

12.30 MRI Characteristics of Intracranial Contents

1. Normal

Cerebrospinal fluid: T_1W, dark (long T1, low signal)
T_2W bright (long T2, high signal)

Grey matter: T_1W dark grey (long/intermediate T1)
T_2W light grey (long/intermediate T2)

White matter: T_1W light grey (short/intermediate T1)
T_2W dark grey (short/intermediate T2)

Areas with high iron content (anterior white matter, basal ganglia, red nuclei etc.) T_2W very dark grey (short T2)

2. Pathological

Meningioma T_1W Isointense with grey matter hyperintense after gadolinium
T_2W Isointense or slightly hyperintense with grey matter. Perifocal hyperintensity due to oedema

Glioma T_1W Mixed hypointense (cystic areas) and isointense (solid areas) May contain hyperintense areas due to haemorrhage.
Variable enhancement after gadolinium according to malignancy: malignant gliomas enhance in solid areas. Some more benign lesions also enhance.

Metastases T_1W Hypointense (cystic areas) or isointense (solid areas). Perifocal

		hypointensity due to oedema. Solid areas usually enhance to a marked degree after gadolinium
	T_2W	Iso- or hyperintense, with marked perifocal hyperintensity due to oedema
Cranio-pharyngioma, dermoid, lipoma	T_1W	Fat containing areas very hyperintense. Calcified areas very hypointense. Solid areas isointense
	T_2W	Fat containing areas hypointense. Calcified areas very hypointense

Further Reading

Gado M. (1992) MRI of the brain: signal intensity patterns. In: *ARRS Neuroradiology Categorical Course Syllabus* (ed. M.S. Huckman). Reston: American Roentgen Ray Society, pp. 1–8.

12.31   MRI Brain – Signal Intensities

Hyperintense T1, Hyperintense T2
1. Chronic haematoma.
2. Flowing blood.
3. Normal posterior pituitary.
4. Cholesterol – e.g. in cholesteatoma, craniopharyngioma or dermoid.

Hyperintense T1, Hypointense T2
1. Subacute haematoma.
2. Blood flow.
3. Haemorrhagic metastases – choriocarcinoma, thyroid carcinoma, renal cell carcinoma.
4. Melanoma metastases.

Hypo-/Isointense T1, Hypointense T2
1. Acute haematoma.
2. Blood flow.
3. Calcification.
4. Metastases – colon, prostate, breast.
5. Meningioma.

Hypo-/Isointense T1, Hyperintense T2
1. Glial neoplasms.
2. Metastases.
3. Oedema – infarction, cerebritis, encephalitis, peritumoral.
4. Lymphoma.
5. Gliosis.
6. Meningioma.
7. Neuroma.
8. Pituitary adenoma.

Isointense T1 and T2
1. Haematoma – acute (0.5T), subacute (1.5T).
2. Blood flow.
3. Metastases.

No Signal T1 and T2
1. High flow.
2. Air or gas.
3. Haemosiderin.
4. Metal.
5. Bone.
6. Ligaments and tendons.

Further Reading
Pomeranz S.J. (1990) *Gamuts and Pearls in MRI*. Cincinnati: Images Unlimited Inc.

12.32   Hyperechoic Lesions in the Basal Ganglia of Neonates and Infants

Single punctate, multiple punctate or stripe-like densities.

1. **Congenital infections** – CMV, toxoplasmosis, rubella, HIV and syphilis.
2. **Asphyxia.**
3. **Chromosome disorders.**
4. **Idiopathic.**

Further Reading

Teele R.L., Hernanz-Schulman M. & Sorel A. (1988) Echogenic vasculature in the basal ganglia of neonates: a sonographic sign of vasculopathy. *Radiology*, 169: 423.

Weber K., Riebel Th. & Nasir R. (1992) Hyperechoic lesions in the basal ganglia: an incidental sonographic finding in neonates and infants. *Pediatr. Radiol.*, 22: 182–6.

12.33 Hyperdense Choroid Plexus on CT in a Child

1. **Calcification** – normal in an adult. Unusual < 10 years and when bilateral consider neurofibromatosis*.
2. **Haemorrhage** – in the neonate the incidence is inversely proportional to the gestational age.
3. **Haemangioma**.
4. **Choroid plexus neoplasm**.
5. **Aortic obstruction in the newborn** – upper extremity hypertension results in increased cerebral blood flow.

Further Reading

Doe F.D., Shuangsoti S. & Netsky M.G. (1972) Cryptic hemangioma of the choroid plexus: a cause of intraventricular hemorrhage. *Neurology*, 22: 1232.

Modic M.T., Weinstein M.A., Rothner A.D., Erenberg G., Duchesneau P.M. & Kaufman B. (1980) Calcification of the choroid plexus visualized by computed tomography. *Radiology*, 135: 369.

Rand J.C., Burton E.M., Tonkin I.L.D. & DiSessa T.G. (1990) The hyperdense choroid plexus: a CT finding associated with aortic arch obstruction in the newborn. *Pediatr. Radiol.*, 21: 2–4.

Reeder J.D., Kaude J.V. & Setzer E.S. (1982) Choroid plexus hemorrhage in premature neonates; recognition by sonography. *Am. J. Neuroradiol.*, 3: 619.

12.34   Surface Enhancement of the Brain

Rim or Linear Enhancement

Indicates the presence of an abnormal fluid collection over the surface of the brain. The enhancing rim is either a segment of normal dura displaced by an extradural collection or arachnoid membrane displaced by a subdural collection.

1. Haematoma.
2. Empyema – a thick and/or serpiginous outline differentiates a subdural empyema from an uninfected subdural haematoma.

Gyriform Enhancement

WIDESPREAD i.e. DISSEMINATED MENINGEAL DISEASE
No mass effect; no accompanying oedema.

1. Infection – viral, bacterial or tuberculous.
2. Tumour – primary or secondary.
3. Sarcoidosis*.
4. Lymphoma*.

FOCAL

1. Arteriovenous malformation.
2. Infarction
3. Encephalitis   } parenchymal lesions infiltrating the cortex and obliterating the sulci.
4. Glioma

Basal Cistern Enhancement

1. Tuberculous meningitis – often accompanied by hydrocephalus and infarction which are bad prognostic indicators.
2. Meningeal neoplasms.
3. Torulosis.

Further Reading

Burrows E.H. (1985) Surface enhancement of the brain. *Clin. Radiol.*, 36: 233–9.
Sze G. (1993) Diseases of the intracranial meninges: MR imaging features. *Am. J. Roentgenol.*, 160: 727–33.

12.35 Multiple Cerebral Enhancing Lesions on CT and MRI

Contrast uptake is seen in tumours, inflammatory granulation tissue and in areas of damage to the blood–brain barrier.

1. **Metastases** – a common feature of disseminated malignancy. Breast and bronchial primary tumours are most often responsible. Deposits may be solid or cystic with marginal (ring) enhancement. In these cases the wall of the cysts is sometimes irregular in thickness. Perifocal oedema is often extensive and accounts for much of the mass effect. Solitary metastases occur and are most often seen in the posterior fossa. Calcification is uncommon and msot often seen in adenocarcinoma. Hyperdensity, pre-contrast is seen in melanoma and adenocarcinoma. Haemorrhage is infrequent and seen in melanoma and hypernephroma.
2. **Abscess** – seen in cyanotic congenital heart disease, pulmonary AVMs, bronchiectasis, immunosuppression, intravenous drug abusers and many other causes of septicaemia. Ring enhancing mass lesions with very marked perifocal oedema, with small lesions appearing solid. The wall of the lesion is thinner and more constant in thickness than is the case with metastases.
3. **Cerebral gliomatosis** – most cases are of low histological grade and cause multifocal low density on CT without enhancement. Some contrast uptake may, nevertheless, be seen on MRI.
4. **Infarction** – contrast enhancement after 2 weeks or so following the ictus increases the sensitivity of CT and MRI in the detection of infarction. Unsuspected multiple infarcts may be revealed in cases of recognized single lesions. Enhancement is typically gyral, serpiginous or, in deeper lesions, irregular with nodular areas. Mass effect and perifocal oedema is slight or absent.
5. **Demyelinating plaques** – low density on CT and bright on T_2W MRI. Predominantly seen in periventricular white matter and rarely recognized elsewhere on CT, though seen in the brain-stem and cerebellum on MRI. Contrast uptake, sometimes marginal and sometimes diffuse, on both MRI and CT in the acute phase.

(continued)

6. **Contusion** – as in infarction, contrast studies after 2 weeks
   or so increase the sensitivity of detection of contused areas
   on MR and CT studies.

12.36 Intracranial Infection

Infection may be extradural, subdural, meningeal or intracerebral.

1. **Extradural abscess** – a complication of compound fracture or cranial surgery. Rarely haematogenous or due to direct spread from paranasal sinuses or mastoids. *CT and MRI findings*: lentiform extracerebral fluid collection separated from brain by thick enhancing membrane.

2. **Subdural abscess** – some are due to haematogenous spread but most are due to direct spread from sinuses or mastoid. Some are the result of incompletely treated meningitis. The patient is febrile, toxic, drowsy and epileptic seizures are common. *CT and MRI findings*: hypodense or isodense layer of fluid in the subdural space, crescentic on the convexity, linear in the interhemispheric space. Contrast enhancement is seen but is relatively subtle in the early stages when the membrane is thin and incomplete. The abscess is easily overlooked, especially in unenhanced studies. A high level of suspicion must be maintained as early diagnosis is vital. Neglected cases progress to cortical thrombophlebitis and venous infarction with secondary abscess formation.

3. **Cerebral abscess** – discrete abscess is preceded by diffuse infection (cerebritis). Most follow sinusitis or mastoid infection with some arising by haematogenous spread (intracardiac shunts, pulmonary arteriovenous malformations (AVMs), bronchiectasis, endocarditis, i.v. drug abuse, septicaemia). Haematogenous lesions are usually central; those due to direct spread are most commonly cerebellar, temporal or anterior, inferior frontal. In the latter, brain infection is preceded by cortical thrombophlebitis. *CT and MRI finding*: diffuse irregularly enhancing mass, resolving into a low density (low signal T_1W) cavity with an intensely enhancing margin (dense on CT, bright on T_1W). May be multilocular. Surrounding oedema (low density on CT, low signal on T_1W, bright on T_2W). Intracranial tuberculosis may be meningeal (see below) or focal intracerebral – a tuberculoma. This is a solid or cavitating, intensely enhancing mass often with perifocal oedema. May be multiple.

(continued)

4. **Meningitis** – may be lymphocytic, pyogenic, granulomatous or fungal. The diagnosis of lymphocytic and bacterial types is clinical. Radiology is used only to assess
brain swelling prior to lumbar puncture, to exclude
abscess and ventriculitis, to look at the sinuses and mastoids and to monitor the development of infarction and
hydrocephalus.

CT: may show isodense or hyperdense cisterns with
enhancement. Small ventricles are due to brain swelling
or may dilate if hydrocephalus ensues. Meningeal
enhancement over the convexity is occasionally seen.

In granulomatous meningitis due to tuberculosis or sarcoidosis and in fungal meningitis (cryptococcus, nocardia,
candida, aspergillus, actinomycosis), the exudate is
thicker and enhancement is more intense. Cerebral infarction is common. Enhancing intracerebral mass(es) may be
seen in sarcoidosis and tuberculosis.

5. **Encephalitis** – diffuse inflammation of the brain of viral
origin. Most are due to herpes simplex (HSV-1 in adults,
HSV-2 in neonates). High mortality and morbidity. Early
treatment (with acyclovir) is vital. Diagnosis clinical with
typical findings on electroencephalography. Biopsy for-
merly advocated but now regarded as unnecessarily invasive.

CT: changes confirmatory and prognostic. Early
changes consist of low density, often temporal and unilateral. *MRI*: high signal on T_2W and more sensitive than
CT. Limbic system often involved. In uncontrolled infection, cystic encephalomalacia develops, with gyral
enhancement. In end stage there is severe atrophy.

6. **AIDS** – diffuse infection of the CNS occurs in HIV infection, causing global atrophy. Opportunistic infection is
common and the usual organism is toxoplasma.
Abscesses occur which are often multiple (NB radiologically similar to lymphoma which is also a complication of
HIV infection; biopsy is advocated). Opportunistic viral
infections also occur (herpes simplex and zoster), together
with progressive multifocal leukoencephalopathy. *CT and
MRI findings*: abscesses and acute inflammation but MRI
is more sensitive for white matter disease. Cryptococcal
meningitis is common and may be terminal.

7. **Acute disseminated encephalomyelitis** – an autoimmune

process which follows measles, mumps, varicella, pertussis etc., including vaccinations. *CT and MRI findings*: multifocal white matter changes – low density on CT, high signal on T$_2$W MRI.

8. **Subacute sclerosing encephalomyelitis** – slowly progressive post-measles syndrome of unknown pathology. White matter changes are best seen on MRI; no enhancement.

9. **Progressive multifocal leukoencephalopathy** – papovavirus infection occurring in immunosuppressed patients. Causes demyelination mainly of the posterior hemispheric white matter.

10. **Congenital infection** – cytomegalovirus infection is common and CNS infection occurs in 10% of cases. Periventricular calcification, cerebellar hypoplasia, porencephaly, polymicrogyria and hydraencephaly are seen. Toxoplasmosis is transmitted to pregnant mothers from cats and causes severe fetal infection. Calcifications occur around the ventricles, in basal ganglia and in the hemispheres, where severe necrotizing lesions may also be seen.

11. **Parasitic infections** – cysticercosis (*Taenia solium*) affects the CNS in 90% of cases. In the early stages numerous small low density lesions are seen on CT or MRI, with enhancement. Later, degenerate lesions appear either solid or as small or large cystic structures with ring enhancement after contrast. Calcification common and is seen on CT and plain radiographs but not MRI. Hydrocephalus may occur. Muscle calcifications are a common accompaniment.

Hydatid disease (*Taenia echinococcus*) affects the brain in only 2% of cases. Usual feature is a large cyst; calcification is uncommon; no enhancement.

Further Reading

Stevens J.M. (1990) Infections of the central nervous system. In: Butler P. (ed.) *Imaging of the Nervous System*, Chapter 5. London: Springer-Verlag.

12.37   Posterior Fossa Neoplasms in Childhood

50–60% of paediatric cerebral tumours. Majority arise within the 4th ventricle and cerebellum. Cerebellar astrocytomas, medulloblastomas and ependymomas present with symptoms of raised intracranial pressure and ataxia. Brain-stem gliomas involve the cranial nerve nuclei and long tracts at an early stage.

1. **Cerebellar astrocytoma** – 20–25% of posterior fossa tumours. Vermis (50%) or hemispheres (20%) or both sites (30%) ± extension into the cavity of 4th ventricle. Calcification in 20%.

   CT

   Large lesion displacing 4th ventricle → obstructive hydro-cephalus. Cystic type (80%) – well-defined cyst > CSF attenuation. 50% have a mural nodule (usually iso-dense) which shows enhancement or a multicystic mass with enhancement of the main bulk of the tumour, cyst walls and cerebellum beyond the cysts. Larger tumour at diag-nosis than the solid type. Solid type (20%) – low density lesion with less well-defined margins; more inhomo-geneous. Homogeneous, ring or no enhancement. May only be detected by the surrounding oedema.

   CT will detect recurrence long before onset of symp-toms. Attenuation of recurrent cystic tumour is double that of CSF.

2. **Medulloblastoma** – 50% occur in first decade; second peak in adults. 20–40% of all posterior fossa tumours. In child-hood – 85% are midline; adults – more laterally in the cerebellar hemispheres. Increased incidence in basal cell naevus syndrome.

   CT

   Moderately well-defined, ovoid or spherical mass; slightly > surrounding cerebellum; rim of oedema. Usually uni-form enhancement; non-enhancement rarely. Calcification (in 10%) is usually small, homogeneous and eccentric. Dystrophic calcification occurs after radiotherapy. Small cystic or necrotic areas are unusual.

   Dissemination by (1) seeding of the subarachnoid space, (2) retrograde ventricular extension or (3) extracranial metastases bone, lymph nodes or soft tissues.

Recurrence of tumour is demonstrated by (1) enhancement at the site of the lesion, (2) enhancement of the subarachnoid space (basal cisterns, Sylvian, fissures, sulci and ependymal surfaces of ventricles, or (3) progressive ventricular enlargement.

3. **Ependymoma** – most commonly in the floor of the 4th ventricle. Usually solitary but may be multiple in neurofibromatosis.

   CT

   Variable features. 80% isodense; non-homogeneous or homogeneous enhancement. Calcification in 50% – small round calculi. Calcification within a 4th ventricular mass or adjacent to the 4th ventricle ≡ ependymoma. Small lucencies in 50%.

4. **Brain-stem glioma** – insidious onset because of the location and tendency to infiltrate cranial nerve nuclei and long tracts without producing CSF obstruction until late. Pons > midbrain. They frequently extend down into medulla and cervical cord, up into thalamus or posterolaterally along the cerebellar peduncle into the hemisphere.

   CT

   Usually low density, either same as or lower than adjacent tissue. Non-homogeneous contrast enhancement minimum–moderate. Calcification is extremely uncommon. May be cystic.

5. **Choroid plexus papilloma** – commonest in the lateral ventricle but may be in 4th.

12.38   Extra-axial Posterior Fossa Mass Lesions

The majority lie in the cerebellopontine angle (CPA).

1. **Acoustic neuroma** – (80%). Most present in middle age, commoner in females (2 : 1). Bilateral lesions in neurofibromatosis 2 (NF-2), younger presentation. Low or iso-attenuating mass in the CPA (low or iso-signal on T_1W, iso- or high signal on T_2W MRI), with enhancement (small non-enhanced areas due to necrosis often seen. Entirely cystic tumours are uncommon). Erosion of bony IAM seen in the majority of tumours > 1.5 cm on plain radiography and > 1 cm on CT. Tumours < 1 cm not consistently shown by CT, but essentially all are shown by contrast enhanced MRI, including intracanalicular tumours. Large tumours may cause hydrocephalus.

2. **Meningioma** – (10%). Occurs along posterior surface of petrous temporal bone (including CPA), along the clivus, from the edge of the tentorial hiatus, and in the foramen magnum. General characteristics similar to acoustic neuroma, and in CPA differentiation may be difficult. Erosion of porus and widening of IAM points to acoustic neuroma, hyperostosis suggests meningioma. Meningioma generally more vascular on angiography, but this is not reliable for differentiation. At other sites pathognomonic appearances are generally obtained.

3. **Dermoid** – (5%). Low or mixed attenuation mass, most commonly seen in CPA. MRI may show areas of high signal on T_1W images due to fatty contents. Some components may show contrast enhancement on CT and MRI. Mass often extends forwards and upwards through the tentorial hiatus. Bone erosion commonly seen.

4. **Chordoma** – (1%). Most intracranial chordomas relate to the clivus which they erode and invade. A soft-tissue mass showing areas of amorphous calcification displaces the brain-stem posteriorly. Contrast enhancement is usually seen.

5. **Others** – (4%). Metastases of meningeal or bony origin occur, most often from breast or bronchial primary. A paraganglioma of glomus jugulare may extend into cranial cavity from the jugular fossa, forming an enhancing tumour mass. Arachnoid cysts occur in the CP angle, and must be distinguished from a dermoid tumour (see above).

In addition to acoustic nerve tumours, neuromas of the 5th and 7th nerves are seen.

Further Reading

Hasso A.N. & Smith D.S. (1989) The cerebellopontine angle. *Semin. Ultrasound CT MR*, 10: 280–301.

12.39   Features of Acoustic Neuromas

10% of all intracranial tumours; 80% of cerebellopontine angle (CPA) tumours.

Age range 40–60 years; M : F2 : 1

Isolated lesions, or bilateral in neurofibromatosis 2*. Most are schwannomas of the sheath of the vestibular nerve.

Most present with progressive deafness, tinnitus and, less commonly, vertigo.

Radiological Features

1. Enlargement of the internal auditory meatus (seen on the perorbital radiograph, tomogram or CT scan). Plain film criteria, in case of difficulty: canal on the affected side is 1 mm greater in height and 2 mm greater in length. A flared or trumpet-like shape may be seen.
2. Isodense enhancing mass on CT, closely related to the inner end of the internal auditory canal (porus acousticus internus). Tumours > 1 cm may be seen but below this size are not reliably detected. Necrosis and cyst formation are seen occasionally in large tumours. Calcification is not a feature. Large tumours indent the pons and displace the 4th ventricle, leading in some cases to hydrocephalus.
3. CT–air meatography (using 3–4 ml of air in the CPA introduced by lumbar puncture) will detect very small extra-meatal masses and will show non-filling of the meatus with air in intrameatal lesions. Conventional pneumography is obsolete.
4. MRI is definitive. Most tumours can be shown on axial and coronal images with T_2 weighting. Virtually all are shown on gadolinium-enhanced T_1W images.

Differential Diagnosis

1. **CPA meningioma** – may be difficult to differentiate when related to the porus. Others are more posteriorly placed. Similar characteristics in general to acoustic neuroma but may show 'dural tail' (see 12.42). Less vascular on angiography than supratentorial meningiomas and may be indistinguishable on angiography.

2. **Facial nerve neuroma** – rare when compared with acoustic neuroma but is indistinguishable.
3. **Metastases** – in the CPA are rare but could cause confusion with an acoustic neuroma.

12.40   Midline Supratentorial Masses

1. **Lipoma of corpus callosum** – developmental mass of fat density and attenuation value on CT, with dense marginal calcification, involving genu and a variable amount of the body of the corpus callosum with partial agenesis. Lesion is of high signal intensity on unenhanced T_1W MR images.

2. **Colloid cyst of third ventricle** – isodense or hyperdense spherical mass in anterior 3rd ventricle on unenhanced CT causing hydrocephalus. Reports of enhancement very improbable. Hydrocephalus sparing 3rd and 4th ventricles should alert suspicion, and if the CT is negative (in an isodense lesion), MR should be performed; cysts are of low signal on T_1W and bright on T_2W images.

3. **Giant cell astrocytoma** – tumour associated with tuberous sclerosis is characteristically located close to foramen of Monro. Usually non-enhancing tumour of low histological grade.

4. **Pineal tumours**
   (a) *Germ cell tumours* account for 50%: germinoma is the most common type, mostly male adolescents. Slow growing circumscribed mass, with homogeneous enhancement on CT and MRI. Hydrocephalus results; other symptoms relate to upper midbrain invasion (defective upward gaze and convergence). Teratomas less common: may show soft-tissue, cystic, fatty and calcific material, and may enhance in part.
   (b) *Neuroectodermal tumours* (pinealoma and pineoblastoma) are indistinguishable from germinoma. Equal incidence in males and females. Slow growing except for blast cell type.
   (c) *Small pineal cysts* are a common incidental finding on MR studies.

5. **Basilar artery ectasia and aneurysm** – a dilated basilar artery may extend up into the posterior third ventricle and cause obstruction to the flow of cerebrospinal fluid.

6. **Vein of Galen aneurysm** – present in infancy, and in childhood. Infant type is a high flow AV fistula, with a distended midline venous sac (despite the name probably not the vein of Galen). It presents with rapid head growth due to hydrocephalus, resulting from high cerebral venous pressure; occasionally cardiac failure due to huge shunt.

Older patients are either of the same type, albeit with a smaller shunt, or are local parenchymal arteriovenous malformations, with vein of Galen dilatation.

7. **Tentorial hiatus meningioma** – eccentrically placed, often partially below tentorium, isodense enhancing tumour mass.

12.41   Intraventricular Masses

10% of all intracranial neoplasms.

Atrium of Lateral Ventricle
1. **Meningioma** – most frequent in older women. Enhancement ++ on CT. Tumour blush on angiography. Peritumoral oedema.
2. **Astrocytoma** – less enhancement and less vascular.
3. **Choroid plexus papilloma** – very vascular. Hydrocephalus from excessive CSF production. 1st decade. Tumour dissemination via CSF pathways when more malignant but unusual when benign.
4. **Choroid plexus carcinoma** – 1st decade. Extraventricular extension with peritumoral oedema.
5. **Primitive neuroectodermal tumour (PNET)** – early in first decade.
6. **Metastases.**

Adjacent to the Foramen of Monro
1. **Colloid cyst** – hyper- or isodense on CT. Hyperintense on T_1W and hyper- or hypointense on T_2W MRI.
2. **Giant cell astrocytoma** – in tuberous sclerosis*.
3. **Meningioma.**
4. **Metastases.**

3rd Ventricle
1. **Craniopharyngioma** – child.
2. **Hypothalamic glioma** – child.
3. **Germ cell tumour.**

4th Ventricle
1. **Medulloblastoma.**
2. **Ependymoma** – with calcification.
3. **Choroid plexus papilloma.**

12.42 Features of Meningiomas

Commonest benign intracranial tumour, 15% of all intra-cranial tumours.

Histological types: meningothelial, fibroblastic, mixed (transitional), angioblastic ('malignant': allied to haem-angiopericytoma), atypical (cystic, lipid containing).

Gross morphology: globular, *en plaque*, multicentric (note association with neurofibromatosis 2).

Sites: falx, convexity, sphenoid ridge, subfrontal, parasellar, tentorial, posterior fossa, middle fossa, intraventricular, optic nerve sheath in declining order of frequency of occurrence.

Diagnosis

1. **Plain films** – hyperostosis (commonly seen in vault, sphenoid wing), erosion (uncommon), calcification, enlarged vascular grooves and foramen spinosum, pneumosinus dilatans (local paranasal sinus expansion).
2. **CT** – slightly hyperdense or isodense circumscribed mass with homogeneous contrast uptake. Narrow zone of perifocal oedema. Calcification and cyst formation in some cases. Hyperostosis.
3. **MRI** – T_1W hypointense or isointense circumscribed mass, T_2W isointense or slightly hyperintense mass with zone of surrounding oedema, homogeneous contrast uptake, dural 'tail' of tissue tapering into dural surface from tumour margin.
4. **Angiography** – hypervascular, sunburst pattern of supply, homogeneous tumour stain in venous phase, meningeal supply usual, with or without a pial component (especially seen in large tumours). Middle meningeal artery is a branch of the external carotid via internal maxillary (occasionally ophthalmic), but note that internal carotid artery gives rise to meningeal arteries (dural cavernous, meningohypophyseal, ophthalmic/ethmoidal, anterior falcine), and also vertebral (posterior) meningeal artery.

12.43   Radiological Features of Head Injury

Skull Radiography is Indicated if
1. There is marked scalp swelling or bruising.
2. A suspected penetrating injury.
3. Loss of clear or blood stained fluid from the nose or ear.
4. If there is or has been disturbance of consciousness.
5. If there are abnormal neurological signs.
6. If the neurological state cannot be assessed because of uncooperation or the influence of drugs or alcohol.

Skull Radiography may Show
1. Fractures and sutural diastasis.
2. Intracranial air.
3. Fluid in the paranasal sinuses or mastoids.
4. Foreign material in the scalp or within the cranium.

CT Scanning is Indicated if
1. The skull is fractured (the risk of associated intracranial damage is much higher). NB Particularly important in suspected compound fracture including skull base fracture.
2. Abnormal neurological symptoms or signs, especially if progressive.
3. Persistent confusion.
4. Coma or severe drowsiness.

CT Scanning may Show
1. Fracture (may not be shown if parallel or near parallel to slice plane). Presence of depressed fragment is important.
2. Scalp swelling (may indicate site of injury).
3. Fluid in mastoid or sinuses (fluid level in sphenoidal sinus points to skull base fracture).
4. Air in subarachnoid space or ventricles (compound injury, often through cribriform plate region).
5. Extradural blood (lentiform opacity related to vault underlying fracture site, usually temporal, temporoparietal or frontal). A fracture related to the middle meningeal artery is at risk from this point of view.
6. Subdural blood (crescentic superficial opacity which may be related to injury site or may lie in a contre coup position).

7. Intracerebral blood: small foci, typically at grey/white matter interface, or more centrally in the white matter with shearing injuries (diffuse axonal injury). This has a poor prognostic significance. Large haematomas relate to direct or contre coup injury. Intraventricular bleeding may be present.
8. Swelling is often a major feature, particularly in association with subdural haematomas, and relates to associated cortical vein injury.
9. Contusion: a combination of focal swelling with associated haemorrhage.
10. Foreign material, intracranial or in scalp.

MR Imaging May Show

1. Surface collections of blood or fluid with greater sensitivity than CT, partly due to absence of artefact at the bone/brain interface. Sensitivity particularly improved in middle and posterior cranial fossa.
2. Contusions not seen on CT.

Further Reading

Teasdale E. (1990) Radiological aspects of head and spinal trauma. In: *Imaging of the Nervous System* (Ed. P. Butler), Reston: American Roentgen Ray Society, pp. 85–105.

12.44   CT Appearances of Cerebral Haematoma

Stage	Image type	Appearances	Nature of haematoma
Acute	Unenhanced	Circumscribed hyperdense mass	Freshly clotted red cells
3–7 days	Unenhanced	Mass becomes ill defined with margin of low density	Contraction of clot with red cell lysis and absorption
7–28 days	Unenhanced	Hyperdensity fades leaving area of low density	Further lysis and absorption
	Enhanced	Rim of contrast uptake around margins of lesion	Blood brain barrier damage in haematoma margin
Over 1 month	Unenhanced	Further reduction in density	Maturation of infarct

12.45 MRI Appearances of Cerebral Haematoma

Stage	Image type	Appearances	Nature of haematoma
Acute	T_1W	Dark	Intracellular
	T_2W	Dark	oxyhaemoglobin
1–2 days	T_1W	Intermediate	Intracellular deoxyhaemoglobin
	T_2W	Dark: bright margin	Perifocal oedema
3–4 days	T_1W	Bright rim appears	Commencing formation of methaemoglobin in the haematoma
	T_2W	Dark with marginal increased signal due to oedema	
5–7 days	T_1W	Bright with dark marginal zone of oedema	Methaemoglobin with rim of fluid and oedema
	T_2W	Bright with darker centre	
2nd week	T_1W	As above	As above
	T_2W	Bright with dark rim	Methaemoglobin in centre with haemosiderin rim
2 months	T_2W	Bright with very dark rim	Gliotic or cystic centre. Ring of haemosiderin in macrophages

Further Reading

Hackney D.B. (1992) Location and age of intracranial haemorrhage. *ARRS Neuroradiology Categorical Course Syllabus* (Ed. M.S. Huckman), Reston: American Roentgen Ray Society, pp. 37–45.

12.46 Subarachnoid Haemorrhage

Aetiology
1. **Ruptured aneurysm** – 75%.
2. **Arteriovenous malformation** – 5%.
3. **Hypertensive intracerebral haemorrhage** – 5%.
4. **Miscellaneous** – 5–8%; trauma, anticoagulant therapy, tumours, vasculopathy, spinal arteriovenous malformation.
5. **'No cause'** – 7–10%. In this group, if the angiogram is complete and of good quality, not compromised by the presence of spasm, blood clot or artefact, no repeat study is required and the prognosis is good.

Aneurysms

PRESENTATION
Acute onset of severe headache, accompanied by nausea and vomiting, decrease in level of consciousness and variable neurological deficit. Specific deficit (3rd nerve palsy) in posterior communicating aneurysm.

CT DIAGNOSIS
Uncontrasted 5 mm sections through the basal cisterns, 10 mm sections through the rest of the brain. High density material in the fissures and sulci, often maximal near to the source of bleeding; intraventricular blood; mass lesion in large aneurysms. Localizing clues include:
   (a) Anterior and midline blood, inferior frontal haematoma, intraventricular blood – anterior communicating aneurysm.
   (b) Ipsilateral suprasellar cisterns, medial and subtemporal blood, 3rd nerve palsy – posterior communicating aneurysm.
   (c) Sylvian fissure, intratemporal haematoma, hemiparesis – middle cerebral aneurysm.
   (d) Blood only in prepontine cistern in a relatively well patient – idiopathic bleeding, ?microaneurysm, ?focal angiodysplasia.

Accuracy about 90% in the first day after onset, declining thereafter, with persistence of blood after 4 days only in massive haemorrhage. MRI is relatively insensitive in the acute stage but may show haemosiderin staining of the brain surface (dark on T_2W) after repeated bleeding.

ANGIOGRAPHIC DIAGNOSIS

The study must be '3 vessel' if reflux into the contralateral vertebral artery is seen; otherwise '4 vessel'.

(a) Anterior communicating artery – 35%.
(b) Posterior communicating artery – 30%.
(c) Middle cerebral artery – 25%.
(d) Others – 10%; internal carotid bifurcation, basilar tip, posterior inferior cerebellar artery, pericallosal artery, peripheral etc.

NB 20% are multiple, most notably bilateral middle cerebral aneurysms.

If multiple, which aneurysm has bled?
(a) Largest aneurysm (if < 5 mm bleeding is rare).
(b) Loculated aneurysms.
(c) Anterior communicating aneurysms.
(d) Adjacent arterial spasm.
(e) Adjacent haematoma (CT).

COMPLICATIONS

Early: brain swelling; acute hydrocephalus.
Late: infarction (due to spasm, seen from 3 days to 2 weeks following bleed); late onset hydrocephalus (may present after discharge from hospital).

Further Reading

Atlas S.W. (1988) Intracranial vascular malformations and aneurysms. *Radiol. Clin. North Am.*, 26: 821–838.

12.47   Intracranial Vascular Malformations

Arteriovenous malformations (AVMs) are the commonest type (pial or intracerebral, and dural); venous malformations are less common (medullary venous anomalies, cavernous malformations); rare types (congenital arteriovenous fistulas including vein of Galen malformation, traumatic arteriovenous fistula, Sturge–Weber, Osler–Rendu–Weber, Wyburn–Mason syndromes).

Arteriovenous Malformation

A small or large network of pathological vessels of developmental origin, allowing arteriovenous communication without intervening capillaries and resulting in enlargement of supplying arteries and draining veins.

PRESENTATION
Haemorrhage (40%), seizures (30%), progressive neurological deficit (due to 'steal' phenomenon) (10%), headache (10%), incidental finding (10%). Most AVMs present in adult life; only 10% present < 20 years of age. 90% are supratentorial.

DIAGNOSIS
Non-contrast CT: non-space-occupying lesion containing high and low-density components, often with calcification.
Contrast CT: higher density components enhance, often showing serpiginous opacities due to dilated vessels. Low density components are due to focal gliosis due to ischaemia (the AVM 'steals' blood from normal tissue) or to previous haemorrhage.
MRI: shows equivalent features to CT but with low signal in vessels due to dephasing of protons in fast flowing blood ('flow voids'). Evidence of old bleeding may be clear (dark haemosiderin rings or amorphous deposits on T_2W images). Contrast enhancement is not required. MR angiography is effective in mapping the morphology of the lesion in three dimensions.
Angiography: all the supplying vessels must be examined, with selective external carotid studies where dural components are found or suspected. Features consist of enlarged supplying arteries (sometimes with aneurysms on feeding vessels), a nidus of small vessels, often quite tightly packed and

enlarged draining veins (again sometimes with venous aneurysms). Purely dural AVMs are most commonly seen in relation to the cavernous sinus (where a large shunt with a cavernous sinus syndrome may develop) and the lateral sinus (where they may be complicated by progressive venous occlusion of unknown cause).

Medullary Venous Anomalies

Now recognized as a common incidental finding on CT and other types of study, but with occasional associated haemorrhage (usually benign in clinical course) or seizures. A prominent transcerebral vein is seen, flowing either centrifugally (superficial type) or centripetally (deep type). An 'umbrella' or 'bicycle spoke' like group of veins enter this vessel, and may be recognized on angiography and occasionally on CT or MRI. Focal gliosis around the anomaly may be seen on CT (low attenuation) or MRI (high signal on T_2W). Intervention is rarely, if ever, warranted.

Cavernous Malformations

A collection, usually but not always small, of dilated venous compartments, with surrounding gliosis and evidence of old haemorrhage. Usually subcortical, occasionally deep, sometimes in the brain-stem. They present with haemorrhage or less commonly seizures. Diagnosable by CT or MRI but not by angiography (the rate of flow is too slow).

CT: shows a well demarcated, often calcified, enhancing lesion, without mass effect, often with surrounding low density.

MRI: shows mixed signal on T_1W and T_2W images, with prominent bright areas on T_2W due to vascular spaces containing almost stagnant blood, and surrounding very low signal on T_2W due to haemosiderin residue from previous haemorrhage. The latter sign is even seen in patients with no history of previous bleeding. The lesions are thought to leak blood in small quantities over long periods.

Further Reading

Atlas S.W. (1988) Intracranial vascular malformations and aneurysms. *Radiol. Clin. North Am.*, 26: 821–38.

12.48 CT and MRI Appearances of Cerebral Infarction

CT

ACUTE

1. Unless accompanied by haemorrhage, in the first 24 hours CT will detect only 50% of infarcts but may show subtle signs of cerebral swelling (obliteration of sulci) and vague reduction of attenuation in a vascular territory.

SUBACUTE

1. Low attentuation due to oedema because of tissue necrosis. Present at 24 hours and maximal at 3–5 days.
2. Mass effect due to oedema. Maximal at 3–5 days, decreasing by 7 days and resolved by 3 weeks.
3. Contrast enhancement (when given) is gyriform or ring-like and is maximal between 2 and 4 weeks.
4. Haemorrhage may occur after a few days to 2 weeks. Most frequently gyriform and due to bleeding from reperfused, damaged capillaries. Haemorrhage may become mass-like but is more heterogeneous and less well defined than primary intracerebral haemorrhage.

CHRONIC

1. Well-defined CSF density associated with brain loss (dilatation of adjacent sulci and ventricles) by 2–3 months after the event.

MRI

ACUTE

1. More sensitive than CT and 90% will have high signal on proton density or T_2W images within 24 hours. Signal changes may be evident at 8 hours.
2. Prior to signal intensity changes being evident there may be absent flow voids (within minutes) or gyral swelling (from 2 hours on T_1W).

SUBACUTE

1. As for CT but the gyriform enhancement with gadolinium is not as marked as the T_2W signal changes and acute haemorrhage is less easily identified. MRI is more sensitive than CT in diagnosing subacute and chronic haemorrhage.
2. Meningeal enhancement may be evident from day 2–6.

Further Reading
Bryan R.N. (1992) Role of the radiologist in the early diagnosis of stroke. In: *ARRS Neuroradiology Categorical Course Syllabus* (Ed. M.S. Huckman), Reston: American Roentgen Ray Society, pp. 137–45.
Felsberg G.J. (1994) Cerebrovascular disease. In: *Review of Radiology* (Eds. C.E. Ravin, C. Cooper & R.A. Leder), 2nd edn., pp. 249–52. Philadelphia: Saunders.

12.49 White Matter Disease

White matter diseases show low density on CT, low signal on T_1W and high signal on T_2W MRI. T_2W MRI is the most sensitive method for detection. The early echo on multiple echo sequences shows periventricular lesions in greater relief against lower signal ventricular CSF. Acute lesions may show focal contrast uptake due to blood brain barrier damage. Conditions can be considered under two main categories – dysmyelinating diseases (primary abnormalities of formation of myelin) and demyelinating diseases (which are the result of myelin loss after its normal formation).

Dysmyelination (Leukodystrophies)

Enzyme deficiencies prevent the normal formation or maintenance of myelin. They are disorders of children and present with variable mental retardation.

LYSOSOMAL DISORDERS

1. **Metachromatic leukodystrophy** – arylsulphatase-A deficiency. AR. Usually presents at 2–3 years but may be later. Rapidly progressive. Diffuse symmetrical abnormalities but with sparing of the subcortical arcuate fibres. Cerebellar lesions may be present. Cerebral atrophy.

2. **Krabbe's (globoid) leukodystrophy** – galactosylceramide β-galactosidase deficiency. AR. Presentation in the first 6 months of life with death in early childhood. Symmetrical abnormalities in the posterior white matter of the optic radiations, centrum semiovale, thalami and caudate nuclei. Severe atrophy is common late in the disease.

PEROXISOMAL DISORDERS

1. **Adrenoleukodystrophy** – four recognizable forms, inherited as X-linked recessive traits (i.e. boys only). Classic type presents between 5 and 10 years. Initial changes are most common in the peritrigonal white matter. Enhancement may be evident at the leading edges of the lesions indicating demyelination. Calcification rarely seen in the parieto-occipital regions.

2. **Zellweger's (cerebrohepatorenal) syndrome** – presentation in the newborn. Hepatomegaly, polycystic kidneys and stippled calcification, particularly of the patellae. Extensive

white matter changes with pachygyria and, in some cases, vermian hypoplasia.

MITOCHONDRIAL DYSFUNCTION

Defects of respiratory chain enzymes which are expressed as myopathic diseases or multisystem disorders with encephalopathy. Among the latter group are:

1. **Leigh's disease** – mostly AR. lesions in the grey and white matter but predominantly the former. CT and MRI abnormalities in the midbrain, pons, periaqueductal grey matter, substantia nigra, floor of 4th ventricle, dentate nuclei. lesions in the caudate nucleus and putamen are common and may show cavitation.

2. **MELAS (mitochondrial myopathy, encephalopathy, lactic acidosis and stroke-like episodes)** – focal cortical and brain-stem white matter changes with basal ganglia calcification ± cerebral and cerebellar atrophy.

3. **MERFF (myoclonus epilepsy with ragged red fibres).**

4. **Alper's disease** – primarily affects cerebral grey matter.

5. **Kearns–Sayre syndrome** – onset in childhood or adolescence of progressive external ophthalmoplegia and pigmentary retinal degeneration and at least one of heart block, elevated CSF protein and cerebellar dysfunction. White matter disease is associated with cortical and/or cerebellar atrophy and calcification in the basal ganglia or deep white matter.

AMINO ACID AND ORGANIC ACID METABOLIC DISORDERS

1. **Canavan's disease** – AR and found predominantly in children of Ashkenazi Jewish descent. Manifests in the first few months of life; progressive increase in head size, hypotonia, seizures, progressing to spasticity and death by 2 years of age. Increased urine and plasma N-acetylaspartic acid. Bilaterally symmetrical changes, most severe in the subcortical white matter and globus pallidus with relative sparing of the brain-stem and internal capsule. Cerebral atrophy is late.

2. **Maple syrup urine disease.**

UNKNOWN METABOLIC DEFECT

1. **Pelizaeus–Merzbacher disease** – rare. X-linked recessive (i.e. girls only). Onset in infancy with nystagmus, ataxia and spasticity. Death in adolescence. Generalized white matter disease.

2. **Alexander's disease** – Presentation in the first year with developmental delay, macrocephaly, spasticity and seizures. Death in early childhood. Frontal involvement occurs earliest and is most severe. Enhancement may occur in the caudate nuclei, periventricular white matter and optic radiations. Megalencephaly and ventricular dilatation.

NB A useful mnemonic for the differential diagnosis of the common dysmyelinating leukodystrophies is 'LACK Proper Myelin' (Hatten, 1991).

L	=	Leigh's disease
A	{	Alexander's disease Adrenoleukodystrophy
C	=	Canavan's disease
K	=	Krabbe's disease
P	=	Pelizaeus–Merzbacher disease
M	=	Metachromatic leukodystrophy

Demyelination

INFLAMMATORY

1. **Multiple sclerosis** – in patients aged 20–50 years. F > M. Fluctuating disease activity; positive oligoclonal bands; optic neuritis; bowel or bladder dysfunction. *MRI findings*: ovoid lesions of various sizes whose long axis is perpendicular to the AP dimension of the brain or perpendicular to the ventricular system and which have little or no mass effect. Large acute lesions may resemble tumours. Lesions predominate in the periventricular regions and are seen in the corpus callosum. White matter tracts of the mid- and hindbrain and of the cerebellum are also affected. Lesions in the cervical cord (15%). Optic nerve lesions seen occasionally. Central atrophy. Increased brain iron.

2. **Acute disseminated encephalomyelitis (ADEM)** – following a recent childhood viral infection or vaccination. Bilaterally asymmetrical abnormalities. Mainly a white matter disease but lesions can be found in grey matter. The former is more responsive to steroids than the latter. The site of the lesions on T_2W MRI correlates well with the clinical disease. Basal ganglia involvement is associated with a worse prognosis.

3. **Acute haemorrhagic encephalomyelitis** – as for ADEM but with foci of haemorrhage which are hyperintense on T_1W.

INFECTIOUS

1. **Congenital and perinatal viral infections**
   (a) Cytomegalovirus – dilated lateral ventricles and sub-arachnoid spaces, pachygyria, polymicrogyria, delayed myelination, periventricular cysts (usually occipital) and calcification (see 12.36).
   (b) Rubella – microcephaly, intracranial calcifications and delayed myelination.
   (c) Herpes simplex – widespread, patchy abnormalities in the cortical white matter, basal ganglia, thalamus and cerebellum. The temporal lobe predilection seen in older children and adults is not seen in the neonate. Rapid development of encephalomalacia. Calcification in the basal ganglia and periventricular white matter. ± gyriform high attenuation (CT) or $\uparrow T_1W$ signal (MRI). Linear thalamic echogenicities on ultrasound.

2. **Acute encephalitis**
   (a) Epidemic encephalopathies – patchy demyelination.
   (b) Herpes simplex – temporal lobe involvement ± haemorrhage and streaky contrast enhancement. May progress to more generalized involvement, multicystic encephalomalacia and gyriform high attenuation. Imaging findings do not correlate with the clinical course.
   (c) Mumps – meningitis much more common than encephalitis. *MRI findings*: foci of perivascular inflammation and demyelination.
   (d) Rubella, measles and chickenpox.

3. **AIDS encephalitis** – diffuse white matter disease but atrophy is the most common manifestation.

4. **Progressive multifocal leukoencephalopathy (PML)** – fatal subacute demyelinating condition occurring in immunocompromised patients and probably due to reactivated papovavirus. Affects the white matter of the centrum semiovale, asymmetrically and predominantly posteriorly. Contrast enhancement not seen.

5. **Subacute sclerosing panencephalitis** – years after measles

infection. Patients aged 5–20 years. Lesions are subcortical and periventricular. Progressive atrophy occurs.
6. **Creutzfeldt–Jakob disease** – progressive dementia caused by sub-viral particles called prions. Diffuse white matter changes with atrophy.

METABOLIC

1. **Central pontine myelinolysis** – history of alcoholism, hypothermia, uncontrolled diabetes and rapid correction of hyponatraemia. Confluent central T_2W hyperintensity in the pons and midbrain with peripheral rim-sparing.
2. **Marchiafava–Bignami syndrome** – following the drinking of alcohol from iron- or lead-containing stills. Changes in the corpus callosum ± atrophy.
3. **Malnutrition.**
4. **Vitamin B_{12} deficiency.**

VASCULAR

1. **Subcortical arteriosclerotic encephalopathy (SAE, Binswanger's disease)** – affects patients with chronic hypertension, causing dementia, spasticity, seizures, gait apraxia and incontinence. Multifocal white matter lesions in the periventricular and deep white matter, extending more peripherally with increasing severity. Often associated with lacunar infarcts in the central grey matter and with atrophy.

TRAUMA

1. **Radiation and/or chemotherapy** – disseminated necrotizing leukoencephalopathy (DNL) occurs secondary to combined radiation and chemotherapy. Deep white matter lesions which may enhance and show mass effect. ± calcification in basal ganglia and grey/white matter junction.

   Radiation necrosis develops following doses ≥ 5800 rads 6–8 months previously. Lesions focal or widespread in the irradiated field. Variable mass effect with irregular enhancement. PET and SPECT scans may be helpful in differentiating radiation injury from residual/recurrent tumour.

Further Reading

Brant-Zawadzki M. (1992) Multiple sclerosis and its imitators. In: *ARRS Neuroradiology Categorical Course Syllabus* (Ed. M.S. Huckman) pp. 229–32.

Greenberg S.B., Faerber E.N., Riviello J.J., de Leon G. & Capitanio M.A. (1990) Subacute necrotizing encephalomyelopathy (Leigh disease): CT and MRI appearances. *Pediatr. Radiol.*, 21: 5–8.

Hatten H.P. Jr (1991) Dysmyelinating leukodystrophies: 'LACK Proper Myelin'. *Pediatr. Radiol.*, 21: 477–482.

Heier L. (1992) What importance should be attached to white matter 'dots'. In: *ARRS Neuroradiology Categorical Course Syllabus* (Ed. M.S. Huckman). Reston: American Roentgen Ray Society, pp. 57–69.

Shaw D.W.W. & Cohen W.A. (1993) Viral infections of the CNS in children: imaging features. *Am. J. Roentgenol.*, 160: 125–133.

Tien R.D., Felsberg G.J., Ferris N.J. & Osumi A.K. (1993) The dementias: correlation of clinical features, pathophysiology, and neuroradiology. *Am. J. Roentgenol.*, 161: 245–55.

12.50   Disorders of Neuronal Migration

The neuronal population of the normal cerebral cortex arrives by a process of outward migration from the periventricular germinal matrix between the 8th and 16th weeks of gestation. This complex process of cell migration can be interfered with by many causes, sporadic and unknown, chromosomal or genetic. Best imaged by MRI but CT is effective in many cases.

1. **Agyria–pachygyria** – poorly formed gyri and sulci, the former being more severe. Focal pachygyria may be the cause of focal epilepsy. Polymicrogyria (see below) may coexist with pachygyria. Extreme cases with a smooth brain may be termed lissencephaly. Complete lissencephaly ≡ agyria. Several distinct forms are recognized.
   Type I lissencephaly – small brain with few gyri; smooth, thickened four layer cortex resembling that of a 13 week fetus with diminished white matter and shallow vertical sylvian fissures (figure-of-eight appearance on axial images). ± agenesis of the corpus callosum. Severe mental retardation, diplegia, seizures, microcephaly and limited survival. Some infants have specific dysmorphic features – Miller–Dieker syndrome and Norman–Roberts syndrome. Pachygyria may also be observed in Zellweger syndrome and prenatal CMV infection.
   Type II lissencephaly (Walker–Warburg syndrome) – smooth cortex, cerebellar hypoplasia and vermian aplasia and hydrocephalus (in 75%) due to cisternal obstruction by abnormal meninges or aqueduct stenosis.
2. **Polymicrogyria** – the neurons reach the cortex but are distributed abnormally. Macroscopically the surface of the brain appears as multiple small bumps. Localized abnormalities are more common than generalized and often involve arterial territories, especially the middle cerebral artery. The most common location is around the sylvian fissure. The cortex is isointense to grey matter but in 20% of cases the underlying white matter has high signal on T_2W. Linear flow voids due to anomalous venous drainage may be present. Polymicrogyrias may be present in the vicinity of a porencephalic cyst, be associated with heterotopic grey matter or agenesis of the corpus callosum or

with evidence of fetal infection such as intracranial calcification. Symptoms and signs depend on the size, site, and presence of associated abnormalities. Majority have mental retardation, seizures and neurological signs.

3. **Schizencephaly** – clefts which extend through the full thickness of the cerebral mantle from ventricle to subarachnoid space. The cleft is lined by heterotopic grey matter and microgyrias indicating that the cleft existed prior to the end of neuronal migration. Unilateral or bilateral (usually asymmetrical) and usually near the sylvian fissure. May be associated with absence of the septum pellucidum or, less commonly, dysgenesis of the corpus callosum. Variable clinical manifestations varying from profound retardation to isolated partial seizures.

4. **Heterotopic grey matter** – collections of neurons in a subependymal location, i.e. at the site of the germinal matrix or arrested within the white matter on their way to the cortex. Isointense to normal grey matter on all imaging sequences. Nodules or bands and may have mass effect. Frequently a part of complex malformation syndromes or, when isolated, may be responsible for focal seizures which are amenable to surgical treatment. Small heterotopias are probably asymptomatic.

5. **Cortical dysplasia** – focal disorganization of the cerebral cortex. A single enlarged gyrus resembling focal pachygyria. Usual presentation is with partial epilepsy.

Further Reading

Aicardi J. (1992) *Clinics in Developmental Medicine No. 115/118. Diseases of the Nervous System in Childhood*, Chapter 3, pp. 108–202. London: MacKieth Press.

Barkovich A.J. (1990) *Pediatric Neuroimaging*. New York: Raven Press.

Byrd S.E. & Naidich T. (1988) Common congenital brain anomalies. *Radiol. Clin. North Am.*, 26: 755–65.

13
Nuclear Medicine
Keith Harding

13.1 Increased Uptake on Bone Scans

1. **Metastatic disease** – multiple, randomly scattered lesions especially in the axial skeleton.
2. **Joint disease** – commonly degenerative in the cervical spine, hips, hands, knees. Also inflammatory joint disease.
3. **Traumatic fractures**
   (a) Aligned fractures in ribs are traumatic.
   (b) Single lesions elsewhere – always ask if history of trauma.
   (c) Stress fractures.
4. **Post surgery** – after joint replacement. Increased uptake lasts 1 year.
5. **Paget's disease*** – diffuse involvement with much increased uptake. Commonly affects the pelvis, skull, femur, and spine. Involvement of the whole of the vertebra is typical.
6. **Superscan** – high uptake throughout the skeleton often due to disseminated secondary disease with poor or absent renal images but often with bladder activity. Look carefully at the skull and ribs where the inhomogeneity may be apparent.
7. **Metabolic bone disease** – high uptake in the axial skeleton, proximal long bones, with prominent calvarium and mandible. Faint or absent kidney images.
8. **Dental disease** – inflammation, recent extraction.
9. **Infection** – increased uptake in vascular and blood pool phases also.
10. See 13.2.

13.2 Increased Uptake on Bone Scans Not Due to Skeletal Abnormality

Artefacts

These are common.

1. **Patient**
   (a) Beware spots of urine in the pelvic area and urine on handkerchiefs.
   (b) Sweat – axillae.
   (c) Injection site.
   (d) Scars of recent operations.
   (e) Breast – accentuation of ribs at the lower border of the breast due to small angle scatter.
2. **Equipment**
   (a) Edge effect – increase in intensity at the edge of the field of view, especially in vertebrae.
   (b) Contamination of the collimator or crystal – check using a uniformity source.

Physiological Variants

1. **Epiphyses in children.**
2. **Inferior angle of the scapula.**
3. **Calcification of cartilages** – especially those in the ribs and anterior neck.
4. **Bladder diverticulum.**
5. **Nipples** especially confusing if at different heights.
6. **Renal pelvis.**

Soft-tissue Uptake

1. **Calcification**
   (a) Myositis ossificans.
   (b) Soft-tissue osseous metaplasia.
   (c) Soft-tissue tumours with calcification.
   (d) Vascular calcification.
   (e) Calcific tendinitis.
   (f) Abscess.

(*continued*)

2. **Others**
   (a) Acute infarction of the myocardium, cerebrum, skeletal muscle.
   (b) Malignant pleural effusion.
   (c) Inflammatory carcinoma of the breast.
   (d) Hepatic necrosis.
   (e) Hepatic metastases – colon, breast, oat cell carcinoma.
   (f) Tumour uptake.

Visualization of Normal Organs
1. **Free pertechnetate** – thyroid, stomach, salivary glands.
2. **Colloid formation** – liver, spleen and sometimes lung.
3. **Study on the previous day.**

13.3 Photopenic Areas (Defects) on Bone Scans

1. **Artefacts** – the commonest cause.
   (a) External – metal objects – coins, belts, lockets, buckles.
   (b) Internal – joint prosthesis, pace makers.
2. **Avascular lesions** – for example cysts.
3. **Multiple myeloma*** – may show increased uptake.
4. **Leukaemia** – may show increased uptake.
5. **Haemangiomas** of the spine – occasionally slightly increased uptake.
6. **Radiotherapy fields** – usually oblong in shape.
7. **Advanced cancer** – especially breast. Possibly related to chemotherapy.
8. **Spina bifida.**

Further Reading
Fogelman I. (ed.) (1987) *Bone Scanning in Clinical Practice*. London: Springer-Verlag.

13.4 Abnormal Bone Scan with Normal or Minimal Radiographic Changes

1. Early disease
   (a) Metastatic.
   (b) Paget's.
   (c) Osteomyelitis.
   (d) Asceptic necrosis.
   (e) Arthritides.
2. Fractures
   (a) Ribs.
   (b) Hands or feet.
3. Lymphoma*.
4. Myelofibrosis.
5. Primary hyperparathyroidism*.
6. Osteodystrophy
   (a) Renal.
   (b) Pulmonary.

Further Reading
Silberstein E.B. & McAfee J.G. (eds) (1984) *Differential Diagnosis in Nuclear Medicine*. New York: McGraw-Hill.

13.5 Positive Radiograph with Normal Bone Scan

1. Benign conditions
   (a) Bone cyst.
   (b) Bone island.
   (c) Exostoses.
2. Recent fractures – within 48 h.
3. Multiple myeloma*.
4. Osteoporosis – q.v.
5. Metastases – very rare but occurs if there is no osteoblastic reaction.

Further Reading
Silberstein E.B. & McAfee J.G. (eds) (1984) *Differential Diagnosis in Nuclear Medicine*. New York: McGraw-Hill.

13.6   Bone Marrow Imaging

Technique: $^{99}Tc^m$ nanocolloid injected with imaging at 1–2 h.

Focal Defects
1. Metastases – may be increased uptake.
2. Infarction.
3. Fractures – healed, in the ribs or compression.
4. Osteomyelitis.
5. Lymphoma*.
6. Myeloproliferative disorders.
7. Paget's disease*.
8. Radiation.

Reduced Central Marrow Activity
1. Myelofibrosis.
2. Aplastic anaemia.
3. Chronic myeloid leukaemia.
4. Lymphomas*.
5. Multiple myeloma*.
6. Extensive metastases.
7. Chronic renal disease.
8. Radiotherapy.

13.7 Localization of Infection

Technique: ^{111}In leucocytes or ^{99}Tc^m HMPAO leucocytes

1. Collection of pus.
2. False positive
   (a) Surgical scars.
   (b) Drip sites and drainage tubes.
   (c) i.v. injection sites.
   (d) Lung accumulation in early images.
   (e) Gastrointestinal bleeding.
   (f) Sites of bone marrow aspiration.
   (g) Swallowed WBC from lung, sinuses, mouth.
   (h) Fractures within the first 2 weeks.
   (i) Inflammatory arthritis.
   (j) Biliary and renal tract (HMPAO only).
3. False negative
   (a) Walled off avascular pus.
   (b) Chronic inflammatory (lymphocytic) reaction.
   (c) Acute osteomyelitis – especially spinal.
   (d) Chronic infection of joint prosthesis.
   (e) Agranulocytosis.
4. Inflammatory bowel disease – uptake at 2 h and reduces by 24 h. Image at 1 h using ^{99}Tc^m HMPAO.
   (a) Crohn's disease.
   (b) Ulcerative colitis.
   (c) Infective colitis.
5. Infected prosthesis.
6. Sinusitis.
7. Acute infarcts – including bowel, myocardial, cerebral.
8. Myocarditis.
9. Rejected transplant – kidney.
10. Pancreatitis.
11. Infected tumour – especially bronchial.

Further Reading

Mello A.M., Blake K. & McDougall I.R. (1992) Cold lesions on indium^{111} white blood cell scintigraphy. *Semin. Nucl. Med.* 22: 292–4.

13.8   Gallium Uptake

Technique: Imaging 24 h after ^{67}Ga injection for inflammatory lesions; up to 72 h for tumour.

Inflammatory
1. **Inflammation or abscess.**
2. **Sarcoidosis** – lacrimal and salivary gland uptake are typical.
3. **Diffuse lung disease** – interstitial fibrosis, scleroderma, asbestosis.
4. **Heart** – myocarditis, pericarditis, systemic lupus erythematosus.

Tumours
1. **Lymphoma** – positive in 90% of patients and 80% of affected sites.
2. **Bronchial carcinoma** – (90%). Used for staging.
3. **Gastrointestinal tumours** – (20%).
4. **Hepatoma.**
5. **Other malignant tumours.**

Normal Variants
1. **Nasopharynx.**
2. **Bowel** – diffuse or outlining the colon.
3. **Breast** – often due to antiemetics or oral contraceptives. Intense uptake if recent breast feeding.

13.9 Somatostatin Receptor Scintigraphy

Technique: Octreotide is a somatostatin receptor. Images are taken 24 hours after injection of ^{111}indium-labelled radionuclide.

1. **Neuroendocrine tumours**
   (a) Pituitary tumours – GH or TSH secreting or non-functioning.
   (b) Gastrinoma, insulinoma, glucagonoma. Some insulinomas are negative, as are exocrine pancreatic tumours.
   (c) Paragangliomas – it is important to image the whole body.
   (d) Neuroblastoma and phaeochromocytoma – MIBG preferred for phaeochromocytoma because of kidney accumulation of octreotide.
   (e) Medullary thyroid carcinoma. Poor results for metastases in the liver, or for intra-thyroidal tumours.
   (f) Carcinoid tumour – liver metastases may be difficult to visualize.
   (g) Small cell lung cancer.
2. **Brain tumours especially meningiomas and astrocytomas.**
3. **Breast cancer.**
4. **Lymphomas.**
5. **Sarcoidosis.**
6. **Autoimmune diseases** – thyroid in Graves disease and joints in rheumatoid arthritis.
7. **False positive**
   (a) Lung uptake after irradiation or bleomycin.
   (b) Recent operation sites.
8. **Visualization of normal organs**
   (a) Pituitary, thyroid.
   (b) Spleen, liver (occasionally gallbladder).
   (c) Kidneys, urinary bladder.
   (d) Nasal region and lung hila with the common cold.

Further Reading

Krenning ER, Kwekkeboom DG, Bakker WH *et al.* (1993) Somatostatin receptor scintigraphy with [^{111}In-DTPA-D-Phe] and [^{123}-Tyr^3]-octreotide: the Rotterdam experience with more than 1000 patients. *Eur. J. Nucl. Med.* 20: 716–31.

13.10 Whole Body Iodine Scan for Localizing Metastases

Technique: The test is usually undertaken when there is a rising level of thyroglobulin. Transfer patient to T3 one month and stop the T3 for 4 days before imaging.

1. **Metastases** – visualization depends on the amount of ^{131}I given. A low activity gives false negative results.
2. **Thyroid bed** – a small amount of uptake is normal.
3. **Normal thyroid tissue**
   (a) Ectopic, retrosternal, sublingual.
   (b) Aberrant – liver, thyroid lymph nodes (unless an ablative dose of iodine has already been given).
4. **Normal uptake** – genitourinary tract, nasopharynx, salivary glands, stomach, breasts.

Further Reading

Wu S., Brown T., Milne N., Egbert R., Kebok A., Lyons K.P. & Hickey J. (1986) Iodine 131 total body scan – extrathyroidal uptake of radioiodine. *Semin. Nucl. Med.*, 16: 82–4.

13.11 Photopenic (Cold) Areas in Thyroid Imaging

Localized
1. Colloid cyst.
2. **Adenoma** – non-functioning.
3. **Carcinoma** – medullary may be bilateral.
4. **Multinodular goitre.**
5. **Local thyroiditis** – may be increased uptake also
   (a) Acute.
   (b) De Quervain's.
   (c) Hashimito's.
   (d) Riedel's.
6. **Vascular** – haemorrhage or infarct.
7. **Artefacts.**
8. **Abscesses.**

Generalized reduction in uptake
1. **Medication** – thyroxine, glucocorticoids, phenylbutazone sulphonylureas.
2. **Hypothyroidism** – primary or secondary.
3. **Ectopic hormone production.**
4. **De Quervain's thyroiditis.**
5. **Ectopic thyroid** – lingual or retrosternal.

Further Reading
Fogelman I. & Maisey M. (1988) *An Atlas of Clinical Nuclear Medicine*, pp. 160–216. London: Martin Dunitz.

13.12   Parathyroid Imaging

Technique: ^{201}Tl, ^{99}Tc^m subtraction or ^{99}Tc^m, ^{123}I subtraction.
  The technique should be limited to localizing adenomas.
Diagnosis is made using clinical information, serum calcium
and parathyroid hormone levels.

1. **Parathyroid adenomas** – approximately two-thirds are
   demonstrated – related to size.
2. **Thyroid nodules** – adenoma or carcinoma.
3. **Hyperplasia** – several areas of uptake evident. More difficult to demonstrate than adenomas.
4. **Parathyroid carcinoma.**
5. **False positive results** – may occur in patients on thyroxine,
   or with thyroiditis.
6. **Other disease**
   (a) Lymphoma*.
   (b) Metastases.
   (c) Sarcoidosis*.

Further Reading

Winzelberg G.G. (1987) Thallium 201/^{99m}Tc parathyroid subtraction
        scintigraphy of the neck: single area of increased thallium
        uptake. *Semin. Nucl. Med.*, 17: 273–5.
Winzelberg G.G. (1987) Thallium 201/^{99m}Tc parathyroid subtraction
        scintigraphy of the neck: multiple areas of increased thallium
        uptake. *Semin. Nucl. Med.*, 17: 276–7.
Winzelberg G.G. (1987) Thallium 201/^{99m}Tc parathyroid subtraction
        scintigraphy of the mediastinum. *Semin. Nucl. Med.*, 17:
        278–9.

13.13 Indications for ⁹⁹Tc-HMPAO Brain Scanning

Technique: Patient lying comfortably in darkened room. HMPAO when given during an event (e.g. fits) is fixed in brain during first pass, and images are acquired later (up to 2 hours).

1. **Stroke** – defect larger than CT or MR lesion.
2. **Transient ischaemic attack (TIA)** – can demonstrate reduced perfusion before CT changes.
3. **Epilepsy** – increased during seizure and reduced inter-ictally for localization prior to surgery.
4. **Alzheimer dementia** – reduced uptake in temporal, parietal and later on in frontal lobes.
5. **Multi-infarct dementia** – random distribution.
6. **Pick's disease** – frontal deficit.
7. **HIV encephalitis** – subcortical or cortical defects and reduced cerebral/cerebellar ratio.
8. **Parkinson's disease** – diffuse decrease in cerebral perfusion (but not cerebellar).
9. **Huntington's disease** – reduced uptake in basal ganglia.
10. **Schizophrenia and other affective disorders** – reduced uptake in frontal and/or temporal regions.
11. **Tumours** – limited value, variable uptake with different tumours.

Further Reading
Semin. Nucl. Med. (1990) 20: 4 and (1991) 21: 1.

13.14   Brain Isotope Angiogram

Technique: Dynamic injection of $^{99}Tc^m$.

Increased Vascularity

1. **Tumours** – glioblastoma multiforme, meningioma, astro-cytoma.
2. **Metastases** – thyroid, kidney, lung, breast, melanoma.
3. **Lesions of skin or scalp** – Paget's disease, fibrous dysplasia, metastases, primary tumours, myeloma, sinusitis.
4. **Arteriovenous malformations.**
5. **Jugular reflux** – reflux up the jugular vein if the patient holds their breath at the time of injection.

Vascularity – Localized Decreased Vascularity

1. **Cerebrovascular occlusion.**
2. **Carotid stenosis or occlusion.**
3. **Subdural haematoma.**
4. **Avascular brain masses**
   (a)   Tumour.
   (b)   Cysts.
   (c)   Haematoma.
   (d)   Abscess.
   (e)   Gliomas (occasionally).
5. **Ventricular enlargement.**
6. **Cortical atrophy** – if marked.

Bilaterally Decreased Vascularity

1. **Poor bolus.**
2. **Low cardiac output.**
3. **Venous return** – obstruction of venous return to the heart.
4. **Raised intracranial pressure** – marked increase.
5. **Brain death.**

Further Reading

Lin D.S. (1986) Hypervascularity on cerebral radionuclide angiogram. *Semin. Nucl. Med.*, 16: 74–6.
Lin D.S. (1986) Hypovascularity on cerebral radionuclide angiogram. *Semin. Nucl. Med.*, 16: 77–9.

13.15 Ventilation Perfusion Mismatch

Mismatched Perfusion Defects
Perfusion defect greater than ventilation defect.
1. **Pulmonary embolus** – especially if multiple and segmental.
2. **Bronchial carcinoma** – but more commonly matched.
3. **Tuberculosis** – typically affecting an apical segment.
4. **Vasculitis** – polyarteritis nodosa, systemic lupus erythematosus, etc.
5. **Tumour embolus.**
6. **Fat embolus.**
7. **Post radiotherapy.**
8. **Pulmonary hypertension.**

Mismatched Ventilation Defects
Bronchial obstruction with normal blood supply. Ventilation defect greater than perfusion defect.
1. **Chronic obstructive airways disease.**
2. **Pneumonia.**
3. **Carcinoma** – the rarest appearance with bronchial carcinoma.
4. **Lung collapse** – of any cause.
5. **Pleural effusion.**

Further Reading
Carvandho P. & Lavender J.P. (1988) Incidence and aetiology of the reverse (V/Q) mismatch defect. *Nucl. Med. Commun.*, 9: 167.

13.16   Multiple Matched Ventilation/Perfusion Defects

Refer to 13.15.

1. **Chronic bronchitis.**
2. **Pulmonary infarct** (do not confuse with the mismatched perfusion defect of embolus).
3. **Asthma or acute bronchitis** – may also show mismatched ventilation or perfusion defects.
4. **Collagen vascular disease.**
5. **Lymphangitis carcinomatosa.**
6. **Pulmonary hypertension.**
7. **Sarcoidosis.**
8. **Intravenous drug abuse.**

Further Reading

Benson M.L. & Balseiro J. (1993) Multiple matched ventilation–perfusion defects in illicit drug use. *Semin. Nucl. Med.*, 23: 180–3.

13.17   Myocardial Perfusion Imaging

Technique: Inject ^{201}Tl (thallium) during exercise test with immediate exercise images and reperfusion images 3 h later, after resting.

Alternatively use separate rest and exercise injections of ^{99}Tc^m agent (MIBI, Tretrafosmin).

Focal Defect on Exercise but not on Reperfusion
1. Exercise induced ischaemia.
2. Hypertrophic cardiomyopathy.
3. Aortic stenosis.
4. Mitral valve prolapse.
5. Myocarditis.

Focal Defect on Exercise and Reperfusion Images
1. Myocardial infarct – old or recent.
2. Peri-infarct ischaemia.
3. Angina pectoris – during pain (also reported when free of pain).
4. Sarcoidosis*.
5. Mitral valve prolapse.
6. Cardiomyopathy – congestive or restrictive.
7. Artefact – breast, diaphragm.

Further Reading
Gerson M.C. & Gelford M.J. (1984) ^{201}Tl-thallium myocardial perfusion imaging. In: Silberstein E.B. & McAfee J.G. (eds), *Differential Diagnosis in Nuclear Medicine*, pp. 17–22. New York: McGraw-Hill.

13.18 Non-Cardiac Uptake of ^{99}Tc-Isonitrile

1. **Physiological**
   (a) Liver, spleen, gallbladder.
   (b) Heart.
   (c) Intestine.
   (d) Kidney and bladder.
   (e) Lung.
   (f) Thyroid and thyroid adenomas.
   (g) Skeletal muscle (especially after exercise).
2. **Parathyroid adenoma***
3. **Malignancy**
   (a) Lung.
   (b) Thyroid.
   (c) Breast.
   (d) Osteosarcoma, chondrosarcoma, or Ewing's sarcoma.
4. **Secondary malignancy**
   (a) Lung.
   (b) Mediastinum.
   (c) Bone.
   (d) Lymph nodes.

Further Reading
Sutter C.W., Joshi M.J. & Stadalnick R.C. (1994) Non-cardiac uptake of technetium-99m MIBI. *Semin. Nucl. Med.*, 24: 84–6.

13.19 Gated Blood Pool Imaging

Technique: ^{99}Tc^m labelled red blood cells.

Dyskinesia Focal
1. Myocardial infarct or contusion.
2. Ischaemic cardiomyopathy.
3. Unstable angina pectoris.
4. Aneurysm – paradoxical movement.

13.20 Photopenic (Cold) Areas in Colloid Liver Scans

Single
1. Single metastasis.
2. Cyst.
3. Abscess.
4. **Primary tumour** – haemangioma, adenoma. Hepatoma may be multiple.
5. Subphrenic abscess.
6. **Adjacent organs** – kidney, stomach, pancreas, especially if involved by tumour.
7. **Non-pathological**
   (a) Contrast media – in the bowel.
   (b) Breast – on anterior view and less apparent on the right lateral view.
   (c) Gallbladder fossa.
   (d) Costal margin indentation.
   (e) Porta hepatis.

Multiple
1. **Metastases** – commonly from the bowel.
2. **Hepatoma** – see above.
3. **Dilated intrahepatic ducts** – obstructive jaundice.
4. **Non-uniformity of the gamma camera** – producing hexagonal defects.

Diffuse
1. **Cirrhosis** – with increased bone marrow and spleen uptake, and a large left lobe of liver.
2. **Metastases** – if extensive.
3. Acute hepatitis.
4. Fatty liver.
5. Amyloid infiltration.
6. **Budd–Chiari** – especially over the right lobe with an enlarged caudate lobe.

13.21 Non-visualization of the Gallbladder with TBIDA

Technique: $^{99}Tc^{m}$-trimethylbromo-iminodiacetic acid (TBIDA) with images up to 90 min if necessary.

No Bowel Activity
1. Common bile duct obstruction – of any cause.
2. Severe hepatitis.
3. Opiates – because of their effect on the sphincter of Oddi.

With Bowel Activity
1. Acute cholecystitis.
2. Chronic cholecystitis – usually fills after 1 h.
3. Cholecystectomy.
4. Inadequate fasting – including i.v. feeding.
5. Biliary pancreatitis.
6. Severe diffuse hepatocellular disease.

Further Reading
Lecklitner M.L. & Growcock G. (1984) Hepatobiliary scintigraphy: non-visualization of activity in the area of the gallbladder associated with intestinal activity. *Semin. Nucl. Med.*, 14: 345–6.

13.22 Spleen Imaging

Technique: For almost all purposes a colloid image of the liver and spleen provides perfectly satisfactory spleen images. However, $^{99}Tc^m$ heat damaged red blood cells required after splenectomy or with equivocal colloid images.

Splenunculus
Post splenectomy – more uptake than in the liver. Note that the liver may fall into the splenic bed. There is normally some activity in the renal tract.

Photopenic Areas (Defects) in the Spleen
1. **Trauma** – leak of the radiopharmaceutical into the abdomen proves that bleeding is currently taking place.
2. **Infarct**
   (a) Infective endocarditis.
   (b) Vasculitis.
   (c) Tumour invasion.
   (d) Pancreatitis.
3. **Involvement by other disease**
   (a) Lymphoma*.
   (b) Melanoma.
   (c) Secondaries, usually from lung or breast.
4. **Artefact** – breast, barium, metal objects.

Absent or Much Reduced Splenic Uptake
Using heat damaged red blood cells or $^{99}Tc^m$ colloid.
1. Splenectomy.
2. Vascular occlusion.
3. Haemoglobinopathies.
4. Polycythaemia rubra vera.
5. Infiltrative – tumour, amyloid.
6. Coeliac disease.
7. Chronic active hepatitis.
8. Lymphomas*.

13.23   Meta Iodo Benzyl Guanidine (MIBG) Imaging

Technique: Images at 4 and 24 h after ^{123}I MIBG; 1–3 days after ^{131}I MIBG.

Normal
1. Myocardium.
2. Liver and spleen.
3. Bladder.
4. Adrenal glands – more marked with ^{123}I MIBG.
5. Salivary glands.
6. Nasopharynx.
7. Thyroid.
8. Colon.

Abnormal
1. Phaeochromocytoma.
2. Neuroblastoma.
3. Carcinoid tumour.
4. Paraganglioma.
5. Medullary thyroid carcinoma.
6. Ganglioneuroma.

Further Reading

McEwan A.H., Shapiro B., Sisson J.C., Beierwaltes W.H. & Ackery D.M. (1985). Radioiodobenzylguanidine for the scintigraphic localisation and therapy of adrenergic tumours. *Semin. Nucl. Med.*, 15: 132–53.
Standalick R.C. (1992) The biodistribution of metaiodobenzylguanidine. *Semin. Nucl. Med.*, 22: 46–7.

13.24 Unilateral Adrenal Visualization

Technique: Images at 3–10 days after injection of ^{75}Se selenocholesterol.

1. **Adenoma** – suppressing the other adrenal.
2. **Metastases** – breast or lung commonly.
3. **Aldosteronism** – after dexamethasone suppression.
4. **Carcinoma.**
5. **Adrenalectomy** – unilateral.
6. **Infarct.**

Further Reading

Standalik R.C. (1981) Unilateral visualisation of the adrenal gland. *Semin. Nucl. Med.*, 11: 224–5.

13.25 Cortical Defects in Renal Images

Technique: ^{99}Tc^m DMSA or MAG3 but may be apparent with other renal imaging agents.

1. **Scars** – note that apparent scars present during infection may resolve later. Oblique views are required.
2. **Hydronephrosis.**
3. **Trauma** – subcapsular or intra-renal.
4. **Renal cysts.**
5. **Carcinoma.**
6. **Infarct or ischaemia.**
7. **Abscesses.**
8. **Metastases.**
9. **Wilms' tumour.**

Further Reading

Fogelman I. & Maisey M. (1988) *An Atlas of Clinical Nuclear Medicine*, pp. 217–373. London: Martin Dunitz.

13.26 Localization of Gastrointestinal Bleeding

Technique: For acute or continuous bleeding image for 30 min using $^{99}Tc^m$ colloid (or DTPA) which can detect a blood loss of 0.1 ml/min. If this is negative or the blood loss is known to be intermittent use $^{99}Tc^m$ labelled red blood cells and image for up to 24 h. This is sensitive to 0.5 ml/min blood loss.

1. **Ulcers** – benign or malignant.
2. **Vascular lesions** – telangiectasia, haematoma, fistula, angiodysplasia.
3. **Tumours** – leiomyoma, adenoma.
4. **Inflammatory lesions** – gastritis, duodenitis.
5. **Varices** – oesophageal or stomach.
6. **Surgical anastomosis.**
7. **Meckel's diverticulum** (q.v.).
8. **Intussusception.**
9. **Metastatic disease.**
10. **Diverticula.**
11. **False positive**
    (a) Renal tract, liver, spleen, small bowel vascularity.
    (b) Uterus.
    (c) Accessory spleen.
    (d) Marrow uptake of colloid, especially if irregular.

Further Reading

Silberstein E.B. & McAfee J.G. (eds) (1984) *Differential Diagnosis in Nuclear Medicine*, pp. 191–3. New York: McGraw-Hill.

13.27 Meckel's Diverticulum

Technique: $^{99}Tc^m$ pertechnetate (perchlorate must not be given).

Meckel's Diverticulum
Appears at the same time as the stomach and the activity increases in intensity with the stomach. May change in position during the study and may empty its contents into the bowel.

Gastrointestinal Bleeding
Any blood leaking into the bowel would be apparent, although it would not show the rounded appearance of a Meckel's diverticulum.

False Positive Results
1. **Physiological**
   (a) Gastric emptying.
   (b) Renal tract – pelvis, ureter, bladder diverticulum.
   (c) Iliac vessels.
   (d) Uterus.
2. **Pathological**
   (a) Ectopic gastric mucosa in the small bowel.
   (b) Infection – for example acute appendicitis.
   (c) Intussusception.
   (d) Haemangioma of the bowel – gradual reduction in activity.

False Negative
1. No ectopic gastric mucosa in the diverticulum.
2. Hidden by bladder or stomach.

Further Reading
Merrick M.V. (1986) In: P.J.A. Robinson (ed.), *Nuclear Gastroenterology*, pp. 163–8. Edinburgh: Churchill Livingstone.

14
Obstetric and Gynaecological Ultrasonography

Josephine McHugo

Obstetric ultrasound can broadly be divided into four sections:

1. Normality/abnormality of the first trimester.
2. Assessment of gestational age and fetal number.
3. Structural abnormalities.
4. Growth and fetal well being throughout pregnancy.

For simplicity these will be dealt with separately but an accurate knowledge of gestational age is essential before abnormal growth can be implied and gestational age is often vital in assessing structural abnormalities.

14.1 Measurements for Dating (in weeks post LMP)

		range
Sac volume	5 wks	± 1.5 wks
Crown–rump length	6½ wks	± 0.7 wks
Biparietal diameter	12 wks	± 1 wk < 20 wks
		± 1.5 wks at 20–26 wks
		± 2–3 wks at 26–30 wks
		3–4 wks after 30 wks
Femur length	12 wks	± 22 day > 34 wks
Cerebellar width	15–16 wks	
Foot length	14 wks	

From the above it can be seen that gestational age measurements are less variable in early pregnancy. Gestational age can be assessed up to approx. 22 weeks. After this, growth becomes the major factor in fetal size.

14.2 Ultrasound Features of a Normal Intrauterine Pregnancy

Using Abdominal Scanning

The earliest ultrasound sign of pregnancy is fundal endometrial thickening.

AT 5 WEEKS
1. Gestational sac should be visible.
2. The gestational sac is surrounded by an echo dense ring.
3. Asymmetry of this ring is apparent.

AT 6 WEEKS
Embryonic structures apparent (the yolk sac and developing amniotic sac).

AT 6½ WEEKS
Cardiac movement identifiable in the fetus.
Crown rump length approximately 5 mm.

These dates will not always apply in obese patients where ultrasound images are not ideal. In these cases ultrasound evidence of a normal pregnancy will not be seen so readily. The above appearances are easily seen using transvaginal scanning.

NORMAL SAC GROWTH
A normal gestational sac grows at a rate of 0.7–1.75 mm/day (mean = 1.33) from 5 to 11 weeks.

Using Transvaginal Ultrasound

Gestational sac – seen as early as 32 days and present in all normal pregnancies with HCG level of 1000 mIU ml^{-1}.

Yolk sac – seen in 100% of normal pregnancies with HCG level of 7200 mIU ml^{-1}. Yolk sac first seen in every pregnancy between 36 and 40 days and when the gestational sac is between 6 and 9 mm.

Embryo with a heart beat – in all pregnancies greater than 40 days and when the gestational sac diameter is greater than 9 mm.

14.3 Indications for Ultrasound Scanning in the First Trimester

Common
1. Threatened abortion.
2. Suspected ectopic pregnancy.
3. Uncertain dates (LMP), size discrepancy.
4. Evaluation of retained products post spontaneous abortion.

Less Common
1. Assessment of success of ovulation induction.
2. Assessment of multiple pregnancies.
3. Guidance for chorionic villus sampling.
4. Retained intrauterine contraceptive device.
5. Adjunct for therapeutic abortion.
6. Evaluation for pelvic masses in early pregnancy.

It should be noted that ultrasound should not simply be used to diagnose an uncomplicated pregnancy.

14.4 Threatened Abortion

Definition (clinical)
Blood loss per vaginam with a closed cervical os.

Incidence
25% pregnancies (clinically apparent)
50% of these go on to abort.

Demonstration of a Living Fetus
90–97% favourable outcome.

Ultrasound Findings in Threatened Abortion
1. Intact pregnancy approx 50%. Fetal viability depends on imaging a fetal heart beat or fetal movements.
2. Blighted ovum 20–25%.
3. Missed abortion 25–30%.
4. Incomplete abortion 2–5%.
5. Ectopic pregnancy 1–3%.
6. Hydatidiform mole < 1%.

14.5 Blighted Ovum (Anembryonic Pregnancy)

Definition
A fertilized ovum in which development has been arrested. The majority have chromosomal abnormalities.

Ultrasound Signs of an 'Empty' Sac
1. No fetal parts seen with a sac diameter > 30 mm.
2. No yolk sac seen with a sac > 20 mm.
3. Irregular sac contour.

14.6   Ectopic Pregnancy

Risk Factors
1. Previous ectopic.
2. IUCD *in situ*.
3. History of pelvic inflammatory disease.
4. Previous tubal surgery.
5. *In vitro* fertilization.

Ultrasound Findings
1. Ultrasound evidence of an intrauterine pregnancy excludes the diagnosis if there are no risk factors. (1 : 30 000 approx. rate of concomitant intra- and extrauterine pregnancy. This increases to 1 : 7000 following ovulation induction).
2. Endometrial thickening (decidual cast/pseudogestational sac).
3. Adnexal mass (complex).
4. Fluid in the pouch of Douglas.
5. Demonstration of a living fetus outside the uterus (demonstrated in approx. 10% of cases of ectopic pregnancy).
6. Absence of any ultrasound abnormality does not exclude the diagnosis (approx. 20% of proven cases have no ultrasound abnormalities).
7. HCG level > 1800 mIU/ml with no evidence of an intrauterine pregnancy strongly suggests an ectopic.
   Sensitivity 44%.
   Specificity 100%.

14.7   Absent Intrauterine Pregnancy with Positive Pregnancy Test

1. Ectopic.
2. Early intrauterine pregnancy < 5 weeks.
3. Recent complete/incomplete abortion.

14.8 Liquor Volume

The liquor volume increases in normal pregnancy until approx. 34/40 and then decreases towards term (approx 400 ml at 20 weeks).

Assessment of liquor volume is usually subjective; (accurate and reproducible with experienced observers). < 2 cm pools in any direction indicates a reduction; > 8 cm indicates an increase.

Differential Diagnosis of Abnormal Liquor Volume
1. **Severe oligohydramnios**
   - (a) Renal agenesis/bilaterally nonfunctioning kidneys.
   - (b) Premature rupture of membranes.
   - (c) Severe growth retardation.
2. **Moderate oligohydramnios**
   - (a) Renal anomalies (bilateral).
   - (b) Premature rupture of membranes.
   - (c) Growth retardation.
3. **Polyhydramnios**
   - (a) Diabetes (maternal).
   - (b) Fetal anomaly (30% cases) – fetus may be hydropic. See 14.9.

     Cardiovascular decompensation.

     Obstructive malformations of the gastrointestinal tract, e.g. TOF, duodenal stenosis/atresia.

     Diaphragmatic hernia.

     Anencephaly/other severe cranial anomalies.
   - (c) Rarer causes, e.g. bone dysplasis, neuromuscular abnormalities.

14.9 Fetal Hydrops

Defined as excessive fluid accumulation in the extravascular compartment = subcutaneous oedema, plus at least one of the following – ascites, pleural or pericardial effusions.

In the fetus ascites and pericardial effusions occur earlier than pleural fluid in cardiac failure.

Immune Hydrops
1. Rhesus incompatibility.
2. Other blood group incompatibility.

Non-immune Hydrops
(late manifestations of many severe diseases)
1. **Cardiovascular**
   (a) Arrhythmias.
   (b) Anatomic defects.
   (c) Cardiomyopathies.
2. **Chromosomal**
   (a) Trisomies.
   (b) Turner's syndrome.
   (c) Triploidy
3. **Infections**
   (a) CMV (cytomegalovirus).
   (b) Toxoplasmosis.
   (c) Rubella.
   (d) Syphilis.
   (e) Other congenital infections.
4. **Twin pregnancies**
   (a) Twin to twin transfusion.
5. **Haematological**
   (a) Alpha–thalassaemia.
   (b) Arteriovenous shunts (large).
6. **Thoracic mass lesions**, e.g.
   (a) Diaphragmatic hernia.
   (b) Cystic adenoma of the lung.
   (c) Pulmonary lymphangiectasia.
7. **Gastrointestinal**
   (a) Atresias.
   (b) Volvulus.
   (c) Perforation.

8. **Umbilicus/placenta**
   (a) Chorioangioma.
   (b) Fetomaternal transfusion.
9. **Urinary**
   (a) Congenital nephrosis.
10. **Miscellaneous**
    (a) Skeletal dysplasias.
    (b) Sacrococcygeal teratoma, etc.

14.10   Raised Serum Alphafeto Protein (AFP)

(This protein is produced by the fetus and crosses the placenta to enter the maternal blood. The level rises during normal pregnancy. Discrimination between normal and abnormal is best between 16 and 18 weeks when termination for lethal abnormalities can be offered).

1. **Wrong dates** – (a normal pregnancy which is more advanced).
2. **Twins.**
3. **Missed abortion.**
4. **CNS abnormalities**
   (a) Anencephaly.
   (b) Spina bifida (open).
   (c) Encephalocele.
   (d) Hydrocephalus.
5. **Renal anomalies**
   (a) Renal agenesis.
   (b) Multicystic dysplasia.
   (c) Hydronephrosis.
6. **Anterior wall defects**
   (a) Omphalocele.
   (b) Gastroschisis.

14.11   Ultrasound Signs Suggesting Chromosomal Abnormality

1. Cystic hygroma.
2. Hydrops.
3. Omphalocele.
4. Gross renal anomalies.
5. Major structural cardiac defects – particularly cushion defects.
6. Multiple structural abnormalities involving separate systems.
7. Symmetrical growth retardation.
8. Severe growth retardation.
9. Duodenal stenosis/atresia.
10. Single umbilical artery – associated with any structural anomaly.
11. Abnormal placenta – (cystic).
12. Nuchal membrane – ≥ 6 mm at 2 trimester.

14.12   Cystic Structures Seen in the Fetal Abdomen

1. Renal
   (a) Multicystic dysplasia.
   (b) Hydronephrosis.
   (c) Bladder in outflow obstruction.
2. Gut obstruction
   (a) Duodenal (double bubble) ⎫ with
   (b) Jejunal (multiple fluid filled loops) ⎭ polyhydramnios.
3. Ovarian cyst
   (a) Simple.
   (b) Complex associated with torsion.
4. Mesenteric cysts.
5. Reduplication cysts.
6. Hepatic cysts.
7. Pancreatic cysts.
8. Lymphangioma.

14.13 Major Structural Abnormalities Diagnosable Antenatally

Renal
1. Hydronephrosis.
2. Multicystic dysplastic kidney.
3. Other causes of macrocysts – in particular those associated with named syndromes: see section 8.
4. Autosomal recessive polycystic disease – bilaterally enlarged, highly reflective kidneys. Usually associated with oligohydramnios.
5. Autosomal dominant polycystic disease – a few cases have been reported in which US has demonstrated cysts or large kidneys with accentuation of the cortico-medullary junction.

Central Nervous System
1. Anencephaly – 50–60% of all neural tube defects. Approx. 50% have an associated spinal anomaly.
2. Spina bifida – failure of fusion of the posterior vertebral arch. It may be open or closed (membrane covers the lesion).
   Myelocele – only CSF is present in the sac.
   Meningomyelocele – neural tissue in the sac.
   Site: 90% lumbosacral; 6% thoracic; 3% cervical.
   Associated Arnold–Chiari malformation in 90% (100% with open lesions).
   US signs of the Arnold–Chiari malformation are:
   (a) Hydrocephalus.
   (b) Abnormally pointed frontoparietal region (lemon sign).
   (c) Abnormally shaped cerebellum (banana sign) due to downward displacement of the cerebellum.

Anterior Abdominal Wall Defects
1. Gastroschisis – a defect separate to the cord insertion through which small bowel herniates. No covering membrane. Umbilical vessels not involved. Defect is usually on the right side and liver may, rarely, be involved. Low incidence of chromosome abnormalities. Incidence 1 : 10 000 – 1 : 15 000 live births.

(continued)

2. **Omphalocele** – abdominal wall defect due to failure of
   small bowel to reenter the abdomen. Membrane (amnion)
   covers the eventrated viscera (small bowel ± liver). Umbilical vessels pass through the defect. High incidence of chromosomal abnormalities. Other malformations in 30–60%.
   Incidence 1 : 2 280–1 : 10 000.

Congenital Diaphragmatic Hernia

Incidence: 1 : 2100–1 : 5 000 live births.
High association (16–56%) with other anomalies:

Chromosomal abnormality	30%.
Cardiac	13%.
Neural tube defects	28%.
Omphalocele	20%.
Renal	15%.

Mortality is 80%; secondary to pulmonary hypoplasia.
US signs:
   Displaced heart.
   Bowel within the thorax.
   Polyhydramnios after 25 weeks.

Cardiac Anomalies

Major structural cardiac defects are potentially diagnosable
antenatally.
The examination is best performed at 20 weeks with a repeat
at 24 weeks. For screening a four chamber view only is usually obtained.
A normal examination requires visualization of
1. Four chambers with an intact ventricular septum.
2. Normal AV valves.
3. Normal semilunar valves.
4. Normal connections of the great vessels.
(The patent ductus arteriosus and foramen ovale are normal
structures in the fetus).
A fetal tachycardia, > 200 beats/min, has a high association
with structural abnormalities.
A fetal bradycardia may be due to complete heart block but
is more likely found in a structurally normal heart.
Complete heart block is associated with maternal SLE and
positive Rh antibodies (maternal).

Skeletal Dysplasias

The diagnosis depends on identifying
1. Abnormal bone growth for gestational age.
2. Abnormal bone architecture.
   In the majority of cases femoral shortening is marked.

LETHAL
1. Achondrogenesis.
2. Thanatophoric dwarfism.
3. Asphyxiating thoracic dysplasia – severe form.
4. Short rib polydactyly syndromes.
5. Campomelic dysplasia.
6. Homozygous achondroplasia*.

SOMETIMES LETHAL
1. Chondroectodermal dysplasia.
2. Chondrodysplasia punctata – rhizomelic type.
3. Diastrophic dwarfism.
4. Metatropic dwarfism.
5. Osteogenesis imperfecta*.
6. Hypophosphatasia* – infantile type.
7. Osteopetrosis* – AR congenita type.

NOT USUALLY LETHAL
1. Achondroplasia* – this shows a late fall in growth after 22–24 weeks.
2. Spondyloepiphyseal dysplasia congenita.
3. Mesomelic dysplasia.

14.14   Fetal Growth

Fetal measurements of growth
1. **Abdominal circumference (AC).**
2. **Head circumference (HC).**
3. **Thigh circumference** (not easy to reproduce therefore little used).

Growth Retardation

Definition
≤ 5th centile for weight.

Incidence
approx 5% births.

Risk factors
Maternal
    Hypertension.
    Renal disease.
    Heart disease.
Placental bleeding in early pregnancy.
Multiple pregnancy.
Previous growth retarded baby.

One-third of cases have no known risk factors. Perinatal mortality/morbidity 4–8 × of normally grown babies. Higher incidence of abnormal physical and neurological development.

Types of Growth Retardation

TYPE 1

Time of onset
2nd trimester.

Form
Symmetrical the whole of the body being affected.

Causes
1. **Genetic** (low growth potential).
2. **Chromosomal abnormalities.**
3. **Malformations.**

4. **Intrauterine infections.**
5. **Drugs,** e.g. alcohol, smoking, etc.

TYPE 2

Time of Onset
3rd trimester.

Form
Asymmetric the trunk being more affected than the head.

Causes
1. **Hypertension.**
2. **Maternal renal or vascular disease.**
3. **Placental insufficiency.**
4. **Impairment of placental maturation** (failure of invasion of the spiral arteries).
5. **Idiopathic.**
   Cases of early onset of growth retardation or cases where a structural anomaly is apparent in association with growth retardation should be karyotyped (amniocentesis/placental biopsy/fetal blood sample).

Asymmetrical growth results in an elevated HC/AC ratio.

Doppler velocity waveform in the uterine and umbilical arteries shows changes that can indicate fetal compromise. The fetal circulation (aorta, neck vessel, etc.) similarly show changes. (Increasing vascular resistance in the abnormal shows a decreased or absent diastolic flow.)

14.15 Normal Placental Development

	Gestation age (weeks)
Entire surface of the placenta is covered with villi	implantation to 6–7
Villous placenta (chorion frondosum) develops	7–11
Atrophy of the remaining villi (chorion laeve)	7–11
Three layers of the placenta identifiable	12

1. Basal plate.
2. Placental substance.
3. Chorionic plate.

14.16 Placenta and Membranes in Twin Pregnancies

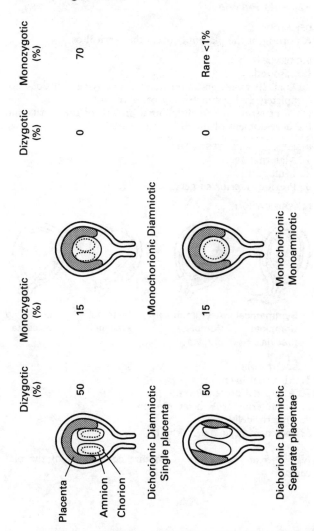

14.17   Abnormalities of the Placenta

Placenta Praevia

DEFINITION
A portion of the placenta covers the cervical os.

INCIDENCE
(ultrasound)
20% at 20 weeks gestation (termed low lying if it does not completely and symmetrically cover the os).
0.5% at term (due to differential growth of the uterus and the development of the lower segment).

INCIDENCE INCREASES WITH
1. Maternal age.
2. Multiparity.
3. Previous uterine surgery.

CLASSIFICATION

Symmetrical Complete praevia   Asymmetrical Complete praevia   Marginal Praevia   Low lying placenta

ASSOCIATIONS
1. Maternal haemorrhage.
2. Abnormal presentation.
3. Intrauterine growth retardation.
4. Preterm delivery.
5. Increased perinatal mortality.

NB   3–5 are related to premature detachment of the placenta.

14.18 Placental Haemorrhage

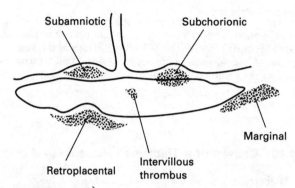

1. **Retroplacental** }
2. **Marginal** } both result in abruption.
3. **Preplacental** – may be either subamniotic or subchorionic but it is often impossible to distinguish this with US.
4. **Intervillous thrombosis** – on US – intraplacental sonolucencies. Incidence increases as the placenta matures. Differential diagnosis – maternal venous lakes.

Placental Abruption

DEFINITION
Premature separation of the normally sited placenta.

INCIDENCE
Clinically apparent in 1% of pregnancies.

CLASSIFICATION
1. Marginal.
2. Retroplacental.

MATERNAL RISK FACTORS
1. Hypertension.
2. Vascular disease.
3. Smoking.
4. Drug abuse (cocaine etc.).

(*continued*)

5. Fibroids.
6. Trauma.

US signs – variable, related to the size, site and time since the event. Acutely a hyperreflective focus relative to the placenta which becomes echo free by 8–14 days. Placental thickness at the site of haemorrhage increases by > 4–4.5 cm. **Outcome** – < 20 weeks gestation 80% normal outcome.

14.19   Causes of a Thickened Placenta (> 4 cm)

1. Diabetes.
2. Rhesus isoimmunization.
3. Fetal hydrops.
4. Triploidy.
5. Intrauterine infections.

14.20   Causes of a Thin Placenta

Intrauterine growth retardation (IUGR).

14.21 Gestational Trophoblastic Disease

DEFINITION
Proliferative disease of the trophoblast.

CLASSIFICATION
1. Hydatidiform mole.
2. Invasive mole.
3. Choriocarcinoma.

INCIDENCE
Geographical variation.
1 : 1200–2000 pregnancies USA.
1 : 100 Hospital patients Indonesia.

RISK FACTORS
Increasing maternal age.
Previous hydatidiform mole.

GENETICS
Two distinct genetic types.
1. Complete (classic) mole 46XX of paternal origin.
2. 46 XY of paternal origin (rare).

Ultrasound Appearances
Large echogenic mass occupying the uterine cavity with numerous small fluid-filled spaces < 15 mm.
(These features are classically seen in the second trimester).

No fetal parts except in a partial mole.

First trimester may simulate a blighted ovum.

Raised Human Chorionic Gonadotrophin (hCG) – in 100% of cases

ASSOCIATION
Theca–lutein cysts (multiseptate). In 20–50% patients.

DIFFERENTIAL DIAGNOSIS
1. Missed abortion with hydropic degeneration of the placenta.
2. Retained products.

(continued)

Incomplete Mole

ULTRASOUND FEATURES
1. Fetal parts seen.
2. Thickened placenta with multiple fluid spaces.
3. Multiple fetal anomalies.
4. Severe intrauterine growth retardation.

Invasive Mole
Develops in approx. 12–15% of cases.

Metastatic Choriocarcinoma
5–8% of cases.

Choriocarcinoma
50% assoc. molar pregnancy.
25% following abortion.
22% following a normal pregnancy.
 3% following an ectopic.

14.22   The Normal Uterus

Size
(length × depth × width).
Nullip. postpubertal – 7 × 4 × 5 cm.
Multiparity – increases the uterine size approx 1 cm in all directions.
Postmenopausal – 3 × 2 × 2 cm.
The neonatal uterus is larger than the prepubertal uterus due to maternal hormones. The endometrial cavity is visualized in 97% of babies and endometrial fluid in 23%.
In childhood the cervix is larger than the uterine body.
The endometrium thickens during the normal menstrual cycle. No endometrium is discernible in the prepubertal or post-menopausal state.

14.23 Endometrial Thickness

Normal
Proliferative phase – 3–5 mm; seen as a thin continuous line early and then as an interrupted line.
Secretory phase – 5–6 mm.
Postmenopausal – < 6 mm.

Increased
1. Early intrauterine pregnancy.
2. Ectopic pregnancy.
3. Oestrogen excess – e.g. polycystic ovary syndrome.
4. Endometrial carcinoma/hyperplasia } > 1 cm is abnormal in postmenopausal women.
5. Endometrial polyp. } Usually irregular.
6. Hormone replacement in postmenopausal women.
7. Ultrasound screening for carcinoma – diagnosis suggested by endometrium > 1 cm and uterine pulsatility index (PI) < 1.6.

14.24 Enlarged Uterus

1. Pregnancy.
2. Leiomyoma.
3. Carcinoma (endometrial).
4. Sarcoma – rare.

14.25   The Normal Ovary

Volume

Length × width × depth × 0.5223 = volume of an ellipse.
Volume increases from the antenatal period to puberty.

Child	1 ml
Normal postpubertal state	5.3–7.6 ml
Normal postmenopausal state	4.3 ml (range 1.5–10.3 ml)

In the normal menstrual cycle one follicle becomes dominant
with a follicular growth of 2 mm/day.

Ovulation

Occurs at a follicular size of 20–24 mm (maximum diameter)
in normal cycles. Smaller in clomiphene cycles; smaller still in
Pergonal cycles.

Ultrasound Signs of Ovulation

1. Collapse of the follicle.
2. Free fluid in the pouch of Douglas.
3. Echo-free zone around the endometrium.

Definition of Simple Cystic Structures in the Ovary

Developing follicle	0.4–1.4 cm
Mature follicle	1.5–2.9 cm
Follicular cyst	> 3 cm

14.26 Ovarian Masses

Ultrasonography is 80–90% accurate in demonstrating the size, consistency and location of pelvic masses. Gross morphology correlates well with ultrasound but poorly with histology.

Intraovarian Doppler velocities (PI < 1) suggest malignancy. This differentiation holds true for postmenopausal women but is less accurate in pre- or perimenopausal women.

Simple Cystic Structures
1. Follicular cyst.
2. Cystadenoma.
3. Polycystic ovaries
   (a) large volume, mean 14 ml,
   (b) multiple (> 10) cysts, 5–8 mm in diameter,
   (c) echogenic stroma relative to the myometrium
       (a) and (b) are seen in 35–40% of cases. 30% have normal volume ovaries, 25% have hyperechoic ovaries and 5% have enlarged ovaries with no cysts. ↑ risk of carcinoma of the endometrium.
4. Cystic teratoma – rare.

Complex (Mainly Cystic)
1. Cystadenocarcinoma.
2. Dermoid.
3. Abscess.
4. Endometriosis.
5. Ectopic pregnancy.

Complex (Mainly Solid)
1. Cystadenocarcinoma.
2. Dermoid.
3. Granulosa cell tumour.
4. Ectopic pregnancy.

(continued)

Solid
1. Adenocarcinoma.
2. Solid teratoma – malignant.
3. Fibroma.
4. Lymphoma.
5. Metastases.
6. Arrhenoblastoma.

Further Reading
Dewbury K., Meire H. & Cosgrove D. (1993) *Ultrasound in Obstetrics and Gynaecology*. Edinburgh: Churchill Livingstone.
Nyberg D.A., Hill L.M., Böhm-Vélez M. & Mendelson E.B. (1992) *Transvaginal Ultrasound*. St Louis: Mosby Year Book.
Rumack C.M., Wilson S.R. & Charboneau J.W. (1991) *Diagnostic Ultrasound*. St Louis: Mosby Year Book.

15
Evaluating Statistics – Explanations of Terminology in General Use

1. **Reliability:** reproducibility of results. (These may be from the same observer or from different observers.) Assessment of this can be built into a study of diagnostic accuracy of a technique, or evaluated beforehand.
2. **Accuracy:** 'proportion of results (positive and negative) which agree with the final diagnosis'.

   i.e. $$\frac{\text{true positives} + \text{true negatives}}{\text{total number of patients in the study.}}$$

   NB This does not take false positive and false negatives into account, and is therefore less meaningful than sensitivity and specificity.
3. **Sensitivity:** 'proportion of diseased patients who are reported as positive'.

   i.e. $$\frac{\text{true positives}}{\text{total number of final diagnosis positive.}}$$

4. **Specificity:** 'proportion of disease-free patients who are reported as negative'.

   i.e. $$\frac{\text{true negatives}}{\text{total number of final diagnosis negative.}}$$

5. **Positive predictive value:** 'proportion of patients reported positive who have the disease'.

   i.e. $$\frac{\text{true positives}}{\text{true positives} + \text{false positives.}}$$

6. **Negative predictive value:** 'proportion of patients reported negative who do not have the disease'.

$$\text{i.e.} \quad \frac{\text{true negatives}}{\text{true negatives} + \text{false negatives}}.$$

Differences in the prevalence of the disease in different studies can affect sensitivity and specificity. For example, if a study is conducted in a tertiary referral hospital the patients will be highly selected and this can alter the way that subtle abnormalities are interpreted as there is a high likelihood of disease being present.

Predictive values are now in common use to indicate the usefulness of an imaging test. However, these depend on sensitivity, specificity *and* prevalence and therefore only apply to settings with a similar prevalence. Formulae are available for calculation of predictive values for different prevalences – see Further Reading.

7. **Receiver operating characteristic (ROC) curves:** In many situations it is not possible to be definitely positive or definitely negative when reporting. With this method approximately five or six levels of certainty may be used in reporting (e.g. 1 = definitely positive, 2 = probably positive etc.). Using each of these levels in turn as the point of cut off between a 'definitely positive' and a 'definitely negative' result, the sensitivity and specificity for each level are then plotted in the form of a graph of sensitivity against 1− specificity. The area under the curve will be 1.0 for a perfect technique (or observer) and 0.5 for an absolutely useless technique (or observer!) (see figure).

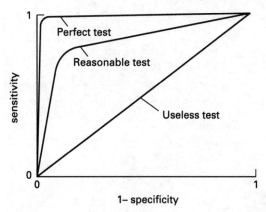

Further Reading
Freedman L.S. (1987) Evaluating and comparing imaging techniques: a review and classification of study designs. *Br. J. Radiol.*, 60: 1071–81.

PART 2

Achondroplasia

A primary defect of enchondral bone formation. Autosomal dominant (but 80% are spontaneous mutations).

Skull
1. Large skull. Small base. Small sella. Steep clivus. Small funnel-shaped foramen magnum.
2. Hydrocephalus – of variable severity.

Thorax
1. Thick, stubby sternum.
2. Short ribs with deep concavities to the anterior ends.

Axial Skeleton
1. Decreasing interpedicular distance caudally in the lumbar spine.
2. Short pedicles with a narrow sagittal diameter of the lumbar spinal canal.
3. Posterior scalloping.
4. Anterior vertebral body beak at T12/L1/L2.

Pelvis
1. Square iliac wings.
2. 'Champagne-glass' pelvic cavity.
3. Short, narrow sacrosciatic notch.
4. Horizontal sacrum articulating low on the ilia.

Appendicular Skeleton
1. Rhizomelic micromelia with bowing of long bones.
2. Widened metaphyses.
3. Ball-and-socket epiphyseal/metaphyseal junction.
4. Broad and short proximal and short proximal and middle phalanges.
5. Trident shaped hands.

Acquired Immune Deficiency Syndrome (AIDS) in Adults

A. Chest

– > 50% present with pulmonary symptoms.
– Bronchoscopy, lavage ± transbronchial biopsy should be considered in all patients as CXR is not pathognomonic.
– The presence of mediastinal/hilar nodes or pleural effusions is serious and often indicates a serious complication such as infections (TB, fungal) or tumours (lymphoma, Kaposi's). Mediastinal/hilar nodes are not a common feature of AIDS or pneumocystis.

1. **Opportunist infections**
   (a) *Pneumocystis carinii* – most common life-threatening infection. Affects 60% of all AIDS patients at least once, and 25% of initial episodes are fatal (it requires intubation, 90% fatality).
   CXR – typically bilateral perihilar and/or basal reticulonodular infiltrates.
   – rapid progression to alveolar consolidation in 3–5 days.
   – rarely
   (i) asymmetrical, upper lobe,
   (ii) 7% have cystic parenchymal changes which can lead to a pneumothorax,
   (iii) mediastinal/hilar nodes or effusions,
   (iv) miliary nodules or solitary nodule (mimics rounded consolidation).
   (b) CMV – found in 80% of autopsies but rarely the only pathogen.
   CXR – typically indistinguishable from pneumocystis or fibrosis.
   (c) *Mycobacterium* – affects 10%, and can occur long before other features of AIDS.
   (d) Bacterial – e.g. *H. influenzae* and *Streptococcus*.
2. **Neoplasms**
   (a) Kaposi's sarcoma – lung involvement occurs in 20% of Kaposi's, and is almost always preceded by cutaneous and/or visceral involvement. It can mimic the appearance of an opportunist infection. Transbronchial and open lung biopsy is often not diagnostic.

    (b) Pulmonary lymphoma – rare.

B. Abdomen
1. **Dysphagia** – common. Usually due to candidiasis, but occasionally due to viral oesophagitis or Kaposi's sarcoma.
2. **Diarrhoea** – common. Usually CMV colitis if mild, or cryptosporidium (protozoa) if severe. The latter produces thick mucosal folds and mild dilatation with a predilection for the duodenum and jejunum. *Giardia*, *Clostridium difficile* and *Mycobacterium* may also occur.
3. **Retroperitoneal/mesenteric lymphadenopathy**
   - (a) Progressive generalized lymphadenopathy syndrome – i.e. two or more extra-inguinal nodes persisting for more than 3 months with no obvious cause. Biopsy reveals benign hyperplasia, and CT shows clusters of small nodes less than 1 cm in diameter in the mesentery and retroperitoneum.
   - (b) Kaposi's sarcoma – stomach is the commonest site but may be multi-centric and involve gut and liver.
   - (c) Lymphoma – usually aggressive form of non-Hodgkin's lymphoma. Peripheral nodes are present in 50% and extranodal involvement is common, particularly bowel, viscera and marrow.
   - (d) *Mycobacterium*.

C. CNS
- 30% of AIDS have neurological signs during their illness.
- 10% of AIDS present with neurological signs, and at autopsy 80% have CNS pathology.
1. **Cerebral atrophy** – probably due to diffuse encephalitis produced by HIV (occasionally toxoplasmosis, CMV) leading to dementia.
2. **Cerebral masses** – occur in 20% of AIDS patients with neurological signs. Commonest causes are
   - (a) Toxoplasmosis – affects 10% of AIDS and causes abscesses. They are commonly multiple thin-walled with necrotic hypodense centres and display ring or nodular enhancement.
   - (b) Lymphoma – affects 6% of AIDS. They are isodense or slightly hyperdense. 50% display uniform contrast enhancement, and 50% show ring enhancement. Solitary lesions are present in 50% of cases.

3. **Other** – white matter disease (progressive multifocal leukoencephalopathy), chronic meningitis (HIV, *Cryptococcus*, *Mycobacterium*) and myelopathy may also occur.

Further Reading

Federle M.P. (1988) A Radiologist Looks at A.I.D.S.: Imaging Evaluation Based on symptom Complexes. *Radiology*, 166: 553–62.

Acquired Immune Deficiency Syndrome (AIDS) in Children

Majority of cases are due to transmission from an infected mother (i.v. drug user, partner of an i.v. drug user, or past history of contact with a bisexual partner) or from transfusions (in the neonatal period or because of diseases such as thalassaemia and haemophilia). 50% of those infected congenitally will present in the first year of life.

AIDS in children differs from AIDS in adults in the following ways:
1. Shorter incubation period.
2. Children are more likely to have serious bacterial infections or CMV.
3. They develop pulmonary lymphoid hyperplasia (PLH)/lymphocytic interstitial pneumonia (LIP), which is rare in adults.
4. They almost never develop Kaposi's sarcoma.
5. They are less likely to be infected with *Toxoplasma, Mycobacterium tuberculosis, Cryptococcus* and *Histoplasma*.
6. Two patterns of presentation and progression can be recognized:
   (a) In the 1st year of life with serious infections, and encephalopathy. Poor prognosis.
   (b) Preschool and school age with bacterial infections and lymphoid tissue hyperplasia. Survival is longer, to adolescence.

Prognostic factors are severity of disease in the mother, the age of onset and the severity at onset.

Generalized Features
Failure to thrive; weight loss; fever; generalized lymphadenopathy; hepatosplenomegaly; recurrent infections; chronic diarrhoea; parotitis.

Chest
1. *Pneumocystis carinii* pneumonia (PCP) – may be localized initially but typically there is rapid progression to generalized lung shadowing which is a mixed alveolar and interstitial infiltrate. 50% of infections occur at age 3–6

months. Two–thirds of infections are the first and only infective episode.

2. Cytomegalovirus (CMV) pneumonia.

3. LIP/PLH. – in 50% of patients. Insidious onset of clinical symptoms. CXR shows a diffuse, symmetrical reticulonodular or nodular pattern (2–3 mm in diameter) which is most easily seen at the bases and periphery of the lungs, ± hilar or mediastinal lymphadenopathy. The nodules consist of collections of lymphocytes and plasma cells without any organisms. Children with LIP are more likely to have generalized lymphadenopathy, salivary gland enlargement and finger clubbing than those whose CXR changes are due to opportunistic infection and the prognosis for LIP is better. Longstanding LIP may be complicated by lower lobe bronchiectasis or cystic lung disease (resembling that seen in histiocytosis).

4. Mediastinal or hilar adenopathy may be secondary to PLH, *M. tuberculosis*, *M. avium-intracellulare*, CMV, lymphoma or fungal infection.

5. Cardiomyopathy, dysrhythmias and unexpected cardiac arrest.

Abdomen

1. Hepatosplenomegaly – due to chronic active hepatitis, hepatitis A or B, CMV, Epstein–Barr virus and *M. tuberculosis*, generalized sepsis, tumour (fibrosarcoma of the liver) or congestive cardiac failure.

2. *Candida* oesophagitis.

3. Chronic diarrhoea – infectious agents are only infrequently found but include *Candida*, CMV and *Cryptosporidium*. Radiological findings are non-specific and include a malabsorption type pattern with thickening of bowel wall and mucosal folds and dilatation. Fine ulceration may be seen.

4. Peumatosis coli.

5. Mesenteric, para-aortic and retroperitoneal lymphadenopathy – due to *M. avium-intracellulare*, lymphocytic proliferation (lymph node syndrome), lymphoma or Kaposi's sarcoma.

6. Renal failure, nephrotic syndrome and urinary tract infections.

Head

1. Typical manifestations are developmental delay, apathy, spastic paraparesis, movement disorders, ataxia and microcephaly. Seizures are uncommon. Imaging may show:
   (a) Cerebral atrophy.
   (b) White matter of ↓ attenuation (CT) or ↑ T_2W signal (MRI).
   (c) Basal ganglia, frontal lobe or thalamic calcification.
2. Meningitis – severe manifestations of common organisms or atypical organisms.
3. Chronic otitis media and sinusitis.

Further Reading

Amodio J.B., Abramson S. & Berdon W.E. & Levy J. (1987) Pediatric AIDS. *Semin. Roentgenol.*, 22: 66–76.

Berdon W.E., Mellins R.E., Abramson S.J. & Ruzal-Shapiro C. (1993) Pediatric HIV infection in its second decade – the changing pattern of lung involvement. *Radiol. Clin. North Am.*, 31: 453–63.

Bradford B.F., Abdenour Jr G.E., Frank J.L., Scott G.B. & Beerman R. (1988) Usual and unusual radiologic manifestations of acquired immunodeficiency syndrome (AIDS) and human immunodeficiency virus (HIV) infection in children. *Radiol. Clin. North Am.*, 26: 341–53.

Faloon J., Eddy J., Wiener L. & Pizzo P.A. (1989) HIV in children. *J. Pediatr.*, 114: 1–30.

Haller J.O. & Cohen H.L. (1994) Pediatric HIV infection: an imaging update. *Pediatr. Radiol.*, 24: 224–30.

Acromegaly

The effect of excessive growth hormone on the mature skeleton.

Skull
1. Thickened skull vault.
2. Enlarged paranasal sinuses and mastoids.
3. Enlarged pituitary fossa because of the eosinophilic adenoma.
4. Prognathism (increased angle of mandible).

Thorax and spine
1. Increased sagittal diameter of the chest with a kyphosis.
2. Vertebral bodies show an increase in the AP and transverse dimensions with posterior scalloping.

Appendicular Skeleton
1. Increased width of bones but unaltered cortical thickness.
2. Tufting of the terminal phalanges.
3. Prominent muscle attachments.
4. Widened joint spaces – especially the metacarpo-phalangeal joints – because of cartilage hypertrophy.
5. Premature osteoarthritis.
6. Increased heel pad thickness (>21.5 mm in female; >23 mm in male).
7. Generalized osteoporosis.

Alkaptonuria

The absence of homogentisic acid oxidase leads to the
accumulation of homogentisic acid and its excretion in sweat
and urine. The majority of cases are inherited as an autosomal
recessive trait.

Axial Skeleton
1. Osteoporosis.
2. Intervertebral disc calcification – predominantly in the
   lumbar spine.
3. Disc space narrowing with vacuum phenomenon.
4. Marginal osteophytes and end-plate sclerosis.
5. Symphysis pubis – joint-space narrowing, chondrocalcinosis, eburnation and, rarely, bone ankylosis.

Appendicular Skeleton
1. Large joints show joint-space narrowing, bony sclerosis,
   articular collapse and fragmentation and intra-articular
   loose bodies.
2. Calcification of bursae and tendons.

Extraskeletal
Ochronotic deposition in other organs may have the following results
1. Cardiovascular system – atherosclerosis, myocardial
   infarction, calcification of aortic and mitral valves.
2. Genitourinary system – renal calculi, nephrocalcinosis,
   prostatic enlargement with calculi.
3. Upper respiratory tract – hoarseness and dyspnoea.
4. Gastrointestinal tract – dysphagia.

Aneurysmal Bone Cyst

1. Age – 10–30 years (75% occur before epiphyseal closure)
2. Sites – ends of long bones, especially in the lower limbs. Also flat bones and vertebral appendages.
3. Appearances
   (a) Arises in unfused metaphysis or in metaphysis and epiphysis after fusion.
   (b) Well-defined lucency with thin but intact cortex.
   (c) Marked expansion (ballooning).
   (d) Thin internal strands of bone.
   (e) ± new bone in the angle between original cortex and the expanded part.
   (f) Fluid level(s) on CT and MRI.
   (g) In the spine they involve the posterior elements.

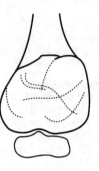

Ankylosing Spondylitis

A mesenchymal disease mainly manifest as an inflammatory arthritis affecting synovial and cartilaginous joints and as an enthesopathy.

Axial Skeleton

1. Involved initially in 70–80%. Initial changes in the sacro-iliac joints followed by the thoracolumbar and lumbosacral regions. The entire spine may be involved eventually.
2. The radiological changes in the sacroiliac joints (see 3.14) are present at the time of the earliest spinal changes.
3. Disco-vertebral junction
    (a) Osteitis – resulting in the squaring of vertebral bodies.
    (b) Syndesmophytes – eventually leading to the 'bamboo spine' (see section 2.14).
    (c) Disc calcification.
    (d) Erosions and destruction – which can be central, peripheral or extensive (pseudarthrosis).
    (e) Osteoporosis – with long-standing disease.
    (f) Kyphosis.
4. Apophyseal joints ⎫ haziness, erosions, subchondral
5. Costotransverse joints ⎬ sclerosis and eventually anky-
6. Costovertebral joints ⎭ losis.
7. Posterior ligament calcification and ossification.

Appendicular Skeleton

1. Involved initially in 10–20% but eventually in 50% of cases. Mild and transient. Asymmetrical involvement of few joints, most frequently hips and shoulders.
2. Similar changes to rheumatoid arthritis, but synovitis is more discrete and less severe. Subchondral bone sclerosis and chondral ossification lead to bony ankylosis. (In adult rheumatoid arthritis, bony ankylosis only occurs in the carpus and tarsus.)
3. No periarticular osteoporosis.

Extraskeletal

1. Iritis in 20% – more frequent with a peripheral arthropathy.

2. Pulmonary upper lobe fibrosis and cavitation (1%).
3. Heart disease – aortic incompetence, conduction defects and pericarditis.
4. Amyloidosis.
5. Inflammatory bowel disease.

Asbestos Inhalation

Lung and/or pleural disease due to the inhalation of asbestos fibres. Disease is more common with crocidolite (blue asbestos) than chrysotile (white asbestos). Pleural disease alone 50%; pleura and lung parenchyma 40%; lung parenchyma alone 10%.

Pleura
1. Plaques or pleural thickening. Most frequent in the lower half of the thorax and tend to follow rib contours. Parietal pleura is affected. Do not occur with less than 20 years exposure.
2. Calcified plaques (in 25%) – probably related to the type of fibre. Usually diaphragmatic.
3. Effusions (in 20%) – frequently recurrent, usually bilateral and often associated with chest pain. Usually associated with pulmonary involvement.

Lung Parenchyma
1. Small nodular and/or reticular opacities which progress through three stages
   (a) Fine reticulation in the lower zones → ground glass appearance.
   (b) More prominent interstitial reticulation in the lower zones.
   (c) Reticular shadowing in the mid and upper zones with obscured heart and diaphragmatic outlines.
2. Large opacities (1 cm or greater), associated with widespread interstitial fibrosis.

Complications
1. Carcinoma of the bronchus – 6–10 × increased incidence in smokers with asbestosis and accounts for 35% of deaths.
2. Mesothelioma – 80% of all mesotheliomas are associated with asbestosis. Accounts for 10% of deaths.
3. Peritoneal mesothelioma.
4. Gastrointestinal carcinomas.
5. Laryngeal carcinoma.

Calcium Pyrophosphate Dihydrate Deposition Disease

1. Three manifestations which occur singly or in combination
   - (a) Crystal-induced acute synovitis (pseudogout).
   - (b) Cartilage calcification (chondrocalcinosis).
   - (c) Structural joint abnormalities (pyrophosphate arthropathy).
2. Associated conditions are hyperparathyroidism and haemochromatosis (definite) and gout, Wilson's disease and alkaptonuria (less definite).
3. Chondrocalcinosis involves
   - (a) Fibrocartilage – especially menisci of the knee, triangular cartilage of the wrist, symphysis pubis and annulus fibrosus of the intervertebral disc.
   - (b) Hyaline cartilage – especially the wrist, knee, elbow and hip.
4. Synovial membrane, joint capsule, tendon and ligament calcification.
5. Pyrophosphate arthropathy is most common in the knee, wrist, metacarpophalangeal joint and acromioclavicular joint. It has similar appearances to osteoarthritis but with several differences
   - (a) Unusual articular distribution – the wrist, elbow and shoulder are uncommon sites for osteoarthritis.
   - (b) Unusual intra-articular distribution, e.g. the patello-femoral compartment of the knee and the radiocarpal compartment of the wrist.
   - (c) Numerous, prominent subchondral cysts.
   - (d) Marked subchondral collapse and fragmentation with multiple loose bodies simulating a neuropathic joint.
   - (e) Variable osteophyte formation.

Chondroblastoma

1. Age – 5–20 years.
2. Sites – upper humerus, lower femur, upper tibia and greater tuberosity (50% occur in the lower limb).
3. Appearances
   (a) Arises in the epiphysis prior to fusion and may expand to involve the metaphysis.
   (b) Well-defined lucency with a thin sclerotic rim.
   (c) Internal calcification in 60%.

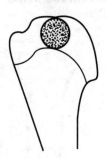

Chondromyxoid Fibroma

1. Age – 10–30 years.
2. Sites – upper end of tibia (50%); also femur and ribs.
3. Appearances
   (a) Metaphyseal ± extension into epiphysis, but never only in the epiphysis.
   (b) Round or oval, well-defined lucency with a sclerotic rim.
   (c) Eccentric expansion.
   (d) Internal calcification is uncommon.

Chondrosarcoma

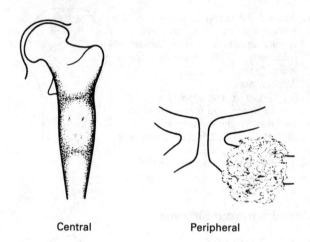

Central   Peripheral

Central

1. Age – 30–60 years.
2. Sites – femur and humerus.
3. Appearances
    (a) Metaphyseal or diaphyseal.
    (b) Lucent, expansile lesion with a sclerotic margin.
    (c) Endosteal cortical thickening or thinning.
    (d) ± cortical destruction and a soft-tissue mass.
    (e) Amorphous or punctate internal calcification.

Peripheral

1. Age – 30–60 years.
2. Sites – pelvic and shoulder girdle, upper femur and humerus.
3. Appearances
    (a) Soft-tissue mass, often arising from the cartilage tip of an osteochondroma.
    (b) Multiple calcific densities.
    (c) Ill-defined margins.
    (d) In the later stages, destruction of underlying bone.

Cleidocranial Dysplasia

Autosomal dominant. One-third are new mutations.

Skull
1. Brachycephaly. Wormian bones. Frontal and parietal bossing.
2. Wide sutures and fontanelles with delayed closure.
3. Broad mandible. Small facial bones. Delayed eruption and supernumerary teeth.
4. Basilar invagination.

Thorax
1. Aplasia or hypoplasia of the clavicles, usually the lateral portion but occasionally the middle portion.
2. Small, high scapulae.
3. Neonatal respiratory distress because of thoracic cage deformity.

Pelvis
1. Absent or delayed ossification of the pubic bones, producing apparent widening of the symphysis pubis.

Appendicular Skeleton
1. Short or absent fibulae.
2. Coxa vara or coxa valga.
3. Congenital pseudarthrosis of the femur.
4. Hand
   (a) Long 2nd and 5th metacarpals; short 2nd and 5th middle phalanges.
   (b) Cone-shaped epiphyses.
   (c) Tapered distal phalanges.
   (d) Supernumerary ossification centres.

Coal Miner's Pneumoconiosis

The effect of the inhalation of coal dust in coal workers.

Simple
1. Small round opacities, 1–5 mm in size. Widespread throughout the lungs but sparing the extreme bases and apices.
2. Less well defined than silicosis.
3. Generally less dense than silicosis, but calcification occurs in at least a few of the nodules in 10% of older coal workers.
4. 'Eggshell' calcification of lymph nodes in 1%.

Complicated, i.e. Progressive Massive Fibrosis
(see Silicosis)

Complications (see Silicosis)

Cretinism (Congenital Hypothyroidism)

Appendicular Skeleton
1. Delayed appearance of ossification centres which may be (a) slightly granular, (b) finely stippled; (c) coarsely stippled or (d) fragmented. The femoral capital epiphyses may be divided into inner and outer halves.
2. Delayed epiphyseal closure.
3. Short long-bones with slender shafts, endosteal thickening and dense metaphyseal bands.
4. Coxa vara with shortened femoral neck and elevated greater trochanter.

Skull
1. Brachycephaly.
2. Multiple wormian bones.
3. Delayed development of vascular markings and diploic differentiation.
4. Delayed sutural closure.
5. Poorly developed sinuses and mastoids.

Axial Skeleton
1. Kyphosis at the thoracolumbar junction, usually associated with a hypoplastic or 'bullet-shaped' body of LV1 or LV2.

The bone changes may have completely regressed in adults.

Crohn's Disease

Colon and small bowel are affected equally. Gastric involvement is uncommon and is usually affected in continuity with disease in the duodenum. Oesophageal involvement is rare.

Small Bowel

1. Terminal ileum is the commonest site.
2. Asymmetrical involvement and skip lesions are characteristic. The disease predominates on the mesenteric border.
3. Aphthoid ulcers – the earliest sign in the terminal ileum and colon.
4. Fissure ulcers – typically they are distributed in a longitudinal and transverse fashion. They may progress to abscess formation, sinuses and fistulae.
5. Blunting, thickening or distortion of the valvulae conniventes – the earliest sign in the small bowel proximal to the terminal ileum. Due to hyperplasia of lymphoid tissue producing an obstructive lymphoedema of the bowel wall.
6. 'Cobblestone' pattern – two possible causes.
   (a) A combination of longitudinal and transverse fissure ulcers bounding intact mucosa. Or
   (b) The bulging of oedematous mucosal folds that are not closely attached to the underlying muscularis.
7. Separation of bowel loops – due to thickened bowel wall.
8. Strictures – which may be short or long, single or multiple. Significant clinical obstruction is less commonly observed.
9. Pseudosacculation.

Colon

1. Asymmetrical involvement and skip lesions. The rectum is involved in 30–50%.
2. Aphthoid ulcers.
3. Deeper fissure ulcers which may produce a 'cobblestone' pattern.
4. Strictures.
5. Pseudosacculation.
6. Inflammatory pseudopolyps.
7. The ileocaecal valve may be thickened, narrowed and ulcerated.

Complications

1. Fistulas.
2. Perforation – which is usually localized and results in abscess formation.
3. Toxic megacolon.
4. Carcinoma
   (a) Colon – less common than in ulcerative colitis, but this may be because more patients with Crohn's disease undergo colectomy at an early stage.
   (b) Small bowel – 300 × increased incidence.
5. Lymphoma.
6. Associated conditions.
   (a) Erythema nodosum.
   (b) Arthritis
      (i) Spondyloarthritis mimicking ankylosing spondylitis. It follows a course independent of the bowel disease and precedes it in 25% of cases.
      (ii) Enteropathic synovitis, the activity of which parallels the bowel disease. The weight-bearing joints of the lower limbs, wrist and fingers are affected.
   (c) Cirrhosis.
   (d) Chronic active hepatitis.
   (e) Gallstones.
   (f) Oxalate urinary tract calculi.
   (g) Pericholangitis.
   (h) Cholangiocarcinoma.
   (i) Sclerosing cholangitis.

Cushing's Syndrome

Cushing's syndrome results from increased endogenous or exogenous cortisol.

Spontaneous Cushing's syndrome is rare and due to

Pituitary disease (Cushing's disease)   80%
    90% of these are due to adenoma and 20%
    have radiological evidence of an intrasellar
    tumour.

Adrenal disease – adenoma
             – carcinoma

Ectopic ACTH, e.g. from a carcinoma   20%
    of the bronchus

Iatrogenic Cushing's syndrome is common and due to high doses of corticosteroids. The effects of excessive amounts of corticosteroids are:

1. Growth retardation in children.
2. Osteoporosis.
3. Pathological fractures which show excessive callus formation during healing; vertebral end-plate fractures, in particular, show prominent bone condensation.
4. Avascular necrosis of bone.
5. Increased incidence of infection – including osteomyelitis and septic arthritis (the knee is affected most frequently).
6. Hypertension.
7. Water retention resulting in oedema.

Cystic Fibrosis

AR condition (gene located in the middle of the long arm of chromosome 7) in which the basic problem is one of excessively viscid mucus. 1 in 2000 live births.

Cardiopulmonary
1. Bronchial wall thickening and mucus-filled bronchi.
2. Atelectasis – subsegmental, segmental or lobar (especially the right upper lobe).
3. Recurrent pneumonia.
4. Bronchiectasis.
5. Focal emphysema in generally overinflated lungs.
6. 'Honeycomb lung' (q.v.), ± pneumothorax (rare before puberty).
7. Low incidence of pleural effusion or empyema at all ages.
8. Cor pulmonale – more common in the older age group and often precedes death.

Gastrointestinal
1. Meconium ileus (10%), meconium peritonitis and meconium ileus equivalent (5–10%).
2. Thickened mucosal folds, nodular filling defects and small-bowel dilatation.

Hepatobiliary
1. Hepatomegaly with texture changes on US and CT.
2. Fatty liver, cirrhosis and portal hypertension.
3. Gallstones, contracted gallbladder, dilatation of intrahepatic bile ducts, intrahepatic bile duct strictures and retention of radionuclide on dynamic biliary scintigraphy.

Pancreas
1. Calcification and calculi.
2. Fibrosis and/or fatty replacement.

Skeletal
1. Retarded maturation.
2. Clubbing and hypertrophic osteoarthropathy.

(*continued*)

Sinuses

1. Chronic sinusitis – opaque maxillary antra in nearly all children over 2 years of age.
2. Nasal polyps (10–15%).
3. Mucocele.

Down's Syndrome (Trisomy 21)

Craniofacial
1. Brachycephaly and microcephaly.
2. Hypoplasia of facial bones and sinuses.
3. Wide sutures and delayed closure. Multiple wormian bones.
4. Hypotelorism.
5. Underdeveloped teeth. No. 2| |2. Less caries than usual.

Central Nervous System
1. Bilateral basal ganglia calcification.

Axial Skeleton
1. Increased height and decreased AP diameter of lumbar vertebrae.
2. Atlantoaxial subluxation.
3. Atlanto-occipital subluxation.
4. Hypoplasia of the posterior arch of C1.
5. Incomplete fusion of vertebral arches of the lumbar spine.

Pelvis
1. Flared iliac wings with small acetabular angles resulting in an abnormal iliac index (iliac angle + acetabular angle).

Chest
1. Congenital heart disease (40%) – mainly endocardial cushion defects and aberrant right subclavian artery.
2. Eleven pairs of ribs.
3. Two ossification centres for the manubrium (90%).

Hands
1. Short tubular bones, clinodactyly (50%) and hypoplasia of the middle phalanx of the little finger (60%).

Gastrointestinal
1. Umbilical hernia.
2. Duodenal atresia or stenosis.

(continued)

3. Tracheo-oesophageal fistula.
4. Anorectal anomalies.

Further Reading

Stein S.M., Kirchner S.G., Horev G. & Hernanz-Schulman M. (1991) Atlanto-occipital subluxation in Down syndrome. *Pediatr Radiol.*, 21: 121–4.

Enchondroma

1. Age – 10–50 years.
2. Sites – hands and wrists predominate (50%). Any other bones formed in cartilage.
3. Appearances
    (a) Diaphyseal or diametaphyseal.
    (b) Well-defined lucency with a thin sclerotic rim.
    (c) Often expansile; cortex preserved.
    (d) Internal ground-glass appearance ± calcification.
    (e) Especially in long bones, may be multilocular.

Syndromes

Ollier's disease – multiple enchondromata.
Maffucci's syndrome – enchondromata + haemangiomata.

Eosinophilic Granuloma

See Langerhans cell histiocytosis.

Ewing's Sarcoma

1. Age – 5–15 years.
2. Sites – femur, pelvis and shoulder girdle.
3. Appearances
   (a) Diaphyseal or, less commonly, metaphyseal.
   (b) Ill-defined medullary destruction.
   (c) ± small areas of new bone formation.
   (d) Periosteal reaction – lamellated (onion skin), Codman's triangle or 'sunray' spiculation.
   (e) Soft-tissue extension.
   (f) Metastases to other bones and lungs.

Extrinsic Allergic Alveolitis

An allergic reaction in the alveoli of sensitized individuals following repeated exposure to one of a number of specific antigens (see 4.21).

Acute Exposure

1. Symptoms 4–8 hours after exposure (dyspnoea, dry cough, fever, malaise and myalgia).
2. The chest X-ray may be normal.
3. When radiological changes are present they usually parallel the severity of clinical symptoms. Changes consist of
   (a) Ground-glass, nodular or miliary shadows, 1–several mm in diameter, diffusely throughout both lungs but with some sparing of the apices and bases. Usually poorly defined.
   (b) Alveolar shadows, particularly in the lower zones, following heavy exposure to antigen.
   (c) Septal lines.
   (d) Hilar lymphadenopathy is rare but may be more frequent in mushroom-worker's lung.
4. Removal from antigen exposure results in resolution of the radiological changes over 1–several weeks.

Chronic Exposure

1. Persistent exposure to low doses of antigen.
2. The diffuse nodular pattern is replaced by the changes characteristic of diffuse interstitial fibrosis.
   (a) Reticular pattern
   (b) Loss of lung volume   } but with marked upper-zone predominance.
   (c) 'Honeycomb' pattern

Fibrous Dysplasia

Unknown pathogenesis. Medullary bone is replaced by fibrous tissue.
1. Diagnosis usually made between 3 and 15 years.
2. May be monostotic or polyostotic. In polyostotic cases the lesions tend to be unilateral; if bilateral then asymmetrical.
3. Most frequent sites are femur, pelvis, skull, mandible, ribs (most common cause of a focal expansile rib lesion) and humerus. Other bones are less frequently affected.
4. Radiological changes include
   (a) A cyst-like lesion in the diaphysis or metaphysis with endosteal scalloping ± bone expansion. No periosteal new bone. The epiphysis is only involved after fusion. Thick sclerotic border – 'rind' sign. Internally the lesion shows a ground-glass appearance ± irregular calcifications together with irregular sclerotic areas.
   (b) Bone deformity, e.g. shepherd's crook deformity of the proximal femur.
   (c) Growth disparity.
   (d) Accelerated bone maturation.
   (e) Skull shows mixed lucencies and sclerosis mainly on the convexity of the calvarium and the floor of the anterior fossa.
   (f) Leontiasis ossea is a sclerosing form affecting the face ± the skull base and producing leonine facies. In such cases extracranial lesions are rare. Involvement may be asymmetrical.
5. Associated endocrine abnormalities include
   (a) Sexual precocity (+ skin pigmentation) – in 30% of females with the polyostotic form. This constitutes the McCune–Albright syndrome.
   (b) Acromegaly, Cushing's syndrome, gynaecomastia and parathyroid hyperplasia (all rare).

Giant Cell Tumour

1. Age – 20–40 years (only 3% occur before epiphyseal closure).
2. Sites – long bones, distal femur especially; occasionally the sacrum or pelvis. Spine rarely.
3. Appearances

   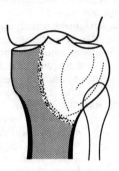

   (a) Epiphyseal and metaphyseal, i.e. subarticular.
   (b) A lucency with an ill-defined endosteal margin.
   (c) Eccentric expansion ± cortical destruction and soft-tissue extension.
   (d) Cortical ridges or internal septa produce a multilocular appearance.

Further Reading

Manaster B.J. & Doyle A.J. (1993) Giant cell tumours of bone. *Radiol. Clin. North Am.*, 31(2): 299–323.

Gout

Caused by monosodium urate monohydrate or uric acid crystal deposition. Idiopathic (in the majority of patients) or associated with many other disorders, e.g. myeloproliferative diseases, drugs and chronic renal disease. Idiopathic gout may be divided into three stages.

Asymptomatic Hyperuricaemia
1. No radiological signs but renal calculi or arthritis will develop in 20%.

Acute Gouty Arthritis
1. Mono- or oligoarticular; occasionally polyarticular.
2. Predilection for joints of the lower extremities, especially the 1st metatarsophalangeal joint (70%), intertarsal joints, ankles and knees. Other joints are affected in long-standing disease.
3. Soft-tissue swelling and joint effusion during the acute attack, with disappearance of the abnormalities as the attack subsides.

Chronic Tophaceous Gout

1. In 50% of patients with recurrent acute gout.
2. Eccentric, asymmetrical nodular deposits of calcium urate (tophi) in the synovium, subchondral bone, helix of the ear and in the soft tissues of the elbow, hand, foot, knee and forearm. Calcification of tophi is uncommon; ossification is rare.
3. Joint space is preserved until late in the disease.
4. Little or no osteoporosis until late, when there may be disuse osteoporosis.

(continued)

5. Bony erosions are produced by tophaceous deposits and may be intra-articular, periarticular or well away from the joint. The latter two may be associated with an obvious soft-tissue mass. Erosions are round or oval, with the long axis in line with the bone. They may have a sclerotic margin. Some erosions have an overhanging lip of bone, which is strongly suggestive of the condition.
6. Severe erosive changes result in an arthritis mutilans.

Complications
1. Urolithiasis – in 10% of gout patients (higher in hot climates).
2. Renal disease
   (a) Acute urate nephropathy – precipitation of uric acid in the collecting ducts. Usually follows treatment with cytotoxic drugs.
   (b) Chronic urate nephropathy – rare.

Haemangioma of Bone

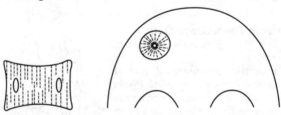

1. Age – 10–50 years.
2. Sites – vertebra (dorsal lumbar) or skull vault.
3. Appearances
   (a) Vertebra – coarse vertical striations, usually affecting only the body but the appendages are, uncommonly, also involved.
   (b) Skull – radial spiculation ('sunburst') within a well-defined vault lucency. 'Hair-on-end' appearance in tangential views.

Haemochromatosis

A genetically determined primary abnormality of iron metabolism. Also occurs secondary to alcohol cirrhosis or multiple blood transfusions, e.g. in thalassaemia or chronic excessive oral iron ingestion.

Clinically – cirrhosis, skin pigmentation, diabetes (bronze diabetics), arthropathy and, later, ascites and cardiac failure.

Bones and Joints
1. Osteoporosis.
2. Chondrocalcinosis – due to calcium pyrophosphate dihydrate deposition (q.v.).
3. Arthropathy – resembles the arthropathy of calcium pyrophosphate deposition disease (q.v.), but shows a predilection for the metacarpophalangeal joints (especially the 2nd and 3rd), the midcarpal joints and the carpometacarpal joints. It also exhibits distinctive beak-like osteophytes and is less rapidly progressive.

Liver and Spleen
1. Mottled increased density of liver and spleen due to the deposition of iron.

Haemophilia

Classical (Factor VIII deficiency) or Christmas disease (Factor IX deficiency). Both are X-linked recessive traits, i.e. manifest in males and carried by females.

Joints
1. Knee, elbow, ankle, hip and shoulder are most frequently affected.
2. Soft-tissue swelling due to haemarthrosis which may appear to be unusually dense owing to the presence of haemosiderin in the chronicaly thickened synovium.
3. Periarticular osteoporosis.
4. Erosion of articular surfaces, with subchondral cysts.
5. Preservation of joint space until late.
6. Accelerated maturation and growth of epiphyses resulting in disparity of size between epiphysis and diaphysis.
7. Contractures.

Bones
1. Osteonecrosis – especially in the femoral head and talus.
2. Haemophilic pseudotumour – in the ilium, femur and tibia most frequently
   (a) Intraosseous – a well-defined medullary lucency with a sclerotic margin. It may breach the cortex. ± periosteal reaction and soft-tissue component.
   (b) Subperiosteal – periosteal reaction with pressure resorption of the cortex and a soft-tissue mass.
   3. Fractures – secondary to osteoporosis.

Soft Tissues
1. Pseudotumour – slow growing.
2. Ectopic ossification.

Further Reading
Stoker D.J. & Murray R.O. (1974) Skeletal changes in haemophilia and other bleeding disorders. *Semin. Roentgenol.*, 9: 185–93.

Homocystinuria

An autosomal recessive inborn error of metabolism. A lack of cystathionine synthetase results in the accumulation of homocystine and methionine, with a deficiency of cystathionine and cystine.

1. Mental defect (60%).
2. Tall, stature, slim build and arachnodactyly, with a morphological resemblance to Marfan's syndrome.
3. Pectus excavatum or carinatum, kyphoscoliosis, genu valgum and pes cavus.
4. Osteoporosis.
5. Medial degeneration of the aorta and elastic arteries.
6. Arterial and venous thromboses.
7. Lens subluxation – usually downward.

Hurler's Syndrome

A mucopolysaccharidosis transmitted as an autosomal recessive trait. Clinical features become evident at the end of the first year – dwarfism, mental retardation, coarse facial features, corneal opacification, deformed teeth and hepatosplenomegaly. Respiratory infections and cardiac failure usually lead to death in the first decade.

Craniofacial
1. Scaphocephalic macrocephaly.
2. J-shaped sella (prominent sulcus chiasmatus).

Central Nervous System
1. Hydrocephalus due to cystic arachnoiditis in the hypothalamic region.
2. Symmetrical low attenuation of white matter on CT (high signal on T_2W, MRI).

Axial Skeleton
1. Oval vertebral bodies with an antero-inferior beak.
2. Kyphosis and a thoracolumbar gibbus.
3. Posterior scalloping with widened interpedicular distance.
4. Short neck.

Appendicular Skeleton

1. Thickened diaphyses.
2. Angulated, oblique growth plates, e.g. those of the distal radius and ulna are angled toward each other.
3. Coxa valga (common). Genu valgum (always).
4. Trident hands with a corase trabecular pattern. Proximal tapering of metacarpals.

Cardiovascular System
1. Cardiac failure due to intimal thickening of coronary arteries or valves.

NB Hunter's syndrome is very similar clinically and radiologically, but the differences are:
   (a) X-linked recessive transmission (i.e. no affected females).
   (b) Later onset (2–6 yrs) and slower progression (death in the 2nd or 3rd decade).
   (c) No corneal clouding.

Hyperparathyroidism, Primary

Causes
1. Adenoma of one gland (90%). (2% of adenomas are multiple).
2. Hyperplasia of all four glands (5%). (More likely if there is a family history.)
3. Carcinoma of one gland.
4. Ectopic parathormone – e.g. from a carcinoma of the bronchus.
5. Multiple endocrine adenopathy syndrome (type 1) – hyperplasia or adenoma associated with pituitary adenoma and pancreatic tumour.

Bones
1. Osteopenia – uncommon. When advanced there is loss of the fine trabeculae and sometimes a ground-glass appearance.
2. Subperiosteal bone resorption – particularly affecting the radial side of the middle phalanx of the midde finger, medial proximal tibia, lateral and occasionally medial end of clavicle, symphysis pubis, ischial tuberosity, medial femoral neck, dorsum sellae, superior surface of ribs and proximal humerus. Severe disease produces terminal phalangeal resorption and, in children, the 'rotting fence-post' appearance of the proximal femur.
3. Diffuse cortical change – cortical tunnelling eventually leading to a 'basketwork' appearance. 'Pepper-pot skull'.
4. Brown tumours – the solitary sign in 3% of cases. Most frequent in the mandible, ribs, pelvis and femora.
5. Bone softening – basilar invagination, wedged or codfish vertebrae, kyphoscoliosis, triradiate pelvis. Pathological fractures.

Soft tissues
1. Calcification in soft tissues, pancreas, lung and arteries.

Joints
1. Marginal erosions – predominantly the distal interphalangeal joints, the ulnar side of the base of the little-finger metacarpal and the hamate. No joint-space narrowing.

2. Weakened subarticular bone, leading to collapse.
3. Chondrocalcinosis (calcium pyrophosphate dihydrate deposition disease) and true gout.
4. Periarticular calcification, including capsular and tendon calcification.

Kidney
1. Nephrocalcinosis.
2. Calculi (in 50%).

Hypercalcaemia
1. Asymptomatic (in 15%) or overt (in 8%).

Gastrointestinal Tract
1. Peptic ulcer.
2. Pancreatitis.

Hypoparathyroidism

1. Short stature, dry skin, alopecia, tetany ± mental retardation.
2. Skeletal changes affecting the entire skeleton.
3. Minimal, generalized increased density of the skeleton, but especially affecting the metaphyses.
4. Calcification of paraspinal ligaments (secondary to elevation of plasma phosphate, which combines with calcium, resulting in heterotopic calcium phosphate deposits).
5. Basal ganglia calcification – uncommon.

Hypophosphatasia

Autosomal recessive. Deficiency of serum and tissue alkaline phosphatase, with excessive urinary excretion of phospho-ethanolamine, 50% die in early infancy.

Neonatal Form
1. Most severely affected. Stillborn or die within 6 months.
2. Clinically – hypotonia, irritability, vomiting respiratory insufficiency, failure to thrive, convulsions and small stature with bowed legs.
3. Radiologically
   (a) Profoundly deficient mineralization with increased liability to fractures.
   (b) Irregular lack of metaphyseal mineralization affecting especially the wrists, knees and costochondral junctions.

Infantile Form
1. Initially asymptomatic, but between 2 weeks and 6 months shows the same symptoms as the neonatal form. Most survive.
2. Radiologically
   (a) Cupped and frayed metaphyses with widened growth-plates.
   (b) Demineralized epiphyses.
   (c) Defective mineralization of skull, including sutures which appear widened.
   (d) Premature sutural fusion → craniostenosis with brachycephaly.

Childhood Form
1. Presents 6 months to 2 years with bowed legs, genu valgum, delayed walking, bone pain, dental caries and premature loss of teeth.
2. Radiologically
   (a) Mild rickets.
   (b) No craniostenosis.

Adult Form

1. Osteomalacia – both clinically and radiologically.

Hypothyroidism

See 'Cretinism'.

Juvenile Chronic Arthritis

Three main clinical subgroups account for 70% of cases.

Systemic Onset
1. Most common at 1–5 years. M = F.
2. Severe extra-articular clinical manifestations include pyrexia, rash, lymphadenopathy and hepatosplenomegaly.
3. Joint involvement is late, but eventually a polyarthritis affects especially the knees, wrists, carpi, ankles and tarsi.

Polyarticular Onset
1. Onset at any age. More common in females.
2. Arthritis predominates with a similar distribution to the systemic onset, but also including the small joints of the fingers and toes. The cervical spine is involved frequently and early.
3. Prolonged disease leads to growth retardation and abnormal epiphyseal development.

Pauciarticular or Monoarticular Onset (most common presentation)
1. Most commonly presents at 1–5 years.
2. Four or less joints involved at the onset – knees, ankles and hips most commonly.
3. ± iridocyclitis.

Less Common Chronic Arthritides in Children
1. Seropositive juvenile onset rheumatoid arthritis – closely resembles the adult disease. Most common over 10 years of age and more common in girls.
2. Juvenile ankylosing spondylitis.
3. Juvenile psoriatic arthritis.
4. Enteropathic arthritis.

Radiological changes
1. Periarticular soft-tissue swelling.
2. Osteopenia – juxta-articular, diffuse or band-like in the

metaphyses, the latter particularly in the distal femur, proximal tibia, distal radius and distal tibia.
3. Accelerated bone growth with large epiphyses and early fusion of growth-plates.
4. Over- or undergrowth of diaphyses.
5. Periostitis – common. Mainly periarticular in the phalanges, metacarpals and metatarsals, but when diaphyseal will eventually result in enlarged rectangular tubular bones.
6. Erosions and joint-space narrowing are late manifestations.
7. Epiphyseal compression fractures.
8. Subluxation and dislocation – most commonly in the hip leading to protrusio acetabuli. Atlanto-axial subluxation is most frequent in seropositive juvenile onset rheumatoid arthritis.
9. Bony ankylosis – especially in the carpus and tarsus.

Langerhans Cell Histiocytosis

Known previously as histiocytosis X. A disease characterized by intense proliferation of reticulohistiocytic elements. Younger patients have more disseminated disease. There are three clinical subgroups.

Eosinophilic Granuloma

1. Accounts for 60–80% of histiocytosis.
2. Commonest in 4–7 year olds, who present with bone pain, local swelling and irritability.
3. 50–75% have solitary lesions. When multiple, usually only two or three. Long bones, pelvis, skull and flat bones are the most common sites involved. 20% of solitary lesions become multiple.
4. Radiological changes in the skeleton include
   (a) Well-defined lucency in the medulla ± thin sclerotic rim. ± endosteal scalloping. True expansion is uncommon except in ribs and vertebral bodies. ± overlying periosteal reaction.
   (b) Multilocular lucency, without expansion, in the pelvis.
   (c) Punched-out lucencies in the skull vault with little or no surrounding sclerosis. May coalesce to give a 'geographical skull'.
   (d) Destructive lesions in the skull base, mastoids, sella or mandible ('floating teeth').
   (e) Vertebra plana, with intact intervertebral discs.
5. Lung involvement in <10% and associated with a worse prognosis.
   (a) Hilar lymphadenopathy.
   (b) Miliary shadowing.
   (c) 'Honeycomb lung'.

Hand–Schüller-Christian Disease

1. Commonest in 1–3 year olds.
2. Osseous lesions together with mild to moderate visceral involvement which includes lymphadenopathy, hepatosplenomegaly, skin lesions, diabetes insipidus, exophthalmos and pulmonary disease.

3. Bone lesions are similar to eosinophilic granuloma, but more numerous and widely distributed.

Letterer–Siwe Disease
1. Major visceral involvement with less prominent bone involvement during the first year of life.
2. Bone lesions are poorly defined.

Lymphoma

Intrathoracic Lymphadenopathy

1. 66% of patients with Hodgkin's disease have intrathoracic disease and 99% of these have intrathoracic lymphadenopathy.
2. 40% of patients with non-Hodgkin's lymphoma have intrathoracic disease and 90% of these have intrathoracic lymphadenopathy.
3. Nodes involved are (in order of frequency) anterior mediastinal, paratracheal, tracheobronchial, bronchopulmonary and subcarinal. Involvement tends to be bilateral and asymmetrical, although unilateral disease is not uncommon.
4. Nodes show a rapid response to radiotherapy and 'eggshell' calcification of lymph nodes may be observed following radiotherapy.

Pulmonary Disease

1. More common in Hodgkin's disease than non-Hodgkin's lymphoma.
2. Very unusual without lymphadenopathy, but may be the first evidence of recurrence after radiotherapy.
3. Most frequently one or more large opacities with an irregular outline. ± air bronchogram.
4. Collapse due to endobronchial lymphoma or, less frequently, extrinsic compression. (Collapse is less common than in bronchial carcinoma.)
5. Lymphatic obstruction → oedema or lymphangitis carcinomatosa.
6. Miliary or larger opacities widely disseminated throughout the lungs.
7. Cavitation – eccentrically within a mass and with a thick wall. (More common than in bronchial carcinoma.)
8. Calcification following radiotherapy.
9. Soft-tissue mass adjacent to a rib deposit.
10. Pleural and pericardial effusions.

Gastrointestinal Tract

Involvement may be the primary presentation (5% of all lymphomas) or be a part of generalized disease (50% at autopsy). In descending order of frequency, the stomach, small intestine, rectum and colon may be involved.

Stomach

1. Primary lymphoma accounts for 2.5% of all gastric neoplasms and 2.5% of lymphomas present with a stomach lesion. Non-Hodgkin's lymphoma accounts for 80%.
2. The radiological manifestations comprise
   (a) Diffuse mucosal thickening and irregularity ± decreased distensibility and peristaltic activity. ± multiple ulcers.
   (b) Smooth nodular mass ± central ulceration. Surrounding mucosa may be normal or show thickened folds.
   (c) Single or multiple ulcers with irregular margins.
   (d) Thickening of the wall with narrowing of the lumen. If the distal stomach is involved there may be extension into the duodenum.
   (e) Duodenal ulcer associated with a gastric mass.

Small Intestine

1. Usually secondary to contiguous spread from mesenteric lymph nodes. Primary disease only in non-Hodgkin's lymphoma.
2. Usually more than one of the following signs is evident
   (a) Irregular mucosal infiltration → thick folds ± nodularity.
   (b) Irregular polypoid mass ± barium tracts within it or central ulceration.
   (c) Annular constriction – usually a long segment.
   (d) Aneurysmal dilatation, with no internal mucosal pattern.
   (e) Polyps – multiple and small or solitary and large. The latter may induce an intussusception.
   (f) Multiple ulcers.
   (g) Non-specific malabsorption pattern.
   (h) Fistula.
   (i) Perforation.

Colon and Rectum

1. Rarely involved. Caecum and rectum more frequently involved than the rest of the colon.

2. Radiologically the disease may show
   (a) Polypoidal mass – which may induce an intussusception.
   (b) Diffuse infiltration of the wall.
   (c) Constricting annular lesion.

Retroperitoneal Lymphadenopathy

1. The typical lymphographic appearances are
   (a) Enlarged nodes.
   (b) Foamy or 'ghost-like' internal architectural pattern.
   (c) Discrete filling defects.
   (d) Non-filling of lymph nodes.

Skeleton

1. Radiological involvement in 10–20% of patients with Hodgkin's disease (50% at autopsy).
2. Involvement arises either from direct spread from contiguous lymph nodes or infiltration of bone marrow (spine, pelvis, major long bones, thoracic cage and skull are sites of predilection).
3. Patterns of bone involvement are
   (a) Predominantly osteolytic.
   (b) Mixed lytic and sclerotic.
   (c) Predominantly sclerotic – *de novo* or following radiotherapy to a lytic lesion.
   (d) 'Moth-eaten' – characteristic of round cell malignancies.
4. In addition the spine may show
   (a) Anterior erosion of a vertebral body due to involvement of an adjacent paravertebral lymph node.
   (b) Solitary dense vertebral body (ivory vertebra).
5. Hypertrophic osteoarthropathy.

Central Nervous System

1. Primary lymphoma of brain (microgliomatosis) accounts for 1% of brain tumours.
2. The cerebrum, brain-stem and cerebellum are affected (in order of frequency).
3. Two patterns may be recognized at CT
   (a) Large round or oval space-occupying lesion showing

increased attenuation and surrounding oedema. Marked homogeneous enhancement (although avascular at angiography). Multifocal in 50%.

(b) Cuff of tissue around the lateral ventricles with marked enhancement.

Further Reading

Craig O. & Gregson R. (1981) Primary lymphoma of the gastrointestinal tract. *Clin. Radiol.*, 32: 63–71.

Felson B. (ed.) (1980) The lymphomas and leukaemias. Part I. *Semin. Roentgenol.*, 15 (3).

Felson B. (ed.) (1980) The lymphomas and leukaemias. Part 2, *Semin. Roentgenol.*, 15 (4).

Libshitz H.I. (ed.) (1990) Imaging the lymphomas. *Radiol. Clin. North Am.*, 28 (4).

Privett J.T.J., Rhys Davies E. & Roylance J. (1977) The radiological features of gastric lymphoma. *Clin. Radiol.*, 28: 457–63.

Strickland B. (1967) Intrathoracic Hodgkin's disease. Part II. Peripheral manifestations of Hodgkin's disease in the chest. *Br. J. Radiol.*, 40: 930–8.

Thomson J.C.G. & Brownell B. (1981) Computed tomographic appearances in microgliomatosis. *Clin. Radiol.*, 32: 367–74.

Marfan's Syndrome

A connective tissue disorder transmitted as an autosomal dominant trait, but with variable expression. 15% spontaneous mutations.

1. Tall stature, long slim limbs and arachnodactyly (metacarpal index 8.4–10.4).
2. Joint laxity.
3. Dislocations of sternoclavicular joint and hip and perilunate dislocation.
4. Scoliosis (60%) and kyphosis.
5. Protrusio acetabuli.
6. Pectus excavatum or carinatum.
7. Rib notching.
8. Narrow facies with a narrow, high arched palate.
9. Lens subluxation – usually upwards.
10. Mitral valve abnormalities – large annulus, regurgitation and prolapse.
11. Aortic sinus dilatation and aortic regurgitation.
12. Cystic medial necrosis of the aorta; aortic dissection.
13. Pulmonary emphysema and bullae.
14. Ascending aortic dilatation ± dissection. Less commonly aneurysms of the descending thoracic or abdominal aorta or pulmonary artery.

Morquio's Syndrome

A mucopolysaccharidosis transmitted as an autosomal recessive trait. Clinical presentation during the second year, with decreased growth, progressive skeletal deformity, corneal opacities, lymphadenopathy, cardiac lesions and deafness.

Axial Skeleton
1. Universal vertebra plana. Wide discs.
2. Hypoplastic dens.
3. Hypoplastic dorsolumbar vertebra which may be displaced posteriorly.
4. Central anterior vertebral body beaks.
5. Short neck.
6. Dorsal scoliosis and dorsolumbar kyphosis.

Appendicular Skeleton
1. Defective irregular ossification of the femoral capital epiphyses leading to flattening.
2. Genu valgum.
3. Short, wide tubular bones with irregular metaphyses. Proximal tapering of the metacarpals.
4. Irregular carpal and tarsal bones.

Cardiovascular System
1. Late onset aortic regurgitation.

Multiple Endocrine Neoplasia (MEN) Syndromes

Autosomal dominant. Classification.

MEN I (Werner's syndrome)
1. Hyperparathyroidism (90%).
2. Pancreatic islet cell tumours (60%).
   Gastrinomas (60%) – usually slow growing: → Zollinger–Ellison syndrome.
   Insulinomas – symptoms of hypoglycaemia.
   VIPomas – secreting vasoactive intestinal peptide → explosive, watery diarrhoea with hypokalaemia and achlorhydria.
   Glucagonomas – produce a syndrome of diabetes mellitus, necrolytic migratory erythema, anaemia, weight loss and thromboembolic complications.
3. Pituitary tumours (5%) – hormone secreting and non-secreting.
4. Thyroid adenoma.
5. Adrenal adenoma.
6. Carcinoid tumour.

MEN IIa (Sipple's syndrome)
1. Medullary carcinoma of the thyroid (100%).
2. Phaeochromocytoma (50%).
3. Hyperparathyroidism (10%).

MEN IIb
1. Marfanoid appearance (100%).
2. Multiple mucosal neuromas (100%).
3. Medullary carcinoma of the thyroid (100%).
4. Phaeochromocytoma (50%).

Multiple Myeloma/Plasmacytoma

Plasma cell neoplasms of bone are solitary (plasmacytoma; 3% of all plasma cell tumours) or multiple (multiple myeloma; 94% of all plasma cell tumours). 3% of all plasma cell tumours are solely extraskeletal.

Plasmacytoma
1. A well-defined, grossly expansile bone lesion arising, most commonly, in the spine, pelvis or ribs.
2. It may also exhibit soft-tissue extension, internal septa or pathological fracture.

Multiple Myeloma
Radiological manifestations are skeletal and extraskeletal.

SKELETAL
1. 80–90% have an abnormal skeleton at the time of diagnosis.
2. The skeleton may
   (a) be normal – uncommon;
   (b) show generalized osteopenia only – rare;
   (c) show osteopenia with discrete lucencies
      (i) The lucencies are usually
         – widely disseminated at the time of diagnosis (spine, pelvis, skull, ribs and shafts of long bones);
         – uniform in size (cf. metastases, which are usually of varying size);
         – well-defined, with a narrow zone of transition.
      (ii) Vertebral body collapse, occasionally with disc destruction. ± paravertebral shadow. Involvement of pedicles is late.
      (iii) Rib lesions tend to be expansile and associated with extrapleural soft-tissue masses.
      (iv) Pathological fractures occur and healing is accompanied by much callus.
   (d) show a permeating, mottled pattern of bone destruction similar to other round cell malignancies, e.g.

(continued)

Ewing's sarcoma, anaplastic metastatic carcinoma, leukaemia and reticulum cell sarcoma.

(e) show multiple sclerotic lesions which mimic osteoblastic metastases (2%).

EXTRASKELETAL

1. Hypercalcaemia (30%).
2. Soft-tissue tumours in sinuses, the submucosa of the pharynx and trachea, cervical lymph nodes, skin and gastrointestinal tract.
3. Hepatosplenomegaly.

Further Reading

Meszaros W.T. (1974) The many facets of multiple myeloma. *Semin. Roentgenol.*, 9: 21–28.

Myasthenia Gravis

An autoimmune disorder characterized by muscle weakness and fatigability. Confirmed clinically by a positive response to intravenous edrophonium chloride (Tensilon test) and the presence of acetylcholine receptor antibodies.

1. Thymus is normal or involuted in 20%, hyperplastic in 65% and 15% have a thymoma. Hyperplasia is more common in the young; thymoma more common after the 4th decade.
2. 60% of thymomas are benign and well encapsulated; 40% are locally invasive and show subpleural deposits.

Further Reading

Moore N.R. (1989) Imaging in myasthenia gravis. *Clin. Radiol.*, 40: 115–16.

Neurofibromatosis

Neurofibromatosis 1 (NF-1; von Recklinghausen disease)

90% of all cases. Prevalence 1 in 4000 persons. 50% are new mutations, 30% are AD inherited. Gene is located on chromosome 17. May be diagnosed if two or more of the following criteria are present:

- Six or more *café-au-lait* spots >5 mm in diameter in prepubertal patients and >15 mm in postpubertal patients.
- Two or more neurofibromas.
- Axillary freckling.
- One plexiform neurofibroma.
- Two or more iris hamartomas (Lisch nodules).
- Optic glioma.
- Typical bone lesions such as sphenoid dysplasia or tibial pseudarthrosis.
- One or more first degree relatives with NF-1.

Neurofibromatosis 2 (NF-2)

10% of all cases. Rare in childhood. Prevalence 1 in 50 000 persons. AD with the gene located on chromosome 22. Manifestations include VIIIth nerve tumours or schwannomas, other intracranial or spinal tumours such as neurinomas and meningiomas. May be diagnosed if one of the following criteria are present:

- Bilateral VIIIth nerve tumours.
- Unilateral VIIIth nerve tumour in association with any two of the following – meningioma, neurofibroma, schwannoma, juvenile posterior subcapsular cataracts.
- Unilateral VIIIth nerve tumour with other spinal or brain tumour as above in a first degree relative.

Skull

1. Dysplastic sphenoid – absent greater wing ± lesser wing (empty orbit), absent posterolateral wall of the orbit. May result in proptosis.
2. Lytic defects in the calvarium, especially in or near the lambdoid suture.
3. Enlargement of foramina.
4. Mandibular abnormalities.   (*continued*)

5. Enlarged internal auditory meati – due to acoustic neuromas or dural ectasia without associated neuroma.

Brain

1. Macrocephaly.
2. Hydrocephalus, of insidious onset – usually due to aqueduct stenosis caused by gliosis but may be secondary to a tumour.
3. Cerebral and cerebellar calcification. Heavy calcification of the choroid plexuses is rare but classical.
4. Tumours.
   (a) Optic tract, chiasm and nerve gliomas (common). 10–30% of optic gliomas are associated with NF-1. The association is higher with optic nerve gliomas and bilateral optic nerve gliomas are found almost exclusively in NF-1. Optic nerve glioma is not found in NF-1.
   (b) Optic nerve sheath meningiomas (rare).
   (c) Cranial nerve (V–XII) schwannomas. Frequently multiple and bilateral in NF-2. Acoustic neuromas (schwannomas) are bilateral in at least 90% of NF-2.
   (d) Brain-stem and supratentorial gliomas.
   (e) Intracranial meningiomas – often multiple in NF-2.
5. Focal or multifocal ↓ T_1W and/or ↑ T_2W signal without mass effect, most often in the basal ganglia, cerebellum and cerebral peduncles. No enhancement. ? Due to hamartomas and probably not progressive. More common in younger patients and in those with an optic glioma.
6. Arachnoid cyst.
7. Arterial occlusive disease, including moyamoya.

Spine

1. Scoliosis (typically acute and thoracic) and kyphosis.
2. Dural ectasia with posterior scalloping.
3. Absent or hypoplastic pedicles.
4. Spondylolisthesis.
5. Lateral meningocele (rare).
6. Multiple neurofibromas (enhancing) ± dumbbell. Enlargement of intervertebral foramina. Most common in the cervicothoracic region.
7. Paraspinal plexiform neurofibromas.

Thorax
1. Rib notching, 'twisted ribbon' ribs and splaying of ribs.
2. Interstitial pulmonary fibrosis progressing to a 'honey-comb' lung.

Appendicular Skeleton
1. Overgrowth or, less commonly, undergrowth of long bones.
2. Overtubulation or undertubulation (due to cortical thickening).
3. Anterior and lateral bowing of the tibia with irregular peri-osteal thickening is common and is usually evident in the first year. It frequently progresses to no. 4.
4. Pseudarthrosis.
5. Intraosseous neurofibromas present as subperiosteal or cortical lucencies with a smooth expanded outer margin.
6. Cortical pressure resorption from an adjacent soft-tissue neurofibroma.
7. Cortical defects may also be due to dysplastic periosteum.
8. Association of non-ossifying fibromas and neurofibrom-atosis.

Other
1. Soft-tissue neurofibromas and plexiform neurofibromas. The latter may be associated with partial gigantism.
2. Renal artery stenosis or aneurysm.
3. Phaeochromocytoma (in 1%).
4. Osteomalacia.

Further Reading
Aoki S., Barkovich A.J., Nishimura K. *et al.* (1989) Neurofibrom-atosis types 1 and 2: cranial MR findings. *Radiology*, 172: 527–34.
Klatte E.C., Franken E.A. & Smith J.A. (1976) The radiographic spec-trum in neurofibromatosis. *Semin. Roentgenol.*, 11: 17–33.
Menor F., Martí-Bonmatí L., Mulas F., Cortina H. & Olagüe R. (1991) Imaging considerations of central nervous system mani-festations in paediatric patients with neurofibromatosis type 1. *Pediatr. Radiol.*, 21: 389–94.
Shu H.H., Mirowitz S.A. & Wippold II F.J. (1993) Neurofibrom-atosis: MR imaging findings involving the head and spine. *Am. J. Roentgenol.*, 160: 159–64.

Neuropathic Arthropathy

Disease	Sites of involvement
Diabetes mellitus	Metatarsophalangeal, tarsometatarsal and intertarsal joints
Steroid treatment	Hips and knee
Syringomyelia	Shoulder, elbow, wrist and cervical spine
Tabes dorsalis	Knee, hip, ankle and lumbar spine
Congenital insensitivity to pain	Ankle and intertarsal joints
Myelomeningocele	Ankle and intertarsal joints
Leprosy	Hands (interphalangeal), feet (metatarsophalgeal) and lower limbs
Chronic alcoholism	Metatarsophalangeal and interphalangeal joints

Radiological changes include
1. Variable progression, but often rapid. In the early stages can resemble osteoarthritis.
2. Joint effusion.
3. Osteochondral fractures and fragmentation of articular surfaces.
4. Intra-articular bony debris.
5. Excessive callus formation.
6. Subluxations and dislocations.
7. Bone density is normal but in diabetes and syringomyelia superadded infection is not uncommon, resulting in juxta-articular osteoporosis.
8. Bone resorption can produce a 'cup and pencil' appearance.

Non-accidental Injury

Skeletal

1. Fractures in 11–55% and significantly more common in the younger child. Typically multiple, in varying stages of healing and explained by an implausible history.
2. Shaft fractures are more common than metaphyseal fractures although the latter are characteristic.
3. Metaphyseal fractures are due to tractional and torsional stresses on limbs and histologically there is a transmetaphyseal disruption of the most immature metaphyseal primary spongiosa. The most subtle indication of injury is a transverse lucency within the subepiphyseal region of the metaphysis. It may be visible in only one projection and its appearance is influenced by the severity of the bony injury, the degree of displacement of the fragments and the chronicity of the process. Peripherally the fracture line may undermine and isolate a thicker fragment of bone and it is this thick peripheral margin of bone that produces the corner fractures and bucket handle configurations.
4. Rib fractures comprise 5–27% of all fractures in abused children. Posterior rib fractures have a higher specificity for abuse than antero-lateral fractures. In the absence of prematurity, birth injury, metabolic disorders, bone dysplasias and major trauma, e.g. road traffic accidents, rib fractures may be considered specific for abuse. 80% are occult.
5. Skull fractures which are linear and in the parietal bone are most common but others are more suggestive of non-accidental injury:
   (a) Multiple fractures.
   (b) Non-parietal fractures.
   (c) Complex fractures.
   (d) Depressed fractures.
   (e) Diastatic fractures greater than 5 mm in width.
   (f) Growing fractures (leptomeningeal cysts).
   A depressed occipital fracture is virtually pathognomonic of abuse.
6. In infants and young children certain fractures have a high specificity for abuse owing to their unusual locations. These include scapular injuries, injuries involving the small bones of the hands and feet and spinal injuries.

(continued)

7. Dislocations are rarely encountered in abused children. Malalignment of bones sharing an articulation usually indicates a growth plate injury rather than dislocation. When dislocations do occur they are likely secondary to massive injury and are accompanied by adjacent fracture.

Intracranial Injuries

Shaking is the most important mechanism in the production of intracranial injury in child abuse. The spectrum of injuries includes:

(a) Subdural haematoma, especially posterior interhemispheric collections due to tearing of the small bridging veins which cross the subdural space.

(b) Intraventricular haemorrhage – when gross is usually associated with massive intracranial injury.

(c) Subarachnoid haemorrhage.

(d) Cerebral oedema – generalized or focal and is the most common CT alteration in all types of paediatric head injury.

(e) Contusional tears – pathognomonic of shaking in the first 6 months of life.

(f) Cerebral contusion – seen usually along the cerebral convexities, particularly in the frontal and parasagittal regions, conforming to the sites of greatest stress during acceleration–deceleration movements.
Commonly associated with subdural haematomas.

(g) Cerebral atrophy – depending on the site of the original injury may be focal or diffuse and evident as early as 1 month following the acute injury.

(h) Post-traumatic hydrocephalus.

Visceral Trauma

Commonly occurs after the child is able to move about. Mortality of 50% for visceral injuries associated with child abuse. The most likely mechanism of injury is a direct blow or the effect of rapid deceleration after being hurled. The most common injuries involve the hollow viscera, mesenteries, liver and pancreas.

Further Reading

Hobbs C.J. (1984) Skull fracture and the diagnosis of abuse. *Arch. Dis. Childh.* 59: 246–52.

Jaspan T., Narborough G., Punt J.A.G. & Lowe J. (1992) Cerebral contusional tears as a marker of child abuse – detection by cranial sonography. *Pediatr. Radiol.,* 22: 237–45.

Kleinman P. (1987) *Diagnostic Imaging of Child Abuse.* Baltimore: Williams & Wilkins.

Merten, D.F., Radkowski M.A. & Leonidas J.C. (1983) The abused child: a radiological reappraisal. *Radiology,* 148: 377–81.

Worlock P., Stower M. & Barbor P. (1986) Patterns of fractures in accidental and non-accidental injury in children: a comparative study. *Br. Med. J.,* 293: 100–3.

Zimmerman R.A., Bilaniuk L.T., Bruce D., Schut L., Uzzell B. & Goldberg H.I. (1979) Computed tomography of craniocerebral injury in the abused child. *Radiology,* 130: 687–90.

Non-ossifying Fibroma (Fibrous Cortical Defect)

1. Age – 10–20 years.
2. Sites – femur and tibia.
3. Appearances
   (a) Diametaphyseal, becoming diaphyseal as the bone grows.
   (b) Well-defined lucency with a sclerotic margin.
   (c) Eccentric ± slight expansion; in thin bones, e.g. fibula, it occupies the entire width of the bone.

Ochronosis

See 'Alkaptonuria'.

Osteoblastoma

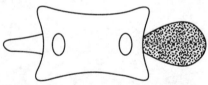

1. Age – 10–20 years.
2. Sites – vertebra (neural arch predominantly) and, less commonly, in the long bones.
3. Appearances
   (a) Well-defined lucency with a sclerotic rim.
   (b) May be expansile, but the cortex is preserved.
   (c) ± internal calcification.
   (d) May be purely sclerotic in the spine.
   (e) In long bones it is metaphyseal or diaphyseal.

Osteochondroma (Exostosis)

1. Age – 10–20 years. M > F.
2. Sites – distal femur, proximal tibia, proximal humerus, pelvis and scapula. When there are multiple osteochondromata the condition is termed diaphyseal acalasis (AD).
3. Appearances
   (a) Metaphyseal.
   (b) Well-defined eccentric protrusion with the parent cortex and trabeculae continuous with that of the tumour.
   (c) Tumour is usually directed away from the end of the bone and migrates away from the end as growth proceeds.
   (d) The cartilage cap is not visible in childhood, but becomes calcified in the adult.
   (e) If large → failure of correct modelling.
   (f) Rapid growth of a stable lesion suggests transformation to a chondrosarcoma (less than 1% of cases).

Osteogenesis Imperfecta

A clinically heterogeneous condition due to disorders of collagen. There are several distinct genetic entities and the current classification is as shown below:

Type 1
Osseous fragility (variable from minimal to severe); blue sclerae; presenile deafness due to otosclerosis (in 20%). Multiple fractures and intracranial bleeding may result in stillbirth or perinatal death. Gracile, osteoporitic bones often with deformity secondary to fractures and mechanical stresses. Rapid fracture healing ± exuberant callus. Flattened or biconcave vertebral bodies. Wormian bones, although these may be obliterated in adulthood. Autosomal dominant.
   Subgroup A: with normal teeth.
   Subgroup B: with dentinogenesis imperfecta.

Type II
Lethal perinatal. Extremely severe osseous fragility.
   Subgroup A: extremely osteopenic skull; broad beaded ribs; short, broad 'concertina' shaped long bones; platyspondyly. New mutation, autosomal dominant.
   Subgroup B: better ossification of skull; thin, wavy ribs with only a few fractures; short, broad 'concertina' shaped long bones; vertebral body height similar to or greater than disc space. Autosomal recessive.
   Subgroup C: poor ossification of skull; thin, irregularly shaped ribs, short, poorly modelled long bones with multiple angulations; normal vertebral body height. Autosomal recessive or new dominant mutation.

Type III
Rare. Moderate to severe osseous fragility; normal sclerae; severe deformity of long bones and spine result in severe dwarfing; cystic expansion of ends of long bones with increasing age. Wormian bones. Markedly elongated lumbar pedicles. White sclerae. Autosomal recessive, or new dominant mutation.

Type IV
Rare. Osseous fragility with normal sclerae and severe deformity of long bones and spine. Autosomal dominant.

Further Reading
Sillence D.O. (1981) Osteogenesis imperfecta. An expanding panorama of variants. *Clin. Orthop.*, 159: 11–25.
Sillence D.O., Senn A. & Danks D.M. (1979) Genetic heterogeneity in osteogenesis imperfecta. *J. Med. Genet.*, 16: 101–16.
Smith R., Francis M.J.O. & Houghton G.R. (1983) *The Brittle Bone Syndrome: Osteogenesis Imperfecta.* Butterworth: London.
Thompson E.M., Young I.D., Hall C.M. & Pembrey M.E. (1987) Recurrence risk and prognosis in severe sporadic osteogenesis imperfecta. *J. Med. Genet.*, 24: 390–405.

Osteoid Osteoma

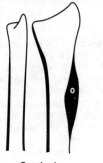 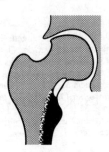

Cortical   Cancellous

1. Age – 10–30 years.
2. Sites – most commonly femur and tibia.
3. Appearances
   Cortical
   (a) Central lucent nidus (less than 1 cm) ± dense calc-
       ified centre.
   (b) Dense surrounding bone.
   (c) Eccentric bone expansion ± periosteal reaction.

   Cancellous
   (a) Usually femoral neck.
   (b) Lucent lesion with bone sclerosis a distance away. The
       head and neck may be osteoporotic.

Osteomalacia

Increased uncalcified osteoid in the mature skeleton.
1. Decreased bone density.
2. Looser's zones – bilaterally symmetrical transverse lucent bands of uncalcified osteoid which, later in the disease, have sclerotic margins. Common sites are the scapulae, femoral necks and shafts, pubic rami and ribs.
3. Coarsening of the trabecular pattern with ill-defined trabeculae.
4. Bone softening – protrusio acetabuli, bowing of long bones, biconcave vertebral bodies and basilar invagination.

Osteopetrosis

A defect of bone resorption due to decreased osteoclastic activity. A number of forms have been recognized.

Benign or Tarda, AD

1. Often asymptomatic individuals in whom a chance diagnosis is made on radiographs taken for some other purpose. Some have a mild anaemia and there may be cranial nerve compressions. Predisposition to fractures. Tooth extraction may be complicated by osteomyelitis.
2. Increasing bone sclerosis during childhood, with some sparing of the peripheral skeleton.
3. 'Bone-within-bone' appearance – usually disappearing by the end of the second decade.
4. 'Rugger jersey' spine.

Malignant or Congenita, AR

1. Manifestations during infancy – failure to thrive and evidence of marrow failure due to bone overgrowth, i.e. anaemia, thrombocytopenia and hepatosplenomegaly. Pathological fractures. Cranial nerve palsies due to bony compression. Death in the first decade.
2. Generalized bone sclerosis with transverse metaphyseal bands.
3. 'Bone-within-bone' appearance.
4. 'Rugger jersey' spine.
5. Later, flask-shaped ends of the long bones.

Intermediate, AR

With Renal Tubular Acidosis, AR

1. Presents in early childhood with failure to thrive and hypotonia due to renal tubular acidosis. Anaemia, cranial nerve lesions and fractures are variable features.
2. Radiology is similar to the benign form but tends to normality in later childhood. Basal ganglia and periventricular calcification are consistent findings which differentiate this form from the others.

Further Reading

Beighton P. (1988) *Inherited Disorders of the Skeleton*, pp. 163–9. Edinburgh: Churchill Livingstone.

Beighton P. & Cremin B.J. *Sclerosing Bone Dysplasias*, pp. 19–31. Berlin: Springer-Verlag.

Osteosarcoma

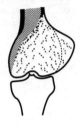

1. Age – 10–25 years with a second peak in the 7th decade (flat bones).
2. Sites – distal femur, proximal tibia, proximal humerus and pelvis.
3. Predisposing factors – Paget's disease, radiotherapy, osteochondroma, fibrous dysplasia, retinoblastoma, osteopetrosis and bone infarct.
4. Association – bilateral retinoblastoma.
5. Appearances
   (a) Metaphyseal; epiphyseal (< 1%) and diaphyseal (10%) are unusual.
   (b) May be predominantly lytic, sclerotic or mixed.
   (c) Wide zone of transition with normal bone.
   (d) Cortical destruction with soft tissue extension.
   (e) ± internal calcification of bone.
   (f) Periosteal reaction – 'sunray' spiculation, lamellated and/or Codman's triangle.
6. Unusual variants
   (a) Telangiectatic – 5% of osteosarcomas. Aggressive. Characterized by large blood-filled cavities and thin septations within the tumour. Similar presentation to conventional osteosarcoma but pathological fracture is more common. Diaphyseal > metaphyseal. Majority in femur and tibia. Usually entirely osteolytic. Fluid levels on CT and MRI.
   (b) Small cell – 1% of osteosarcomas. Similar appearance and presentation to conventional osteosarcoma but prognosis is much worse.
   (c) Low grade or intraosseous well-differentiated – 1–2%. Older age at presentation and more chronic history. More benign looking radiological appearance.
   (d) Parosteal – 5%. Attached to the surface of the bone by a stalk (early) or a broad base (late) with a tendency to encircle it. Older age group, 20–40 years. Femur is most common site.

(e) Extraosseous – buttocks and thighs. Ossification or calcification in a soft-tissue mass.
(f) Multicentric – rapidly fatal.

Further Reading

Bloem J.L. & Kroon H.M. (1993) Osseous lesions. *Radiol. Clin. North Am.*, 31(2): 261–78.
Dahlin D.C. (1967) Osteogenic sarcoma. A study of 600 cases. *J. Bone Joint Surg.*, 49(A): 101–10.
Kumar R., David R., Madewell J.E. & Lindell Jr M.M. (1987) Radiographic spectrum of osteogenic sarcoma. *Am. J. Roentgenol.*, 148: 767–72.

Paget's Disease

A condition characterized by excessive abnormal remodelling of bone. Increasing prevalence with age – rare in patients less than 40 years old, 3% of the population in middle age and 10% of the population in old age. The disease predominates in the axial skeleton – spine (75%), skull (65%), pelvis (40%) – and proximal femur (75%). (The percentages represent patients with Paget's disease in whom these sites are affected.) Monostotic disease does occur. There are three stages.

Active (Osteolytic)
1. Skull – osteoporosis circumscripta, especially in the frontal and occipital bones.
2. Long bones – a well-defined, advancing radiolucency with a V-shaped margin which begins subarticularly.

Osteolytic and Osteosclerotic
1. Skull – osteoporosis circumscripta with focal areas of bone sclerosis.
2. Pelvis – mixed osteolytic and osteosclerotic areas.
3. Long bones – epiphyseal and metaphyseal sclerosis with diaphyseal lucency.

Inactive (Osteosclerotic)
1. Skull – thickened vault. 'Cotton wool' areas of sclerotic bone. The facial bones are not commonly affected (cf. fibrous dysplasia).
2. Spine – especially the lumbar spine. Enlargement of vertebrae and coarsened trabeculae. Cortical thickening produces the 'picture frame' vertebral body. Ivory vertebra.
3. Pelvis – widening and coarsened trabeculation of the pelvic ring, with splitting of the iliopectineal line may progress to widespread changes in the pelvis which are commonly asymmetrical.
4. Long bones – sclerosis due to coarsened, thickened trabeculae. Cortical thickening with encroachment on the medullary canal. The epiphyseal region is nearly always involved.

Complications

1. Bone softening – bowed bones, basilar invagination and protrusio acetabuli.
2. Fractures – transverse with a predilection for the convex aspect of the bone and which usually only partially traverse the bone.
3. Sarcomatous change – in 1% of patients (5–10% if there is widespread involvement). Femur, pelvis and humerus most commonly affected. Osteogenic sarcoma (50%), fibrosarcoma (25%) and chondrosarcoma (10%) are the most common histological diagnoses. They are predominantly lytic.
4. Degenerative joint disease – most frequent in the hip and knee.
5. Neurological complications – nerve entrapment and spinal-cord compression.
6. High output cardiac failure.
7. Extramedullary haemopoiesis.
8. Osteomyelitis.

Paraneoplastic Syndromes

Endocrine Disorders

1. **Cushing's syndrome** – carcinoma of the bronchus, malignant epithelial thymoma, islet cell carcinoma, small cell carcinoma, medullary thyroid carcinoma.
2. **Hypercalcaemia** – osseous metastases; carcinoma of lung, oesophageal carcinoma, squamous carcinomas of the head and neck, lymphomas and leukaemia.
3. **Hypocalcaemia and osteomalacia** – non-ossifying fibroma, giant cell tumour, osteoblastoma (and fibrous dysplasia, neurofibromatosis and melorheostosis bone).
4. **Hypoglycaemia** – sarcomas, mesotheliomas, lymphomas, gastrointestinal carcinomas.
5. **Hyperglycaemia** – glucagon-producing islet cell tumours, enteroglucagon-producing renal carcinoma.
6. **Inappropriate antidiuretic hormone** – carcinoma of bronchus, adenocarcinomas of the gastrointestinal tract.
7. **Carcinoid syndrome** – adenocarcinoma of pancreas, islet cell tumours, small cell carcinoma of the lung, medullary carcinoma of the thyroid, APUD tumours.
8. **Gynaecomastia** – non-seminomatous tumours of the testis, liver and renal cell carcinomas, carcinoma of bronchus.
9. **Hyperthyroidism** – hydatidiform mole or choriocarcinoma, non-seminomatous tumours of testis.
10. **Hypertension** – phaeochromocytoma, neuroblastoma, aldosterone secreting tumours, renal tumours (Wilms' tumour, renal cell carcinoma, haemangiopericytoma).

Haematological Disorders

1. **Polycythaemia** – renal tumours (Wilms' tumour, renal cell carcinoma), liver cell carcinoma, cerebellar haemangioblastoma, uterine fibroids, renal cystic disease.
2. **Red cell aplasia** – thymoma, carcinomas of the bronchus, stomach or thyroid.
3. **Haemolytic anaemia** – lymphoid malignancies, carcinomas of the ovary, stomach, colon, bronchus, cervix and breast.
4. **Thrombocytosis and leukocytosis** – bone marrow metastases.

Digestive Disorders
1. **Zollinger–Ellison syndrome** – non-beta cell adenomas or carcinomas of the pancreas or duodenum, mucinous adenocarcinoma of the ovary.
2. **Multiple endocrine neoplasia (MEN)** (q.v.)
3. **Tumour-related diarrhoea** – Zollinger–Ellison syndrome, carcinoid syndrome, non-beta cell tumour of the pancreas, vasoactive intestinal peptide secreting tumours (VIPomas).

Renal Dysfunction
1. **Nephrotic syndrome** – lymphomas, carcinomas of the bronchus, stomach, colon and ovary.
2. **Tubular dysfunction** – multiple myeloma.

Musculoskeletal Disorders
1. **Hypertrophic osteoarthropathy** (see 1.37) – carcinoma of bronchus, metastases, lymphomas, pleural fibroma.
2. **Dermatomyositis** – carcinomas of the breast, bronchus, ovary or stomach, leukaemias, lymphomas and sarcomas.

Skin Disorders
1. **Acanthosis nigricans** – adenocarcinoma of the stomach.
2. **Pellagra-like lesions** – carcinoid syndrome.
3. **Porphyria cutanea tarda** – liver cell carcinoma or adenoma.
4. **Pemphigus vulgaris** – adenocarcinoma of the pancreas.

Neurological Disorders
1. **Progressive multifocal leukoencephalopathy** – leukaemia, lymphoma, myeloma.
2. **Cerebellar atrophy** – carcinomas of the lung, breast, ovary and kidney; lymphomas.
3. **Myelopathy** – visceral carcinomas.
4. **Myasthenia gravis** – thymoma, thymic hyperplasia.
5. **Myasthenic syndrome** – small cell carcinoma of the lung (Lambert–Eaton syndrome).
6. **Opsimyoclonus (dancing eyes)** – neuroblastoma (usually cervico-thoracic).

Further Reading
Lachman R.S. & Taybi H. (1990) *Radiology of Syndromes, Metabolic Disorders, and Skeletal Dysplasias*, pp. 630–1. Chicago: Year Book Medical Publishers.

Plasmacytoma

See 'Multiple myeloma/plasmacytoma'.

Polycystic Disease, Recessive

Polycystic kidneys, with periportal hepatic fibrosis and bile duct obstruction. Neonatal and infantile/juvenile forms.

Polycystic Disease of the Newborn
1. Presents in the first few days with renal failure and/or respiratory distress because of elevated diaphragms. Majority die in a few days.
2. Bilateral large smooth kidneys with dense striated nephrograms (because of dilated tubules).
3. Calyces are not usually demonstrated but are normal.
4. Markedly hyperechoic kidneys on US with loss of corticomedullary differentiation. May be some macrocysts.

Polycystic Disease of Childhood
1. Presents at 3–5 years.
2. Renal cysts are less prominent and hepatic fibrosis is greater. Presentation is, therefore, with portal hypertension.
3. Kidneys may be similar to the newborn type (although not so massive) or to the adult type. Multiple hepatic cysts.

Polycystic Disease, Dominant

Presents in 3rd–4th decade and terminal renal failure occurs within 10 years. May be diagnosed by screening family members and has been identified antenatally.

Kidneys
1. Bilateral, but asymmetrical, enlarged lobulated kidneys. Unilateral in 8%.
2. Multiple smooth defects in the nephrogram with elongation and deformity of calyces giving a 'spider leg' appearance. Cysts may produce filling defects in the renal pelvis. ± calcification in cyst walls.
3. Multiple cysts on US, CT and MRI.
4. Increased incidence of renal cell carcinoma (may be bilateral).

Other Organs
1. Cystic changes in the liver (in 30%) and, less commonly, in the pancreas and spleen.
2. Displacement of bowel.
3. Intracranial aneurysms in 10%.

Pseudohypoparathyroidism

End organ unresponsiveness to parathormone. X-linked dominant transmission.
1. Short stature, round face, thickset features, mental retardation and hypocalcaemia.
2. Short 4th and 5th metacarpals and metatarsals.
3. Basal ganglia calcification (50%).
4. Soft-tissue calcification.

Pseudopseudohypoparathyroidism

Similar clinical and radiological features to pseudohypoparathyroidism but with a normal plasma calcium.

Psoriatic Arthropathy

Occurs in 5% of psoriatics and may antedate the skin changes. There are five clinical and radiological types.
1. Polyarthritis with predominant involvement of the distal interphalangeal joints.
2. Seronegative polyarthritis simulating rheumatoid arthritis.
3. Monoarthritis or asymmetrical oligoarthritis.
4. Spondyloarthritis which can mimic ankylosing spondylitis.
5. Arthritis mutilans (commonly associated with severe skin changes).

The radiological changes comprise

1. Involvement of synovial and cartilaginous joints and entheses.
2. Joints most frequently affected are the interphalangeal joints of the hands and feet, the metacarpophalangeal and metatarsophalangeal joints, the sacroiliac joints and those in the spine. The large joints are relatively spared. Involvement is asymmetrical.
3. Preserved bone density.
4. Soft-tissue swelling – periarticular or fusiform of a digit.
5. The joint space is narrowed in the large joints and widened in the small joints because of severe destruction of subchondral bone.
6. Erosions which are initially periarticular and progress to involve the entire articular surface. 'Cup and pencil' deformity. Severe destructive changes result in an arthritis mutilans. Erosions also occur at entheses.
7. Bony proliferation (a) adjacent to the erosions and (b) at tendon and ligament insertions.
8. Periosteal new bone – particularly in the hands and feet.
9. Ankylosis – especially at the interphalangeal joints of the hands and feet.
10. Distal phalangeal tuft resorption – almost always with severe nail changes.
11. Sacroiliitis and spondylitis with paravertebral ossification.

Pulmonary Embolic Disease

Clinical conditions which predispose to venous thromboembolism are
1. Surgical procedures, especially major abdominal and gynaecological surgery and hip operations.
2. Trauma.
3. Prolonged bed-rest.
4. Neoplastic disease.
5. Pregnancy and the puerperium.
6. Oestrogens.

Pulmonary embolism is massive if more than 50% of the major pulmonary arteries are involved and minor if less than 50% are involved. Duration of embolism in the pulmonary arteries may be acute (<48 hours), subacute (several days or weeks) or chronic (months or years).

Acute or Subacute Massive Embolism
1. The chest X-ray is most commonly normal.
2. Asymmetrical oligaemia – often best diagnosed by comparison with a previous chest X-ray. The main pulmonary artery may be enlarged.

Acute Minor
1. Although segmental oligaemia ± dilatation of the segmental artery proximal to the obstruction may be observed, this is uncommon and the chest X-ray is often normal.
2. Pulmonary infarction follows in about 33%. The signs are non-specific but include
   (a) Subpleural consolidation – segmental or subsegmental. Single or multiple.
   (b) Segmental collapse and later linear (plate) atelactasis.
   (c) Pleural reaction with a small effusion.
   (d) Elevation of the hemidiaphragm on the affected side.
   (e) Cavitation of the infarct.
3. Infarction is more common the right side and in the lower zones.

NB   The ventilation–perfusion radionuclide lung-scan is an extremely useful investigation for the diagnosis of pulmonary embolism, especially as the chest X-ray is so commonly normal. The characteristic abnormality is a segmental perfusion defect at the periphery of the lung with no corresponding ventilation defect, i.e. a mismatched defect. This is pathognomonic of pulmonary embolism. When the chest X-ray shows collapse or infarction the lung scan shows a corresponding ventilation and perfusion defect, i.e. a matched effect. This is a non-specific finding seen with any pulmonary mass lesion.

Pulmonary arteriography is reserved for those patients in whom embolectomy is being considered.

Chronic

1. 'Plump' hila with peripheral arterial pruning, i.e. the signs of pulmonary arterial hypertension.
2. ± multiple areas of linear atelactasis.

Further Reading

Bedont R.A. & Armstrong II J.D. (1989) Imaging of venous thromboembolic disease. *Current Imaging*, 1: 154–60.

Kerr I.H., Simon G. & Sutton G.C. (1971) The value of the plain radiograph in acute massive pulmonary embolism. *Br. J. Radiol.*, 44: 751–7.

Robinson P.J. (1989) Lung scintigraphy – doubt and certainty in the diagnosis of pulmonary embolism. *Clin. Radiol.*, 40: 557–60.

Reiter's Syndrome

Sexually transmitted or following dysentery. Males predominate.

1. Urethritis ± cystitis ± prostatitis.
2. Circinate balanitis (30%).
3. Conjunctivitis (30%).
4. Keratoderma blennorrhagica.
5. Arthritis (radiological changes in 80% of cases)
    (a) Involvement of synovial and cartilaginous joints and entheses.
    (b) Asymmetrical involvement of the lower limbs – most commonly the knees, ankles, small joints of the feet and calcaneum. The spine and sacroiliac joints are involved less frequently.
    (c) Soft-tissue swelling.
    (d) Osteoporosis is a feature of the acute disease but not of recurrent or chronic disease.
    (e) Erosions which are initially periarticular and progress to involve the central portion of the articular surface.
    (f) Periosteal new bone.
    (g) New bone formation at ligament and tendon insertions.
    (h) Sacroiliitis and spondylitis with paravertebral ossification.

Renal Osteodystrophy

Due to renal glomerular disease – most bilateral reflux nephropathy pyelonephritis and chronic glomerulonephritis. It consists of osteomalacia or rickets + secondary hyperparathyroidism + osteosclerosis.

Children
1. Changes most marked in the skull, pelvis, scapulae, vertebrae and metaphyses of tubular bones.
2. Vertebral sclerosis may be confined to the upper and lower thirds of the bodies – 'rugger jersey' spine.
3. Soft-tissue calcification – less common than in adults.
4. Rickets – but the epiphyseal plate is less wide and the metaphysis is less cupped than in vitamin-D dependent rickets.
5. Secondary hyperparathyroidism – subperiosteal erosions and a 'rotting fence-post' appearance of the femoral necks. ± slipped upper femoral epiphysis.
6. Delayed skeletal maturation.

Adults
1. Hyperparathyroidism (q.v.)
2. Soft-tissue calcification is common, especially in arteries.
3. Osteosclerosis, including 'rugger jersey' spine.
4. Osteomalacia is mainly evident as Looser's zones.

Rheumatoid Arthritis

A multisystem collagen disorder in which joint disease is variably associated with other systemic manifestations.

1. A symmetrical arthritis of synovial joints, especially the metacarpophalangeal and proximal interphalangeal joints of the hands and feet, wrists, knees, ankles, elbows, glenohumeral and acromioclavicular joints and hips. The synovial articulations of the axial skeleton may also be affected, especially the apophyseal and atlantoaxial joints of the cervical spine. Less commonly the sacroiliac and temporomandibular joints are involved.

2. Cartilaginous joints, e.g. discovertebral junctions outside the cervical spine, symphysis pubis and manubriosternal joints, and entheses are less frequently and less severely involved (cf. seronegative spondyloarthropathies).

3. The sequence of pathological/radiological changes at synovial joints is

    (a) Synovial inflammation and effusion → soft-tissue swelling and widened joint space.

    (b) Hyperaemia and disuse → juxta-articular osteoporosis; later generalized.

    (c) Destruction of cartilage by pannus → joint-space narrowing.

    (d) Pannus destruction of unprotected bone at the insertion of the joint capsule → periarticular erosions.

    (e) Pannus destruction of subchondral bone → widespread erosions and subchondral cysts.

    (f) Capsular and ligamentous laxity → subluxation, dislocation and deformity.

    (g) Fibrous and bony ankylosis.

4. Periosteal reaction – uncommon.

5. Secondary degenerative arthritis in the major weight-bearing joints.

Complications

1. Joint complications

    (a) Deformity and subluxation.

    (b) Pyogenic arthritis.

    (c) Tendon rupture.

    (d) Baker's cyst – which may rupture.

   (e) Cord or root compression due to cervical subluxation.
   (f) Hoarseness – due to involvement of the cricoary-
       tenoid joints.
2. Subcutaneous nodules.
3. Anaemia.
4. Pulmonary complications
   (a) Pleural effusion.
   (b) Rheumatoid nodules.
   (c) Fibrosing alveolitis.
   (d) Caplan's syndrome.
5. Cardiac complications
   (a) Pericarditis ± effusion.
6. Ocular complications
   (a) Episcleritis.
   (b) Uveitis.
   (c) Sjögren's syndrome.
7. Arteritis
   (a) Raynaud's phenomenon.
   (b) Leg ulcers.
   (c) Visceral ischaemia.
8. Felty's syndrome (splenomegaly, leucopenia and rheumatoid arthritis).
9. Peripheral and autonomic neuropathy.
10. Amyloidosis.
11. Complications of therapy.

Rickets

Increased uncalcified osteoid in the immature skeleton.

Changes at the Growth Plate and Cortex

1. Widened growth plate (a).
2. Fraying, splaying and cupping of the metaphysis, which is of reduced density (b).
3. Thin bony spur extending from the metaphysis to surround the uncalcified growth plate (c).
4. Indistinct cortex because of uncalcified subperiosteal osteoid (d).
5. Rickety rosary – cupping of the anterior ends of the ribs and, on palpation, abnormally large costochondral junctions.
6. Looser's zones uncommon in children.

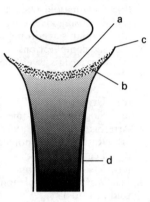

Changes Due to Bone Softening (Deformities)

1. Bowing of long bones.
2. Triradiate pelvis.
3. Harrison's sulcus – indrawing of the lower part of the chest wall because of soft ribs.
4. Scoliosis.
5. Biconcave vertebral bodies.
6. Basilar invagination.
7. Craniotabes – flattening of the occiput and accumulating osteoid in the frontal and parietal regions.

General Changes

1. Retarded bone maturation and growth.
2. Decreased bone density – uncommon.

Sarcoidosis

A multisystem granulomatous disorder of unknown aetiology.
Commonest presentations are:

erythema nodosum	30%
routine chest X-ray	25%
respiratory symptoms	20%
ocular symptoms	8%
other skin lesions	5%

Intrathoracic Sarcoidosis (in 90%)

The chest X-ray at presentation may be:

normal	8%
bilateral hilar lymphadenopathy (BHL)	50%
bilateral hilar lymphadenopathy + pulmonary infiltrate	30%
pulmonary infiltrate ± fibrosis	12%

1. Lymphadenopathy – bilateral hilar ± uni- or bilateral paratracheal lymphadenopathy. Anterior mediastinal lymph
   nodes are also involved in 16%. Unilateral hilar lymphadenopathy in 1–5%. 'Eggshell' calcification occurs in 1–
   5% and takes about 6 years to develop.
2. Parenchymal shadowing includes
   (a) Micronodular shadows < 2 mm ⎤
   (b) Larger shadows < 5 mm, ill- ⎬ predominantly
       defined, mimicking consoli- ⎪ mid
       dation or oedema   ⎦ zones.
   (c) Large nodules, 1–4 cm, ill-defined, multiple, bilateral
       and in any zone.
   (d) Coarse fibrosis – typically in the mid and upper zones.
3. Pleural involvement in 5–7%. Effusion in 2%.
4. Pneumothorax – secondary to chronic lung fibrosis.
5. Bronchostenosis in 1–2% – extrinsic compression or endobronchial granuloma.

Skin Sarcoidosis

1. Erythema nodosum – almost always in association with
   bilateral hilar lymphadenopathy.
2. Lupus pernio, plaques, subcutaneous nodules and scar
   infiltration.

Ocular Sarcoidosis

1. Most commonly manifests as acute uveitis + bilateral hilar lymphadenopathy + erythema nodosum.

Hepatic and Gastrointestinal Sarcoidosis

1. Hepatic granulomas in 66%, but symptomatic hepatobiliary disease is rare.
2. Gastric and peritoneal granulomas occur but are asymptomatic.

Neurologic Sarcoidosis

1. Neuropathies – especially bilateral lower motor neuron VIIth nerve palsies.
2. Cerebral sarcoidosis is evident in 14% of autopsies of patients dying of sarcoidosis, but in only 1–5% clinically. Most commonly it produces nodular granulomatous masses in the basal meninges or adhesive meningitis, which result in cranial nerve palsies and/or hydrocephalus. Granulomas in the brain parenchyma present as space-occupying lesions. (On CT scanning they have a high attenuation, are homogeneously enhancing and peripherally situated.)

Joint Sarcoidosis

1. A transient, symmetrical arthropathy involving knees, ankles and, less commonly, the wrists and interphalangeal joints.

Bone Sarcoidosis

1. In 3% of patients and most frequently associated with skin lesions.
2. Hands and feet are most commonly affected.
   (a) Enlarged nutrient foramina in phalanges and, occasionally, metacarpals and metatarsals.
   (b) Coarse trabeculation, eventually assuming a lacework, reticulated pattern. Initially metaphyseal and eventually affecting the entire bone.
   (c) Larger, well-defined lucencies.
   (d) Resorption of distal phalanges.
   (e) Terminal phalangeal sclerosis.

    (f) Periarticular calcification.
    (g) Subperiosteal bone resorption – simulating hyperpara-
         thyroidism.
    (h) Periosteal reaction.
    (i) Soft-tissue swelling – dactylitis.
3. In the remainder of the skeleton
    (a) Well-defined lucencies with a sclerotic margin.
    (b) Paraspinal masses with an extradural block at myelo-
         graphy.
    (c) Destructive lesions of the nasal and jaw bones.

Sarcoidosis Elsewhere

1. Peripheral lymphadenopathy in 15%.
2. Hypercalcaemia (10%) and hypercalciuria (60%).
3. Splenomegaly in 6%.
4. Uveoparatid fever (uveitis, cranial nerve palsy, fever and
   parotitis).

Further Reading

Freundlich I.M., Libshitz H.I., Glassman L.M. & Israel H.L. (1970)
    Sarcoidosis: typical and atypical thoracic manifestations and
    complications. *Clin. Radiol.*, 21: 376–83.
Kendall B.E. (1978) Radiological findings in neurosarcoidosis. *Br. J.
    Radiol.*, 51: 81–92.
Rockoff S.D. & Rohatgi P.K. (1985) Unusual manifestations of tho-
    racic sarcoidosis. *Am. J. Roentgenol.*, 144: 513–28.

Scleroderma (Progressive Systemic Sclerosis)

A multisystem connective tissue disorder, the course of which varies from acute and fulminating to mild and chronic.

Soft Tissues
1. Raynaud's phenomenon (60%).
2. Skin thickening – initially of the fingers (and less often the toes) and of the mouth; progresses to shiny taut skin.
3. Subcutaneous calcification – especially in the fingertips and over bony prominences.
4. Myopathy or myositis.

Joints
1. Eventually 50% of patients have articular involvement. Fingers, wrists and ankles are commonly affected.
2. Terminal phalangeal resorption is associated with soft- tissue atrophy.
3. Erosions at the distal interphalangeal, 1st carpometacarpal, metacarpophalangeal and metatarsophalangeal joints.

Mandible
1. Thickening of the periodontal membrane ± loss of the lamina dura.

Ribs
1. Symmetrical erosions on the superior surfaces which predominate along the posterior aspects of the 3rd–6th ribs.

Respiratory System
1. Lung involvement in 10–25%.
2. Aspiration pneumonitis secondary to gastro-oesophageal reflux.
3. Interstitial lung disease and fibrosis, more marked in the lower zones.

Gastrointestinal System
1. Oesophageal abnormalities (50%) – dilatation, atonicity, poor or absent peristalsis and free gastro-oesophageal reflux through a widely open gastro-oesophageal junction.

2. Small bowel (75%) – dilated, atonic, thickened mucosal folds and pseudosacculation.
3. Colon (75%) – atonic with pseudosacculations on the anti-mesenteric border.

Heart

1. Cardiomegaly (30%) – due to myocardial ± pericardial involvement. ± pericardial effusion.
2. Cor pulmonale may develop secondary to the interstitial lung disease.

Scurvy

The result of vitamin C deficiency.

1. Onset at 6 months–2 years. Rare in adults.
2. Earliest signs are seen at the knees.
3. Osteoporosis (usually the only sign seen in adults).
4. Loss of epiphyseal density with a pencil-thin cortex (Wimberger's sign) (a).
5. Dense zone of provisional calcification – due to excessive calcification of osteoid (b).
6. Metaphyseal lucency. (Trümmerfeld zone) (c).
7. Metaphyseal corner fractures through the weakened lucent metaphysis (Pelkan spurs) resulting in cupping of the metaphysis (d).
8. Periosteal reaction due to subperiosteal haematoma (e).

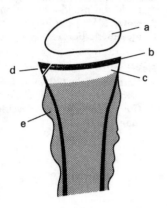

Sickle-cell Anaemia

Skeletal
1. Marrow hyperplasia produces widening of medullary cavities, decreased bone density, coarsening of the trabecular pattern, and cortical thinning and expansion. The changes are most marked in the axial skeleton.
   (a) Skull – coarse granular osteoporosis with widening of the diploë which spares the occiput below the internal occipital protuberance. 'Hair-on-end' appearance (5%). Focal lucencies (but probably due to infarcts).
   (b) Spine – osteoporosis, exaggerated vertical trabeculae and biconcave vertebral bodies (but see also 2(c) below).
2. Vascular occlusion due to sickling results in osteonecrosis.
   (a) Sickle-cell dactylitis (hand–foot syndrome) – in children aged 6 months–2 years. Symmetrical soft-tissue swelling, patchy lucency and sclerosis of the shafts of metacarpals, metatarsals and phalanges, and periosteal reaction.
   (b) Long bones – diaphyseal or epiphyseal infarcts. The femoral head is affected in 12% of patients (60% in sickle/haemoglobin C (SC) disease).
   (c) Spine – square-shaped compression infarcts of the vertebral end-plates are virtually diagnostic.
3. Growth disturbances – retarded growth, delayed closure of epiphyses and tibiotalar slant.
4. Fractures.
5. Osteomyelitis and pyogenic arthritis – due to salmonellae in over 50% of cases.

Extraskeletal
1. Extramedullary haemopoiesis – but more common in thalassaemia.
2. Cholelithiasis.
3. Splenic infarction.
4. Cardiomegaly and congestive cardiac failure – because of anaemia.
5. Renal papillary necrosis.

Silicosis

Occurs in miners, quarry workers, masons, pottery workers, sand blasters, foundry workers and boiler scalers. The duration and degree of exposure determine the time of onset of disease

(a) Chronic silicosis – disease after 20–40 years of exposure.

(b) Accelerated silicosis – disease after 5–15 years of exposure.

(c) Acute silicoproteinosis – heavy exposure over a short period of time (several months to 5 years), e.g. in sand blasters.

Simple

1. Nodular shadows, pin-point to pea-sized, which are first seen around the right hilum but later are disseminated throughout both lungs within relative sparing of the extreme bases and apices. Exceptionally, they may be restricted to the upper zones.

2. Inhalation of pure silica produces very sharp, dense nodules. Mixed dusts are less well defined and of lower density. Density increases with the size of the nodule. Goldminers have very dense nodular shadows.

3. Nodules may calcify, especially in goldminers.

4. Minor hilar lymph-node enlargement, but only obvious when calcification occurs (in 5%). Anterior and posterior mediastinal lymph nodes may also enlarge.

5. Kerley A and B lines – more pronounced with mixed dusts.

6. Silicoproteinosis presents as diffuse alveolar disease.

Complicated, i.e. Progressive Massive Fibrosis (PMF)

1. Superimposed on the changes of simple silicosis.

2. The rapid development of massive, ill-defined, dense, oval or round shadows. Usually bilateral and fairly symmetrical in the upper two-thirds of the lungs.

3. They begin peripherally and increase in size and density as they move towards the hilum, leaving emphysematous lung at the periphery.

4. May cavitate or calcify.

Complications

1. Infections – chronic bronchitis and tuberculosis.
2. Pneumothorax – but usually limited by thickened pleura.
3. Cor pulmonale – a common cause of death.
4. Caplan's syndrome – in patients with rheumatoid disease. Well-defined, peripheral nodules 0.5–5 cm in diameter. Calcification and cavitation may occur.

Simple Bone Cyst

1. Age – 5–15 years.
2. Sites – proximal humerus and femur (75% of cases) and apophysis of the greater trochanter.
3. Appearances
   (a) Metaphyseal, extending to the epiphyseal plate. It migrates away from the metaphysis with time.
   (b) Well-defined lucency with a thin sclerotic rim.
   (c) Usually central.
   (d) Thinned cortex with slight expansion (never more than the width of the epiphyseal plate).
   (e) Thin internal septa.

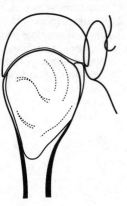

Steroids

See 'Cushing's syndrome'.

Systemic Lupus Erythematosus

Musculoskeletal
1. Polyarthritis – bilateral and symmetrical, involving the small joints of the hand, knee, wrist and shoulder. Soft-tissue swelling and periarticular osteoporosis of the proximal interphalangeal and metacarpophalangeal joints simulate rheumatoid arthritis, but periarticular erosions are not a usual feature.
2. Easily correctable deformities of the hand which cause little functional disability.
3. Osteonecrosis – most frequently of the femoral head.
4. Terminal phalangeal sclerosis and resorption.

Cardiorespiratory
1. Pleural effusion (60%), which is often recurrent. Often accompanied by a pleurisy resulting in elevation of a hemidiaphragm and plate atelectasis at the base.
2. Uraemic pulmonary oedema.
3. Acute lupus pneumonitis.
4. Diffuse interstitial disease – uncommon.
5. Cardiomegaly – due to pericarditis with effusion, myocardial disease or fluid overload in renal failure.

Abdomen
1. Hepatosplenomegaly.
2. Renal disease eventually results in small, smooth, non-functioning kidneys.

Thalassaemia

Skeletal

1. Marrow hyperplasia is more pronounced than in sickle-cell anaemia (q.v.). The changes in thalassaemia major are more severe than in thalassaemia minor. Initially both axial and appendicular skeleton are affected but as marrow regresses from the appendicular skeleton at puberty the changes in the latter diminish.
   (a) Skull – granular osteoporosis, widening of the diploë, thinning of the outer table and 'hair-on-end' appearance. Involvement of the facial bones produces obliteration of the paranasal sinuses, hypertelorism and malocclusion of the teeth. These changes are rarely a feature of other haemoglobinopathies and are important differentiating signs.
   (b) Spine – osteoporosis, exaggerated vertical trabeculae and fish-shaped vertebrae.
   (c) Ribs, clavicles and tubular bones of the hands and feet show the typical changes of marrow hyperplasia (see Sickle-cell anaemia).
2. Growth disturbances.
3. Fractures.

Extraskeletal

1. Extramedullary haemopoiesis – including hepatosplenomegaly.
2. Cardiomegaly.

Tuberous Sclerosis

AD with variable expression and a high incidence of fresh mutations (50%). Gene is located on the long arm of chromosome 11. Clinical features include seizures, mental retardation and skin lesions (adenoma sebaceum, hypomelanotic macules, fibrous plaques, shagreen patches and subungual fibromas). *Café-au-lait* spots are not more frequent in tuberous sclerosis (TS) than in the general population.

Central Nervous System

1. Subependymal nodules – *CT*: calcified or non-calcified; increase in number and degree of calcification with time. *MRI*: low or intermediate signal, ± high signal rim on T_2W, ± enhancement with gadolinium.
2. Parenchymal tubers – *CT*: low attenuation, less commonly high attenuation, rarely calcified, non-enhancing; associated with gyral broadening; minimal progression with time. *MRI*: prolonged T1 and T2 signal; no enhancement. however, signal intensity changes with age:
   Newborn: T1 hyperintense, T2 hypointense.
   Young child: T1 hypointense, T2 hyperintense.
   Older child: T1 isointense, T2 hyperintense.
3. Hydrocephalus.
4. Cerebral neoplasms – giant cell astrocytoma, typically near the foramen of Monro. Marked enhancement on CT and MRI.
5. Retinal astrocytomas (phakomas) – an asymptomatic calcified retinal nodule(s).
6. Arterial ectasia and occlusion.

Kidneys

1. Angiomyolipomas (AML) – in 40–80% of patients with TS. 50% of patients with AML have TS. May be the only lesion of TS in some patients. Detected after infancy. Asymptomatic or cause haematuria. Multiple, bilateral and variable size. *US*: multiple echogenic nodules. *IVU*: stretching of calyces. *CT*: masses containing fat. *MRI*: high T_1W signal masses. *Angiography*: hypervascularity and irregular outpouchings from interlobar and interlobular arteries.

(*continued*)

2. Cysts – in 50%. ± angiomyolipomas. May be present in the neonatal period. Similar appearance to dominant polycystic kidney disease.
3. Increased incidence of renal cell carcinoma and Wilms' tumour.
4. Intratumoral and perirenal haemorrhage.
5. Aneurysms of intrarenal arteries.

Skeleton

1. Lesions are asymptomatic. Present 1–50% of TS patients.
2. Patchy, localized, sclerotic lesions in the skull, vertebrae, pelvis and long bones.
3. Irregular periosteal new bone formation.
4. Distal phalangeal erosion by subungual fibroma.
5. Cyst-like defects in phalanges, metacarpals and metatarsals.
6. Rib expansion and sclerosis.

Lungs

1. In 0.1–1% of TS patients. Majority are female. First respiratory symptoms at 18–34 years. Similar to lymphangiomyomatosis of lung but less pleural disease, especially chylothorax.
2. *CXR*: non-specific coarse generalized reticulonodular shadowing which progresses to honeycomb lung. *HRCT*: well-defined cystic spaces with thin walls, few mm to 5 cm in diameter.

Heart

1. Cardiac rhabdomyomas are the earliest detectable lesions in TS. May be diagnosed as early as 22 weeks gestation. Multiple tumours in 80–90%. At least 80% of those with cardiac rhabdomyomas have TS and 60% of TS patients < 18 years have cardiac rhabdomyomas. Presentation with cardiac failure, murmur and/or arrhythmias. The tumours do not increase in size and most regress spontaneously (within weeks of birth). *CXR*: normal or non-specific cardiomegaly.

Further Reading

Medley B.E., McLeod R.A. & Wayne Houser O. (1976) Tuberous sclerosis. *Semin. Roentgenol.*, 11: 35–54.

Menor F., Martí-Bonmatí L., Mulas F., Poyatos C. & Cortina H. (1992) Neuroimaging in tuberous sclerosis: a clinicoradiological evaluation in paediatric patients. *Pediatr. Radiol.*, 22: 485–9.

Turner's Syndrome

Females with XO chromosome pattern.
1. Small stature with retarded bone maturation.
2. Mental retardation in 10%.
3. Osteoporosis.

Chest
1. Cardiovascular abnormalities – present in 20%, and 70% are coarctation.
2. Broad chest, mild pectus excavatum; widely spaced nipples.

Abdomen
1. Ovarian dysgenesis.
2. Renal anomalies – 'horseshoe kidney' and bifid renal pelvis are the most common.

Axial Skeleton
1. Scoliosis and kyphosis.
2. Hypoplasia of the cervical spine.

Appendicular Skeleton
1. Cubitus valgus in 70%.
2. Short 4th metacarpal and/or metatarsal in 50%, ± short 3rd and 5th metacarpals.
3. Madelung's deformity.
4. Enlargement of the medial tibial plateau ± small exotosis inferiorly.
5. Pes cavus.
6. Transient congenital oedema of the dorsum of the feet.

Ulcerative Colitis

1. Diseased colon is affected in continuity with symmetrical involvement of the wall.
2. Rectum involved in 95%. The rectum may appear normal if steroid enemas have been administered.
3. Granular mucosa and mucosal ulcers.
4. 'Thumbprinting' due mucosal oedema.
5. Blunting of haustral folds progresses to a narrowed, shortened and tubular colon if the disease becomes chronic.
6. Widening of the retrorectal space.
7. Inflammatory pseudopolyps due to regenerating mucosa. Found in 10–20% of ulcerative colitics and usually following a previous severe attack. Filiform polyps occur in quiescent phase.
8. Patulous ileocaecal valve with reflux ileitis (dilated terminal ileum).

Complications

1. Toxic megacolon – in 7–10%.
2. Strictures – much less common than in Crohn's disease and must be differentiated from carcinoma.
3. Carcinoma of the colon – 20–30 × increased incidence if extensive colitis has been present for more than 10 years.
4. Associated conditions
   (a) Erythema nodosum, aphthous ulceration and pyoderma gangrenosum.
   (b) Arthritis – similar to Crohn's disease (q.v.).
   (c) Cirrhosis.
   (d) Chronic active hepatitis.
   (e) Pericholangitis.
   (f) Sclerosing cholangitis.
   (g) Bile duct carcinoma.
   (h) Oxalate urinary calculi.

Further Reading

General
Cockshott P. & Middlemass J.H. (1979) *Clinical Radiology in the Tropics*. Edinburgh: Churchill Livingstone.
Grainger R.G. & Allison D.J. (eds) (1991) *Diagnostic Radiology – an Anglo-American Textbook of Imaging*, 2nd edn. Edinburgh: Churchill Livingstone.
Putman C.E. & Ravin C.E. (eds) (1994) *Textbook of Diagnostic Imaging*, 2nd edn. Philadelphia: WB Saunders.
Reeder M.M. (1993) *Reeder and Felson's Gamuts in Radiology*, New York: Springer-Verlag.
Sutton D. (1993) *A Textbook of Radiology and Imaging*, 5th edn. Edinburgh: Churchill Livingstone.
Thompson W.M. (ed) (1994) Staging neoplasms. *Radiol. Clin. North Am.*, 32 (1).

Paediatrics
Barkovich A.J. (1990) *Contemporary Neuroimaging. Volume 1: Pediatric Neuroimaging*. New York: Raven Press.
Kirks D.R. (1991) *Practical Pediatric Imaging*, 2nd edn. Edinburgh: Churchill Livingstone.
Swischuk L.E. (1984) *Differential Diagnosis in Paediatric Radiology*. Baltimore: Williams & Wilkins.

Ultrasound
Cosgrove D., Meire H., Dewbury K. & Wilde P. (1993) *Clinical Ultrasound – A Comprehensive Text*. Edinburgh: Churchill Livingstone.

MRI
Edelman R.R. & Hesselink J.R. (1990) *Clinical Magnetic Resonance Imaging*. Philadelphia: Saunders.

Musculoskeletal
Beighton P. (1988) *Inherited Disorders of the Skeleton*, 2nd edn. Edinburgh: Churchill Livingstone.

Beighton P. & Cremin B.J. (1980) *Sclerosing Bone Dysplasias*. Berlin: Springer-Verlag.

Bradford D.S. & Hensinger R.M. (1985) *The Pediatric Spine*. New York: Thieme.

Greenfield G.B. (1986) *Radiology of Bone Disease*, 4th edn. Philadelphia: Lippincott.

Kozlokski K. & Beighton P. (1984) *Gamut Index of Skeletal Dysplasias*. Berlin: Springer-Verlag.

Modic M.T. (ed.) (1991) Imaging of the spine. *Radiol. Clin. North Am.*, 29 (4).

Moser R.P. (ed.) (1993) Imaging of bone and soft tissue tumors. *Radiol. Clin. North Am.*, 31 (2).

Murray R.O., Jacobson H.G. & Stoker D.J. (1990) *The Radiology of Skeletal Disorders: Exercises in Diagnosis*. Edinburgh: Churchill Livingstone.

Poznanski A.K. (1984) *The Hand in Radiologic Diagnosis*, 2nd edn. Philadelphia: Saunders.

Resnick D. & Niwayama G. (1988) *Diagnosis of Bone and Joint Disorders*, 2nd edn. Philadelphia: Saunders.

Spranger J.W., Langer L.O. & Wiedmann H.R. (1974) *Bone Dysplasias: An Atlas of Constitutional Disorders of Skeletal Development*. Philadelphia: Saunders.

Wynne-Davies R., Hall C.M. & Apley A.G. (1985) *Atlas of Skeletal Dysplasias*. Edinburgh: Churchill Livingstone.

The Chest

Felson B. (1973) *Chest Roentgenology*. Philadelphia: Saunders.

Fraser R.G., Paré J.A.P., Paré P.D., Fraser R.S. & Genereux G.P. (1988) *Diagnosis of Diseases of the Chest*, 3rd edn. Philadelphia: Saunders.

McLoud T.C. (ed.) (1992) Occupational lung disease. *Radiol. Clin. North Am.* 30 (6).

Müller N.L. (ed.) Imaging of diffuse lung diseases. *Radiol. Clin. North Am.* 29 (5).

Newman B. (ed.) (1993) The pediatric chest. *Radiol. Clin. North. Am.* 31 (3).

Potchen E.J., Grainger R.G. & Greene R. (1993) *Pulmonary Radiology*. Philadelphia: Saunders.

Woodring J.H. (ed.) (1990) Lung cancer. *Radiol. Clin. North. Am.* 28 (3).

Cardiovascular System

Felson B. (ed.) (1969) The myocardium. *Semin. Roentgenol.*, 4 (4).

Felson B. (ed.) (1979) Acquired valvular disease of the heart. *Semin. Roentgenol.*, 14 (2).

Hipona F.A. (ed.) (1971) Cardiac radiology, medical aspects. *Radiol. Clin. North Am.*, 9 (3).

Hipona F.A. (ed.) (1971) Cardiac radiology, surgical aspects. *Radiol. Clin. North Am.*, 9 (2).

Jefferson K. (1970) The plain chest radiograph in congenital heart disease. *Br. J. Radiol.*, 43: 753–70.

Jefferson K. & Rees S. (1980) *Clinical Cardiac Radiology*, 2nd edn. London: Butterworths.

Möes C.A.F. (1975) Analysis of the chest in the neonate with congenital heart disease. *Radiol. Clin. North Am.*, 13: 251–76.

The Abdomen

Bernardino M.E. (ed.) (1991) Imaging of the liver and biliary tree. *Radiol. Clin. North Am.*, 29 (6).

Coleman B.G. (ed) (1992) The female pelvis. *Radiol. Clin. North Am.*, 30 (4).

Feczko P.J. & Halpert R.D. (eds) (1987) *Radiol. Clin. North Am.*, 25 (1).

Feczko P.J. & Mezwa D.G. (eds) (1993) The alimentary tract. *Radiol. Clin. North Am.*, 31 (6).

Freeny P.C. (ed) (1989) Radiology of the pancreas. *Radiol. Clin. North Am.*, 27 (1).

Gore R.M. (ed) CT of the Gastrointestinal Tract. *Radiol. Clin. North Am.*, 27 (4).

Laufer I. & Levine M.S. (1992) *Double Contrast Gastrointestinal Radiology*, 2nd edn. Philadelphia: Saunders.

Sherwood T. (1980) *Uroradiology*. Oxford: Blackwell.

Index

Part 1 is indexed by sections
Part 2 is indexed by page numbers
References to **bold** type are to principal sections